Scott Foresman • Addison Wesley

enVisionMATH™

Authors

Randall I. Charles
Professor Emeritus
Department of Mathematics
San Jose State University
San Jose, California

Janet H. Caldwell
Professor of Mathematics
Rowan University
Glassboro, New Jersey

Mary Cavanagh
Mathematics Consultant
San Diego County Office of Education
San Diego, California

Dinah Chancellor
Mathematics Consultant with Carroll ISD
Southlake, Texas
Mathematics Specialist with Venus ISD
Venus, Texas

Juanita V. Copley
Professor
College of Education
University of Houston
Houston, Texas

Warren D. Crown
Associate Dean for Academic Affairs
Graduate School of Education
Rutgers University
New Brunswick, New Jersey

Francis (Skip) Fennell
Professor of Education
McDaniel College
Westminster, Maryland

Alma B. Ramirez
Sr. Research Associate
Math Pathways and Pitfalls WestEd
Oakland, California

Kay B. Sammons
Coordinator of Elementary Mathematics
Howard County Public Schools
Ellicott City, Maryland

Jane F. Schielack
Professor of Mathematics
Associate Dean for Assessment and
Pre K-12 Education, College of Science
Texas A&M University
College Station, Texas

William Tate
Edward Mallinckrodt Distinguished
University Professor in Arts & Sciences
Washington University
St. Louis, Missouri

John A. Van de Walle
Professor Emeritus, Mathematics Education
Virginia Commonwealth University
Richmond, Virginia

Consulting Mathematicians

Edward J. Barbeau
Professor of Mathematics
University of Toronto
Toronto, Canada

Sybilla Beckmann
Professor of Mathematics
Department of Mathematics
University of Georgia
Athens, Georgia

David Bressoud
DeWitt Wallace Professor of Mathematics
Macalester College
Saint Paul, Minnesota

Gary Lippman
Professor of Mathematics and Computer Science
California State University East Bay
Hayward, California

PEARSON

Glenview, Illinois • Boston, Massachusetts • Chandler, Arizona • Upper Saddle River, New Jersey

Consulting Authors

Charles R. Allan
Mathematics Education Consultant
(Retired)
Michigan Department of Education
Lansing, Michigan

Verónica Galván Carlan
Private Consultant Mathematics
Harlingen, Texas

Stuart J. Murphy
Visual Learning Specialist
Boston, Massachusetts

Grant Wiggins
Researcher and Educational Consultant
Hopewell, New Jersey

ELL Consultants/Reviewers

Jim Cummins
Professor
The University of Toronto
Toronto, Canada

Alma B. Ramirez
Sr. Research Associate
Math Pathways and Pitfalls WestEd
Oakland, California

National Math Development Team

Cindy Bumbales
Teacher
Lake in the Hills, IL

Ann Hottovy
Teacher
Hampshire, IL

Deborah Ives
Supervisor of Mathematics
Ridgewood, NJ

Lisa Jasumback
Math Curriculum Supervisor
Farmington, UT

Rebecca Johnson
Teacher
Canonsburg, PA

Jo Lynn Miller
Math Specialist
Salt Lake City, UT

Patricia Morrison
Elementary Mathematics Specialist K-5
Upper Marlboro, MD

Patricia Horrigan Rourke
Mathematics Coordinator
Holliston, MA

Elise Sabaski
Teacher
Gladstone, MO

Math Advisory Board

John F. Campbell
Teacher
Upton, MA

Enrique Franco
Coordinator Elementary Math
Los Angeles, CA

Gladys Garrison
Teacher
Minot AFB, ND

Pat Glubka
Instructional Resource Teacher
Brookfield, UT

Shari Goodman
Math Specialist
Salt Lake City, UT

Cathy Massett
Math Facilitator
Cobb County SD, GA

Mary Modene
Math Facilitator
Belleville, IL

Kimya Moyo
Math Manager
Cincinnati, OH

Denise Redington
Teacher
Chicago, IL

Arlene Rosowski
Supervisor of Mathematics
Buffalo, NY

Darlene Teague
Director of Core Data
Kansas City, MO

Debbie Thompson
Elementary Math Teaching Specialist
Wichita, KS

Michele Whiston
Supervisor
Curriculum, Instruction, and Assessment
Mobile County, AL

Scott Foresman·Addison Wesley
enVisionMATH™

ISBN-13: 978-0-328-48975-6
ISBN-10: 0-328-48975-1

2 3 4 5 6 7 8 9 10 V082 13 12 11 10 09

enVisionMATH™

Topic Titles

Contents

MATH STRAND COLORS

- Number and Operations
- Algebra
- Geometry
- Measurement
- Data Analysis and Probability
- Problem Solving

Topic 3 Operations with Decimals

Topic 4 Solving Equations

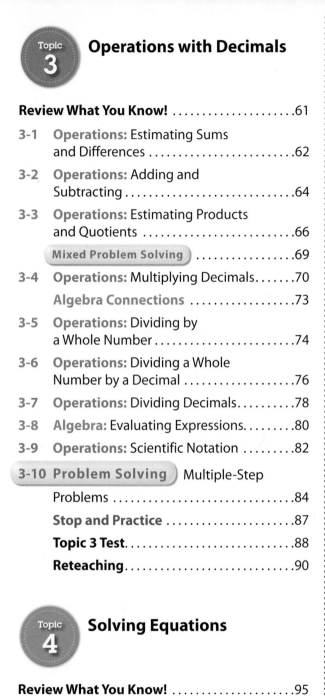

Topic 5 Number and Fraction Concepts

Topic 6 Decimals, Fractions, and Mixed Numbers

Topic 7 Adding and Subtracting Fractions and Mixed Numbers

Topic 8 Multiplying Fractions and Mixed Numbers

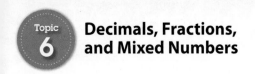

Topic 9 Dividing Fractions and Mixed Numbers

Topic 10 Integers

Topic 11 Properties of Two-Dimensional Figures

Topic 12 Ratios, Rates, and Proportions

Topic 13 Solving Proportions

Topic 14 Understanding Percent

Topic 15 Equations and Graphs

Topic 16 Measurement

Topic 17 Perimeter and Area

Topic 18 Volume and Surface Area

Topic 19 Data and Graphs

Topic 20 Probability

Student Resources

enVisionMATH Across the U.S.A.

Problem Solving Using Number and Operations

New Jersey State Bug

In 1974 the honeybee became the state bug of New Jersey. Honeybees are helpful insects. They make honey and they pollinate many types of plants that people use for food. Without pollination these plants would not produce fruits or seeds. Tiny insects called fairyflies are related to honeybees. Fairyflies destroy the eggs of many insects that damage crops. Fairyflies are about 0.008 to 0.04 inch long. The smallest of them can fly through the eye of a needle!

Fort Moultrie, Charleston, South Carolina

Fort Moultrie is located in Charleston, South Carolina. It is on an island in the harbor. It was the site of a Revolutionary War battle. The Americans built a fort of spongy palmetto logs. British cannonballs did little damage to the fort. They either bounced off the logs or sank into them. The Americans were able to take shelter inside the fort and fire cannonballs at British ships. The Americans won the battle. South Carolina is now known as the Palmetto State.

Missouri State Capitol

Jefferson City is the capital of Missouri. The city has had three state Capitol buildings. The first Capitol burned in 1837. The second Capitol burned in 1911 after it was hit by lightning. The present Capitol was completed in 1917. The building is 437 feet long. Much of the building is made of Missouri limestone. The south entrance has large bronze doors. They are each 18 feet high and 13 feet wide.

TEST PREP

Directions: Carefully read questions 1–20. Write your answers on a separate sheet of paper.

1. What is the difference in length between a honeybee that is 0.5 inch long and a fairyfly that is 0.04 inch long?

A 0.1 inch
B 0.06 inch
C 0.46 inch
D 0.041 inch

2. A honeybee can be $1\frac{3}{10}$ centimeters long. Which improper fraction is equal to $1\frac{3}{10}$?

A $\frac{13}{10}$
B $\frac{23}{13}$
C $\frac{13}{3}$
D $\frac{23}{10}$

3. The roots of a palmetto are 5.8 meters deep. Which is equivalent to 5.8?

A $5\frac{2}{3}$
B $5\frac{5}{9}$
C $5\frac{3}{7}$
D $5\frac{4}{5}$

4. The fruit of a palmetto can be $\frac{1}{3}$ inch in diameter. Which decimal would be to the right of $\frac{1}{3}$ on a number line?

A 0.05
B 0.2
C 0.31
D 0.4

5. The Missouri Capitol is about 145.67 yards long. What is the value of the 7 in this measurement?

A 7 tenths
B 7 hundredths
C 7 thousandths
D 7 hundred

6. The Missouri Capitol cost about $4,215,000 to build. Round 4,215,000 to the nearest million.

A 4
B 4,000,000
C 4,200,000
D 4,215,000

enVisionMATH Across the U.S.A.

Problem Solving Using Geometry

Norfolk County, Massachusetts

Four U.S. Presidents have been born in Norfolk County, Massachusetts. John Adams was the second U.S. President. He was born in 1735 in the town of Braintree. John Quincy Adams became the sixth President. He was a son of John Adams. John Quincy Adams was born in 1767 in Braintree. The part of Braintree where John Adams and John Quincy Adams were born later became part of the town of Quincy. John F. Kennedy was the thirty-fifth President. He was born in 1917 in the town of Brookline. George H. W. Bush, the forty-first President, was born in the town of Milton in 1924.

7. Suppose you drew a triangle on the map connecting the cities of Brookline, Milton, and Boston. If the angle at Brookline measures about 85°, and the angle at Milton measures about 35°, what is the measure of the angle at Boston?

A About 120° **C** About 60°
B About 105° **D** About 45°

8. The distance from Braintree to Brookline is about 11 miles. From Braintree to Boston it is about 10 miles. Boston is about 3 miles from Brookline. What is the perimeter of the triangle that connects these three cities?

A About 24 miles **C** About 48 miles
B About 35 miles **D** About 55 miles

9. Suppose you drew a polygon whose vertices are at Brookline, Milton, Quincy, and Boston. What is the sum of the interior angles of this polygon?

A 180° **C** 300°
B 240° **D** 360°

Quincy, Massachusetts

Problem Solving Using Measurement

The National Aquarium

The National Aquarium is located in Baltimore, Maryland. In addition to many fish, it also has other types of animals, such as birds, mammals, amphibians, and reptiles. One species is the giant Pacific octopus. Some giant Pacific octopuses can grow to weigh more than 400 pounds. An octopus is not a type of fish. It is more closely related to clams and snails.

The Nation's First Subway System

The first subway system in the United States was built in Boston, Massachusetts. It was begun in 1897. Boston needed a subway because its streets were crowded with vehicles. Sometimes there were so many vehicles on the streets that they could barely move. Some people at the time joked that it would be quicker to climb out of a street trolley and walk over the tops of stalled vehicles. They said that people could walk to where they were going faster than the trolley could move.

10. The arm span of a giant Pacific octopus can be 24 feet. How many yards is that?

A 2
B 4
C 6
D 8

11. Which metric unit would be best to use to weigh an adult giant Pacific octopus?

A milligrams
B grams
C kilograms
D metric tons

12. Suppose a person gets on the Boston subway at Riverside Station at 11:50 A.M. and leaves the subway at Park Street Station 12:28 P.M. How much time did the subway trip take?

A 22 minutes
B 38 minutes
C 1 hour 18 minutes
D 1 hour 32 minutes

enVisionMATH Across the U.S.A.

Problem Solving Using Data Analysis and Probability

Antique oil well pump engine wagon

Drake Well, Titusville, Pennsylvania

In 1859, Edwin Drake drilled a successful oil well in Titusville, Pennsylvania. The well was the start of the U.S. oil industry. Drake thought that he could find oil because there were places nearby where oil rose naturally to the surface of the ground. Native Americans had been using this oil for a long time. Today there is a museum at the site of Drake's well. Pennsylvania produces large amounts of oil each year.

Oil Production in Pennsylvania

Year	Millions of Barrels
2001	1.62
2002	2.23
2003	2.43
2004	2.54
2005	3.95

13. Look at the table showing the amount of oil production in Pennsylvania. What is the range of the data?

A 0.61 million barrels
B 0.92 million barrels
C 1.72 million barrels
D 2.33 million barrels

14. Based on the table, between which two years did oil production in Pennsylvania change the most?

A 2001–2002 **C** 2003–2004
B 2002–2003 **D** 2004–2005

15. Which is the best measure of the mean number of barrels of oil produced in Pennsylvania during 2003, 2004, and 2005?

A 2.16 million barrels
B 2.49 million barrels
C 2.97 million barrels
D 3.26 million barrels

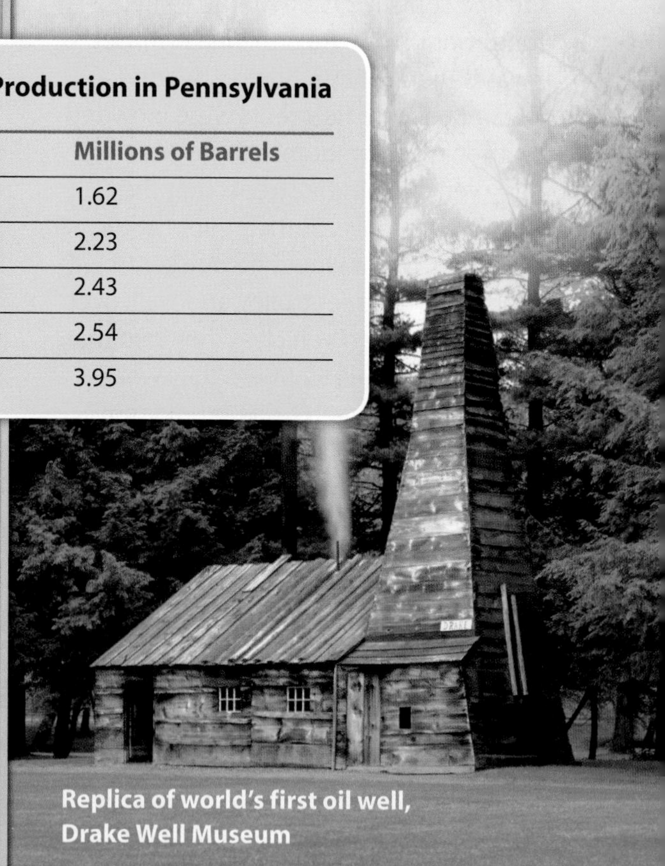

Replica of world's first oil well, Drake Well Museum

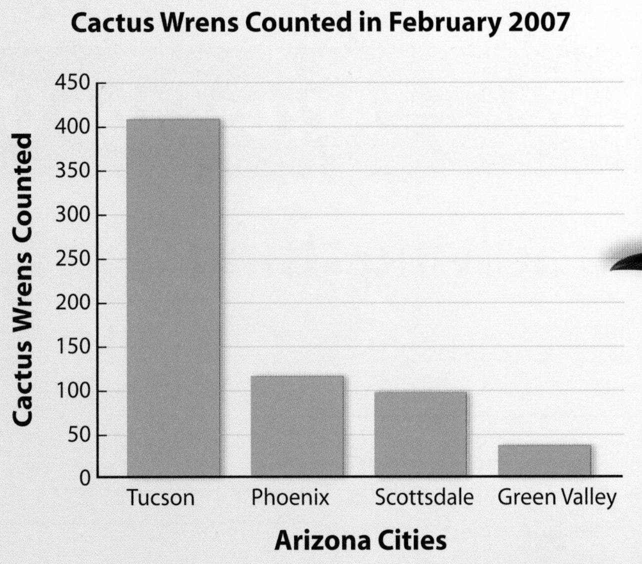

Arizona State Flower and Bird

The state flower of Arizona is the saguaro cactus blossom. The saguaro cactus can grow to a height of 50 feet, and it can live about 150 to 200 years. The saguaro grows slowly. At first it grows straight up. After at least 50 years, the trunk starts producing branches. The state bird of Arizona is the cactus wren. These birds commonly build nests in desert plants such as the saguaro.

New Jersey State Quarter

The New Jersey quarter was made in 1999. It shows a scene from the Revolutionary War. The scene shows George Washington standing in a boat. The boat is crossing the Delaware River. Other members of the Colonial army are in the boat too. They are on their way to an important battle.

16. Look at the graph above. It shows the number of cactus wrens counted in Arizona during February 16–19, 2007. About how many more cactus wrens were counted in Tucson than in Scottsdale?

A 300 **C** 150

B 225 **D** 75

17. Look at the graph showing the number of cactus wrens counted in Arizona during February 16–19, 2007. Which is the best estimate for the number of cactus wrens counted in Phoenix and Green Valley?

A 530 **C** 220

B 440 **D** 150

18. Suppose two New Jersey quarters are tossed into the air. What is the probability that they will both land showing tails?

A 0 **C** $\frac{1}{2}$

B $\frac{1}{4}$ **D** 1

enVisionMATH **Across the U.S.A.**

Problem Solving Using Algebra

New Presque Isle Lighthouse, Michigan

Michigan is called the "Great Lakes State." The state has more than 100 lighthouses and navigational lights. One of the lighthouses is the New Presque Isle Lighthouse. It was built in 1870 to replace an older lighthouse. The tower of the lighthouse is about 110 feet tall. In 1970 the lighthouse was set up to run automatically. A person who was responsible for running the lighthouse used to live in a building next to the lighthouse. The building is now a museum and gift shop.

19. The light of the New Presque Isle Lighthouse flashes four times each minute. Which algebraic expression shows the number of flashes in m minutes?

A $4m$
B $m - 4$
C $4 + m$
D $m \div 4$

20. The tower of the New Presque Isle Lighthouse is about 70 feet taller than the tower of the Old Presque Isle Lighthouse. If the height of the new tower is h, which algebraic expression shows the height of the old tower?

A $70 \div h$
B $70h$
C $70 + h$
D $h - 70$

Problem-Solving Handbook

Scott Foresman·Addison Wesley

enVisionMATH™

Problem-Solving Handbook

Use this Problem-Solving Handbook throughout the year to help you solve problems.

Don't give up!

Everybody can be a good problem solver!

There's almost always more than one way to solve a problem!

Don't trust key words.

Pictures help me understand!

Explaining helps me understand!

Problem-Solving Process

Read and Understand

What am I trying to find?
- Tell what the question is asking.

What do I know?
- Tell the problem in my own words.
- Identify key facts and details.

Plan and Solve

What strategy or strategies should I try?

Can I show the problem?
- Try drawing a picture.
- Try making a list, table, or graph.
- Try acting it out or using objects.

How will I solve the problem?

What is the answer?
- Tell the answer in a complete sentence.

Strategies
- Show What You Know
  - Draw a Picture
  - Make an Organized List
  - Make a Table
  - Make a Graph
  - Act It Out/ Use Objects
- Look for a Pattern
- Try, Check, Revise
- Write an Equation
- Use Reasoning
- Work Backward
- Solve a Simpler Problem

Look Back and Check

Did I check my work?
- Compare my work to the information in the problem.
- Be sure all calculations are correct.

Is my answer reasonable?
- Estimate to see if my answer makes sense.
- Make sure the question was answered.

Using Bar Diagrams

Use a bar diagram to show how what you know and what you want to find are related. Then choose an operation to solve the problem.

Problem 1

Carrie helps at the family flower store in the summer. She keeps a record of how many customers come into the store. How many customers came into the store on Monday and Wednesday?

Customers

Data

Days	Customers
Monday	124
Tuesday	163
Wednesday	151
Thursday	206
Friday	259

Bar Diagram

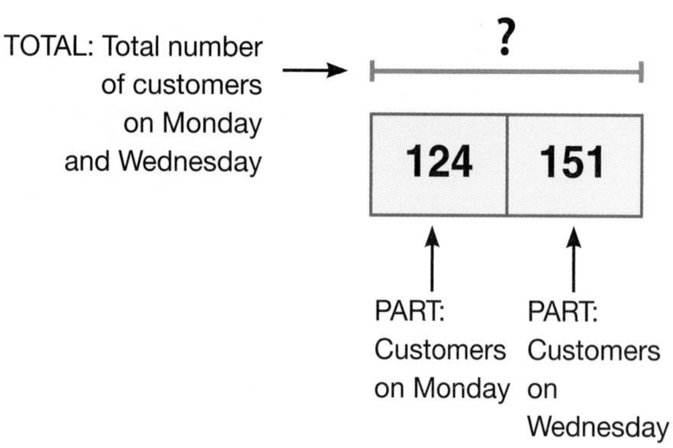

124 + 151 = ☐

Think I can add to find the total.

Problem 2

Kim is saving to buy a sweatshirt for the college her brother attends. She has $18. How much more money does she need to buy the sweatshirt?

Bar Diagram

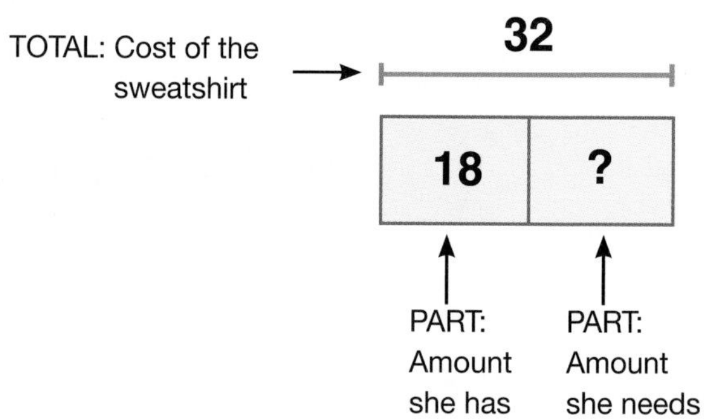

32 − 18 = ☐

Think I can subtract to find the missing part.

Pictures help me understand!

Don't trust key words!

Problem 3

Season tickets to the community theater cost only $105 each no matter what age you are. What is the cost of tickets for four people?

Bar Diagram

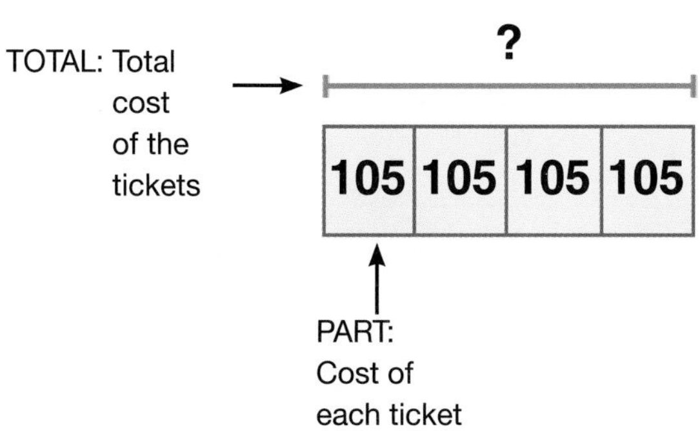

$4 \times 105 = \square$

Think: I can multiply because the parts are equal.

Problem 4

Thirty students traveled in 3 vans to the zoo. The same number of students were in each van. How many students were in each van?

Bar Diagram

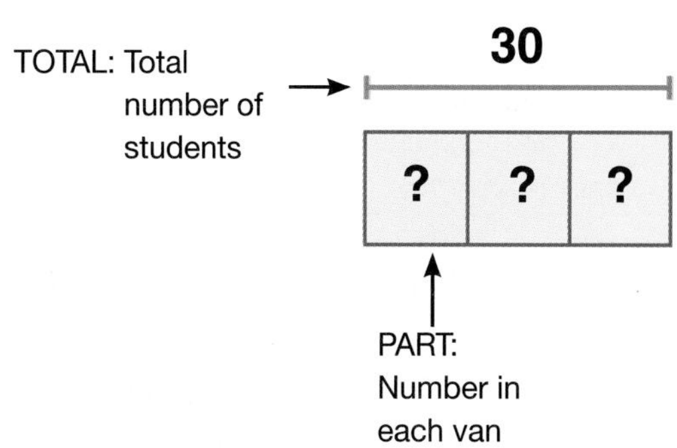

$30 \div 3 = \square$

Think: I can divide to find how many are in each part.

Problem-Solving Strategies

Strategy	Example	When I Use It

Draw a Picture

Example: The race was 5 kilometers. Markers were at the starting line and the finish line. Markers showed each kilometer of the race. Find the number of markers used.

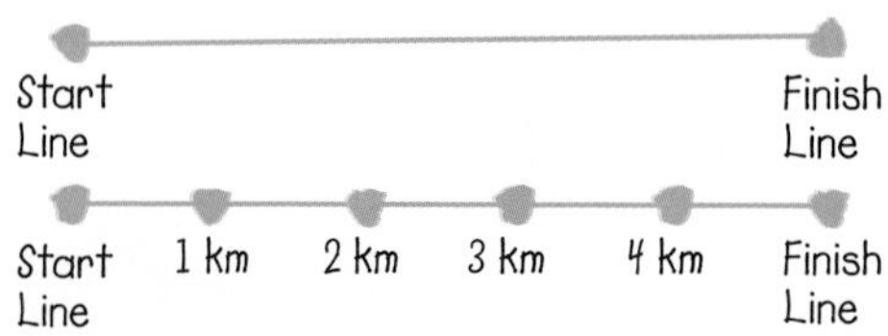

When I Use It: Try drawing a picture when it helps you visualize the problem or when the relationships such as joining or separating are involved.

Make a Table

Example: Phil and Marcy spent all day Saturday at the fair. Phil rode 3 rides each half hour and Marcy rode 2 rides each half hour. How many rides had Marcy ridden when Phil rode 24 rides?

Rides for Phil	3	6	9	12	15	18	21	24
Rides for Marcy	2	4	6	8	10	12	14	16

When I Use It: Try making a table when:

- there are 2 or more quantities,
- amounts change using a pattern.

Look for a Pattern

Example: The house numbers on Forest Road change in a planned way. Describe the pattern. Tell what the next two house numbers should be.

When I Use It: Look for a pattern when something repeats in a predictable way.

Everybody can be a good problem solver!

Strategy	Example	When I Use It
Make an Organized List	How many ways can you make change for a quarter using dimes and nickels?	Make an organized list when asked to find combinations of two or more items.
Try, Check, Revise	Suzanne spent \$27, not including tax, on dog supplies. She bought two of one item and one of another item. What did she buy? $\$8 + \$8 + \$15 = \$31$ $\$7 + \$7 + \$12 = \$26$ $\$6 + \$6 + \$15 = \$27$	Use Try, Check, Revise when quantities are being combined to find a total, but you don't know which quantities.
Write an Equation	Maria's new CD player can hold 6 discs at a time. If she has 204 CDs, how many times can the player be filled without repeating a CD? Find $204 \div 6 = n$.	Write an equation when the story describes a situation that uses an operation or operations.

1 quarter =
1 dime + 1 dime + 1 nickel
1 dime + 1 nickel + 1 nickel + 1 nickel
1 nickel + 1 nickel + 1 nickel + 1 nickel + 1 nickel

Dog Supplies Sale!
Leash \$8
Collar \$6
Bowls \$7
Medium Beds \$15
Toys \$12

Even More Strategies

Strategy	Example	When I Use It
Act It Out	How many ways can 3 students shake each other's hand? 	Think about acting out a problem when the numbers are small and there is action in the problem you can do.
Use Reasoning	Beth collected some shells, rocks, and beach glass. **Beth's Collection** 2 rocks 3 times as many shells as rocks 12 objects in all  How many of each object are in the collection?	Use reasoning when you can use known information to reason out unknown information.
Work Backward	Tracy has band practice at 10:15 A.M. It takes her 20 minutes to get from home to practice and 5 minutes to warm up. What time should she leave home to get to practice on time? 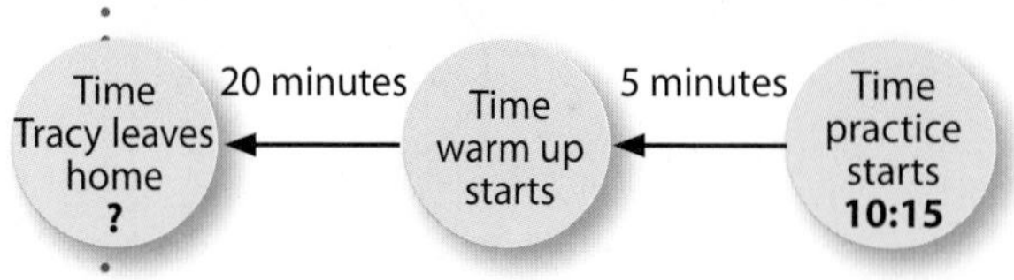	Try working backward when: • you know the end result of a series of steps, • you want to know what happened at the beginning.

I can think about when to use each strategy.

Strategy	Example	When I Use It
Solve a Simpler Problem 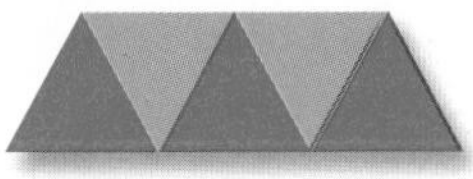	Each side of each triangle in the figure at the left is one centimeter. If there are 12 triangles in a row, what is the perimeter of the figure? I can look at 1 triangle, then 2 triangles, then 3 triangles.  perimeter = 3 cm 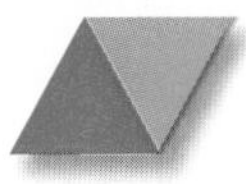 perimeter = 4 cm  perimeter = 5 cm	Try solving a simpler problem when you can create a simpler case that is easier to solve.
Make a Graph	Mary was in a jump rope contest. How did her number of jumps change over the five days of the contest? 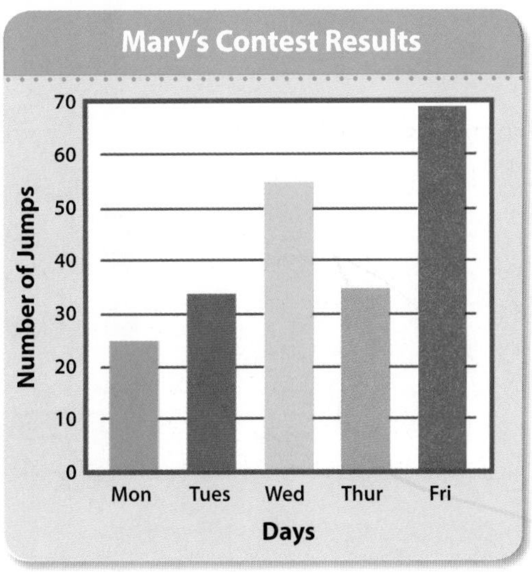	Make a graph when: • data for an event are given, • the question can be answered by reading the graph.

Writing to Explain

Here is a good math explanation.

Writing to Explain What happens to the area of the rectangle if the lengths of its sides are doubled?

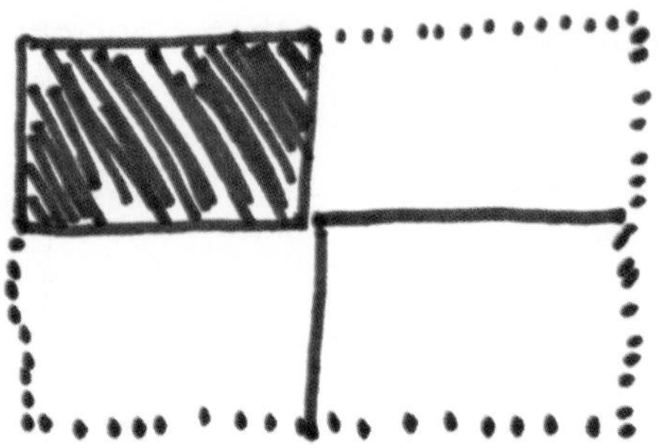

■ = $\frac{1}{4}$ of the whole rectangle

The area of the new rectangle is 4 times the area of the original rectangle.

Tips for Writing Good Math Explanations....

A good explanation should be:

- correct
- simple
- complete
- easy to understand

Math explanations can use:

- words
- pictures
- numbers
- symbols

Explaining helps me understand!

This is another good math explanation.

Writing to Explain Use blocks to show 13×24. Draw a picture of what you did with the blocks.

First we made a row of 24 using 2 tens and 4 ones. Then we made more rows until we had 13 rows. Then we said 13 rows of 2 tens is 13×2 tens = 26 tens or 260. Then we said 13 rows of 4 ones is $13 \times 4 = 52$. Then we added the parts $260 + 52 = 312$ So, $13 \times 24 = 312$.

Problem-Solving Recording Sheet

Name Jane

Teaching Tool
1

Problem-Solving Recording Sheet

Problem:
On June 14, 1777, the Continental Congress approved the design of a national flag. The 1777 flag had 13 stars, one for each colony. Today's flag has 50 stars, one for each state. How many stars were added to the flag since 1777?

Find?

Number of stars added to the flag

Know?

Original flag
13 stars

Today's flag
50 stars

Strategies?

Show the Problem
- ☑ Draw a Picture
- ☐ Make an Organized List
- ☐ Make a Table
- ☐ Make a Graph
- ☐ Act It Out/Use Objects

- ☐ Look for a Pattern
- ☐ Try, Check, Revise
- ☑ Write an Equation
- ☐ Use Reasoning
- ☐ Work Backwards
- ☐ Solve a Simpler Problem

Show the Problem?

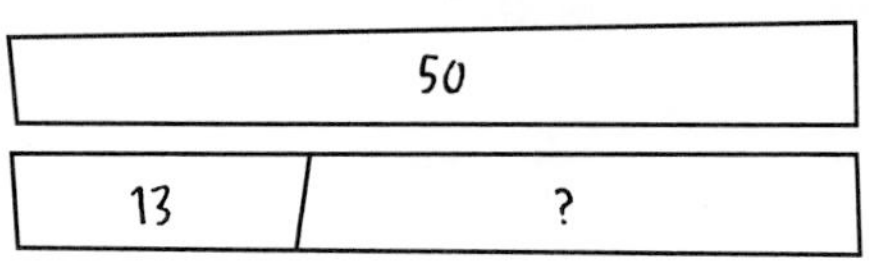

Solution?

I am comparing the two quantities.
I could add up from 13 to 50. I can also subtract 13 from 50. I'll subtract.

$$\begin{array}{r} 50 \\ -\ 13 \\ \hline 37 \end{array}$$

Answer?

There were 37 stars added to the flag from 1777 to today.

Check? Reasonable?

37 + 13 = 50 so I subtracted correctly.

50 − 13 is about 50 − 10 = 40
40 is close to 37. 37 is reasonable.

Teaching Tools • 1

Here's a way to organize my problem-solving work

Name Benton

Teaching Tool 1

Problem-Solving Recording Sheet

Problem:

Suppose your teacher told you to open your math book to the facing pages whose page numbers add to 85. To which two pages would you open your book?

Find?

Two facing page numbers

Know?

Two pages.
Facing each other.
Sum is 85.

Strategies?

Show the Problem
- ☑ Draw a Picture
- ☐ Make an Organized List
- ☐ Make a Table
- ☐ Make a Graph
- ☐ Act It Out/Use Objects

- ☐ Look for a Pattern
- ☑ Try, Check, Revise
- ☑ Write an Equation
- ☐ Use Reasoning
- ☐ Work Backwards
- ☐ Solve a Simpler Problem

Show the Problem?

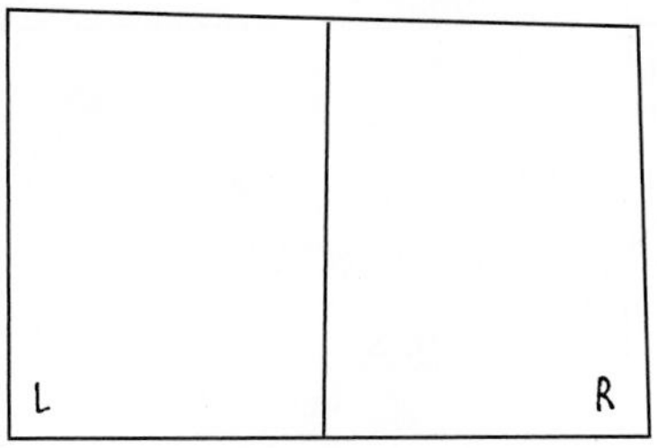

L + R = 85
L is 1 less than R

Solution?

I'll try some numbers in the middle.
40 + 41 = 81, too low
How about 46 and 47?
46 + 47 = 93, too high
Ok, now try 42 and 43.
42 + 43 = 85.

Answer?

The page numbers are 42 and 43.

Check? Reasonable?

I added correctly.
42 + 43 is about 40 + 40 = 80
80 is close to 85.
42 and 43 is reasonable.

Topic 1

Numeration

1 How high can the Helios Prototype airplane fly in comparison to other aircraft? You will find out in Lesson 1-2.

2 Coral Reefs are formed by tiny marine animals, known as coral polyps, that live in colonies. About how many coral polyps could form 1 square foot of coral reef? You will find out in Lesson 1-5.

3 The Milky Way Galaxy may have about 200 billion stars. How do you write very large numbers such as this? You will find out in Lesson 1-1.

Review What You Know!

Vocabulary

Choose the best term from the box.

- place
- decimal point
- digits

1. A period placed in a number to separate whole number values from values less than one is called a __?__.
2. The value of the position of any digit in a number is called its __?__.
3. The symbols used to write numbers 0, 1, 2, 3, 4, 5, 6, 7, 8, and 9 are __?__.

Writing Numbers

Write each word form in standard form.

4. nineteen
5. thirty-seven
6. three hundred five
7. two thousand twelve
8. forty thousand
9. one hundred thousand

Write the word form of each number.

10. 49 **11.** 112 **12.** 10,465

Decimals

Writing to Explain Write an answer for the question.

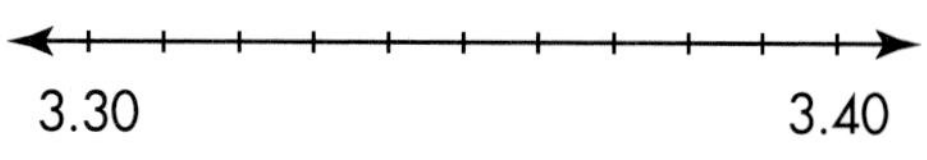

13. How would you locate 3.33 on the number line? Explain.

Lesson
1-1

Understand It!
The place and period of each digit of a number help to find the values of very large numbers.

Place Value

How can you read very large numbers?

In astronomy, a light-year is the distance that light can travel in one year. One light-year is equal to about 9,500,000,000,000 kilometers. Use a place-value chart to help you find the value of the digit 9 and read the number.

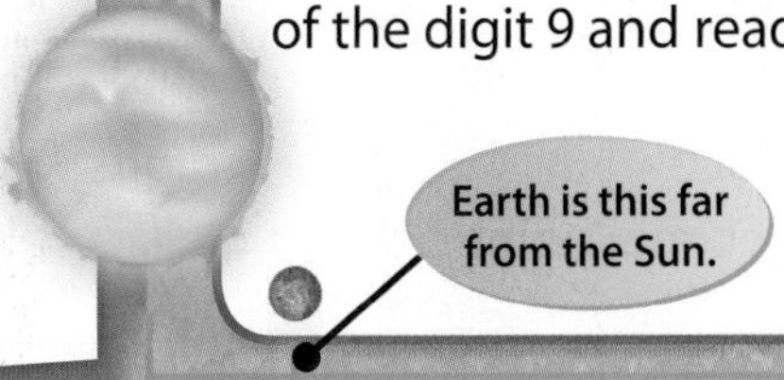

Another Example What are different ways to write very large numbers?

A place-value chart can help you write a very large number, such as 44,600,000,000, in different forms.

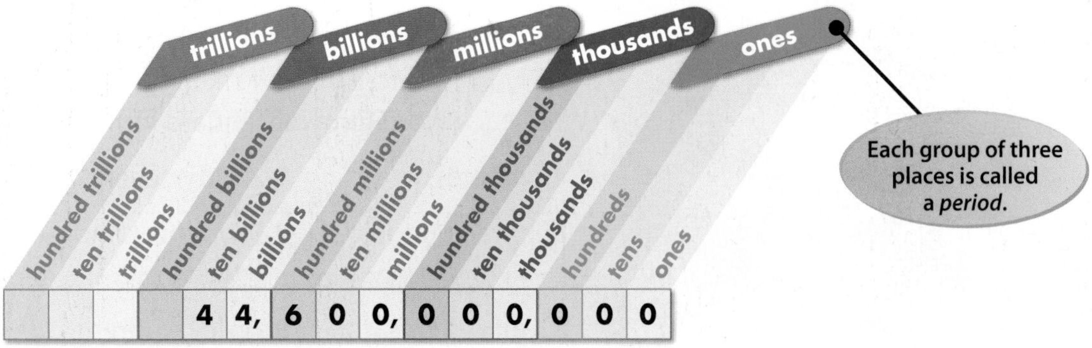

Standard form: 44,600,000,000

Word form: forty-four billion, six hundred million

Short word form: 44 billion, 600 million

Expanded form: 40,000,000,000 + 4,000,000,000 + 600,000,000 **or**
(4 × 10,000,000,000) + (4 × 1,000,000,000) + (6 × 100,000,000)

Explain It

1. What is the relationship between the commas in a number and the periods in a place-value chart?
2. In the example above, how do you know what the addends are for a number written in expanded form?

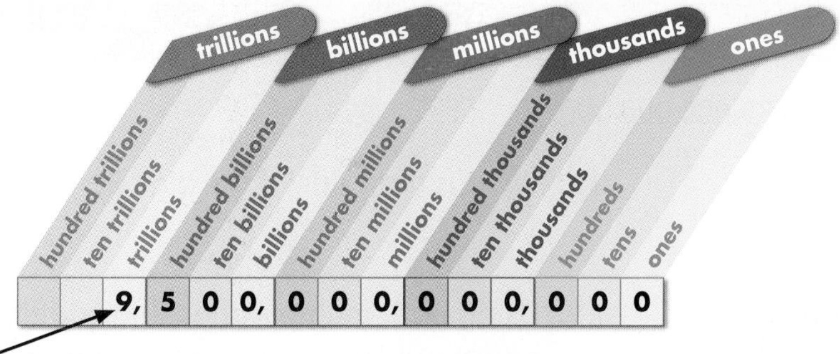

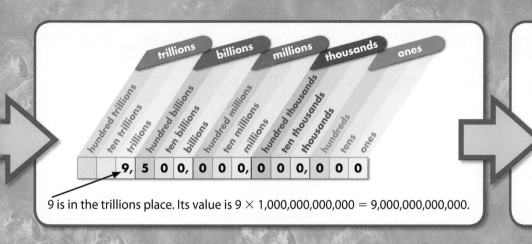

9 is in the trillions place. Its value is $9 \times 1,000,000,000,000 = 9,000,000,000,000$.

You can use the word form to read the number.

Word form: nine trillion, five hundred billion

Guided Practice*

Do you know HOW?

In **1** through **4**, write the place and value of the underlined digit.

1. 1,234,567 (digit 3 underlined)

2. 9,870,563,142,000 (digit 9 underlined)

3. 36,192,748 (digit 6 underlined)

4. 82,765,432,109,497 (digit 8 underlined)

In **5** and **6**, write each number in the form indicated.

5. 57,000,000,009 in expanded form

6. 321 trillion, 705 thousand in standard form

Do you UNDERSTAND?

7. How do you use periods to read and write very large numbers?

8. In the example at the top, how would you write the number in expanded form?

9. When writing 136,000,000 in expanded form, why would you skip the hundred thousands, ten thousands, thousands, hundreds, tens, and ones?

Independent Practice

In **10** through **12**, write the place and value of the digit 3 in each number?

10. 3,476

11. 384,400

12. 5,437,200,184,400

In **13** through **15**, write each number in short-word form.

13. 18,429,000,050,000

14. 10,007,000,000,000

15. 8,507,004,041

DIGITAL Animated Glossary **www.pearsonsuccessnet.com**

For another example, see Set A on page 28.

Independent Practice

For **16** through **19**, use the number 1,435,600,000,000.

16. What is the place and value of the digit 5?

17. What is the value of the digit 3?

18. Write the number in word form.

19. Using both multiplication and addition, how would you write this number in expanded form?

Problem Solving

20. How do you write the number of stars in the Milky Way Galaxy in standard form?

The Milky Way galaxy is thought to have about 200 billion stars.

21. Writing to Explain Describe how you would use the standard form of a number to write the short-word form.

In a recent year, the world used an estimated 15,850,000,000 kilowatt hours of electricity. Use this information to answer **22** through **24**.

22. What is the value of each non-zero digit in the number.

23. Number Sense From left to right, what is the place of the second 5 in this number?

A trillions

B hundred millions

C ten millions

D hundred thousands

24. Algebra At this rate, about how many kilowatt hours of electricity might the world use over a 10-year period?

A 160 million

B 160 billion

C 16 trillion

D 160 trillion

25. Which of these numbers represents seventy-six trillion, two hundred seven thousand?

A 76,000,000,207,000

B 76,000,000,007,200

C 76,000,207,000,000

D 76,000,207,000

26. Which of these numbers is ten million more than three billion, four hundred twenty-nine million?

A 3,419,000,000,000

B 3,439,000,000,000

C 3,419,000,000

D 3,439,000,000

Mixed Problem Solving

Ancient Civilizations in Today's World

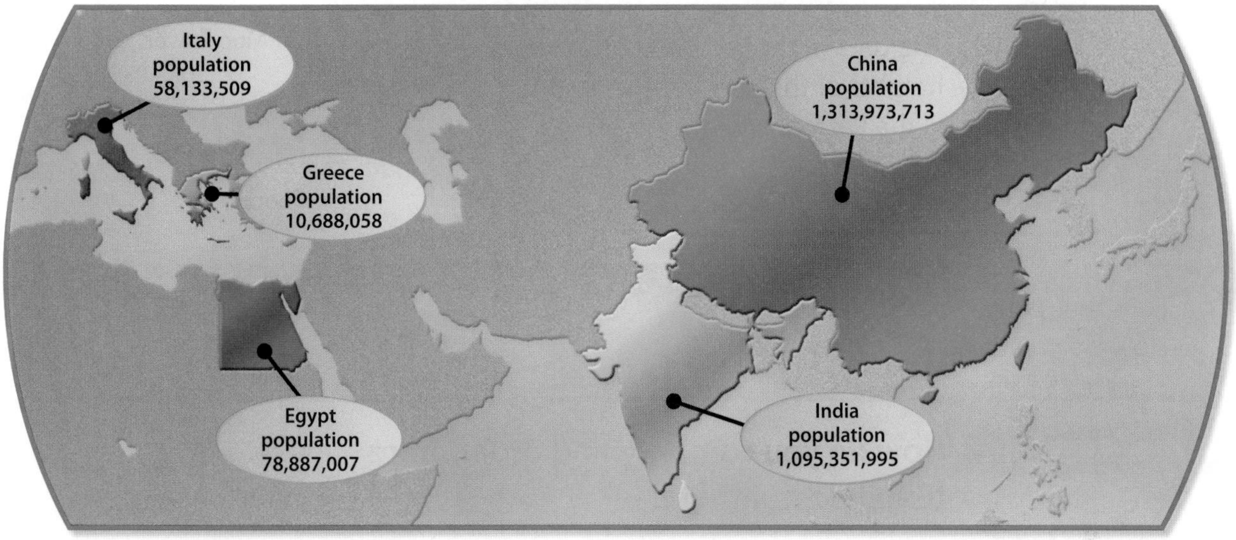

Use the estimated populations shown on the map above to answer **1** through **10**.

1. Which countries have a population in the billions?

2. Which value does the digit 1 have in Greece's population?

3. Which places does the digit 3 occupy in China's population?

4. Which country has a population close to 80 million?

5. Which countries have a population between ten million and one hundred million?

6. Draw a place-value chart to show the place and value of each of the digits in India's population.

Tip *You might want to use a calculator to do calculations with very large numbers.*

7. Which country has the least population? How much less is its population than the greatest population shown?

8. How many people would India need to gain for its population to equal that of China?

9. In a recent year, the population of Italy's capital, Rome, was about 2,553,873. About how many times larger was Italy's population than the population of Rome?

10. It is projected that China's population will increase approximately 20% by 2025. Approximately how many more people will China have?

    A 130,000,000 **C** 260,000,000

    B 89,000,000 **D** 3,190,000,000

Lesson

1-2

Understand It!
Place value is used to compare and order numbers.

Comparing and Ordering Whole Numbers

How can you compare numbers?

Use the data in the table to compare the heights of the buildings. Which is taller, the Petronas Towers or the Sears Tower?

Data

Tall Buildings	Height (ft)
Jin Mao Tower	1,380
Taipei 101	1,670
Petronas Towers	1,483
Sears Tower	1,450

Another Example **How do you compare and order more than two numbers?**

Order the heights of the buildings in the above table from least to greatest.

Step 1

Write the numbers, lining up the places. Compare the digits.

1,483

1,380 → least

1,670 → greatest

1,450

Step 2

Write the remaining numbers, lining up the places. Compare.

1,483 → greater

1,450

Step 3

Order the numbers and the heights of the buildings from least to greatest.

1,380; 1,450; 1,483; 1,670

Jin Mao Tower, Sears Tower, Petronas Towers, Taipei 101

Guided Practice*

Do you know HOW?

In **1** and **2**, use $<$ or $>$ to compare.

1. 27,318 ◯ 28,001

2. 1,000,001 ◯ 1,000,010

In **3**, order the numbers from least to greatest.

3. 3,964 4,160 3,395 4,000

Do you UNDERSTAND?

4. In the example at the top, where do you begin comparing digits?

5. Two International Finance Centre is 1,362 feet tall. Use the table above to find which is taller, Two International Finance Centre or the Jin Mao Tower?

For another example, see Set A on page 28.

Step 1

Write the numbers in a column to line up the places.

1,483
1,450

Compare the digits from left to right.

Step 2

Find the first place where the digits are different.

1,483
1,450

Use > or < to compare.

8 > 5

So, 1,483 > 1,450.

Step 3

Write your answer.

1,483 > 1,450

or

1,450 < 1,483

The Petronas Towers are taller than the Sears Tower.

Independent Practice

For **6** through **8**, use < or > to compare.

6. 8,867 ◯ 8,896 **7.** 102,086 ◯ 100,266 **8.** 5,743,834 ◯ 5,745,618

For **9** and **10**, order the numbers from least to greatest.

Tip *Compare each place from left to right.*

9. 85,634; 86,364; 86,446; 68,989

10. 4,088,777; 4,221,000; 4,202,006

For **11** and **12**, order the numbers from greatest to least.

11. 400 billion; 857 thousand; 3 trillion

12. 5,743,834; 5,754,618; 5,900,962

Problem Solving

13. Writing to Explain The SR-71 spy plane can fly at an altitude of 85,000 feet. Explain how you would compare this altitude with the altitude of the Helios shown below. Tell which plane could fly higher.

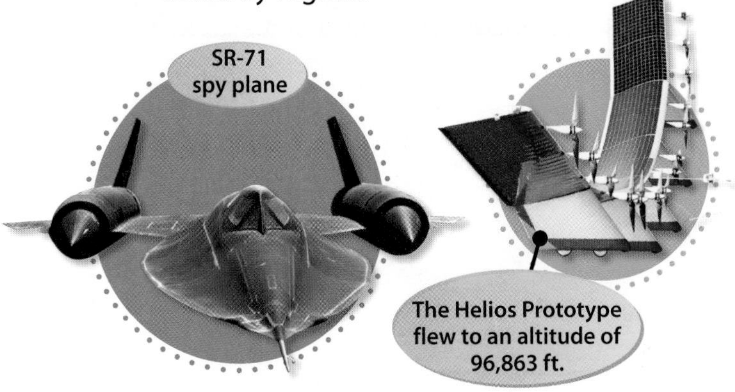
SR-71
spy plane
The Helios Prototype flew to an altitude of 96,863 ft.

14. Number Sense When comparing 1,290 km and 1,130 km, which place do you use to determine which number is greater?

15. Geometry Which measurement of this rectangular vegetable garden has the greatest value?

A length

B width

C perimeter

D length + width

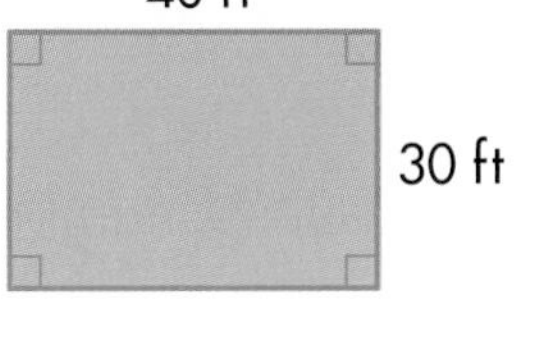
40 ft
30 ft

Lesson
1-3 Exponents and Place Value

Understand It!
Exponents show the number of times a factor is repeated.

How can you write a number using exponents?

Each place in a place-value chart has a value that is 10 times as great as the place to its right. Use this pattern to write 1,000,000 as repeated multiplication.

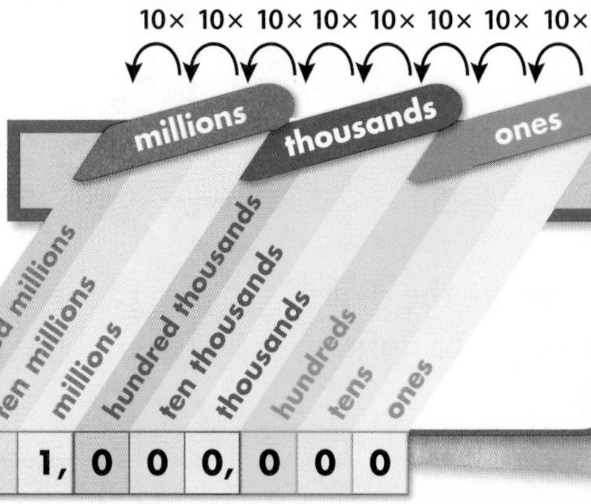

Another Example How do you write the expanded form of a number using exponents?

Standard form: 562,384

Expanded form: $(5 \times 100{,}000) + (6 \times 10{,}000) + (2 \times 1{,}000) + (3 \times 100) + (8 \times 10) + (4 \times 1)$

Expanded form using exponents: $(5 \times 10^5) + (6 \times 10^4) + (2 \times 10^3) + (3 \times 10^2) + (8 \times 10^1) + (4 \times 10^0)$

Any number raised to the first power always equals that number. $10^1 = 10$

Explain It

1. How many times is 9 used as a factor in the exponent 9^8?

2. Why does $3 \times 10^0 = 3$?

Other Examples

Write each in exponential form.

$36 = 6 \times 6 = 6^2$ — **6^2 is read as six squared.**

$10 \times 10 \times 10 = 10^3$ — **10^3 is read as ten cubed.**

Evaluate numbers in exponential form.

$5^3 = 5 \times 5 \times 5 = 125$

$3^4 = 3 \times 3 \times 3 \times 3 = 81$

10 is used as a factor six times.

1,000,000 = 10 × 10 × 10 × 10 × 10 × 10

You can write the repeated multiplication of a number in exponential form.

1,000,000 = 10^6

The base is the number that is repeatedly multiplied.

The exponent or power is the number of times the base is used as a factor.

Each place in the place-value chart can be written using an exponent.

Value	*Exponential Form*
100,000	10^5
10,000	10^4
1,000	10^3
100	10^2
10	10^1
1	10^0

Guided Practice*

Do you know HOW?

1. Write 10,000 as repeated multiplication.

2. Write 7 × 7 × 7 × 7 in exponential form.

3. Write 37,169 in expanded form using exponents.

4. Write 5^3 in standard form.

Do you UNDERSTAND?

5. In the example at the top, why was the number 10 used as the base to write 1,000,000 in exponential form?

6. How many times would 10 be repeatedly multiplied to equal 100,000?

7. How many zeros are in 10^7 when it is written in standard form?

Independent Practice

Leveled Practice What number is the base?

8. 4^9 **9.** 17^6

What number is the exponent?

10. 31^9 **11.** 2^{100}

Write each in exponential form.

Tip *Count the number of zeros in each number.*

12. 1,000 **13.** 1,000,000,000 **14.** 10 × 10 × 10 × 10 × 10

Write each number in expanded form using exponents.

15. 841 **16.** 5,832 **17.** 1,874,161 **18.** 22,600,000

Evaluate **19** through **22**.

19. $6^2 =$ ☐ **20.** $10^8 =$ ☐ **21.** $4^3 =$ ☐ **22.** $2^7 =$ ☐

DIGITAL Animated Glossary **www.pearsonsuccessnet.com**

*For another example, see Set B on page 28.

23. The population of one U.S. state is approximately 33,871,648. What is this number in expanded form using exponents?

24. Reasoning What number raised to both the first power and the second power equals 1?

25. Writing to Explain Explain how to compare 2^4 and 4^2.

26. In Exercise 23, what is the place of the digit 7?

A hundreds

B thousands

C ten thousands

D millions

27. Writing to Explain Kalesha was asked to write 80,808 in expanded form using exponents. Her response was $(8 \times 10^2) + (8 \times 10^1) + (8 \times 10^0)$. Explain where she made mistakes and write the correct response.

28. Think About the Process You invest $1 in a mutual fund. Every 8 years, your money doubles. If you don't add more money, which expression shows how much your investment is worth after 48 years?

A 1^{48}

B $1 \times 2 \times 2 \times 2 \times 2 \times 2$

C $1 + 2 + 2 + 2 + 2 + 2 + 2$

D $1 \times 2 \times 2 \times 2 \times 2 \times 2 \times 2$

29. Number Sense Using the map, write the population of the United States in expanded form using exponents.

30. In 1900, there were 76,803,887 people in the United States. How many more people were there in the United States in a recent year than in 1900?

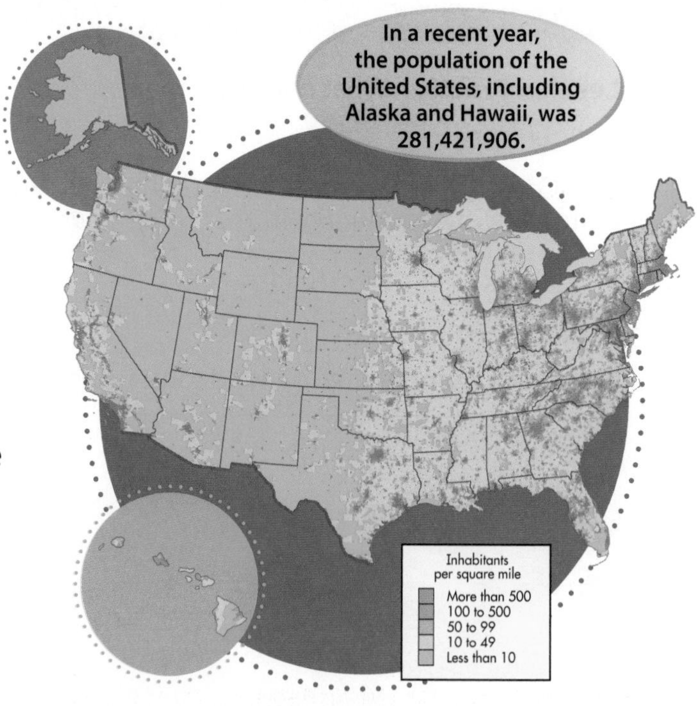

Algebra Connections

Solution Pairs

An equation is a mathematical sentence that uses an equals sign to show that two expressions are equal. Any values that make an equation true are solutions to the equation.

An inequality is a mathematical sentence that contains <, >, ≤, or ≥. Any value that makes the inequality true is a solution. You can graph the solutions of an inequality on a number line.

Tip *Read ≥ as "is greater than or equal to."*
Read ≤ as "is less than or equal to."

Example: Find two values for each variable that make the equation, $y = x + 3$, true.

If $x = 1$, then $y = 1 + 3 = 4$ is true.
If $x = 5$, then $y = 5 + 3 = 8$ is true.
(1, 4) and (5, 8) are solution pairs.

Example: Graph three values that make the inequality, $x > 3$, true.

$x = 3.1, x = 4, x = 5$

Draw a number line. Plot three points that are greater than 3.

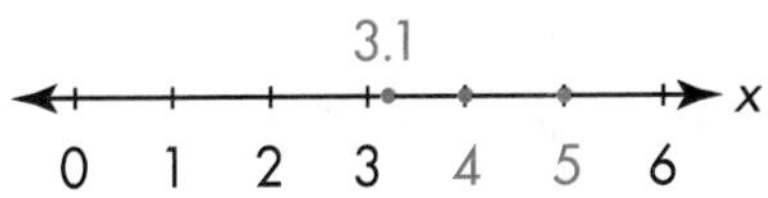

For **1** through **4**, copy the table and find two values for each variable that make the equation true.

1. $y = 4 + x$

x		
y		

2. $b = a - 2$

a		
b		

3. $t = 3w$

w		
t		

4. $y = x \div 2$

x		
y		

5. Copy the number line and graph three values that make the inequality, $d \geq 9$, true.

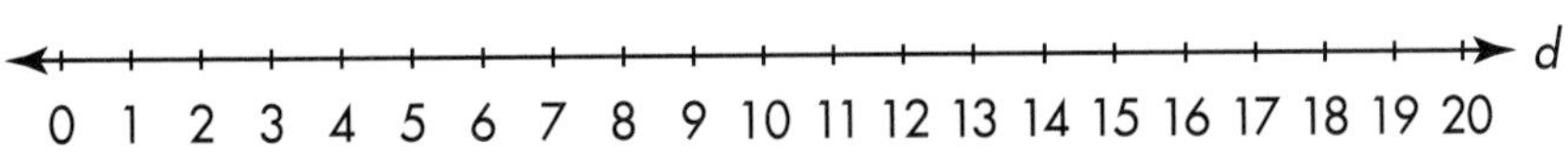

6. Copy the number line and graph three values that make the inequality, $\frac{x}{3} < 4$, true.

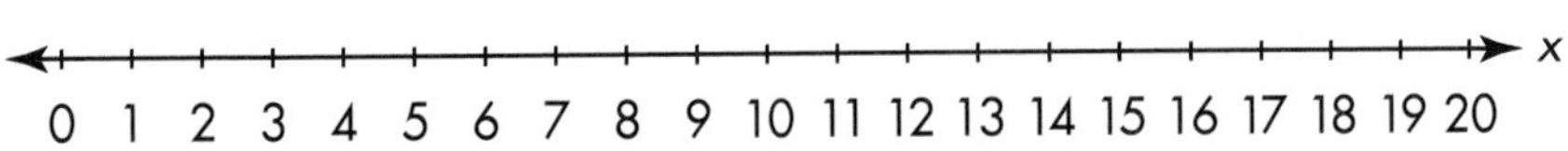

Lesson

1-4

Understand It!
The place-value system can be extended to include numbers between whole numbers.

Decimal Place Value

How can you read very small decimal numbers?

One gallon equals 3.7854 liters. How do you read this number?

A decimal is a number that uses a decimal point and has one or more digits to the right of the decimal point.

One bottle is filled with exactly 1 liter.
The other bottle is filled with exactly 1 gallon.

Another Example What are different ways to write decimals?

The atomic mass of the chemical chromium is 51.9961.
Use a place-value chart to write the decimal in different forms.

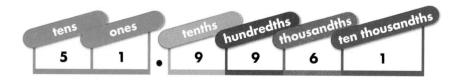

tens	ones		tenths	hundredths	thousandths	ten thousandths
5	1	.	9	9	6	1

Standard form: 51.9961

Short-word form: 51 and 9,961 ten thousandths

Word form: fifty-one and nine thousand nine hundred sixty-one ten thousandths

Expanded form: $(5 \times 10) + (1 \times 1) + (9 \times 0.1) + (9 \times 0.01) + (6 \times 0.001) + (1 \times 0.0001) =$
$50 + 1 + 0.9 + 0.09 + 0.006 + 0.0001$

Explain It

1. What is the purpose of the decimal point in a decimal number?

2. If the first digit to the right of the decimal was changed to "0" in the number above, how would you write the new number in different forms?

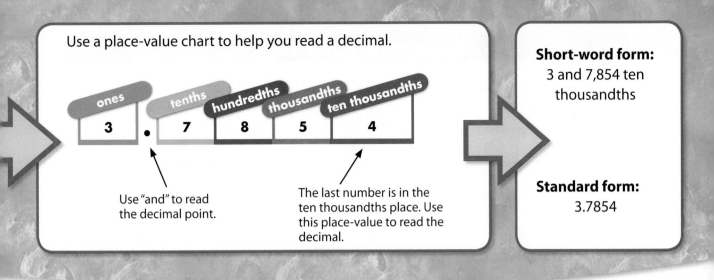

Use a place-value chart to help you read a decimal.

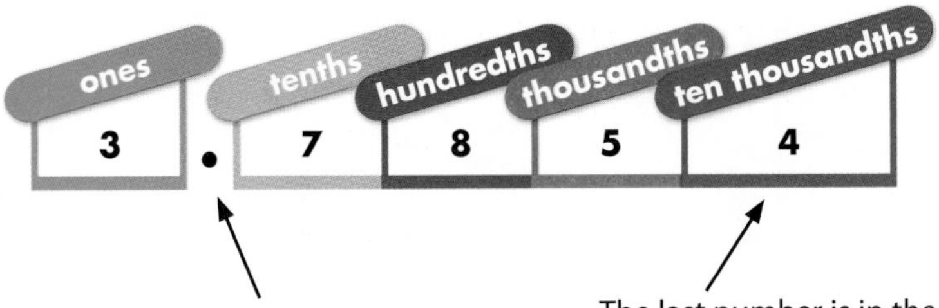

Use "and" to read the decimal point.

The last number is in the ten thousandths place. Use this place-value to read the decimal.

Short-word form:
3 and 7,854 ten thousandths

Standard form:
3.7854

Guided Practice*

Do you know HOW?

In **1** through **4**, write the place and value of the underlined digit.

1. $17.00\underline{1}$ **2.** $987.654\underline{2}$

3. $14.9\underline{2}84$ **4.** $7.291\underline{6}$

In **5** through **7**, write the number in the form indicated.

5. 1.5629 in word form

6. 568.0101 in short-word form

7. 27.6003 in expanded form

Do you UNDERSTAND?

8. How do you use a decimal point to read and write very small numbers?

9. In the example at the top of the page, how do you know that 0.005 is the value of the digit 5?

10. What is the decimal portion of 63.029? What is the whole number portion?

Independent Practice

Tip *All digits to the left of the decimal point are whole numbers, and all digits to the right of the decimal point are decimals.*

Write the place and value of the underlined digit.

11. $1{,}957.0\underline{1}$ **12.** $647.47\underline{6}$ **13.** $84.\underline{4}8$ **14.** $327.0\underline{0}94$

15. $0.05\underline{2}1$ **16.** $78.\underline{6}67$ **17.** $\underline{3}.016$ **18.** $8.591\underline{4}$

DIGITAL Animated Glossary
www.pearsonsuccessnet.com

**For another example, see Set C on page 28.*

Independent Practice

Use the place-value chart to answer **19** through **23**.

tens	ones	.	tenths	hundredths	thousandths	ten thousandths
2	2	.	9	8	0	8

19. What is the place value of the last digit?

20. From left to right, what is the value of the second 8 in the number?

21. How would you write the number in short-word form?

22. How would you write the number in word form?

23. How would you write the number in expanded form?

Problem Solving

24. **Number Sense** Write a decimal that has the digit 9 in the tenths place and the ten-thousandths place.

25. **Writing to Explain** What would happen if you removed the decimal point from a number?

Use this data table to answer items **26** through **29**.

Downhill Skiing Records

Old Record	New Record
154.165 mph	154.25 mph

26. **Number Sense** Which place do you use to tell that the new record is faster?

A tens **B** tenths **C** hundreds **D** thousandths

27 Which is the word form of the new record?

A one hundred fifty-four and one hundred sixty-five thousandths

B one hundred fifty-four and twenty-five thousandths

C one hundred fifty-four and twenty-five hundredths

D one hundred fifty-four

28. **Think About the Process** Which expression tells how to find how much faster the new record was?

A $154.165 + 154.25$ **C** 154.165×154.25

B $154.25 - 154.165$ **D** $154.25 \div 154.165$

29. **Writing to Explain** Explain why writing the new record as 154.250 mph does not change its value.

Mixed Problem Solving

Math and Science

Some Facts About the Grizzly Bear

Mass (adult)	681.82 kg
Height (adult)	2.1 m
Claw Length (adult)	10.16 cm

Use the table above to answer **1** through **3**.

1. Write the height of an adult grizzly bear in short-word form.

2. Write the length of an adult grizzly bear's claw length in expanded form.

3. If newborn grizzlies weigh about 0.45 kg, how many kilograms do grizzly bears gain from the time they are newborns until they are adults?

4. If a bear ran at a speed of 54.078 km/h, then increased its speed two-hundredths of a kilometer per hour, how fast would it be running?

5. A male grizzly can weigh twice as much as a female grizzly. How much would a female weigh if the male weighed 681.82?

6. The female grizzly has one to four cubs every other year. If a female has four cubs every other year for 12 years, how many cubs would she have given birth to?

7. If one cub weighed 0.45 kg and another cub weighed 1.23 kg, how much more would the heavier cub weigh than the lighter one?

Lesson
1-5

Understand It!
Place value and patterns can help you multiply and divide by powers of 10.

Multiplying and Dividing by 10, 100, and 1,000

How can you multiply by powers of 10?

The sailfish has been recorded swimming at speeds greater than 100 kilometers per hour. About how many miles per hour is this? Use 1 km ≈ 0.62 mi.

Choose an Operation Multiply 0.62 × 100 to convert 100 kilometers to miles.

Another Example How can you divide by powers of 10?

Find 5.7 ÷ 1,000 or 5.7 ÷ 10^3.

A relationship exists between divisors that are powers of 10, their exponential forms, and the number of places the decimal point is moved to the left to find the quotient.

Divisor	*Exponential Form*	*Decimal Point Moves Left*
10	10^1	1 place
100	10^2	2 places
1,000	10^3	3 places

5.7 ÷ 1,000 = 0.005.7

Move the decimal point 3 places to the left. Annex zeros in the tenths and hundredths places.

5.7 ÷ 10^3 = 0.005.7

5.7 ÷ 1,000 = 0.0057 or 5.7 ÷ 10^3 = 0.0057

Explain It

1. Use the pattern in the table above. How many places to the left would you move the decimal point in the dividend to divide by 10,000?

2. If the dividend is 641.2 and the quotient is 6.412, what is the divisor in standard form and in exponential form?

The table shows the relationship between the number of zeros in factors that are powers of 10, their exponential forms, and the number of places the decimal point of another factor is moved to the right to find the product.

Factor	Exponential Form	Decimal Point Moves Right
10	10^1	1 place
100	10^2	2 places
1,000	10^3	3 places

Find 0.62 × 100.

To multiply by 100, or 10^2, move the decimal point 2 places to the right. Annex zeros if needed.

0.62 × 100 = .62

The decimal point moves 2 places to the right.

0.62 × 100 = 62

100 kilometers is about 62 miles. Sailfish can swim faster than 62 miles per hour.

Guided Practice*

Do you know HOW?

In **1** through **4**, find each missing number.

Tip *Make sure you move the decimal point in the correct direction.*

1. 3.98 × 10 = ▢

2. 95.2 × ▢ = 9,520

3. 1,342.9 ÷ ▢ = 1.3429

4. 2.601 ÷ 10^2 = ▢

Do you UNDERSTAND?

5. Explain how to move the decimal point when you are multiplying by a power of 10.

6. Suppose a jet is flying 1,000 kilometers per hour. How many zeros would you need to annex to multiply 0.62 × 1,000? What is the product?

Independent Practice

In **7** through **18**, find each missing number.

7. 60.014 × ▢ = 600.14

8. 34.12 × 100 = ▢

9. 80.9 × 100 = ▢

10. 127.3 × 1,000 = ▢

11. 5,100 ÷ ▢ = 51

12. 8,231 ÷ 10,000 = ▢

13. 41.2 ÷ 10^1 = ▢

14. 1,304.25 ÷ 10^3 = ▢

15. 8 ÷ ▢ = 0.008

16. 0.0603 × ▢ = 603

17. 905.01 ÷ ▢ = 9.0501

18. 459.532 × ▢ = 459,532

For another example, see Set D on page 29.

Problem Solving

19. Number Sense What number do you get when you divide 504 by 1,000?

20. Writing to Explain Jimmy says that if you multiply any whole number or decimal by 100, all you have to do is move the decimal point to the hundreds place. Is he right?

21. Which 5 in 32,535,832,708 has the greatest value? How do you know?

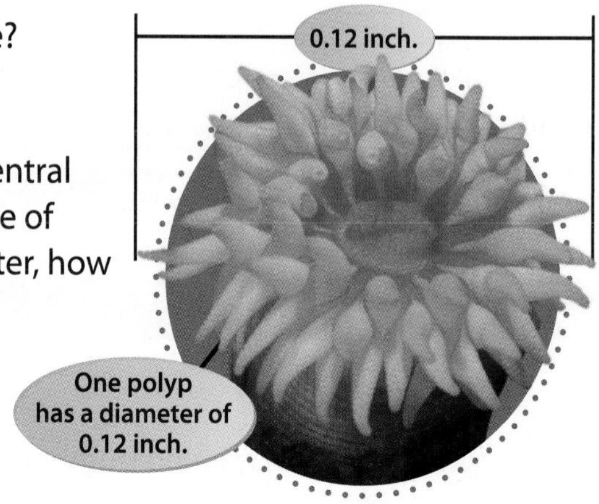
0.12 inch.
One polyp has a diameter of 0.12 inch.

22. A coral polyp is a tubular saclike animal with a central mouth surrounded by a ring of tentacles. The size of polyps varies. If each polyp is 0.12 inch in diameter, how many polyps would fit in a row 12 inches long?

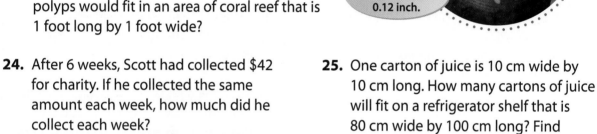

23. If each polyp is 0.12 inch in diameter, how many polyps would fit in an area of coral reef that is 1 foot long by 1 foot wide?

24. After 6 weeks, Scott had collected $42 for charity. If he collected the same amount each week, how much did he collect each week?

25. One carton of juice is 10 cm wide by 10 cm long. How many cartons of juice will fit on a refrigerator shelf that is 80 cm wide by 100 cm long? Find $(80 \times 100) \div (10 \times 10)$.

26. In 2005, the estimated population of Jacksonville, FL, was 782,623; of Indianapolis, IN, was 784,118; and of Columbus, OH, was 730,657. Order the populations of the three cities from greatest to least.

27. Writing to Explain Why can you just move the decimal point to find a solution when you multiply or divide by 10, 100, or 1,000, but not when you multiply or divide by a number that is not a power of 10?

28. A *googol* is described as 10^{100}. How many zeros are in a googol written in standard form?

29. A megabyte of computer memory can be estimated as 10^6 bytes. Write 10^6 in standard form.

30. Think About the Process A bottle contains 1,500 milliliters of water. Which expression can be used to find the number of 100-milliliter glasses that can be filled with water?

A 1.5×100

B $1{,}500 \div 100$

C $1.5 \div 100$

D $150 \div 100$

31. Think About the Process Suppose that one bacterial cell divides every 30 minutes to make 2 cells. Which expression will find how many cells there will be after 3 hours?

A $1 \times 2 \times 2 \times 2 \times 2 \times 2$

B 2×30

C $1 \times 2 \times 2 \times 2 \times 2 \times 2 \times 2$

D $2 \times 2 \times 30$

Enrichment

Roman Numerals

The numbers we use every day are part of the decimal number system. In ancient Rome, a system of letters, called *Roman numerals*, was used to represent numbers. Roman numerals are based on adding and subtracting.

The seven Roman numerals are shown in the table below. These letters can be combined.

Data

Roman Numeral	Value
I	1
V	5
X	10
L	50
C	100
D	500
M	1,000

Rules for Roman Numerals

1. If the value of a letter is greater than or equal to the value of the letter to its right, add. Write the values of VI and CCC.

V ↓ 5, I ↓ 1: 5 + 1 = 6

C ↓ 100, C ↓ 100, C ↓ 100: 100 + 100 + 100 = 300

2. If the value of a letter is less than the value of the letter to its right, subtract. Write the values of IV and XL.

I V: 5 − 1 = 4

X L: 50 − 10 = 40

3. A letter cannot be repeated more than three times in a row. There is no such numeral as CCCC; 400 is written as CD (500 − 100).

Example: Write the value of CMXXIX.

Think CM XX IX

= (1,000 − 100) + (10 + 10) + (10 − 1)

= 900 + 20 + 9 = 929

Practice

1. Write each missing Roman numeral in the table at the right.

Data

Number	Roman Numeral
3	
8	
13	
29	
105	
2,009	

For **2** through **9**, use the rules for reading and writing Roman numerals to write the value of each.

2. XIV **3.** MLX **4.** CCLIV **5.** MXVII

6. XLV **7.** XXIX **8.** XCVII **9.** LXXXIV

For **10** through **12**, tell whether each statement is true or false.

10. 33 = XXXIII **11.** DCCXXI = 721 **12.** 102 = IIC

Lesson

1-6

Understand It!
Comparing and ordering decimals is similar to comparing and ordering whole numbers.

Comparing and Ordering Decimals

How can you compare decimals?

Batting averages for a single season are shown for some baseball players. Which of the two batting averages circled is greater?

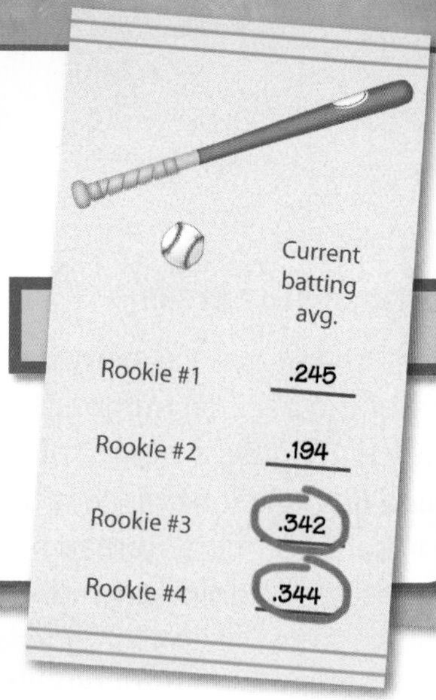

Another Example How do you order decimals using place value?

One Way Use a number line to order 4.002, 3.985, and 4.01 from least to greatest.

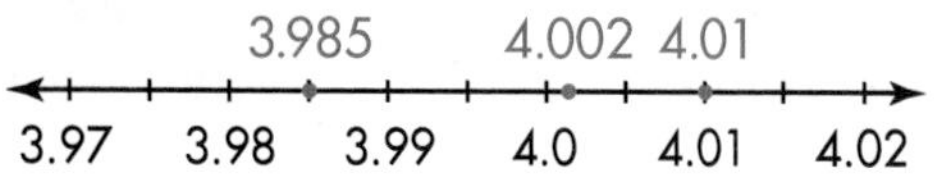

3.985 is left of 4.002 and 4.002 is left of 4.01. So, $3.985 < 4.002 < 4.01$.

Another Way Order 4.002, 3.985, and 4.01 from least to greatest by lining up the numbers so their decimal points align. Then compare digits from left to right and order the digits of each place value.

Order ones.	The tenths digits are the same.	Order hundredths.
4.002	3.985	3.985
3.985 ← Least	4.002	4.002
4.010	4.010	4.010 ← Greatest

Write your answer: 3.985, 4.002, 4.01

Guided Practice*

Do you know HOW?

In **1** through **4**, use $>$, $<$, or $=$.

1. 1.09 ◯ 1.9 **2.** 18.001 ◯ 18.01

3. 7.25 ◯ 7.3 **4.** 0.1 ◯ 0.1000

5. Order 7.08, 6.257, 7.6, 6.1, 6.29 from least to greatest.

Do you UNDERSTAND?

6. Explain why 46.69 is less than 46.7.

7. In the example at the top of the page, what place value determines which batting average is greater?

*For another example, see Set E on page 29.

One Way

Compare 0.342 and 0.344 by locating them on a number line.

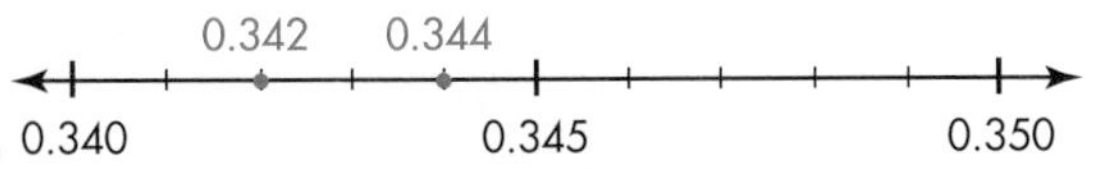

0.344 is right of 0.342 on the number line.

So, 0.344 > 0.342.

Another Way

Line the numbers up so their decimal points align.

0.342
0.344

Compare the digits from left to right.

0.342
0.344
4 > 2

So, 0.344 > 0.342.

Independent Practice

In **8** through **15**, use >, <, or = to compare each pair of numbers.

8. 5.084 ◯ 5.84 **9.** 52.01 ◯ 51.99 **10.** 0.721 ◯ 0.7021 **11.** 1.22 ◯ 1.222

12. 2.99 ◯ 2.9900 **13.** 438.783 ◯ 438.738 **14.** 3.1428 ◯ 3.1420 **15.** 3.35 ◯ 2.44

Order these numbers from least to greatest.

16. 12.23, 12.223, 12.322

17. 1.01, 1.0, 1.011, 1.001

18. 35.43, 35.435, 35.44, 35.451

19. 0.7841, 0.834, 0.705, 0.81

Problem Solving

20. Writing to Explain A redwood tree has a diameter of 30.2 ft. Lyndell says this tree has a smaller diameter than a tree with a diameter of 30.20 because 2 is less than 20. Is Lyndell correct? Explain.

21. Arliss ran the fitness run in 9.65 seconds. Bonita ran it in 9.9 seconds. Cory ran it in 9.625 seconds, and Darla ran it in 10 seconds. Who ran it in the least amount of time?

A Arliss
B Bonita
C Cory
D Darla

22. Reasoning Is a decimal with 4 digits always greater than a decimal with 3 digits? Give an example to explain.

23. Number Sense Name three decimals between 0.55 and 0.56.

Lesson
1-7

Understand It!
Some problems can be solved by making organized lists of the possible outcomes to the problem.

Problem Solving

Make an Organized List

Suppose you throw three darts at the target pictured on the right. All of the darts hit the target. How can you find all of the different total points that you could score?

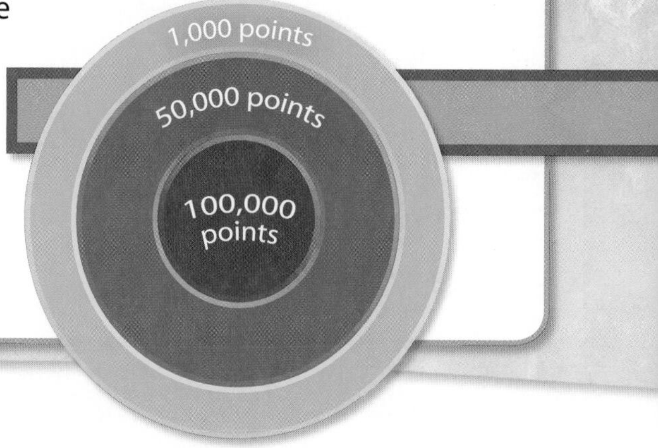

Guided Practice*

Do you know HOW?

Suppose two darts hit a target that has two rings. The outer ring is worth 50 points, and the inner ring is worth 150 points. Use this information to answer **1** and **2**.

1. Make an organized list to show all of the possible scores.

2. How many possible totals are there?

Do you UNDERSTAND?

3. In the example at the top, how is the list organized?

4. **Write a Problem** Write a problem that you can solve by making an organized list.

Independent Practice

Solve **5** by making an organized list. The list has been started for you.

5. Yolanda needs a 3-digit code for her locker. She wants to use the first three digits of her phone number, 763. How many different combinations using each of these digits does Yolanda have to choose from?

7	6	3
763	673	376

Stuck? Try this....

- What do I know?
- What am I asked to find?
- What diagram can I use to help understand the problem?
- Can I use addition, subtraction, multiplication, or division?
- Is all of my work correct?
- Did I answer the right question?
- Is my answer reasonable?

*For another example, see Set F on page 29.

Read and Understand

What do you know? There are 3 different point values on the target. All 3 darts hit the target.

What are you trying to find? What are the different total points that you could score?

Plan and Solve

Make an organized list to find all the possible scores.

There are ten different totals possible.

1,000	50,000	100,000	Total
✓✓✓			3,000
✓✓	✓		52,000
✓✓		✓	102,000
✓	✓✓		101,000
✓		✓✓	201,000
✓	✓	✓	151,000
	✓✓✓		150,000
	✓✓	✓	200,000
	✓	✓✓	250,000
		✓✓✓	300,000

Solve **6** using the art on the right.

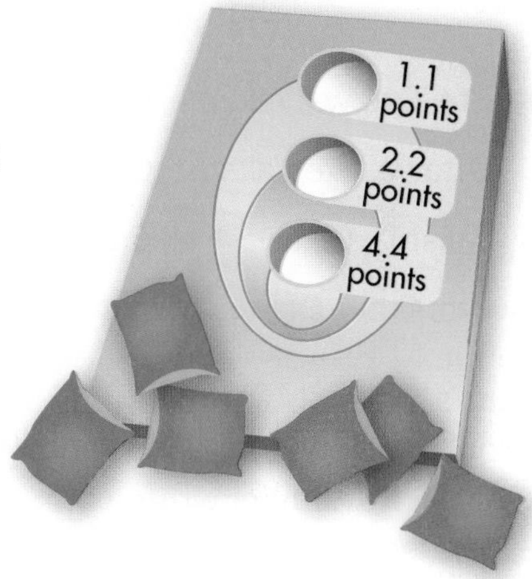

6. Randy went to the school fun fair and played the beanbag toss. He tossed 3 beanbags, and each went into a hole on the board. What are the possible total points he could have scored?

7. Ariana, Mia, Ethan, and Nick are planning a one-on-one basketball tournament. In the tournament, each player will play the other three just once. How many games will be played?

8. **Estimate** About how many eggs would be laid by 7 chickens if each chicken lays 36 eggs?

9. Is your estimate of the number of eggs 7 chickens could lay more or less than the actual answer? Explain.

10. Look for a pattern in the table of values at the right. Find a rule for the table.

Input	−2	3	9	17
Output	3	8	14	22

11. **Writing to Explain** How could you find the number of different ways to arrange 4 students in a row for a photo?

12. Dani has only quarters, dimes, and nickels in her bank. She needs $0.60 for the bus. She wants to use at least one quarter. How many different ways can Dani combine the coins to pay for the bus?

13. **Think About the Process** Cassie is making an organized list of all the different ways to arrange the letters WXYZ. Following Cassie's organization, which arrangement of letters will she place on the list next?

WXYZ
WXZY
WYXZ
WYZX
WZXY

A WZYX **B** XWYZ **C** YWXZ **D** ZWYZ

1. The table gives the number of members in some Native American tribes. Which lists the tribes from the least to the greatest membership? (1-2)

Tribe	Membership
Crow	13,394
Ottawa	10,677
Ute	10,385
Yakama	10,851

A Ute, Ottawa, Yakama, Crow

B Ottawa, Ute, Yakama, Crow

C Yakama, Ottawa, Ute, Crow

D Ute, Crow, Ottawa, Yakama

2. Pluto's mean distance from the Sun is about 5 billion 900 million kilometers. What is the number written in expanded form? (1-3)

A $(5 \times 10^9) + (9 \times 10^8)$

B $(5 \times 10^6) + (9 \times 10^5)$

C $(5 \times 10^9) + (9 \times 10^7)$

D $(5 \times 10^{12}) + (9 \times 10^8)$

3. Mario has 320 new plants to landscape 10 flowerbeds of a new office complex. If each flowerbed has the same number of plants, how many plants go in each flowerbed? (1-5)

A 3,200 plants

B 310 plants

C 32 plants

D 3 plants

4. What is the value of the 6 in 196,937,000? (1-1)

A 6 billion

B 6 million

C 6 hundred million

D 6 hundred thousand

5. Which of the following is equal to 5^4? (1-3)

A $4 \times 4 \times 4 \times 4 \times 4$

B 5×4

C $(4 \times 5)^4$

D $5 \times 5 \times 5 \times 5$

6. Which of the following is between 0.007 and 0.016? (1-6)

A 0.0008

B 0.070

C 0.0015

D 0.010

7. Which of the following is a way to write four and eight hundred two ten-thousandths? (1-4)

A 4.802

B 4.082

C 4.0802

D 4.0082

8. Which of the following lists the numbers in order from greatest to least? (1-6)

A 2.1027, 2.1127, 2.0127

B 2.1027, 2.0127, 2.1127

C 2.1127, 2.0127, 2.1027

D 2.1127, 2.1027, 2.0127

9. The record for the fastest car belongs to a British jet car that traveled at 763.035 miles per hour. What is this number written in expanded form? (1-4)

A $700 + 60 + 3 + 0.03 + 0.05$

B $700 + 60 + 3 + 0.3 + 0.5$

C $700 + 60 + 3 + 0.3 + 0.05$

D $700 + 60 + 3 + 0.03 + 0.005$

10. The maximum climbing speed of a three-toed sloth is 0.15 miles per hour. Which speed is less than 0.15 mph? (1-6)

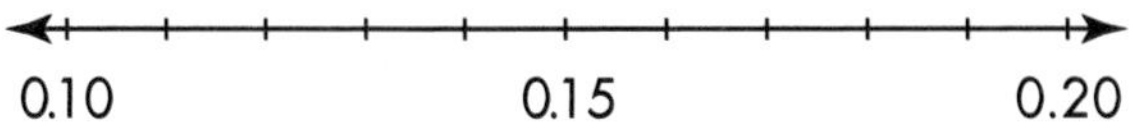

A 0.146 mph

B 0.162 mph

C 0.157 mph

D 0.153 mph

11. Which country listed in the table has a population greater than 188,078,227? (1-2)

Data

Country	Population
Bangladesh	147,365,352
Indonesia	245,452,739
Pakistan	165,803,560
Russia	142,893,540

A Bangladesh

B Indonesia

C Pakistan

D Russia

12. What is 0.043×100? (1-5)

A 43

B 4.3

C 0.43

D 0.0043

13. Which is 10,000,000 written in exponential form? (1-3)

A 7^{10}

B 10^7

C 10^8

D 8^{10}

14. In a recent year, the United States had about two trillion, two hundred two billion, six hundred million dollars in outstanding consumer credit. What is this number in standard form? (1-1)

A $2,202,600,000

B $2,000,202,600,000

C $2,202,600,000,000

D $200,202,600,000,000

15. Make a list to determine all the possible combinations of pennies, nickels, dimes, and quarters that total 25 cents. How many combinations are possible? (1-7)

A 13

B 11

C 9

D 4

Topic 2

Variables, Expressions, and Properties

1 How many flowers can decorate one float for the Tournament of Roses Parade®? You will find out in Lesson 2-1.

2 One of the world's tallest fountains is located in Fountain Hills, Arizona. How high does the fountain spray water into the air? You will find out in Lesson 2-5.

3

There have been 12 astronauts who have walked on the surface of the Moon. How many pounds of lunar rock and soil did theses astronauts bring back to Earth? You will find out in Lesson 2-6.

4

This superflag hung over Hoover Dam during the 1996 Olympic Torch relay. How many grommets does it take to hang the flag over the dam? You will find out in Lesson 2-3.

Review What You Know!

Vocabulary

Choose the best term from the box.

- algebraic expression
- exponential form
- variable
- compatible

1. A(n) __?__ is a mathematical phrase that includes at least one variable and one operation.
2. The __?__ of a number uses exponents to write the repeated multiplication of the number called the base.
3. Numbers that are easy to compute mentally are called __?__ numbers.
4. A(n) __?__ is a symbol, such as n, that takes the place of a number or value.

Evaluating Expressions

Evaluate each expression for $x = 4$ and $x = 7$.

5. $3x + 8$
6. $24 - 3x$
7. $5 + 5 + x$
8. $84 \div x$
9. $2x + 5 - x$
10. $9x$
11. $2x + 4$
12. $28 \div x$

Answer Terms

Writing to Explain Write an answer for each question.

13. How are these terms alike: differences, sums, quotients, and products?
14. What does it mean to evaluate an algebraic expression?

Lesson

2-1

Understand It!
An algebraic expression involves at least one variable and one operation.

Using Variables to Write Expressions

How can you write an algebraic expression?

Donnie bought CDs for $10 each. How can you represent the total cost of the CDs?

A variable is a quantity that can change or vary and is often represented with a letter. Variables help you translate word phrases into algebraic expressions.

Other Examples

The table shows algebraic expressions for given situations.

Word Phrase	Operation	Algebraic Expression
three dollars more than cost *c*	addition	$c + 3$
twelve pencils decreased by a number *n*	subtraction	$12 - n$
five times a distance *d*	multiplication	$5 \times d$ or $5d$
a apples divided by four	division	$a \div 4$ or $\frac{a}{4}$
five less than three times an amount *x*	multiplication and subtraction	$3x - 5$

Guided Practice*

Do you know HOW?

Write an algebraic expression for each situation.

1. the difference of a number *t* and 22
2. *m* bicycles added to 18 bicycles
3. 11 times a number *z*
4. 4 less than 5 times a number *g*

Do you UNDERSTAND?

5. In the example at the top of the page, what does the variable *n* represent?
6. Identify the variable and the operation in the algebraic expression 8*y*.
7. Write an algebraic expression for this situation: *n* more students than the 8 students sitting in each of the 3 rows.

DIGITAL Animated Glossary **www.pearsonsuccessnet.com**

For another example, see Set A on page 56.

CDs cost $10 each. The operation is multiplication.

Number of CDs	*Total Cost*
1	$\$10 \times 1$
2	$\$10 \times 2$
3	$\$10 \times 3$
4	$\$10 \times 4$

Use the variable n to represent the number of CDs and write an algebraic expression.

$$\$10 \times n$$

An algebraic expression is a mathematical phrase that has at least one variable and one operation. The total cost of the CDs is represented by

$$10 \times n$$

or $10n$.

The operation is multiplication. The variable is n.

Independent Practice

For **8** through **13**, write algebraic expressions.

8. A number p increased by 22

9. 15 divided by a number r

10. 12 more points than a number p times 8

11. 6 less than 7 times a number b

12. 5 more than the product of x and 9

13. 7 times the difference of y and 4

Problem Solving

14. The distance around a closed shape can be expressed as 3 times side s, or $3s$. Draw an example of this geometric shape.

15. Manuel sold a cartons of apple juice and r cartons of raisins. Write an algebraic expression to represent how many cartons were sold.

16. One float for the Tournament of Roses parade uses as many flowers as a florist usually uses in 5 years. If x is the number of flowers a florist uses in 1 year, write an algebraic expression for the number of flowers used to make a float.

17. **Writing to Explain** Devin's DVD case has 3 rows of slots, but 5 slots are broken. If x equals the number of slots in a row, explain how the expression $3x - 5$ relates to Devin's DVD case.

18. A group of hens laid the same number of eggs each day for a week. Kelly collected the eggs for six days. Write an expression to show the number of eggs Kelly did not collect.

19. **Think About the Process** Which expression shows a quantity of rolls, r, added to 8 bagels?

A $8 - r$

B $8r$

C $8 + r$

D $r \div 8$

Lesson
2-2

Understand It!
Properties of operations can help you rewrite expressions and simplify computations.

Properties of Operations

How can you use properties of operations to rewrite expressions?

The Commutative Property of Addition states the order in which numbers are added does not change the sum of the numbers. The Commutative Property of Multiplication states the order in which numbers are multiplied does not change the product of the numbers.

Commutative Properties

Addition

$a + b = b + a$

$8 + 18 = 18 + 8$

Multiplication

$a \times b = b \times a$

$5 \times 12 = 12 \times 5$

Guided Practice*

Do you know HOW?

Find each missing number. Tell what property is shown.

1. $19 + (42 + 8) = (\square + 42) + 8$
2. $12 + 8 = \square + 12$
3. $42 \times 8 \times 3 = 42 \times 8 \times \square \times 3$
4. $32 \times 85 = 85 \times \square$

Do you UNDERSTAND?

5. For the Identity Property, why does addition involve a zero and multiplication involve a one? Why don't they both use one or both use zero?
6. Yuen Lee put 3 cartons of markers in the closet. Each carton contains 3 rows of 7 boxes. Use one of the Associative Properties to show two different ways of finding the number of marker boxes.

Independent Practice

Find each missing number. Tell what property or properties are shown.

7. $\square \times (14 \times 32) = (5 \times 14) \times 32$
8. $5 + 23 + 4 = 23 + 4 + \square$
9. $25 + 0 + (3 + 16) = (25 + \square) + 3$
10. $(7 + 12) + 4 = (7 + \square) + 12$
11. $(5 \times 7) \times (3 \times 8) = (5 \times 3) \times (8 \times \square)$
12. $(43 \times 1) \times 4 = \square \times 43$
13. $(6 + 3) + 4 = 6 + (3 + \square)$
14. $(8 \times 9) \times \square = 8 \times (9 \times 10)$
15. $7 \times \square = 6 \times 7$
16. $15 + 48 = \square + 15$
17. $8 + \square = 4 + 8$
18. $(1 \times 2) \times 3 = \square \times (2 \times 3)$

DIGITAL
Animated Glossary
www.pearsonsuccessnet.com

For another example, see Set B on page 56.

The Associative Property of Addition states that the way numbers are grouped does not affect the sum.

$$a + (b + c) = (a + b) + c$$

$$2 + (8 + 10) = (2 + 8) + 10$$

The Associative Property of Multiplication states that the way numbers are grouped does not affect the product.

$$a \times (b \times c) = (a \times b) \times c$$

$$2 \times (4 \times 5) = (2 \times 4) \times 5$$

The Identity Property of Addition states that the sum of any number and zero is that number.

$$a + 0 = a$$

$$24 + 0 = 24$$

The Identity Property of Multiplication states that the product of a number and one is that number.

$$a \times 1 = a$$

$$36 \times 1 = 36$$

Find each missing number. Tell what property or properties are shown.

19. $(41 \times 43) \times (3 \times 19) = (41 \times \square) \times (19 \times 43)$

20. $(5 \times 3) \times \square = 5 \times (8 \times 3)$

21. $328 \times 1 = \square$

22. $(12 + 0) \times (1 \times 12) = \square \times \square$

Problem Solving

For **23** and **24**, use the table to the right.

23. Donnie and Pete live in Bluewater. They rode their bikes to Zink and then to Riverton. Then they rode back home, using the same route. Write a number sentence using the Commutative Property of Addition to show the distances each way.

24. Once they rode from Riverton to Red Rock, from Red Rock to Curry, and then rode back to Riverton. How many miles did they ride that time?

Data

Where Donnie and Pete Rode	Distance
Bluewater to Zink	13 miles
Zink to Riverton	9 miles
Riverton to Red Rock	12 miles
Red Rock to Curry	11 miles

25 **Think About the Process** Stage 15 of the Tour de France bicycle race includes legs from Gap to Embrun, Embrun to Guillestre, and Guillestre to Arvieux. One way to express the distance of these legs is 33.5 + (20.5 + 21.5). Which expression below is another way to express these legs?

A (23 + 33.5) + (20.5 − 21.5)

B (33.5 + 20.5) + 21.5

C 33.5 + (20.5 × 21.5)

D (33.5 × 21.5) + 20.5

26. Write the standard form for 6.45 billion.

27. **Writing to Explain** Can you use the Associative Properties with subtraction and division? Use (14 − 8) − 2 and 24 ÷ (4 ÷ 2) to explain.

Lesson
2-3

Understand It!
There are rules that organize the sequence of operations to follow when simplifying an expression.

Order of Operations

How do you know which operation to perform first?

Evaluate $14 + 8 \times 6$.

Adding first gives:

$14 + 8 \times 6$

22×6

132

Multiplying first gives:

$14 + 8 \times 6$

$14 + 48$

62

Other Examples

Evaluate $20 + (30 - 10) \div 5$.

Using order of operations:

$20 + (30 - 10) \div 5$ ← **Compute inside the parentheses first.**

$20 + 20 \div 5$ ← **Next, divide.**

$20 + 4$ ← **Finally, add.**

24

Using a scientific calculator:

Press:

20 [+] [(] 30 [−] 10 [)] [÷] 5 [ENTER =]

Display will read: 24

Evaluate $4^2 - (4 + 6) \div 2$.

Using order of operations:

$4^2 - (4 + 6) \div 2$ ← **Compute inside the parentheses first.**

$4^2 - 10 \div 2$ ← **Evaluate exponents.**

$16 - 10 \div 2$ ← **Then divide.**

$16 - 5$ ← **Finally, subtract.**

11

Using a scientific calculator:

Press:

4 [^] 2 [−] [(] 4 [+] 6 [)] [÷] 2 [ENTER =]

Display will read: 11

Explain It

1. To evaluate $3 \times (7 + 5)$, what should you do first and why?

2. In the second example using the scientific calculator, what is the purpose of the [^] key?

Mathematicians use a set of rules known as order of operations, the order in which to perform operations in calculations.

1. Compute inside parentheses.
2. Evaluate terms with exponents.
3. Multiply and divide from left to right.
4. Add and subtract from left to right.

Using the correct order of operations, $14 + 8 \times 6 = 62$.
A scientific calculator uses order of operations.

Press: 14 [+] 8 [×] 6 [ENTER =]

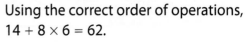

Display will read: 62

Guided Practice*

Do you know HOW?

Evaluate each expression.

1. $36 \div 6 + 6$

2. $36 \div (6 + 6)$

3. $24 \div (4 + 8) + 2$

4. $48 \div (4 + 8) + 2^2$

5. $24 \div 4 + 8 + 2$

6. $48 \div 4 + 8 + 2^2$

Do you UNDERSTAND?

7. Where could you insert parentheses to make this number sentence true?
$80 \div 8 \times 5 + 4 = 90$

8. Donavan entered $12 + 4 \times 3 - 6$ into Lidia's scientific calculator. The display showed 18. In what order did the calculator complete the operations?

Independent Practice

Evaluate each expression.

9. $3^3 - 8 \times 3$

10. $(5^2 + 7) \div 4$

11. $6 \times 4 - 4 + 2$

12. $18 - 3 \times 5 + 2$

13. $49 - 4 \times (49 \div 7)$

14. $(64 \div 8) \times 3 + 6$

15. $72 \div (4 + 4) \times 5$

16. $(3 \times 3) \times (2 \times 2) \div 36$

Use parentheses to make each number sentence true.

17. $5 + 4 \times 3 \times 3 = 41$

18. $9 \times 0 + 4 = 36$

19. $5^2 - 6 \times 0 = 25$

20. $8 \times 9 - 2 - 3 = 32$

21. $5 + 4 \times 3 \times 3 = 81$

22. $9 \times 0 + 4 = 4$

23. $5^2 - 6 \times 0 = 0$

24. $8 \times 9 - 2 - 3 = 53$

25. $1 + 2 \times 3 + 4 = 21$

26. $2^2 + 4 \times 6 = 48$

27. $5 \times 6 \times 8 - 7 = 30$

28. $6^2 + 7 + 9 \times 10 = 133$

DIGITAL Animated Glossary
www.pearsonsuccessnet.com

**For another example, see Set C on page 57.*

29. **Number Sense** Use the symbols +, −, ×, and ÷ to make the number sentence true.

(3 ☐ 5) ☐ 4 ☐ (14 ☐ 2) = 12

30. Meredith bought 3 T-shirts for $12.00 each. Her grandmother paid for half the total cost. To find how much Meredith paid, evaluate the expression: $(3 \times 12) \div 2$.

31. Luke needs a new fence around his garden, but the gate across the narrow end of the garden will not be replaced. To find how many feet of fencing Luke needs, evaluate the expression: $12 + (2 \times 14)$.

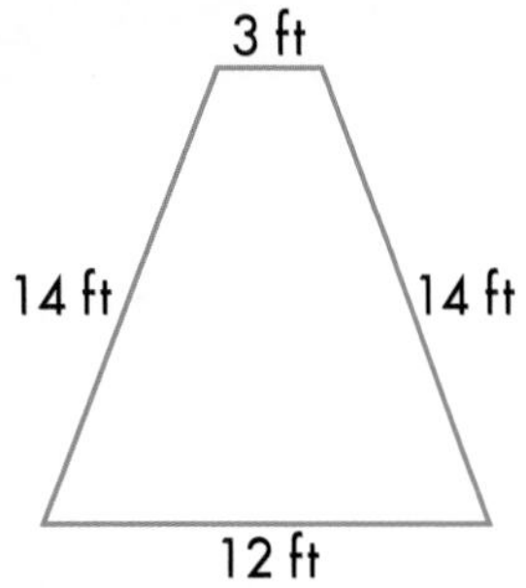

32. **Writing to Explain** If p is greater than zero, tell which of these expressions will result in the higher number: $(2 \times p) + 5$ or $2 \times (p + 5)$. Explain how you know.

33. Jaron walked 15 blocks north and then 3 blocks west to school. Marisol walked 3 blocks east and then 15 blocks south to school. Write an equation to show that each traveled the same distance.

34. On Saturday, every seat in Mazen Theater was full. The balcony has 10 rows with 22 seats in each. The main floor has 25 rows with 30 seats each. To find the number of people at the theater, evaluate the following expression: $(10 \times 22) + (25 \times 30)$.

A 16 **C** 970

B 87 **D** 14,100

35. On her math test, Bianca scored 5 points on each of 5 questions, 2 points on each of 2 questions, and 3 points on each of 4 questions. To find the number of points she scored, evaluate the expression: $5^2 + 2^2 + (3 \times 4)$.

A 26 **C** 41

B 40 **D** 84

36. The world's largest flag measures 505 ft by 225 ft. The flag hangs by a cable through grommets on one of the shorter sides. There is a grommet every 30 in. If there is a grommet at each end, evaluate the expression $1 + (225 \times 12) \div 30$ to find out how many grommets are used to hang the flag.

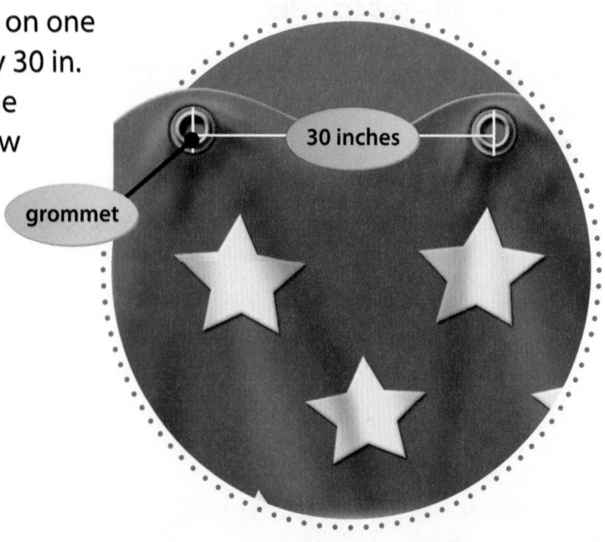

Going Digital

Exponents and Order of Operations

Evaluate 5^6 on a calculator two ways.

Step 1 Use the exponent key [^].

Press: 5 [^] 6 [ENTER =]

Display: 15625

Step 2 Use repeated multiplication.

5 [×] 5 [×] 5 [×] 5 [×] 5 [×] 5 [ENTER =]

Display: 15625

Evaluate $9^3 + (27 \div 3 + 47)$ on a calculator two ways.

Step 1 Use the calculator's order of operations.

9 [^] 3 [+] [(] 27 [÷] 3 [+] 47 [)] [ENTER =]

Display: 785

Step 2 Follow order of operations to verify that the calculator used the correct order of operations.

27 [÷] 3 [ENTER =] [+] 47 [ENTER =]

Display: 9 56

9 [^] 3 [ENTER =] [+] 56 [ENTER =]

Display: 729 785

Practice

Evaluate each expression two ways.

1. 8^5

2. 7^4

3. $8 \times 19 - 36 + 12^5$

4. $(72 \div 9) + 6 \times 3^5$

5. 3^7

6. $1204 \div 14 - 2^5 + 178$

Lesson

2-4

Understand It!
You can use the Distributive Property to compute some products mentally.

The Distributive Property

How can you use the Distributive Property to evaluate expressions?

The Distributive Property states that multiplying a sum (or difference) by a number gives the same result as multiplying each number in the sum (or difference) by the number and adding (or subtracting) the products.

Distributive Property

$a(b+c) = a(b) + a(c)$ $a(b-c) = a(b) - a(c)$

Guided Practice*

Do you know HOW?

In **1** through **4**, find each missing number.

1. 8(7 + 23) = 8(7) + 8( )
2. 4(28) = 4(20) + 4 ( )
3. 8(57) − 8(7) = 8( )
4. 5(26 − 3) = 5 ( ) − 5(3)

Do you UNDERSTAND?

5. Why is it easier to evaluate 7 × 60 than to evaluate 7 × 55 + 7 × 5?
6. Tony read 22 pages in the morning and 28 pages in the afternoon for 5 days. Lois read 47 pages each day for 5 days. Explain how to use the Distributive Property to find how many pages each of them read.

Independent Practice

Leveled Practice In **7** through **16**, use the Distributive Property to find each missing number.

7. 6(32) = 6( ) + 6(2)
8. 20(5) − 20(2) = 20( )
9. 3(28) + (3)2 = ( )(30)
10. 9(23) = 9( ) + 9(3)
11. 6(46) − 6(6) = 6( )
12. 4(33) = 4(30) + 4( )
13. 30(22 − 10) = 30(22) − 30( )
14. 8(99) = 8(100) − 8( )
15. 20(33 − 5) = 20( )
    = 20( ) + 20(8)
16. 5(42) + 5(5) = 5( )
    = 5( ) + 5(7)

DIGITAL Animated Glossary **www.pearsonsuccessnet.com**

*For another example, see Set D on page 57.

Use the Distributive Property to break apart a number to find the product for 5×27.

5×27 ← **Break 27 apart.**

$5(20 + 7)$ ← **27 =** 20 7

$5(20) + 5(7)$ ← **Multiply each addend.**

$100 + 35$ ← **Add.**

135

$\mathbf{5 \times 27 = 135}$

Use the Distributive Property to join numbers together to find $8(32) - 8(2)$.

$8(32) - 8(2)$

$8(32 - 2)$ ← **Join factors.**

$8(30)$ ← **Subtract.**

240 ← **Multiply.**

$\mathbf{8(32) - 8(2) = 240}$

Independent Practice

Use the Distributive Property and mental math to evaluate.

Tip *When doing mental math, choose to join or break apart based on which is easier.*

17. $7(29)$ **18.** $6(21) + 6(31)$ **19.** $5(22) + 5(8)$ **20.** $8(47)$

21. $6(41) + 6(9)$ **22.** $30(3) + 30(5)$ **23.** $3(21) - 3(11)$ **24.** $5(25 - 3)$

Problem Solving

25. **Writing to Explain** The 6th graders ordered lunch from the Big Group Menu. They ordered 22 organic chilis and 8 veggie plates. Their order can be expressed as $6(22) + 6(8)$. Explain what mental math steps you would use to find the total cost of the order.

Data

Big Group Menu	
Organic Chili	$6.00
Chicken Tacos	$4.00
Fruit Salad	$5.00
Organic Salad	$5.00
Veggie Plate	$6.00

26. Using the Big Group Menu, write and solve a problem where you can use the Distributive Property.

27. **Writing to Explain** Jamal said that 9.45 is greater than 9.8 because 45 is greater than 8. Is he correct? Explain.

28. Hiroko put money in a savings account each week. After 9 weeks, there was $49.50 in the account. If Hiroko put the same amount in each week, how much did she save each week?

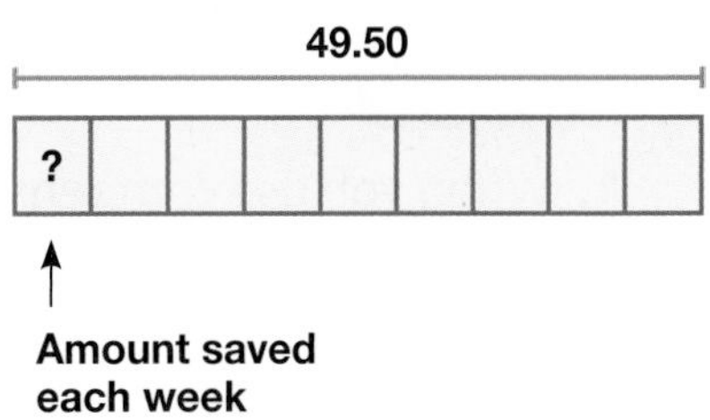

29. **Think About the Process** Which choice shows a problem with common factors that could be used for mental math?

A $3(45) + 3(5)$ **B** $4(18) - 7(8)$ **C** $2(22) + 3(33)$ **D** $8(39) + 4(40)$

Lesson

2-5

Understand It!
You can compute mentally by breaking apart numbers, using compatible numbers, and applying properties of operations.

Mental Math

How can you break apart numbers to compute mentally?

Jo has to read 45 history pages and 46 science pages by the end of next week.

How many total pages must Jo read?

Another Example What other strategies can you use to compute mentally?

Look for compatible numbers and use properties of operations to compute mentally.

$5 \times 28 \times 20$
$(5 \times 20) \times 28$
100×28
$2{,}800$

$42 + 39 + 8$
$(42 + 8) + 39$
$50 + 39$
89

Tip *Use the Commutative and Associative Properties when multiplying or adding.*

Use compensation to create compatible numbers that are easy to compute mentally.

$57 + 698$
$(57 - 2) + (698 + 2)$
$55 + 700$
755

$355 - 297$
$355 - (297 + 3)$
$355 - 300$
$55 + 3$
58

$5(89)$
$5(90 - 1)$
$5(90) - 5(1)$
$450 - 5$
445

Explain It

1. When you use compensation to subtract, why must you add to the difference you find?

2. When you use compensation to multiply, which property are you using?

Use mental math.

Break apart the numbers into tens and ones.

$$\begin{array}{r} 45 = 40 + 5 \\ \underline{+\ 46} = \underline{40 + 6} \end{array}$$

Do simpler calculations: Add the tens and add the ones.

$$\begin{array}{r} 40 + 5 \\ \underline{+\ 40 + 6} \\ 80 + 11 \end{array}$$

Combine the sums. $80 + 11 = 91$

So, $45 + 46 = 91$.

Explain why breaking apart the numbers works.

$(40 + 5) + (40 + 6)$ ← **Break apart numbers.**

$(40 + 40) + (5 + 6)$ ← **Use Commutative and Associative Properties.**

$80 + 11$ ← **Add.**

91 ← **Add.**

Jo has 91 pages to read.

Guided Practice*

Do you know HOW?

Compute mentally.

1. $89 + 32 + 8$

2. $76 + 59 + 6$

3. $2 \times 9 \times 20$

4. $5 \times 31 \times 2$

5. 8×39

6. $48 + 52$

7. $453 - 397$

8. $6(42)$

Do you UNDERSTAND?

9. When you use the Compensation Strategy in a problem such as 5×698, you turn one multiplication problem into two and then combine them. Why does this idea make sense?

10. Jo has to read 2 science chapters for each of the next 5 weeks. Each chapter is 45 pages long. How many pages does she have to read?

Independent Practice

Compute mentally.

11. $10 + 23 + 130$

12. $721 - 395$

13. $2 \times 38 \times 5$

14. $28 + 26 + 32 + 14$

15. $5 \times 3 \times 40$

16. $(856 - 400) - 3$

17. $6(69)$

18. $80 \times 10 \times 5$

19. $44 + 56$

20. $840 + 260 + 72$

21. $495 + 75 + 14$

22. $397 + 255$

23. $8(82)$

24. $4 \times 5 \times 25$

*For another example, see Set E on page 58.

Problem Solving

Use the data table for **25** and **26**. Find the answers mentally.

Jacob's earnings on his paper route this month	
Week 1	$45
Week 2	$32
Week 3	$55
Week 4	$64

25. How much did Jacob make during the first three weeks?

26. Jamal earned $5 for every dollar Jacob earned during week 4 on his paper route. How much money did Jamal earn?

27. Writing to Explain Avis swam her first lap in 32 seconds and her second lap in 45 seconds. Explain the steps you can use to mentally calculate her total time.

28. Use the break-apart strategy to mentally solve 81 + 43 + 2.

29. Draw It Copy and complete the bar diagram to show how to use the Distributive Property to mentally compute the problem below.

Four friends are having a snack. They each have 8 strawberries and 22 blueberries. How many berries do they have altogether?

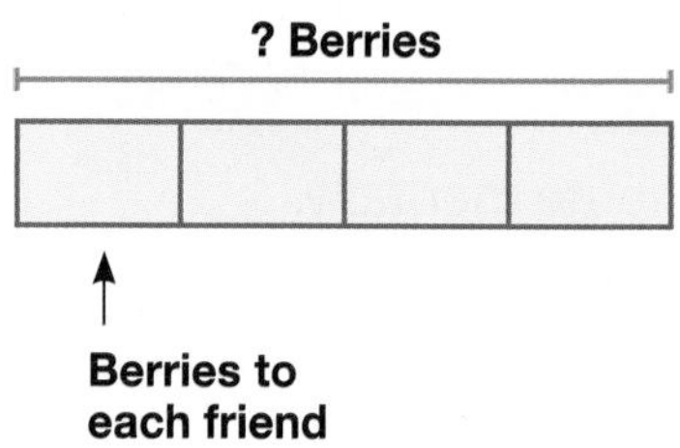

30. Number Sense What kind of numbers would make 3-factor multiplication problems easy to do mentally?

31. Writing to Explain Explain how you can use the Distributive Property to multiply 6 and 82.

One of the world's tallest fountains shoots water 171 m into the air once per hour. Use this information for **32** and **33**.

32. Think About the Process Which expression shows a break-apart strategy to mentally calculate the total of the heights of the water this fountain shoots in the air in 5 hours?

A 171×5 **B** $5(100 \times 71)$ **C** $170 \times 5 + 1$ **D** $5(100 + 70 + 1)$

33. The fountain sprays water for 15 minutes during every hour between 10:00 A.M. and 9:00 P.M. If the fountain sprayed water 10 times higher than it does, how high would the water shoot up? Solve mentally, and then check your answer.

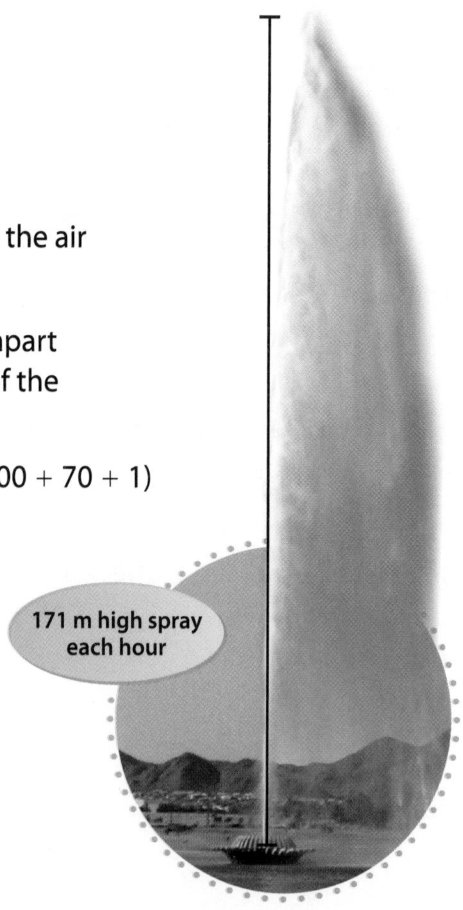

Mixed Problem Solving

Counting Calories

Calories come from the food you eat. Your body converts those calories into the energy you need every day.

After class, the sixth grade had the snack foods shown in the chart. For **1** through **5**, write an expression to show how many calories the person ate. Then, evaluate each expression.

Tip *Make sure to watch the units on the chart compared to the units in the problems.*

Data

Calories in Snack Foods

Snack Food	Calories	Snack Food	Calories
Dried Fruit (oz)		**Fruit (med)**	
raisins	115	apple	80
apricots	40	banana	105
dates	70	orange	60
Other (cup)		peach	35
pretzels	60	**Veggies (cup)**	
plain popcorn	25	carrots	70
Cheese (oz)		celery	20
cheddar	105	**Nuts (tbsp)**	
low fat cottage cheese	25	almonds	55
		Brazil nuts	60
Swiss	105	cashews	50
		peanuts	50

1. Wen-Wei ate a peach and an apple for lunch. After class, he ate 2 cups of celery and 8 tablespoons of peanuts. How many calories did he eat after class?

2. Andrea ate 3 tablespoons of Brazil nuts. Then she ate 2 more tablespoons. Later, she ate another 4 tablespoons.

3. Gloria ate 2 ounces of low fat cottage cheese, a cup of carrots, and 6 tablespoons of cashews. Then, she went back and got 4 more tablespoons of cashews and an orange. She ate everything but half of the orange.

4. Ayesha ate 4 cups of celery, 3 oranges, and 2 ounces of Swiss cheese.

5. Daryl took 2 oz dried apricots, 4 tbsp almonds, and 2 cups of pretzels. He ate all of it, except for 1 oz of apricots.

For **6** and **7**, write an expression that describes the situation, and then evaluate the expression.

6. Paulo took 4 bananas, 6 ounces of dates, 4 ounces of cheddar cheese, and 2 ounces of Swiss cheese. He split it all evenly with Alex. How many calories did Paulo eat?

7. Kyle filled a basket with 10 cups of plain popcorn. He shared it equally with 4 other people. Then, he got an apple and shared it equally with 1 other person. On his last trip to the snack table, he took 3 ounces of raisins, but he tripped and dropped 1 ounce of them. How many calories did Kyle eat?

Lesson
2-6

Understand It!
Expressions can be evaluated by substituting given values for the variables.

Evaluating Expressions

How can you evaluate an algebraic expression?

Willie has one large case that holds 20 miniature racecars. He also has 3 smaller cases with miniature racecars.

The number of miniature cars Willie has can be expressed as $20 + 3x$. How many miniature cars does he have if each smaller case holds 14 cars?

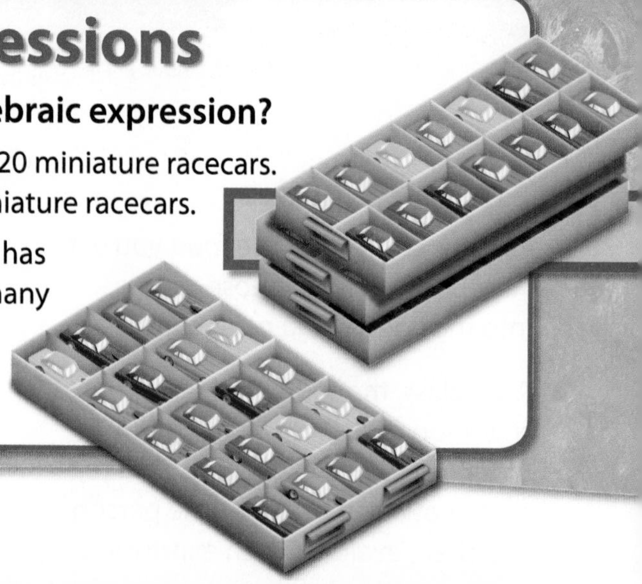

Guided Practice*

Do you know HOW?

Use substitution to evaluate.

Tip *Remember that substituting means to replace the variable with a value.*

1. $t - 8; t = 18$

2. $6(w) + 9; w = 3$

3. $2x \div 4; x = 12$

4. $3z + 4 - 2z; z = 5$

5. $p + (8p - 4); p = 9$

Do you UNDERSTAND?

6. Why is it important to use order of operations to evaluate algebraic expressions?

7. Suppose that Willie's large case holds 36 cars, and the 3 small cases each hold 18 cars. Write an algebraic expression to represent the number of cars. Then, evaluate the expression for $x = 18$.

Independent Practice

For **8** through **22**, evaluate each expression for 3, 4, and 10.

Tip *Remember to keep the order of operations in mind.*

8. $9x$

9. $3x + 6$

10. $48 \div x$

11. $x(0)$

12. $1x$

13. $x(4) \div 2$

14. $x - 3$

15. $x^2 + 1$

16. $x \div x$

17. $100 - x^2$

18. $3x + 4x$

19. $2x + 7$

20. $3x + 9$

21. $5x + 6x$

22. $x^2 - 1$

23. Evaluate the expression for the values of n.

n	3	5	8	12	25
$2 + 3n$					

24. Evaluate the expression for the values of k.

k	6	9	12
$2(k - 4)$			

DIGITAL
Animated Glossary
www.pearsonsuccessnet.com

For another example, see Set F on page 58.

Evaluate $20 + 3x$.

Evaluate means to find a value of an expression. To evaluate an algebraic expression, use substitution to replace the variable with a number.

If x equals the number of miniature cars in each smaller case, then evaluate for $x = 14$.

$$20 + 3(14)$$

$$20 + 42$$

$$62$$

Willie has 62 miniature racecars.

Suppose that the smaller cases each hold 10 miniature cars. How many cars would he have then?

$$20 + 3x$$

$$20 + 3(10)$$

$$50$$

Willie would have 50 cars.

x	$20 + 3x$
14	62
10	50

Problem Solving

Use the table at right for **25** and **26**.

Data

Vehicle	Week	Day
Small car	$250	$100
Medium car	$290	$110
Luxury car	$325	$120
Small van	$350	$150
Large van	$390	$170

25. Corinne wants to rent a small white car. It will cost the weekly fee plus 30¢ per mile. Write an expression that shows the amount Corinne will owe for her car. Then solve for 100 miles.

26. Trey is renting a luxury car for a week and a few days. He does not have to pay a per-mile fee. Write an expression that shows the amount Trey will owe for his car. Then solve for an 11-day rental.

27. **Writing to Explain** What operations are involved in the expressions $2x + 7$ and $3x + 6$?

28. There have been more than 70 spacecrafts to the Moon and 12 astronauts have walked on the surface on the Moon. They have brought back 842 pounds of lunar rock and soil back to Earth. If x equals the average number of pounds of lunar rock and soil brought back by each astronaut, evaluate $12x = 842$ to find the value of x.

29. The Moon is about 238,900 miles from Earth. Which expression best shows the distance, d, to the Moon from a spacecraft that is directly between the Earth and the Moon and is 50,000 miles from Earth?

A $50{,}000 + d = 238{,}900$

B $50{,}000 - d = 238{,}900$

C $d + 238{,}900 = 50{,}000$

D $50{,}000d = 238{,}900$

Lesson

2-7

Understand It!
Recognizing the pattern that relates to quantities represented in a table helps to extend the table.

Using Expressions to Describe Patterns

How can you write expressions to describe patterns?

Delvin saves a part of everything he earns. The table at the right shows Delvin's savings pattern.

The INPUT column shows the money he has earned. The OUTPUT column shows the money he has saved.

Write an expression to describe the pattern.

INPUT	*OUTPUT*
\$84	\$42
\$66	\$33
\$50	\$25
\$22	
\$30	

Guided Practice*

Do you know HOW?

Use the input/output table for **1** and **2**.

INPUT	0	1	2	3	4
OUTPUT	3	4	5	6	7

1. If the input number is 8, what is the output number?

2. Write an algebraic expression that describes the output pattern.

Do you UNDERSTAND?

3. Suppose that Delvin earned \$36 mowing lawns. What input and output entries would you add to his table?

4. **Reasonableness** Is it reasonable for an output to be greater than the input in the table above? Explain.

5. What algebraic expression using division also describes the output pattern for the table above?

Independent Practice

Use this table for **6** and **7**.

Apple Weight	1 lb	2 lb	3 lb	4 lb	5 lb	10 lb
Apple Price	\$2	\$4	\$6			

6. What is the cost of 4 lb, 5 lb, and 10 lb of apples?

7. Write an algebraic expression that describes the output pattern if the input is a variable a.

Use this table for **8** and **9**.

Total Students	12	18	24	27	36	39
Number of Study Groups		6	8		12	

8. Copy and complete the table.

9. Write an algebraic expression that describes the relationship between the input and output values.

DIGITAL Animated Glossary **www.pearsonsuccessnet.com**

*For another example, see Set G on page 59.

An input/output table is a table of related values. Identify the pattern.

What is the relationship between the values?

$\frac{1}{2}(84) = 42 \rightarrow$ 42 is half of 84.

$\frac{1}{2}(66) = 33 \rightarrow$ 33 is half of 66.

$\frac{1}{2}(50) = 25 \rightarrow$ 25 is half of 50.

The pattern is: $\frac{1}{2}$(INPUT) = OUTPUT

Let x = INPUT.

So, the pattern is $\frac{1}{2}x$.

Use the pattern to find the missing values.

$\frac{1}{2}(22) = 11$

$\frac{1}{2}(30) = 15$

INPUT	*OUTPUT*
\$84	\$42
\$66	\$33
\$50	\$25
\$22	\$11
\$30	\$15

Problem Solving

Use the input/output table at right for **10** and **11**.

INPUT	*OUTPUT*
\$12	\$5
\$27	\$10
\$36	
\$48	\$17

10. Hazem keeps $\frac{1}{3}$ of the tips he earns. Also, he gets \$1 each night to reimburse his parking fee. This information is shown in the input/output table. Write an algebraic expression that describes the output pattern if the input is the variable *k*.

11. How much money would Hazem keep in a night if he takes in \$36 in tips?

Use the input/output table at right for **12** and **13**.

INPUT (tiles)	*OUTPUT (stars)*
4	1
8	2
12	3

12. Ms. Windsor's classroom has a tile floor. The students are making stars to put in the center of 4-tile groups. This input/output chart shows the pattern. Write an algebraic expression that describes the output pattern if the input is the variable *t*.

13. **Writing to Explain** There are 30 rows with 24 tiles in each row on a floor. Explain how to find the number of stars needed to complete the pattern for the floor.

Use the table at right for **14**.

Data

Number of Books	**Total Cost**
1	\$2.50
2	\$5.00
3	\$7.50

14. **Think About the Process** Which algebraic expression shows the cost of a chosen number of books *b*?

A *b* + \$2.50 **C** \$*b* − \$2.50

B \$2.50*b* **D** *b* ÷ \$2.50

Test

1. Tickets cost $30 each plus a one-time $2 postage fee. Which expression shows the cost for n tickets? (2-1)

A $30n + 2$

B $30n - 2$

C $30(n + 2)$

D $30 + 2n$

2. Luis bought 5 boxes of ceramic tiles with 20 tiles in each. Each tile covers 36 square inches. Use mental math to evaluate $20 \times 36 \times 5$ and find the total square inches. (2-5)

A 1,360 in^2

B 3,600 in^2

C 7,200 in^2

D 9,000 in^2

3. What number makes the number sentence true? (2-5)

$4 \times 8 \times 25 = 100 \times \square$

A 200

B 32

C 25

D 8

4. At the Jacovic family reunion, 42 tables each had 6 people. To find the number of people, Ivan did the computation shown below. What number makes the number sentence true? (2-4)

$6(40 + 2) = 240 + \square$

A 62

B 42

C 14

D 12

5. What is the value of the expression in the table when $m = 6$? (2-6)

m	$50 - 4m$
2	42
4	34
6	

A 24

B 26

C 44

D 52

6. Large balloons are sold in packages of 12. Which expression can represent the total number of balloons in a packages of large balloons? (2-1)

A $12a$

B $12 \div a$

C $a \div 12$

D $12 + a$

7. Which algebraic expression can be used to describe the output pattern in the table if the input is a variable p? (2-7)

Data

Boxes of Pens and Total Number of Pens				
Input	4	6	8	10
Output	32	48	64	80

A $p + 14$

B $2p$

C $8p$

D $p \div 9$

8. Use the expression shown to find how many people attended the field trip. (2-3)

$15 \times 4 + 10 \times 5$

A 110 people

B 350 people

C 810 people

D 1,050 people

9. Which of the following shows a way to find $127 + 396$ using compensation? (2-5)

A $127 + 400 + 4$

B $127 - 400 + 4$

C $127 - 400 - 4$

D $127 + 400 - 4$

10. Alita sells necklaces for $3 each. She spent $14 on supplies. The expression $3x - 14$ can be used to find the amount Alita earns for selling x necklaces. How much will Alita earn if she sells 12 necklaces? (2-6)

A $36

B $24

C $22

D $6

11. The expression shown below can be used to find the total cost of violin lessons for a year. What is the first step to evaluate the expression? (2-3)

$25 + 14 \times (52 - 6)$

A Add $25 + 14$.

B Multiply 14×52.

C Subtract $52 - 6$.

D Multiply 14×6.

12. Which property is shown below? (2-2)

$2 \times 32 \times 5 = 2 \times 5 \times 32$

A Associative Property of Multiplication

B Commutative Property of Multiplication

C Identity Property of Multiplication

D Multiplication Property of Zero

13. If the input number is 20 in the table shown, what is the output number? (2-7)

Input	Output
6	12
8	14
10	16

A 26

B 24

C 22

D 18

14. A machine can make 375 bales of hay in 3 hours. At this rate, how long does it take the machine to make 875 bales of hay? (2-8)

Time, h	1	3	
Bales, $125 \times h$	125	375	875

A 9 hours

B 8 hours

C 7 hours

D 6 hours

Set A, pages 32–33

Variables represent values that can change.

The expression $24 + n$ means "the sum of 24 and a number." The unknown number is a variable that is expressed by a letter, n.

Operation Terms

Addition → Sum

Subtraction → Difference

Multiplication → Product

Division → Quotient

Remember that you can use any letter as a variable that stands for an unknown value.

Write the phrases as algebraic expressions.

1. 22 less forks than a number, f
2. 48 times a number of game markers, g
3. a number of eggs, e, divided by 12
4. 3 times the number of milk cartons, m, used by the 6th grade class

Set B, pages 34–35

The properties of operations help you evaluate expressions.

Properties of Operations	
Commutative Property of Addition	$7 + 5 = 12$ So, $5 + 7 = 12$.
Commutative Property of Multiplication	$3 \times 8 = 24$ So, $8 \times 3 = 24$.
Associative Property of Addition	$2 + (3 + 5) = 10$ So, $(2 + 3) + 5 = 10$.
Associative Property of Multiplication	$4 \times (3 \times 5) = 60$ So, $(4 \times 3) \times 5 = 60$.
Identity Property of Addition	Adding zero does not change a number. So, $435 + 0 = 435$.
Identity Property of Multiplication	Multiplying by one does not change a number. So, $84 \times 1 = 84$.

Evaluate the expression: $4 + 8 + 3 + 2$

Following properties of operations:

$4 + 8 + 3 + 2 = 4 + 3 + 8 + 2$
$= 7 + 10$
$= 17$

Remember that when the properties of operations are not followed, numerical expressions are computed incorrectly.

Tell what properties are shown.

1. $3(4 \times 32) = (3 \times 4)32$
2. $21 \times 1 = 21$
3. $9 + 8 + 4 = 8 + 4 + 9$
4. $9 + 0 = 9$
5. $6 \times 8 = 8 \times 6$
6. $5 + 4 = 4 + 5$
7. $6 \times (4 \times 3) = (6 \times 4) \times 3$
8. $8 + (2 + 4) = (8 + 2) + 4$
9. $9 \times 5 \times 4 = 9 \times 4 \times 5$
10. $12 + 0 = 12$
11. $425 \times 1 = 425$
12. $(8 \times 5) \times 4 = 4 \times (5 \times 8)$

Set C, pages 36–38

The order of operations helps you get the correct answer. The order of operations rules are:

Step 1 Compute inside parentheses.

Step 2 Evaluate terms with exponents.

Step 3 Multiply and divide from left to right.

Step 4 Add and subtract from left to right.

Evaluate $8 + 6 \times 9 - 4 \div 2$.

First, multiply and divide. $8 + 54 - 2$

Then, add and subtract. 60

Remember that when the order of operations rules are followed, it helps you get the correct answer.

Use parentheses to make each sentence true.

1. $9 + 8 - 2 \times 7 + 1 = 1$

2. $40 - 4 \times 4^2 \div 2 = 8$

3. $5 \times 5 - 3 - 2 = 0$

4. $8 + 12 \div 4 + 6 = 11$

5. $9 + 8 \div 2 \times 4 + 3^2 = 19$

6. $6 \times 2 - 1 + 5^2 = 31$

7. $8 \times 3 + 8 - 2^2 = 84$

8. $50 - 3 \times 6 + 2 + 4^2 = 42$

Set D, pages 40–41

Use the Distributive Property to evaluate mentally.

8(42)

Break the numbers apart to find numbers that are easier to multiply mentally.

8(40 + 2)

Apply the Distributive Property.

8(40) + 8(2)

Multiply the separate terms. Add the products.

320 + 16 = 336

Remember that the Distributive Property says that multiplying a sum by a number is the same as multiplying each addend by the number and adding the products.

Use the Distributive Property to evaluate mentally.

1. 5(41) + 5(9)

2. 3(45)

3. 4(23)

4. 9(32) + 9(8)

5. 3(27)

6. 6(7) + 6(23)

Set E, pages 42–44

Find $4 \times 18 \times 25$ using compatible numbers to compute mentally.

Look for compatible numbers that are easy to compute. $4 \times 18 \times 25$

$4 \times 25 \times 18$

Then do the remaining calculation. $100 \times 18 = 1{,}800$

So, $4 \times 18 \times 25 = 1{,}800$.

Remember to find compatible numbers to make your mental math easier.

Compute mentally.

1. $15 + 67 + 25$
2. $463 - 333$
3. $6 \times 23 \times 5$
4. $250 \times 6 \times 4$
5. $921 + 529$
6. $297 - 100$
7. $2 \times 8 \times 5$
8. $20 \times 16 \times 5$

Set F, pages 46–47

Evaluate each expression for $x = 2$.

1. $7x - 3$

   $7(2) - 3$ ← Use substitution.

   $14 - 3 = 11$ ← Compute.

2. $4x + 2$

   $4(2) + 2$ ← Use substitution.

   $8 + 2 = 10$ ← Compute.

3. $9x \div 3$

   $9(2) \div 3$ ← Use substitution.

   $18 \div 3 = 6$ ← Compute.

Remember that using *substitution* means to replace the variables with the chosen values.

Evaluate each expression for $x = 4$.

1. $12x - 7$
2. $3x + 18$
3. $11x + 4$
4. $8x + 2$
5. $6x \div 2$
6. $8x - 5$
7. $7x \div 4$
8. $4x - 9$
9. $22x + 6$
10. $9x - 3$
11. $4x \div (x - 2)$
12. $10x - 8$

Set G, pages 48–49

You can write an algebraic expression that explains an input/output relationship. If x is 4, how can you express 9?

Try: $2x + 1 = 9$

See if that works for the other input values.

$2 \times 8 + 1 = 17$

$2 \times 11 + 1 = 23$

Yes, it works!

INPUT	*OUTPUT*
4	9
8	17
11	23

Remember that input/output tables can help you see patterns in expressions.

Use this input/output table for **1** and **2**.

Dollars Sold	*Prize Points*
\$20	4
\$40	8
\$60	12
\$115	■

1. Students earn prize points for selling fundraising items. Write an algebraic expression that explains the relationship between input dollars sold, d, and output prize points.

2. How many prize points would a student earn for selling \$115 worth of items?

Set H, pages 50–52

Making a table to organize your data helps to identify patterns and quickly find solutions. When making a table, include labels for the variable and the expression. Enter the values of x you want to find. Then solve the expression for each value.

Ginny is paid \$12 a week for doing chores. She puts the money in her savings account. If she started out with \$112, find out how much money she has in her account after 3 weeks and after 8 weeks.

Step 1 Identify the expression.
$112 + 12x$

Step 2 Make a table.

x	$112 + 12x$
3	\$148
8	\$208

Remember to choose labels based on the information to be found.

Write an expression for each problem. Then make a table to solve it.

1. Anna walks her dog 2 miles a day, 5 days a week. Write an expression describing how far Anna and her dog walked after x weeks.

2. Todd earns \$500 a week, plus \$50 every time he sells a computer. Write an expression to show how much money Todd earns per week when he sells x computers. Then make a table to show how much Todd earns in a week if he sells 2, 4, or 5 computers.

Topic 3

Operations with Decimals

1 The wings of a ruby-throated hummingbird beat an average of 52 times per second. How many times would its wings beat in a minute? You will find out in Lesson 3-4.

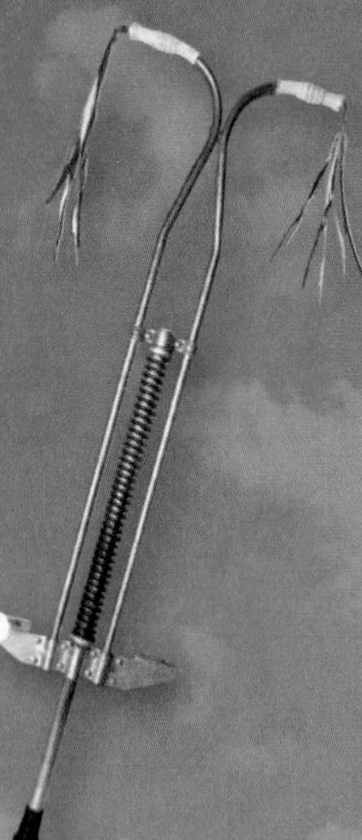

2 What is the world record for jumping the farthest distance on a pogo stick? You will find out in Lesson 3-3.

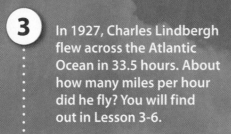

3 In 1927, Charles Lindbergh flew across the Atlantic Ocean in 33.5 hours. About how many miles per hour did he fly? You will find out in Lesson 3-6.

4 The longest spin of a basketball on one finger is 255 minutes. How many hours is this? You will find out in Lesson 3-5.

Review What You Know!

Vocabulary

Choose the best term from the box.

- dividend
- decimal
- base
- exponent

1. An ___?___ tells you how many times to multiply a base by itself.

2. A number that is being divided by another number is called the ___?___.

3. A number that uses a decimal point and has one or more digits to the right of the decimal point is a ___?___.

4. The repeated factor raised to a power in exponential form is called the ___?___.

Whole Number Operations

Calculate each value.

5. 9,007 − 3,128

6. 7,964 + 3,872

7. 35×17

8. 181×42

9. $768 \div 6$

10. $506 \div 22$

Order of Operations

Evaluate each expression.

11. $6 \times 2 + 4$

12. $45 - 24 \div 6$

13. $(20 + 19) \div 3$

14. $5^2 - 5 \times 2$

Decimals

15. **Writing to Explain** What decimal does this model represent? Explain.

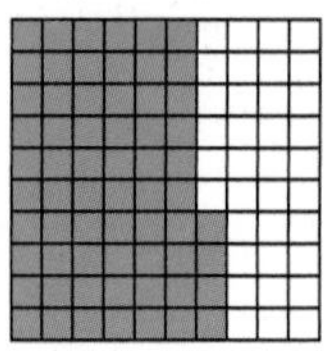

Lesson

3-1

Understand It!
Changing numbers to other numbers that are easy to compute can help you estimate the sums or differences of decimals.

Estimating Sums and Differences

How can you estimate with decimals?

To estimate means to find an approximate answer or solution.

The 10-second barrier in the 100-meter dash was broken in the 1968 Olympics, when the winning time was 9.95 seconds. Mrs. Johnson, the gym teacher, ran the 100 meters in 14.7 seconds. About how much faster was the 1968 Olympic time than Mrs. Johnson's time?

Guided Practice*

Do you know HOW?

In **1** and **2**, complete each estimate by rounding to the nearest tenth.

1. 1.769 + 0.686
1.▢ + 0.▢ = ▢.5

2. 20.45 − 13.15
▢ − 13.2 = ▢

Round each number to the nearest whole number to estimate the answer.

3. 1.456 + 5.4 + 14.08 =

4. 72.43 − 59.8 =

Do you UNDERSTAND?

5. When might you want to estimate an answer?

6. In the problem above, how does comparing the remaining digits in the original numbers tell you whether the estimate is an overestimate or an underestimate?

7. Write your own real-world problem that would be appropriate for estimating the sum or difference of decimals.

Independent Practice

In **8** through **10**, round each number to the nearest whole number to estimate each answer.

8. 20.791 + 5.25 + 3.84 **9.** $10.10 − $3.69 **10.** 376.52 − 9.14

In **11** through **13**, use front-end estimation to estimate each answer.

11. 7.12 + 2.501 + 9.2 **12.** 91.26 − 30.463 **13.** $3.79 − $1.22

DIGITAL Animated Glossary
www.pearsonsuccessnet.com

For another example, see Set A on page 90.

One Way

Use rounding to quickly estimate sums and differences. Round each number to the same place value.

Round each number to the nearest whole number.

$$\begin{array}{r} 14.7 \\ -\ 9.95 \\ \hline \end{array} \rightarrow \begin{array}{r} 15 \\ -\ 10 \\ \hline 5 \end{array}$$

The difference is about 5 seconds.

Another Way

Use the front-end digits to make a front-end estimate, and then adjust the estimate using the remaining digits.

$$\begin{array}{r} 14.7 \\ -\ 9.95 \\ \hline \end{array} \rightarrow \begin{array}{r} 14 \\ -\ 9 \\ \hline 5 \end{array}$$

Since $0.7 < 0.95$, the difference is less than 5.

The 1968 Olympic time is less than 5 seconds faster than Mrs. Johnson's time.

Problem Solving

14. Rachel is shopping and needs to buy bread, lunchmeat, and pretzels to make lunch. She has a ten-dollar bill. Will she have enough money for her purchases? Use estimation to find whether she will have enough money. Explain your reasoning.

15. **Writing to Explain** Kira and Jerome want to go to a movie and have popcorn and a drink. A movie ticket costs \$7.75, and the snack and drink combo costs \$2.85. Kira says if they each bring \$10, it will be enough. Jerome says they each need more than \$10. Who is correct and why?

16. Which of the following is the best estimate for $0.375 + 2.46$?

A 2.5 **B** 3 **C** 3.5 **D** 4

17. **Number Sense** In baseball, an earned run average (ERA) is the average of earned runs given up by a pitcher per nine innings pitched.

a Order the ERAs in the table from greatest to least.

b About how many tenths difference is there between the lowest and highest ERAs in the table?

Data

Player	Earned Run Average (ERA)
Eddie	1.82
John	2.10
Mario	2.06
Scott	2.04
Josh	1.89

18. **Think About the Process** Which expression will give an answer of 10?

A $(5 + 3) \times 9 - 2 \div 5$

B $5 + (3 \times 9 - 2) \div 5$

C $2 \times (9 - 5) + 3 \div 5$

D $2 + 9 \times (5 - 3) \div 5$

Lesson
3-2

Understand It!
Adding and subtracting decimals is similar to adding and subtracting whole numbers.

Adding and Subtracting

How can you add whole numbers and decimals?

Kim and Martin swam 50 meters. Martin took 0.26 seconds longer than Kim. What was Martin's time in the race?

Choose an Operation Add to find Martin's time.

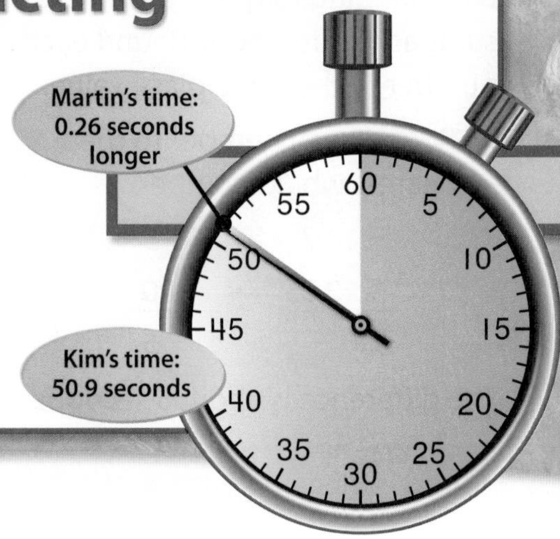

Another Example How can you subtract whole numbers and decimals?

Asha ran a race in 20.7 seconds. Katie ran the same race 0.25 seconds faster. How fast did Katie run the race?

Subtract to find Katie's time. Find 20.7 − 0.25. Estimate the difference by rounding.

$$20.7 - 0.3 = 20.4$$

To find the difference, line up the decimal points.

$$\begin{array}{r} 20.70 \\ -\ \ 0.25 \\ \hline \end{array}$$

← Annex a zero as a placeholder.

Subtract each place. Regroup the seven tenths to subtract the hundredths.

$$\begin{array}{r} {\scriptstyle 6\ 10} \\ 20.\not{7}\not{0} \\ -\ \ 0.25 \\ \hline 20.45 \end{array}$$

Katie ran the race in 20.45 seconds. 20.45 is close to the estimate 20.4.

Guided Practice*

Do you know HOW?

In **1** through **6**, find each sum or difference.

1. 5.9 + 2.7

2. 4.01 − 2.95

3. 2.57 + 7.706

4. 1.5 − 1.056

5. 10 + 3.284

6. 15 − 6.108

Do you UNDERSTAND?

7. How is adding and subtracting decimals similar to and different from adding and subtracting whole numbers?

8. In Another Example, how does the estimate help you determine if the answer is reasonable?

*For another example, see Set B on page 90.

Find 50.9 + 0.26. Estimate first by rounding each addend.

$51 + 0.3 = 51.3$

To find the sum, line up the decimal points.

$$\begin{array}{r} 50.90 \\ +\ 0.26 \\ \hline \end{array}$$

Annex a zero to 50.9 so that each place has a digit.

Add each place. You can regroup the sum of nine tenths and two tenths.

$$\begin{array}{r} \overset{1}{5}0.90 \\ +\ 0.26 \\ \hline 51.16 \end{array}$$

Martin swam the race in 51.16 seconds. The sum 51.16 is close to the estimate, 51.3.

Independent Practice

Find each sum or difference.

9. 2.17 − 0.8 **10.** 4.3 + 4.16 **11.** 7.62 − 3.867 **12.** 4.815 + 2.17

13. 5.187 − 0.48 **14.** 5.78 + 16.597 **15.** 9.501 − 9.45 **16.** 14 + 9.8

17. 46.91 − 28.7 **18.** 5.61 + 2.4 **19.** 27 + 0.185 **20.** 0.46 − 0.333

Problem Solving

21. The U.S. Census Bureau tracks the time it takes people to travel to work.

Data

Location	Average Travel Time to Work (minutes)
United States	25.5
Los Angeles, CA	29.6
Chicago, IL	35.2
New York, NY	40.0

How does the average travel time for New Yorkers compare to the United States?

A 14.5 minutes longer

B 14.5 minutes shorter

C 4.8 minutes longer

D 10.4 minutes longer

22. **Writing to Explain** Mr. Smith gave a cashier a \$50 bill for a purchase of \$38.70. The cashier gave him a \$10 bill, two \$1 bills, and three dimes back. Did Mr. Smith get the correct change? Why or why not?

23. **Estimation** Minh wrote the following number sentence: 2.6 + 0.33 = 5.9. Use estimation to show that Minh's answer is incorrect.

24. **Algebra** Copy and complete the sequence of numbers.

7.5, 6.25, 5, ▢, ▢

Lesson
3-3 Estimating Products and Quotients

Understand It!
Rounding and using compatible numbers that are easy to compute with mentally can help you estimate the products or quotients of decimals.

How can you use estimation to find a product?

The students at Waldron Middle School are selling tins of popcorn to raise money for new uniforms. They sold 42 tins in the first week. Estimate how much money the students have raised selling popcorn in the first week.

Another Example
How can you use estimation to find a quotient?

One Way

Estimate 7.83 ÷ 3.8 by rounding each factor.

$$7.83 \div 3.8$$

↓ ↓

$$8.0 \div 4.0$$

$$8.0 \div 4.0 = 2$$

So, $7.83 \div 3.8 \approx 2$.

Another Way

Estimate 44.3 ÷ 6.7 using compatible numbers.

$$44.3 \div 6.7$$

44.3 is close to 42 and 6.7 is close to 7.

↓ ↓

$$42 \div 7 = 6$$

So, $44.3 \div 6.7 \approx 6$.

Tip *The symbol ≈ is read "is approximately equal to."*

Explain It

1. Explain when you would use rounding or compatible numbers to estimate a product or quotient.

2. **Reasonableness** Would it be reasonable to use 60 and 6 as compatible numbers in the Another Way problem above? Explain.

3. When estimating a quotient such as 44.3 ÷ 6.7, why is using compatible numbers easier than rounding each factor?

One Way

Estimate by rounding each factor.

42 × $9.25
↓ ↓
40 × $9 = $360

So, 42 × $9.25 ≈ $360.

The students raised about $360 the first week.

Another Way

Estimate by using compatible numbers. Compatible numbers are close to the actual numbers, but they are easier to compute mentally.

42 × $9.25
↓ ↓
42 × $10 = $420

$9.25 is close to 10 and it is easy to multiply by 10.

So, 42 × $9.25 ≈ $420.

The students raised about $420 the first week.

Guided Practice*

Do you know HOW?

Estimate each answer using rounding.

1. 6.8 × 53

2. 3,520 ÷ 6.82

3. 65.13 × 2.89

4. 2,386.25 ÷ 40.1

Estimate each answer by using compatible numbers.

5. 9.34 × 0.68

6. 35.7 ÷ 8.9

7. 20.6 × 3.7

8. 52.3 ÷ 9.7

Do you UNDERSTAND?

9. Which method is easier to use to estimate the total amount of money the students will raise if they sell 112 tins of popcorn?

10. In the examples at the top of the page, are the estimates overestimates or underestimates? Explain.

Independent Practice

For **11** through **26**, estimate each product or quotient.

11. 615 ÷ 5.3

12. 12.10 ÷ 3.69

13. 376.52 × 9.94

14. 20.2 × 1.96

15. 412 × 2.421

16. 98.2 × 33.46

17. 73.6 ÷ 7.16

18. $73.09 ÷ 0.88

19. 11.3 × 0.8

20. $26.15 ÷ $3.29

21. 973 ÷ 4.8

22. 2.06 × 15.5

23. 240 ÷ 3.5

24. 9.3 × 52.7

25. $29.95 ÷ 4

26. 2.875 × 12.5

27. Which compatible numbers could you use to estimate 636.2 ÷ 91.702?

DIGITAL
Animated Glossary
www.pearsonsuccessnet.com

For another example, see Set C on page 90.

Problem Solving

28. Writing to Explain Javier used compatible numbers to estimate that 328 ÷ 49 is about 10. Do you think this is a good estimate? Explain.

29. Number Sense In the number 24.543, why is the value of each 4 different?

30. Julie estimates that she can produce 28 puzzles in one week. She sells each puzzle for $12.25. Estimate the amount of money Julie can earn in a month.

31. Use the Distributive Property to rewrite the following expression: $22 \times 3 + 11 \times 3 = 99$.

32. Number Sense Use rounding to estimate 32.782×99.898. Will the estimate be greater or less than the exact product?

33. The sixth grade ordered 19 medium veggie pizzas. Each pizza cost $8.49. Estimate the cost of the pizzas.

34. The diagram at the right shows the distance and time records set in 1997 for pogo-stick jumping. Estimate the number of miles jumped each hour.

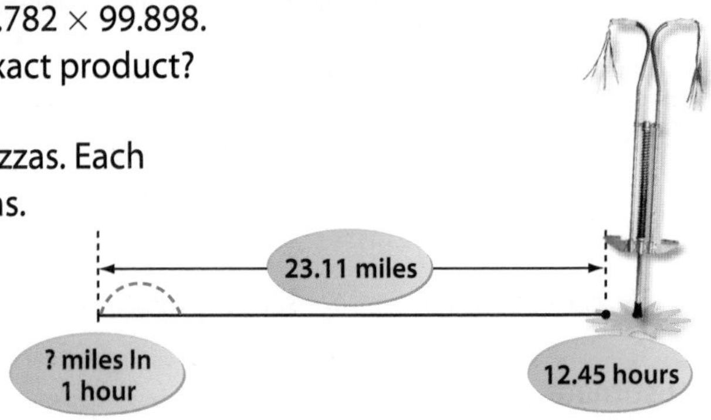

35. Algebra Use your estimate of the number of miles jumped per hour from Exercise 34 to estimate how many miles were jumped after 5 hours.

36. Copy and complete the sequence of numbers.

6.5, 5.25, 4, ▢, ▢

37. Think About the Process Latrell is buying clothes for school. He has $150. He wants to buy two pairs of jeans for $38 each and 2 shirts for $25 each. Which expression shows how to find whether he has enough money?

A $(150 \times 2) - 38 + (2 + 25)$

B $150 - (2 \times 38) - (2 \times 25)$

C $150 + (2 \times 38) \div (2 \times 25)$

D $150 \div (2 + 38) \times (2 \times 25)$

38. Number Sense Charlie practiced his clarinet for 1.5 hours on Monday and 2.25 hours on Tuesday. If he promised his teacher that he would practice 6 hours a week, about how much more time does he need to practice this week?

A About 1 hour

B About 2 hours

C About 3 hours

D About 4 hours

Mixed Problem Solving

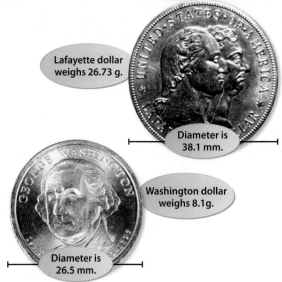

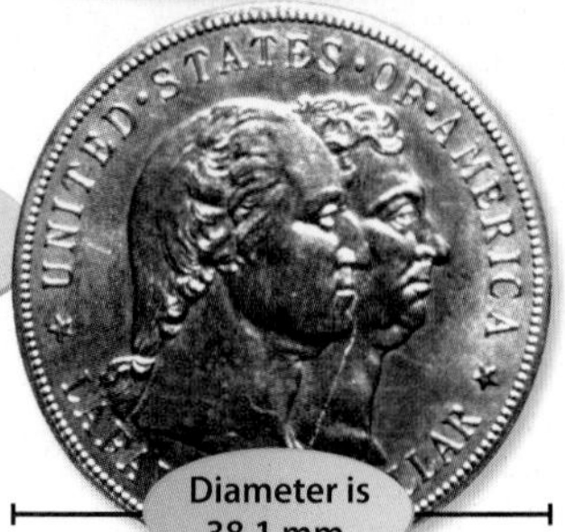
Lafayette dollar weighs 26.73 g.
Diameter is 38.1 mm.

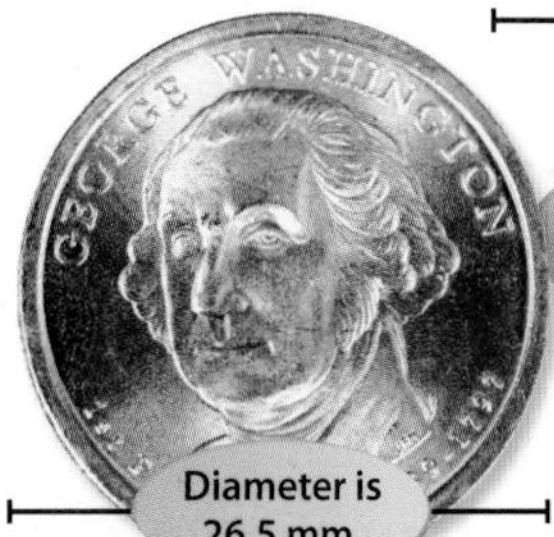
Washington dollar weighs 8.1g.
Diameter is 26.5 mm.

The United States Mint makes coins called commemorative coins. Commemorative coins honor people, places, or events. The Lafayette dollar, issued in 1900, was the first commemorative dollar coin. One side shows an image of both George Washington and General Lafayette, the French nobleman who served with George Washington in the Revolutionary War. In 2007, the United States Mint issued a George Washington dollar coin, the first in a series of Presidential dollar coins.

Coins are minted to exact specifications. Use the information in the pictures for **1** through **5**.

1. The Lafayette dollar was $\frac{9}{10}$ silver. Estimate the weight of 12 Lafayette dollars.

2. Estimate how many Washington dollars, laid side by side, it would take to equal the length of a meter stick. Explain.

3. How much heavier is a Lafayette dollar than a Washington dollar?

4. The Washington dollar has a thickness of about 0.0787 inches. Round 0.0787 to the nearest hundredth.

5. Patti used rounding to estimate the length of six Lafayette dollars laid side by side. Is her estimate an overestimate or an underestimate? Explain.

$$38.1 \times 6 \approx 40 \times 6$$
$$\approx 240 \text{ mm}$$

6. The United States Mint has been producing and distributing coins since 1792. How many years passed between 1792 and 1900, when it issued the first commemorative dollar coin?

7. Presidents are elected for 4-year terms. George Washington served as President from 1789 to 1797. How many terms did George Washington serve as President?

8. When George Washington was elected President, the population of the United States was about 4 million. Write 4 million in standard form.

9. Which expression shows the total weight of *W* Washington dollars and *L* Lafayette dollars?

A $8.1(W + L)$ **C** $8.1W + 26.73L$

B $26.73(W + L)$ **D** $26.73W + 8.1L$

10. George Washington was one of the tallest Presidents. He was about 6 feet 2 inches tall. How many inches is 6 feet 2 inches?

Lesson
3-4 Multiplying Decimals

Hands-On: grid paper

Understand It!
Multiplying decimals is similar to multiplying whole numbers. Place-value relationships help you determine where to place the decimal point in the product.

How can you multiply whole numbers and decimals?

Bari displayed four paintings side-by-side in one row. Each painting has the same width. What is the total width of the 4 paintings?

Choose an Operation Multiply to find the total width of the four paintings.

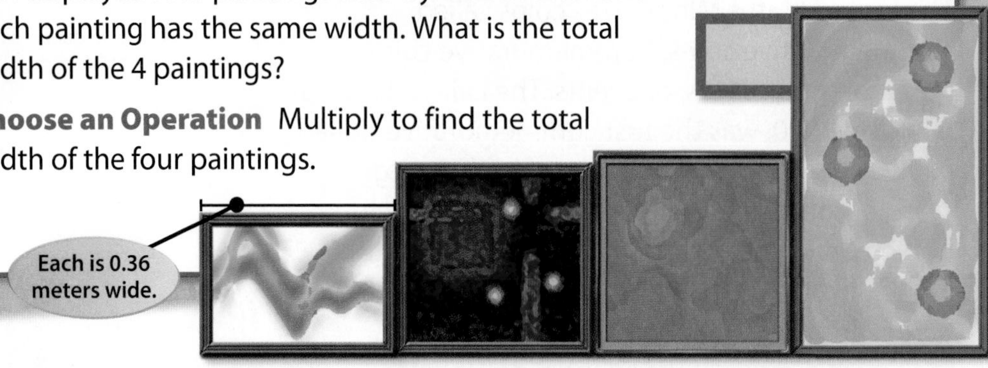

Another Example How can you multiply a decimal by a decimal?

Find 0.5 × 0.3. Use what you know about multiplying whole numbers to multiply decimals.

What You Think

Think of 0.5 as shading the first five columns of a decimal model. Think of 0.3 as shading the first 3 rows of the decimal model.

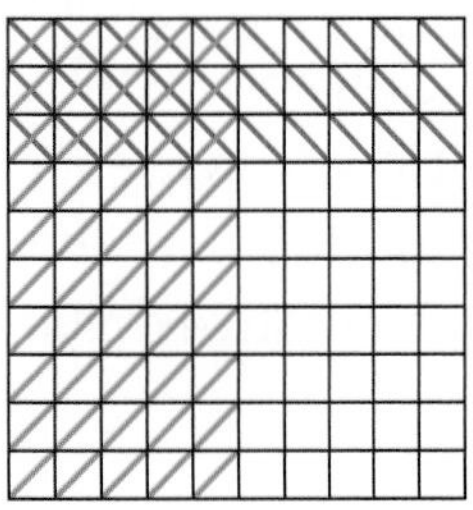

The product is the area where the shading overlaps.

$0.5 \times 0.3 = 0.15$

What You Write

Multiply. Count the number of decimal places in each factor to place the decimal in the product.

```
   1
  0.5  ←   1 decimal place
× 0.3  ←  +1 decimal place
 0.15  ←   2 decimal places
```

You can multiply using a calculator.

Press: 0.5 [×] 0.3 [ENTER =]

Display: 0.15

Explain It

1. How can you place the decimal in the product when you multiply with decimals?

What You Think

Find 0.36 × 4. Multiplying 0.36 × 4 is like adding 0.36 four times on a decimal model.

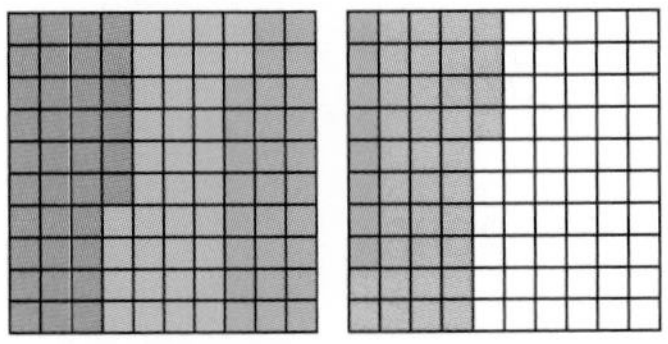

The product is the total area shaded.

$0.36 \times 4 = 1.44$

What You Write

Multiply. Add the number of decimal places to place the decimals.

$\overset{1\ 2}{0.36}$	←	2 decimal places
× 4	←	+ 0 decimal places
1.44	←	2 decimal places

The total width is 1.44 meters. You can also multiply using a calculator.

Press: 0.36 [×] 4 [ENTER =]

Display: 1.44

Other Examples

Place the decimal in a product.

Find 48.2 × 3.9.

Estimate: $50 \times 4 = 200$

48.2	←	1 decimal place
× 3.9	←	+ 1 decimal place
4338		
14460		
187.98	←	2 decimal places

The answer is reasonable because 187.98 is close to 200.

Annex zeros to the left of a product.

Sometimes you need to add zeros to the left of a product in order to place the decimal point correctly.

Find 0.43 × 0.2.

0.43	←	2 decimal places
× 0.2	←	+ 1 decimal place
0.086	←	3 decimal places

You can multiply using a calculator.

Press: 0.43 [×] 0.2 [ENTER =]

Display: 0.086

Guided Practice*

Do you know HOW?

In **1** through **4**, place the decimal point in the product. You may use grids to help.

1. 2 × 0.302 = 604 **2.** 3 × 0.92 = 276

3. 4.2 × 5.4 = 2268 **4.** 5.7 × 0.03 = 171

In **5** and **6**, find the product.

5. 0.8 × 4 **6.** 0.7 × 21

Do you UNDERSTAND?

7. Explain when you need to add zeros to the left of a product.

8. In the example at the top, which method is easier to use to find the product, paper and pencil or a calculator?

DIGITAL eTools www.pearsonsuccessnet.com

*For another example, see Set D on page 91.

Independent Practice

Leveled Practice In **9** through **14**, place the decimal point in each product.

9. $0.7 \times 12 = 84$ **10.** $4 \times 0.27 = 108$ **11.** $6 \times 0.13 = 078$

12. $3 \times 0.134 = 0402$ **13.** $0.78 \times 5 = 390$ **14.** $0.232 \times 9 = 2088$

In **15** through **25,** find the product. You may use grids to help.

15. 10×0.32 **16.** 3×0.232 **17.** 0.7×0.8 **18.** 22.3×1.2

19. 100×0.129 **20.** 18×2.987 **21.** 33.3×0.3 **22.** 1.235×4.8

23. $3.2 \times 2.8 \times 6.1$ **24.** $1.8 \times 0.5 \times 100$ **25.** $74.3 \times 0.1 \times 2.1$

Problem Solving

26. **Writing to Explain** Why does multiplying numbers by 10 move the decimal point to the right, but multiplying by 0.10 move the decimal point to the left?

27. **Number Sense** Jen solved this math sentence: $9 \times 0.989 = 89.01$. How can you use estimation to show that Jen's answer is wrong? What mistake do you think she made?

28. The wings of a ruby-throated hummingbird beat an average of 52 times per second.

a If a ruby-throated hummingbird hovers for 35.5 seconds, on average how many times does its wings beat?

b Estimate about how many times its wings would beat in a minute.

29. Think About the Process Which expression does this decimal model show?

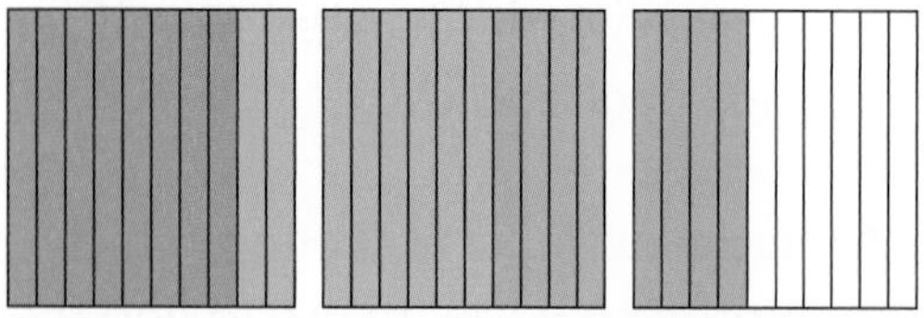

A 0.8×3 **C** $0.8 \div 3$

B $0.8 + 3$ **D** $0.8 - 3$

30. Think About the Process Which expression does this decimal model show?

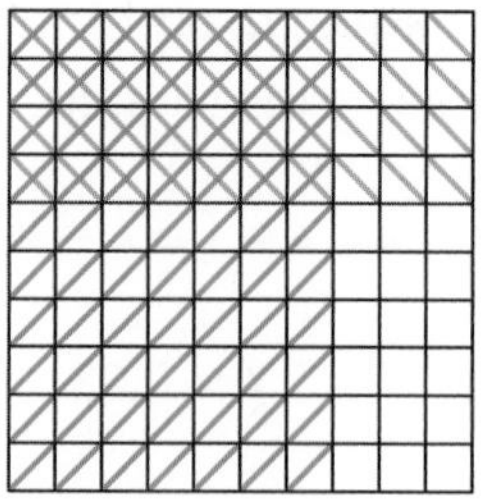

A $0.7 \div 0.4$ **C** $0.7 - 0.4$

B 0.7×0.4 **D** $0.7 + 0.4$

Algebra Connections

True or False?

Remember that a variable is a value that can change and is often represented by a letter. If you are given the value of the variable, you can substitute the value for the letter to evaluate an expression or equation.

Example: Evaluate $x - 0.5 = 0.8$ for $x = 1.3$.

Substitute 1.3 for the variable.

$1.3 - 0.5 = 0.8$

$0.8 = 0.8$

The equation is **true** when $x = 1.3$.

In **1** through **8**, evaluate for the variable. Write **true** or **false** for each equation.

1. $x + 7 = 8.3; x = 1.3$

2. $x - 2.88 = 7.11; x = 4$

3. $6x = 12.6; x = 21$

4. $0.5 + x = 1.2; x = 0.7$

5. $x \div 3 = 4.8; x = 14.4$

6. $x - 4.5 = 5.9; x = 9.4$

7. $7x = 21.35; x = 3.5$

8. $27.6 \div x = 9.2; x = 3$

In **9** through **12**, evaluate the equations to find the answers.

9. If $b = 5.7$, which equation is true?

A $3 + b = 6$

B $b - 2 = 5.5$

C $b + 4.4 = 9.1$

D $6 - b = 0.3$

10. If $s = 8.9$, which equation is true?

A $0.1 + s = 8.8$

B $s - 0.01 = 8.807$

C $s + 1.1 = 10$

D $11.1 - s = 3.2$

11. If $g = 0.29$, which equation is true?

A $g - 0.02 = 0.27$

B $g - 0.22 = 0.7$

C $g + 0.2 = 0.31$

D $g + 2 = 0.49$

12. If $n = 1.78$, which equation is true?

A $n - 0.3 = 2.08$

B $2.3 + n = 4.08$

C $n + 0.3 = 1.48$

D $5 - n = 4.22$

Lesson **3-5**

Understand It!
Dividing a decimal is similar to dividing a whole number. The place value of the dividend helps you determine where to place the decimal point in the quotient.

Dividing by a Whole Number

How can you write a quotient for a decimal dividend?

Three friends received $2.58 for aluminum cans they recycled. They decided to share the money equally. How much will each friend get?

Choose an Operation Divide to find how much each friend will get.

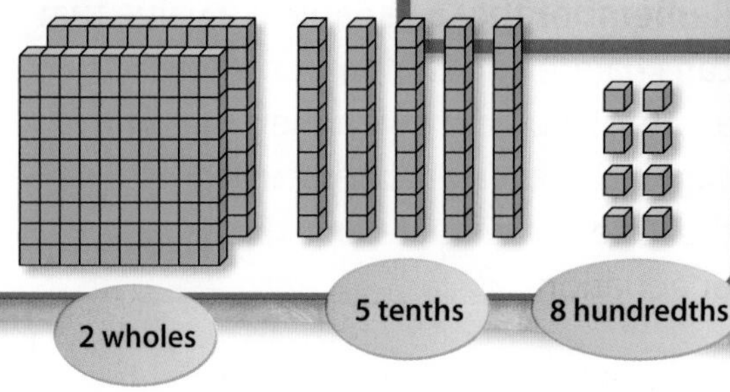

Another Example

How can you write a decimal quotient when dividing whole numbers?

Find 180 ÷ 8.

Step 1

Estimate.
Since 180 ÷ 10 = 18, start dividing in the tens place.

```
    2
8)180
 - 16
    2
```

Compare: 2 < 8

Step 2

Divide the ones.

```
   22
8)180
 - 16↓
    20    Bring down.
  - 16
     4
```

Compare: 4 < 8

Step 3

Divide the tenths.

```
   22.5    Place the decimal.
8)180.0    Annex a zero.
 - 16↓ |
    20 |
  - 16 ↓
     40    Bring down.
   - 40
      0
```

Guided Practice*

Do you know HOW?

Copy and complete.

1.

```
      __.2__
49)306.25
 - __9__
     1____
   - 98
     ______
   - 245
       __
```

2.

```
      0.____
15)14.4
 - ______
        9__
  -   __0
        __
```

Do you UNDERSTAND?

3. How do you know where to place the decimal point in long division with decimals?

4. Estimation How would you estimate the quotient of $180 ÷ 62 and in which place would you start dividing?

DIGITAL eTools **www.pearsonsuccessnet.com**

*For another example, see Set E on page 91.

What You Think

Find 2.58 ÷ 3. Estimate using compatible numbers. Since 3 ÷ 3 = 1, then 2.58 ÷ 3 < 1.

Divide the models into 24 tenths and 18 ones to share equally.

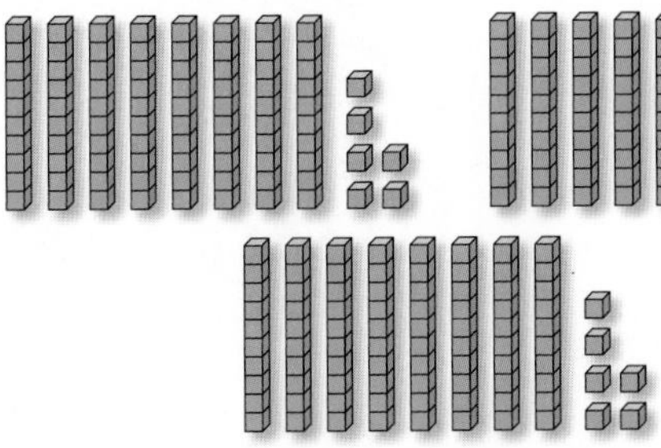

What You Write

Use the estimate to start dividing in the tenths place.

```
   0.86
3)2.58
 - 24
    18
```

Place the decimal point in the quotient above the decimal point in the dividend. Divide as usual.

Each of the three friends will get $0.86.

Independent Practice

In **5** through **20**, find each quotient.

5. $99.09 ÷ 3 **6.** 97.5 ÷ 6 **7.** 71.2 ÷ 8 **8.** 151.2 ÷ 6

9. 1.57 ÷ 10 **10.** 2.4 ÷ 8 **11.** $350 ÷ 40 **12.** 248.60 ÷ 50

13. 5 ÷ 5,000 **14.** 5.68 ÷ 8 **15.** $23.10 ÷ 11 **16.** 60.3 ÷ 9

17. $92.55 ÷ 5 **18.** 396 ÷ 88 **19.** 100 ÷ 1,000 **20.** 5.43 ÷ 15

Problem Solving

21. Admission to an amusement park cost $107.25 for three friends. If the price was the same for each friend, what was the cost of each admission?

22. **Number Sense** If Brand A dog food costs $29.95 for 30 pounds and Brand B dog food costs $50 for 45 pounds, which costs less per pound?

23. **Writing to Explain** Is the work below correct? If not, explain why and give a correct response.

Find 0.9 ÷ 30.

```
    0.30
30)0.90
  - 90
     0
```

24. **Think About the Process** How might you best estimate the quotient of 352.25 ÷ 33?

A Round 352.25 to 352.

B Round 352.25 to 352 and 33 to 30.

C Round 352.25 to 400 and 33 to 30.

D Use compatible numbers 350 and 35.

25. The longest spin of a basketball on one finger is 255 minutes. How many hours is this?

Lesson
3-6

Understand It!
To divide a whole number by a decimal, change the divisor to a whole number by multiplying the divisor and the dividend by the same power of 10.

Dividing a Whole Number by a Decimal

How can you divide a whole number by a decimal?

A band was deciding how many songs could fit on a CD. They bought blank CDs for recording their songs. If their average song is 3.2 minutes long, how many songs can fit on each CD?

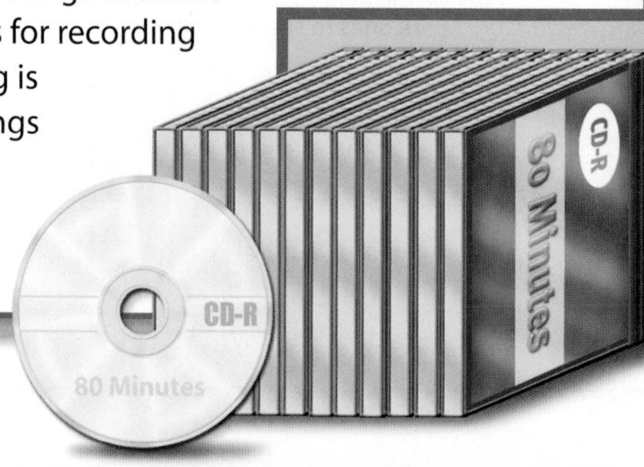

Choose an Operation
Find 80 ÷ 3.2.

Guided Practice*

Do you know HOW?

In **1** through **4**, find a power of 10 that will make the divisor a whole number and write the equivalent problem.

1. 426 ÷ 0.6
2. 216 ÷ 0.03
3. 2,800 ÷ 0.007
4. 720 ÷ 1.2

Do you UNDERSTAND?

5. When changing the divisor to a whole number, why do you multiply both the divisor and the dividend by the same power of 10?

6. In the problem above, why might the band not be able to put a full 25 songs on the CD?

Independent Practice

Leveled Practice In **7** through **14**, find a power of 10 that will make the divisor a whole number and write the equivalent problem.

7. 2,466 ÷ 0.9
8. 65 ÷ 0.005
9. 143 ÷ 0.22
10. 164 ÷ 2.05
11. 32 ÷ 8.9
12. 512 ÷ 2.56
13. 36 ÷ 0.009
14. 4,221 ÷ 0.7

In **15** though **26**, find each quotient. Show your work.

15. $0.03\overline{)24}$
16. $0.006\overline{)18}$
17. $0.05\overline{)12}$
18. $0.0008\overline{)3}$
19. 114 ÷ 0.04
20. 51 ÷ 0.06
21. 126 ÷ 0.9
22. 11 ÷ 0.0025
23. 180 ÷ 0.40
24. 756 ÷ 0.70
25. 2,550 ÷ 0.25
26. 110 ÷ 0.002

*For another example, see Set F on page 91.

Step 1

Estimate. 90 ÷ 3 = 30

$3.2\overline{)80}$

Think of a power of 10 that will make the divisor a whole number.

3.2 × 10 = 32

Step 2

Multiply the divisor and dividend by the same power of 10. Write the equivalent division problem.

3.2 × 10 = 32
80 × 10 = 800

$3.2\overline{)80.0} = 32\overline{)800}$

Step 3

Place the decimal in the quotient. Divide.

```
    25
32)800
  - 64
   160
  -160
     0
```

25 is close to the estimate of 30.

The band can fit 25 songs on a CD.

Problem Solving

27. In 1927, Charles Lindbergh made the first solo, non-stop flight 3,610 miles across the Atlantic Ocean. The flight lasted about 33.5 hours. About how many miles per hour did he fly? Divide 3,610 by 33.5 and round to the nearest whole number.

28. **Writing to Explain** Is the quotient for 41 ÷ 0.8 greater or less than 41? Explain.

29. **Estimation** In a timed typing test, Lara typed 63 words per minute. Estimate the number of words she should be able to type in half an hour.

30. The fence next to the creek near Adam's house leans a little more each year because the bank of the creek is eroding. If the fence leans about 3.7 degrees more each year, estimate how many more degrees the fence will lean after 5 years.

Use the information in the table for **31** and **32**.

Data

Animal	Speed (miles per hour)
Sea horse	0.01
Sloth	0.17
Snail	0.03
Tortoise	0.23

31. **Number Sense** Arrange the animals at the right in order from fastest to slowest.

32. **Think About the Process** At the average speed shown, the expression 2 ÷ 0.03 equals how long it would take the snail to travel 2 miles. Which expression is equivalent to 2 ÷ 0.03?

A 2 ÷ 3

B 20 ÷ 3

C 200 ÷ 3

D 2,000 ÷ 3

Lesson

3-7

Understand It!
Dividing decimals is similar to dividing a whole number by a decimal. Change the divisor to a whole number by multiplying the divisor and the dividend by the same power of 10.

Dividing Decimals

How can you divide using a decimal divisor?

Michelle purchases several bottles of water. Before tax is added, the total cost is \$3.60 and the cost of each bottle is \$1.20. How many bottles did she buy?

Choose an Operation
Divide 3.60 by 1.20.

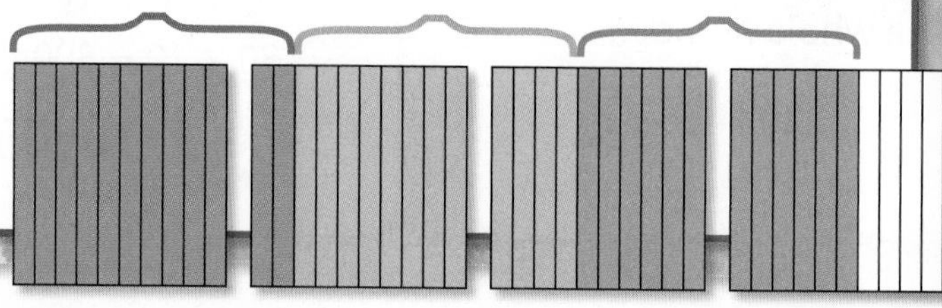

Another Example How can you divide a decimal by a decimal?

Find $0.021 \div 0.35$.

Step 1

Use multiplication to estimate.
$\square \times 0.35 = 0.021$.
You know:
$1 \times 0.35 = 0.35$ and
$0.1 \times 0.35 = 0.035$.
So, the quotient is < 0.1.

Step 2

Multiply the divisor and dividend by the same power of 10 to make the divisor a whole number, and place the decimal in quotient.

$0.35\overline{)0.021} = 35\overline{)2.1}$

Step 3

Divide. Annex zeros as needed.

$$\begin{array}{r} 0.06 \\ 35\overline{)2.10} \\ -\,2\,10 \\ \hline 0 \end{array}$$

Since $0.06 < 0.1$, the answer is reasonable.

Guided Practice*

Do you know HOW?

Find each quotient.

Tip *Use estimation to check answers for reasonableness.*

1. $2 \div 0.5$

2. $1.25 \div 0.25$

3. $2.1 \div 0.7$

4. $6.6 \div 0.3$

Do you UNDERSTAND?

5. When dividing by a decimal, why can you multiply the divisor and dividend by the same power of 10?

6. Why is a zero added to the dividend in Step 3 of the example above?

*For another example, see Set G on page 92.

Step 1

Estimate.

$4 \div 1 = 4$

Think of a power of 10 that will make the divisor a whole number.

1.20)3.60

Multiply 1.20 by 100.

Step 2

Multiply the divisor and dividend by the same power of 10 and place the decimal in the quotient.

1.20)3.60

Find: 120)360.

Step 3

Divide.

$$\begin{array}{r} 3 \\ 120\overline{)360} \\ -360 \\ \hline 0 \end{array}$$

3 is close to 4. The answer is reasonable.

Michelle purchased 3 bottles of water.

Independent Practice

Leveled Practice In **7** through **10**, estimate each quotient.

7. $3.6 \div 0.7$ **8.** $9.8 \div 0.2$ **9.** $17.8 \div 3.1$ **10.** $89.05 \div 4.8$

In **11** through **22,** find each quotient.

11. $62 \div 0.25$ **12.** $48.4 \div 0.02$ **13.** $0.02 \div 0.005$ **14.** $182.88 \div 0.08$

15. $107.25 \div 0.03$ **16.** $5.68 \div 8$ **17.** $624 \div 0.6$ **18.** $23.1 \div 0.7$

19. $24.2 \div 55$ **20.** $0.3567 \div 8.7$ **21.** $3.6 \div 9$ **22.** $4.788 \div 0.42$

Problem Solving

23. Writing to Explain Susan solves $1.4 \div 0.2$ using the diagram below. Is her reasoning correct? Explain her thinking.

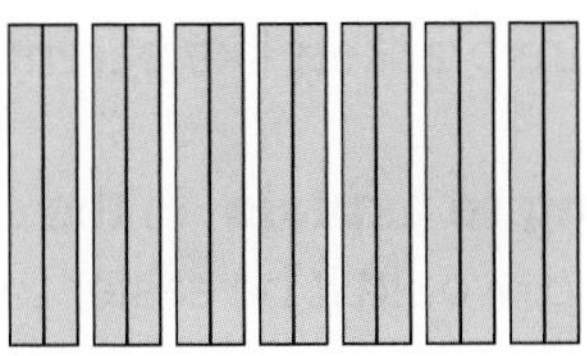

24. Number Sense Tim estimates that $60 \div 5.7$ is about 10. Will the actual quotient be greater than or less than 10? Explain.

25. Reasonableness Dex estimates that $49{,}892 \div 0.89$ is about 5,000. Is his estimate reasonable? Why or why not?

26. Think About the Process What value can you multiply the divisor and dividend by to begin dividing this problem?
$89 \div 0.004$

A 1 **B** 10 **C** 100 **D** 1,000

Lesson
3-8 Evaluating Expressions

Understand It!
You can use order of operations to evaluate the bracketed parts of numerical expressions.

How can you evaluate with brackets?

Evaluate $3.2 \times 12 - [2 + (3.6 \div 0.6)]$

Some expressions look difficult because they include parentheses and brackets. You can think of brackets as "outside" parentheses.

You evaluate inside parentheses first.

Order of Operations

1. Evaluate inside parentheses and brackets.
2. Evaluate terms with exponents.
3. Multiply and divide from left to right.
4. Add and subtract from left to right.

Another Example How can you evaluate expressions with brackets and variables?

Evaluate $[6(x - 3.5)] \div 12 + 4.2$ for $x = 9.5$.

Step 1

Substitute a number for the variable; $x = 9.5$.

$[6(x - 3.5)] \div 12 + 4.2$
$[6 \times (9.5 - 3.5)] \div 12 + 4.2$

Step 2

Evaluate inside parentheses and brackets.

$[6 \times (9.5 - 3.5)] \div 12 + 4.2$
$[6 \times 6] \div 12 + 4.2$
$36 \div 12 + 4.2$

Step 3

Continue to follow order of operations.

$36 \div 12 + 4.2$
$3 + 4.2$
7.2

Guided Practice*

Do you know HOW?

Evaluate each expression.

1. $2.3 + (4.5 - 2.1)$

2. $(9.8 + x) \times 2.8; x = 6.2$

3. $[(5.5 + 2.3) - 2.1] + 2.3$

4. $[(7.9 + 13.5) - (y + 10.4)]; y = 9.8$

Do you UNDERSTAND?

5. How are brackets like parentheses?

6. **Writing to Explain** In the example at the top, would it be easier to evaluate the expression using mental math, paper and pencil, or a calculator?

For another example, see Set H on page 92.

Step 1

Evaluate inside parentheses and brackets.

$3.2 \times 12 - [2 + (3.6 \div 0.6)]$

$3.2 \times 12 - [2 + 6]$

$3.2 \times 12 - 8$

Step 2

There are no exponents, so you can multiply next.

$3.2 \times 12 - 8$

$38.4 - 8$

Remember to work from left to right.

Step 3

Lastly, subtract.

$38.4 - 8 = 30.4$

When you evaluate expressions, follow the rules of the order of operations.

Independent Practice

Evaluate each expression.

7. $3.1 + (9.6 - 2.3)$

8. $(9.9 + x) \div 0.25; x = 3.6$

9. $112.5 - (3.3 \div 0.6) \times 2$

10. $[(2 + 9.8) - 2.5] + 7.7$

11. $[2.1 \times (125 \div 5)] - 2.5$

12. $[(16 \times 3.5) \div 0.25] + 1 - 10^2$

13. $14.6 + [(42 - 21.4) \times 3.5]$

14. $18.9 - [(33.3 \div 11.1) \times 6]$

15. $3 \times [(18 \times 5.5) \div y]; y = 0.3$

Problem Solving

16. Writing to Explain How do you know which part of the expression to solve first? Explain.

$(26 + 2.5) - [(8.3 \times 3) + (1 - 0.25)]$

17. Estimation Explain how you could use estimation to get an approximate answer for the expression below.

$(11.6 + 7.3) - (6.2 \times 2.1)$

18. Theresa bought three containers of tennis balls at $2.98 each. She had a coupon for $1 off. Her mom paid for half of the remaining cost. Evaluate the expression $[(3 \times 2.98) - 1] \div 2$.

19. Soledad solves the problem below and thinks that the answer is 92.3. Jill solves the same problem, but thinks that the answer is 67.5. Who is correct?

$[(65 + 28.2) - (7.8 + 5.5)] - 12.4$

20. **Think About the Process** Using order of operations, which is the last operation you should perform to evaluate this expression?

$(1 \times 2.5) + (52 \div 13) + (5 + 6.7) - (98 - 8)$

A Addition

B Subtraction

C Multiplication

D Division

21. How long of a piece of tape would be needed to go around the perimeter of the triangle below?

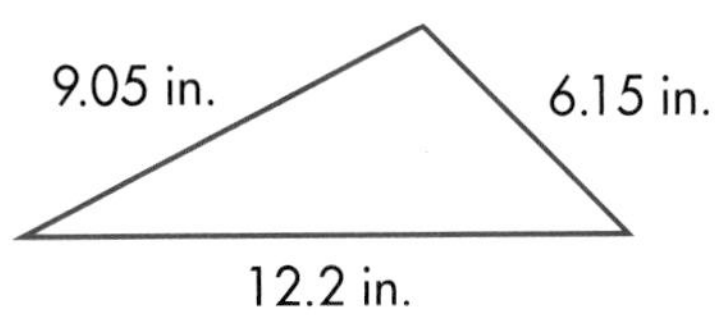

1. The table gives the size of some park areas. Which is the best estimate of the difference between the sizes of Shady Heights and Pine Island? (3-1)

Park Area	Size in Acres
Shady Heights	58.38
Pine Island	27.5
Oak Woods	792.84

A 30 acres

B 35 acres

C 38 acres

D 40 acres

2. If eight ounces of canned pumpkin has 85 calories, how many calories are in one ounce? (3-5)

A 16.25 calories

B 16.025 calories

C 10.625 calories

D 10.025 calories

3. What is the sum of 23.7 and 6.912? (3-2)

A 7.149

B 16.778

C 30.919

D 30.612

4. Which of the following is equal to 4.2? (3-8)

A $2.4 + 3 \times 4 - 2 \div 2$

B $2.4 + [3 \times (4 - 2)] \div 2$

C $[(2.4 + 3) \times 4 - 2] \div 2$

D $[2.4 + 3 \times (4 - 2)] \div 2$

5. One day, 2,149 people visited an amusement park. If the cost of admission for each person is $28.95, which is the best estimate of the total cost of admissions for the day? (3-3)

A $60,000

B $55,000

C $600,000

D $6,000

6. Kimberly scored a total of 35.104 points in four events for her gymnastic competition. If she scored the same amount on each event, how many points did she score on each? (3-5)

A 0.8776 points

B 8.0776 points

C 8.776 points

D 87.76 points

7. The average annual rainfall in Tucson, Arizona, is 12.17 inches. If Tucson receives 14.1 inches in one year, how many inches above average is that amount? (3-2)

A 12.03 inches

B 2.93 inches

C 1.93 inches

D 1.07 inches

8. Which of the following is equal to $2 \div 0.008$? (3-6)

A $2{,}000 \div 8$

B $2 \div 8$

C $2{,}000 \div 80$

D $0.002 \div 8$

9. What is 1.61 ÷ 2.3? (3-7)

A 0.8

B 0.7

C 0.08

D 0.07

10. The unit used to measure the height of a horse is called a hand. One hand is equal to 10.16 centimeters. If a horse is 15 hands tall, how many centimeters tall is it? (3-4)

A 60.96 centimeters

B 151.14 centimeters

C 152.04 centimeters

D 152.4 centimeters

11. The Earth orbits the Sun at an average distance of about 92,960,000 miles from the Sun. Which expresses the distance in scientific notation? (3-9)

A 10×9.296^7

B 10×9.296^6

C 9.296×10^6

D 9.296×10^7

12. Russ has a car that averages 9.8 miles per gallon while Mike's car averages 39.2 miles per gallon. How many times more miles per gallon does Mike's car get than Russ's car? (3-7)

A 4.1

B 4

C 3.5

D 3

13. To ship a package, a shipping company charges $1.68 for each pound. How much would it cost to ship a 5.5 pound package? Find $1.68 × 5.5. (3-4)

A $8.40

B $9.24

C $16.80

D $92.40

14. The table shows the entrance prices at a museum. The Rodriguez family has 2 adults and 5 children. If they have a coupon for $10 off, what is the total cost of admission for the family? (3-10)

Data

Type of Ticket	Cost
Adult	$12.50
Child	$4.00
Senior	$5.00

A $35

B $45

C $50

D $58

15. What is the first step in evaluating the expression shown below? (3-8)

$[3 \times (12.4 + 2.1)] - 14 + 7.9$

A Multiply 3 and 12.4.

B Add 14 and 7.9.

C Add 12.4 and 2.1.

D Multiply 3 and 2.1.

Reteaching

Set A, pages 62–63

Jesse has $20 to buy school supplies. The items he wants to buy cost $5.49, $4.39, $6.99, and $4.96. Does he have enough money?

Use rounding to estimate the sum. Round each number to the same place value.

5.49 + 4.39 + 6.99 + 4.96

↓ ↓ ↓ ↓

5 + 4 + 7 + 5 = 21

Jesse does not have enough money.

Remember that you can estimate sums and differences of decimals by rounding or using front-end estimation.

Estimate each answer.

1. 91.2 + 89.9 **2.** 902.3 − 8.8

3. 62.99 − 10.83 **4.** 423.22 + 98.30

5. 24.52 − 9.6 **6.** 369.45 + 32.42

7. 16 + 19.234 **8.** 62.54 − 32.92

Set B, pages 64–65

Lucy bought 3 pounds of pears and 9.12 pounds of apples. Find the number of pounds of pears and apples Lucy bought.

Write the numbers. Add a decimal to the whole number and annex zeros as placeholders. Then add.

$$\begin{array}{r} 3.00 \\ +\ 9.12 \\ \hline 12.12 \end{array}$$

Lucy bought 12.12 pounds of pears and apples.

Remember to line up the decimal points and to annex zeros as placeholders before calculating sums and differences.

1. 523.2 + 25.2

2. 902.3 − 7.8

3. 98.23 − 42.33

4. 178.23 + 220.34

5. 2.93 + 7.24

Set C, pages 66–68

Estimate 27.183 ÷ 3.2.

Use compatible numbers to estimate a product or quotient.

27.183 ÷ 3.2

↓ ↓

27 ÷ 3 = 9

27.183 and 3.2 are close to the compatible numbers 27 and 3.

So, 27.183 ÷ 3.2 ≈ 9.

Remember that you can estimate products and quotients using rounding or compatible numbers.

Estimate each answer. Tell which method you used.

1. 6.42 ÷ 2.96 **2.** 15.23 × 9.15

3. 495.12 ÷ 74.5 **4.** 12.421 × 3.17

5. 132 × 820 **6.** 998 ÷ 12

7. 9,032 ÷ 289 **8.** 68 × 31

Set D, pages 70–72

Find 52.5 × 1.9. Estimate: 50 × 2 = 100.

```
   52.5  ←   1 decimal place
×   1.9  ←  + 1 decimal place
   4725
   5250
  99.75  ←   2 decimal places
```

The answer is reasonable because 99.75 is close to 100.

Remember to count the number of decimal places in both factors in order to place the decimal correctly in the product.

Find each product.

1. 5 × 98.2 **2.** 4 × 0.21

3. 4.4 × 6 **4.** 7 × 21.6

5. 12.5 × 163.2 **6.** 16 × 52.3

7. 0.8 × 0.11 **8.** 0.07 × 0.44

9. 6.4 × 3.2 **10.** 31.5 × 0.01

Set E, pages 74–75

Divide 333.37 ÷ 53. Estimate: 300 ÷ 50 = 6.

```
      6.29
53)333.37
  − 318
     153    Bring down 3.
   − 106
     477    Bring down 7.
   − 477
       0
```

Remember to place the decimal point in the quotient above the decimal point in the dividend.

Find each quotient.

1. $1.89 ÷ 3 **2.** 638.4 ÷ 7

3. 116 ÷ 8 **4.** 110.7 ÷ 9

5. 511.2 ÷ 6 **6.** $24.60 ÷ 8

7. 35.75 ÷ 55 **8.** 120.4 ÷ 602

Set F, pages 76–77

Divide 54 ÷ 2.5. Estimate: 50 ÷ 2 = 25.

Multiply the divisor and dividend by the same power of 10 and place the decimal in the quotient. Then divide.

```
                   21.6    21.6 is close to
2.5)54.0  →    25)540.0    the estimate 25.
                − 50
                   40
                 − 25
                  150
                − 150
                    0
```

54 ÷ 2.5 = 21.6

Remember to move the decimal point in the dividend the same number of places it was moved for the divisor.

Find each quotient.

1. 115 ÷ 0.04 **2.** 51 ÷ 0.006

3. 126 ÷ 0.9 **4.** 11 ÷ 0.0025

5. 5 ÷ 0.05 **6.** 16 ÷ 1.6

7. 28 ÷ 0.07 **8.** 65 ÷ 1.3

9. 450 ÷ 1.25 **10.** 21 ÷ 1.05

Set G, pages 78–79

Find $2.75 \div 0.05$.

Step 1 Use multiplication to estimate.
You know $100 \times 0.05 = 5$.
So $2.75 \div 0.05 < 100$.

Step 2 Multiply the divisor and dividend by the same power of 10 and place the decimal in the quotient.

$0.05\overline{)2.75} \rightarrow 5\overline{)275.}$

Step 3 Divide.

$$\begin{array}{r} 55. \\ 5\overline{)275.} \\ -25 \\ \hline 25 \\ -25 \\ \hline 0 \end{array}$$

Since $55 < 100$, the answer is reasonable.
$2.75 \div 0.05 = 55$

Remember to think of a power of 10 that will make the divisor a whole number.

Find the power of 10 that will make the divisor a whole number.

1. $9.6 \div 1.6$

2. $48.4 \div 0.4$

3. $13.2 \div 0.006$

4. $10.8 \div 0.09$

Find each quotient.

5. $80.1 \div 0.9$

6. $12.8 \div 0.4$

7. $1.26 \div 0.2$

8. $1.68 \div 0.8$

9. $2.24 \div 3.2$

10. $3.78 \div 4.2$

11. $42.5 \div 0.05$

12. $75.5 \div 0.5$

13. $117.3 \div 2.3$

14. $132.68 \div 2.14$

Set H, pages 80–81

Use the order of operations to evaluate expressions with brackets.

Order of Operations

1. Compute inside parentheses and brackets.
2. Evaluate terms with exponents.
3. Multiply and divide from left to right.
4. Add and subtract from left to right.

Remember that you can think of brackets as outside parentheses and evaluate the inside parentheses first.

Evaluate each expression.

1. $(7.8 + 4.7) \div 0.25$

2. $92.3 - (3.2 \div 0.4) \times 2^3$

3. $[(8 \times 2.5) \div 0.5] + 120$

4. $31.2(40 + 60) \div 0.6$

5. $(8.7 - 3.2) \div 0.5$

Use the values given for variables to evaluate each expression.

6. $4.2 + 5 \times x \div 0.10; x = 4$

7. $2^2 \times (4.2 - y); y = 1.2$

8. $12 + (4^2 \div z); z = 0.04$

Topic 3

Reteaching

Set I, pages 82–83

Write 1,800,000,000 in scientific notation.

1,800,000,000 → First Factor 1.8

The decimal point moved left, 9 places.

When the decimal point moves to the left, use a positive exponent to write the power-of-10 factor.

Power-of-10 factor → 10^9

$1{,}800{,}000{,}000 = 1.8 \times 10^9$

Write 0.0000617 in scientific notation.

0.0000617 → First Factor 6.17

The decimal point moved right 5 places.

When the decimal point moves to the right, use a negative exponent to write the power-of-10 factor.

Power-of-10 factor → 10^{-5}

$0.0000617 = 6.17 \times 10^{-5}$

Remember to count the number of places you move the decimal point to the right or left to find the exponent for the power-of-10 factor.

Find the power-of-10 factor.

1. $167{,}233{,}000 = 1.67233 \times$ ☐
2. $0.000872 = 8.72 \times$ ☐
3. $27{,}834{,}000 = 2.7834 \times$ ☐
4. $0.0000761 = 7.61 \times$ ☐
5. $3{,}415{,}617{,}893{,}400 =$ $3.4156178934 \times$ ☐
6. $0.000000056 = 5.6 \times$ ☐

Write each number in scientific notation.

7. 0.000123
8. 978,636,545,232
9. 2,056,105
10. 0.00940051
11. 0.000234
12. 869,545,464,121
13. 31,562,163
14. 0.0830242

Set J, pages 84–86

Find and answer the hidden questions to solve multiple-step word problems.

Each layer of a box will hold 16 toys. If a box has 4 layers, will 3 boxes be enough to hold 180 toys?

Hidden Question 1: How many toys does one box hold?

You know each layer holds 16 toys and each box has 4 layers.

So, 16 toys $\times$ 4 layers = 64 toys per box.

Hidden Question 2: How many toys are in 3 boxes?

64 toys per box $\times$ 3 boxes = 192 toys

Yes, 3 boxes will hold 180 toys.

Remember to find and answer the hidden questions to solve the problem.

1. Melina is in charge of buying 30 snack packs of dried fruit for the picnic. Where should she buy the dried fruit for the lowest cost?

Data

Dried Fruit Snack Pack Prices	
Fresh Foods Market	5/$4
Karmel's Fruit Stand	3/$2.50

2. One weekend, Franco hiked 3 miles on Saturday and twice as many miles on Sunday. How many total miles did Franco hike?

Topic 4

Solving Equations

1 How high do hot-air balloons fly? The world record is about 65,000 feet. How much higher is this than a normal flight? You will find out in Lesson 4-2.

The world's largest fish is a whale shark. How many times longer is this fish than you? You will find out in Lesson 4-4.

2

3

How do scientists measure the mass of objects when doing experiments? You will find out in Lesson 4-1.

Review What You Know!

Vocabulary

Choose the best terms from the box.

- equal
- equation
- opposite
- variable

1. In the expression 6*x*, *x* is a(n) __?__.

2. The __?__ of –6 is 6.

3. A(n) __?__ is a math statement that shows that two parts are __?__.

Equality

Tell whether the equation is true.

4. $6 + 2 = 2 + 6$

5. $4 + 5 = 3 + 6$

6. $10 - 8 = 2 + 0$

Expressions

Evaluate each expression.

7. $x - 2$ when $x = 8$

8. $2b$ when $b = 9$

9. $\frac{15}{x}$ when $x = 3$

Order of Operations

10. **Writing to Explain** Explain in which order you should compute the operations in the expression. Then evaluate the expression.

$(\frac{33}{3}) + 1$

Lesson

4-1

Understand It!
Properties of equality are used to keep equations balanced.

Properties of Equality

How can you keep an equation balanced?

An equation is a sentence that uses an equals sign to show that two expressions have the same value.

$$5 + 3 = 8$$

Think of an equation as a pan balance. To keep the pans balanced, you do the same thing to both sides. Use the Addition Property of Equality to add the same amount to both sides of an equation.

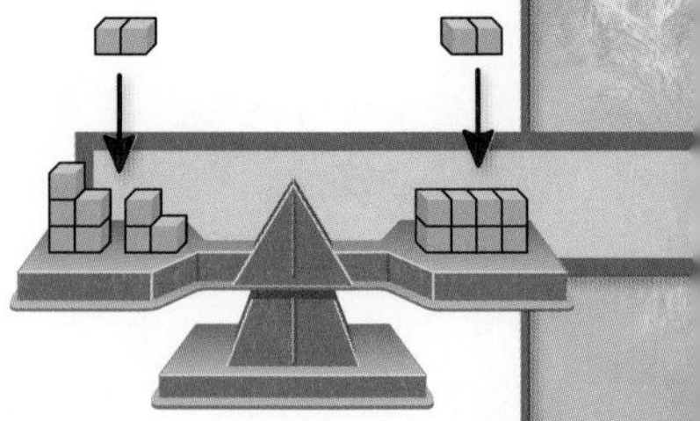

$(5 + 3) + 2 = 8 + 2$

Other Examples

Addition Property of Equality

If $12 + 18 = 30$, does $12 + 18 + 5 = 30 + 5$? Why or why not?

Yes; the same number, 5, was added to both sides of the equation.

Division Property of Equality

If $4x = 20$, does $4x \div 4 = 20 \div 5$? Why or why not?

No; both sides of the equation are divided by different numbers, not by the same amount.

Guided Practice*

Do you know HOW?

In **1** through **4**, analyze each set of equations.

1. If $23 + 37 = 60$, does $23 + 37 + 9 = 60 + 9$? Why or why not?

2. If $7m = 63$, does $7m - 9 = 63 - 9$? Why or why not?

3. If $35 - 7 = 28$, does $(35 - 7) \div 7 = 28 \div 28$? Why or why not?

4. If $8x - 2 = 34$, does $(8x - 2) \times 8 = 34 \times 2$? Why or why not?

Do you UNDERSTAND?

5. A pan balance shows $7 + 5 = 12$. If 4 units are removed from one side, what needs to be done to the other side to keep the pans balanced?

6. For the equation $23 + 43 = 66$, if one side is multiplied by 3, what needs to be done to the other side of the equation to keep them equal?

DIGITAL
Animated Glossary
www.pearsonsuccessnet.com

For another example, see Set A on page 116.

The Subtraction Property of Equality lets you subtract the same amount from both sides of the equation.

$5 + 3 = 8$

$(5 + 3) - 2 = 8 - 2$

The Multiplication Property of Equality lets you multiply both sides of the equation by the same non-zero amount.

$5 + 3 = 8$

$(5 + 3) \times 2 = 8 \times 2$

The Division Property of Equality lets you divide both sides of the equation by the same non-zero amount.

$5 + 3 = 8$

$(5 + 3) \div 2 = 8 \div 2$

Independent Practice

In **7** through **12**, analyze each set of equations.

7. If $10 \times 3 = 30$, does $10 \times 3 + 4 = 30 + 5$? Why or why not?

8. If $8n = 180$, does $8n \div 8 = 180 \div 8$? Why or why not?

9. If $78 - 7 = 71$, does $78 - 7 + 23 = 71 + 23$? Why or why not?

10. If $12 - 2 = 10$, does $12 - 2 - 3 = 10 - 2$? Why or why not?

11. If $102 \div 2 = 51$, does $102 \div 2 \times 3 = 51 \times 3$? Why or why not?

12. If $d \div 3 = 10$, does $d \div 3 + 3 = 10 + 3$? Explain.

Problem Solving

13. Scientists often use a pan balance to measure mass when doing experiments. Draw a picture of a pan balance to show $4 + 3 - 1 = 7 - 1$ if a scientist takes one unit of mass from each side of a pan balance.

14. You use a \$20 bill to pay for a purchase of \$18.60. The cashier gives you two \$1 bills and four dimes back. Were you given the correct change? Why or why not?

15. Writing to Explain Jim wrote that $5 + 5 = 10$. Then he wrote that $5 + 5 + n = 10 + n$. Are his equations balanced? Explain.

16. Think About the Process Which property was used below?

If $7m = 49$, then $7m \div 7 = 49 \div 7$

A Addition Property of Equality

B Subtraction Property of Equality

C Multiplication Property of Equality

D Division Property of Equality

Lesson
4-2

Understand It!
Inverse relationships between addition and subtraction and properties of equality can be used to solve some equations.

Solving Addition and Subtraction Equations

George bought 7 more figures.

How can you get the variable alone in an addition equation?

George had x plastic figures. After he bought 7 more figures, he had 25. How many plastic figures did George have before he bought more?

Solve the equation $x + 7 = 25$ to find the answer.

Another Example How can you get the variable alone in a subtraction equation?

Solve: $x - 19.1 = 34.4$.

What You Think

How can I get x alone on one side of the equation $x - 19.1 = 34.4$?

Adding 19.1 will undo subtracting 19.1. That will leave the x alone.

Think: Adding 19.1 is the inverse of subtracting 19.1.

What You Write

$$x - 19.1 = 34.4$$
$$x - 19.1 + 19.1 = 34.4 + 19.1$$
$$x = 53.5$$

To check, substitute 53.5 for x.

$$x - 19.1 = 34.4$$
$$53.5 - 19.1 = 34.4$$
$$34.4 = 34.4 \quad \text{It checks.}$$

Explain It

1. Explain how addition and subtraction have an inverse relationship.
2. Explain which Property of Equality was used to solve the subtraction equation above.

What You Think

Think How can I get x alone on one side of the equation $x + 7 = 25$?

Operations that undo each other have an inverse relationship. Subtracting 7 is the inverse of adding 7.

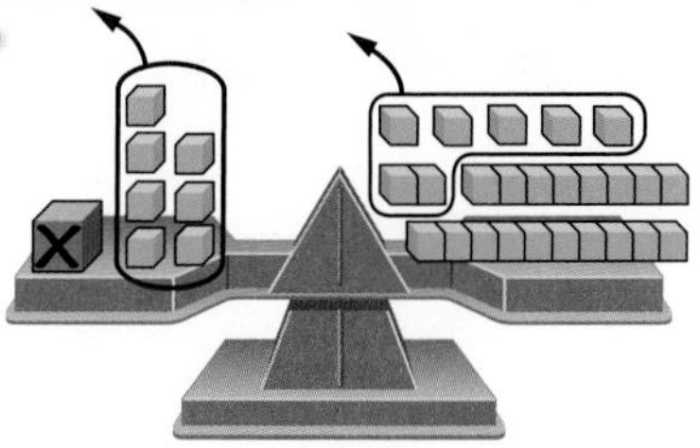

Take 7 away from each side. That will leave the x alone.

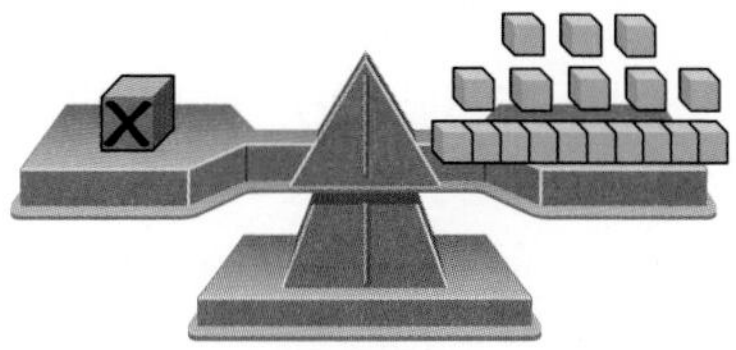

x is 18.

What You Write

$x + 7 = 25$

$x + 7 - 7 = 25 - 7$

$x = 18$

To check, substitute 18 for x.

$x + 7 = 25$

$18 + 7 = 25$

$25 = 25$ It checks.

George started with 18 figures.

Guided Practice*

Do you know HOW?

In **1** and **2**, explain how to get the variable alone in each equation.

1. $25 + m = 49$ **2.** $t - 40.5 = 3.7$

In **3** and **4**, solve each equation and check your answer.

3. $12 = x - 11$ **4.** $22.7 = 13.3 + x$

Do you UNDERSTAND?

5. In the example above, which Property of Equality was used to solve the equation?

6. Claire had x books. After she bought 8 more books, she had 24 books. How many books did Claire start with?

Solve $x + 8 = 24$.

Independent Practice

Leveled Practice Explain how to get the variable alone in each equation.

7. $y - 12 = 89$
$y - 12 + \square = 89 + 12$

8. $80.5 + r = 160$
$80.5 + r - \square = 160 - \square$

9. $60.6 = x - 16.8$
$60.6 + \square = x - 16.8 + \square$

Complete solving each equation and check your answer.

10. $20 = y + 12$
$20 - 12 = y + 12 - 12$

11. $x + 0.2 = 1.9$
$x + 0.2 - 0.2 = 1.9 - 0.2$

12. $z - 31.3 = 17.6$
$z - 31.3 + 31.3 = 17.6 + 31.3$

13. $55 = x - 48$
$55 + 48 = x - 48 + 48$

14. $19.5 = x + 8.8$
$19.5 - 8.8 = x + 8.8 - 8.8$

15. $76 = y - 18$
$76 + 18 = y - 18 + 18$

DIGITAL Animated Glossary **www.pearsonsuccessnet.com**

For another example, see Set B on page 116.

Independent Practice

Solve each equation and check your answer.

16. $y + 13 = 98$ **17.** $r - 80 = 160$ **18.** $t + 2.7 = 3.3$ **19.** $c - 8.9 = 4.6$

20. $r + 2.3 = 40$ **21.** $67.2 = s - 18.6$ **22.** $4.9 = x - 3.8$ **23.** $29 = c + 0.8$

24. $x + 13.9 = 98.9$ **25.** $m - 21.34 = 22.51$ **26.** $s - 90.9 = 43.45$ **27.** $d + 15.5 = 56.03$

Problem Solving

28. Lila would like to take a ceramics class. The class costs $120. She has saved $80 so far. Solve the equation $80 + d = 120$ to find the amount that Lila still needs.

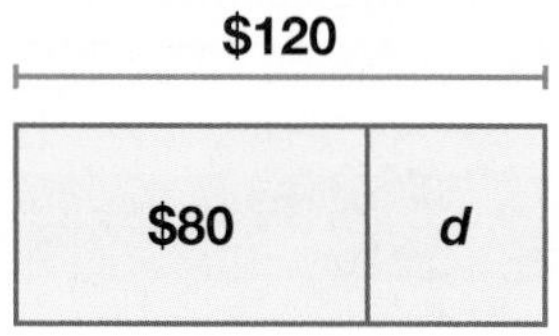

29. Every 2 weeks, Manny mows a total of 43 lawns in his neighborhood. He has 27 lawns left to mow this time. Solve the equation $43 - n = 27$ to find the number of lawns that Manny has mowed.

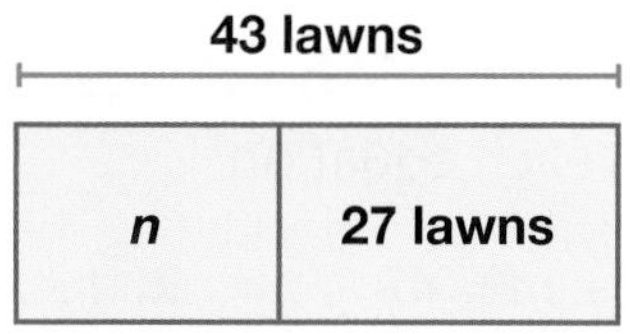

30. Give the standard form for 85 million, 16 thousand, twelve.

31. Alma pays $26.88 each week for gas and $24.95 every three months to change the oil in her car. How much does Alma pay in total for these every year?

32. The world record for a hot-air balloon flight is 65,000 feet high. Most hot-air balloons fly 62,150 feet below this height. At what height do most hot-air balloons fly? Use the equation $h + 62{,}150 = 65{,}000$.

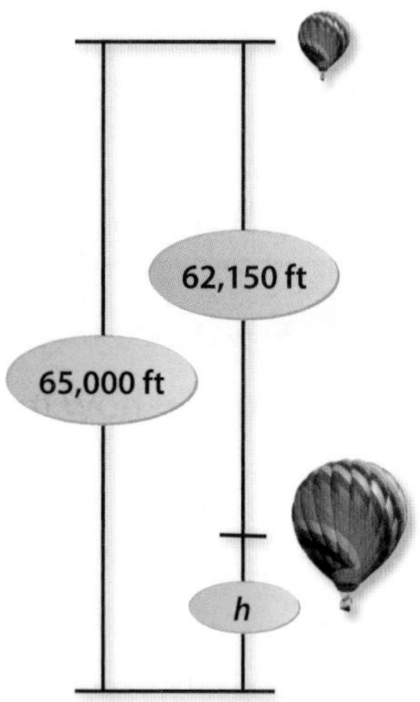

33. **Think About the Process** How could you find the solution to $c - 35.2 = 40$?

A Add 35.2 to one side.

B Subtract 35.2 from one side.

C Add 35.2 to both sides.

D Subtract 35.2 from both sides.

34. **Number Sense** Will the solution of the equation $x - 14 = 7$ be greater than or less than 7? Use number sense to decide.

35. **Writing to Explain** Explain how to get n alone in the equation $n + 25 = 233$.

Enrichment

Other Properties of Equality

When you solve equations, you apply the Addition, Subtraction, Multiplication, and Division Properties of Equality. There are three more properties that can help you to solve equations: the Reflexive, Symmetric, and Transitive Properties of Equality.

Property	Mathematical Statement	What It Means
Reflexive Property	$a = a$	A number equals itself.
Symmetric Property	If $a = b$, then $b = a$.	If numbers are equal, they remain equal if their order is changed.
Transitive Property	If $a = b$ and $b = c$, then $a = c$.	If numbers equal the same number, they equal each other.

Tip *When using the Transitive Property of Equality, make sure that both equations have equal values in common.*

Examples:

Reflexive Property
$4 = 4$
$9h = 9h$

Symmetric Property
If $4 = y$, then $y = 4$.
If $1 + 2 = 3$, then $3 = 1 + 2$.

Transitive Property
If $3 + 2 = 5$, and $8 - 3 = 5$,
then $3 + 2 = 8 - 3$.

Practice

For **1** through **3**, identify each property.

1. If $\frac{12}{6} = \frac{4}{2}$ and $\frac{4}{2} = 2$, then $\frac{12}{6} = 2$.

2. If $12 = 3x$, then $3x = 12$.

3. $9 + 3 = 9 + 3$

For **4** through **9**, name the property that describes each situation.

4. Jessica is the same height as Juan, and Juan is the same height as Lina. So, Lina and Jessica are the same height.

5. While doing a science experiment, Ali found that 12 mL $+ x = y$ and $y =$ 16 mL, so 12 mL $+ x =$ 16 mL.

6. Twelve thousand dollars equals twelve thousand dollars.

7. Wendy's dog is the same weight as Mike's dog, so Mike's dog is the same weight as Wendy's dog.

8. $d + 25 = 25 + d$

9. A number to the second power equals the same number to the second power.

Lesson
4-3

Understand It!
Learning how and when to draw a picture can help you write equations to solve problems.

Problem Solving

Draw a Picture and Write an Equation

Jaron and Max sell pens and notebooks for the student council. Their total sales this year are \$170. If they sold \$48 worth of pens, how many dollars worth of notebooks did they sell?

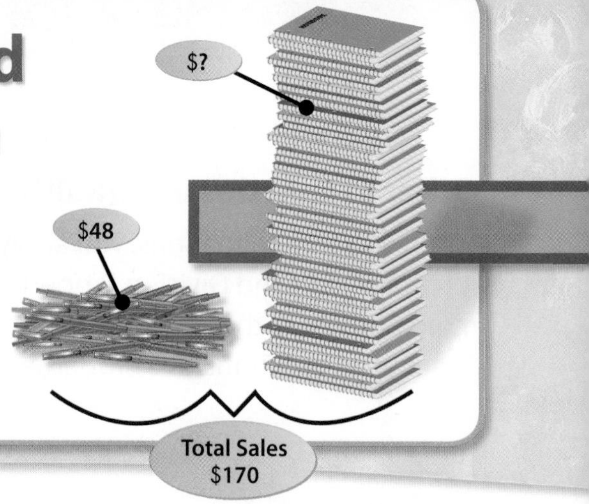

Another Example How can you translate words into subtraction equations?

Nina buys lunch for herself and her sister. She pays \$7.50. Nina has \$5.25 left over. How much money did she begin with?

Read and Understand

What do I know? Nina pays \$7.50 for lunch for herself and her sister. She has \$5.25 left.

What am I asked to find? How much money did Nina have before she bought lunch?

Plan and Solve

Draw a Picture Use the picture to represent the problem, and write an equation. Let b = the money Nina began with.

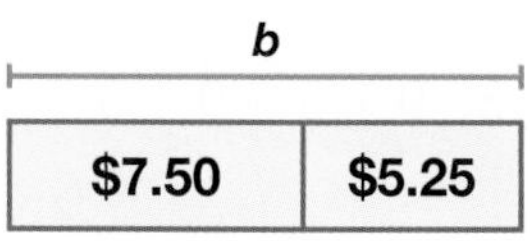

Solve $b - 7.50 = 5.25$.

$b - 7.50 + 7.50 = 5.25 + 7.50$

$b = 12.75$

Nina began with \$12.75.

Explain It

1. **Reasonableness** How can you use estimation to know if the answer is reasonable?
2. Tell how to check the problem.

Read and Understand

What do I know?

Jaron and Max sold \$170 worth of pens and notebooks. They sold \$48 worth of pens.

What am I asked to find?

How many dollars worth of notebooks did they sell?

Plan and Solve

Draw a Picture Use a picture to represent the problem, and write an equation.

Let s = the sales of notebooks in dollars.

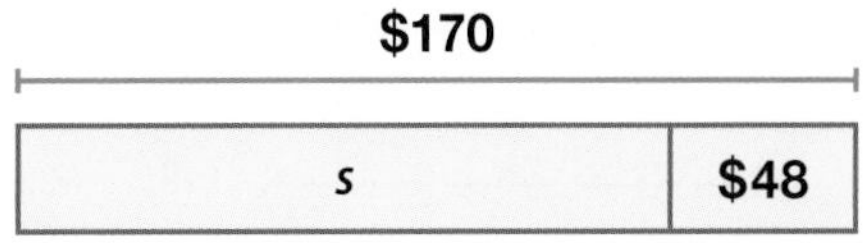

Solve $s + 48 = 170$.

$s + 48 - 48 = 170 - 48$

$s = 122$

They sold \$122 worth of notebooks.

Guided Practice*

Do you know HOW?

Draw a picture and write an equation to solve.

1. Drew sold lemonade and apples at the school fair. She sold a total of \$64. If she sold \$21 in lemonade, how many dollars worth of apples did she sell?

Do you UNDERSTAND?

2. In the example at the top of the page, how can you use estimation to know if the answer is reasonable?

3. In the example at the top of the page, how can you check the answer?

Independent Practice

Solve.

4. Raquel and Mark want to buy their mom a gift that costs \$32.95. Raquel earns \$18.20 babysitting. How much does Mark need to earn to pay for the gift? Draw a picture and write an equation to solve.

5. Steven bicycled 126 miles in a month. He bicycled 17 miles less than Jessica. Write and solve an equation to find how far Jessica went.

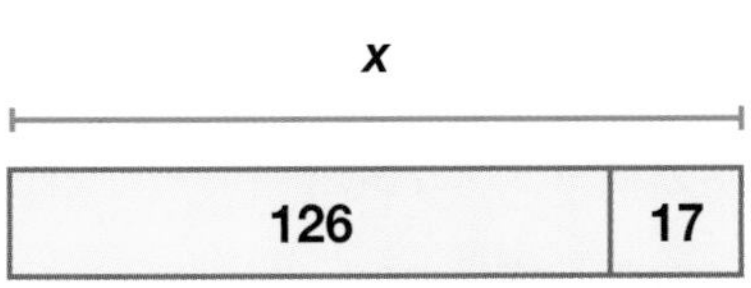

Stuck? Try this....

- What do I know?
- What am I asked to find?
- What diagram can I use to help understand the problem?
- Can I use addition, subtraction, multiplication, or division?
- Is all my work correct?
- Did I answer the right question?
- Is my answer reasonable?

*For another example, see Set C on page 116.

Independent Practice

6. The band has sold 184 tickets for their concert. They want to sell 31 more. How many tickets do they want to sell?

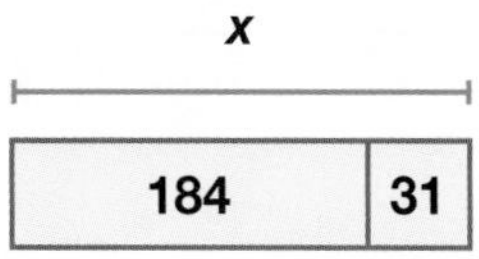

7. Mike knows that it will cost $66.34 to get his bike fixed. He has $42.68. How much more money does Mike need?

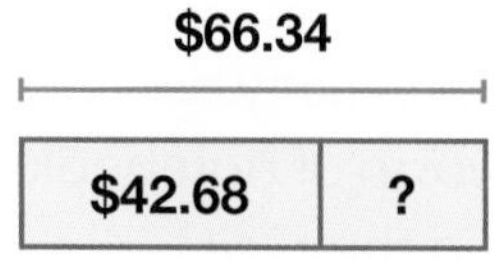

8. Lake Victoria in Africa is 26,828 square miles. It is 26,635 square miles larger than Lake Tahoe in the United States. How big is Lake Tahoe? Use the equation $x + 26{,}635 = 26{,}828$.

9. Anya pays the bus fare for herself and her brother. She pays $3.50. Anya is left with $6.25. How much money did she begin with? Use the equation $x - \$3.50 = \$6.25$.

10. Mirabel is thinking of a number. She tells her friend if she subtracts 87 from the number, she will get 37. What is the number?

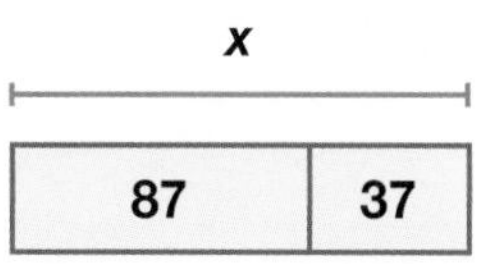

11. A sequoia known as Tall Tree measures about 368 feet. Another sequoia known as General Grant measures about 267 feet. How much would General Grant have to grow to be as tall as Tall Tree?

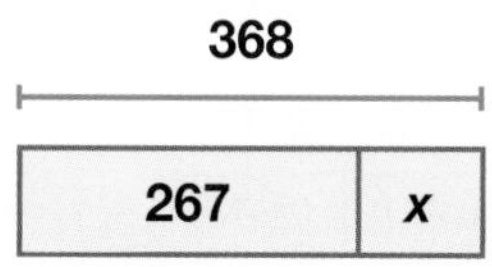

Think About the Process

12. Simon has collected 27 pairs of glasses for charity. He wants to collect a total of 55 pairs. If x equals the number of pairs of glasses Simon still wants to collect, which equation best describes the total number of pairs he wants to collect?

A $27 + x = 55$

B $x - 27 = 55$

C $x - 55 = 27$

D $27 + 55 = x$

13. In a survey of pet owners, 267 people owned only dogs. The remaining 258 people owned only cats. Which equation could you use to find the total number of pet owners, T?

A $T + 258 = 267$

B $T - 267 = 258$

C $267 - T = 258$

D $267 + T = 258$

Going Digital

Solving Addition Equations

Use e tools

Place-Value Blocks

Use the Place-Value Blocks eTool to solve $x + 35 = 52$.

Step 1 Go to the Place-Value Blocks eTool. Select the Two-part workspace. Think of the top space as representing the left side of the equation and the bottom space as representing the right side. Click on the long vertical block. Then, click in the top part of the workspace 3 times to show 30. Click on the small cube and click in the top part of the workspace 5 times to show 5. The odometer should read 35. Use blocks to show 52 in the bottom part of the workspace, similarly. Imagine an x in the top part.

Step 2 Use the Erase tool to remove a vertical block from both the top and the bottom part of the workspace. This is like subtracting 10 from both sides of the equation. Remove as many pairs of 10 as you can. Erase two pairs of small cubes, similarly. You should have 3 ones in the top workspace and 2 tens in the bottom work space. Use the Hammer tool to break apart one of the tens in the bottom part into 10 ones. Then remove 3 more pairs of ones from the top and bottom. The bottom part of the workspace now has 17. Thus, $x = 17$ is the solution to the equation $x + 35 = 52$.

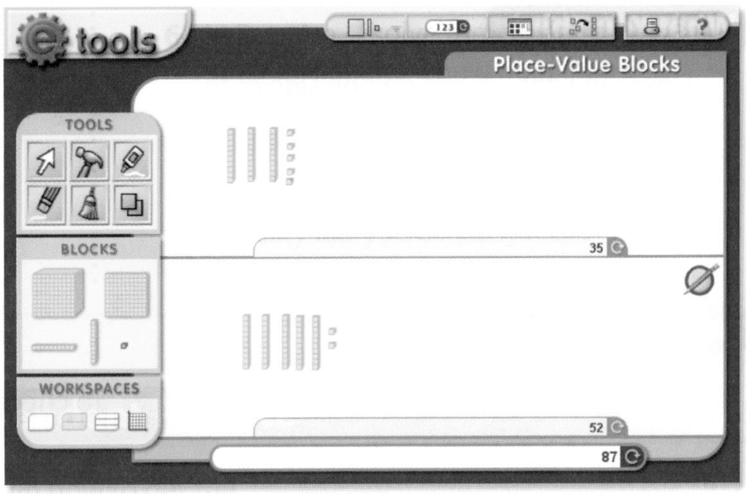

Practice

Solve each equation.

1. $x + 43 = 61$

2. $x + 28 = 74$

3. $x + 29 = 85$

4. $38 + x = 105$

5. $41 + x = 163$

6. $176 + x = 326$

Problem Solving

24. **Writing to Explain** How can you find the solution to the equation $4x = 20$?

25. A female whale shark is 35 feet long. An average 12-year-old is 5 feet tall. How many times longer is this fish than an average 12-year-old? Solve the equation $35 = 5x$.

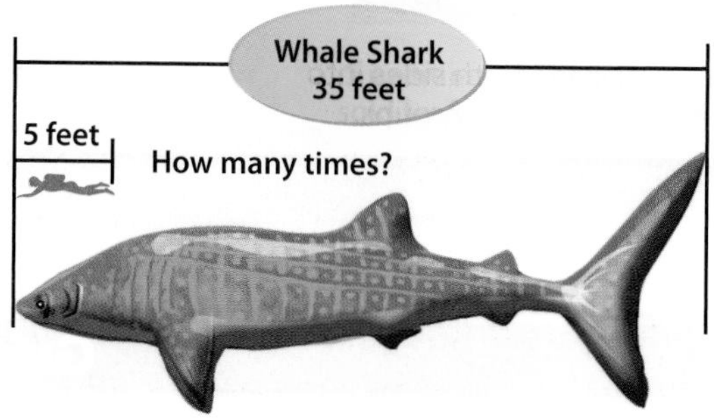

26. Two teams of students earned money by washing cars. Team 1 washed 19 cars at $4.25 each. Team 2 washed 17 cars for a total of $82.50. Which team earned more money? By how much?

27. A supertaster can have about 4.5 times more taste buds than a nontaster. If a supertaster has 425 taste buds per square centimeter, how many taste buds might a nontaster have per square centimeter? Use the equation $4.5t = 425$.

28. **Estimation** About how much is the value of x in the equation $254 = 75x$?

29. **Number Sense** Is 280 the solution of $x \div 4 = 70$? Explain your answer.

30. Josh's class is planting a garden. Josh divided seeds so that 20 students had 35 seeds each.

    a How many seeds did Josh start with? Use the equation $y \div 20 = 35$.

    b How many seeds would each student get if there were 25 students to divide the same number of seeds?

31. **Think About the Process** What is the first step in solving the equation below?

    $x \div 30 = 8$

    A Add 30 to both sides.

    B Subtract 30 from both sides.

    C Multiply both sides by 30.

    D Divide both sides by 30.

32. Which algebraic equation best describes total weight (T) of four baskets of strawberries, if w equals the weight of one box of strawberries?

    A $T = 4 + w$ **C** $T = 4 \div w$

    B $T = w \div 4$ **D** $T = 4w$

33. Eric paid a library fine (f) for returning a book 4 days late. If the library charges $0.15 per day for late returns, which equation best describes his fine?

    A $f \times 4 = 0.15$ **C** $4 \div f = 0.15$

    B $f \div 4 = 0.15$ **D** $4 - f = 0.15$

Square Roots

A *square number* is any number that can be written as the product of a whole number multiplied by itself. For example, $9 = 3 \times 3$, so 9 is a square number. The square of 3 is 3^2, or 9.

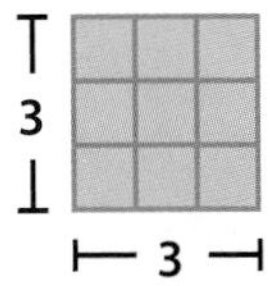

Square numbers can be modeled as the area of square arrays.

$3^2 = 9$

Finding the *square root* of a number is the inverse of squaring a number. To find the square root of a number, ask, "What number times itself equals the given number?" The symbol for a square root is $\sqrt{\ }$. It's called a radical sign.

Find the square root of 16, or $\sqrt{16}$. What number times itself is 16?

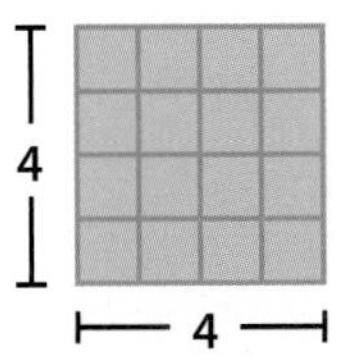

$4 \times 4 = 16$

The square root of 16 is 4, or $\sqrt{16} = 4$.

Example: Find the square root of 25, or $\sqrt{25}$.

Ask, "What number times itself is 25?"

$5 \times 5 = 25$

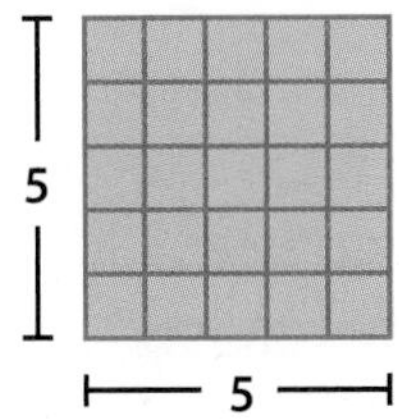

The square root of 25 is 5, or $\sqrt{25} = 5$.

Notice that the length of one of the sides of the array is the same as the square root.

Practice

For **1** through **5**, write the square number for each array. Then find the square root.

1. 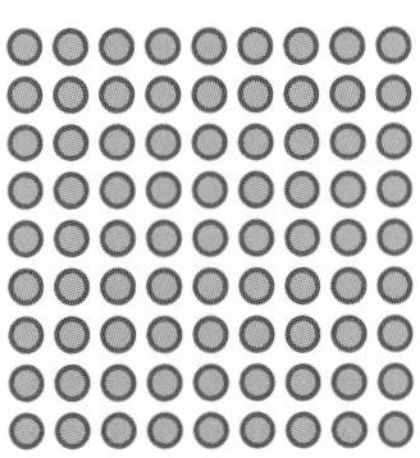

2. 

3. 

4. 

5. 

For **6** through **11**, find each square root.

6. $\sqrt{4}$ **7.** $\sqrt{169}$ **8.** $\sqrt{1}$ **9.** $\sqrt{400}$ **10.** $\sqrt{324}$ **11.** $\sqrt{484}$

12. Writing to Explain Gina says that the square root of 100 is 50. She says that finding a square root of a number is easy; all you need to do is add two of the same number to get the answer. Is she right? Explain.

Lesson

4-5

Understand It!
Learning how and when to draw a picture can help you write equations to solve problems.

Problem Solving

Draw a Picture and Write an Equation

Min and her 4 friends had a garage sale to help pay for their choir trip. They divided their total earnings so that each person had $37. How much was the total earnings from the garage sale?

Another Example How can you translate words into multiplication equations?

Gary collects minerals. His friend Elli has 5 times as many minerals as he does. If Elli has 125 minerals, how many does Gary have?

Read and Understand

What do I know? Elli has 5 times more minerals than Gary has. Elli has 125 minerals.

What am I asked to find? How many minerals Gary has.

Plan and Solve

Draw a Picture Use the picture to represent the problem, and write an equation. Let x equal the minerals Gary has.

Solve $5x = 125$.

$5x \div 5 = 125 \div 5$

$x = 25$

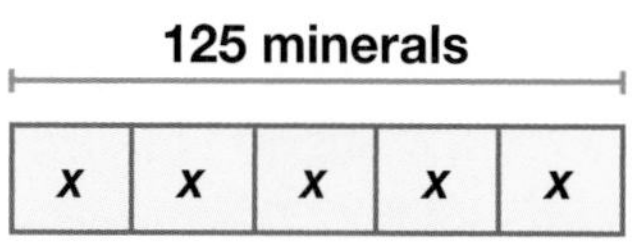

Gary has 25 minerals.

Explain It

1. **Reasonableness** How can you use estimation to know if the answer is reasonable?
2. Tell how to check the problem.

Read and Understand

What do I know?

Min and 4 friends had a garage sale and each earned $37.

What am I asked to find?

How much was the total earnings from the garage sale?

Plan and Solve

Draw a Picture Use a picture to represent the problem and write an equation.

Let t = the total earnings in dollars.

t = total earnings

$37	$37	$37	$37	$37

Solve $t \div 5 = 37$.

$t \div 5 \times 5 = 37 \times 5$

$t = 185$

The garage sale raised $185.

Guided Practice*

Do you know HOW?

Draw a picture and write an equation to solve.

1. Ryan made a CD of his favorite songs. There are 42 minutes of time on the CD. He records 14 songs. What is the average length of each song?

Do you UNDERSTAND?

2. In the example at the top of the page, how can you use estimation to know if the answer is reasonable?

3. In the example at the top of the page, how can you check the answer?

Independent Practice

Solve.

4. David saves $15 each week that he earns babysitting. After 8 weeks, how much money will he have saved? Draw a picture and write an equation to solve.

5. The Technology Club pools their money to buy robot parts. They divide the parts among the 13 members. Each gets 24 parts. Write an equation to find the total number of parts.

t = total number of parts

24	24	24	24	24	24	24	24	24	24	24	24	24

Stuck? Try this....

- What do I know?
- What am I asked to find?
- What diagram can I use to help understand the problem?
- What operation should I use in my equation?
- Is all my work correct?
- How can I check my answer?

*For another example, see Set E on page 117.

Independent Practice

6. In a lunch survey, 3 times as many students preferred soft tacos as preferred pizza. If 324 students preferred soft tacos, how many students preferred pizza?

7. A charity group divides donated items among 19 families. Each family receives 14 items. How many items were donated in total? Use the picture to help solve.

i = total items

14	14	14	14	14	14	14	14	14	14	14	14	14	14	14	14	14	14	14

8. Vicki hands out stickers to 23 preschool students. If each child gets 9 stickers, how many stickers were there to begin with? Solve the equation $s \div 23 = 9$.

9. Darby rents in-line skates for 4.5 hours. His total bill is \$27. How much did he pay per hour to rent the skates? Solve the equation $4.5x = \$27$.

10. In an orchestra, there are 5 times as many string instruments as percussion instruments. If there are 45 string instruments, how many percussion instruments are there?

11. Raffle tickets are sold to 435 people attending the school fair. If 6 tickets were sold per person, how many tickets were sold? Solve the equation $t \div 435 = 6$.

Think About the Process

12. Raquel walks dogs for her neighbors. She worked for 11 hours and earned \$71.50.

    If x equals how much Raquel charges per hour, which equation best describes how much she earned?

    A $x - 11 = \$71.50$

    B $x \div 11 = \$71.50$

    C $11x = \$71.50$

    D $x + 11 = \$71.50$

13. Among 65 people at a Strawberry Festival, each person eats an average of 13 strawberries. If s equals the total number of strawberries eaten, which equation best shows how the total strawberries were divided among the people?

    A $s - 65 = 13$

    B $65 \div 13 = s$

    C $13s = 65$

    D $s \div 65 = 13$

Stop and Practice

Skills Review Complete the equations.

1. $12 + 15 = 27$
$12 + 15 + 6 = 27 + \square$
$\square = \square$

2. $57 - 9 = 48$
$57 - 9 - 7 = 48 - \square$
$\square = \square$

3. $6 \times 6 = 36$
$6 \times 6 \div 4 = 36 \div \square$
$\square = \square$

4. $64 \div 8 = 8$
$64 \div 8 \times 3 = 8 \times \square$
$\square = \square$

Solve each equation.

5. $15 + x = 34$ **6.** $s + 1.7 = 30$ **7.** $u - 12 = 45$ **8.** $n - 5.7 = 7.5$

9. $40y = 360$ **10.** $1.5z = 10.5$ **11.** $g \div 10 = 15$ **12.** $k \div 7.25 = 8$

13. $6.12 + t = 66$ **14.** $p \div 5.5 = 11$ **15.** $0.8z = 48$ **16.** $m - 9.45 = 2.7$

Error Search Find each solution that is not correct. Write it correctly and explain the error.

17. $w - 15 = 35$
$w = 20$

18. $27 + r = 56$
$r = 29$

19. $7p = 63$
$p = 56$

20. $v \div 4 = 32$
$v = 8$

21. $12q = 60$
$q = 5$

Number Sense

Estimating and Reasoning Write whether each statement is true or false. Explain your answer.

22. In the equation $4 + c = 18$, the value of c will be less than 18.

23. In the equation $18h = 108$, h will be less than 5.

24. The value of x in the equation $12 + x = 30$ will be less than the value of p in the equation $15 + p = 30$.

25. In the equation $9.9c = 119$, the value of c will be greater than 10.

26. The value of k will be the same in all of these equations:
$k + 5 = 62$ $k - 5 = 62$ $5k = 62$

Topic 4

Test

1. If $2x = 12$, which of the following is also true? (4-1)

   A $2x - 7 = 12 - 7$

   B $2x - 7 = 12 + 7$

   C $2x - 7 = 12$

   D $2x + 7 = 12 - 7$

2. The local animal shelter has 3 times as many cats as dogs. If there are 27 cats at the shelter, solve the equation $3x = 27$ to find the number of dogs. (4-4)

   A $x = 81$

   B $x = 24$

   C $x = 9$

   D $x = 3$

3. The choir had 50 members after 3 students joined. The equation shown can be used to find the membership, x, before the students joined. What step should be taken to get x alone on one side of the equation? (4-2)

   $x + 3 = 50$

   A Multiply each side of the equation by 3.

   B Add 3 to each side of the equation.

   C Subtract 3 from each side of the equation.

   D Divide each side of the equation by 3.

4. If $3x = 15 + 3$, which of the following is also true? (4-1)

   A $3x \div 3 = (15 + 3) \times 3$

   B $3x \div 3 = (15 + 3) \div 3$

   C $3x - 3 = (15 + 3) \div 3$

   D $3x + 3 = 15 + 3$

5. The math club is selling popcorn for a fundraiser. Gina sold 9 boxes for a total of $108 in sales. Which equation can be used to find c, the cost of each box? (4-5)

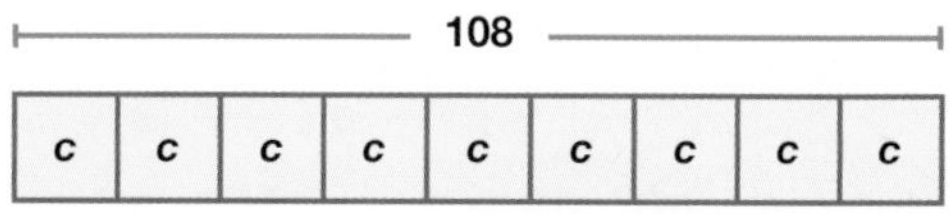

   A $c \div 9 = 108$

   B $9c = 108$

   C $c - 9 = 108$

   D $c + 9 = 108$

6. Some animals have different blood types. Dogs have 13 blood types, which is 10 more than cats have. Which picture and equation can be used to find c, the number of blood types cats have? (4-3)

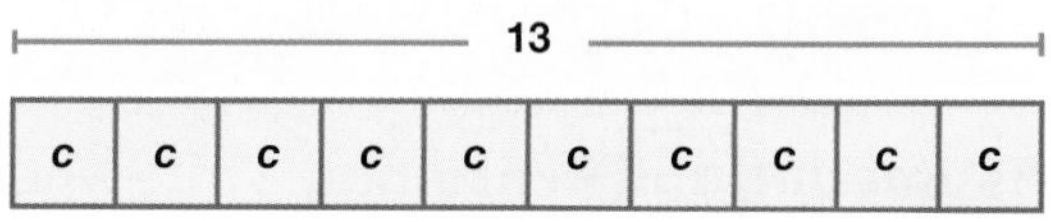

   A $10c = 13$

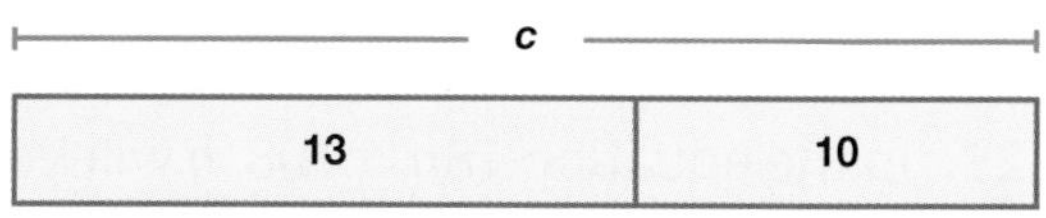

   B $c - 13 = 10$

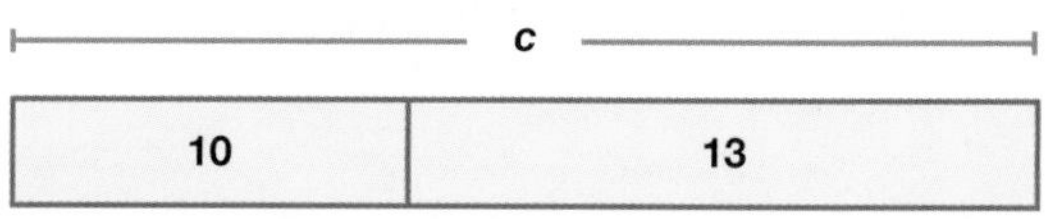

   C $c - 10 = 13$

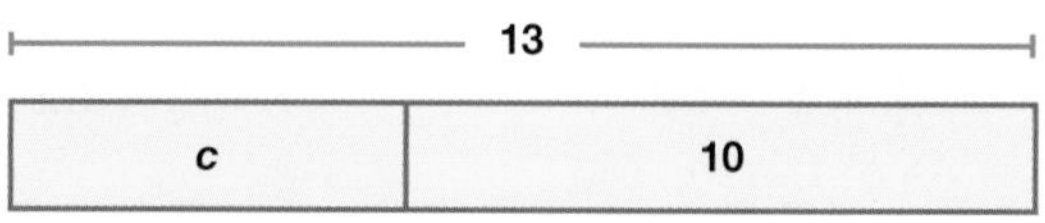

   D $c + 10 = 13$

7. Which value of m makes the following equation true? (4-4)

$m \div 1.5 = 6$

A $m = 9$

B $m = 6$

C $m = 3$

D $m = 1.5$

8. A baseball team won 36 games this season, 6 more games than last season. Solve the equation $n + 6 = 36$ to find n, the number of games they won last season. (4-2)

A $n = 6$

B $n = 30$

C $n = 40$

D $n = 42$

9. What step should be taken to get x alone in the equation shown? (4-4)

$4.2x = 60$

A Add 4.2 to each side of the equation.

B Subtract 4.2 from each side of the equation.

C Multiply each side of the equation by 4.2.

D Divide each side of the equation by 4.2.

10. Which value of t makes the following equation true? (4-2)

$t - 15.5 = 25.5$

A $t = 10$

B $t = 15.5$

C $t = 25.5$

D $t = 41$

11. Amy's horse eats 3 bales of hay each week. Which picture and equation can be used to find w, the number of weeks that 36 bales of hay will feed the horse? (4-5)

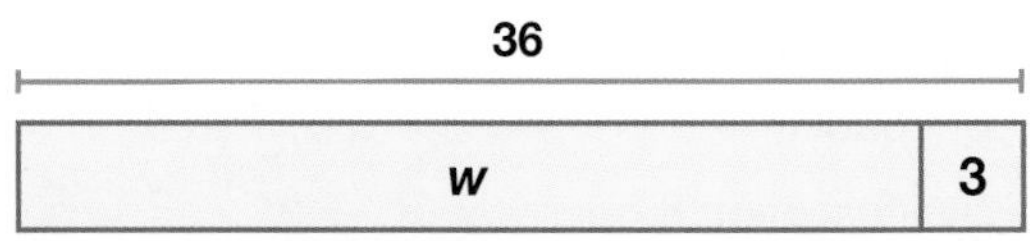

A $w + 3 = 36$

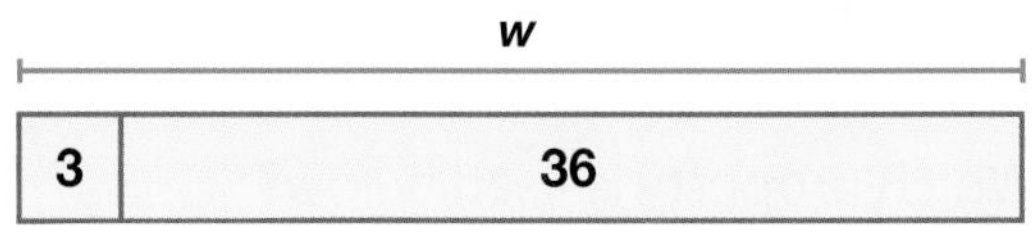

B $w - 3 = 36$

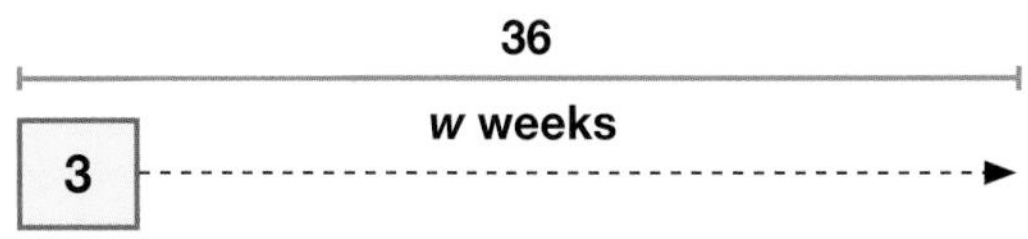

C $3w = 36$

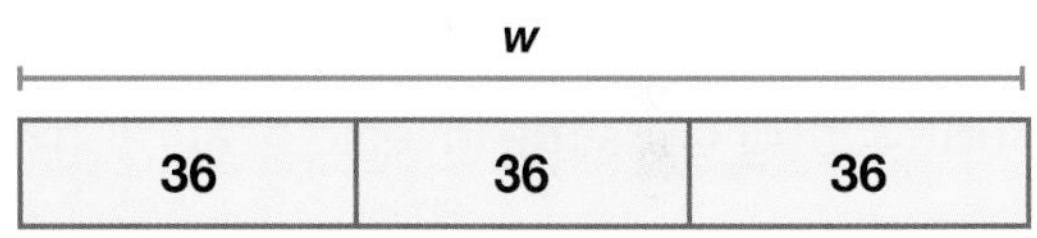

D $w \div 3 = 36$

12. There are 53 countries in Africa, including 6 countries that are islands off the coast of the main continent. Which equation can be used to find c, the number of countries that are on the main continent? (4-3)

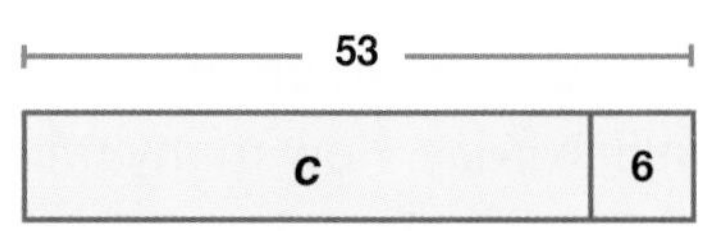

A $c + 6 = 53$

B $c - 6 = 53$

C $6c = 53$

D $c \div 6 = 53$

Topic 4

Reteaching

Set A, pages 96–97

The properties of equality are illustrated in the table.

Properties of Equality	
Addition Property of Equality	$4 + 3 = 7$ So, $4 + 3 + 2 = 7 + 2$
Subtraction Property of Equality	$9 + 8 = 17$ So, $9 + 8 - 5 = 17 - 5$
Multiplication Property of Equality	$3 \times 5 = 15$ So, $3 \times 5 \times 2 = 15 \times 2$
Division Property of Equality	$16 + 2 = 18$ So, $(16 + 2) \div 2 = 18 \div 2$

Which property is used below?

$2 \times 3 = 6 \qquad (2 \times 3) - 4 = 6 - 4$

The Subtraction Property of Equality is used.

Remember that the properties of equality allow you to apply the same operation with the same amount to both sides of an equation.

1. If $6 + 2 = 8$, does $6 + 2 + 3 = 8 + 3$? Why or why not?
2. If $8 - 1 = 7$, does $8 - 1 - 2 = 7 - 3$? Why or why not?
3. If $8x = 56$, does $8x \div 8 = 56 \div 56$? Why or why not?
4. If $y - 6 = 13$, does $(y - 6) \times 7 = 13 \times 7$? Why or why not?

Set B, pages 98–100

Solve for x in $x + 4.8 = 19$.

Subtracting 4.8 is the inverse of adding 4.8.

$x + 4.8 = 19$	←	Solve the equation.
$x + 4.8 - 4.8 = 19 - 4.8$	←	Use the Subtraction Property of Equality.
$x = 14.2$	←	Simplify.

Remember that addition and subtraction have an inverse relationship. To check, substitute your answer back into the original equation.

Solve for x.

1. $x + 29 = 11$
2. $x + 3.4 = 15.2$
3. $x - 2.1 = 4.2$
4. $x - 17 = 13$

Set C, pages 102–104

Daniel hiked 13 miles on the weekend. He hiked 8 miles on Saturday. How many miles did he hike on Sunday? Draw a picture to represent the problem.

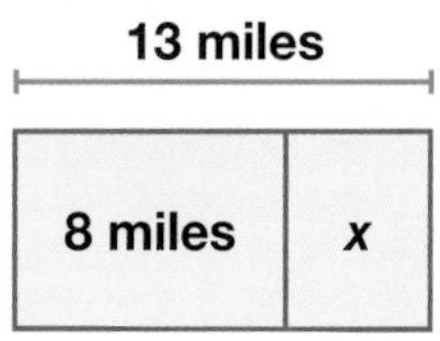

Remember that drawing a picture can help translate words into addition and subtraction equations to solve problems.

1. Use the picture to write an equation for the hiking problem.
2. Solve the equation you wrote.

Topic 4

Reteaching

Set D, pages 106–108

Solve for x in $9x = 1.8$.

Dividing by 9 is the inverse of multiplying by 9.

$9x = 1.8$ ← Solve the equation.

$9x \div 9 = 1.8 \div 9$ ← Use the Division Property of Equality.

$x = 0.2$ ← Simplify.

Remember that multiplication and division have an inverse relationship. To check, substitute your answer back into the original equation.

Solve for x.

1. $8x = 64$

2. $x \div 20 = 120$

3. $x \div 1.2 = 2$

4. $7x = 7.7$

5. $2.6 = 1.3x$

6. $24.2 = x \div 2.2$

7. $x \div 5 = 110$

8. $40x = 1{,}000$

9. $11x = 264$

10. $x \div 10 = 70$

Set E, pages 110–112

Raphael and 3 friends raised money for a band trip. If each person raised $21, what was the total amount that the 4 friends raised?

Let x be the total amount of money the 4 friends raised. Draw a picture to represent the problem.

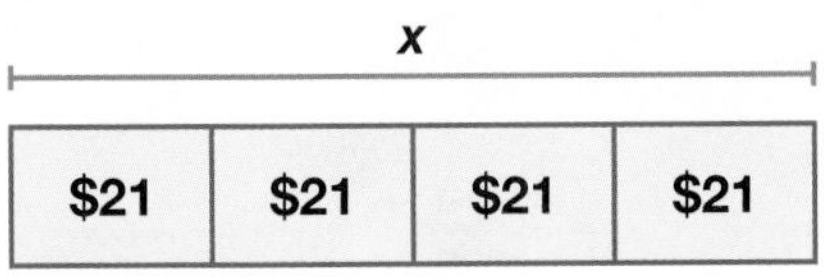

Use the drawing to write an equation and solve the problem.

$x \div 4 = 21$ ← Write the equation.

$(x \div 4) \times 4 = 21 \times 4$ ← Solve the equation.

$x = 84$ ← Simplify.

The 4 friends raised a total of $84.

Remember that drawing a picture can help translate words into multiplication and division equations to solve problems.

Solve.

1. Tyler buys cinder blocks to build a garden wall. A cinder block weighs 25 pounds. How many blocks should Tyler buy if he wants to buy 500 pounds?

2. Chris buys snacks after school. After 12 weeks, he spent $60. If he spent the same amount each week, how much did he spend each week?

3. Kyle buys 3 erasers and 1 pen. The pen costs $4.50, which is 3 times the cost of 1 eraser. How much does 1 eraser cost?

Topic 5

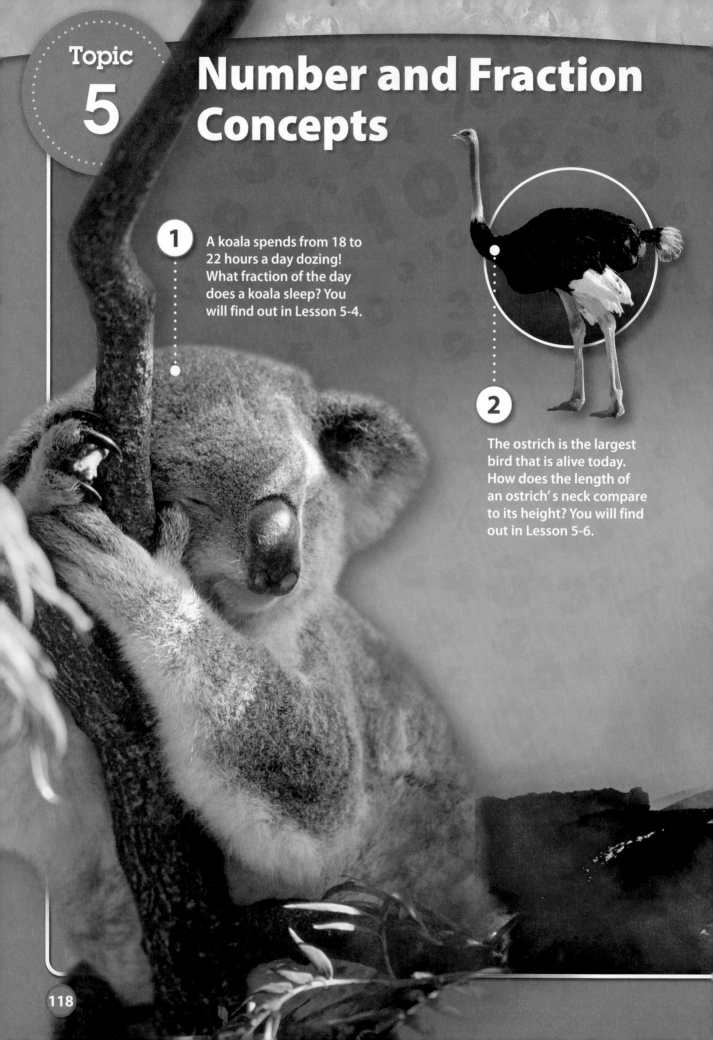

Number and Fraction Concepts

1 A koala spends from 18 to 22 hours a day dozing! What fraction of the day does a koala sleep? You will find out in Lesson 5-4.

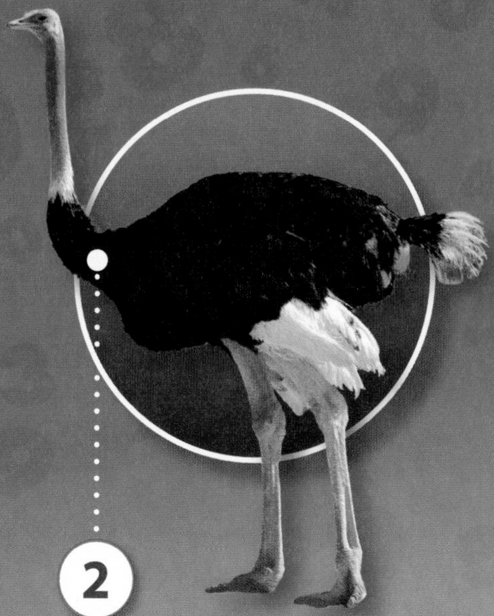

2 The ostrich is the largest bird that is alive today. How does the length of an ostrich's neck compare to its height? You will find out in Lesson 5-6.

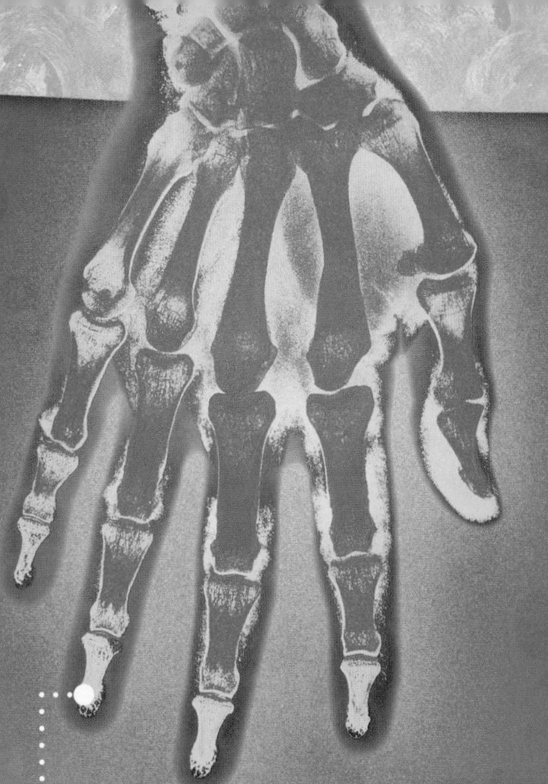

3

There are 206 bones in the human body. How many of these bones are in your hands? You will find out in Lesson 5-5.

4

In the world, 1,500 volcanoes could possibly be active. About how many of these erupt every year? You will find out in Lesson 5-3.

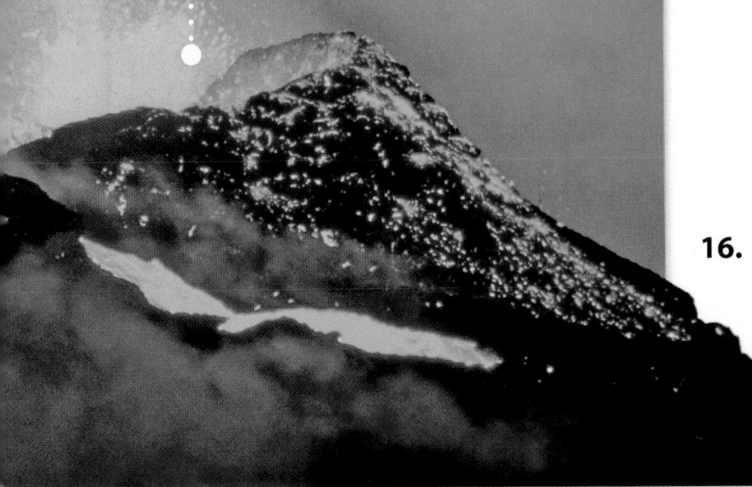

Review What You Know!

Vocabulary

Choose the best term from the box.

• divisor	• array
• factors	• multiples

1. A (an) __?__ is an arrangement of objects in rows and columns.

2. 2 and 5 are __?__ of 10.

3. The number used to divide another number is the __?__.

4. 10 and 20 are __?__ of 5.

Finding Factors

List all the factors of each number.

5. 5 **6.** 6 **7.** 14

8. 25 **9.** 32 **10.** 48

11. 56 **12.** 67 **13.** 100

Fractions

Write the fraction shown by the shaded part or region.

14. 

15. 

Exponents

16. **Writing to Explain** How can the expression $11 \times 11 \times 11 \times 11$ be written in exponential form? Explain.

Lesson
5-1 Factors, Multiples, and Divisibility

Understand It!
There are rules you can use to tell if one number is divisible by another number.

How are factors and divisibility related?

How many different ways can Raul build a dog pen that has an area of 36 square meters and has sides measured in whole meters.

Choose an Operation Divide to find the possible measurements.

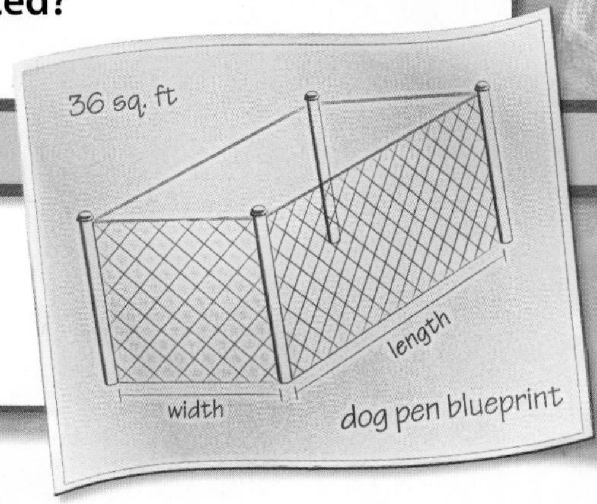

Another Example

How can you use divisibility rules?

Is 126 divisible by 2, 3, 4, 6, 9, or 10? You can use divisibility rules to find out.

Divisibility Rules

A whole number is divisible by	Examples:	Is 126 divisible by the number?
2 if the ones digit is an even number.	10; 6; 108	Yes, the ones digit is even.
3 if the sum of the digits is divisible by 3.	3; 627; 891	Yes, 1 + 2 + 6 = 9. 9 is divisible by 3.
4 if the last two digits of the number are divisible by 4.	64; 5,888	No, 26 is not divisible by 4.
5 if the ones digit is 0 or 5.	380; 9,005	No, the ones digit is 6.
6 if the number is divisible by both 2 and 3.	240; 8,982	Yes, 126 is divisible by both 2 and 3.
9 if the sum of the digits is divisible by 9.	189; 1,035	Yes, 1 + 2 + 6 = 9. 9 is divisible by 9.
10 if the ones digit is 0.	170; 1,380	No, the ones digit is not 0.

What is a multiple of a number?

Is 126 a multiple of 7? A multiple of a given number is a product of that number and a whole number greater than 0.

Since $126 \div 7 = 18$, 126 is the product of 7 and 18. So, 126 is a multiple of 7. Other multiples of 7 are 7, 14, 21, 28, 35, 42, 49, and so on.

Explain It

1. Is 53,802 a multiple of 9? Explain your answer.

A number is divisible by another number when the quotient is a whole number and the remainder is 0.

The divisors and quotients are factors of 36.

$36 \div 1 = 36$	**1 and 36 are factors.**
$36 \div 2 = 18$	**2 and 18 are factors.**
$36 \div 3 = 12$	**3 and 12 are factors.**
$36 \div 4 = 9$	**4 and 9 are factors.**
$36 \div 5 = 7$ R1	**5 and 7 are not factors of 36.**
$36 \div 6 = 6$	**6 is a factor.**

All the factors have been found. The factors of 36 are 1, 2, 3, 4, 6, 9, 12, 18, and 36.

Use each pair of factors to find the possible measurements of the dog pen.

1 and 36	4 and 9	12 and 3
2 and 18	6 and 6	18 and 2
3 and 12	9 and 4	36 and 1

There are 9 different ways Raul can build the dog pen.

Guided Practice*

Do you know HOW?

In **1** through **4**, tell whether each number is divisible by 2, 3, 4, 5, 6, 9, or 10.

1. 60 **2.** 228

3. 78 **4.** 117

In **5** through **8**, tell whether the first number is a multiple of the second.

5. 72; 3 **6.** 368; 2

7. 2,102; 5 **8.** 1,780; 10

Do you UNDERSTAND?

9. In the example at the top of the page, how can you tell if 36 is divisible by 2?

10. **Writing to Explain** How can you tell that 189 is divisible by 3 without doing the division?

11. If a number is divisible by 10, will it always be divisible by 4? Explain.

Independent Practice

In **12** through **15**, use the divisibility rules to tell if each number is divisible by 2, 3, 4, 5, 6, 9, or 10.

12. 63 **13.** 225 **14.** 399 **15.** 4,090

In **16** through **23**, name at least three factors of each number that are greater than 1.

16. 70 **17.** 84 **18.** 98 **19.** 75

20. 150 **21.** 333 **22.** 3,000 **23.** 1,200

DIGITAL Animated Glossary **www.pearsonsuccessnet.com**

For another example, see Set A on page 140.

Independent Practice

In **24** through **31**, tell whether the first number is a multiple of the second.

24. 50; 10 **25.** 92; 3 **26.** 123; 9 **27.** 289; 5

28. 1,099; 3 **29.** 6,012; 6 **30.** 10,235; 2 **31.** 31,233; 6

Problem Solving

Use the table for **32** and **33**.

32. One game of Four-Square needs exactly 4 players. Which schools can divide their participants exactly by 4?

33. **Writing to Explain** Can the total number of participants in the Four-Square Tournament be divided evenly by 4? Why? Explain your answer.

Data

Four-Square Tournament

School	Number of Participants
Almont Junior High	244
Sheridan Elementary	189
Kellogg Elementary	437
Dalton Middle School	178

34. **Writing to Explain** Is the number 10,387 divisible by 3? Why or why not?

35. Leah is helping her mother paint the exterior of the house. She knows that paint rollers come in packages of 3. If her mother needs 20 rollers, how many packages will she need to buy?

36. A Venn diagram shows groups and how they are related. What does the area of overlap in the Venn diagram below show?

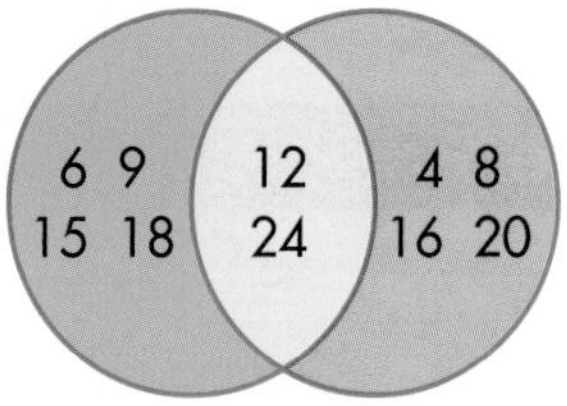

A factors of 3

B factors of 4

C multiples of 3 and 4

D multiples of 8

37. Maury notes that 31 and 41 are not divisible by any number except themselves and 1. He concludes that if a number ends in 1, it cannot be divided by any number other than itself and 1. Which number disproves this rule?

A 91 **C** 71

B 61 **D** 81

38. **Algebra** If x is a whole number greater than 0, which is always true?

A $6x$ is divisible by 3.

B $6x$ is divisible by 4.

C $6x$ is divisible by 5.

D $6x$ is divisible by 9.

Enrichment

Venn Diagrams

A Venn diagram uses circles, loops, or other shapes to show relationships between sets. Sets are described by the data or objects they contain. Circles overlap, or intersect, when some data belong to more than one set. The Venn diagram below relates parallelograms. Notice that squares are a subset of both rectangles and rhombuses.

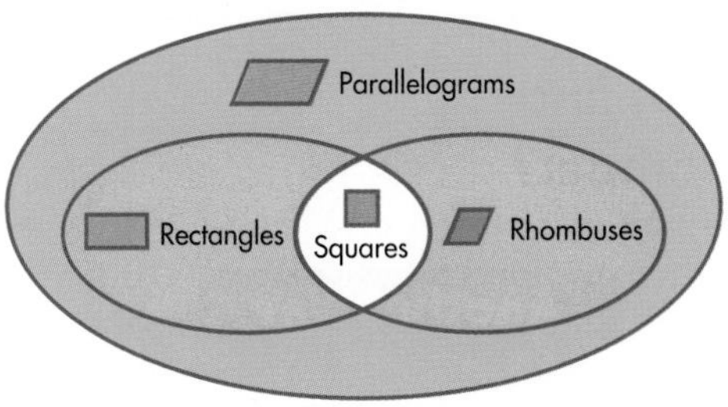

Example: Describe the sets shown in the Venn diagram below.

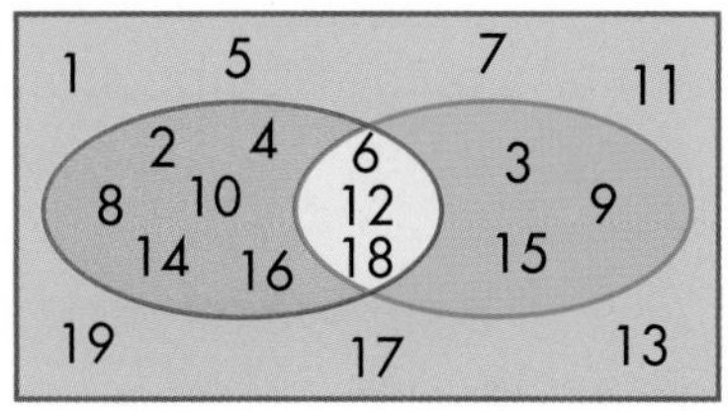

Counting numbers less than 20 are shown in the rectangle. The numbers in the red loop are divisible by 2. The numbers in the green loop are divisible by 3. The numbers divisible by both 2 and 3 are a subset of both loops.

Practice

1. In the Venn diagram of parallelograms above, is the set of rectangles a subset of parallelograms? Explain.

2. In the example above, what other divisibility rule is true of the subset of numbers divisible by both 2 and 3?

For **3** through **5**, describe the sets shown.

3.

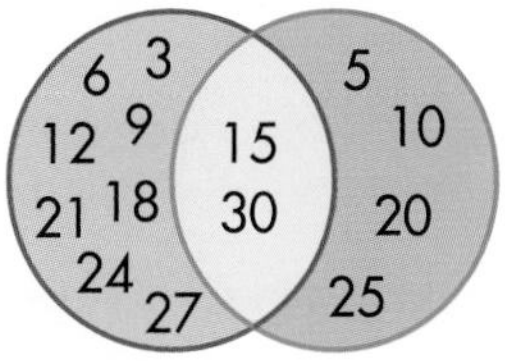

4.

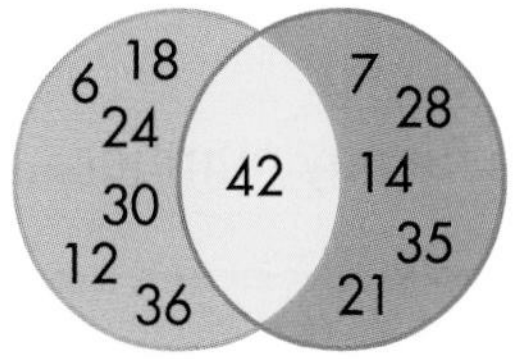

5.

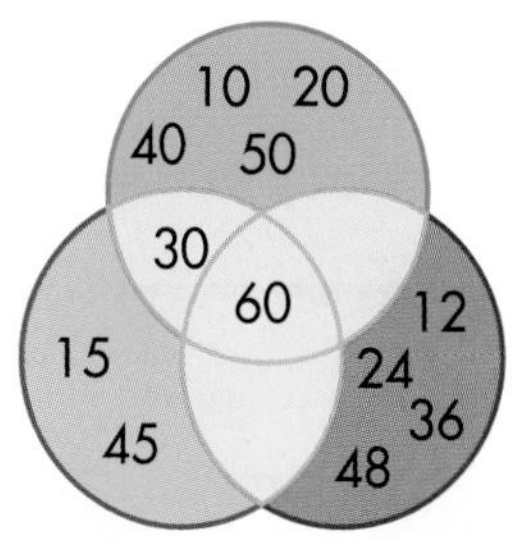

6. Draw a Venn diagram with two sets: one set of numbers divisible by 10 and the other set of numbers divisible by 25. Use at least 10 numbers in the diagram.

7. Draw a Venn diagram with three sets. One set of numbers is divisible by 5. The second set of numbers is divisible by 10. The third set of numbers is divisible by 15. Use at least 10 numbers and tell which sets are subsets of other sets.

Lesson
5-2 Prime Factorization

Understand It!
Every whole number greater than 1 is either a prime number or a composite number.

How can you write the prime factorization of a number?

Whole numbers greater than 1 are either prime or composite numbers.

A prime number has exactly two factors, 1 and itself. The numbers 2, 3, and 5 are prime numbers.

Model	Dimension	Factors
	1×2	1, 2
	1×3	1, 3
	1×4	1, 4
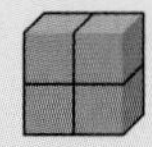	2×2	2
	1×5	1, 5

Another Example How can you use a factor tree to find the prime factorization of a number?

One Way

To find the prime factorization of 72, begin with the smallest prime factor. Write factors until all the factors are prime numbers.

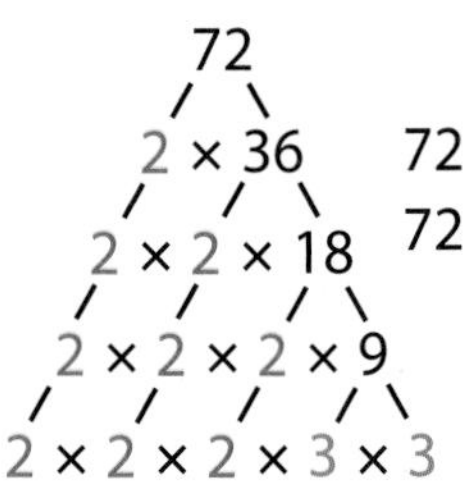

$72 = 2 \times 2 \times 2 \times 3 \times 3$

$72 = 2^3 \times 3^2$

Another Way

To find the prime factorization of 72, begin with any two factors of 72. Write factors until all the factors are prime numbers.

Arrange prime factors in order.

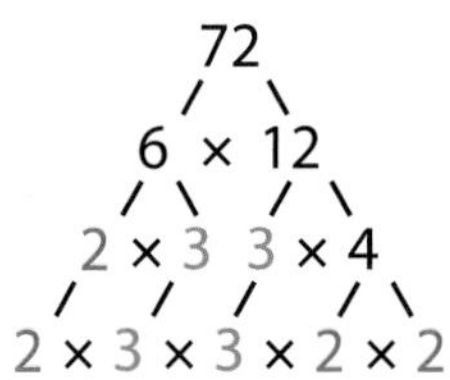

$72 = 2 \times 2 \times 2 \times 3 \times 3$

$72 = 2^3 \times 3^2$

There is only one prime factorization for any number.

Guided Practice*

Do you know HOW?

In **1** through **8**, write the prime factorization of each number. If it is prime, write *prime*.

1. 18 **2.** 23 **3.** 32 **4.** 45

5. 89 **6.** 169 **7.** 216 **8.** 243

Do you UNDERSTAND?

9. How do the two factor trees above show that there is only one prime factorization for 72?

10. Is 1 prime or composite?

*For another example, see Set B on page 140.

A composite number has more than two factors and can be written as the product of its prime factors. This is called its prime factorization.

4 is a composite number. The factors of 4 are 1, 2, and 4. 2 is its only prime factor. The prime factorization of 4 is 2×2, or 2^2.

To find the prime factorization of 60, write its factors, beginning with the smallest prime factor.

$60 = 2 \times 30$ ← 2 is a factor of 60.

$= 2 \times 2 \times 15$ ← 2 is a factor again.

$= 2 \times 2 \times 3 \times 5$ ← 3 and 5 are factors.

$= 2^2 \times 3 \times 5$ ← Use exponents.

Independent Practice

In **11** through **25**, write the prime factorization of each number. If it is prime, write *prime*.

Tip *Choose easy factors. For example, for 1,300, start with 1,300 = 13 x 100.*

11. 26 **12.** 47 **13.** 68 **14.** 125 **15.** 490

16. 750 **17.** 210 **18.** 2,100 **19.** 120 **20.** 65

21. 300 **22.** 27 **23.** 38 **24.** 99 **25.** 57

Problem Solving

26. Geometry A triangle has 63° and 30° angles. What is the measure of the third angle? Is it acute, right, or obtuse?

27. Which is a prime number?

A 33 **B** 35 **C** 37 **D** 39

28. Writing to Explain Raul makes a conjecture that every odd number greater than 3 can be expressed as the sum of two primes. Use the number 11 to explain that Raul is wrong.

A famous unsolved problem referred to as *Goldbach's conjecture* states that every even number greater than 2 can be written as the sum of two prime numbers. For example, $4 = 2 + 2$, $6 = 3 + 3$, $8 = 3 + 5$, and so on. Computers have shown that Goldbach's conjecture is true for all even numbers up to 100,000,000,000,000!

In **29** through **33**, use *Goldbach's conjecture*. Show that each number can be written as the sum of two primes.

29. 18 **30.** 30 **31.** 32 **32.** 46 **33.** 66

DIGITAL Animated Glossary **www.pearsonsuccessnet.com**

Lesson
5-3

Understand It!
There are different ways to find the greatest factor that is common to a set of two or more numbers.

Greatest Common Factor

How can you find the GCF of a set of numbers?

Keesha is putting together bags of supplies. She has 42 craft sticks and 12 glue bottles. If she puts an equal number of craft sticks and an equal number of glue bottles in each bag, what is the greatest number of bags Keesha can make so that nothing is left over?

Another Example How can you use prime factorization to find the GCF of a set of numbers?

Find the GCF of 60 and 84.

Step 1

Find the prime factorization of each number.

Tip *You can use factor trees to find the prime factorizations.*

$60 = 2 \times 2 \times 3 \times 5 = 2^2 \times 3 \times 5$

$84 = 2 \times 2 \times 3 \times 7 = 2^2 \times 3 \times 7$

Step 2

Multiply the common prime factors.

$2^2 \times 3 = 2 \times 2 \times 3 = 12$

12 is the GCF of 60 and 84.

Guided Practice*

Do you know HOW?

Find the GCF for each set of numbers.

1. 18, 36
2. 14, 35
3. 22, 55
4. 25, 100
5. 15, 44
6. 27, 81
7. 39, 69
8. 99, 121

Do you UNDERSTAND?

9. Why can the greatest common factor also be called the *greatest common divisor*?

10. How are the two ways shown to find the GCF for a set of numbers alike and different?

DIGITAL Animated Glossary **www.pearsonsuccessnet.com**

For another example, see Set C on page 140.

Step 1

List and compare all the factors of each number in the set.

Factors of 12: 1, 2, 3, 4, 6, 12

Factors of 42: 1, 2, 3, 6, 7, 14, 21, 42

1, 2, 3 and 6 are factors of both 12 and 42. These are called common factors.

Step 2

Identify the greatest common factor (GCF). The greatest common factor is the greatest number that is a factor of two or more numbers.

You can see that 6 is the GCF of 12 and 42.

This means that 6 is the greatest number that can be divided evenly into 12 and 42. So, Keesha can make 6 bags.

Independent Practice

In **11** through **22**, find the greatest common factor for each set of numbers.

11. 21, 49 **12.** 8, 52 **13.** 20, 35 **14.** 15, 36

15. 30, 66 **16.** 52, 78 **17.** 32, 81 **18.** 45, 120

19. 34, 51, 85 **20.** 56, 63, 72 **21.** 20, 32, 44 **22.** 46, 92, 138

Problem Solving

The Venn diagram to the right shows the factors of 24 and 40.

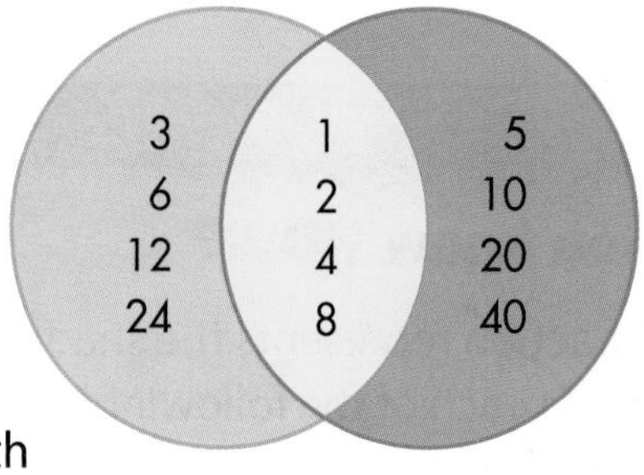

23. What is the meaning of each of the three shaded regions? Which factor is the GCF?

24. Draw a Venn diagram to show the common factors of 36 and 54. What is the GCF?

25. About 50 of the 1,500 possibly active volcanoes on Earth erupt every year. What is the GCF of 50 and 1,500?

26. **Algebra** Amy bought 4 T-shirts and used a $10 coupon to reduce the total. If p equals the price of one T-shirt, write an expression to show the amount Amy paid.

27. **Writing to Explain** How does finding the prime factorization of a group of numbers help you to find their GCF?

28. What is the GCF of 45 and 60?

A 5 **B** 10 **C** 15 **D** 20

Lesson
5-4

Understand It!
A fraction names equal parts of a whole. The whole can be a region, a set, or a number line.

Understanding Fractions

How can fractions be used?

Fractions are numbers that describe the division of a whole into equal parts. Sometimes the whole is a region. The numerator tells the number of equal parts or objects being considered. The denominator tells the total number of equal parts or objects.

$\frac{2}{6}$ numerator / denominator

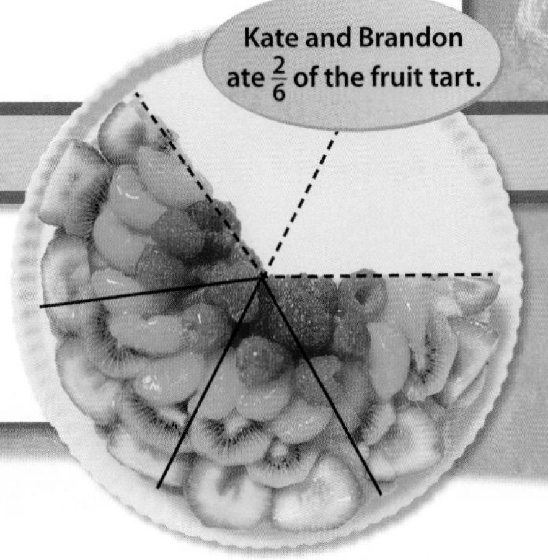

Kate and Brandon ate $\frac{2}{6}$ of the fruit tart.

Other Examples

A fraction is relative to the size of the whole.

In each circle, $\frac{1}{4}$ is shaded. Since the circles are not the same size, the shaded areas are not the same size.

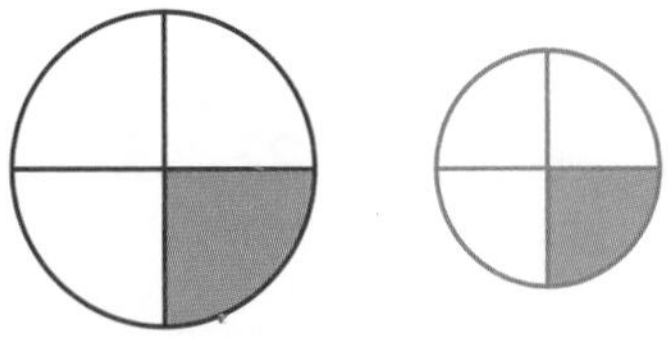

The fraction $\frac{1}{2}$ of each line segment is shaded. Since the line segments are different lengths, the shaded segments are not the same lengths.

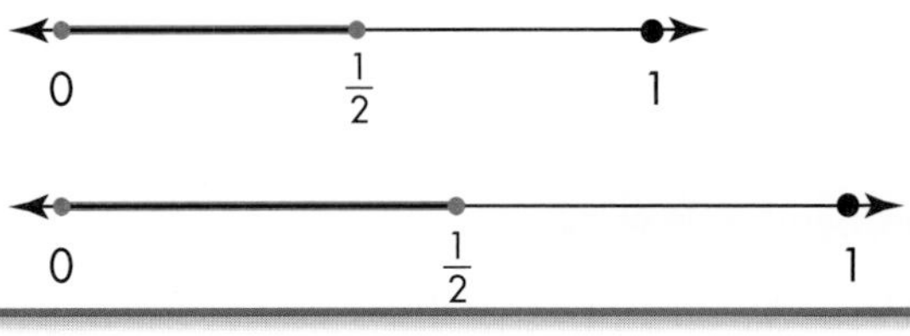

Guided Practice*

Do you know HOW?

What fraction represents the shaded portion in each of the following?

1.  **2.** 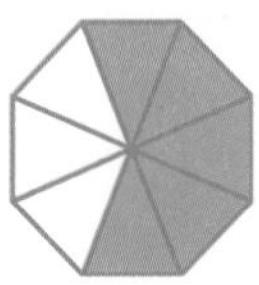

What fraction represents each point on the number line below?

3. 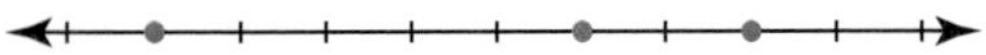

Do you UNDERSTAND?

4. How are the parts of a region described by a fraction like the segments of a number line described by a fraction?

5. Draw pictures to represent the fraction $\frac{2}{5}$ as a region, a set, and a segment of a number line.

6. There are 16 boys and 14 girls in the 6th grade class. What fraction represents the boys?

*For another example, see Set D on page 141.

Sometimes the whole is a set. Fractions can describe part of a set of things.

$\frac{7}{8}$ of the baseball gloves are for right-handed players.

Fractions also can describe a segment of a number line. The number 1 represents a whole unit. This unit on the number line is divided into 7 equal segments.

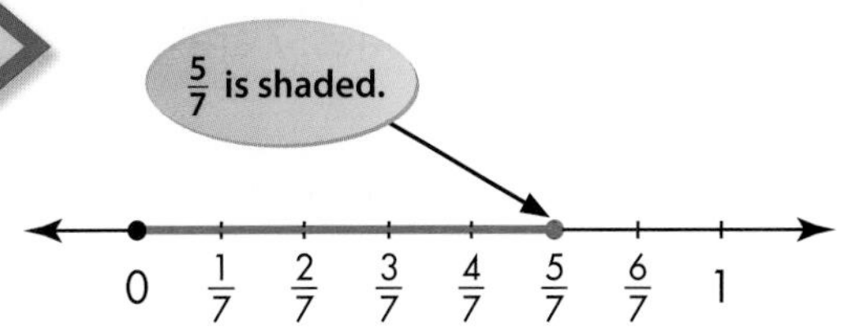

Independent Practice

In **7** through **10**, write the fraction that represents the shaded portion.

7. 

8. 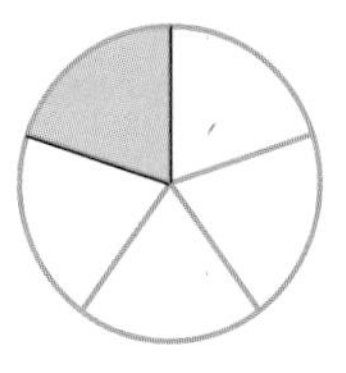

9. 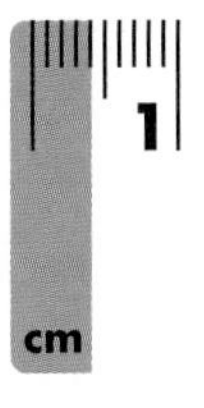

10. 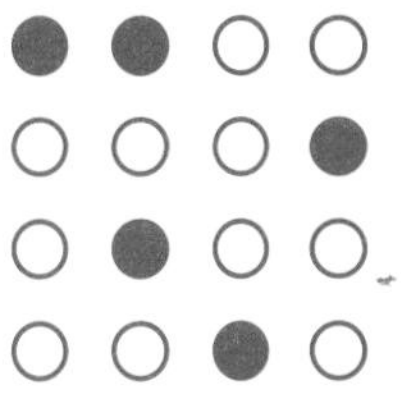

In **11** and **12**, identify the fraction representing each point on the number line.

11. 

12. 

In **13** through **17**, draw models to show the fractions.

13. Draw a number line to represent $\frac{7}{12}$.

14. Draw a number line to represent $\frac{5}{8}$.

15. Draw a set to represent $\frac{2}{3}$.

16. Draw a region to represent $\frac{6}{9}$.

17. Draw a set to represent $\frac{7}{9}$.

Animated Glossary
www.pearsonsuccessnet.com

Problem Solving

Draw a Picture For **18** through **21**, draw a picture to show how you would represent each of the following fractions.

18. Jay picks up 15 stones. 7 are gray.

19. Shi-An mows $\frac{3}{4}$ of her lawn.

20. In a line of 10 towels on a clothesline, 8 are striped.

21. Joan runs $\frac{2}{5}$ of the distance to the car.

Estimation For **22** through **25**, estimate the fraction of the circle that is shaded.

22. 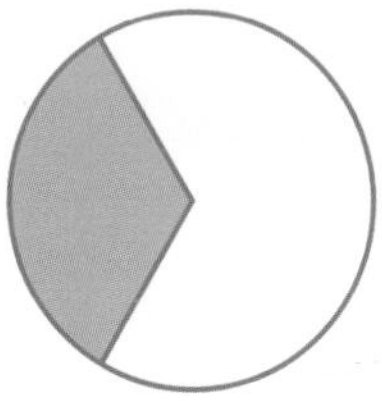

23. 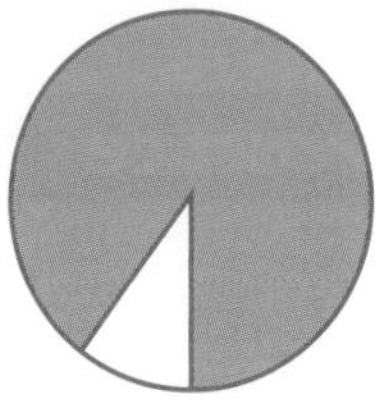

24. 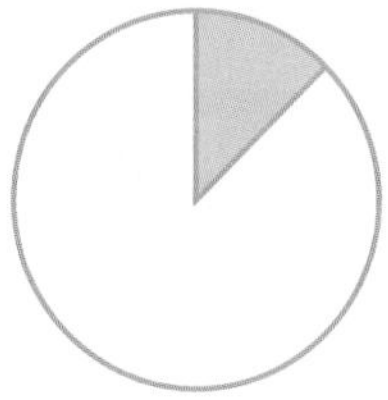

25. 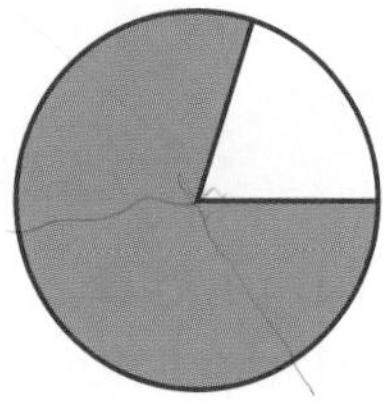

26. A koala often sleeps 18 hours in one day. Write the fraction of the day that a koala often sleeps.

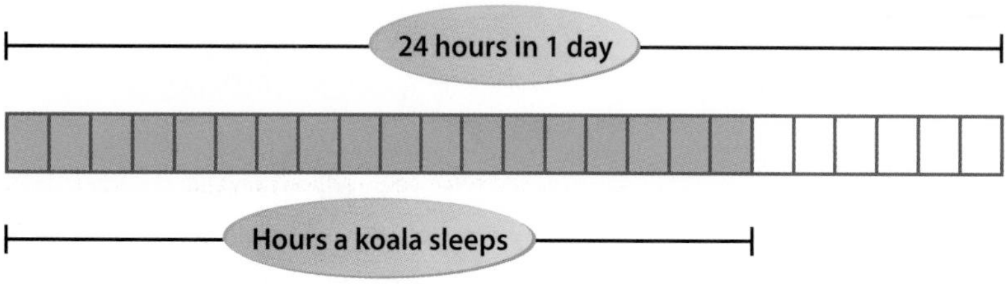

27. What fraction represents the point shown on the number line?

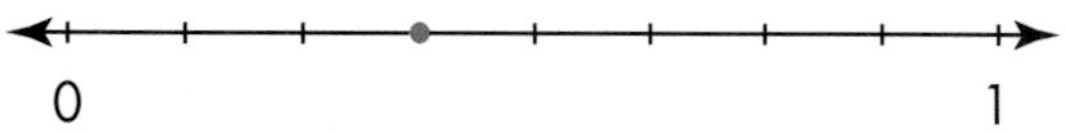

A $\frac{3}{9}$ **B** $\frac{4}{9}$ **C** $\frac{3}{8}$ **D** $\frac{4}{8}$

28. **Think About the Process** In which picture does the blue shaded portion NOT represent the fraction $\frac{4}{7}$?

A 

B 

C 

D 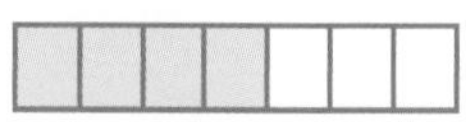

Algebra Connections

Completing Tables

Remember that you can make and use a table to solve a problem that relates one quantity to another.

Example: At the market, a pound of fruit costs \$2. If *x* equals the number of pounds of fruit, make a table to show the total cost of 1, 2, 3, or 4 pounds of fruit.

Pounds of fruit x	*Total cost* $2x$
1	\$2
2	\$4
3	\$6
4	\$8

For **1** through **3**, copy and complete each table.

1. Becca saved \$150. Now, she saves \$15 more each week. If *x* equals the number of weeks Becca saves, find her total savings after 3, 4, 6, and 10 weeks.

Weeks Becca saves x	*Total savings* $15x + 150$
3	■
4	■
6	■
10	■

2. An adult takes some children to the movies. A child's ticket costs \$4.25. An adult ticket costs \$6.50. If *x* equals the number of children, find the total cost of the tickets for 1, 2, 3, or 4 children taken.

Children x	*Total cost* $6.50 + 4.25x$
1	■
2	■
3	■
4	■

3. Three friends are sharing a pizza equally. If *x* equals the number of same-size pieces into which the pizza is cut, find the number of pieces each friend will get if the pizza is cut into 3, 6, 9, or 12 pieces.

Total number of pieces x	*Pieces per friend* $\frac{x}{3}$
3	■
6	■
9	■
12	■

Lesson
5-5

Understand It!
Different fractions can be used to name the same amount.

Equivalent Fractions

Hands-On
fraction strips

How can you find equivalent fractions?

Fractions that have different numerators and denominators but name the same amount are called equivalent fractions.

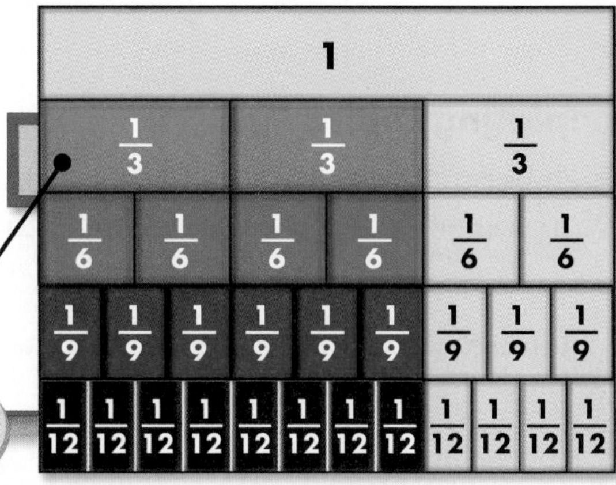

The fraction strips show equivalent fractions.
$\frac{2}{3}=\frac{4}{6}=\frac{6}{9}=\frac{8}{12}$

Guided Practice*

Do you know HOW?

In **1** through **5**, write two fractions that are equivalent to the one fraction given. You may use fraction strips to help.

1. $\frac{2}{4}$ $\frac{2\times 2}{4\times 2}=\frac{\square}{\square}$ $\frac{2\div 2}{4\div 2}=\frac{\square}{\square}$

2. $\frac{24}{48}$

3. $\frac{10}{35}$

4. $\frac{6}{10}$

5. $\frac{4}{9}$

Do you UNDERSTAND?

6. Why is multiplying or dividing the numerator and denominator by the same nonzero number the same as multiplying or dividing the fraction by 1?

7. Why wouldn't you use division to find an equivalent fraction for $\frac{7}{15}$?

Independent Practice

Leveled Practice In **8** through **21**, write two fractions that are equivalent to each fraction given. You may use fraction strips to help.

8. $\frac{3}{12}$ $\frac{3\times 2}{12\times 2}=\frac{\square}{\square}$ $\frac{3\div 3}{12\div 3}=\frac{\square}{\square}$

9. $\frac{6}{12}$ $\frac{6\div 3}{12\div 3}=\frac{\square}{\square}$ $\frac{6\div 6}{12\div 6}=\frac{\square}{\square}$

10. $\frac{6}{9}$

11. $\frac{35}{56}$

12. $\frac{32}{40}$

13. $\frac{5}{7}$

14. $\frac{3}{15}$

15. $\frac{7}{21}$

16. $\frac{9}{10}$

17. $\frac{25}{30}$

18. $\frac{14}{35}$

19. $\frac{121}{132}$

20. $\frac{28}{36}$

21. $\frac{1}{1000}$

DIGITAL
Animated Glossary, eTools
www.pearsonsuccessnet.com

For another example, see Set E on page 141.

One Way

You can multiply both the numerator and the denominator by the same nonzero number.

$$\frac{10 \times 2}{15 \times 2} = \frac{20}{30}$$

$\frac{10}{15}$ and $\frac{20}{30}$ are equivalent fractions.

Another Way

You can divide the numerator and denominator by the same nonzero number if they can both be divided evenly.

$$\frac{10 \div 5}{15 \div 5} = \frac{2}{3}$$

$\frac{10}{15}$ and $\frac{2}{3}$ are equivalent fractions.

Problem Solving

22. **Number Sense** How can you use equivalent fractions to know that $\frac{43}{200}$ is between $\frac{1}{5}$ and $\frac{1}{4}$?

23. Kai says that $\frac{3}{7} = \frac{9}{14}$. Is Kai correct? Explain.

24. **Writing to Explain** Jenna claims that no matter how many equivalent fractions are found for any fraction, she can always find one more. Is she right? Explain.

25. **Algebra** Find the value of x that makes the fractions equivalent.

a $\frac{10}{14} = \frac{x}{42}$ **b** $\frac{x}{200} = \frac{3}{4}$

26. There are 206 bones in the body. The fraction $\frac{54}{206}$ represents the number of bones in both hands compared to the total number of bones in the body. Write an equivalent fraction.

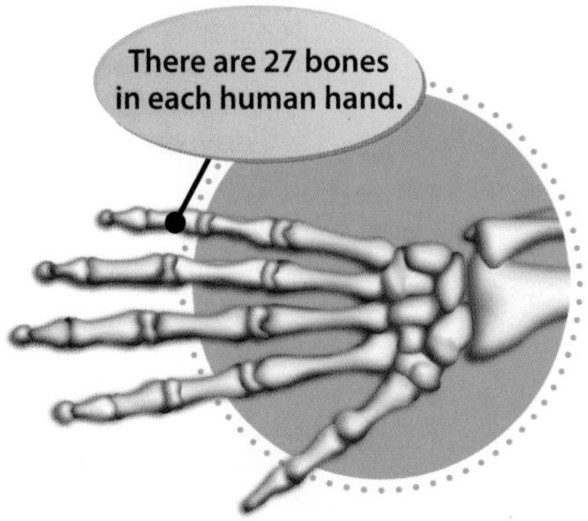

There are 27 bones in each human hand.

27. Which of the following fractions is NOT equivalent to the others?

A $\frac{1}{3}$ **B** $\frac{4}{12}$ **C** $\frac{5}{21}$ **D** $\frac{3}{9}$

28. **Writing to Explain** How does this diagram help show that $\frac{2}{7} = \frac{8}{28}$?

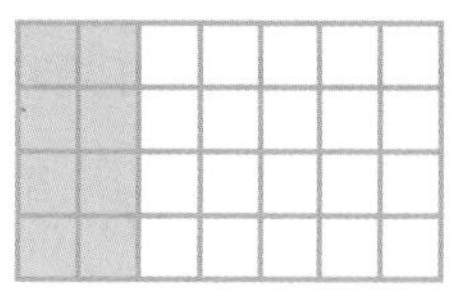

29. Draw a grid like the one in Exercise 28 to show that $\frac{5}{6} = \frac{15}{18}$.

Lesson
5-6

Understand It!
A fraction can be expressed in simplest form by dividing the numerator and denominator by their greatest common factor.

Fractions in Simplest Form

How do you write fractions in simplest form?

Thirty-six out of the 48 sixth graders at Lincoln Middle School are going on a field trip to the Museum of Art. Write the fraction $\frac{36}{48}$ in simplest form.

A fraction is in simplest form if the only common factor of the numerator and denominator is 1.

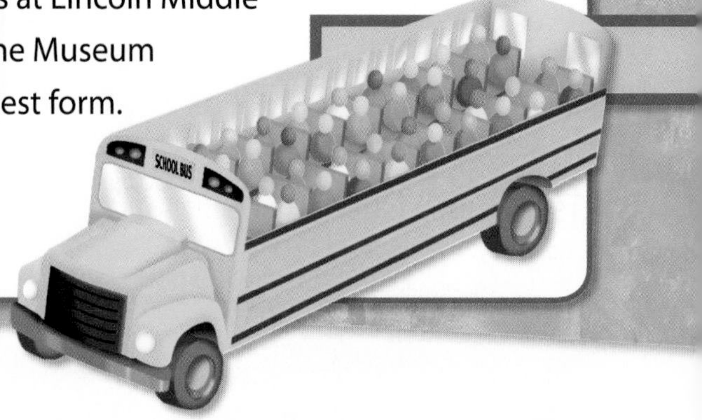

Guided Practice*

Do you know HOW?

In **1** and **2**, find the GCF of the numerator and denominator. Use the GCF to write each fraction in its simplest form.

1. $\frac{18}{24}$ **2.** $\frac{12}{36}$

Write each fraction in simplest form.

3. $\frac{35}{49}$ **4.** $\frac{4}{24}$

5. $\frac{180}{200}$ **6.** $\frac{24}{27}$

Do you UNDERSTAND?

7. Which way do you prefer to use to find the simplest form of a fraction? Why?

8. Of the 36 students who went to the art museum, 18 had been there before. What is the simplest form for the fraction of students on the trip who had been there before?

Independent Practice

Leveled Practice In **9** through **15**, find the GCF of the numerator and denominator. Use the GCF to write each fraction in its simplest form.

9. $\frac{15}{24}$ The GCF is 3. $\frac{15 \div 3}{24 \div 3} = \frac{\square}{\square}$ **10.** $\frac{16}{32}$ The GCF is 16. $\frac{16 \div 16}{32 \div 16} = \frac{\square}{\square}$

11. $\frac{14}{63}$ **12.** $\frac{40}{64}$ **13.** $\frac{27}{45}$ **14.** $\frac{24}{72}$ **15.** $\frac{35}{55}$

Write each fraction in simplest form.

16. $\frac{9}{36}$ **17.** $\frac{8}{96}$ **18.** $\frac{12}{78}$ **19.** $\frac{72}{81}$ **20.** $\frac{9}{63}$

21. $\frac{4}{92}$ **22.** $\frac{10}{75}$ **23.** $\frac{75}{165}$ **24.** $\frac{39}{300}$ **25.** $\frac{30}{108}$

DIGITAL Animated Glossary **www.pearsonsuccessnet.com**

*For another example, see Set E on page 141.

One Way

Use common factors to do repeated division of the numerator and denominator until 1 is the only common factor.

$$\frac{36 \div 2}{48 \div 2} = \frac{18 \div 6}{24 \div 6} = \frac{3}{4}$$

I can divide by 2. Next I can divide by 6. Now 1 is the only common factor.

Another Way

Divide the numerator and denominator by the GCF (greatest common factor).

$$\frac{36 \div 12}{48 \div 12} = \frac{3}{4}$$

$36 = 2 \times 2 \times 3 \times 3$
$48 = 2 \times 2 \times 2 \times 2 \times 3$
$GCF = 2 \times 2 \times 3 = 12$

$\frac{3}{4}$ of the students are going on the trip.

Problem Solving

26. The table shows Aaron's batting averages for four years. How much did Aaron's batting average improve between years 1 and 4?

Data

Year	Batting Average
1	.279
2	.281
3	.287
4	.295

27. Writing to Explain How do you know that a fraction is in simplest form?

28. Place the decimal point in each product.

a $3 \times 0.476 = 1428$ **b** $5.8 \times 6.32 = 36656$

29. Algebra If $\frac{x}{24}$ is a fraction in simplest form, which could be a value for x?

A 3 **B** 6 **C** 7 **D** 9

30. Which of the following fractions is in simplest form?

A $\frac{12}{15}$ **B** $\frac{39}{65}$ **C** $\frac{27}{98}$ **D** $\frac{11}{121}$

31. Ostriches have very long necks. The ostrich pictured at the right is 91 inches tall. Its neck is 39 inches. Write a fraction in simplest form to compare the length of the ostrich's neck to its height.

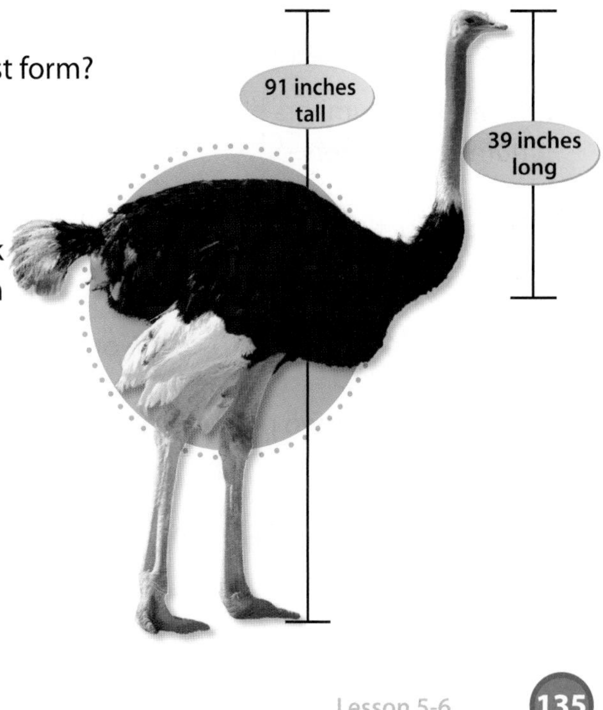

Lesson
5-7

Understand It!
Conjectures about math need to be tested to determine if they are correct.

Problem Solving

Make and Test Conjectures

A conjecture is a generalization that you think is true.
A question can help you make a conjecture.

How many factors do perfect square numbers have?

16 is a perfect square. Other perfect squares are: 4, 9, 25, 36, 49, 64, 81, 100.

Find the factors of some perfect squares.

Guided Practice*

Do you know HOW?

Test these conjectures. Explain whether they are correct or incorrect.

1. The difference of two odd numbers is always even.

2. The sum of a negative integer and a positive integer is always negative.

Do you UNDERSTAND?

3. How can you test or check a conjecture to see if it is correct?

4. **Write a Problem** Write a conjecture about the sum of three odd numbers. Then test your conjecture.

Independent Practice

In **5** through **9**, test these conjectures. Explain whether they are correct or incorrect.

5. Composite numbers have an even number of factors.

6. The product of two prime numbers is never an even number.

7. All multiples of 6 end in 0, 2, 4, 6 or 8.

8. The sum of any two perfect squares is an even number.

9. A GCF cannot always be found for a set of whole numbers.

Stuck? Try this....

- What do I know?
- What am I asked to find?
- What diagram can I use to help understand the problem?
- Can I use addition, subtraction, multiplication, or division?
- Is all my work correct?
- Did I answer the right question?
- Is my answer reasonable?

*For another example, see Set F on page 141.

Try several cases to help you make a conjecture.

Factors of 4: 1, 2, 4
3 factors

Factors of 9: 1, 3, 9
3 factors

Make a Conjecture
All perfect square numbers have exactly 3 factors.

Test Your Conjecture
Find the factors of other perfect squares.

16: 1, 2, 4, 8, 16
5 factors

25: 1, 5, 25
3 factors

36: 1, 2, 3, 4, 6, 9, 12, 18, 36
9 factors

The conjecture is not right. Use reasoning to make another conjecture.

Make a Conjecture
All perfect squares have an odd number of factors.

Test Your Conjecture
100: 1, 2, 4, 5, 10, 20, 25, 50, 100
9 factors

The conjecture works for the numbers tested.

In **10** through **13**, make a conjecture about each of the following. Then test your conjecture.

10. Adding two odd numbers.

11. Multiplying two odd numbers.

12. Adding an even number and an odd number.

13. Multiplying an even number and an odd number.

14. **Writing to Explain** How can you test the following conjecture: all fractions have an equivalent fraction?

15. **Geometry** A rhombus has three angles that combine to measure 300°. How much does the fourth angle measure?

16. **Algebra** Hector deposits $153.32 into his savings account, raising the balance to $3,126.70. Use an algebraic equation to find how much was in Hector's account before the deposit.

17. Leela is making jumps on her skateboard at the skate park. One ramp is at an 18° angle. Another ramp is at an angle 7° greater. What is the angle of the steeper ramp?

18. Sekino is going skiing in the mountains. When he left his home, it was 25° Celsius. When he arrived at the ski lodge, it was –5° Celsius. What was the difference in temperature?

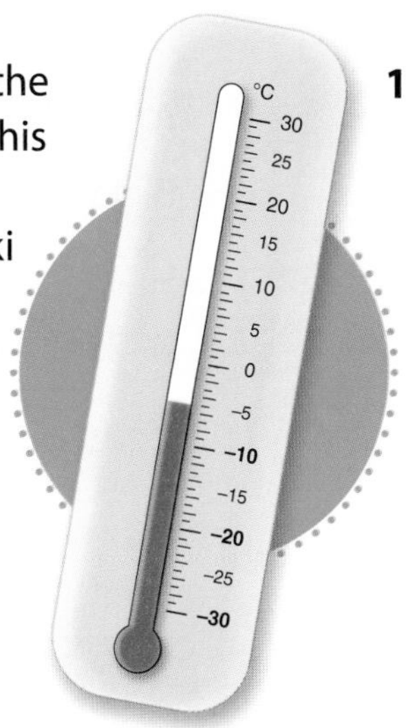

19. Which fraction is equivalent to $\frac{3}{4}$?

A $\frac{7}{8}$ **B** $\frac{8}{12}$ **C** $\frac{12}{16}$ **D** $\frac{16}{20}$

DIGITAL
Animated Glossary
www.pearsonsuccessnet.com

Topic 5
Test

1. The 20 students in Ms. Roho's class and the 16 students in Mr. Wann's class are going on a field trip. The teachers want to divide the students in each class into groups that are the same size, and no group has students from both classes. What is the largest size possible for each group? Find the greatest common factor of 20 and 16. (5-3)

A 2 students

B 4 students

C 5 students

D 10 students

2. At the beginning of the school year, Adrienne's class had 4 new students out of 20 students enrolled. What is $\frac{4}{20}$ written in simplest form? (5-6)

A $\frac{4}{5}$

B $\frac{2}{10}$

C $\frac{1}{5}$

D $\frac{1}{4}$

3. Todd has run two of the nine laps he needs to run. Which point on the number line represents $\frac{2}{9}$? (5-4)

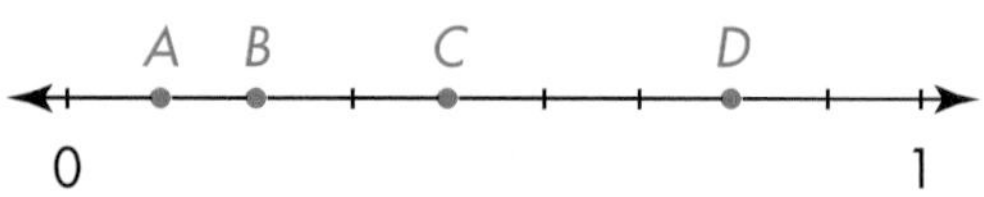

A Point *A*

B Point *B*

C Point *C*

D Point *D*

4. Three-twelfths of the girls on Jamila's softball team missed practice. Which of the following is equal to $\frac{3}{12}$? (5-5)

A $\frac{1}{10}$

B $\frac{1}{4}$

C $\frac{9}{24}$

D $\frac{5}{14}$

5. What is the greatest common factor (GCF) of 36 and 54? (5-3)

A 2

B 6

C 9

D 18

6. Which step can be used to write $\frac{10}{15}$ in simplest form? (5-6)

A Divide 10 and 15 by their GCF, 5.

B Divide 10 and 15 by their GCF, 10.

C Multiply 10 and 15 by their GCF, 5.

D Multiply 10 and 15 by their GCF, 10.

7. Which of the following numbers is prime? (5-2)

A 9

B 15

C 21

D 23

8. Which is the prime factorization of 75? (5-2)

A 3×25

B 5×3^2

C 3×5^2

D $3^2 \times 5^2$

9. Aaron made a conjecture that any number ending in zero will be divisible by 4. Which of the following best describes whether or not the conjecture is correct? (5-7)

A No, it is not correct because 10 is not divisible by 4.

B No, it is not correct because 4, 8, 12, and 16 do not end in 0.

C Yes, it is correct because 100 is divisible by 4.

D Yes, it is correct because 20, 160, and 200 are all divisible by 4.

10. What portion of the football field, including the end zones, is shaded blue? (5-4)

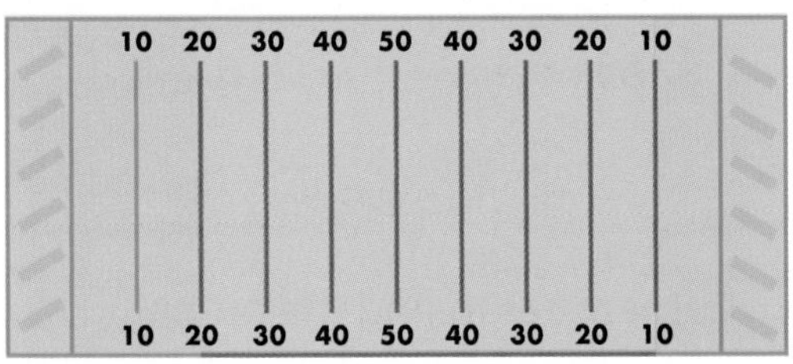

A $\frac{12}{7}$

B $\frac{7}{7}$

C $\frac{7}{10}$

D $\frac{7}{12}$

11. Which step should be taken to find the value of x that makes the fractions equivalent? (5-5)

$\frac{5}{7} = \frac{x}{21}$

A Add 3 to 5.

B Add 14 to 5.

C Multiply 5 by 3.

D Multiply 5 by 7.

12. Which divisibility rule would you apply to tell whether a number is divisible by 3? (5-1)

A The last digit is divisible by 3.

B The sum of the digits is divisible by 3.

C The last two digits are divisible by 3.

D The sum of the digits is divisible by 9.

13. Which two fractions can be used to represent point M? (5-5)

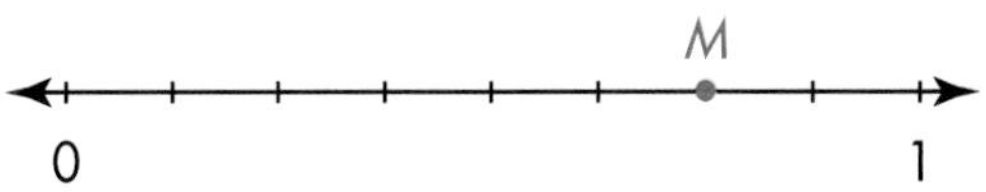

A $\frac{6}{8}$ and $\frac{3}{4}$

B $\frac{6}{8}$ and $\frac{3}{5}$

C $\frac{2}{3}$ and $\frac{6}{9}$

D $\frac{2}{6}$ and $\frac{3}{4}$

Topic 5

Reteaching

Set A, pages 120–122

Tell whether 63 is divisible by 2, 3, 4, 5, 6, 9, or 10.

Use divisibility rules.

- 2: **Is the ones digit even?** No
- 3: **Is the sum of the digits divisible by 3?** Yes
- 4: **Are the last two digits divisible by 4?** No
- 5: **Is the ones digit 0 or 5?** No
- 6: **Is the number divisible by both 2 and 3?** No
- 9: **Is the sum of the digits divisible by 9?** Yes
- 10: **Is the ones digit a 0?** No

So, 63 is divisible by 3 and 9.

Remember that you can use divisibility rules to tell whether a number is divisible by another number.

Tell whether each number is divisible by 2, 3, 4, 5, 6, 9, or 10.

1. 40 **2.** 33

3. 75 **4.** 113

Tell whether the first number is a multiple of the second.

5. 25; 5 **6.** 81; 9

7. 310; 3 **8.** 29; 7

Set B, pages 124–125

Find the prime factorization of 140. Use a factor tree to write factors beginning with the smallest factor. Write factors until all the factors are prime numbers.

140
/ \
2 × 70
/ / \
2 × 2 × 35
/ / / \
2 × 2 × 5 × 7

$140 = 2 \times 2 \times 5 \times 7$

$= 2^2 \times 5 \times 7$

Remember to order factors from least to greatest and to use exponents.

Find the prime factorization of each number. Write *prime*, if the number is prime.

1. 24 **2.** 56

3. 81 **4.** 37

5. 83 **6.** 48

Set C, pages 126–127

Find the greatest common factor, or GCF, of 24 and 132 by using prime factorization.

24 and 132

Step 1 Find the prime factorization of each number.

$24 = 2 \times 2 \times 2 \times 3$ $132 = 2 \times 2 \times 3 \times 11$

Step 2 Multipy the common prime factors. The GCF of 24 and 132 is $2 \times 2 \times 3 = 12$.

Remember to find the prime factorization of each number and then multiply common factors to find the GCF for each set of numbers.

Find the GCF of each pair of numbers.

1. 30, 105 **2.** 8, 52

3. 28, 126 **4.** 35, 63

5. 75, 128 **6.** 120, 168

Set D, pages 128–130

Write a fraction to describe the shaded part of the whole.

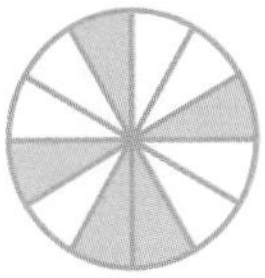

$\frac{5}{12}$ of the circle is shaded.

Remember that a set of objects or a number line can represent a whole. Write each fraction represented.

1. 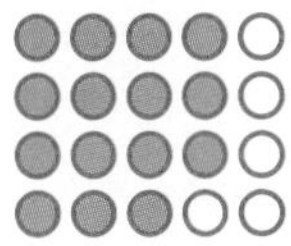

2. 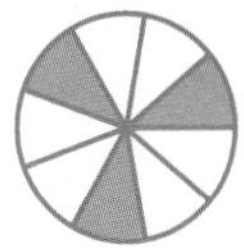

3. 

Set E, pages 132–135

Write two equivalent fractions for $\frac{4}{18}$.

One Way

$$\frac{4 \div 2}{18 \div 2} = \frac{2}{9}$$

Another Way

$$\frac{4 \times 2}{18 \times 2} = \frac{8}{36}$$

Write $\frac{28}{70}$ in simplest form.

$\frac{28}{70}$ ← The GCF of 28 and 70 is 14.

$\frac{28 \div 14}{70 \div 14} = \frac{2}{5}$ ← Simplest form

Remember to divide or multiply the numerator and denominator by the same nonzero number. Write two equivalent fractions for each.

1. $\frac{6}{20}$ **2.** $\frac{7}{11}$

3. $\frac{1}{11}$ **4.** $\frac{98}{100}$

Write each fraction in simplest form.

5. $\frac{13}{39}$ **6.** $\frac{12}{63}$ **7.** $\frac{18}{49}$

8. $\frac{1}{48}$ **9.** $\frac{90}{150}$ **10.** $\frac{8}{72}$

Set F, pages 136–137

A conjecture is a generalization that you think is true.

Make a Conjecture The product of two odd numbers is an odd number.

Test your conjecture.

$3 \times 3 = 9$ $5 \times 7 = 35$

$9 \times 9 = 81$ $11 \times 13 = 143$

The conjecture works for the numbers tested.

Remember to try several cases to test a conjecture. Explain whether these conjectures are correct or incorrect.

1. If a number is divisible by 8, it is divisible by 2 and 4.
2. The difference of two odd numbers is always odd.
3. The product of a negative integer and a positive integer is always negative.

Topic 6

Decimals, Fractions, and Mixed Numbers

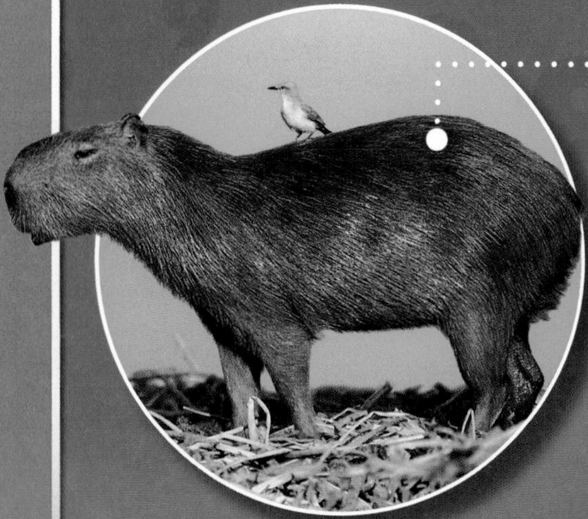

1 The capybara is the world's largest rodent. It is related to the guinea pig. How long is a capybara? You will find out in Lesson 6-3.

2 Alaska is the largest state. What part of the total area of the United States does Alaska make up? You will find out in Lesson 6-2.

3

The Green Darner dragonfly is an excellent flier. How fast can a Green Darner fly? You will find out in Lesson 6-4.

Review What You Know!

Vocabulary

Choose the best term from the box.

- denominator
- numerator
- fraction

1. The top value of a fraction, which names the number of objects or equal parts being considered, is the __?__.

2. The bottom value of a fraction, which tells the number of equal parts in all, is the __?__.

3. A number used to name a part of a whole, such as a region or a set, is a __?__.

Simplifying Fractions

Write each fraction in simplest form.

4. $\frac{6}{10}$ **5.** $\frac{2}{4}$ **6.** $\frac{10}{12}$

7. $\frac{3}{9}$ **8.** $\frac{18}{24}$ **9.** $\frac{10}{24}$

Equivalent Fractions

Find an equivalent fraction for each of the following fractions.

10. $\frac{2}{3}$ **11.** $\frac{1}{2}$ **12.** $\frac{10}{100}$

13. $\frac{5}{9}$ **14.** $\frac{14}{42}$ **15.** $\frac{4}{5}$

Number Lines

16. Writing to Explain How can you draw a number line that shows the point 0.6? Draw an example.

Lesson

6-1

Understand It!
Fractions can be written as division expressions by using the numerator as the dividend and the denominator as the divisor.

Fractions and Division

How are fractions related to division?

Eleven members of the 6th grade Science Club stayed after school to help their teacher, Ms. Oliva, set up the laboratory. Afterwards, Ms. Oliva bought two large pizzas. If all twelve people divide the pizza equally, what fraction of a large pizza will each person get?

Another Example **How can you use a number line to show fractions are related to division?**

Use number lines to show $\frac{2}{3} = 2 \div 3$.

One Way

$\frac{2}{3}$ Think: 2 groups of $\frac{1}{3}$

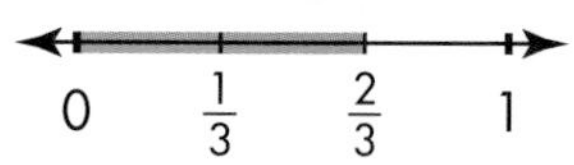

Another Way

$2 \div 3$ Think: $\frac{1}{3}$ of 2 wholes

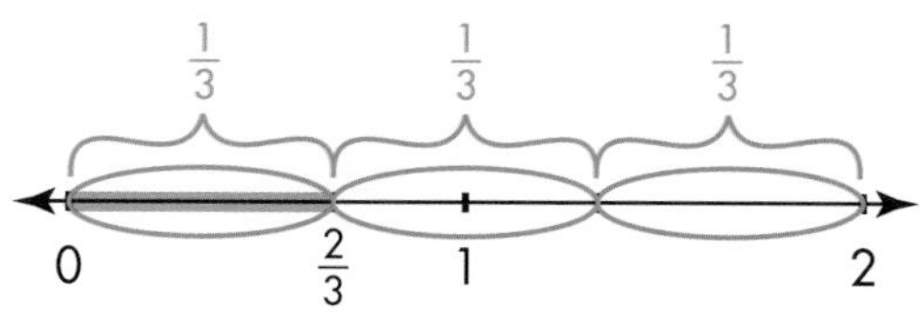

One way to think about a fraction is the division of the numerator by the denominator.

Guided Practice*

Do you know HOW?

Write a division expression for the following fractions.

1. $\frac{3}{4}$ **2.** $\frac{5}{6}$

Write each division expression as a fraction.

3. $4 \div 7$ **4.** $8 \div 9$

Do you UNDERSTAND?

5. How do the numerator and denominator of a fraction compare with the dividend and divisor of a division expression?

6. Copy the number line below and use it to show $3 \div 4$.

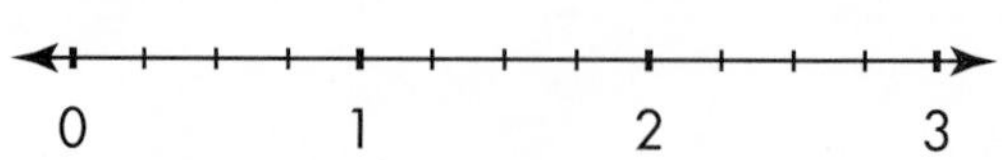

*For another example, see Set A on page 158.

One Way

Divide each pizza into 12 equal parts. Then each person would get two slices of one of the pizzas.

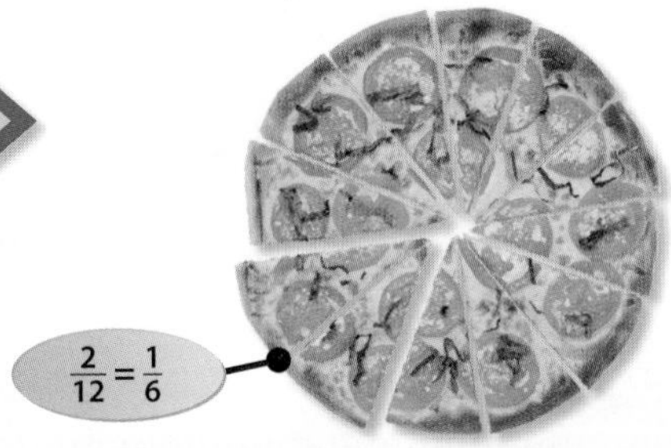

Another Way

Divide the two pizzas into 12 equal parts: $2 \div 12$. Each pizza has six equal parts.

You can think of fractions as division:

$$\frac{2}{12} = 2 \div 12$$

Independent Practice

Write a division expression for the following fractions.

7. $\frac{7}{8}$ **8.** $\frac{1}{2}$ **9.** $\frac{3}{5}$ **10.** $\frac{6}{7}$ **11.** $\frac{15}{29}$

12. $\frac{4}{9}$ **13.** $\frac{6}{11}$ **14.** $\frac{9}{15}$ **15.** $\frac{1}{4}$ **16.** $\frac{14}{21}$

Write each division expression as a fraction.

17. $9 \div 11$ **18.** $1 \div 10$ **19.** $4 \div 9$ **20.** $7 \div 13$ **21.** $5 \div 8$

22. $3 \div 7$ **23.** $12 \div 23$ **24.** $8 \div 30$ **25.** $11 \div 17$ **26.** $25 \div 75$

Problem Solving

27. **Writing to Explain** Into how many sections would you divide this number line to graph $\frac{7}{10}$? Why?

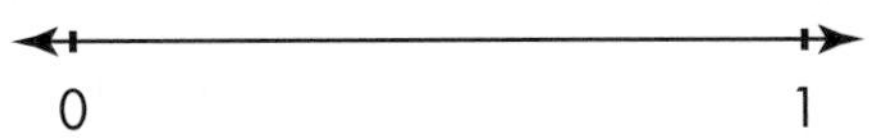

The table at the right shows the weights of different materials used to build a bridge. Use the table to answer **28** and **29**.

Data

Bridge	Materials
Concrete	1,000 tons
Steel structure	400 tons
Glass and granite	200 tons

28. Write a division expression that represents the weight of the steel structure compared to the total weight of the bridge's materials.

29. Which of the following fractions equals the amount of glass and granite in the bridge divided by the amount of steel, written in simplest form?

A $\frac{1}{2}$ **B** $\frac{1}{3}$ **C** $\frac{1}{4}$ **D** $\frac{1}{8}$

Lesson
6-2 Fractions and Decimals

Understand It!
A fraction and a decimal can be used to represent the same value.

How can you write equivalent fractions and decimals?

A banana slug moves through forests in northern California at a rate of about $\frac{1}{20}$ of an inch per minute. Which decimal is equivalent to $\frac{1}{20}$?

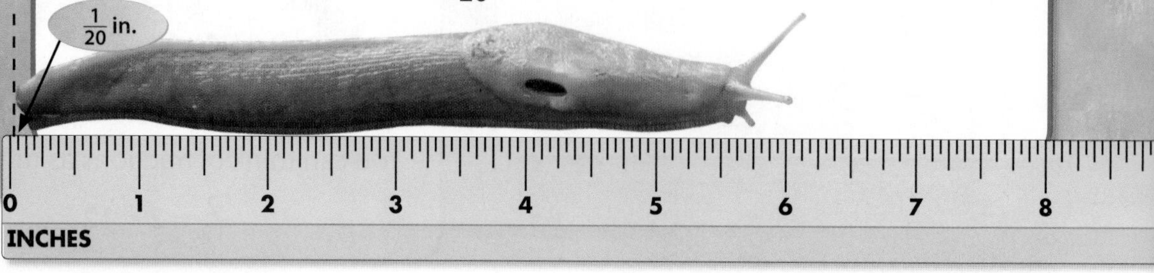

Guided Practice*

Do you know HOW?

In **1** and **2**, write a decimal and a fraction in simplest form for each shaded area.

1. 

2. 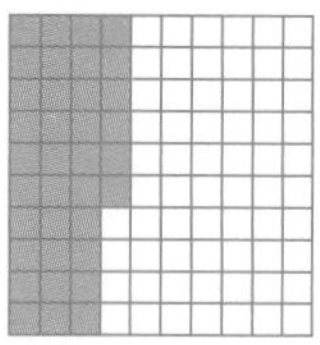

Write each fraction as a decimal.

3. $\frac{3}{4}$ **4.** $\frac{13}{20}$ **5.** $\frac{9}{1000}$

Do you UNDERSTAND?

6. Describe how you could use mental math to write a decimal as a fraction.

7. Describe how you would use an equivalent fraction with a denominator that is a multiple of 10 to solve Exercise 3.

Independent Practice

Leveled Practice Write a decimal and a fraction in simplest form for each shaded portion.

8. 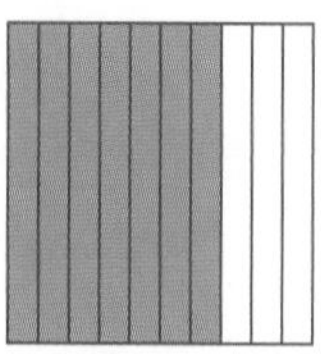

9. 

10. 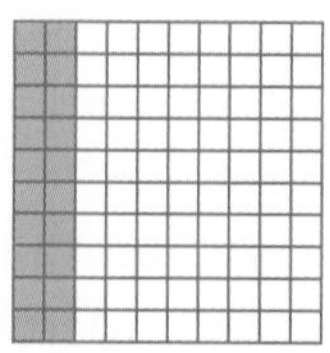

In **11** through **18**, write each decimal as a fraction in simplest form.

11. 0.4 **12.** 0.06 **13.** 0.08 **14.** 0.35

15. 0.75 **16.** 0.43 **17.** 0.025 **18.** 0.999

*For another example, see Set B on page 158.

One Way

Fractions can be written in equivalent forms. A fraction with a denominator of 10, 100, 1,000, and so on can also be written as a decimal.

You can change $\frac{1}{20}$ to an equivalent fraction in 100ths:

$$\frac{1 \times 5}{20 \times 5} = \frac{5}{100}$$

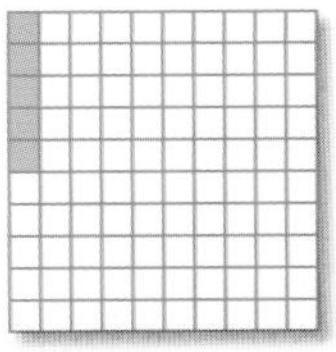

So, $\frac{1}{20} = 0.05$.

Another Way

Divide the numerator by the denominator:

$$\frac{1}{20} = 1 \div 20$$

$$\begin{array}{r} 0.05 \\ 20\overline{)1.00} \\ -\ \ 100 \\ \hline 0 \end{array}$$

You can use division to change any fraction to a decimal.

$$\frac{1}{20} = 0.05$$

Independent Practice

In **19** through **33**, convert each fraction to a decimal.

19. $\frac{3}{8}$ **20.** $\frac{1}{2}$ **21.** $\frac{1}{4}$ **22.** $\frac{6}{15}$ **23.** $\frac{9}{10}$

24. $\frac{3}{5}$ **25.** $\frac{18}{100}$ **26.** $\frac{27}{50}$ **27.** $\frac{15}{20}$ **28.** $\frac{19}{38}$

29. $\frac{9}{25}$ **30.** $\frac{7}{8}$ **31.** $\frac{1}{200}$ **32.** $\frac{4}{125}$ **33.** $\frac{39}{40}$

Problem Solving

34. **Number Sense** How can you show $\frac{1}{4}$ on a hundredths grid? What decimal does the model show?

35. **Writing to Explain** Kirsten thinks that $\frac{2}{5}$ and $\frac{10}{25}$ both convert to the same decimal. Is she right? Explain.

36. Kennedy Space Center, located on Merritt Island, is also a National Wildlife Refuge. Only about 0.04 of the total area is used for space shuttle operations. Which fraction best represents the area used for space shuttle operations?

A $\frac{2}{5}$ **C** $\frac{1}{25}$

B $\frac{1}{4}$ **D** $\frac{1}{200}$

37. Alaska is the largest state, with an area that is about $\frac{163}{1,000}$ of the area of the United States. Write this number as a decimal.

38. **Geometry** Use the information in the triangle to find the measure of $\angle x$.

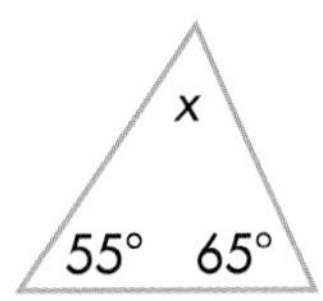

Lesson
6-3

Understand It!
A fraction that is greater than 1 can be written as an improper fraction or as a mixed number.

Improper Fractions and Mixed Numbers

How can you represent quantities that are greater than or equal to 1?

Jenny and Tyler are baking bread. How do the measurements they make relate to fractions and mixed numbers?

Another Example **How can you change between improper fractions and mixed numbers?**

Write $\frac{12}{9}$ as a mixed number.

- Divide the numerator by the denominator.

$$\begin{array}{r} 1\text{ R}3 \\ 9\overline{)12} \\ -\ 9 \\ \hline 3 \end{array}$$

- Write the remainder as a fraction in simplest form.

$$\frac{3}{9} = \frac{1}{3}$$

- So, $\frac{12}{9} = 1\frac{1}{3}$.

Write $3\frac{5}{8}$ as an improper fraction.

$3\frac{5}{8} = 3 + \frac{5}{8}$ **Write 3 as a fraction using a denominator of 8.**

$= \frac{24}{8} + \frac{5}{8}$

$= \frac{29}{8}$

Shortcut

- **Multiply the whole number by the fraction denominator.**
  $3 \times 8 = 24$
- **Add the fraction numerator to this product. This is the new numerator.**
  $24 + 5 = 29$
- **Keep the same denominator.** $\frac{29}{8}$

Guided Practice*

Do you know HOW?

Write each improper fraction as a mixed number in simplest form.

1. $\frac{7}{3}$ **2.** $\frac{41}{9}$ **3.** $\frac{9}{5}$

Do you UNDERSTAND?

4. Why can you divide the numerator of an improper fraction by its denominator?

DIGITAL Animated Glossary **www.pearsonsuccessnet.com**

For another example, see Set C on page 158.

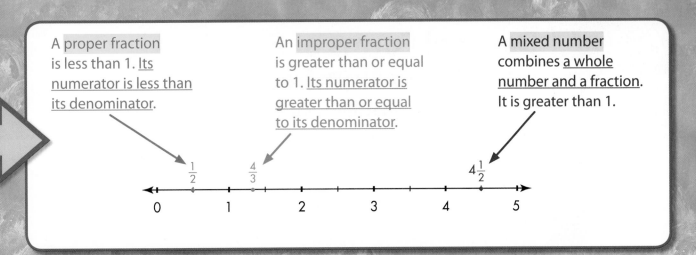

A proper fraction is less than 1. Its numerator is less than its denominator.

An improper fraction is greater than or equal to 1. Its numerator is greater than or equal to its denominator.

A mixed number combines a whole number and a fraction. It is greater than 1.

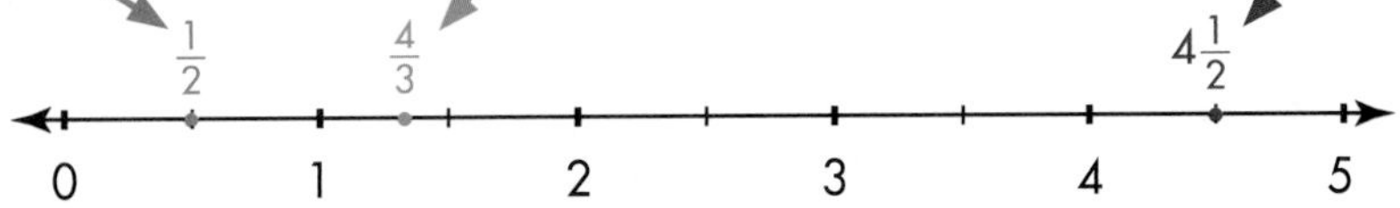

Independent Practice

Write each improper fraction as a whole number or mixed number in simplest form.

5. $\frac{38}{7}$ **6.** $\frac{14}{8}$ **7.** $\frac{8}{3}$ **8.** $\frac{42}{6}$ **9.** $\frac{17}{5}$ **10.** $\frac{21}{9}$

Write each mixed number as an improper fraction.

11. $1\frac{1}{8}$ **12.** $4\frac{8}{15}$ **13.** $3\frac{1}{11}$ **14.** $5\frac{3}{5}$ **15.** $2\frac{7}{12}$ **16.** $8\frac{1}{4}$

For **17** through **21**, which letter on the number line corresponds to each number?

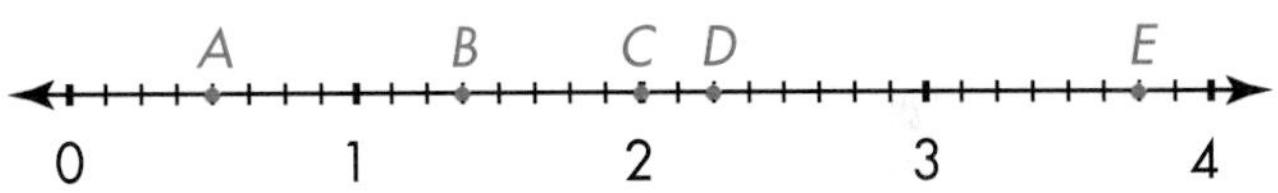

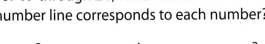

17. $1\frac{3}{8}$ **18.** $\frac{4}{2}$ **19.** $3\frac{3}{4}$ **20.** $\frac{1}{2}$ **21.** $\frac{9}{4}$

Problem Solving

22. A capybara is the world's largest rodent. It can grow to be $1\frac{3}{10}$ m long. Which improper fraction represents the length of the capybara?

A $\frac{36}{13}$ m

B $\frac{13}{10}$ m

C $\frac{29}{10}$ m

D $\frac{11}{10}$ m

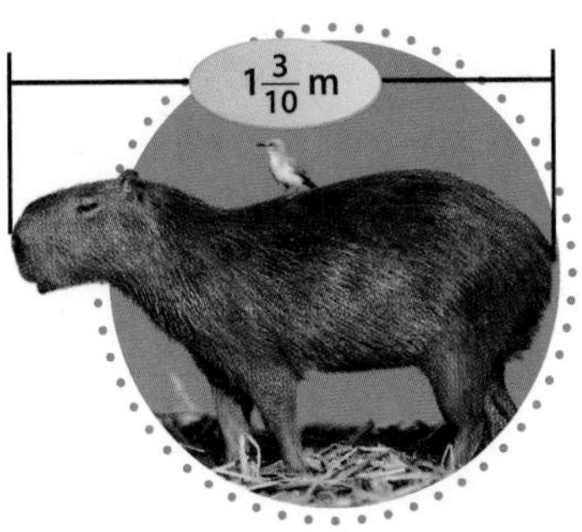

23. Writing to Explain Diego said that $\frac{9}{4}$ and $1\frac{1}{4}$ are equivalent. Is he right? Explain.

24. Geometry A quadrilateral has 3 angles that measure 47°, 110°, and 85°. What is the measurement of the fourth angle?

25. Reasoning Should $\frac{15}{15}$ be expressed as a mixed number or a whole number? How do you know?

Lesson
6-4

Understand It!
The digits in the decimal form of a fraction or mixed number may terminate or keep repeating.

Decimal Forms of Fractions and Mixed Numbers

How can you write fractions as decimals?

Recall that a fraction can represent division of the numerator by the denominator. Write $\frac{3}{8}$ and $2\frac{5}{11}$ as decimals.

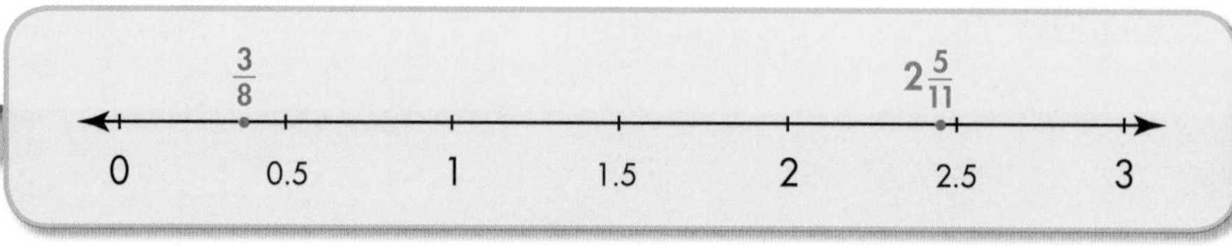

Another Example

How can you write decimals as fractions or mixed numbers?

Convert decimals to fractions by writing the decimal as a fraction with a denominator of tenths, hundredths, or thousandths. Then write the fraction in simplest form. Use a similar approach to convert a decimal greater than 1 to a mixed number.

Write 0.28 as a fraction.

Think $0.28 = 28$ hundredths

$$0.28 = \frac{28}{100}$$

Simplify. $\frac{28}{100} = \frac{7}{25}$

So, $0.28 = \frac{7}{25}$.

Write 4.125 as a mixed number.

Think $4.125 = 4 + 0.125$

$4 + 0.125 = 4$ and 125 thousandths

$$4 + 0.125 = 4 + \frac{125}{1{,}000}$$

$$= 4\frac{125}{1{,}000}$$

Simplify. $4\frac{125}{1{,}000} = 4\frac{1}{8}$

So, $4.125 = 4\frac{1}{8}$.

Explain It

1. When simplifying $\frac{28}{100}$, why were the numerator and denominator divided by 4?

2. When writing 4.125 as a mixed number, why should you first think of 4.125 as $4 + 0.125$?

Divide to write $\frac{3}{8}$ as a decimal.

$$8\overline{)3.000} = 0.375$$

The decimal 0.375 is a terminating decimal because the digits in the quotient end and there is no remainder.

$\frac{3}{8} = 0.375$

Think of $2\frac{5}{11}$ as $2 + \frac{5}{11}$.

Divide the numerator and denominator of the fraction to find the decimal portion of the number.

$$\begin{array}{r} 0.4545 \\ 11\overline{)5.0000} \\ -\underline{44} \\ 60 \\ -\underline{55} \\ 50 \\ -\underline{44} \\ 60 \\ -\underline{55} \\ 5 \end{array}$$

The decimal 0.4545… is a repeating decimal because the digits in the quotient repeat. A bar is written over the repeating digits: $0.\overline{45}$.

So, $2\frac{5}{11} = 2.4545\ldots = 2.\overline{45}$.

Guided Practice*

Do you know HOW?

Write each decimal as a fraction or a mixed number in simplest form.

1. 0.8 **2.** 3.125 **3.** 2.75

Write each fraction or mixed number as a decimal.

4. $\frac{7}{10}$ **5.** $1\frac{5}{8}$ **6.** $4\frac{5}{9}$

Do you UNDERSTAND?

7. In the example at the top of the page, why is there a bar over the 45?

8. How could you check your answer to Exercise 2 in Do you know HOW?

Independent Practice

Write each fraction or mixed number as a decimal.

9. $\frac{2}{3}$ **10.** $1\frac{1}{2}$ **11.** $\frac{1}{11}$ **12.** $\frac{9}{10}$ **13.** $\frac{5}{4}$

14. $3\frac{3}{8}$ **15.** $\frac{1}{16}$ **16.** $\frac{4}{3}$ **17.** $\frac{2}{15}$ **18.** $5\frac{7}{8}$

Write each decimal as a fraction or a mixed number in simplest form.

19. 0.4 **20.** 1.6 **21.** 0.375 **22.** 4.45 **23.** 0.032

24. 0.08 **25.** 0.68 **26.** 2.25 **27.** 12.875 **28.** 0.002

DIGITAL Animated Glossary **www.pearsonsuccessnet.com**

For another example, see Set D on page 159.

Problem Solving

Mercury, Venus, Earth, and Mars are the inner planets in our solar system. The table shows the volume of each inner planet as a decimal, compared to the volume of Earth. Use the table for **29** and **30**.

Data

Planet	Volume Compared to Earth
Mercury	0.054
Venus	0.88
Earth	1
Mars	0.15

29. What is the fraction equivalent for the volume of Mars compared to Earth?

30. What is the fraction equivalent for the volume of Venus compared to Earth?

31. Julie found an arrowhead that measured 2.625 in. Write the length of the arrowhead as a mixed number.

32. A radio station broadcasts news 1.75 hours each weekday. On Saturday and Sunday, the news broadcasts are twice as long. How many hours of news are broadcast each week?

33. **Writing to Explain** If you know the decimal equivalent of $\frac{1}{8}$, explain how you could use that to find the decimal equivalent of $\frac{3}{8}$.

34. The Green Darner dragonfly is one of the largest dragonflies. It has a wingspan of about 4 inches and weighs about 0.04 ounces. Write its weight as a fraction in simplest form.

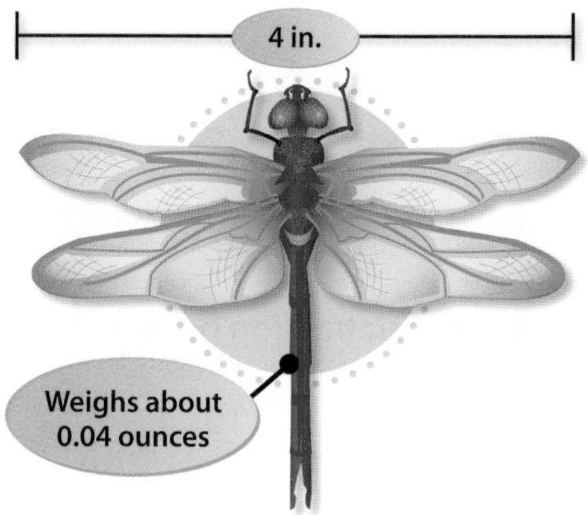

35. The Green Darner dragonfly is an excellent flier. It can fly at speeds of greater than 50 miles per hour. If a Green Darner is flying at $50\frac{3}{16}$ miles per hour. What is its speed written as a decimal?

36. **Number Sense** What do the decimal forms of the fractions $\frac{1}{3}$, $\frac{5}{6}$, and $\frac{7}{11}$ have in common?

37. Which of the following fractions can be changed to a terminating decimal?

A $\frac{1}{5}$ **C** $\frac{1}{3}$ **B** $\frac{5}{11}$ **D** $\frac{7}{9}$

Algebra Connections

What's the Rule?

Remember that you can find a rule for a table of values by looking for a mathematical relationship between the two variables.

Example:

Speed of Car A	*Speed of Car B*
40 mph	37 mph
72 mph	69 mph
25 mph	22 mph
57 mph	54 mph

Find a rule relating the speeds of the cars.

Subtract 3 mph from the speed of Car *A* to get the speed of Car *B*. So, Car *A* is always 3 mph faster than Car *B*.

Find a rule for each table. Then write a sentence that tells the rule.

1.

Number of races Jessica ran	*Number of miles Jessica ran*
4	12
2	6
9	27
5	15

2.

Scotty's allowance	*Clint's allowance*
$8.50	$17.00
$3.00	$6.00
$6.25	$12.50
$2.20	$4.40

3.

Mya's age	*Sabrina's age*
4	29
2	27
7	32
11	36

4.

Apples	*Plums*
24	6
12	3
32	8
16	4

5.

Speed of Car A	*Speed of Car B*
36 mph	18 mph
42 mph	21 mph
60 mph	30 mph
112 mph	56 mph

6.

Height of bean plant	*Height of corn plant*
3 in.	5 in.
6 in.	8 in.
12 in.	14 in.
15 in.	17 in.

Topic 6

Test

1. Which of the fractions is equal to $4 \div 10$? (6-1)

A $\frac{5}{2}$

B $\frac{6}{4}$

C $\frac{4}{6}$

D $\frac{2}{5}$

2. Eduardo has won 5 out of the 8 swim meets in which he has participated. Which decimal is equal to $\frac{5}{8}$? (6-2)

A 0.5

B 0.525

C 0.625

D 1.6

3. Which point represents $\frac{21}{8}$ on the number line? (6-3)

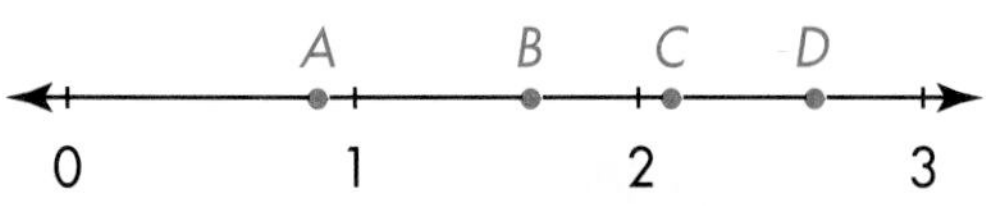

A Point *A*

B Point *B*

C Point *C*

D Point *D*

4. The largest hailstone on record had a diameter of $17\frac{4}{5}$ centimeters. What is $17\frac{4}{5}$ written as a decimal? (6-4)

A 17.8

B 17.5

C 17.45

D 17.4

5. Which number is equivalent to $3\frac{5}{6}$? (6-3)

A $\frac{33}{6}$

B $\frac{23}{6}$

C 18

D 4

6. The table shows the measures recorded by several groups of students as they did a science experiment. Which of the following shows the Group D measurement as a decimal? (6-4)

Data

Group	Measures
A	$21\frac{3}{4}$ in.
B	$22\frac{1}{8}$ in.
C	$21\frac{15}{16}$ in.
D	$21\frac{5}{8}$ in.

A 21.625

B 21.58

C 21.85

D $21.8\overline{3}$

7. What is $3\frac{1}{4}$ written as an improper fraction? (6-3)

A $\frac{13}{4}$

B $\frac{12}{4}$

C $\frac{8}{4}$

D $\frac{7}{4}$

8. Tracy purchased 5.32 gallons of gasoline. What is 5.32 written as a fraction? (6-4)

A $5\frac{8}{100}$

B $5\frac{8}{25}$

C $5\frac{32}{50}$

D $5\frac{32}{10}$

9. Seventeen of the 34 students in Ms. Randall's class walk to school. Which decimal is equal to $\frac{17}{34}$? (6-2)

A 0.34

B 0.5

C 0.17

D 0.2

10. Five siblings are dividing 2 acres of land evenly between them. Which number sentence can be used to find the amount of land each sibling will receive? (6-1)

A $5 \div 2 = \frac{5}{2}$

B $2 \div 5 = \frac{5}{2}$

C $5 \div 2 = \frac{2}{5}$

D $2 \div 5 = \frac{2}{5}$

11. Which of the following is equal to 0.65? (6-2)

A $\frac{65}{10}$

B $\frac{13}{2}$

C $\frac{13}{20}$

D $\frac{13}{200}$

12. Mrs. Francisco is making a walkway out of steppingstones. The walkway is 7.2 yards long and has stones every 0.9 yard. She has placed the first stone, the middle stone, and the last stone, as shown in the diagram below.

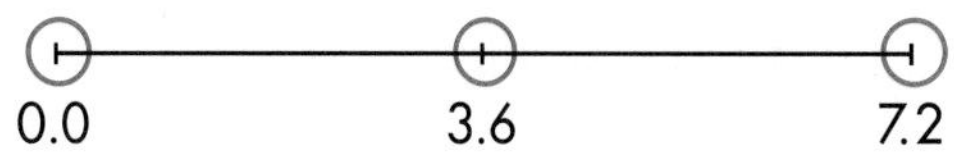

Which picture shows how she should place the other stones? (6-5)

A
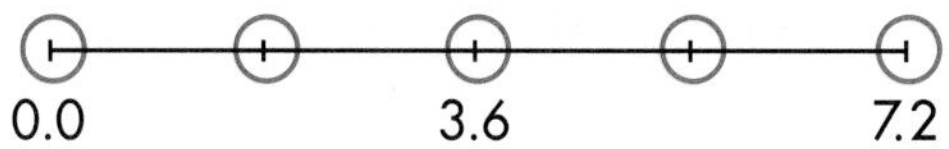

B
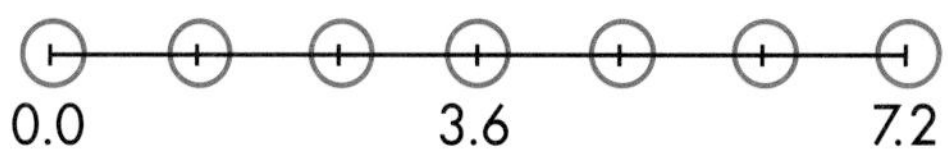

C
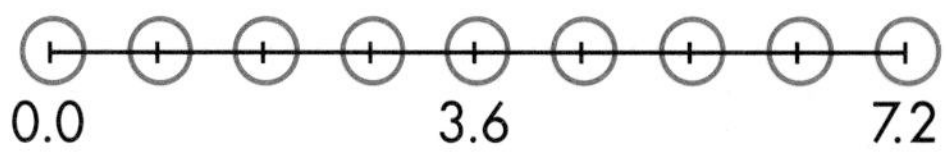

D
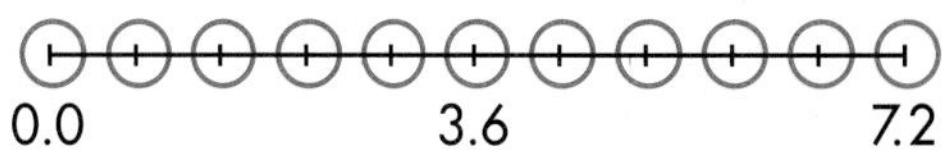

13. Which is equivalent to $\frac{93}{4}$? (6-3)

A $20\frac{3}{4}$

B $23\frac{1}{4}$

C $9\frac{3}{4}$

D 89

Reteaching

Set A, pages 144–145

You can represent the fraction $\frac{2}{3}$ as division.

Think $\frac{1}{3}$ of 2 wholes

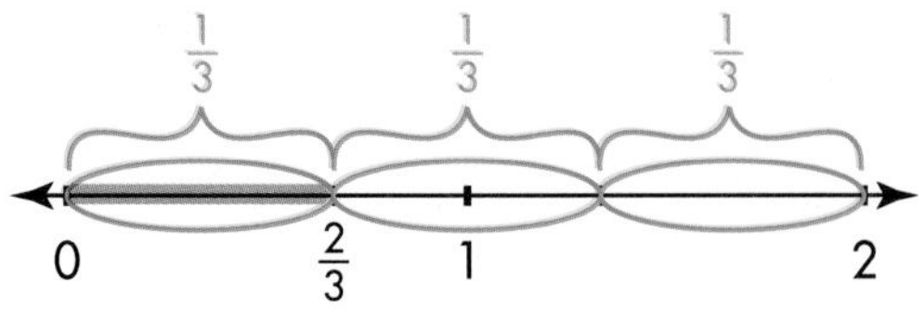

$$\frac{2}{3} = 2 \div 3$$

Remember that any fraction can be represented as division of the numerator by the denominator.

Write a division expression for each.

1. $\frac{7}{9}$ **2.** $\frac{2}{3}$ **3.** $\frac{11}{17}$

Write each expression as a fraction.

4. $7 \div 12$ **5.** $17 \div 20$

Set B, pages 146–147

You can write equivalent decimals for fractions.

Convert $\frac{1}{25}$ to a decimal. Change $\frac{1}{25}$ to an equivalent fraction in 100ths.

$$\frac{1 \times 4}{25 \times 4} = \frac{4}{100} = 0.04$$

Or, divide the numerator by the denominator.

$$\begin{array}{r} 0.04 \\ 25\overline{)1.00} \\ -100 \\ \hline 0 \end{array}$$

So, $\frac{1}{25} = 0.04$.

Remember that any decimal can be written as a fraction by using the place value of the decimal as the denominator of the fraction.

Write each decimal as a fraction in simplest form.

1. 0.7 **2.** 0.125 **3.** 0.69

4. 0.015 **5.** 0.501 **6.** 0.34

Write each fraction as a decimal.

6. $\frac{1}{20}$ **7.** $\frac{7}{10}$ **8.** $\frac{41}{250}$

Set C, pages 148–149

Write $\frac{19}{3}$ as a mixed number.

- Divide the numerator by the denominator. $\begin{array}{r} 6\text{ R}1 \\ 3\overline{)19} \end{array}$
- Write the remainder as a fraction in simplest form. $\frac{19}{3} = 6\frac{1}{3}$

Write $9\frac{5}{8}$ as an improper fraction.

$9\frac{5}{8} = 9 + \frac{5}{8}$ and $9 + \frac{5}{8} = \frac{72}{8} + \frac{5}{8}$

So, $9\frac{5}{8} = \frac{77}{8}$.

Remember to always write the answer in simplest form.

Write each improper fraction as a mixed number or whole number.

1. $\frac{16}{6}$ **2.** $\frac{24}{9}$ **3.** $\frac{9}{2}$

Write each as an improper fraction.

4. $4\frac{5}{9}$ **5.** $2\frac{7}{11}$ **6.** $8\frac{5}{7}$

7. $5\frac{1}{3}$ **8.** $10\frac{4}{5}$ **9.** $8\frac{8}{11}$

Set D, pages 150–152

Write 0.15 as a fraction in simplest form.

$$0.15 = \frac{15}{100} = \frac{3}{20}$$

Write $1\frac{7}{8}$ as a decimal.

Think $1\frac{7}{8} = 1 + \frac{7}{8}$

$$\begin{array}{r} 0.875 \\ 8\overline{)7.000} \\ -64 \\ \hline 60 \\ -56 \\ \hline 40 \\ -40 \\ \hline 0 \end{array}$$

So, $1\frac{7}{8} = 1.875$.

Remember that a repeating decimal has one or more digits that repeat. A bar is written over the repeating digits.

Write each decimal as a fraction or mixed number in simplest form.

1. 0.125 **2.** 0.7 **3.** 0.08

4 0.875 **5.** 0.99 **6.** $6.\overline{6}$

Write each as a decimal.

7. $\frac{3}{8}$ **8.** $1\frac{1}{3}$ **9.** $2\frac{3}{4}$

10. $3\frac{5}{12}$ **11.** $\frac{1}{6}$ **12.** $21\frac{4}{5}$

Set E, pages 154–155

Find the finish line for a race that is 0.7 mile long.

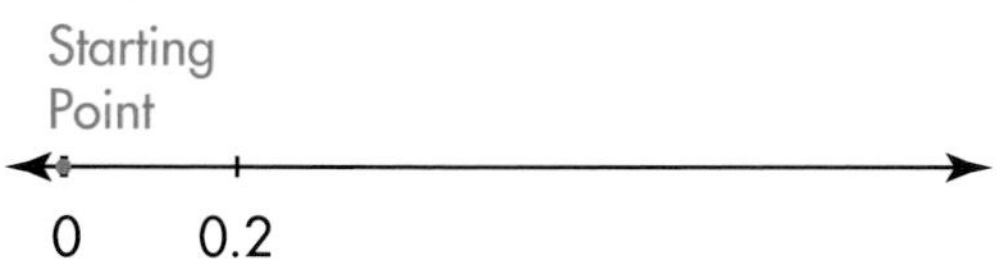

Measure and divide the length into equal segments of 0.1 mile.

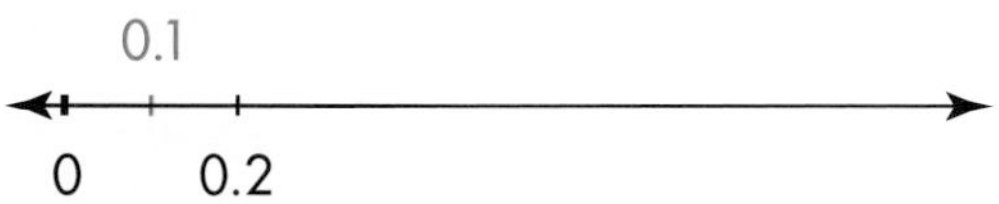

Use the length of 0.1 mile to mark every tenth of a mile to the finish line.

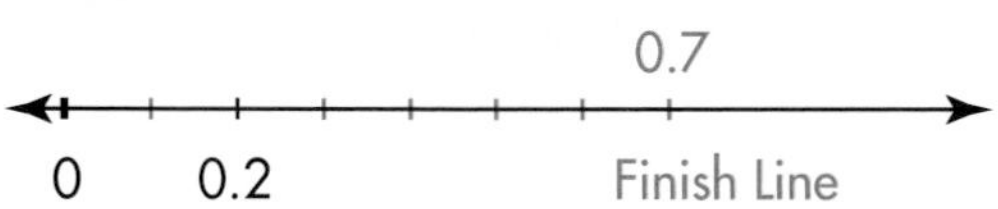

Remember that drawing a picture can help you solve problems.

1. Park planners were designing a straight 2-mile track for dirt bikes. There will be a hill at the 1.75 mile point. Use a ruler to copy their work, find the 2-mile finish, and mark the place of the hill.

Tip *Use the information in the picture to find equal segments of 0.25 miles.*

Topic 7

Adding and Subtracting Fractions and Mixed Numbers

1 Chilies from plants like these are cut up or ground into powder to add flavor to foods like enchiladas and tacos. How do fractions help you measure chili powder? You will find out in Lesson 7-1.

2 The hiking trail around Mirror Lake in Yosemite National Park is 5 miles long. How can adding and subtracting fractions help when you go hiking? You will find out in Lesson 7-3.

3

Fairy penguins are the smallest kind of penguin. They come ashore in large groups at night. How tall are these penguins? You will find out in Lesson 7-6.

Review What You Know!

Vocabulary

Choose the best term from the box.

- equivalent fractions
- mixed number
- improper fraction

1. A(n) __?__ includes both a whole number and a fraction.

2. A(n) __?__ is a fraction in which the numerator is greater than or equal to the denominator.

3. Two or more different fractions that name the same amount are called __?__ .

Factoring

Find the greatest common factor (GCF) for the numbers in each set.

4. 10, 12 **5.** 10, 25 **6.** 7, 21

7. 2, 6, 8 **8.** 2, 5, 10 **9.** 3, 6, 9, 12

Equivalent Numbers

Find each missing value.

10. $1\frac{1}{6} = \frac{\square}{6}$ **11.** $\frac{\square}{10} = \frac{1}{2}$ **12.** $\frac{10}{15} = \frac{\square}{3}$

13. $\frac{4}{8} = \frac{1}{\square}$ **14.** $1\frac{1}{2} = \frac{3}{\square}$ **15.** $\frac{4}{16} = \frac{1}{\square}$

Fractions

Writing to Explain Write an answer for each question.

16. How can you find equivalent fractions?

17. How do you know when a fraction is in simplest form?

4

Mountains near oceans have a rainy side and a dry side. The side facing the ocean gets much more rain than the other side. How much rain does the ocean side get? You will find out in Lesson 7-5.

Lesson

7-1 Adding and Subtracting: Like Denominators

Understand It!
Fractions with like denominators are easy to add and subtract because the sum or difference of the numerators is written over a common denominator.

How can you add fractions with like denominators?

Greg ate $\frac{1}{8}$ of a quesadilla with peppers and $\frac{1}{8}$ of a same-size quesadilla with beans. How much of one whole quesadilla did he eat?

Choose an Operation Add the fractional parts.

Another Example How can you subtract fractions with like denominators?

Step 1

Find $\frac{5}{8} - \frac{1}{8}$.

The fractions have like denominators. Subtract the numerators. Write the difference over the like denominator.

$\frac{5}{8} - \frac{1}{8} = \frac{4}{8}$ The difference is $\frac{4}{8}$.

Step 2

Simplify the answer.

The GCF of 4 and 8 is 4.

$$\frac{4 \div 4}{8 \div 4} = \frac{1}{2}$$

So, $\frac{5}{8} - \frac{1}{8} = \frac{4}{8} = \frac{1}{2}$.

Guided Practice*

Do you know HOW?

Find each sum or difference. Simplify.

1. $\frac{1}{3} + \frac{1}{3}$

2. $\frac{3}{4} - \frac{2}{4}$

3. $\frac{5}{9} + \frac{3}{9}$

4. $\frac{11}{12} - \frac{2}{12}$

Do you UNDERSTAND?

5. When fractions have like denominators, how can you find their sum?

6. Why is $\frac{1}{8} + \frac{1}{8} = \frac{2}{16}$ not correct?

Independent Practice

Find each sum or difference. Simplify your answers.

7. $\frac{1}{4} + \frac{1}{4}$

8. $\frac{3}{5} - \frac{2}{5}$

9. $\frac{3}{4} + \frac{3}{4}$

10. $\frac{8}{9} - \frac{5}{9}$

DIGITAL Animated Glossary **www.pearsonsuccessnet.com**

*For another example, see Set A on page 182.

Step 1

Find $\frac{1}{8} + \frac{1}{8}$. The fractions have the same denominators or like denominators.

Add the numerators. Write the sum over the like denominator.

$$\frac{1}{8} + \frac{1}{8} = \frac{2}{8}$$

Greg ate $\frac{2}{8}$ of one whole quesadilla.

Step 2

Simplify the answer. The greatest common factor (GCF) of 2 and 8 is 2.

$$\frac{2 \div 2}{8 \div 2} = \frac{1}{4}$$

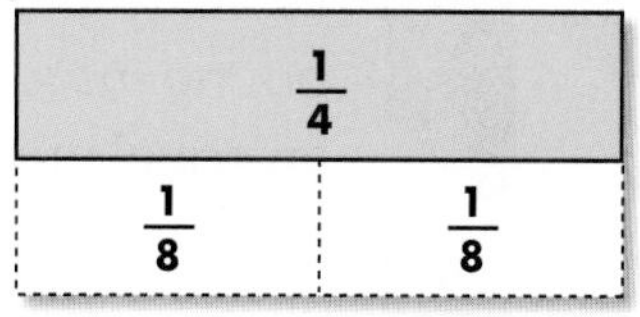

So, $\frac{1}{8} + \frac{1}{8} = \frac{2}{8}$ or $\frac{1}{4}$.

Find each sum or difference. Simplify your answers.

11. $\frac{3}{8} - \frac{1}{8}$

12. $\frac{5}{14} + \frac{6}{14}$

13. $\frac{6}{11} + \frac{5}{11}$

14. $\frac{10}{15} - \frac{6}{15}$

15. $\frac{1}{4} + \frac{1}{4} + \frac{3}{4}$

16. $\frac{3}{16} + \frac{4}{16} + \frac{8}{16}$

17. $\frac{8}{20} + \frac{1}{20} + \frac{3}{20}$

18. $\frac{3}{26} + \frac{3}{26} + \frac{19}{26}$

Evaluate **19** and **20** for $x = \frac{1}{5}$.

19. $\frac{3}{5} - x$

20. $x + \frac{4}{5}$

Evaluate **21** and **22** for $x = \frac{3}{8}$.

21. $\frac{9}{8} - x$

22. $(x - \frac{2}{8}) + \frac{7}{8}$

Problem Solving

23. Many recipes use ingredients that are measured as fractional amounts. Use the recipe to answer the questions.

a What is the total amount of olive oil, flour, and red chili powder in the sauce?

b What is the total amount of cumin and garlic powder in the sauce?

Red Enchilada Sauce Recipe

- *1 tablespoon olive oil*
- *$\frac{1}{2}$ tablespoon flour*
- *$\frac{1}{2}$ tablespoon red chili powder*
- *$\frac{1}{2}$ teaspoon cumin*
- *$\frac{1}{2}$ teaspoon garlic powder*
- *3 ounces tomato paste*
- *1 cup water*

Makes 1–1$\frac{1}{2}$ cups

24. **Writing to Explain** Kari has 8 CDs and Ian has 14 CDs. Write a number sentence that uses the Commutative Property of Addition to show two ways to find how many CDs they have altogether.

25. **Think About the Process** Sarah's book has 100 pages. She read 12 pages on Sunday, 20 pages on Monday, and 13 pages on Tuesday. She wants to know what fraction of the book she has read. Which expression finds the numerator?

A 12 + 20 + 13

B 100 − 45

C 100 − 10

D 12 + 20 + 13 + 100

26. Lynn had $\frac{7}{8}$ of a set of markers. She gave part of the set to her friend Cheryl. Lynn has $\frac{3}{8}$ of a set left. What fraction of a set did she give to Cheryl?

Lesson
7-2

Understand It!
List the multiples or use the prime factorization of two or more numbers to find the common multiple with the least value.

Least Common Multiple

How can you find the least common multiple of two numbers?

Grant is making picnic lunches. He wants to buy as many juice bottles as applesauce cups, but no more than he really needs to get an equal number of each.

How many packages of each should Grant buy?

Guided Practice*

Do you know HOW?

In **1** and **2**, list multiples of each number to find the LCM of each pair of numbers.

1. 2, 5

2. 6, 10

In **3** and **4**, use prime factorization to find the LCM of each set of numbers.

3. 12, 24

4. 3, 6, 9

Do you UNDERSTAND?

5. After 48, what is the next common multiple of 6 and 8?

6. **Number Sense** Grant finds juice bottles that come in packages of 3, but can only find applesauce in packages of 8. Will the LCM change? Explain.

Independent Practice

Find the LCM for each set of numbers.

Tip *You can use a factor tree to find a prime factorization.*

```
     12
    /  \
   3 × 4
  /   / \
 3 × 2 × 2
```

7. 4, 10

8. 3, 4

9. 10, 12

10. 15, 20

11. 3, 13

12. 8, 10

13. 6, 27

14. 4, 11

15. 6, 15

16. 7, 8

17. 5, 7

18. 10, 25

19. 4, 5, 12

20. 6, 8, 10

21. 9, 18, 24

22. 5, 12, 30

DIGITAL Animated Glossary **www.pearsonsuccessnet.com**

For another example, see Set B on page 182.

One Way

List multiples of each pack size.

6: 6, 12, 18, 24, 30, 36, 42, 48 …

8: 8, 16, 24, 32, 40, 48 …

24 and 48 are common multiples of 6 and 8.

The least common multiple (LCM) is 24, the common multiple with the least value.

$6 \times 4 = 24$ — 4 packages of juice bottles

$8 \times 3 = 24$ — 3 packages of applesauce cups

Another Way

Use prime factorization. Circle the greater number of times each different factor appears.

6: $2 \times$ (3)

8: ($2 \times 2 \times 2$)

Then find the product of those circled factors.

$3 \times 2 \times 2 \times 2 = 24$

To get 24 of each, Grant should buy 4 packages of juice bottles and 3 packages of applesauce cups.

Problem Solving

23. Writing to Explain Films play continuously at the museum. If the 3 films shown in the table to the right begin to play at the same time at 8 A.M., what time will it be before they begin playing together again? Explain.

Data

Museum Film Schedule	
Film Title	**Length**
Introduction to the Museum	2 minutes
Profiles of Artists	30 minutes
Art and Architecture	45 minutes

24. Can you use the Associative Property with division or subtraction? Use $30 \div (10 \div 5)$ and $(16 - 8) - 4$ to explain your answer.

25. Linda is sending out cards. If envelopes come in boxes of 25 and stamps come in packs of 10, what is the least number of stamps and envelopes she can buy to get one stamp for each envelope?

26. **Think About the Process** Blue buttons come in packs of 25, and green buttons come in packs of 40. What is the LCM of 25 and 40?

A 100 **C** 200

B 1,000 **D** 400

27. Granola bars are sold in 12-ounce and 36-ounce packages. What is the least number of ounces you can buy of each package to have equal amounts of each of the different sizes?

A 12 **B** 36 **C** 72 **D** 144

28. Reasoning Ron is working to find the LCM of 6, 9, and 10. Is his work shown below correct?

6: (2×3)

9: 3×3

10: (2×5)

$2 \times 3 \times 2 \times 5 = 60$, so the LCM of 6, 9, and 10 is 60.

29. The red kangaroo was 2 years old when it came to the zoo in 2003. How old will the kangaroo be in the year 2015?

Lesson
7-3

Understand It!
Add and subtract fractions with unlike denominators by finding a least common denominator and writing equivalent fractions with like denominators.

Adding and Subtracting: Unlike Denominators

How can you add fractions with unlike denominators?

Abby and Faith each had cereal for breakfast. Abby ate $\frac{1}{2}$ cup of cereal and Faith ate $\frac{1}{3}$ cup of cereal. How much cereal did they eat all together?

Choose an Operation Add the fractional parts.

Another Example How can you subtract fractions with unlike denominators?

Find $\frac{1}{3} - \frac{1}{4}$.

Step 1

To subtract fractions with unlike denominators, find the least common multiple (LCM) of the denominators to use as the least common denominator (LCD).

Multiples of 3: 3, 6, 9, 12...

Multiples of 4: 4, 8, 12...

Since the LCM of 3 and 4 is 12, the LCD is 12.

Step 2

Write the fractions as equivalent fractions with the LCD of 12.

$\frac{1 \times 4}{3 \times 4} = \frac{4}{12}$ and $\frac{1 \times 3}{4 \times 3} = \frac{3}{12}$

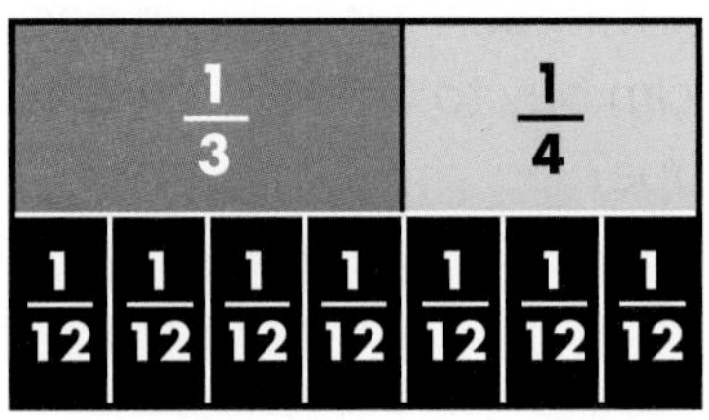

Step 3

Subtract. Simplify if possible.

$\frac{4}{12} - \frac{3}{12} = \frac{1}{12}$

The difference is $\frac{1}{12}$.

Explain It

1. In Step 1, why do you find the LCM of 3 and 4?
2. In Step 2, why do you multiply the numerators and denominators of the different fractions by 4 and by 3?
3. In Step 3, why should you simplify if possible?

Step 1

Find $\frac{1}{2} + \frac{1}{3}$.

To add fractions with different or unlike denominators, find a common denominator.

The least common multiple (LCM) of the denominators is the least common denominator (LCD).

Multiples of 2: 2, 4, 6 ...

Multiples of 3: 3, 6 ...

The LCM is 6, so the LCD is 6.

Step 2

Write the addends as equivalent fractions with the LCD of 6.

$$\frac{1 \times 3}{2 \times 3} = \frac{3}{6}$$

and

$$\frac{1 \times 2}{3 \times 2} = \frac{2}{6}$$

Step 3

Add. Simplify if possible.

$$\frac{3}{6} + \frac{2}{6} = \frac{5}{6}$$

Abby and Faith ate a total of $\frac{5}{6}$ cup of cereal.

Guided Practice*

Do you know HOW?

In **1** and **2**, find the LCD for each pair of fractions.

1. $\frac{3}{4}, \frac{2}{5}$

2. $\frac{2}{7}, \frac{1}{3}$

In **3** through **6**, find each sum or difference. Simplify your answers.

3. $\frac{5}{8} - \frac{1}{2}$

4. $\frac{1}{2} + \frac{1}{5}$

5. $\frac{4}{5} - \frac{3}{10}$

6. $\frac{11}{15} - \frac{2}{3}$

Do you UNDERSTAND?

7. Why do you need to find a common denominator before you can add or subtract fractions with unlike denominators?

8. In Step 1 above, how else could you find the LCM of the denominators?

9. What equivalent fraction would you use for $\frac{2}{3}$ to find $\frac{2}{3} - \frac{1}{4}$?

Independent Practice

Leveled Practice Find the LCD for each pair of fractions.

10. $\frac{3}{5}, \frac{1}{2}$

11. $\frac{5}{8}, \frac{9}{16}$

12. $\frac{4}{9}, \frac{1}{6}$

13. $\frac{3}{4}, \frac{1}{3}$

14. $\frac{1}{3}, \frac{7}{9}$

Find two fractions equivalent to each fraction.

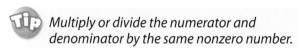

Tip *Multiply or divide the numerator and denominator by the same nonzero number.*

15. $\frac{1}{4}$

16. $\frac{3}{8}$

17. $\frac{6}{9}$

18. $\frac{5}{25}$

19. $\frac{10}{11}$

DIGITAL Animated Glossary **www.pearsonsuccessnet.com**

For another example, see Set B on page 182.

Independent Practice

In **20** through **28**, find each sum or difference. Simplify your answer.

20. $\frac{3}{4} - \frac{1}{3}$

21. $\frac{5}{12} + \frac{5}{10}$

22. $\frac{2}{5} + \frac{1}{6}$

23. $\frac{2}{5} + \frac{1}{7}$

24. $\frac{5}{12} + \frac{5}{15}$

25. $\frac{5}{12} - \frac{5}{15}$

26. $\frac{1}{4} + \frac{1}{4} + \frac{1}{3}$

27. $\frac{3}{10} + \frac{3}{12} + \frac{3}{15}$

28. $\frac{3}{10} - \frac{3}{12} + \frac{3}{15}$

Problem Solving

29. Tom wants to add $\frac{3}{10}$ and $\frac{4}{15}$. Which is the LCM for 10 and 15?

A 5 **B** 25 **C** 30 **D** 60

30. **Draw a Picture** The fractions $\frac{1}{12}$, $\frac{1}{6}$, and $\frac{1}{4}$ have a common denominator of 12. Draw a fraction model to find $\frac{1}{12} + \frac{1}{6} + \frac{1}{4}$. Simplify your answer if possible.

Tip *Draw equivalent fraction strips to make a model.*

31. **Writing to Explain** Two streets intersect, forming vertical angles. What is the measure of angle x? Explain.

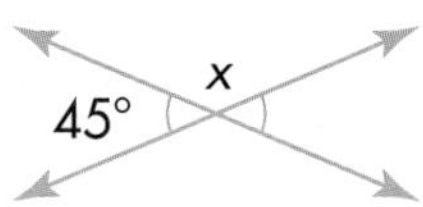

32. A street lighting pole along the road is standing at a 95° angle to the ground. What is the measure of an angle supplementary to the angle of the pole?

Use the table for **33** and **34**.

33. How much more of the trail did Jon hike than Andrea?

34. How much more of the trail did Callie hike than Jon?

Data

Hiker	Fraction of Mirror Lake Trail hiked
Andrea	$\frac{2}{5}$
Jon	$\frac{1}{2}$
Callie	$\frac{4}{5}$

35. **Algebra** Max needs $\frac{3}{4}$ cup of beans to make chili. He already has $\frac{1}{2}$ cup. Write an equation that Max could use to find how many more cups of beans he needs to make the chili.

36. **Think About the Process** Which equivalent fractions would you use to find the sum of $\frac{3}{4}$ and $\frac{1}{3}$?

A $\frac{3}{12}$ and $\frac{1}{12}$ **B** $\frac{9}{12}$ and $\frac{4}{12}$ **C** $\frac{3}{4}$ and $\frac{3}{9}$ **D** $\frac{3}{4}$ and $\frac{4}{3}$

Algebra Connections

Equations with Fractions

Remember that you can evaluate an algebraic expression by substituting a value of the variable and simplifying.

Evaluate each equation for $v = \frac{1}{4}$ to determine whether it is true.

1. $\frac{2}{3} + v = \frac{3}{7}$

2. $v + \frac{1}{2} = \frac{3}{4}$

3. $v - \frac{1}{5} = \frac{1}{20}$

4. $\frac{1}{4} + v = \frac{3}{16}$

5. $\frac{4}{5} - v = \frac{2}{3}$

6. $\frac{3}{4} - v = \frac{1}{2}$

7. $\frac{3}{10} + v = \frac{11}{20}$

8. $v + \frac{1}{6} = \frac{5}{12}$

9. $\frac{1}{3} + v = \frac{1}{2}$

10. $v - \frac{1}{4} = 0$

11. $v - \frac{1}{8} = \frac{1}{8}$

12. $v + \frac{2}{5} = \frac{7}{8}$

Example: If $m = \frac{2}{5}$, which of the three equations listed below are true?

$\frac{1}{2} + m = 1$; $m + \frac{3}{5} = 1$; $\frac{4}{9} - m = \frac{1}{2}$

Think *How can I check to see if each equation is true?*

Substitute $\frac{2}{5}$ for m in each equation.

$\frac{1}{2} + \frac{2}{5} = \frac{5}{10} + \frac{4}{10} = \frac{9}{10} \neq 1$

$\frac{2}{5} + \frac{3}{5} = 1$

$\frac{4}{9} - \frac{2}{5} = \frac{20}{45} - \frac{18}{45} = \frac{2}{45} \neq \frac{1}{2}$

The only true equation is $m + \frac{3}{5} = 1$.

13. It rained $\frac{2}{3}$ inch on Saturday. Find the total amount of rain, t, for the weekend if it rained $\frac{1}{4}$ inch on Sunday. Write and solve an equation to find the answer.

14. Jill walked $\frac{1}{3}$ mile less than Romero walked. If w equals how far Romero walked, which expression describes how far Jill walked?

A $\frac{1}{3} - w$

B $\frac{1}{3} + w$

C $w - \frac{1}{3}$

D $\frac{1}{3} + w$

15. **Write a Problem** Write a real-world problem using the equation $n = \frac{3}{8} - \frac{1}{6}$.

Lesson
7-4

Understand It!
When estimating sums and differences of fractions and mixed numbers use a number line or benchmark fractions to round each fraction or mixed number.

Estimating Sums and Differences of Mixed Numbers

What are some ways to estimate?

Jamila's mom wants to make a size 10 dress and jacket. About how many yards of fabric does she need? Estimate the sum $2\frac{1}{4} + 1\frac{7}{8}$ to find out.

Fabric Required (in yards)

	Size 10	Size 14
Dress	$2\frac{1}{4}$	$2\frac{7}{8}$
Jacket	$1\frac{7}{8}$	$2\frac{1}{4}$

Another Example How can you use benchmark fractions such as $\frac{1}{4}$, $\frac{1}{3}$, $\frac{1}{2}$, $\frac{2}{3}$, and $\frac{3}{4}$ to estimate?

Estimate $\frac{5}{8} - \frac{3}{16}$.

$\frac{5}{8}$ is close to $\frac{6}{8}$, and $\frac{6}{8} = \frac{3}{4}$.

$\frac{3}{16}$ is close to $\frac{4}{16}$, and $\frac{4}{16} = \frac{1}{4}$.

So, $\frac{5}{8} - \frac{3}{16}$ is close to $\frac{3}{4} - \frac{1}{4}$.

$\frac{3}{4} - \frac{1}{4} = \frac{2}{4}$ or $\frac{1}{2}$

So, $\frac{5}{8} - \frac{3}{16} \approx \frac{1}{2}$.

Guided Practice*

Do you know HOW?

Round to the nearest whole number.

1. $\frac{3}{4}$ **2.** $1\frac{5}{7}$ **3.** $2\frac{3}{10}$

Estimate each sum or difference using benchmark fractions.

4. $2\frac{5}{9} - 1\frac{1}{3}$ **5.** $2\frac{4}{10} + 3\frac{5}{8}$

Do you UNDERSTAND?

6. To estimate with mixed numbers, when should you round up to the nearest whole number?

7. Suppose Jamila's mom wants to make a size 14 dress and jacket. About how many yards of fabric does she need?

Independent Practice

Leveled Practice Use the number line to round the mixed numbers to the nearest whole number.

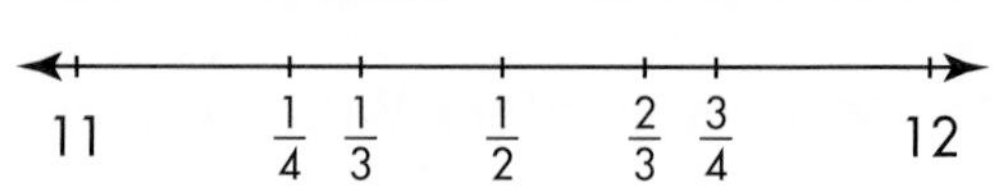

8. $11\frac{4}{6}$ **9.** $11\frac{2}{8}$ **10.** $11\frac{8}{12}$ **11.** $11\frac{4}{10}$

*For another example, see Set C on page 182.

One Way

Use a number line to round fractions and mixed numbers to the nearest whole number.

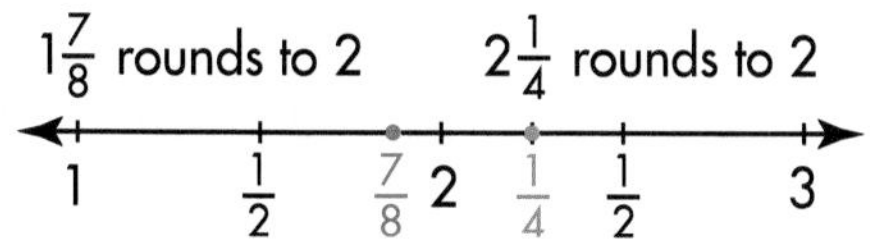

So, $2\frac{1}{4} + 1\frac{7}{8} \approx 2 + 2$, or 4.

Jamila's mom needs about 4 yards of fabric.

Another Way

Use $\frac{1}{2}$ as a benchmark to round fractions to the nearest whole number.

Round fractions less than $\frac{1}{2}$ down. Since $\frac{1}{4} < \frac{1}{2}$, $2\frac{1}{4}$ rounds to 2.

Round fractions greater than or equal to $\frac{1}{2}$ up. Since $\frac{7}{8} > \frac{1}{2}$, $1\frac{7}{8}$ rounds to 2.

So, $2\frac{1}{4} + 1\frac{7}{8} \approx 2 + 2 = 4$.

Estimate each sum or difference.

12. $2\frac{1}{8} - \frac{5}{7}$

13. $12\frac{1}{3} + 2\frac{1}{4}$

14. $2\frac{2}{3} + \frac{7}{8}$

15. $1\frac{10}{15} - \frac{8}{9}$

16. $10\frac{5}{6} - 2\frac{3}{8}$

17. $12\frac{8}{25} + 13\frac{5}{9}$

18. $48\frac{1}{10} - 2\frac{7}{9}$

19. $33\frac{14}{15} + 23\frac{9}{25}$

Problem Solving

20. Use the recipes to answer the questions.

a Estimate how many cups of Fruit Trail Mix this recipe can make.

b Estimate how many cups of Traditional Trail Mix this recipe can make.

c Estimate how much trail mix you would have if you made both recipes.

Fruit Trail Mix
• $\frac{1}{2}$ cup raisins
• $\frac{3}{8}$ cup sunflower seeds
• 1 cup unsalted peanuts
• $\frac{1}{4}$ cup coconut
Traditional Trail Mix
• $1\frac{1}{3}$ cup raisins
• 1 cup sunflower seeds
• $1\frac{3}{4}$ cup unsalted peanuts
• 1 cup cashews

21. Algebra In the equation $5\frac{2}{9} + x = 9\frac{7}{8}$, estimate the value of x.

22. Writing to Explain Scott uses a pattern to collect beetles. The table shows how many of each species he has. Use the pattern to find the missing numbers. Explain Scott's pattern.

Number of Beetles by Species

Species	A	B	C	D	E	F	G
Number	1	3	6	10	15		

23. Think About the Process To round $2\frac{2}{5}$ to the nearest whole number, which two numbers should you compare?

A 2 and $\frac{2}{5}$

B $\frac{2}{5}$ and $\frac{1}{2}$

C $\frac{1}{2}$ and 2

D $2\frac{2}{5}$ and $\frac{1}{2}$

Lesson
7-6

Understand It!
When you subtract mixed numbers, subtract the fractional parts and the whole number parts, then simplify.

Subtracting Mixed Numbers

How can you find the difference of mixed numbers?

North Park has two go-cart paths: the Little Indy and the Grand Prix. How much longer is the Grand Prix than the Little Indy?

Choose an Operation Subtract to find how much longer the Grand Prix is.

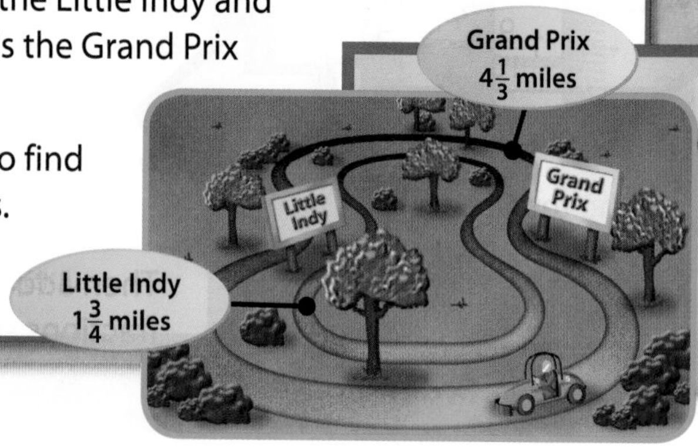

Another Example How can you find the difference between a whole number and a mixed number?

Find $15 - 2\frac{1}{3}$.

Step 1

Estimate. $15 - 2 = 13$

$$\begin{array}{r} 15 \\ -\ 2\frac{1}{3} \\ \hline \end{array}$$

There is no fraction from which to subtract $\frac{1}{3}$.

Step 2

To subtract, rename 15 to show thirds.

Think

$$\begin{array}{r} 15 \\ -\ 2\frac{1}{3} \\ \hline \end{array} = 14 + 1 = \begin{array}{r} 14\frac{3}{3} \\ -\ 2\frac{1}{3} \\ \hline \end{array}$$

Step 3

Subtract and simplify.

$$\begin{array}{r} 14\frac{3}{3} \\ -\ 2\frac{1}{3} \\ \hline 12\frac{2}{3} \end{array}$$

Explain It

1. How is renaming mixed numbers for subtraction like regrouping for whole number subtraction?

2. How is the problem $6 - 2\frac{3}{4}$ different from $6\frac{3}{4} - 2$?

3. **Reasonableness** Was the answer for Another Example reasonable? Explain.

Step 1

Estimate: 4 − 2 = 2.

Then find the LCD to write equivalent fractions.

$$\begin{array}{rcr} 4\frac{1}{3} & = & 4\frac{4}{12} \\ -\ 1\frac{3}{4} & = & -\ 1\frac{9}{12} \\ \hline \end{array}$$

Step 2

To subtract, rename $4\frac{4}{12}$ to show more twelfths.

Think $4\frac{4}{12} = 3 + 1 + \frac{4}{12}$

$= 3 + \frac{12}{12} + \frac{4}{12}$

$= 3\frac{16}{12}$

Step 3

Subtract and simplify.

$$\begin{array}{rcr} 4\frac{4}{12} & = & 3\frac{16}{12} \\ -\ 1\frac{9}{12} & = & -\ 1\frac{9}{12} \\ \hline & & 2\frac{7}{12} \end{array}$$

Check for reasonableness. The Grand Prix is $2\frac{7}{12}$ miles longer.

Guided Practice*

Do you know HOW?

Find each difference. Simplify your answers.

1. $2\frac{3}{4} - 2\frac{1}{4}$

2. $4\frac{1}{4} - 3\frac{1}{3}$

3. $9\frac{3}{4} - 7$

4. $5\frac{5}{8} - 5\frac{1}{8}$

5. $2\frac{3}{4} - 2\frac{1}{3}$

6. $6 - 2\frac{7}{8}$

Do you UNDERSTAND?

7. In the example above, why was $4\frac{4}{12}$ renamed as $3\frac{16}{12}$?

8. The Grand Prix is $4\frac{1}{3}$ miles long. The road around the park is $6\frac{1}{8}$ miles long. How much longer is the road than the Grand Prix?

Independent Practice

Leveled Practice Find each difference. Simplify if possible.

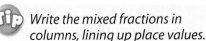

Tip *Write the mixed fractions in columns, lining up place values.*

9. $5\frac{2}{3} - 2\frac{1}{3}$

10. $10\frac{4}{5} - 6\frac{3}{5}$

11. $4\frac{7}{8} - 2\frac{1}{8}$

12. $7\frac{1}{2} - 4\frac{1}{3}$

13. $8\frac{2}{3} - 4\frac{1}{4}$

14. $12\frac{3}{4} - 8\frac{1}{3}$

15. $14\frac{1}{3} - 6\frac{2}{3}$

16. $5\frac{4}{8} - 2\frac{6}{8}$

17. $5\frac{1}{10} - 4\frac{1}{8}$

18. $6\frac{7}{24} - 5\frac{1}{3}$

19. $3\frac{1}{3} - 2\frac{3}{4}$

20. $2\frac{3}{8} - 1\frac{1}{2}$

21. $6\frac{15}{32} - 2\frac{5}{8}$

22. $5\frac{12}{25} + 18\frac{13}{25} - 12\frac{4}{5}$

23. $22\frac{5}{13} - 11\frac{12}{13} - 2\frac{1}{13}$

24. Which of the above exercises could you compute mentally?

*For another example, see Set D on page 183.

Problem Solving

25. **Algebra** Of 1,400 students in the school, 448 play chess. Solve $448 + x = 1{,}400$ to find how many do not play chess.

26. **Writing to Explain** How are the steps different for renaming fractions when adding and subtracting mixed numbers with unlike denominators?

27. During half time, the soccer players drank $2\frac{1}{2}$ pitchers of water. After the game, they drank $4\frac{2}{3}$ pitchers of water.

a How much water did they drink altogether?

b How many more pitchers of water did the players drink after the game than during half time?

28. There is a triangular flowerbed in front of Kimiko's school. Two of its angles are shown in the diagram. What is the size of angle *A*?

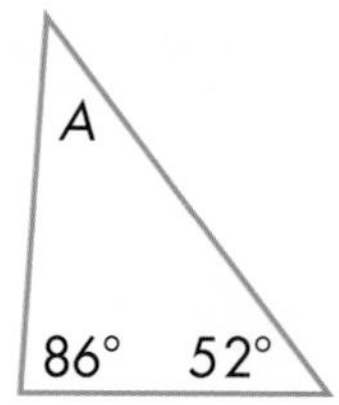

29. Think About the Process Which expression could you use to find the difference between $6\frac{1}{3}$ and $4\frac{1}{2}$?

A $5\frac{8}{6} - 4\frac{3}{6}$

B $6\frac{1}{6} - 4\frac{1}{6}$

C $5\frac{2}{6} - 4\frac{3}{6}$

D $6\frac{8}{6} - 4\frac{3}{6}$

30. Which shows the Commutative Property of Addition?

A $6\frac{2}{3} + 4\frac{1}{2} = 11\frac{1}{6}$

B $6\frac{2}{3} + 4\frac{1}{2} = 4\frac{1}{2} + 6\frac{2}{3}$

C $6\frac{2}{3} = 11\frac{1}{6} - 4\frac{1}{2}$

D $4\frac{1}{2} = 11\frac{1}{6} - 6\frac{2}{3}$

31. Write a number story to add or subtract mixed numbers.

32. Fairy penguins are the smallest kind of penguin. Adults usually range from 13 inches to 16 inches tall. One mother penguin is $13\frac{1}{2}$ inches tall. Her chick is $7\frac{3}{4}$ inches tall. How much taller is the mother than her chick?

33. **Geometry** There is a fence around 3 sides of Ryan's backyard. Two sides are each 55 feet. The back is 27 ft 8 in. How long is the fence in inches? In feet?

34. Trevor has a piece of wood that is $2\frac{2}{3}$ feet long. How much should he cut off to make it $1\frac{3}{4}$ feet long?

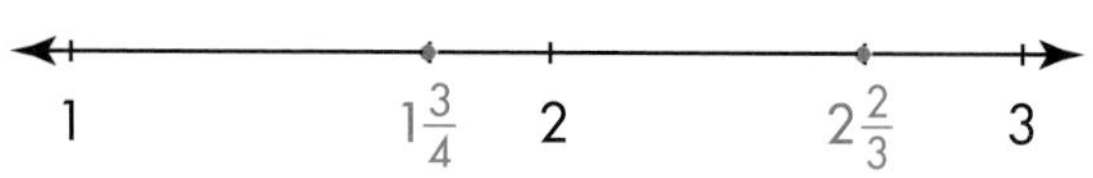

A $\frac{1}{4}$ ft

B $\frac{1}{3}$ ft

C $1\frac{1}{3}$ ft

D $\frac{11}{12}$ ft

Mixed Problem Solving

Math and Literature

Mr. Blake's class is having a formal debate. He keeps track of the time each student speaks in a table.

Use the data at right for **1** and **2**.

1. How much longer did Tim speak than Erik?

2. How many total minutes did Julie and Heather speak?

Student Debate Time

Student	Tim	Erik	Julie	Heather
Time (minutes)	$3\frac{1}{2}$	$1\frac{3}{4}$	$5\frac{1}{3}$	$2\frac{1}{4}$

Use the data at right for **3** and **4**.

3. Micalann presented on Tuesday and Friday. How many minutes did Micalann speak?

4. Lowell was allowed 6 minutes to present his project. How many more minutes could he have spoken?

Presentation Time

Student	Tuesday	Wednesday	Friday
Micalann	$2\frac{1}{3}$ min.		$2\frac{3}{4}$ min.
Lowell		$4\frac{1}{2}$ min.	

5. Three students gave a group presentation. Roberta spoke for $2\frac{1}{2}$ minutes. Alice spoke for $3\frac{1}{3}$ minutes, and Kai spoke for $4\frac{3}{4}$ minutes. How long was their presentation?

6. The teacher wants the students to give a 10-minute group presentation. If Jamie's group has already prepared $6\frac{1}{3}$ minutes, how much do they still need to prepare?

Use the data at right for **7** and **8**.

7. Who presented longer, Group 1 or Group 2? How many more minutes did they present?

8. Group 5 did not finish their 10-minute group presentation. How much of the presentation was left?

A $1\frac{4}{5}$ minutes

B 2 minutes

C $\frac{4}{5}$ minute

D $1\frac{1}{5}$ minutes

Group Presentation Time

Group	Time
Group 1	$9\frac{1}{3}$ min.
Group 2	$9\frac{3}{5}$ min.
Group 3	$5\frac{1}{2}$ min.
Group 4	$6\frac{1}{4}$ min.
Group 5	$8\frac{1}{5}$ min.

Lesson
7-7

Understand It!
Solve problems by making and using a table that represents and organizes needed information.

Problem Solving

Make a Table

Kyle offers to buy 10 of Todd's model airplanes. Kyle offers two plans for payment. Which payment plan should Todd accept?

Plan 1: Pay a single $200 payment for the 10 model airplanes.

Plan 2: Pay $0.50 for one model airplane; then pay enough for each additional model to double the previous total payment.

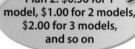

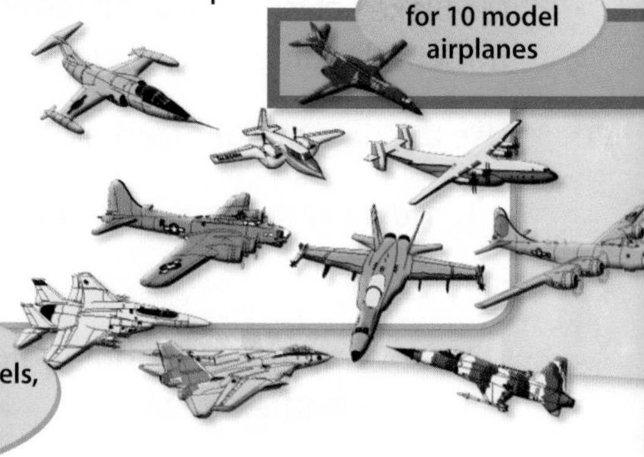

Plan 2: $0.50 for 1 model, $1.00 for 2 models, $2.00 for 3 models, and so on

Guided Practice*

Do you know HOW?

1. Larissa swam $3\frac{1}{2}$ laps the first day. Each day after that she swam $1\frac{1}{2}$ laps more than the previous day. How far will Larissa swim on Day 6? Copy and complete the table.

Day	1	2	3	4	5	6
Laps	$3\frac{1}{2}$					

Do you UNDERSTAND?

2. In the example at the top, how did making a table help answer the question?

3. **Write a Problem** Write a real-world problem that you can solve by making a table.

Independent Practice

Solve. Copy and extend the table for Exercise 4.

4. Skyler wants to buy a pair of inline skates for $75. She earns $10 a week. If she saves $\frac{1}{2}$ of her money each week, how many weeks will she need to save to buy the skates?

Number of Weeks	*Total Savings ($)*
1	5
2	10
3	
4	

Stuck? Try this....

- What do I know?
- What am I asked to find?
- What diagram can I use to help understand the problem?
- Is all my work correct?
- Did I answer the right question?
- Is my answer reasonable?

**For another example, Set E on page 183.*

Read and Understand

What do I know? Plan 1 would pay $200.

What am I being asked to find? Find how much would be paid under Plan 2.

Plan and Solve

Make a table to find the total payment for the 10 models under Plan 2.

Models Bought	1	2	3	4	5	6	7	8	9	10
Total Payments ($)	0.5	1	2	4	8	16	32	64	128	256

Todd would receive $200 under Plan 1 and $256 under Plan 2. He should accept Plan 2.

5. Fabian plans to read for $2\frac{1}{2}$ minutes the first day and then double his reading time each day. How many minutes will Fabian read on Day 6?

6. **Estimate** Ruth wants to earn a prize for reading for 500 minutes. If she reads for $\frac{1}{4}$ hour every day for 15 days, will she earn the prize she wants? Explain.

7. Trevor bought 3 new pairs of jeans and 2 new sweaters for school. How many different clothing combinations can he make? Make an organized list to help you find the answer.

8. Every day, Martha and her mother go for a walk around Lake Andrea. The path is $1\frac{3}{5}$ miles long. How many total miles have Martha and her mother walked after 4 days?

9. **Writing to Explain** Read the problem and Jerome's answer to the problem below. Explain why his answer is incorrect and fix it.

The Grant family is saving for a vacation. They open a savings account with $225 and deposit money each week. The first week, they deposit $15. Each week after that, they deposit $15 more than they deposited the week before. How much money will the Grants have saved after Week 6?

Jerome's answer:

After Week 6, the Grants will have saved $90.

10. Cody is building towers in the shape of a triangle out of cereal boxes for a display in his dad's store. How many boxes will he need to make 3 towers if each tower has 5 boxes in the bottom row and each higher row has one less box than the previous row? Draw a picture to help you find the answer.

11. National Cellular charges $0.75 for the first minute and $0.07 for each additional minute of a cell phone call. American Cellular charges $0.85 for the first minute, but only $0.05 for each additional minute. Which company charges less for an 8-minute cell phone call? How much less?

Test

1. A buttonhole should be $\frac{1}{16}$-inch wider than the button. How wide should a buttonhole be made to fit a button that is $\frac{14}{16}$ inches wide? (7-1)

   A $\frac{15}{32}$

   B $\frac{13}{16}$

   C $\frac{14}{16}$

   D $\frac{15}{16}$

2. What is the least common multiple of 5, 8, and 16? (7-2)

   A 40

   B 80

   C 120

   D 640

3. The table lists the North American records for barometric pressure. What is the difference between the highest and the lowest pressure recorded? (7-6)

Data

Record	Inches of Mercury	Location
Highest pressure	$31\frac{17}{20}$	Northway, Alaska
Lowest pressure	$26\frac{7}{20}$	Key West, Florida

   A $\frac{10}{20}$ inch

   B $\frac{1}{2}$ inch

   C $5\frac{1}{2}$ inch

   D 5 inch

4. Sabrina tried to tighten a $\frac{1}{8}$-inch bolt with a $\frac{3}{16}$-inch wrench. What is the difference in measure between the bolt and the wrench? (7-3)

   A $\frac{1}{16}$ inch

   B $\frac{1}{8}$ inch

   C $\frac{1}{4}$ inch

   D $\frac{5}{16}$ inch

5. What is $7\frac{6}{15} + 4\frac{4}{5}$? (7-5)

   A $11\frac{1}{5}$

   B $11\frac{2}{3}$

   C $12\frac{2}{15}$

   D $12\frac{1}{5}$

6. Hotdogs are sold in packages of 10 and hotdog buns are sold in packages of 8. What is the least number of hot dogs and buns that Angel must buy so that she has the same number of each? (7-2)

   A 20

   B 40

   C 80

   D 100

7. Which expression is the best estimate for $1\frac{3}{4} + 2\frac{3}{8}$? (7-4)

   A 2 + 2

   B 1 + 2

   C 2 + 3

   D 1 + 3

8. The table shows the lengths of some movies. How much longer is the action movie than the comedy movie? (7-6)

Movie	Length (in hours)
Action	$2\frac{3}{4}$
Comedy	$1\frac{5}{6}$
Drama	$2\frac{1}{3}$

A $\frac{1}{6}$ hour

B $\frac{11}{12}$ hour

C $1\frac{1}{12}$ hour

D $1\frac{11}{12}$ hour

9. What is the difference between $\frac{3}{8}$ and $\frac{1}{8}$? (7-1)

A $\frac{1}{2}$

B $\frac{1}{4}$

C $\frac{3}{16}$

D $\frac{1}{8}$

10. Sadie wrote a report for school that was $3\frac{1}{4}$ pages long. Robert's report was $4\frac{9}{10}$ pages long. Which is the best estimate of how much longer Robert's report was than Sadie's? (7-4)

A $\frac{1}{2}$ page

B 1 page

C 2 pages

D 3 pages

11. What is the least common denominator to add $\frac{2}{9} + \frac{4}{15}$? (7-3)

A 45

B 60

C 90

D 135

12. What is $12\frac{11}{18}$ rounded to the nearest whole number? (7-4)

A 11

B 12

C 13

D 18

13. Serafina can choose between two dining halls for a banquet. Hall A charges $200 plus $4 per person. Hall B charges $150 plus $5 per person. How many people would have to attend for the charges to be the same? (7-7)

Dining Hall	Number of People			
	0	10	20	30
A	$200	$240	$280	
B	$150	$200	$250	

A 30

B 40

C 50

D 60

Set A, pages 162–163

Find $\frac{2}{9} + \frac{1}{9}$.   Find $\frac{7}{9} - \frac{1}{9}$.

The fractions have like denominators. Add or subtract the numerators.

$\frac{2}{9} + \frac{1}{9} = \frac{3}{9}$ $\frac{7}{9} - \frac{1}{9} = \frac{6}{9}$

Use the GCF, 3, to simplify.

$\frac{2}{9} + \frac{1}{9} = \frac{3}{9} = \frac{1}{3}$ $\frac{7}{9} - \frac{1}{9} = \frac{6}{9} = \frac{2}{3}$

Remember that when the denominators are the same, you add or subtract only the numerators.

Find each sum or difference. Simplify.

1. $\frac{2}{5} + \frac{1}{5}$ **2.** $\frac{9}{10} - \frac{7}{10}$

3. $\frac{7}{8} + \frac{2}{8}$ **4.** $\frac{12}{13} - \frac{8}{13}$

Set B, pages 164–168

Find the least common multiple (LCM) of 5 and 6.

List multiples of each number.

5: 5; 10; 15; 20; 25; 30 . . .   6: 6; 12; 18; 24; 30 . . .

The LCM is 30. Use this LCM as the least common denominator (LCD) to calculate below.

$$\begin{array}{rcr} \frac{3}{5} & = & \frac{18}{30} \\ +\ \frac{1}{6} & = & +\ \frac{5}{30} \\ \hline & & \frac{23}{30} \end{array} \qquad \begin{array}{rcr} \frac{3}{5} & = & \frac{18}{30} \\ -\ \frac{1}{6} & = & -\ \frac{5}{30} \\ \hline & & \frac{13}{30} \end{array}$$

Remember that the LCM of the denominators in a set of fractions is the LCD for that set of fractions.

Find the LCM for each set of numbers.

1. 10, 20   **2.** 3, 6

3. 8, 10   **4.** 2, 3, 5

Find each sum or difference. Simplify.

5. $\frac{1}{2} + \frac{1}{7}$ **6.** $\frac{1}{3} + \frac{2}{4}$

7. $\frac{3}{4} - \frac{1}{3}$ **8.** $\frac{5}{6} - \frac{1}{2}$

Set C, pages 170–171

Estimate $5\frac{1}{3} + 9\frac{9}{11}$.

Compare fractions to $\frac{1}{2}$ to round to the nearest whole number.

Round fractions that are less than $\frac{1}{2}$ down to the nearest whole number. $5\frac{1}{3}$ rounds to 5.

Round fractions greater than or equal to $\frac{1}{2}$ up to the nearest whole number. $9\frac{9}{11}$ rounds to 10.

So, $5\frac{1}{3} + 9\frac{9}{11} \approx 5 + 10 = 15$.

Remember that you can also use benchmark fractions such as $\frac{1}{4}, \frac{1}{3}, \frac{1}{2}, \frac{2}{3}$, and $\frac{3}{4}$ to help you estimate.

Round to the nearest whole number.

1. $2\frac{9}{10}$ **2.** $9\frac{19}{20}$ **3.** $6\frac{2}{7}$

Estimate each sum or difference.

4. $3\frac{1}{4} - 1\frac{1}{2}$ **5.** $5\frac{2}{9} + 4\frac{11}{13}$

6. $2\frac{3}{8} + 5\frac{3}{5}$ **7.** $9\frac{3}{7} - 6\frac{2}{5}$

Set D, pages 172–176

Find $2\frac{5}{8} + 3\frac{1}{2}$. Find $3\frac{1}{2} - 2\frac{5}{8}$.

Rewrite the fractions as equivalent fractions with like denominators.

$$\begin{array}{rcr} 2\frac{5}{8} & = & 2\frac{5}{8} \\ +\ 3\frac{1}{2} & = & +\ 3\frac{4}{8} \\ \hline \end{array} \qquad \begin{array}{rcr} 3\frac{1}{2} & = & 3\frac{4}{8} \\ -\ 2\frac{5}{8} & = & -\ 2\frac{5}{8} \\ \hline \end{array}$$

Add.

$$\begin{array}{r} 2\frac{5}{8} \\ +\ 3\frac{4}{8} \\ \hline 5\frac{9}{8} \end{array}$$

Rename the improper fraction.

$$5\frac{9}{8} = 5 + 1\frac{1}{8}$$
$$= 6\frac{1}{8}$$

Rename $3\frac{4}{8}$ to make more eighths.

$$\begin{array}{rcr} 3\frac{4}{8} & = & 2\frac{12}{8} \\ -\ 2\frac{5}{8} & = & -\ 2\frac{5}{8} \\ \hline \end{array}$$

Subtract and simplify.

$$\begin{array}{r} 2\frac{12}{8} \\ -\ 2\frac{5}{8} \\ \hline \frac{7}{8} \end{array}$$

Remember to rename improper fractions as mixed numbers in sums.

Also remember to rename the fraction part of a mixed number when necessary to subtract a larger fraction.

Find each sum or difference. Simplify.

1. $3\frac{1}{5} + 2\frac{3}{5}$

2. $3\frac{5}{8} + 3\frac{7}{8}$

3. $5\frac{3}{5} + \frac{2}{3}$

4. $50\frac{3}{4} + 50\frac{4}{5}$

5. $5\frac{11}{12} + \frac{1}{2}$

6. $3\frac{4}{5} + 2\frac{1}{9}$

7. $10\frac{2}{3} - 6\frac{1}{3}$

8. $8\frac{3}{8} - 3\frac{7}{8}$

9. $19\frac{1}{2} - 10\frac{1}{4}$

10. $16\frac{1}{3} - 12\frac{5}{6}$

11. $21\frac{3}{5} - 10\frac{29}{30}$

12. $14\frac{11}{12} - \frac{1}{4}$

Set E, pages 178–179

For every movie you rent you earn 15 points toward a free movie rental. How many movies would you need to rent in order to earn a free rental worth 90 points? Copy and continue the table to solve the problem.

Movies Rented	1	2	3
Points	15	30	45

For 4 movies rented, you earn 60 points.
For 5 movies rented, you earn 75 points.
For 6 movies rented, you earn 90 points.

Remember when making a table to solve a problem, look for a pattern in the data and extend the table to find the answer.

Make a table to solve. Give the answer in a complete sentence.

1. Ramir makes T-shirts to sell. It costs him $3.25 in materials to make a T-shirt. He sells the T-shirts for $5. How many T-shirts does he need to sell to make a profit of $12.25 ?

Topic 8

Multiplying Fractions and Mixed Numbers

1

The frilled lizard has a long tail that is about $\frac{2}{3}$ the length of its body. How long is the frilled lizard's tail? You will find out in Lesson 8-1.

2

If you rode an elevator up $\frac{3}{4}$ of the height of the Sears Tower, about how many feet high would you be? You will find out in Lesson 8-2.

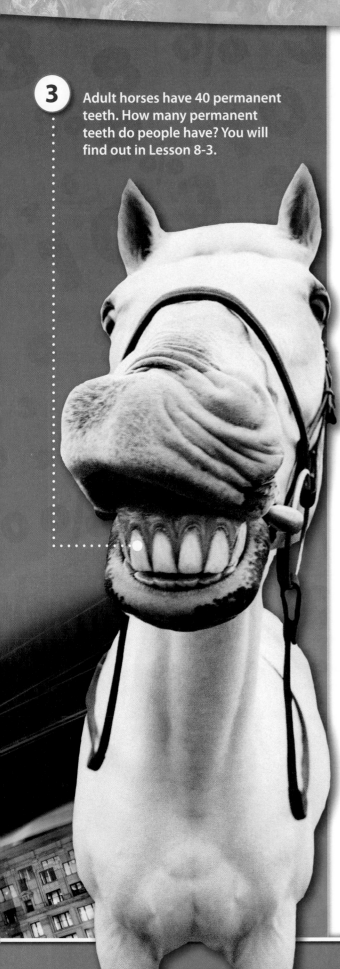

3 Adult horses have 40 permanent teeth. How many permanent teeth do people have? You will find out in Lesson 8-3.

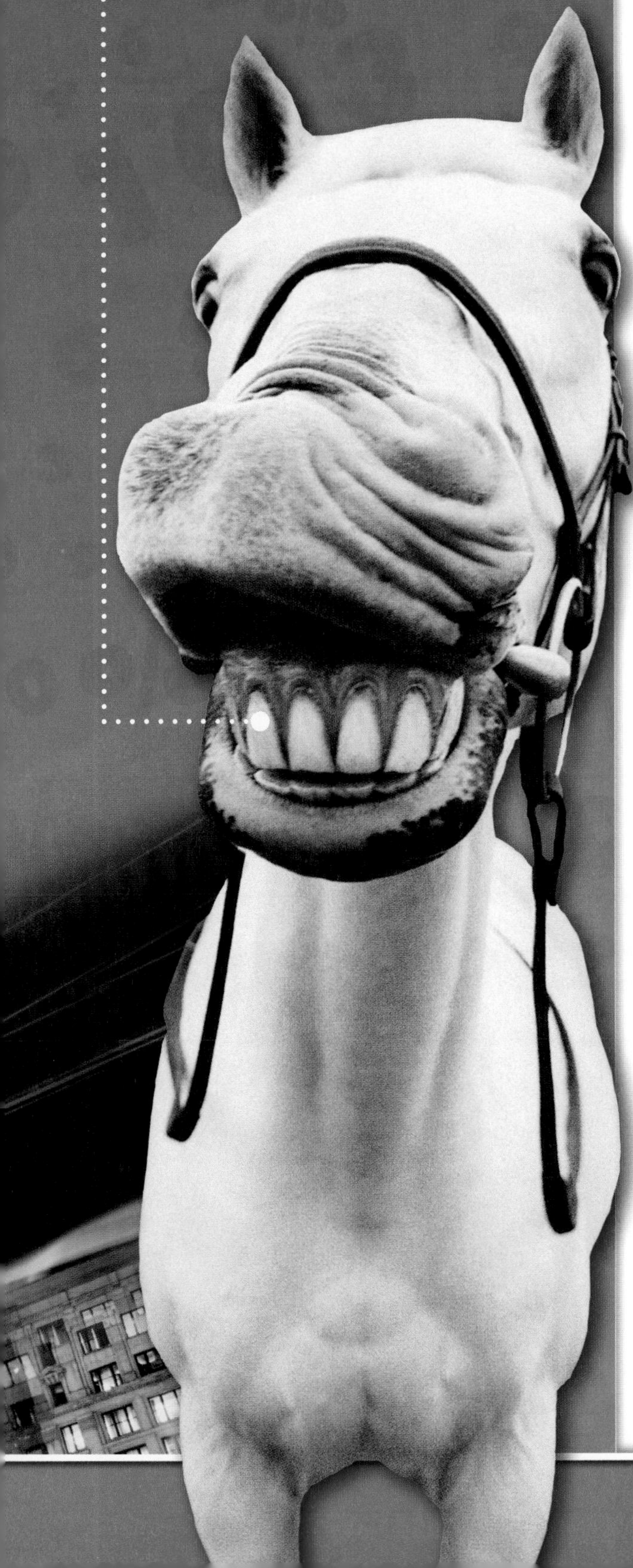

Review What You Know!

Vocabulary

Choose the best term from the box.

- estimate
- like denominators
- greatest common factor

1. The __?__ is the greatest number that is a factor of two or more numbers.

2. To find an approximate answer or solution is to __?__.

3. $\frac{4}{8}$ and $\frac{7}{8}$ have __?__.

Estimation

Estimate each sum, difference, or product.

4. 1,478 + 2,822 **5.** 305 − 197

6. 6,490 − 3,510 **7.** 1,213 + 4,797 + 403

8. 38 × 6 **9.** 59 × 21

Fractions and Decimals

Write the shaded part as a fraction.

10. 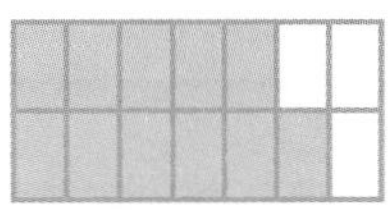 **11.** 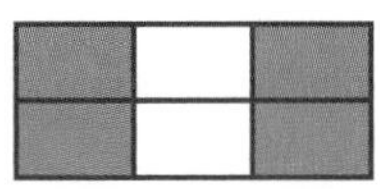

Express each decimal as a fraction or mixed number. Simplify where possible.

12. 0.80 **13.** 5.25 **14.** 15.95

Divisibility

15. **Writing to Explain** How can you tell if 78 is divisible by 2, 3, or 6?

Lesson

8-1

Understand It!
When you multiply a whole number and a proper fraction, the product is less than the whole number.

Multiplying a Fraction and a Whole Number

Hands-On
counters

How can you multiply a fraction and whole number?

A recipe makes 12 soft pretzels. If Ilene sprinkles parmesan cheese as a topping over $\frac{2}{3}$ of the baked pretzels, how many cheese pretzels will Ilene make?

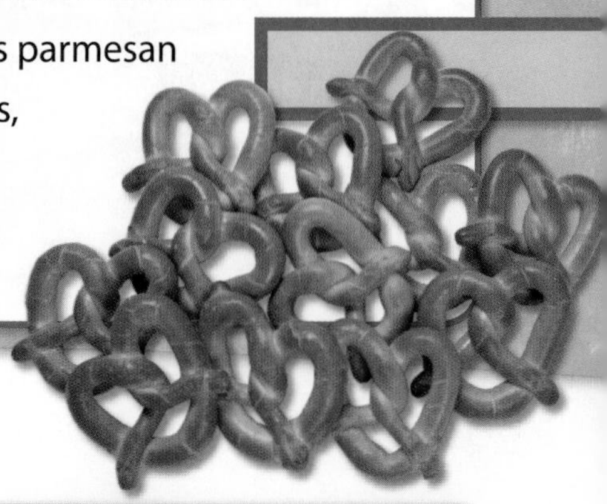

Choose an Operation Multiply to find $\frac{2}{3} \times 12$.

Other Examples

Renaming the Whole Number

Find $10 \times \frac{3}{4}$.

To find $10 \times \frac{3}{4}$, you can change 10 to $\frac{10}{1}$ and then multiply.

$\frac{10}{1} \times \frac{3}{4} = \frac{30}{4}$ ← $10 \times 3 = 30$ ← $1 \times 4 = 4$

Simplify.

$\frac{30}{4} = 7\frac{2}{4} = 7\frac{1}{2}$

So, $10 \times \frac{3}{4} = 7\frac{1}{2}$.

Using a Calculator

Find $81 \times \frac{4}{9}$.

Press: 81 [×] 4 [n] 9 [d] [ENTER =]

Display: $81 \times \frac{4}{9} = 36$

So, $81 \times \frac{4}{9} = 36$.

Guided Practice*

Do you know HOW?

Find each product.

1. $\frac{1}{8} \times 4$

2. $\frac{3}{8} \times 4$

3. $\frac{1}{4} \times 16$

4. $\frac{3}{4} \times 16$

5. $9 \times \frac{1}{6}$

6. $9 \times \frac{5}{6}$

Do you UNDERSTAND?

7. In the example at the top of the page, how does finding $\frac{1}{3}$ of 12 help you find $\frac{2}{3}$ of 12?

8. If $\frac{3}{4}$ of the 12 pretzels were sprinkled with cheese, how many pretzels would be sprinkled?

DIGITAL
eTools
www.pearsonsuccessnet.com

For another example, see Set A on page 198.

You can think of a fraction as division, $\frac{2}{3} = 2 \div 3$.

Use this relationship to find $\frac{2}{3} \times 12$.

If the whole number is divisible by the denominator of the fraction, you can divide first and then multiply.

12 is divisible by 3. So, divide 12 by 3.

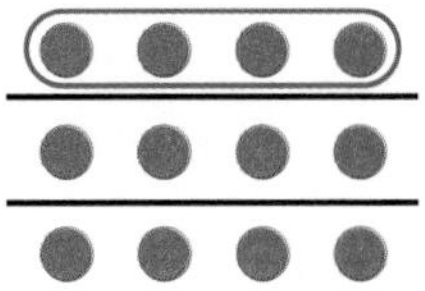

Dividing 12 by 3 is the same as multiplying $\frac{1}{3}$ and 12.

$12 \div 3 = 4$ and $\frac{1}{3} \times 12 = 4$.

You can think of $\frac{2}{3}$ as 2 times $\frac{1}{3}$.
So, multiply by 2:

$\frac{2}{3} \times 12 = 2(\frac{1}{3} \times 12)$

$= 2(4) = 8$

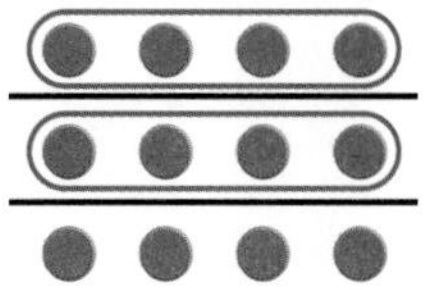

Ilene makes 8 cheese pretzels.

Independent Practice

In **9** through **20**, find the product. You may use counters to help.

9. $5 \times \frac{2}{3}$ **10.** $\frac{7}{8}$ of 24 **11.** $\frac{9}{10}$ of 20 **12.** $18 \times \frac{2}{3}$

13. $\frac{3}{5} \times 30$ **14.** $\frac{9}{20}$ of 40 **15.** $\frac{7}{100}$ of 700 **16.** $\frac{1}{5}$ of 45

17. $\frac{5}{9}$ of 36 **18.** $\frac{3}{4}$ of 200 **19.** $\frac{7}{8}$ of 32 **20.** $\frac{9}{10}$ of 25

Problem Solving

During a nature walk, Jill identified 20 species of plants and animals. Use this information for **21** and **22**.

21. **Reasoning** Jill said that $\frac{1}{3}$ of the species she identified were animals. Can this be correct? Explain.

22. If $\frac{3}{5}$ of the species Jill identified were plants, how many species were plants?

23. **Think About the Process** The cornbread recipe needs to be tripled for the band dinner. If $\frac{2}{3}$ cup of sugar and $\frac{3}{4}$ cup of cornmeal are needed for 1 recipe, which expression shows the total amount of cornmeal and sugar used for the dinner?

A $3(\frac{3}{4} \times \frac{2}{3})$

B $\frac{2}{3}(3 + \frac{3}{4})$

C $(3 \times \frac{2}{3}) + (3 \times \frac{3}{4})$

D $(\frac{2}{3} + \frac{3}{4}) \times (\frac{2}{3} + \frac{3}{4})$

24. Some frilled lizards grow to be 90 cm long. If $\frac{2}{3}$ of this length is its tail, how long is the tail?

25. **Writing to Explain** How can you use mental math to find $250 \times \frac{3}{10}$?

Lesson
8-2

Understand It!
You can use the same methods to estimate with fractions that you use to estimate with decimals.

Estimating Products

How can you use compatible numbers to estimate products of fractions?

Sara has 14 postcards that are each $\frac{3}{8}$ foot wide.
Estimate the width of these postcards placed side by side.

Choose an Operation Multiply to find the width of the postcards side by side.

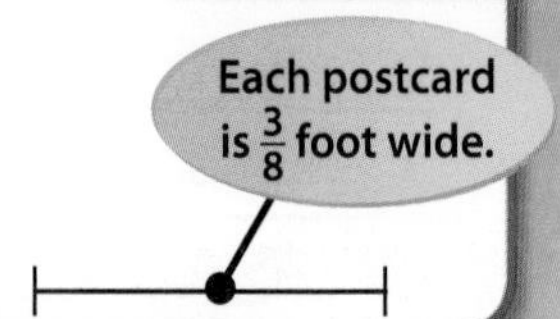
Each postcard is $\frac{3}{8}$ foot wide.

Another Example How can you use rounding to estimate products of fractions and mixed numbers?

Estimate $3\frac{3}{4} \times 14\frac{1}{2}$. Round to the nearest whole numbers.

$$3\frac{3}{4} \times 14\frac{1}{2}$$
$$\downarrow \quad \downarrow$$
$$4 \times 15 = 60$$

So, $3\frac{3}{4} \times 14\frac{1}{2} \approx 60$.

Estimate $\frac{5}{6} \times 3\frac{7}{8}$. Round to the nearest whole numbers.

$$\frac{5}{6} \times 3\frac{7}{8}$$
$$\downarrow \quad \downarrow$$
$$1 \times 4 = 4$$

So, $\frac{5}{6} \times 3\frac{7}{8} \approx 4$.

Guided Practice*

Do you know HOW?

For **1** through **4**, estimate each product.

1. $\frac{3}{4} \times 19$

2. $35 \times \frac{5}{9}$

3. $21\frac{3}{4} \times \frac{1}{5}$

4. $3 \times 6\frac{4}{5}$

Do you UNDERSTAND?

5. In the example at the top, why can you have two different estimates?

6. How can rounding to the nearest whole number help you estimate products?

Independent Practice

For **7** through **14**, estimate each product.

7. $\frac{1}{4} \times 25$

8. $70 \times \frac{5}{8}$

9. $\frac{3}{8} \times 20$

10. $5\frac{5}{6} \times 8\frac{1}{9}$

11. $11\frac{7}{8} \times 4\frac{1}{3}$

12. $\frac{11}{12} \times 4\frac{7}{8}$

13. $2\frac{3}{4} \times 30\frac{1}{16}$

14. $1\frac{4}{5} \times 75\frac{2}{9}$

*For another example, see Set B on page 198.

One Way

Use a compatible whole number to estimate $\frac{3}{8} \times 14$.

Change 14 to the nearest whole number that is compatible with the denominator of the fraction $\frac{3}{8}$.

$$\frac{3}{8} \times 14 \approx \frac{3}{8} \times 16$$

Think $\frac{1}{8} \times 16 = 2$, so $\frac{3}{8} \times 16 = 6$.

The width of 14 postcards would be about 6 feet.

Another Way

Use a compatible benchmark fraction to estimate $\frac{3}{8} \times 14$.

$\frac{3}{8}$ is close to the benchmark fraction $\frac{1}{2}$, and the denominator of $\frac{1}{2}$ is compatible with 14.

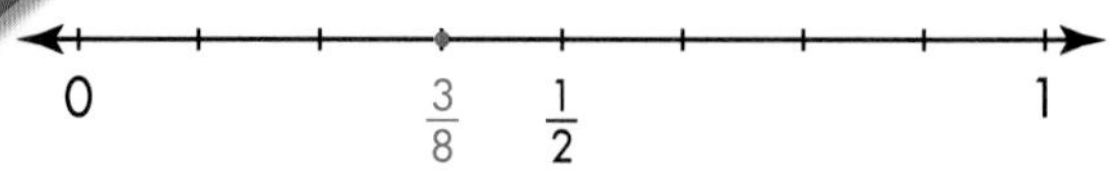

$$\frac{3}{8} \times 14 \approx \frac{1}{2} \times 14, \text{ or } 7$$

The width of 14 postcards would be about 7 feet.

Problem Solving

Millie's cousin is moving to town. Millie wants to make her cousin a personalized sign. The table shows how much space is taken up by different types of letters and numerals. Use the table for **15** and **16**.

Data

Type of lettering	Length (inches)
Capital letter	$\frac{3}{4}$
Lowercase letter	$\frac{5}{9}$

15. Estimate the length needed to spell out "WELCOME" in all capital letters.

16. Estimate the length needed to spell out "welcome" in all lowercase letters.

17. **Writing to Explain** Kwame says the answer to $25 \times \frac{2}{9}$ is $5\frac{5}{9}$. Is Kwame's answer reasonable? Use an estimate to explain.

18. The Sears Tower in Chicago is about 1,400 feet tall. If you took an elevator about $\frac{3}{4}$ the way up the tower, how many feet high would you be?

19. Use estimation to determine which of the following comparisons is true.

A $5\frac{1}{5} \times 3\frac{3}{4} < 14$

B $4\frac{4}{7} \times 4\frac{5}{9} < 16$

C $6\frac{1}{3} \times 7\frac{7}{8} > 42$

D $44\frac{2}{3} \times 2\frac{5}{7} > 150$

20. **Algebra** Which inverse relationship could you use to get x alone on one side of the equation $7\frac{7}{8} + x = 9\frac{1}{4}$?

A Addition

B Subtraction

C Multiplication

D Division

21. **Think About the Process** Which of the following would best help you estimate $6\frac{6}{7} \times 7\frac{1}{3}$?

A Change the mixed numbers to improper fractions.

B Change the mixed numbers to decimals.

C Draw a picture to show the problem.

D Round the factors to the nearest whole numbers.

Lesson
8-3

Understand It!
The product of two fractions can be found by multiplying the numerators and multiplying the denominators.

Multiplying Fractions

How do you find products of fractions?

Paige is planting $\frac{3}{4}$ of her garden with flowers, and $\frac{2}{3}$ of the flowers she plants will be morning-glories. What fraction of the garden will be planted with morning-glories?

Choose an Operation Multiply to find what fraction of the garden will be planted with morning-glories.

Another Example How can you simplify before you multiply?

Find $16 \times \frac{5}{12}$. ← Simplify before you multiply by finding the GCFs of any numerator and any denominator.

$\frac{{}^{4}\cancel{16}}{1} \times \frac{5}{\cancel{12}_{3}}$ ← The GCF of 16 and 12 is 4. Divide 16 and 12 by this GCF. The GCF of 1 and 5 is 1. 1 and 5 are simplified.

$\frac{{}^{4}\cancel{16}}{1} \times \frac{5}{\cancel{12}_{3}} = \frac{20}{3} = 6\frac{2}{3}$ ← Multiply.

Guided Practice*

Do you know HOW?

In **1** through **4**, write a multiplication sentence for each picture.

1. 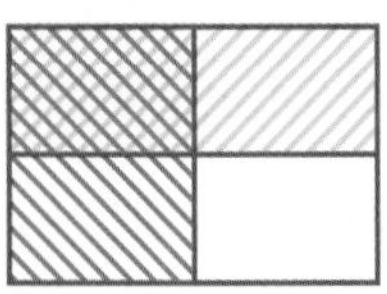

$\frac{1}{2} \times \frac{1}{2} = \square$

2. 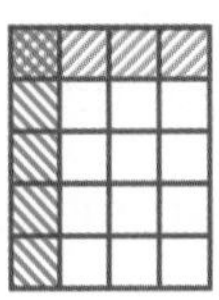

$\frac{1}{4} \times \square = \square$

3. 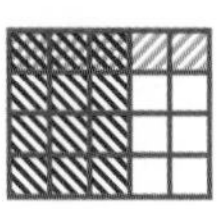

4. 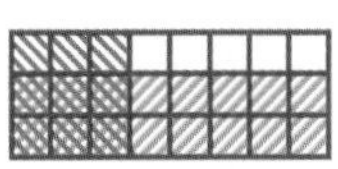

Do you UNDERSTAND?

5. In the morning-glory example, look at the model for multiplying fractions that are both less than 1. Compare the size of the product to the size of each factor.

6. In Another Example, how would the answer to $16 \times \frac{5}{12}$ be different if you did not simplify before multiplying?

*For another example, see Set C on page 198.

This model shows the meaning of multiplying $\frac{3}{4} \times \frac{2}{3}$.

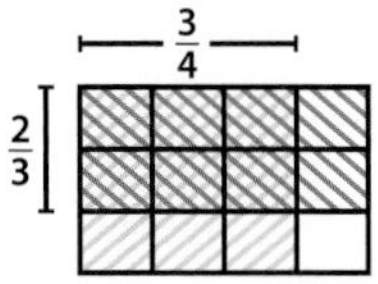

Six of the 12 squares have overlapping colors.

$\frac{3}{4} \times \frac{2}{3} = \frac{6}{12}$

To find the product:

Multiply the numerators.

Multiply the denominators.

Simplify if possible.

$$\frac{3}{4} \times \frac{2}{3} = \frac{3 \times 2}{4 \times 3} = \frac{6}{12} = \frac{1}{2}$$

Use a calculator.

Press:

3 [n] 4 [d] [×]

2 [n] 3 [d] [ENTER =]

[Simp] [ENTER =]

[Simp] [ENTER =]

Display: 3/6 ►S 1/2

Paige will plant $\frac{1}{2}$ of her garden in morning-glories.

Independent Practice

In **7** through **21**, find each product. Simplify if possible.

7. $54 \times \frac{5}{6}$ **8.** $\frac{4}{7} \times 56$ **9.** $16 \times \frac{3}{8}$ **10.** $\frac{5}{9} \times \frac{3}{5}$ **11.** $\frac{1}{2} \times \frac{3}{7}$

12. $\frac{2}{9} \times 72$ **13.** $\frac{3}{4} \times \frac{1}{4}$ **14.** $\frac{5}{11} \times \frac{33}{35}$ **15.** $18 \times \frac{7}{12}$ **16.** $\frac{5}{8} \times 26$

17. $3\frac{3}{5} \times 15$ **18.** $2\frac{1}{3} \times 21$ **19.** $\frac{5}{8} \times \frac{3}{10}$ **20.** $\frac{10}{12} \times \frac{3}{5}$ **21.** $18 \times \frac{3}{4}$

Problem Solving

22. Number Sense Brianna lives $\frac{1}{3}$ mile from school. If she walks to and from school every day for 5 days, how far will she walk?

23. Draw a Picture Mr. Reed is planting peppers in $\frac{2}{5}$ of his garden, and $\frac{4}{5}$ of the peppers are sweet peppers. Draw a picture to show $\frac{2}{5} \times \frac{4}{5}$.

24. A display in a grocery store has 120 pieces of fruit. Apples make up $\frac{3}{5}$ of the display, and oranges make up $\frac{2}{5}$ of the display. If $\frac{1}{2}$ of the apples are green, how many green apples are there?

A 24 **C** 48

B 36 **D** 72

25. Writing to Explain Which is greater, $\frac{3}{8} \times \frac{1}{3}$ or $\frac{3}{8} \times \frac{1}{5}$? Explain how you know.

26. Adult horses have about 40 permanent teeth. If people have $\frac{4}{5}$ this number of permanent teeth, how many permanent teeth do people have?

A 32 **C** 45

B 40 **D** 50

Lesson
8-4

Understand It!
You can find the product of two mixed numbers by changing the mixed numbers to improper fractions and then multiplying the numerators and multiplying the denominators.

Multiplying Mixed Numbers

How can you find the product of mixed numbers?

A small can of tomatoes weighs $7\frac{1}{3}$ ounces.
How much do $4\frac{1}{2}$ cans of tomatoes weigh?

Find $4\frac{1}{2} \times 7\frac{1}{3}$.

Another Example How can you use the Distributive Property to multiply a whole number and a mixed number?

Find $3 \times 4\frac{2}{15}$.

Step 1

Estimate:

$3 \times 4 = 12$

Step 2

Break apart the mixed number; use the Distributive Property:

$3 \times 4\frac{2}{15} = 3 \times (4 + \frac{2}{15})$

$= (3 \times 4) + (3 \times \frac{2}{15})$

Step 3

Multiply each part and add:

$= 12 + \frac{6}{15}$

$= 12\frac{6}{15}$

The answer, $12\frac{6}{15}$, is close to the estimate, 12, so the answer is reasonable.

Guided Practice*

Do you know HOW?

In **1** through **8**, find each product. Simplify if possible.

1. $3\frac{1}{12} \times 6$

2. $5\frac{1}{4} \times 1\frac{4}{7}$

3. $2\frac{5}{6} \times 9$

4. $6\frac{2}{3} \times 4\frac{7}{8}$

5. $5\frac{1}{6} \times 3\frac{3}{4}$

6. $5 \times 7\frac{3}{16}$

7. $1\frac{5}{8} \times 3\frac{4}{5}$

8. $4\frac{2}{9} \times 2\frac{1}{3}$

Do you UNDERSTAND?

9. How could you find $3 \times 4\frac{2}{7}$ without using the Distributive Property?

10. One case of $7\frac{1}{3}$-ounce cans of tomatoes contains 25 cans. How many ounces of tomatoes are in one case?

*For another example, see Set D on page 199.

Estimate. Use rounding.

$$4\frac{1}{2} \times 7\frac{1}{3}$$

$$\downarrow \quad \downarrow$$

$$5 \times 7 = 35$$

So, $4\frac{1}{2} \times 7\frac{1}{3} \approx 35$.

$$4\frac{1}{2} \times 7\frac{1}{3}$$

$$\downarrow \quad \downarrow$$

Then multiply. Write each mixed number as an improper fraction.

$$\frac{^{3}\cancel{9}}{_{1}\cancel{2}} \times \frac{\cancel{22}^{11}}{\cancel{3}_{1}}$$

Look for common factors and simplify.

$$\frac{3}{1} \times \frac{11}{1} = \frac{33}{1} = 33$$

The answer is close to the estimate and reasonable. So, $4\frac{1}{2}$ cans of tomatoes weigh 33 ounces.

Independent Practice

In **11** through **18**, find each product. Simplify if possible.

11. $5\frac{1}{3} \times 6\frac{3}{5}$ **12.** $2\frac{5}{8} \times 3\frac{4}{9}$ **13.** $7\frac{1}{3} \times 4\frac{9}{10}$ **14.** $8 \times 3\frac{3}{4}$

15. $1\frac{3}{8} \times 4\frac{5}{6}$ **16.** $5\frac{7}{9} \times 3\frac{1}{9}$ **17.** $6\frac{2}{3} \times 12$ **18.** $7\frac{4}{5} \times 2\frac{3}{7}$

In **19** through **22**, evaluate each expression for $R = 2\frac{1}{4}$.

19. $7\frac{1}{2}R$ **20.** $2\frac{1}{5}R$ **21.** $3\frac{1}{3}R$ **22.** $1\frac{2}{3}R$

Problem Solving

23. **Geometry** Melba's kitchen has parallelogram-shaped tiles on the floor. What is the measure of angle *w*?

24. Juanita's dog weighs $2\frac{1}{2}$ times as much as Caleb's dog. Caleb's dog weighs $8\frac{3}{4}$ pounds. Solve the equation $w = 8\frac{3}{4} \times 2\frac{1}{2}$ to find the weight, *w*, of Juanita's dog.

25. Mrs. Damico's bookshelf has a set of 16 books on it. Each book is $1\frac{3}{8}$ inches wide. If the books take the full length of the shelf with no space left over, how long is the shelf?

A $11\frac{7}{11}$ inches **C** 20 inches

B $17\frac{3}{8}$ inches **D** 22 inches

26. **Writing to Explain** Explain how to change a mixed number to a fraction.

27. Lakenda divided up her garden plot to have $\frac{1}{8}$ tomatoes, $\frac{1}{4}$ peppers, $\frac{1}{6}$ dill, $\frac{1}{6}$ basil, and the rest flowers. Draw a diagram of her garden.

Lesson
8-5

Understand It!
Some problems can be solved by finding hidden questions to be answered first and then using the answers to solve the original problem.

Problem Solving

Multiple-Step Problems

To solve some problems, you first need to answer one or more hidden questions.

How much larger is the area of the family room than the area of the kitchen?

Remember that you can find the area of a rectangular shape by multiplying its length times its width, or $A = \ell w$.

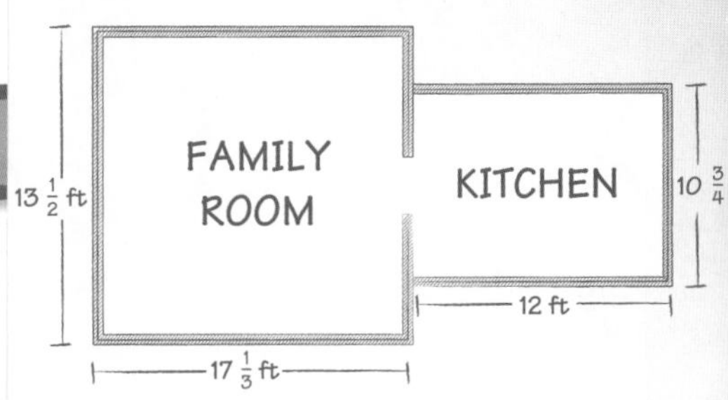

Guided Practice*

Do you know HOW?

1. A Web site has a daily trivia contest. On Mondays, Wednesdays, and Fridays, you have $1\frac{1}{2}$ hours to submit an answer. On Tuesdays and Thursdays, you have $1\frac{1}{4}$ hours. How many total hours in a week do you have to submit an answer?
   a What are the hidden questions?
   b Solve the problem.

Do you UNDERSTAND?

2. How can you find the hidden question in a problem?
3. **Write a Problem** Use a real-life situation to write a problem that contains a hidden question or hidden questions.

Independent Practice

4. Suzy runs $1\frac{1}{4}$ miles a day for a week. Gretchen walks 3 miles a day for a week. How many more miles does Gretchen cover than Suzy in a week?
   a What are the hidden questions?
   b Solve the problem.
5. John has $1\frac{1}{2}$ hours of homework from Monday through Thursday and $2\frac{3}{4}$ hours over the weekend. How much homework does John have in a week?
6. A movie costs $8.50 for adults and $5.75 for children under 13. Enrico's father took Enrico and two of his friends to the movie. If Enrico and his friends are under 13, what was the total cost for the movie?

Stuck? Try this....

- What do I know?
- What am I asked to find?
- What diagram can I use to help understand the problem?
- Can I use addition, subtraction, multiplication, or division?
- Is all of my work correct?
- Did I answer the right question?
- Is my answer reasonable?

*For another example, see Set E on page199.

Read and Understand

What do I know? The family room is $17\frac{1}{3}$ ft × $13\frac{1}{2}$ ft. The kitchen is 12 ft × $10\frac{3}{4}$ ft.

What am I asked to find? How much larger is the family room than the kitchen?

Plan and Solve

Hidden Question 1: What is the area of the family room?

$A = 17\frac{1}{3} \times 13\frac{1}{2}$

$A = \frac{{}^{26}\cancel{52}}{{}_{1}\cancel{3}} \times \frac{\cancel{27}^{9}}{\cancel{2}_{1}} = 234$

Hidden Question 2: What is the area of the kitchen?

$A = 12 \times 10\frac{3}{4}$

$A = \frac{{}^{3}\cancel{12}}{1} \times \frac{43}{\cancel{4}_{1}} = 129$

$234 - 129 = 105$

The family room is 105 square feet larger than the kitchen.

Problem Solving

In **7** and **8**, identify the hidden questions. Then solve the problem.

7. Crystal has a choice of buying either lunch at the right. Which lunch costs less? How much less?

8. Chris has a choice of two cell phone plans. Plan A charges a flat fee of $20 per month for 300 minutes and $0.20 for every minute over 300. Plan B charges $0.10 per minute with no fee. Which plan would be cheaper for 442 minutes?

Use the table at the right for **9** and **10**.

Data

Jellyfish	Length
Thimble jellyfish	1 inch
Lion's Mane jellyfish	7 feet

9. What is the difference in length between a Lion's Mane jellyfish and a Thimble jellyfish?

10. How many times longer is a Lion's Mane jellyfish than a Thimble jellyfish?

11. Kathy is measuring the rainfall in a rain gauge for her science project. The first week, she measured $2\frac{1}{4}$ inches of rain. The second week, she measured twice as much rain, and the third week, she measured half as much rain as the first week. It did not rain at all in the fourth week. How much rainfall did Kathy measure for the entire month? Explain.

12. The Spanish Club is selling folders to advertise their club. Rob, the president of the club, had 50 folders printed. Janice, the vice president of the club, had a different design printed on four and a half times as many folders. How many folders does the Spanish Club have?

A 50 **B** 200

C 250 **D** 275

Test

1. An orchard of fruit trees is 6 acres in size. If $\frac{2}{3}$ of the orchard has apple trees, how many acres are planted with apple trees. (8-1)

   A 2 acres

   B 3 acres

   C 4 acres

   D 5 acres

2. A parking lot has 85 parking spaces. A parking attendant estimates that about $\frac{1}{3}$ of them are empty. Which is the best estimate of the number of empty spaces? (8-2)

   A 20 empty spaces

   B 30 empty spaces

   C 40 empty spaces

   D 42 empty spaces

3. Which of the following expressions is illustrated by the multiplication model pictured below? (8-3)

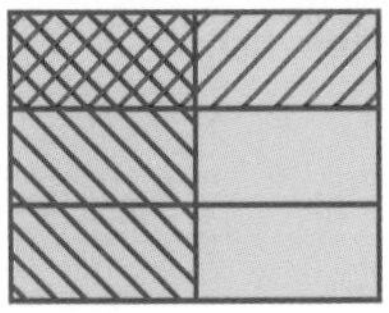

   A $\frac{1}{12} \times \frac{1}{2}$

   B $2 \times \frac{1}{2}$

   C $\frac{1}{3} \times \frac{1}{2}$

   D $\frac{1}{3} \times 2$

4. Identify the hidden question: Tomas's car gets 18 miles per gallon of gas. The gas tank in Tomas's car will hold 15 gallons. Can Tomas make an 800-mile trip on 3 tanks of gasoline? (8-5)

   A How far can Tomas's car travel on one tank of gas?

   B How long will the trip take?

   C How much gasoline is in Tomas's gas tank before the trip?

   D What is the price of gasoline?

5. What is the product of $15 \times \frac{2}{5}$? (8-1)

   A $15\frac{2}{5}$

   B 5

   C 6

   D 30

6. The student desks in Mrs. Miller's room are $2\frac{1}{4}$ feet wide. If she plans to arrange 4 desks as shown, estimate the approximate width of the 4 desks altogether. (8-2)

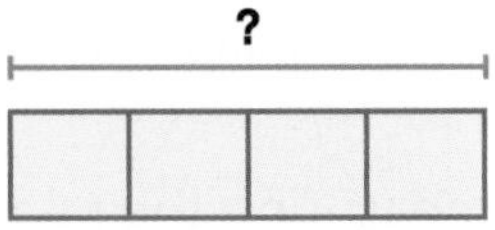

   A 8 feet

   B 14 feet

   C 12 feet

   D 15 feet

7. Which of the following can be used to find $\frac{1}{2} \times 6\frac{2}{7}$? (8-4)

A $(\frac{1}{2} + 6) \times (\frac{1}{2} + \frac{2}{7})$

B $(6 + \frac{1}{2}) \times (6 + \frac{2}{7})$

C $(6 \times \frac{1}{2}) + (6 \times \frac{2}{7})$

D $(\frac{1}{2} \times 6) + (\frac{1}{2} \times \frac{2}{7})$

8. The Cougar volleyball team won $\frac{3}{4}$ of their games this year and $\frac{2}{3}$ of their games last year. They play 24 games each year. How many more games did they win this year than last year? (8-5)

A 2 games

B 4 games

C 16 games

D 18 games

9. Ben used $2\frac{1}{3}$ gallons of paint to paint his bedroom. He needs $1\frac{1}{2}$ times as much to paint the living room. How much paint does Ben need to paint the living room? (8-4)

A $2\frac{1}{6}$ gallons

B $3\frac{1}{6}$ gallons

C $3\frac{1}{3}$ gallons

D $3\frac{1}{2}$ gallons

10. What is $\frac{9}{14} \times \frac{7}{10}$? (8-3)

A $\frac{16}{140}$

B $\frac{9}{20}$

C $\frac{9}{10}$

D $\frac{45}{49}$

11. A meatloaf weighs $\frac{7}{8}$ pounds. If $\frac{2}{3}$ of the meatloaf is ground beef, how much is ground beef? (8-3)

A $\frac{9}{24}$ pounds

B $\frac{7}{12}$ pounds

C $\frac{14}{12}$ pounds

D $\frac{14}{11}$ pounds

12. Which of the following uses a compatible whole number to find an estimate of $\frac{3}{4} \times 47$? (8-2)

A $\frac{3}{4} \times 48$

B $\frac{3}{4} \times 42$

C $\frac{3}{4} \times 45$

D $\frac{4}{3} \times 42$

13. What is $\frac{4}{5}$ of 15? (8-1)

A $18\frac{3}{4}$

B 7

C 11

D 12

Set A, pages 186–187

You can use a model to multiply $6 \times \frac{2}{3}$.

6 is divisible by 3, so divide 6 by 3.

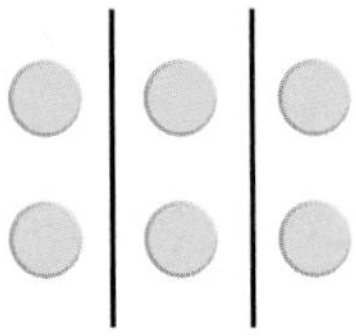

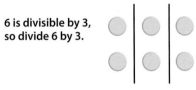

$6 \div 3 = 2$ and $\frac{1}{3} \times 6 = 2$.

$\frac{2}{3} \times 6 = 2(\frac{1}{3} \times 6)$

$= 2(2)$ or 4.

Remember that if the whole number factor is divisible by the denominator of the fraction factor, you can divide first and then multiply.

1. $\frac{2}{3} \times 9$

2. $\frac{1}{3} \times 12$

3. $\frac{2}{7} \times 14$

4. $\frac{2}{5}$ of 20

5. $\frac{1}{20} \times 400$

6. $\frac{3}{16} \times 48$

7. $\frac{3}{8}$ of 4,000

8. $\frac{1}{20}$ of 10,000

Set B, pages 188–189

Estimate $5\frac{1}{3} \times 4\frac{5}{8}$ using rounding and compatible numbers.

Round to the nearest whole numbers:

$5\frac{1}{3} \times 4\frac{5}{8}$

↓ ↓

$5 \times 5 = 25$

Use compatible numbers:

$5\frac{1}{3} \times 4\frac{5}{8}$

↓ ↓

$5 \times 5 = 25$

Using rounding or compatible numbers sometimes gives the same answer.

Remember that you can use the benchmark fraction $\frac{1}{2}$ as a compatible number for fractions close to $\frac{1}{2}$.

1. $\frac{8}{9} \times \frac{5}{8}$

2. $24\frac{7}{10} \times 4$

3. $3\frac{5}{6} \times 8\frac{2}{7}$

4. $27 \times 3\frac{2}{5}$

5. $34\frac{3}{8} \times 12\frac{1}{5}$

6. $3\frac{11}{12} \times 4\frac{4}{5}$

7. $7\frac{3}{8} \times 3\frac{1}{4}$

8. $79\frac{3}{4} \times 4\frac{7}{9}$

Set C, pages 190–191

Find $\frac{3}{8} \times \frac{4}{9}$.

Multiply the numerators and denominators.

$$\frac{3}{8} \times \frac{4}{9} = \frac{3 \times 4}{8 \times 9} = \frac{12}{72}$$

Simplify if possible. Divide the numerator and denominator by their GCF. The GCF of 12 and 72 is 12.

$$\frac{12}{72} = \frac{12 \div 12}{72 \div 12} = \frac{1}{6}$$

Remember that you can also simplify before multiplying by using the GCFs of any numerator and any denominator.

1. $\frac{5}{6} \times \frac{3}{5}$

2. $\frac{2}{7} \times \frac{1}{8}$

3. $\frac{2}{3} \times 45$

4. $\frac{1}{9} \times \frac{4}{7}$

5. $\frac{3}{4} \times \frac{8}{9}$

6. $\frac{5}{8} \times 32$

7. $\frac{3}{12} \times 20$

8. $\frac{1}{3} \times \frac{12}{15}$

Reteaching

Set D, pages 192–193

Find $5\frac{1}{3} \times 2\frac{7}{8}$.

Write the mixed numbers as improper fractions.

$$5\frac{1}{3} \times 2\frac{7}{8} = \frac{16}{3} \times \frac{23}{8}$$

Look for common factors and simplify.

$$\frac{\overset{2}{\cancel{16}}}{3} \times \frac{23}{\underset{1}{\cancel{8}}}$$

Multiply the numerators and denominators. Then write the improper fraction as a mixed number.

$$\frac{2}{3} \times \frac{23}{1} = \frac{46}{3} = 15\frac{1}{3}$$

Remember that when changing a mixed number to an improper fraction, the denominator does not change.

Find each product. Simplify if possible.

1. $3\frac{1}{5} \times 2\frac{1}{4}$
2. $4\frac{1}{6} \times 3\frac{3}{5}$
3. $1\frac{3}{8} \times 4\frac{2}{3}$
4. $5\frac{2}{3} \times 7\frac{1}{2}$
5. $3\frac{1}{6} \times 2\frac{2}{9}$
6. $6\frac{3}{4} \times 3\frac{3}{7}$
7. $8\frac{1}{4} \times 12$
8. $1\frac{2}{5} \times 2\frac{1}{4}$
9. $5\frac{2}{5} \times 1\frac{2}{3}$
10. $4\frac{5}{8} \times 1\frac{7}{9}$

Set E, pages 194–195

Find and answer hidden questions in multiple-step word problems.

A school sells sweatshirts for \$30, T-shirts for \$15, and caps for \$12. At sports games, the school sells all merchandise for half price. How much money could you save if you bought a sweatshirt, T-shirt, and cap at a sports game?

Hidden Question 1: What is the cost of the items at full price?

You know the regular price of each item.

$30 + 15 + 12 = \$57$

Hidden Question 2: What is the cost of the items at the discounted prices?

$(30 \times \frac{1}{2}) + (15 \times \frac{1}{2}) + (12 \times \frac{1}{2})$

$= 15 + 7.50 + 6 = \$28.50$

Subtract the totals to find how much you would save by buying the items at a sports game.

$57 - 28.50 = \$28.50$

You could save \$28.50.

Remember to find and answer the hidden questions to solve multiple-step problems.

For **1** and **2**, identify the hidden questions, and then solve each problem.

1. A store sells 40 sandwiches on Wednesday and 45 on Thursday. On Friday, it sells as many sandwiches as it sold on Wednesday and Thursday. How many sandwiches were sold from Wednesday to Friday?

2. A DJ for the school dance plans to play dance music for two hours. She has 20 requests for songs, and each song plays for $3\frac{1}{2}$ minutes. If she plays all of the requests, how much time will she have to play other songs?

Topic 9

Dividing Fractions and Mixed Numbers

1 How far can a sloth move in an hour? You will find out in Lesson 9-2.

How much fuel does it take to move the space shuttle from its hangar to the Vehicle Assembly Building? You will find out in Lesson 9-6.

2

3

The Cullinan diamond is the largest diamond ever found. How much does this diamond weigh? You will find out in Lesson 9-5.

Review What You Know!

Vocabulary

Choose the best term from the box.

- simplest form
- prime number
- Distributive Property

1. When the only common factor of the numerator and denominator of a fraction is 1, then the fraction is in __?__.

2. Use the __?__ to break apart numbers and make it easier to compute products mentally.

3. A(n) __?__ is a whole number greater than 1 having exactly two factors, 1 and itself.

Solving Equations

Solve each equation.

4. $g \div 7 = 45$

5. $r + 312 = 487$

6. $6m = 252$

7. $538 = a - 108$

Mixed Numbers

Write each mixed number as an improper fraction.

8. $8\frac{1}{3}$

9. $5\frac{3}{5}$

10. $2\frac{5}{8}$

Look for a Pattern

11. **Writing to Explain** What is the next figure in the series below? Explain the pattern.

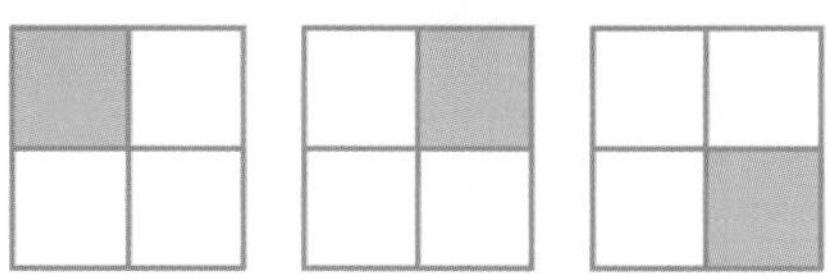

Lesson
9-1 Understanding Division of Fractions

Understand It!
Division of fractions can be represented using models and by performing repeated subtraction.

How can you model division of fractions?

Mr. Roberts uses pieces of wood that are each $\frac{3}{4}$ of a foot long for a set of shelves he is making. How many pieces of wood can he get from a board that is 3 feet long?

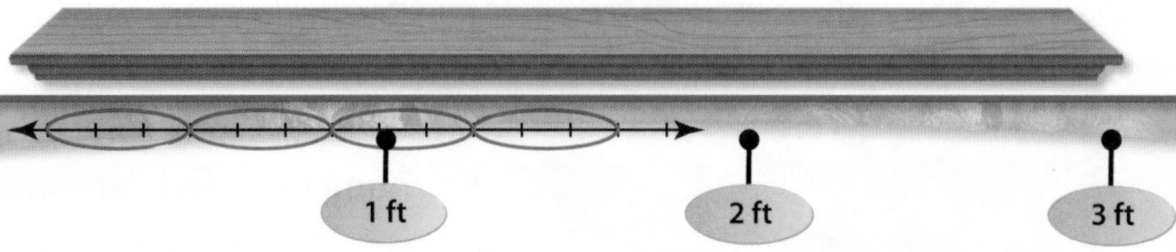

Other Examples

Dividing a Fraction by a Whole Number

Find $\frac{1}{2} \div 3$.
Use a picture to show $\frac{1}{2}$.

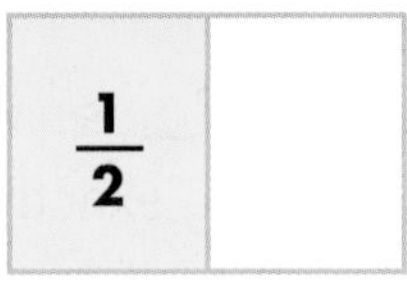

Divide $\frac{1}{2}$ into 3 equal parts.
$\frac{1}{2} \div 3$

Each part contains $\frac{1}{6}$ of the whole.
So, $\frac{1}{2} \div 3 = \frac{1}{6}$.

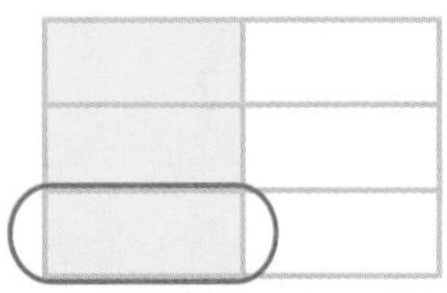

Dividing a Fraction by a Fraction

Find $\frac{3}{4} \div \frac{1}{4}$.

Use a number line to show $\frac{3}{4}$.

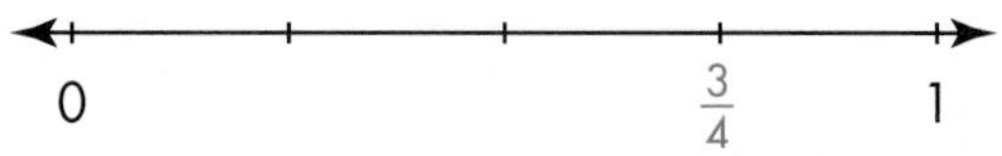

Divide $\frac{3}{4}$ into $\frac{1}{4}$ parts. There are 3 parts.

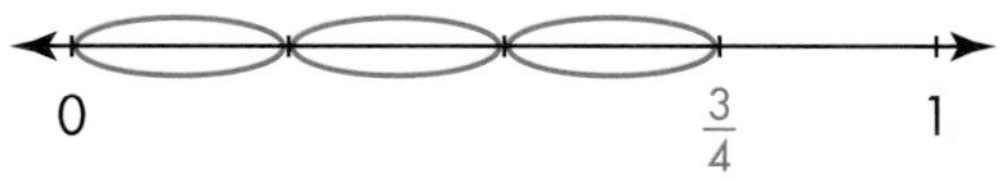

So, $\frac{3}{4} \div \frac{1}{4} = 3$.

Guided Practice*

Do you know HOW?

Write a division sentence to represent each.

1.

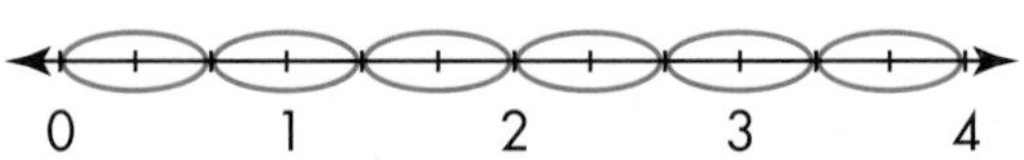

2.

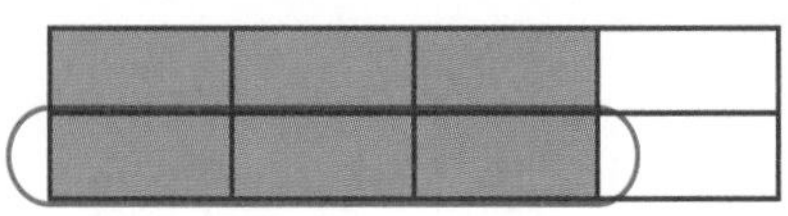

Do you UNDERSTAND?

3. Reasonableness When you divide a whole number by a fraction, will the quotient be larger or smaller than the whole number?

4. How many pieces would you get from cutting a board 10 feet long into pieces that are $\frac{2}{3}$ foot long?

*For another example, see Set A on page 218.

One Way

Think How many $\frac{3}{4}$s are in 3?

Use a number line to show 3 feet.

Divide it into $\frac{3}{4}$-foot parts.

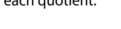

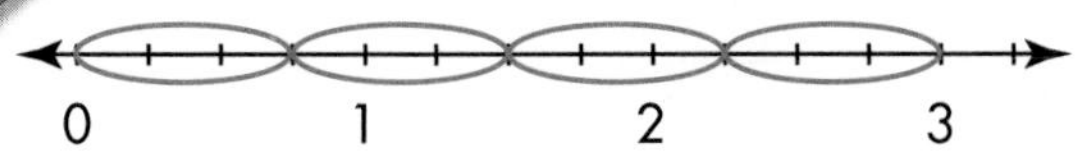

So, $3 \div \frac{3}{4} = 4$.

When the divisor is less than 1, the quotient is larger than the dividend.

Another Way

Think of division as repeated subtraction. Rewrite 3 as an improper fraction, $\frac{12}{4}$. Then, subtract $\frac{3}{4}$ repeatedly:

$$\frac{12}{4} - \frac{3}{4} = \frac{9}{4} \qquad \frac{9}{4} - \frac{3}{4} = \frac{6}{4} \qquad \frac{6}{4} - \frac{3}{4} = \frac{3}{4} \qquad \frac{3}{4} - \frac{3}{4} = 0$$

Mr. Roberts can get 4 pieces.

Independent Practice

Leveled Practice In **5** and **6**, complete each division sentence using the models provided.

5. $6 \div \frac{1}{2} = \square$

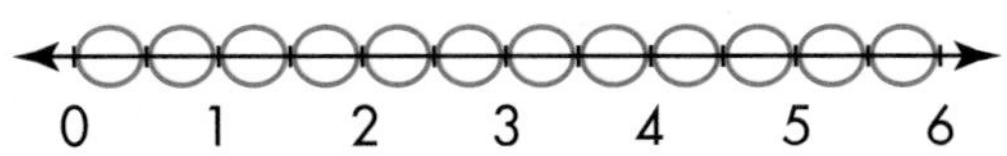

6. $\frac{2}{3} \div 3 = \square$

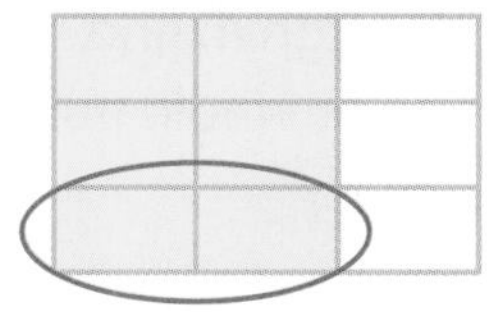

In **7** through **10**, find each quotient. Simplify if possible.

Tip *Draw a model to help you visualize.*

7. $\frac{6}{7} \div \frac{3}{7}$

8. $\frac{7}{8} \div 3$

9. $8 \div \frac{4}{5}$

10. $\frac{5}{9} \div 10$

Problem Solving

11. **Draw a Picture** Keiko divided $\frac{3}{8}$ gallon of milk evenly into 5 glasses. What fraction of a gallon is in each glass?

12. **Writing to Explain** Without solving, explain how you can compare the quotient of $\frac{6}{7} \div \frac{1}{2}$ to $\frac{6}{7}$.

13. **Draw a Picture** A car trip is 6 hours long. Every $\frac{2}{3}$ of an hour, Brian changes the radio station. How many times does Brian change the station during the trip?

14. **Geometry** A regular polygon has a perimeter of 8 units. If each side measures $\frac{4}{5}$ unit, how many sides does the polygon have?

15. For training, Raul runs several miles each day. He runs each $\frac{1}{2}$ mile in 3 minutes.

a How much time does Raul need to run 6 miles?

b How much time does Raul need to run $2\frac{1}{3}$ miles?

16. **Think About the Process** Which division sentence is shown by this model?

A $\frac{3}{8} \div 3$

B $3 \div \frac{3}{8}$

C $8 \div \frac{3}{5}$

D $\frac{3}{5} \div 8$

Lesson
9-2

Understand It!
The inverse relationship between multiplication and division will help you understand how to divide by a fraction.

Dividing a Whole Number by a Fraction

How can you find the quotient of a whole number and a fraction?

Look at the division and multiplication sentences at the right. What is the pattern?

Use the pattern to find the quotient for $4 \div \frac{2}{3}$.

$8 \div \frac{4}{1} = 2$	$8 \times \frac{1}{4} = 2$
$6 \div \frac{2}{1} = 3$	$6 \times \frac{1}{2} = 3$
$5 \div \frac{1}{2} = 10$	$5 \times \frac{2}{1} = 10$
$3 \div \frac{3}{4} = 4$	$3 \times \frac{4}{3} = 4$

Guided Practice*

Do you know HOW?

In **1** through **4**, find the reciprocal of each fraction or whole number.

1. $\frac{3}{5}$

2. $\frac{1}{6}$

3. 9

4. $\frac{7}{4}$

In **5** and **6**, find each quotient. Simplify, if possible.

5. $6 \div \frac{2}{3}$

6. $12 \div \frac{3}{8}$

Do you UNDERSTAND?

7. Is $4 \div \frac{3}{2}$ the same as $4 \div \frac{2}{3}$? Explain.

8. Explain how you would find the reciprocal of a whole number.

9. In the table above, how does the quotient compare to the dividend when the divisor is a fraction less than 1?

Independent Practice

Leveled Practice In **10** through **17**, find the reciprocal of each number.

10. $\frac{3}{10}$

11. 6

12. $\frac{1}{15}$

13. 3

14. $\frac{7}{12}$

15. $\frac{11}{5}$

16. 12

17. $\frac{22}{5}$

Find each quotient. Simplify, if possible.

18. $4 \div \frac{4}{7}$

19. $2 \div \frac{3}{8}$

20. $5 \div \frac{2}{3}$

21. $9 \div \frac{4}{5}$

22. $36 \div \frac{3}{4}$

23. $7 \div 1\frac{3}{4}$

24. $18 \div \frac{2}{3}$

25. $20 \div \frac{1}{2}$

26. $9 \div \frac{3}{5}$

27. $5 \div \frac{2}{7}$

28. $12 \div \frac{1}{3}$

29. $8 \div \frac{3}{8}$

DIGITAL
Animated Glossary
www.pearsonsuccessnet.com

*For another example, see Set B on page 218.

The pattern in the table shows a rule for dividing by a fraction.

Dividing by a fraction is the same as multiplying by its reciprocal.

Two numbers whose product is 1 are called reciprocals of each other. If a nonzero number is named as a fraction $\frac{a}{b}$, then its reciprocal can be named $\frac{b}{a}$.

$\frac{2}{3} \times \frac{3}{2} = 1$ ← **The reciprocal of $\frac{2}{3}$ is $\frac{3}{2}$.**

Find $4 \div \frac{2}{3}$.

Rewrite the problem as a multiplication problem. Simplify, then multiply.

$$4 \div \frac{2}{3} = 4 \times \frac{3}{2}$$
$$= \frac{\overset{2}{\cancel{4}}}{1} \times \frac{3}{\cancel{2}_{1}}$$
$$= \frac{6}{1} = 6$$
$$4 \div \frac{2}{3} = 6$$

Problem Solving

Use this information for **30** and **31**.

A tortoise can move 300 ft in $\frac{1}{3}$ h.
A snail can move 40 ft in $\frac{1}{4}$ h.
A sloth can move 50 ft in $\frac{1}{8}$ h.

30. About how far could each animal move in one hour?

31. Which animal would move the farthest in 3 hours traveling at its maximum speed?

32. Writing to Explain A bowl of soup holds 7 ounces. If a spoonful holds $\frac{1}{6}$ ounce, how many spoonfuls are in 3 bowls of soup? Explain.

33. A recording of the current weather conditions lasts $\frac{3}{4}$ minute. How many times could the recording be played in 1 hour?

34. How many $\frac{1}{4}$-pound burgers can Danny make with 12 pounds of ground turkey?

35. Draw a Picture Draw a picture or number line to show $3 \div \frac{1}{3}$.

36. Reasoning Valeria bought a 9 ft length of ribbon from which she wants to cut $\frac{2}{3}$-ft pieces. How many pieces can she cut?

37. Each health book is $\frac{3}{4}$ inch long. If Mrs. Menes's bookshelf is 2 feet long, how many books can she fit on the shelf?

38. In the number 589,745,162, what is the numerical value in the ten millions place?

A 5 **B** 8 **C** 9 **D** 7

39. Trey is buying 8 notebooks for $1.25 each. How much money will he need?

Lesson
9-3

Understand It!
A division expression containing fractions can be changed to an equivalent multiplication expression to solve.

Dividing Fractions

How can you find the quotient of two fractions?

Andrew has $\frac{3}{4}$ of a gallon of lemonade. He wants to pour it into $\frac{1}{6}$-gallon containers. How many containers can he fill?

Choose an Operation Divide to find the number of containers.

Guided Practice*

Do you know HOW?

In **1** through **4**, find each quotient. Simplify, if possible.

1. $\frac{3}{4} \div \frac{2}{3}$

2. $\frac{3}{12} \div \frac{1}{8}$

3. $\frac{1}{2} \div \frac{4}{5}$

4. $\frac{7}{10} \div \frac{2}{5}$

Do you UNDERSTAND?

5. In the example above, did it change the answer to simplify before multiplying?

6. In the example at the top, how many $\frac{1}{8}$-gallon containers could Andrew fill?

Independent Practice

In **7** through **22**, find each quotient. Simplify, if possible.

7. $\frac{1}{2} \div \frac{1}{2}$

8. $\frac{1}{2} \div \frac{1}{4}$

9. $\frac{7}{8} \div \frac{1}{8}$

10. $\frac{2}{3} \div \frac{3}{4}$

11. $\frac{1}{9} \div \frac{1}{5}$

12. $\frac{2}{7} \div \frac{1}{2}$

13. $\frac{2}{9} \div \frac{4}{5}$

14. $\frac{1}{2} \div \frac{2}{4}$

15. $\frac{3}{8} \div \frac{1}{9}$

16. $\frac{2}{3} \div \frac{1}{4}$

17. $\frac{2}{5} \div \frac{1}{8}$

18. $\frac{5}{6} \div \frac{2}{3}$

19. $\frac{6}{7} \div \frac{1}{3}$

20. $\frac{7}{8} \div \frac{1}{2}$

21. $\frac{12}{14} \div \frac{14}{12}$

22. $\frac{5}{14} \div \frac{4}{7}$

In **23** through **26**, evaluate each expression for $x = \frac{5}{6}$.

23. $x \div \frac{3}{9}$

24. $\frac{10}{13} \div x$

25. $\frac{5}{8} \div x$

26. $x \div \frac{9}{10}$

*For another example, see Set B on page 218.

Step 1

Find $\frac{3}{4} \div \frac{1}{6}$.

To divide by a fraction, rewrite the problem as a multiplication problem using the reciprocal of the divisor.

$\frac{6}{1}$ is the reciprocal of $\frac{1}{6}$.

$$\frac{3}{4} \div \frac{1}{6} = \frac{3}{4} \times \frac{6}{1}$$

Step 2

Look for common factors to simplify. Then multiply.

$$\frac{3}{{}_2\cancel{4}} \times \frac{\cancel{6}^3}{1} = \frac{9}{2}$$

$$\frac{9}{2} = 4\frac{1}{2}$$

Andrew can fill 4 containers, plus $\frac{1}{2}$ of an additional container.

Problem Solving

27. Tomas tiled $\frac{1}{2}$ of his bathroom floor in blue. He tiled $\frac{2}{3}$ of the remaining bathroom floor in green. He used white tiles for the rest of the bathroom. How much of the bathroom had white tiles? Use the picture to help find your solution.

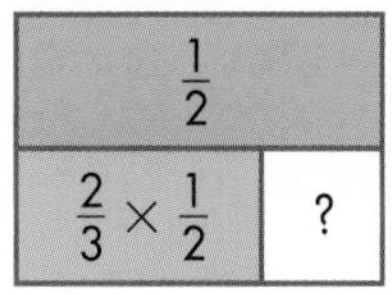

28. Luis has an 8-cup bag of trail mix to share. If he gives 9 friends $\frac{2}{3}$ of a cup each, how much trail mix does he have left?

29. Which fraction has the greatest value?

A $\frac{7}{12}$

B $\frac{2}{3}$

C $\frac{3}{4}$

D $\frac{7}{9}$

30. **Algebra** Write an equation for each statement, then solve.

a One-half of a watermelon was shared among 4 people. How much watermelon did each person get?

b A recipe for cookies calls for $\frac{1}{4}$ cup of almonds. If Sara has $1\frac{1}{2}$ cups of almonds, how many recipes of cookies can she make?

c Reena runs a quarter of a mile and then walks one-eighth mile. If she continues this pattern 10 times, how far will she run?

31. **Make a Table** A restaurant sells 9 daily specials for every 6 full-price meals sold. At this rate, how many daily specials will have been sold when 30 full-price meals have been sold?

32. **Writing to Explain** Write an explanation to a friend telling him or her how to find $\frac{3}{4} \div \frac{2}{3}$.

33. Simplify the following expressions.

a $2 + (10 - \frac{6}{3})$

b $5(6 + 3)$

c $\frac{10}{(25 - 5)}$

Lesson

9-4

Understand It!
You can use the same methods to estimate quotients of mixed numbers that you use to estimate quotients of decimals.

Estimating Quotients

How can you estimate the quotient of mixed numbers?

Lillian and her friends can hike an average of $3\frac{5}{8}$ miles per hour. About how many hours will it take them to hike $15\frac{5}{6}$ miles of the trail?

Estimate the quotient $15\frac{5}{6} \div 3\frac{5}{8}$ to find out.

Other Examples

Estimate $55\frac{1}{3} \div 6\frac{1}{4}$.

Use compatible numbers.

$$55\frac{1}{3} \div 6\frac{1}{4}$$
$$\downarrow \quad \downarrow$$
$$54 \div 6 = 9$$
$$55\frac{1}{3} \div 6\frac{1}{4} \approx 9$$

Estimate $7\frac{3}{4} \div 1\frac{7}{8}$.

Use rounding.

$$7\frac{3}{4} \div 1\frac{7}{8}$$
$$\downarrow \quad \downarrow$$
$$8 \div 2 = 4$$
$$7\frac{3}{4} \div 1\frac{7}{8} \approx 4$$

Estimate $26\frac{3}{4} \div 5\frac{1}{4}$.

Use compatible numbers.

$$26\frac{3}{4} \div 5\frac{1}{4}$$
$$\downarrow \quad \downarrow$$
$$25 \div 5 = 5$$
$$26\frac{3}{4} \div 5\frac{1}{4} \approx 5$$

Guided Practice*

Do you know HOW?

In **1** through **4**, estimate the quotient.

1. $35\frac{1}{3} \div 6\frac{2}{3}$

2. $24\frac{5}{8} \div 5\frac{4}{7}$

3. $11\frac{3}{8} \div 3\frac{7}{9}$

4. $26\frac{1}{3} \div 8\frac{3}{4}$

Do you UNDERSTAND?

5. In the example above, why do you round $7\frac{3}{4}$ to 8? Explain.

6. Estimate the amount of time it would take to hike $20\frac{1}{2}$ miles.

Independent Practice

In **7** through **14**, estimate each quotient.

7. $40\frac{9}{10} \div 20\frac{1}{6}$

8. $35\frac{2}{9} \div 5\frac{8}{9}$

9. $3\frac{7}{8} \div 1\frac{1}{5}$

10. $21\frac{2}{3} \div 6\frac{4}{5}$

11. $13\frac{5}{8} \div 2\frac{1}{3}$

12. $87\frac{4}{7} \div 7\frac{5}{7}$

13. $59\frac{3}{8} \div 11\frac{1}{9}$

14. $18\frac{1}{5} \div 1\frac{5}{9}$

*For another example, see Set C on page 218.

One Way

Round to the nearest whole number by comparing the fractions to $\frac{1}{2}$.

$15\frac{5}{6} \div 3\frac{5}{8}$

$\downarrow \quad \downarrow$

$16 \div 4 = 4$

Both $\frac{5}{6}$ and $\frac{5}{8}$ are greater than $\frac{1}{2}$, so round up to the nearest whole number.

So, $15\frac{5}{6} \div 3\frac{5}{8} \approx 4$.

It will take Lillian and her friends about 4 hours to finish their hike.

Another Way

Use compatible numbers.

$15\frac{5}{6} \div 3\frac{5}{8}$

$\downarrow \quad \downarrow$

$16 \div 4 = 4$

$15\frac{5}{6}$ and $3\frac{5}{8}$ are close to the compatible numbers 16 and 4.

So, $15\frac{5}{6} \div 3\frac{5}{8} \approx 4$.

It will take Lillian and her friends about 4 hours to finish their hike.

In **15** through **22**, estimate each quotient.

15. $32\frac{1}{3} \div 7\frac{2}{3}$

16. $40\frac{1}{4} \div 5\frac{1}{9}$

17. $23\frac{4}{5} \div 11\frac{2}{3}$

18. $49\frac{6}{7} \div 4\frac{2}{3}$

19. $27\frac{2}{3} \div 13\frac{5}{6}$

20. $99\frac{2}{9} \div 4\frac{3}{4}$

21. $74\frac{7}{8} \div 24\frac{2}{5}$

22. $55\frac{2}{3} \div 27\frac{5}{6}$

Problem Solving

23. Geometry What is the perimeter of the parallelogram at right?

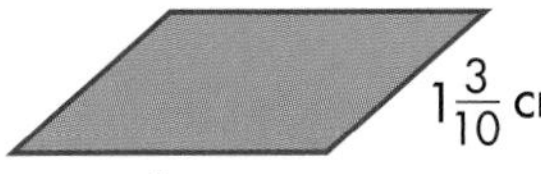

24. The area of a room is $45\frac{3}{4}$ square feet, and the length is $9\frac{1}{8}$ feet. Use the equation $w = 45\frac{3}{4} \div 9\frac{1}{8}$ to estimate the width, w, of the room.

25. Alex is driving to his school reunion 30.5 miles away. He stopped for gas 4.3 miles after he started driving. Then he drove 15.2 miles to the first rest stop. How many miles does he have left to drive to his reunion?

26. Use estimation to determine which of the following comparisons is true.

A $13\frac{5}{7} \div 2\frac{1}{3} > 9$

B $12\frac{1}{2} \div 4\frac{1}{2} > 6$

C $39\frac{8}{9} \div 3\frac{7}{8} > 9$

D $19\frac{4}{5} \div 9\frac{8}{9} > 11$

27. On Monday, John hiked for $24\frac{1}{2}$ miles along the Appalachian Trail. On Tuesday it rained, so he covered only $6\frac{3}{4}$ miles. About how many times farther did John hike on Monday than on Tuesday?

28. Writing to Explain Donna has a $25\frac{1}{2}$-foot roll of crepe paper for streamers. Explain how you would estimate the number of $1\frac{3}{4}$-foot streamers Donna can make.

29. Wanda rents a car for 3 days for $18.95 per day and $0.15 per mile. If Wanda traveled 350 miles, what is her total cost, excluding tax?

30. Algebra Write an equation to show how many quarters are in $10.

Lesson
9-5

Understand It!
Rewrite division of mixed numbers as multiplication problems using improper fractions and the reciprocal of the divisor.

Dividing Mixed Numbers

How can you find the quotient of mixed numbers?

Damon has $37\frac{1}{2}$ inches of space on his car bumper that he wants to use for bumper stickers. How many short bumper stickers can he fit side by side on his car bumper?

Find $37\frac{1}{2} \div 6\frac{1}{4}$.

Bumper Stickers	Type	Length
	Short	$6\frac{1}{4}$"
	Medium	$10\frac{3}{4}$"
	Long	15"

Guided Practice*

Do you know HOW?

In **1** through **6**, find each quotient. Simplify if possible.

Tip *Remember to estimate.*

1. $18 \div 3\frac{2}{3}$

2. $4\frac{1}{3} \div 2\frac{4}{5}$

3. $5 \div 6\frac{2}{5}$

4. $6\frac{5}{9} \div 1\frac{7}{9}$

5. $7\frac{2}{3} \div 5\frac{1}{9}$

6. $3\frac{3}{7} \div 5\frac{6}{7}$

Do you UNDERSTAND?

7. When dividing mixed numbers, why is it important to estimate the quotient first?

8. How many medium bumper stickers could fit on a 76-inch-long bumper?

Independent Practice

Leveled Practice In **9** through **20**, find each quotient. Simplify if possible.

9. $1\frac{3}{8} \div 4\frac{1}{8}$

10. $2\frac{5}{6} \div 6\frac{1}{3}$

11. $3\frac{1}{4} \div 4\frac{2}{7}$

12. $5\frac{1}{2} \div 7\frac{2}{5}$

13. $1 \div 8\frac{5}{9}$

14. $3\frac{5}{6} \div 9\frac{5}{6}$

15. $4\frac{1}{3} \div 3\frac{1}{4}$

16. $8 \div 2\frac{2}{3}$

17. $6\frac{3}{4} \div 1\frac{7}{8}$

18. $2\frac{5}{8} \div 13$

19. $3\frac{6}{7} \div 6\frac{3}{4}$

20. $9\frac{7}{9} \div 8\frac{1}{4}$

In **21** through **28**, evaluate each expression for $n = 2\frac{1}{5}$.

21. $8\frac{1}{2} \div n$

22. $n \div 4$

23. $20\frac{4}{5} \div n$

24. $n \div \frac{5}{8}$

25. $3\frac{4}{5} \div n$

26. $15 \div n$

27. $n \div 2\frac{1}{5}$

28. $n \div 2\frac{4}{9}$

*For another example, see Set D on page 219.

Estimate using compatible numbers.

$$37\frac{1}{2} \div 6\frac{1}{4}$$

$$\downarrow \quad \downarrow$$

$$36 \div 6 = 6$$

So, $37\frac{1}{2} \times 6\frac{1}{4} \approx 6$.

Write each mixed number as an improper fraction.

$$37\frac{1}{2} \div 6\frac{1}{4} = \frac{75}{2} \div \frac{25}{4}$$

$$\frac{75}{2} \times \frac{4}{25}$$ ← **Use the reciprocal of $\frac{25}{4}$ to write a multiplication problem.**

$$\frac{^{3}\cancel{75}}{_{1}\cancel{2}} \times \frac{\cancel{4}^{2}}{\cancel{25}_{1}} = 6$$

Damon can put 6 short bumper stickers on his car bumper.

Problem Solving

29. Writing to Explain Explain why $3\frac{7}{8} \div \frac{1}{8}$ is greater than $3\frac{7}{8} \times \frac{1}{8}$.

30. How many $\frac{3}{4}$-ft pieces can you cut from a $6\frac{1}{2}$-ft ribbon?

31. Number Sense Which number is its own reciprocal? Explain.

32. Number Sense If $9 \times \frac{x}{6} = 9 \div \frac{x}{6}$, then what does x equal? Explain.

33. Which expression would you use to find how many halves there are in $6\frac{3}{8}$?

A $\frac{1}{2} \times 6\frac{3}{8}$

B $6\frac{3}{8} \div \frac{1}{2}$

C $\frac{1}{2} \div 6\frac{3}{8}$

D $6\frac{3}{8} \div 2$

34. Algebra Evaluate each expression if $T = \frac{2}{3}$.

a $\frac{1}{2}T$ **b** $\frac{8}{9} + T$ **c** $2 \div T$

35. Estimation Bus 26 takes $2\frac{3}{4}$ hours to complete its route. Estimate how many times Bus 26 can complete its route in 16 hours.

36. The biggest diamond ever found weighed $1\frac{1}{2}$ pounds uncut. If this diamond were cut into three pieces, how much would each piece weigh?

37. The large room is twice as long as the smaller room.

a How long is the larger room?

b If the length of the smaller room were divided into two equal parts, how long would each part be?

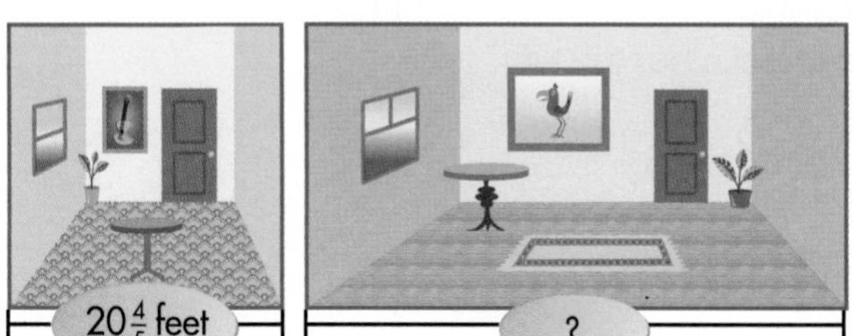

Lesson
9-6

Understand It!
Use inverse relationships and properties of equality to solve equations with fractions.

Solving Equations

How can you solve equations involving fractions and mixed numbers?

Melissa split a 6-foot-long strip of fruit leather into two pieces, as shown below. What is the length of the shorter piece of fruit leather?

Use the equation $3\frac{3}{4} + x = 6$ to solve the problem.

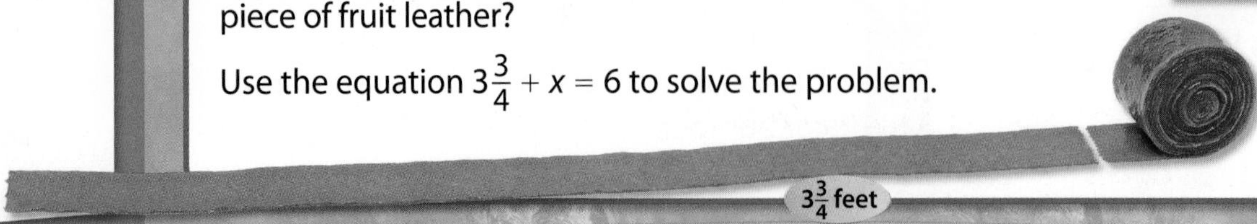

Other Examples

You have learned to solve equations with whole numbers.
Now use what you learned to solve equations with fractions.

Subtraction Equation

Solve: $y - \frac{4}{9} = 5\frac{1}{3}$

$y - \frac{4}{9} + \frac{4}{9} = 5\frac{1}{3} + \frac{4}{9}$

$y = 5\frac{3}{9} + \frac{4}{9}$

$y = 5\frac{7}{9}$

Multiplication Equation

Solve: $\frac{3}{8}n = 15$

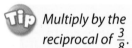

Tip *Multiply by the reciprocal of $\frac{3}{8}$.*

$\frac{3}{8}n = 15$

$\left(\frac{8}{3}\right)\frac{3}{8}n = \left(\frac{8}{3}\right) 15$

$n = \frac{8}{\cancel{3}_1} \times \frac{\cancel{15}^5}{1}$

$n = 40$

Division Equation

Solve: $m \div \frac{2}{5} = 4\frac{3}{4}$

$m \div \frac{2}{5} = \frac{19}{4}$

$m \div \frac{2}{5} \times \frac{2}{5} = \frac{19}{4} \times \frac{2}{5}$

$m = \frac{19}{_2\cancel{4}} \times \frac{\cancel{2}^1}{5}$

$m = \frac{19}{10}$

$m = 1\frac{9}{10}$

Guided Practice*

Do you know HOW?

In **1** through **6**, solve each equation and check your answer.

1. $t - \frac{2}{3} = 25\frac{3}{4}$

2. $v + \frac{5}{8} = 9\frac{1}{3}$

3. $\frac{3}{4}x = 27$

4. $y \div \frac{4}{7} = 8\frac{5}{9}$

5. $\frac{7}{9}g = 49$

6. $r - \frac{3}{5} = 15\frac{5}{8}$

Do you UNDERSTAND?

7. How did subtracting the mixed number help you solve the problem at the top of the page?

8. Check the answer to each equation in Other Examples.

*For another example, see Set E on page 219.

What You Think

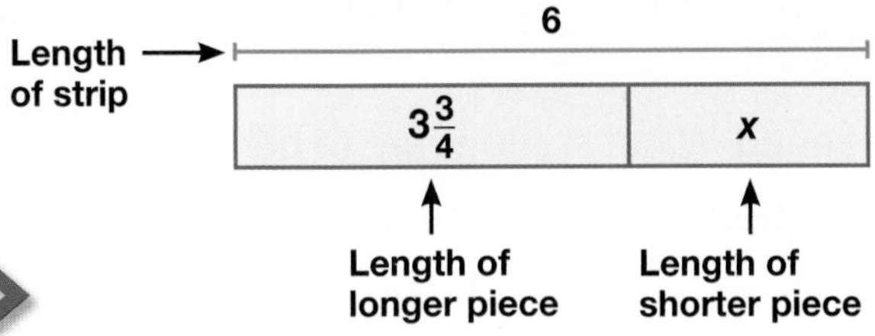

$$3\frac{3}{4} + x = 6$$

Use inverse relationships and properties of equality. Subtract $3\frac{3}{4}$ from both sides of the equation to get x alone.

What You Write

$$3\frac{3}{4} + x = 6$$

$$3\frac{3}{4} + x - 3\frac{3}{4} = 6 - 3\frac{3}{4}$$

$$x = 2\frac{1}{4}$$

The shorter piece is $2\frac{1}{4}$ feet long.
Check.

$$3\frac{3}{4} + x = 6$$

$$3\frac{3}{4} + 2\frac{1}{4} = 6$$

$$6 = 6$$

Independent Practice

In **9** through **16**, solve each equation and check your answer.

9. $s \div \frac{1}{6} = 22\frac{2}{3}$

10. $16 = n \div \frac{3}{4}$

11. $3\frac{1}{6} + f = 7\frac{5}{6}$

12. $p - 6 = 2\frac{7}{12}$

13. $7\frac{1}{9} = 2\frac{4}{5} + m$

14. $a + 3\frac{1}{4} = 5\frac{2}{9}$

15. $\frac{5}{6}b = 7\frac{1}{3}$

16. $k - 6\frac{3}{8} = 4\frac{6}{7}$

Problem Solving

17. **Writing to Explain** A fraction, f, divided by $\frac{2}{5}$ equals $\frac{7}{8}$. Write an algebraic sentence to show the equation. Then solve the equation and explain how you solved it.

18. The Ramirez family spent several days hiking the Rocky Mountains. Every day they hiked $8\frac{1}{3}$ miles. How many days did they hike if they hiked a total of 50 miles?

19. **Number Sense** Is the solution of $b \div \frac{5}{6} = 25$ greater than or less than 25? How can you tell before computing?

20. Choose the expression with the greatest product.

A $3\frac{1}{8} \times \frac{2}{5}$

B $3\frac{1}{8} \times \frac{2}{3}$

C $3\frac{1}{8} \times 5\frac{1}{2}$

D $3\frac{1}{8} \times 5\frac{1}{8}$

21. How many gallons of fuel does it take to move the space shuttle at the right the 3 miles from its hangar to the Vehicle Assembly Building?

Tip *1 mi = 5,280 ft*

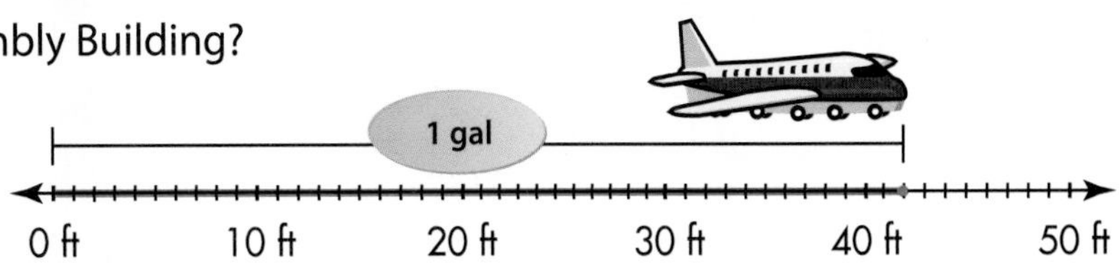

Lesson
9-7

Understand It!
Some problems can be solved by observing patterns and applying the same pattern to the problem.

Problem Solving

Look for a Pattern

A $12\frac{1}{2}$ mile walk-or-run is being planned. Water stations are to be placed at distance markers using a pattern. What are the distances for the five unmarked signs where water stations will be placed?

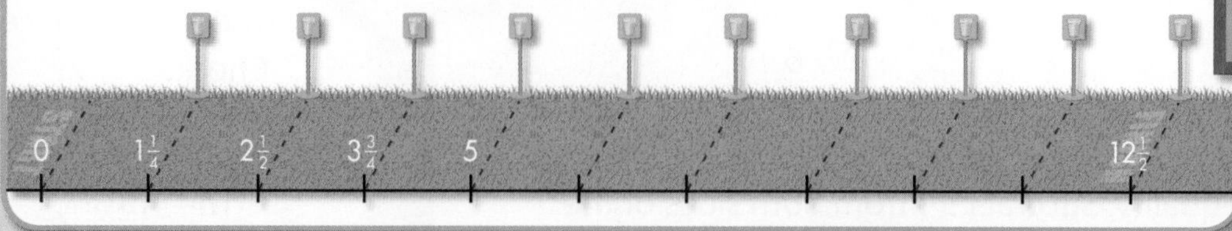

Guided Practice*

Do you know HOW?

Find the pattern.

1. $0, \frac{1}{4}, \frac{2}{4}, \frac{3}{4}, \square, \square, \square, \square, \frac{8}{4}$

2. $0, \frac{2}{3}, \frac{4}{3}, \frac{6}{3}, \square, \square, \square, \square, \frac{16}{3}$

3. $-2, -6, -18, \square, \square, \square, -1{,}458$

Do you UNDERSTAND?

4. Why should you check two other consecutive points after you find a possible pattern?

5. **Write a Problem** Write a problem that starts with $5\frac{1}{2}$, uses a pattern three times, and leaves blanks to fill in.

Independent Practice

Find the missing numbers. Describe the pattern.

6. $\frac{24}{4}, \frac{21}{4}, \frac{18}{4}, \frac{15}{4}, \square, \square, \square, \square, \frac{0}{4}$

7. $12, 10\frac{1}{2}, 9, 7\frac{1}{2}, \square, \square, \square, \square, 0$

8. $-16, -12, -8, \square, \square, \square, \square, 12$

9. $\square, \square, \square, \square, 10, 12\frac{1}{2}, 15, 17\frac{1}{2}$

10. $23, \square, \square, \square, \square, 21\frac{1}{8}, 20\frac{3}{4}, 20\frac{3}{8}$

11. $\frac{9}{2}, \frac{9}{4}, \frac{9}{8}, \square, \square, \square, \square, \frac{9}{256}$

Stuck? Try this....

- What do I know?
- What am I asked to find?
- What diagram can I use to help understand the problem?
- Can I use addition, subtraction, multiplication, or division?
- Is all of my work correct?
- Did I answer the right question?
- Is my answer reasonable?

*For another example, see Set F on page 219.

Plan

Look for a pattern. Choose the first 2 markers. How can you mathematically get from the first value to the second?

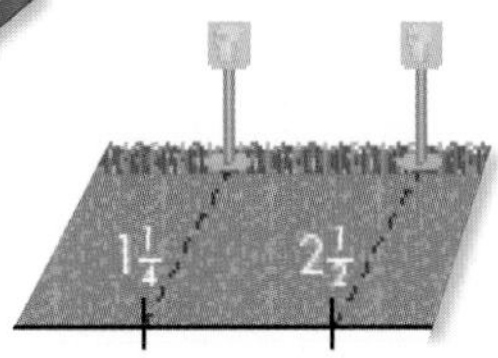

Add $1\frac{1}{4}$.

Plan

Check the pattern using other consecutive markers.

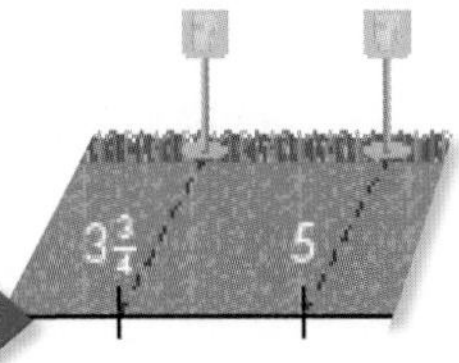

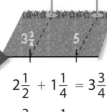

$2\frac{1}{2} + 1\frac{1}{4} = 3\frac{3}{4}$

$3\frac{3}{4} + 1\frac{1}{4} = 5$

The pattern "add $1\frac{1}{4}$" works.

Solve

Copy and complete the pattern by adding $1\frac{1}{4}$ mile.

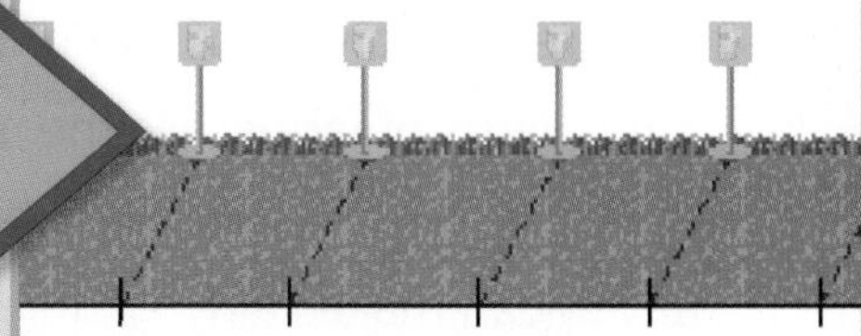

The missing distances are $6\frac{1}{4}$, $7\frac{1}{2}$, $8\frac{3}{4}$, 10, and $11\frac{1}{4}$ miles.

Problem Solving

Use the chart at right for **12** through **14**.

$1 \times 8 + 1 = 9$
$12 \times 8 + 2 = 98$
$123 \times 8 + 3 = 987$
$1{,}234 \times 8 + 4 = 9{,}876$

12. What is the next equation in the pattern?

13. Use the pattern to find $1{,}234{,}567 \times 8 + 7$.

14. **Writing to Explain** How did you find the answer to Exercise 13 without computing?

15. Which figure completes this pattern?

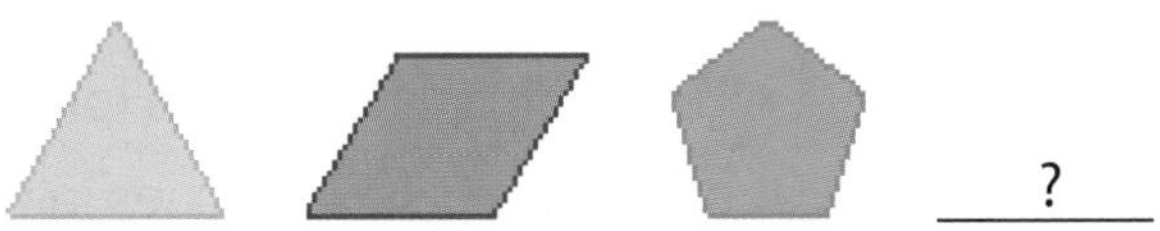

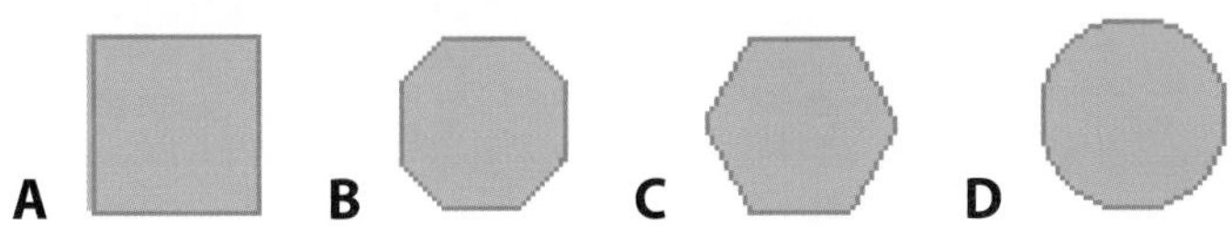

16. Some pairs of numbers make an interesting pattern when they are squared. $12^2 = 144$, and $21^2 = 441$. Explain whether this pattern is the same for 13^2, 31^2, and 112^2, 211^2.

17. Maya and Carlos are growing crystals for the science fair. They check their crystals' growth at certain times based on a pattern. They began at 1:15. Add the missing times and describe the pattern they used.

1:15, 2:30, 3:45, 5:00, ▢, ▢, ▢, ▢, 11:15

Topic 9

Test

1. Raven is making pillows. Each pillow requires $\frac{3}{5}$ of a yard of fabric. If Raven has 6 yards of fabric, use the model to find $6 \div \frac{3}{5}$, the number of pillows Raven can make. (9-1)

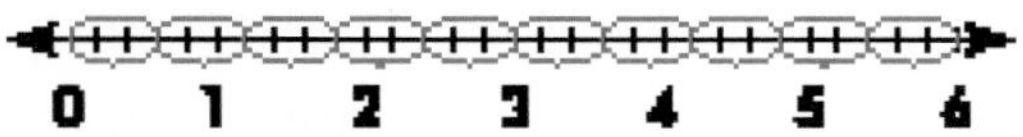

A 10 pillows

B 6 pillows

C 5 pillows

D 3 pillows

2. What step can be taken to find the solution to the equation shown? (9-6)

$\frac{5}{14}x = 20$

A Subtract $\frac{5}{14}$ from both sides.

B Divide both sides by $\frac{14}{5}$.

C Multiply both sides by $\frac{5}{14}$.

D Multiply both sides by $\frac{14}{5}$.

3. Which number sentence is represented by the number line? (9-1)

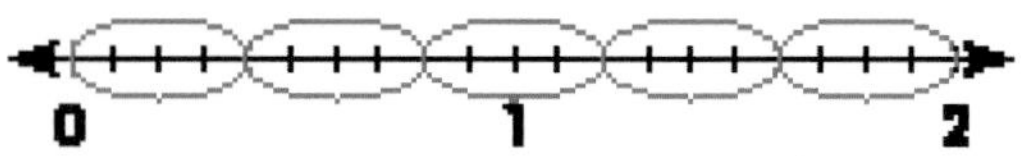

A $2 \div \frac{4}{10} = 5$

B $2 \div \frac{1}{10} = \frac{4}{10}$

C $\frac{4}{10} \div 2 = 5$

D $5 \div \frac{4}{10} = 2$

4. Which has the same value as $\frac{2}{5} \div \frac{5}{9}$? (9-3)

A $\frac{5}{2} \times \frac{5}{9}$

B $\frac{5}{2} \div \frac{5}{9}$

C $\frac{2}{5} \div \frac{9}{5}$

D $\frac{2}{5} \times \frac{9}{5}$

5. Holly is displaying a postcard collection on a bulletin board that is $35\frac{3}{4}$ inches wide. If each postcard is $5\frac{7}{8}$ inches in width, about how many postcards can she display in each row? (9-4)

A about 5 postcards

B about 6 postcards

C about 8 postcards

D about 10 postcards

6. A model train is $15\frac{3}{4}$ inches long. Each car on this train is $2\frac{5}{8}$ inches in length. How many cars are on the train? (9-5)

A 3 cars

B 4 cars

C 5 cars

D 6 cars

7. Mr. Sanchez is making pancakes. Each batch of pancakes uses $\frac{3}{4}$ cup of milk. If he has 9 cups of milk available, how many batches can he make? (9-2)

A 3 batches

B 7 batches

C 12 batches

D 27 batches

8. Find $\frac{3}{4} \div \frac{1}{4}$. (9-3)

A 4

B 3

C 2

D $\frac{3}{16}$

9. How many $\frac{1}{8}$-pint bottles can be filled from a $\frac{3}{4}$-pint bottle of hydrogen peroxide? (9-3)

A 6

B 5

C 4

D 1

10. Hal is stacking some CD cases on a shelf that is $19\frac{7}{8}$ inches wide. If each stack is $4\frac{11}{16}$ inches wide, estimate how many stacks of cases will fit on the shelf. (9-4)

A 3 stacks

B 4 stacks

C 6 stacks

D 12 stacks

11. Find $2\frac{1}{6} \div \frac{2}{3}$. (9-5)

A $1\frac{4}{9}$

B $2\frac{1}{4}$

C $3\frac{1}{4}$

D $6\frac{1}{2}$

12. Solve $t + \frac{1}{4} = 2\frac{7}{12}$. (9-6)

A $t = 10\frac{1}{3}$

B $t = 2\frac{1}{3}$

C $t = 2\frac{5}{6}$

D $t = \frac{31}{48}$

13. Shasta has 3 lbs of wax and uses $\frac{3}{8}$ lb to make one candle. How many candles can she make? (9-2)

A $\frac{1}{8}$ candle

B 5 candles

C 8 candles

D 9 candles

14. The table shows the weight of a small dog each week since it was born. If the pattern continues, what will be the puppy's weight in week 6? (9-7)

Week	1	2	3	4	5	6
Weight in pounds	$\frac{5}{16}$	$\frac{1}{2}$	$\frac{11}{16}$	$\frac{7}{8}$		

A $\frac{3}{16}$ pound

B $1\frac{1}{16}$ pounds

C $1\frac{1}{4}$ pounds

D $1\frac{1}{2}$ pounds

Topic 9

Reteaching

Set A, pages 202–203

Find $4 \div \frac{4}{5}$. Use a number line.

Divide 4 into $\frac{4}{5}$ parts.

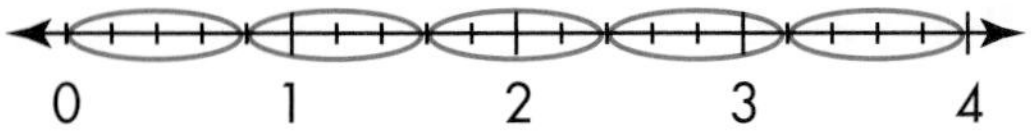

$4 \div \frac{4}{5} = 5$

Remember that when the divisor is less than 1, the quotient is larger than the dividend.

1. $7 \div \frac{1}{2}$

2. $6 \div \frac{2}{5}$

3. $2 \div \frac{1}{8}$

4. $\frac{8}{9} \div \frac{4}{9}$

5. $\frac{2}{3} \div 2$

6. $\frac{3}{4} \div 6$

Set B, pages 204–207

Find $4 \div \frac{8}{13}$.

Dividing by a fraction is the same as multiplying by its reciprocal.

$4 \div \frac{8}{13} = 4 \times \frac{13}{8}$ **Use the reciprocal of the divisor to rewrite the problem.**

$\frac{{}^{1}\cancel{4}}{1} \times \frac{13}{\cancel{8}^{2}} = 6\frac{1}{2}$ **Look for common factors and simplify.**

Find $\frac{3}{4} \div \frac{5}{8}$.

$\frac{3}{4} \div \frac{5}{8} = \frac{3}{4} \times \frac{8}{5}$ **Rewrite the problem as a multiplication problem.**

$\frac{3}{{}^{1}\cancel{4}} \times \frac{\cancel{8}^{2}}{5} = \frac{6}{5}$ or $1\frac{1}{5}$ **Simplify. Then, multiply.**

Remember that the product of a number and its reciprocal is 1.

1. $25 \div \frac{4}{9}$

2. $12 \div \frac{3}{5}$

3. $8 \div \frac{5}{7}$

4. $\frac{7}{8} \div \frac{1}{4}$

5. $\frac{1}{3} \div \frac{3}{5}$

6. $\frac{3}{4} \div \frac{1}{3}$

7. $\frac{5}{6} \div \frac{3}{8}$

8. $\frac{1}{3} \div \frac{1}{2}$

9. $5 \div \frac{5}{16}$

10. $\frac{7}{12} \div \frac{3}{4}$

11. $\frac{8}{9} \div \frac{2}{3}$

12. $\frac{2}{7} \div \frac{2}{7}$

Set C, pages 208–209

Estimate $3\frac{1}{5} \div 8\frac{3}{4}$ using rounding or compatible numbers.

$3\frac{1}{5} \div 8\frac{3}{4} \approx 3 \div 9$

$3 \div 9 = \frac{3}{9}$ or $\frac{1}{3}$

Round to the nearest whole number. $\frac{1}{5} < \frac{1}{2}$ and $\frac{3}{4} > \frac{1}{2}$. $3\frac{1}{5}$ and $8\frac{3}{4}$ round to 3 and 9.

So, $3\frac{1}{5} \div 8\frac{3}{4} \approx \frac{1}{3}$.

Remember that you can estimate using compatible numbers.

1. $\frac{7}{9} \div 16$

2. $24\frac{4}{10} \div 6\frac{1}{3}$

3. $3\frac{5}{6} \div 8\frac{2}{7}$

4. $27 \div 3\frac{2}{5}$

5. $36\frac{3}{8} \div 12\frac{2}{5}$

6. $3\frac{11}{12} \div 4\frac{4}{5}$

Set D, pages 210–211

Find $6\frac{1}{2} \div 1\frac{1}{6}$. Estimate. $6\frac{1}{2} \div 1\frac{1}{6} \approx 6$

$6\frac{1}{2} \div 1\frac{1}{6} = \frac{13}{2} \div \frac{7}{6}$ **Write the mixed numbers as improper fractions.**

$\frac{13}{2} \div \frac{7}{6} = \frac{13}{2} \times \frac{6}{7}$ **Then write the problem as a multiplication problem using the reciprocal of the divisor.**

$\frac{13}{\cancel{2}_1} \times \frac{\cancel{6}^3}{7} = \frac{39}{7}$ or $5\frac{4}{7}$ **Simplify. Then, multiply.**

$5\frac{4}{7}$ is close to the estimate of 6.

Remember to estimate before solving the problem so you can check the reasonableness of your answer.

Find each quotient.

1. $6\frac{3}{8} \div 4\frac{1}{4}$

2. $9 \div 2\frac{2}{7}$

3. $3\frac{3}{5} \div 1\frac{1}{5}$

4. $5\frac{1}{2} \div 3\frac{3}{8}$

5. $3\frac{2}{5} \div 1\frac{1}{5}$

6. $12\frac{1}{6} \div 3$

Set E, pages 212–213

Find $w + 4\frac{1}{3} = 7$.

Subtract $4\frac{1}{3}$ from both sides.

$w + 4\frac{1}{3} - 4\frac{1}{3} = 7 - 4\frac{1}{3}$

$w = 2\frac{2}{3}$

Remember that you can use inverse relationships and properties of equality to solve each equation.

1. $g + 3\frac{5}{8} = 7\frac{1}{4}$

2. $b \div 15 = 8\frac{1}{3}$

3. $\frac{7}{9}y = 49$

Set F, pages 214–215

If the pattern continues, how tall will the plants be at the end of 5 weeks?

Week	1	2	3	4	5
Plant Growth (in.)	$2\frac{1}{2}$	5	$7\frac{1}{2}$		

The plants grew $2\frac{1}{2}$ inches during Week 1.

$2\frac{1}{2} + 2\frac{1}{2} = 5;\ 5 + 2\frac{1}{2} = 7\frac{1}{2}$ **Check the pattern for Weeks 2 and 3.**

$7\frac{1}{2} + 2\frac{1}{2} = 10;\ 10 + 2\frac{1}{2} = 12\frac{1}{2}$ **Use the pattern to solve the problem.**

The plants will be $12\frac{1}{2}$ in. at the end of 5 weeks.

Remember to look for a pattern by finding relationships between numbers, figures, or expressions. Find the missing numbers.

1. $\frac{1}{17}, \frac{3}{17}, \frac{6}{17}, \frac{10}{17}$, ▢

2. 12, $13\frac{1}{3}$, $14\frac{2}{3}$, 16, ▢, ▢

3. $\frac{5}{18}, \frac{4}{18}, \frac{3}{18}$, ▢, ▢

4. 6, 2, −2, −6, ▢, ▢

Topic 10

Integers

1 A commercial airplane cruises at about 30,000 feet. Can a bird fly that high? You will find out in Lesson 10-1.

2 Antartica is the coldest and the windiest continent. How much colder can the wind make temperatures feel? You will find out in Lesson 10-4.

3 How deep is an ocean? You will find out in Lesson 10-5.

4 How are stock prices like integers? You will find out in Lesson 10-6.

Review What You Know!

Vocabulary

Choose the best term from the box.

• evaluate	• addend
• sum	• inverse

1. Multiplying and dividing can undo each other; they have a(n) __?__ relationship.

2. In the equation 8 + 7 = 15, 8 is a(n) __?__ and 15 is the __?__ .

3. When you __?__ an algebraic expression, you substitute a number for the variable.

Order of Operations

Simplify each expression using order of operations.

4. $24 \div (8 - 5)$ **5.** $4 + 7 \times 2$

6. $9 - 9 + 22$ **7.** $8 \times 3 \div 6 - 1$

8. $3 + 12 \div 2$ **9.** $4 + (3 \times 6) - 3$

Evaluating Expressions

Evaluate each expression for $x = 2$ and $x = 8$.

10. $48 \div x$ **11.** $x \times 0$ **12.** $1x$

13. $4x \div 2$ **14.** $x - 2$ **15.** $x^2 + 1$

16. $x \div x$ **17.** $100 - x^2$

Properties

18. **Writing to Explain** How can you find 37×9 using the Distributive Property? Explain.

Lesson
10-1 Understanding Integers

Understand It!
Numbers to the right of 0 on the number line are positive, and numbers to the left of 0 on the number line are negative.

What are integers?

You can compare integers to degrees of temperature measured on a thermometer. When the temperature goes below zero, it is written with a negative sign.

6°C is 6°C warmer than 0°C.

–6°C is 6°C colder than 0°C.

The distance from 0°C is the same.

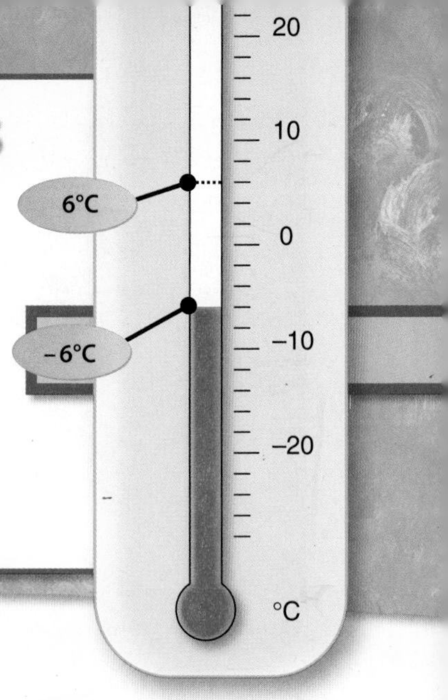

You have learned how to read the counting numbers. This chart shows how to read negative integers.

Integer	How to Read It
–3	Negative three
–(–3)	The opposite of negative three
|–3|	The absolute value of negative three

Guided Practice*

Do you know HOW?

Use the number line below for **1** through **6**. Give the integer that each point represents. Then write its opposite and absolute value.

1. *A* **2.** *B* **3.** *C*

4. *D* **5.** *E* **6.** *F*

Do you UNDERSTAND?

7. What do you know about two different integers that have the same absolute value?

8. Which integers do you use for counting?

9. How would you read the number –17?

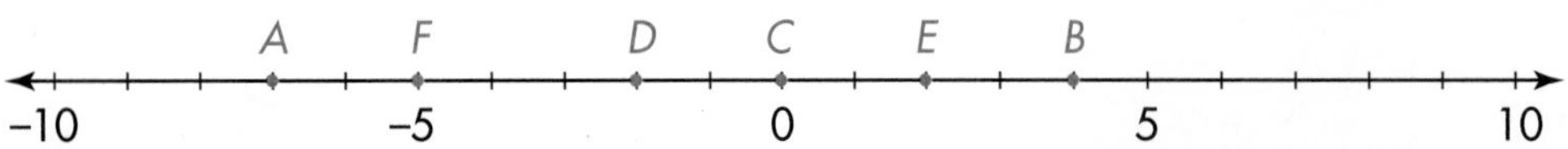

Independent Practice

In **10** through **15**, what is the opposite and absolute value of each integer?

10. 5 **11.** –13 **12.** 22 **13.** –31 **14.** –50 **15.** 66

DIGITAL Animated Glossary **www.pearsonsuccessnet.com**

**For another example, see Set A on page 256.*

A number line can show numbers like on a thermometer. Numbers that are the same distance from 0 are called opposites. –6 and 6 are opposites.

Integers are made up of the counting numbers, their opposites, and zero.

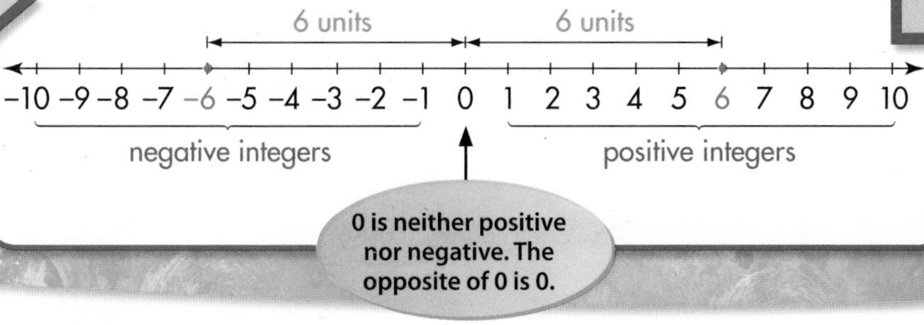

The absolute value of an integer is its distance from zero.

Distance is always positive.

The absolute value of 6 is written $|6| = 6$.

The absolute value of –6 is written $|-6| = 6$.

Problem Solving

16. Geometry Which of the following polygons has the greatest perimeter?

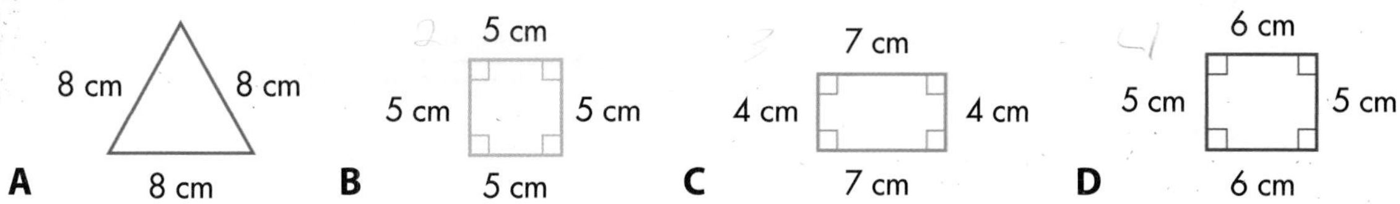

17. Writing to Explain If the opposite of an integer is equal to its absolute value, is the number positive or negative? Explain your answer.

Ruppell's Griffons fly up to 37,000 feet.

18. What is the value of $|-14|$?

A the opposite of 14 **C** 14

B –14 **D** greater than 14

Mexican free-tailed bats fly up to 10,000 feet.

Use the pictures at the right to answer **19** through **21**.

19. Number Sense About how much higher can a Ruppell's Griffon fly than a migrating bird can fly?

A migrating bird flies up to 5,000 feet.

20. Write a negative integer to represent the depth to which a dolphin may dive.

A dolphin can swim to 150 feet below sea level.

21. Which animal can fly or swim at a greater distance from sea level, a sperm whale or a migrating bird?

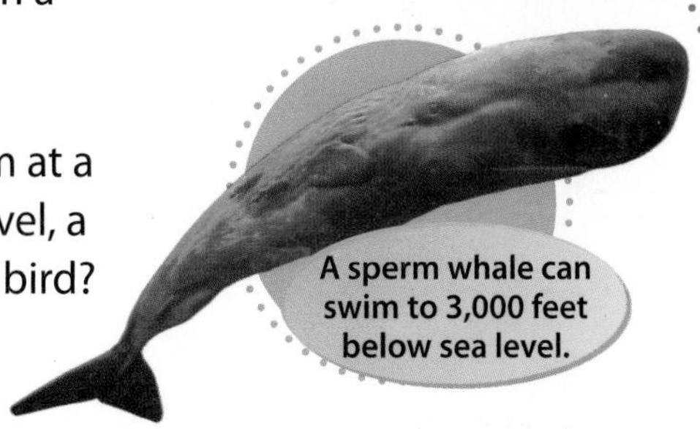

A sperm whale can swim to 3,000 feet below sea level.

Lesson
10-2 Comparing and Ordering Integers

Understand It!
Number values on a number line decrease as you move left and increase as you move right.

How can you compare and order integers?

The table shows the low temperatures during a cold week. Find which day had the lowest temperature. Then order the temperatures from least to greatest.

You can use a number line to help.

Data

Day	Temperature
Monday	3°C
Tuesday	–6°C
Wednesday	5°C
Thursday	1°C
Friday	–5°C

Guided Practice*

Do you know HOW?

In **1** through **4**, use <, >, or = to compare.

1. 7 ◯ –12

2. –3 ◯ –9

3. –8 ◯ 0

4. |–2| ◯ –2

In **5** through **8**, order the numbers from least to greatest.

5. –6, 5, –7

6. 8, –6, –2

7. –21, |–15|, –12

8. |3|, –3, –19, 11

Do you UNDERSTAND?

9. Is –7 to the right or to the left of –2 on a number line? What does that tell you about their values?

10. From greatest to least, what were the three coldest temperatures in the chart at the top of the page?

11. Which day had the highest temperature?

Independent Practice

In **12** through **19**, use <, >, or = to compare.

Tip *You can draw and use a number line.*

12. 5 ◯ –18

13. |–7| ◯ 7

14. 0 ◯ 9

15. 18 ◯ 9

16. –19 ◯ –23

17. 4 ◯ –6

18. |–32| ◯ |7|

19. –1 ◯ 3

In **20** through **28**, order the numbers from least to greatest.

20. –6, 8, –9, 13

21. |–19|, 12, |–21|, –3

22. 17, 14, –10, 4, –2, –4

23. 4.5, –4.66, –5, 7

24. –37, |15|, 11, –3, 8, |–12|

25. 57, –21, 43, –6, 7, 23

26. –6, 1.3, –3.5, 2

27. 2, 0, –8, –11, –5

28. 2.25, –7.5, –7, –3.2

*For another example, see Set A on page 256.

First locate the integers on a number line.

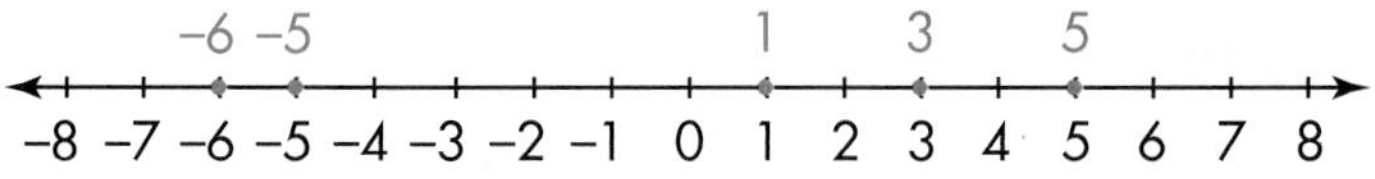

When comparing integers on a number line, the integer that is farther to the left is less.

–6 is farther to the left than –5, so –6 is less. It was colder on Tuesday than on Friday.

You can write this two ways: $-6 < -5$ or $-5 > -6$.

Integer values on a number line decrease as you move left and increase as you move right.

The temperature farthest to the left is –6. Tuesday was the coldest day.

Moving left to right, you can write the temperatures from least to greatest: –6, –5, 1, 3, 5

Problem Solving

29. Writing to Explain If n = any integer, explain why $|n| = |-n|$.

30. In miniature golf, the lowest score wins. Scores can be compared to *par,* a number of strokes set for the course.

a Using the table at right, list the top five finishers in order from first place to fifth place.

b Which students' scores are opposites?

Data

Player	Par Score
Martha	0 (par)
Madison	–2
Tom	–3
Emma	4
Ben	1
Quincy	–4
Jackson	6

31. Shayla has 4 roses, 7 tulips, and 3 daffodils. Fred has 5 roses, 3 morning-glories, and 3 tulips. Nick has 7 roses and 5 tulips. Who has the most flowers? Who has the least?

32. Cheyenne recorded the temperature three times during the day.

left for school	–4°F
lunchtime	2°F
bedtime	–7°F

a Order the temperatures from least to greatest.

b At which of the times was the temperature the coldest?

33. The variables on this number line represent integers. Order the variables from least to greatest.

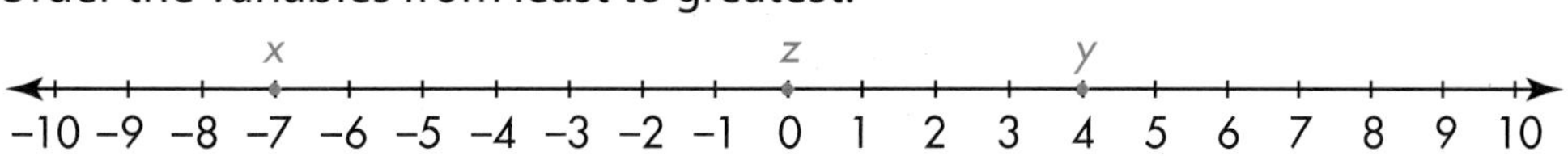

A x, y, z **B** y, z, x **C** x, z, y **D** y, x, z

Problem Solving

24. **Writing to Explain** Why is $-1\frac{3}{8}$ a rational number but not an integer?

25. **Number Sense** Which number is greater: −4.2 or −6.2? Explain.

26. **Number Sense** Name three rational numbers that are between 7 and 8.

27. Write a word phrase for $\frac{1}{5}(3x + 4)$.

28. Craig hiked a 2.625 mi trail and a 1.125 mi trail. Aubra hiked a 3.76 mi trail. Who hiked farther? By how much?

29. Order −3.25, $-3\frac{1}{8}$, $-3\frac{3}{4}$, and −3.1 from least to greatest. Did you write all the numbers as fractions or as decimals?

The animals listed in the table live below the ocean's surface. The table shows possible locations of the animals relative to the ocean's surface. Use the table to answer **30** and **31**.

Animal	Possible Locations Relative to Ocean's Surface
Bloodbelly comb jelly	−0.8 km
Deep sea anglerfish	$-\frac{2}{3}$ km
Fanfin anglerfish	$-2\frac{1}{4}$ km
Gulper eel	−1.19 km
Pacific blackdragon	$-\frac{3}{10}$ km
Slender snipe eel	−0.6 km

30. Order the anglerfish and eels by their possible locations shown in the table, from deepest to shallowest.

31. Which animal's possible location shown in the table is closest to −0.7 km?

A Gulper eel

B Deep sea anglerfish

C Pacific blackdragon

D Fanfin anglerfish

32. The diagram to the right shows how sets of numbers are related. Copy the table below. Indicate the sets to which the numbers belong.

Number	Natural	Whole	Integer	Rational
10	Yes	Yes	Yes	Yes
−6				
0				
2.7				
−3.5				

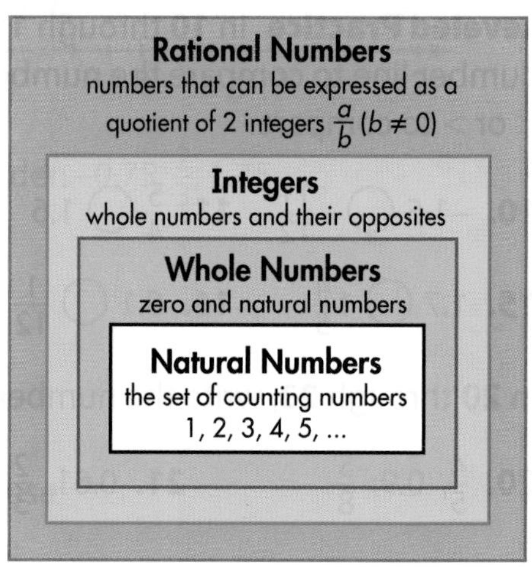

Rational Numbers
numbers that can be expressed as a quotient of 2 integers $\frac{a}{b}$ ($b \neq 0$)
Integers
whole numbers and their opposites
Whole Numbers
zero and natural numbers
Natural Numbers
the set of counting numbers
1, 2, 3, 4, 5, ...

Going Digital

Changing Fractions and Mixed Numbers to Decimal Form

The examples below show two ways you can use your calculator to change fractions and mixed numbers to decimals.

Write $\frac{3}{40}$ in decimal form.

Press: 3 [÷] 40 [ENTER =] Display: 0.075

or

Press: 3 [n/d] 40 [ENTER =] [F↔D] Display: 0.075

Write $4\frac{19}{20}$ in decimal form.

Press: 4 [+] 19 [÷] 20 [ENTER =] Display: 4.950

or

Press: 4 [+] 19 [n/d] 20 [ENTER =] [F↔D] Display: 4.950

Practice

Write each fraction or mixed number in decimal form. Try to predict whether the decimal will terminate or repeat before doing each calculation. Remember, your calculator may round decimals to the nearest thousandth.

1. $\frac{7}{8}$ **2.** $\frac{9}{16}$ **3.** $\frac{4}{9}$ **4.** $2\frac{11}{20}$

5. $5\frac{14}{15}$ **6.** $\frac{31}{40}$ **7.** $\frac{8}{11}$ **8.** $16\frac{17}{80}$

9. $\frac{5}{18}$ **10.** $\frac{37}{200}$ **11.** $7\frac{19}{30}$ **12.** $4\frac{31}{33}$

Lesson
10-4

Understand It!
When adding integers, positive numbers represent a move to the right on the number line, and negative numbers represent a move to the left.

Adding Integers

How can you add integers with the same signs?

It was –2°C when Jack left for school at 7:30 A.M. During the next three hours, the temperature decreased three degrees Celsius. What was the temperature at 10:30 A.M. that morning?

Choose an Operation: Add to find the temperature at 10:30. Find –2 + (–3).

Another Example **How do you add integers with different signs?**

Find –2 + 3.

One Way

Think about walking a number line, walking backward for negative addends and forward for positive addends.

- Start at 0 on the number line, facing the positive integers.
- Walk backward 2 steps for –2 and stop.
- Then walk forward 3 steps for 3. Stop at 1.

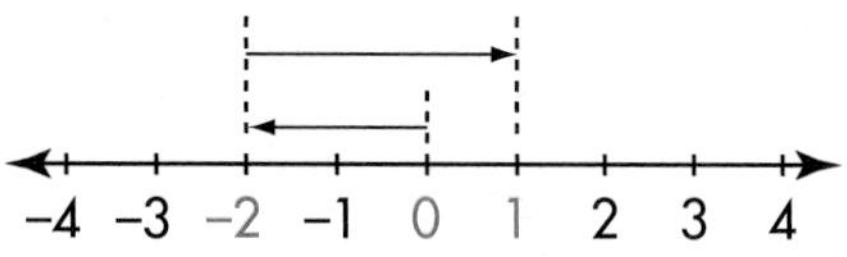

So, –2 + 3 = 1.

Another Way

Use these **rules for adding integers with different signs.**

- Find the absolute value of each addend. |–2| = 2 and |3| = 3
- Subtract the lesser absolute value from the greater. 3 – 2 = 1
- Give the difference of the absolute values the same sign as the addend with the greater absolute value.

Think The addend with the greater absolute value is 3. 3 is positive. The sum, 1, is also positive.

So, –2 + 3 = 1.

Explain It

1. Suppose you were finding 2 + (–3) on a number line. Explain the steps.
2. Suppose you were using the rules to find 2 + (–3). What sign would you give the difference of the absolute values?

One Way

Think about walking a number line.

- Start at 0 on the number line, facing the positive integers.
- Walk backward 2 steps for −2 and stop.
- Walk backward 3 more steps to add −3.

Stop at −5. So, −2 + (−3) = −5.

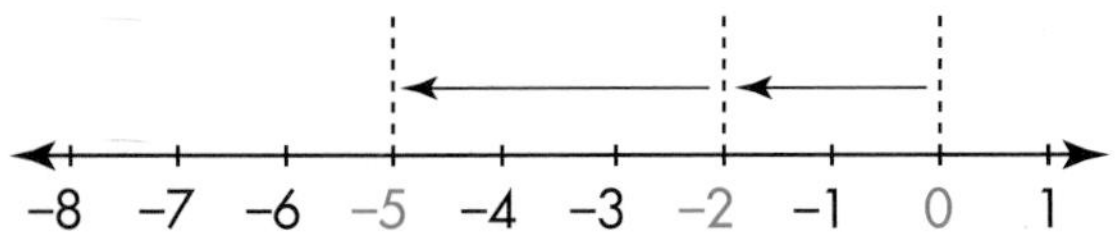

Another Way

Use these **rules for adding integers with the same signs**.

- Find the absolute values of the addends. |−2| = 2 and |−3| = 3
- Add the absolute values. 2 + 3 = 5.
- Give the sum the same sign as the addends.

So, −2 + (−3) = −5.

Guided Practice*

Do you know HOW?

Find each sum. Use a number line or the rules for adding integers.

1. −7 + 4 **2.** 8 + (−3)

3. −5 + 14 **4.** 18 + 13

5. −2 + (−6) **6.** 24 + (−7)

7. 43 + (−19) **8.** −16 + (−12)

Do you UNDERSTAND?

9. When is the sum of a positive integer and a negative integer, positive?

10. It was 5°C when Tricia woke up in the morning. The temperature was 7 degrees higher at lunchtime. What was the lunchtime temperature?

Independent Practice

Leveled Practice In **11** and **12**, use the number lines to find the sum.

11. 4 + (−3)

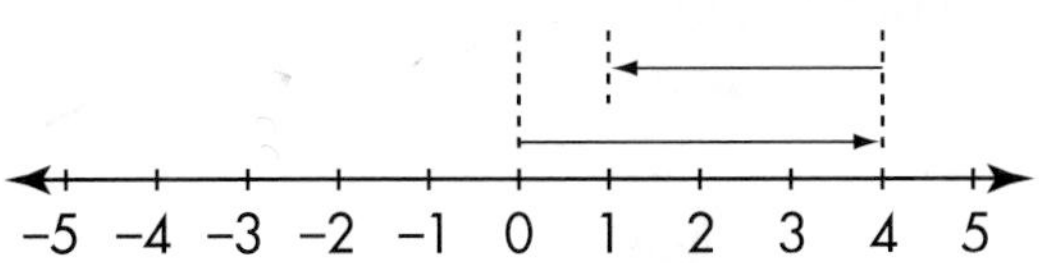

12. −2 + 7

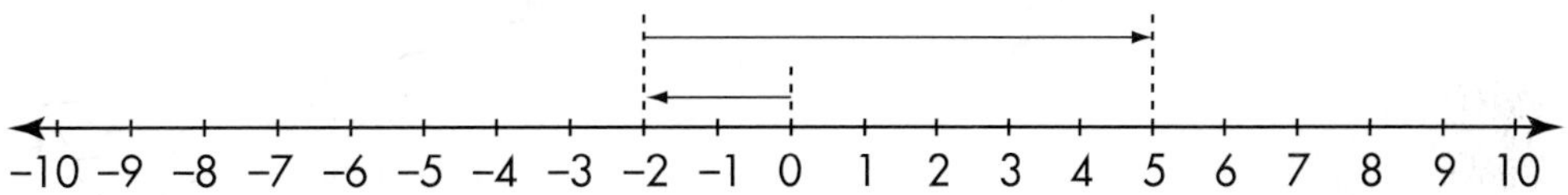

For **13** through **22**, find each sum. **Tip** *Draw a number line to help you add.*

13. −25 + (−1) **14.** −23 + (−6) **15.** 3 + (−13) **16.** −23 + 8 **17.** 32 + (−4)

18. −7 + 15 **19.** 6 + (−19) **20.** −3 + (−7) **21.** −4 + (−8) **22.** −8 + 30

For another example, see Set C on page 257.

Independent Practice

In **23** through **27**, use a number line or the rules for adding integers to find each sum.

23. $3 + (-8)$ **24.** $-9 + 7$ **25.** $-4 + (-8)$ **26.** $-15 + (-23)$ **27.** $19 + (-32)$

In **28** through **32**, evaluate each expression for $b = -18$.

28. $33 + b$ **29.** $b + (-16)$ **30.** $24 + b + (-6)$ **31.** $-11 + |-38| + b$ **32.** $|b| + (-47) + 15$

Problem Solving

33. **Algebra** Use the rule to complete the table.

Rule: Add −7

In	3	−19	22	−43	−7
Out	■	■	■	■	■

34. In Antarctica, the temperature often drops below −40°F, and the wind speed can exceed 40 miles per hour (mph). A 40-mph wind makes −40°F feel 44°F colder. How cold does −40°F feel when the wind is blowing 40 mph?

35. Bandu lost $4 at the swimming pool. Later that week, he and his sister each earned $10. Does Bandu have less or more money than before he went to the swimming pool?

36. **Writing to Explain** Describe a situation that the following expression could represent: $17 + (-9)$.

37. **Reasoning** If you add an integer and its opposite, what is the sum?

38. Which digit is in the thousandths place? 381,427.659

39. **Think About the Process** Which expression has a value of 25?

A $3 + 4 \times 6 - 2$ **B** $(3 + 4) \times (6 - 2)$ **C** $3 + 4 \times (6 - 2)$ **D** $(3 + 4) \times 6 - 2$

40. **Think About the Process** The bus stopped 3 times within the distance of 7 blocks. At the first stop, 2 people got on the bus. At the second stop, 3 people got off. At the third stop, 1 person got off and 4 people got on. Which expression best describes how the number of people on the bus changed?

A $2 + 3 + (1 + 4)$ **B** $2 + 3 + (-1 + 4)$ **C** $2 + (-3) + (-1 + 4)$ **D** $2 + (-3) + (1 + 4)$

41. Mona went to the library and checked out 5 books. She returned 4 books. Evaluate the expression $5 + (-4)$.

A 1 **B** −1 **C** $|1|$ **D** 9

Going Digital

Addition of Integers

Use eTools
Counters
Add $-6 + (-8)$ and $-5 + 9$.

Step 1 Go to the Counters eTool. Let each yellow counter represent positive one and each red counter represent negative one. To show $-6 + (-8)$, show 6 red counters in a row and 8 red counters in another row. Click on the red counter and then click in the workspace to show and make the rows. The result is 14 red counters. So, $-6 + (-8) = -14$.

Step 2 Use the Broom tool to clear the workspace. To show $-5 + 9$, show 5 red counters in one row and 9 yellow counters in a second row. A sum such as $-1 + 1$ or $-5 + 5$ is called a zero pair. The sum of a number and its opposite is always zero and the numbers are called a zero pair. The zero pairs can be removed without changing the sum.

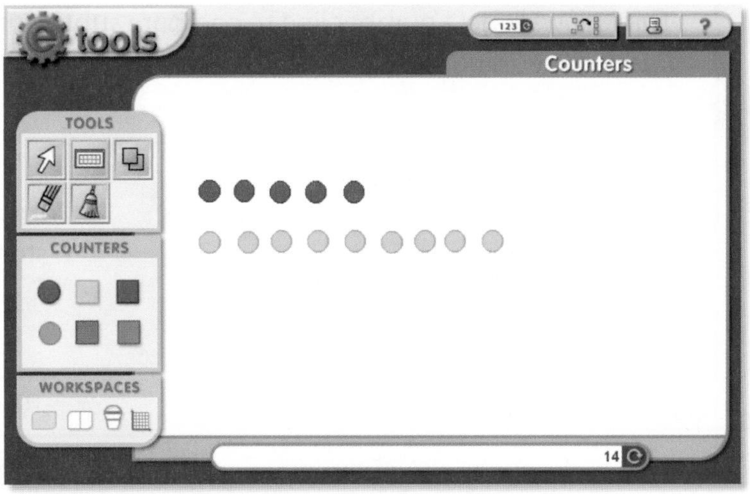

Use the Arrow tool to select 5 red and 5 yellow counters as zero pairs. Remove the zero pairs by using the Erase tool. The result is 4 yellow counters. So, $-5 + 9 = 4$.

Practice

Find each sum.

1. $-7 + (-5)$

2. $-1 + 10$

3. $2 + (-8)$

4. $-3 + 11$

5. $4 + (-14)$

6. $-9 + (-6)$

Lesson
10-5

Understand It!
Subtracting an integer is the same as adding the opposite of the integer.

Subtracting Integers

How can you subtract integers?

Malita is making wind chimes to sell. So far, she has made two. Her first customer liked them so well that she ordered six. How many more does Malita need to make?

Choose an Operation: Subtract to find how many more Malita needs to make. Find 2 − 6.

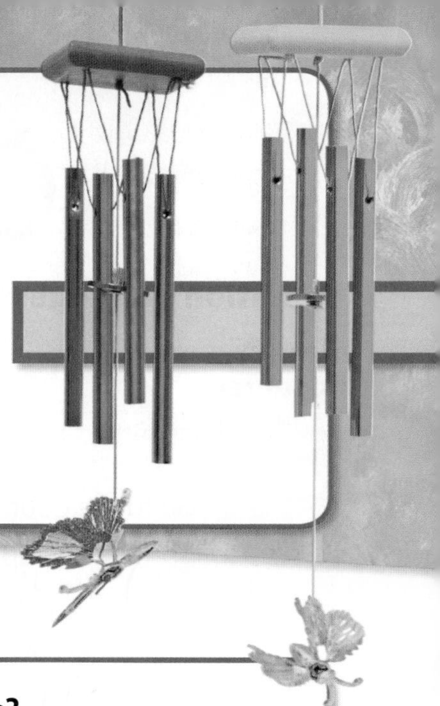

Another Example What is the rule for subtracting integers?

Rule: Subtracting an integer is the same as adding its opposite.

Think of walking a number line to compare subtracting an integer to adding its opposite. Find –3 − 6.

Step 1

Find –3 − 6 by subtracting the integer, 6.

Start at 0. Walk backward 3 steps to –3 and stop.

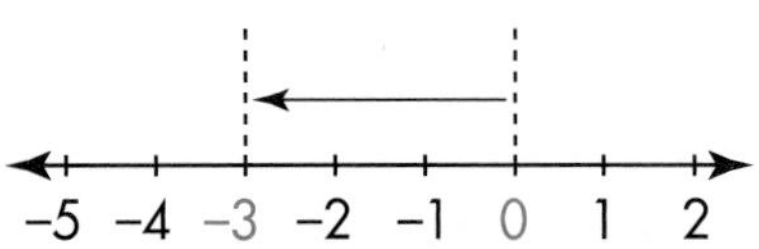

Step 2

Turn around to subtract. Walk forward 6 steps for 6. Stop at –9.

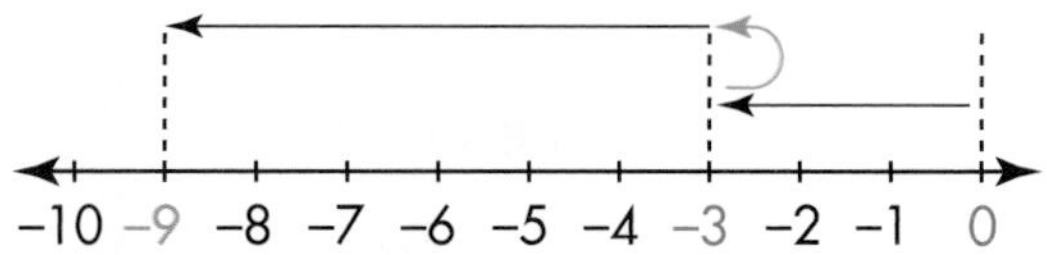

So, –3 − 6 = –9.

Step 1

Find –3 − 6 by adding the opposite of 6, –3 + (–6).

Start at 0. Walk backward 3 steps to –3 and stop.

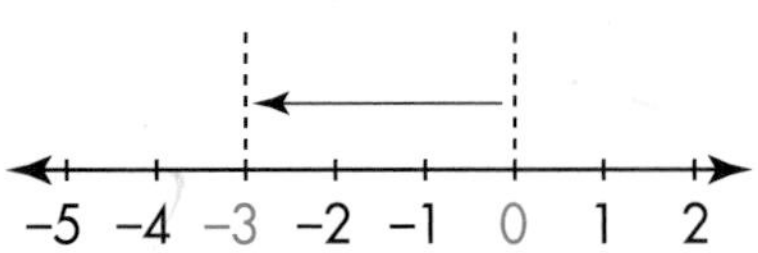

Step 2

Continue to walk backward 6 steps for –6. Stop at –9.

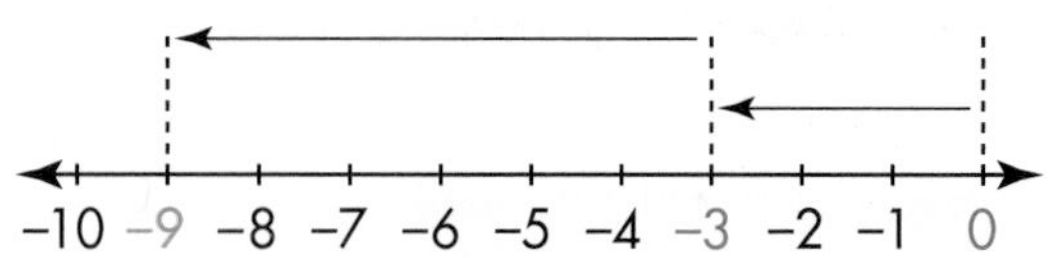

So, –3 + (–6) = –9.

Explain It

1. How does the above example show how to subtract integers?

Step 1

Think about walking a number line to help you subtract integers.

Start at 0, facing the positive integers.

Walk forward 2 steps for 2.

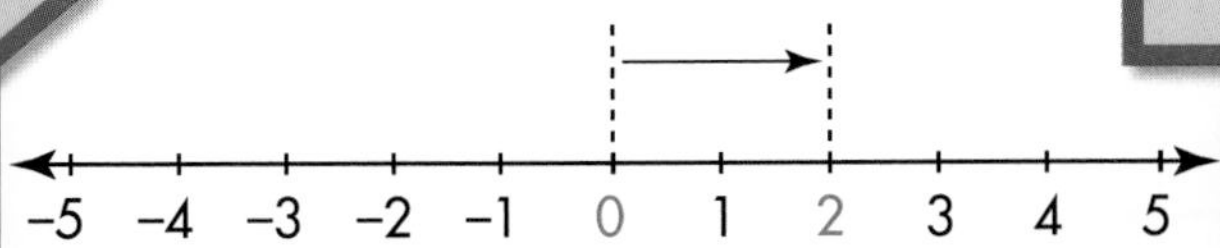

Step 2

The subtraction sign means turn around.

Then walk forward 6 steps for 6. Stop at –4.

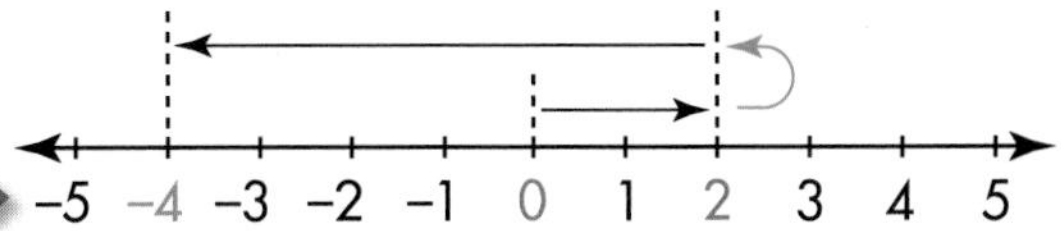

So, 2 – 6 = –4.

Malita still needs to make 4 more wind chimes for her customer.

Guided Practice*

Do you know HOW?

Find each difference.

Tip *Draw a number line or use the rule for subtracting integers.*

1. 5 – 13 **2.** –7 – 4

3. 3 – (–9) **4.** –11 – (–6)

Evaluate each expression for $n = -5$.

5. $n - 6$ **6.** $-15 - n$

7. $n - (-12)$ **8.** $1 - n$

Do you UNDERSTAND?

9. In the example at the top of the page, how can you tell if 2 – 6 is positive or negative before you compute the answer?

10. Explain why 4 – (–3) = 4 + 3 without solving the equation.

11. Can the Commutative Property be used to subtract integers? Explain your answer.

Independent Practice

Leveled Practice In **12** through **15**, use a number line like the one below to find each difference.

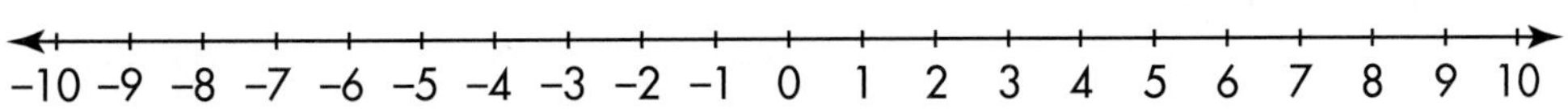

12. 3 – 4 **13.** –7 – 2 **14.** 5 – (–1) **15.** 5 – 10

In **16** through **25**, use a number line or the rule for subtracting integers to find each difference.

16. –6 – (–8) **17.** –6 – (–4) **18.** –11 – 4 **19.** 24 – (–7) **20.** |–3| – |3|

21. –39 – (–39) **22.** 14 – |–20| **23.** –7 – (–9) **24.** –9 – (–6) **25.** –4 – (–7)

**For another example, see Set D on page 257.*

Independent Practice

In **26** through **33**, evaluate each expression for $t = -7$.

26. $41 - t$ **27.** $18 - t - (-11)$ **28.** $t - (-25)$ **29.** $|t| - (-39) - 4$

30. $17 - |-29| - t$ **31.** $-10 - t$ **32.** $t - (-4)$ **33.** $9 - t - |-5|$

Problem Solving

34. Writing to Explain Jeremy said that $5 - (-4)$ is the same as $5 + (-4)$. Is he correct? Explain why or why not.

35. Algebra The temperature was 3°C when Maria went to bed. The temperature fell 7°C during the night. Find the temperature when Maria woke up by evaluating $3 - d$ for $d = 7$.

36. Alfonso was in the elevator of a 45-story building. He went up 24 floors and then went down 30 floors. Which expression shows the difference in number of floors from where he started?

A $24 - 30$

B $24 - (-30)$

C $45 - 30$

D $45 - (-30)$

37. Cherise plans to build a square fence with sides of 15 feet. If she puts up 10 feet of fencing each day, how many days will it take her to complete the fence?

A 3 days

B 6 days

C 10 days

D 15 days

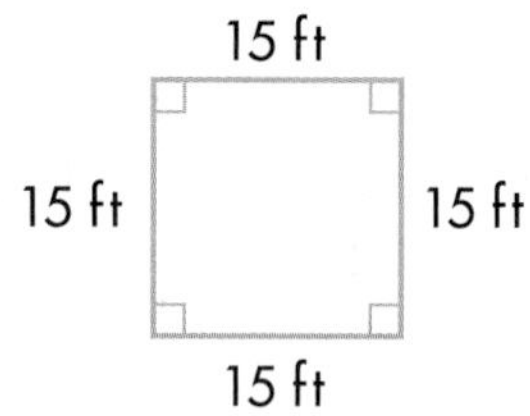

Use the table below to answer **38** and **39**.

Tip *Because distance is always positive, think of distances below sea level as absolute values.*

38. How much deeper is the Atlantic Ocean than the Arctic Ocean? Find the difference between the average depths of the Arctic Ocean and the Atlantic Ocean.

Data

Average Depth of Oceans (compared to sea level)	
Atlantic	12,900 feet below
Pacific	14,000 feet below
Arctic	4,300 feet below
Indian	12,800 feet below

39. A scuba diver is diving in the Pacific Ocean. How far is the diver from the average depth of the ocean floor?

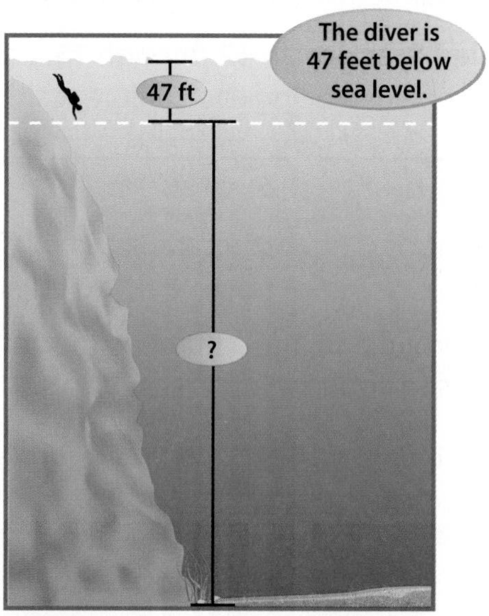

Mixed Problem Solving

Use the diagram to answer **1** through **3**.

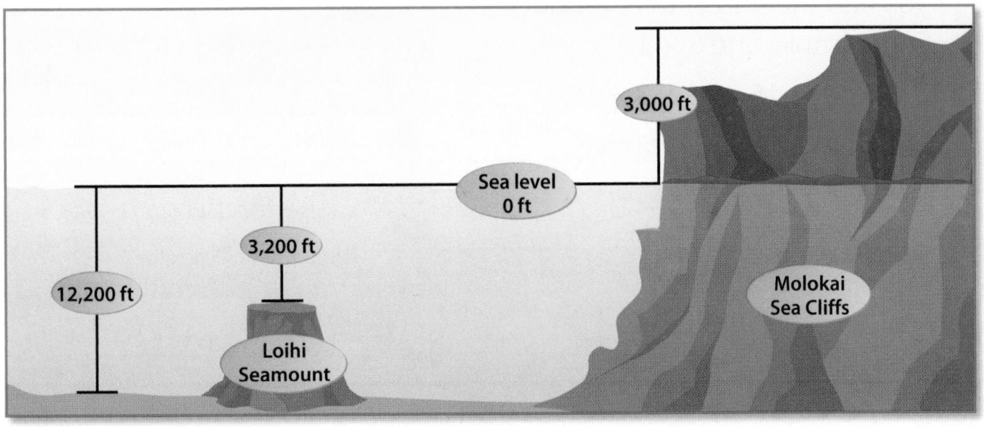

1. What is the difference in elevation between the top of the Molokai Sea Cliffs and the top of the Loihi Seamount?

2. The Loihi Seamount is a volcano located near Hawaii under the surface of the sea. About how tall is the Loihi Seamount?

3. What is the difference in elevation from the top of the Molokai Sea Cliffs to the bottom of the ocean near the Loihi Seamount?

Use the diagram and the diagram above to answer **4** through **7**.

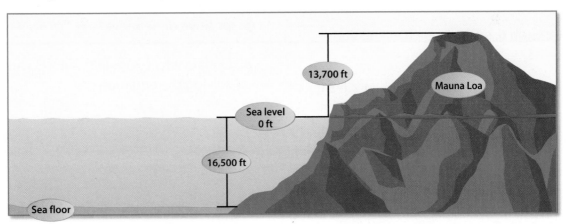

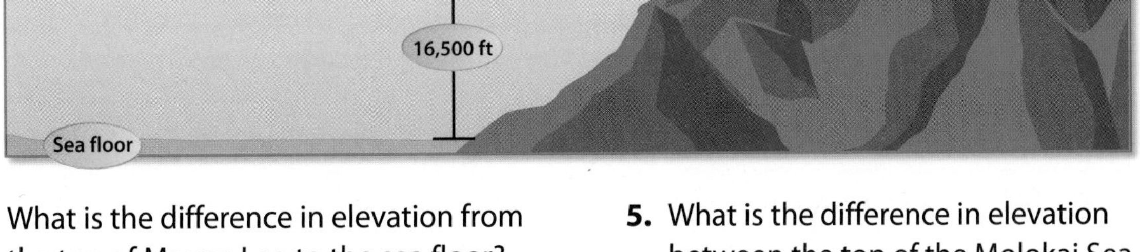

4. What is the difference in elevation from the top of Mauna Loa to the sea floor?

5. What is the difference in elevation between the top of the Molokai Sea Cliffs and the top of Mauna Loa?

6. Mauna Loa depresses the sea floor, resulting in 26,400 more feet added to its height. What is the total height of Mauna Loa?

7. What is the difference in elevation between the top of Mauna Loa and the top of the Loihi Seamount?

Lesson

10-6

Understand It!
When multiplying integers, you can compare the signs of the factors to determine the sign of the product.

Multiplying Integers

How can you identify the sign of the product of two integers?

When multiplying integers, the signs of the factors help you find the sign of their product.
For example, find 5×3.

$5 + 5 + 5 = 15$, so $5 \times 3 = 15$.

The product of two positive integers is positive.

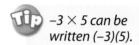

Signs of Factors and Products

First Factor		Second Factor		Product
Positive	×	Positive	=	Positive
Positive	×	Negative	=	Negative
Negative	×	Positive	=	Negative
Negative	×	Negative	=	Positive

Rules for Multiplying Integers

The product of two integers with the same sign is positive.

The product of two integers with different signs is negative.

Tip *-3×5 can be written $(-3)(5)$.*

Guided Practice*

Do you know HOW?

In **1** through **3**, find each product.

1. $(3)(-8)$ **2.** $(-9)(-6)$ **3.** $4 \times (-2)$

In **4** through **6**, evaluate each expression for $n = -3$.

4. $5n$ **5.** $-14n$ **6.** $n \times |-31|$

Do you UNDERSTAND?

7. Using the Rules for Multiplying Integers, is the product of two positive integers and a negative integer positive or negative?

8. Explain why $(-4) \times (-3) = 4 \times 3$ without solving the equation.

Independent Practice

In **9** through **18**, find the product.

9. $3 \times (-7)$ **10.** $(-8)(6)$ **11.** -9×4 **12.** $15 \times (-8)$ **13.** $(-14)^2$

14. $-1 \times (-27)$ **15.** 4×24 **16.** $(7)(-18)$ **17.** $-5 \times (11)$ **18.** $17 \times (-3)$

In **19** through **28**, use order of operations to evaluate each expression for $a = -2$.

19. $a + 7$ **20.** $a - 6$ **21.** $-5a + (3)(-7)$ **22.** $-2a + 4$ **23.** $-8a$

24. $21 + (-a) + 3$ **25.** $17a$ **26.** $a + 27$ **27.** $a - 14$ **28.** $6a$

 *For another example, see Set E on page 258.

Find -3×5 and $5 \times (-3)$.

$-3 \times 5 = (-3) + (-3) + (-3) + (-3) + (-3)$

So, $-3 \times 5 = -15$.

Using the Commutative Property of Multiplication, $5 \times (-3) = -15$, too.

The product of a positive integer and a negative integer is negative.

Find $-5 \times (-3)$.

The products in the table increase by 5.

Continuing the pattern results in 5, 10, 15.

So, $-5 \times (-3) = 15$.

The product of two negative integers is positive.

$-5 \times 3 = -15$
$-5 \times 2 = -10$
$-5 \times 1 = -5$
$-5 \times 0 = 0$
$-5 \times -1 =$ ☐
$-5 \times -2 =$ ☐
$-5 \times -3 =$ ☐

Problem Solving

29. **Algebra** The temperature is decreasing 3°F every hour. Which expression shows the change in temperature for h hours?

A $3h$ **B** $3 + h$ **C** $(-3)h$ **D** $h - 3$

30. **Number Sense** Decide whether each of the following is negative or positive:

a the product of 2 negative integers and 1 positive integer

b the product of 3 negative integers

31. Which shows an expression equal to $8 \times (16 + 7)$?

A $(8 \times 16) + (8 \times 7)$ **C** 8×24

B $8 \times 16 + 7$ **D** $8 \times 7 + 16$

Use the table to answer **32** and **33**.

Data

Stock Name	Change in Value ($ per share)
Red Company	−2
White Company	1
Blue Company	−3

32. Haru has 30 shares of Red Company stock. How has the value of her stock changed? Find $30 \times (-2)$.

33. **Writing to Explain** Kerry owns 15 shares of Red Company stock and 10 shares of Blue Company stock. Explain which of Kerry's stock values changed more.

For **34** and **35**, put numbers in order from least to greatest.

34. 0.324, 0.11, 0.5

35. 1.56, 1.748, 1.009

Lesson

10-7

Understand It!
When dividing integers, you can compare the signs of the divisor and the dividend to determine the sign of the quotient.

Dividing Integers

How can you identify the sign of the quotient of two integers?

You know how to use the relationship between multiplication and division to write division facts.

You can also use the relationship between multiplication and division to identify the sign of the quotient of two integers.

Multiplication FACT	Related Division FACT
$3 \times 4 = 12$	$12 \div 3 = 4$
$4 \times 3 = 12$	$12 \div 4 = 3$

Guided Practice*

Do you know HOW?

In **1** through **4**, find each quotient.

1. $-54 \div (-6)$

2. $-63 \div 7$

3. $35 \div (-5)$

4. $-32 \div (-8)$

In **5** through **8**, evaluate each expression for $n = -24$.

5. $n \div (-3)$

6. $96 \div n$

7. $\frac{-144}{n}$

8. $n \div 12$

Do you UNDERSTAND?

9. How can you tell if the quotient for $-1{,}557 \div 329$ is positive or negative without computing?

10. A hiking club took 2 hours to hike 6 miles down a mountain. Evaluate the expression $-6 \div 2$.

Independent Practice

In **11** through **20**, find each quotient.

Tip *Zero does not have a sign.*

11. $21 \div (-7)$

12. $-105 \div (-5)$

13. $0 \div (-12)$

14. $56 \div (-8)$

15. $14 \div (-14)$

16. $-52 \div (-26)$

17. $144 \div 24$

18. $-121 \div 11$

19. $120 \div (-1)$

20. $150 \div (-15)$

In **21** through **28**, use order of operations to evaluate each expression for $a = -6$.

21. $a \div 2$

22. $-48 \div a$

23. $126 \div a$

24. $25 + (a \div 3)$

25. $0 \div (3a + 27)$

26. $36 \div a + 4$

27. $a^2 \div 6$

28. $(2a - 3) \div 5$

*For another example, see Set F on page 258.

Look for rules for dividing integers in the examples below.

You Know	Related Division Fact	Sign of Quotient
$5 \times 3 = 15$	$15 \div 5 = 3$	+
$-5 \times 3 = -15$	$-15 \div (-5) = 3$	+
$5 \times (-3) = -15$	$-15 \div 5 = -3$	−
$-5 \times (-3) = 15$	$15 \div (-5) = -3$	−

The **rules for dividing integers** are similar to the rules for multiplying:

- The quotient of two integers with the same sign is positive.
- The quotient of two integers with different signs is negative.

Problem Solving

29. Oleg and Nat went scuba diving and dove to 45 feet below the surface. There are 3 feet in a yard. Evaluate $-45 \div 3$ to find how many yards they dove.

30. The coldest temperature ever recorded in Antarctica was −129°F. The warmest recorded temperature was 59°F. How much warmer is the warmest temperature than the coldest?

31. Reasonableness Mrs. Ortiz is planning a turkey dinner for 20 people. She needs to decide how big a turkey to buy. Each person will eat about 0.62 pounds. Should she buy a 10-, 15-, or 20-pound turkey? Explain.

32. Kaden tracked the weather in Anchorage, Alaska, for a week in January.

Data

Day	Lowest Temperature
Monday	−15°F
Tuesday	−8°F
Wednesday	−13°F
Thursday	−13°F
Friday	−14°F
Saturday	−10°F
Sunday	−11°F

a What was the average lowest temperature for the week?

b What was the warmest temperature?

33. Writing to Explain Mia solved the problem below. Is Mia's work correct? If not, explain your answer.
$(-9 \div -3) + (-3) = -6$

34. Number Sense Compute 15×12 mentally by finding the product of twice the first factor and half the second factor.

35. Algebra The water level of a lake dropped 15 inches over a period of 5 weeks. At what rate did the water level change per week? Evaluate $-15 \div 5$.

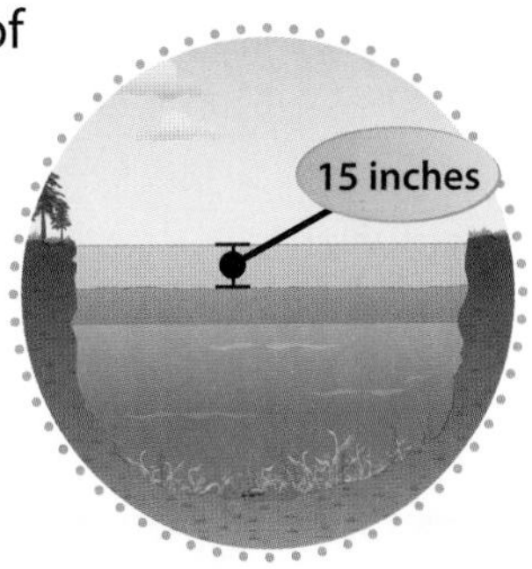

Lesson

10-8

Understand It!
You can solve equations with integers by using the same methods as for solving equations with whole numbers or decimals.

Solving Equations with Integers

How can you solve equations using inverse operations and properties of equality?

The low temperature on Tuesday is 9°C higher than the low temperature on Monday. Tuesday's low temperature is shown on the thermometer.

What was Monday's low temperature?

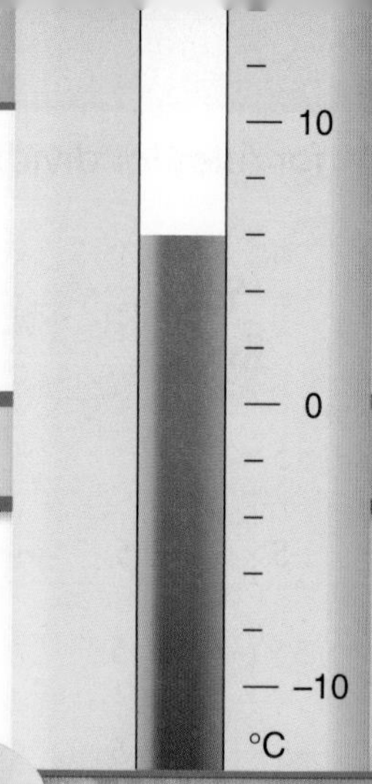

10
0
–10
°C
Tuesday's low temperature was 6°C.

Other Examples

Subtraction Equation

Solve: $n - 11 = -5$

Adding 11 to both sides undoes the subtraction.

$$n - 11 + 11 = -5 + 11$$

$$n = 6$$

Check: $n - 11 = -5$

$6 - 11 = -5$

It checks. $-5 = -5$

Multiplication Equation

Solve: $4x = -24$

Dividing both sides by 4 undoes the multiplication.

$$4x \div 4 = -24 \div 4$$

$$x = -6$$

Check: $4x = -24$

$4(-6) = -24$

It checks. $-24 = -24$

Division Equation

Solve: $r \div 5 = -7$

Multiplying both sides by 5 undoes the division.

$$r \div 5 \times 5 = -7 \times 5$$

$$r = -35$$

Check: $r \div 5 = -7$

$-35 \div 5 = -7$

It checks. $-7 = -7$

Explain It

1. In each of the examples above, what steps did you follow to check your solution?

2. Which property of equality is used to solve the division equation?

Let M = Monday's low temperature.

Solve the equation:

$$M + 9 = 6$$
$$M + 9 - 9 = 6 - 9$$
$$M = -3$$

← Subtract 9 from both sides of the equation.

Subtracting 9 from both sides of the equation undoes the addition and keeps the equation balanced.

Check your answer by substituting it for the variable.

$$M + 9 = 6$$
$$-3 + 9 = 6$$
$$6 = 6$$

It checks. The low temperature on Monday was –3°C.

Guided Practice*

Do you know HOW?

Complete, solve, and check each of these equations.

1. $a - 12 = -37$
$a - 12 + 12 = -37 + 12$
$a = \square$

2. $-6b = -36$
$-6b \div (-6) = -36 \div (-6)$
$b = \square$

3. $m \div 7 = -4$

4. $t + 59 = 3$

Do you UNDERSTAND?

5. In the example above, why was an inverse operation used to solve the equation?

6. Each day of work, Kevin moved 25 pounds of rocks from a large pile. When he was done, the rock pile weighed 150 pounds less. Use the equation $-25d = -150$ to find how many days Kevin worked.

Independent Practice

Leveled Practice In **7** through **9**, complete and check each solution to the equations.

7. $d + 4 = 16$
$d + 4 - \square = 16 - 4$
$d = \square$

8. $p - 5 = 15$
$p - 5 + \square = 15 + 5$
$p = \square$

9. $3g = 18$
$3g \div \square = 18 \div 3$
$g = \square$

In **10** through **21**, solve the equation.

10. $f \div 7 = 7$

11. $r + 9 = -15$

12. $b \div 4 = -9$

13. $6w = -72$

14. $v - (-11) = -27$

15. $-17g = 68$

16. $E + (-34) = -30$

17. $H \div 25 = -6$

18. $k - 17 = 14$

19. $7d = -105$

20. $M \div 21 = 0$

21. $360 \div q = 90$

*For another example, see Set G on page 258.

Problem Solving

In **22** through **25**, specify the base and the exponent; then complete the equation.

22. $3^4 = $ **23.** $6^3 = $ **24.** $12^2 = $ **25.** $1^2 = $

26. Writing to Explain Describe how you would solve $p \div 12 = -3$.

27. Put these numbers in order from least to greatest.

−2, 6, −12, 12, 0, −5

28. Use a variable and the numbers 6 and −72 to write an equation that involves multiplication. Then use inverse operations to solve it.

29. Joanna collected a total of 60 aluminum cans in 2 days for a Science Club fund-raising project. She collected $\frac{8}{15}$ of the total cans on the second day. How many cans did she collect on the first day?

30. In a football game, a team gained 8 yards in the first play. In the second play, the team lost 5 yards. Write an equation to show how to find *n*, the number of yards the team gained overall in these two plays.

31. Terry runs a lemonade stand. One week he spent $12 on ingredients and made a profit of $9. Solve $-12 + p = 9$ to find how many dollars worth of lemonade he sold.

32. Estimation The Cooper River Bridge is the longest suspension bridge for cars in the United States. Its main span stretches 1,546 feet and the total length of the bridge is about 13,200 feet. About how many times longer is the bridge than the length of its main span?

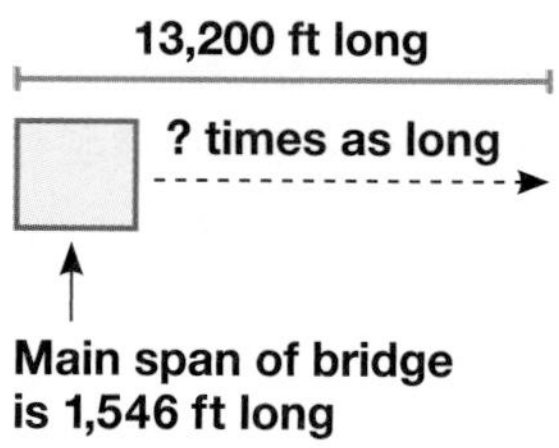

33. Kiera separated some nickels into 12 stacks. Each stack has 8 nickels. Which inverse operation could you use to solve the equation $n \div 12 = 8$ for *n*, the total number of nickels?

A Multiply each side of the equation by 8.

B Subtract 12 from each side of the equation.

C Multiply each side of the equation by 12.

D Divide each side of the equation by 12.

34. Copy the number line and label a point for the value given.

$A\ (4), B\ (-2), C\ |-7|, D\ (-5 + -4)$

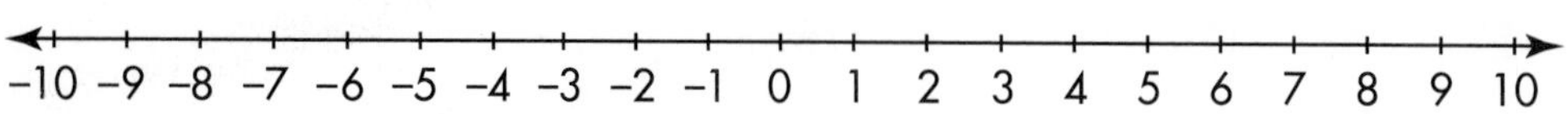

Algebra Connections

Expressions with Integers

Remember that mathematicians use a set of rules called the order of operations:

1. Compute inside parentheses first.
2. Evaluate terms with exponents.
3. Multiply and divide from left to right.
4. Add and subtract from left to right.

Example: Evaluate $5^2 \times (-2 + 3) + 1$.

$5^2 \times (1) + 1$ ← Compute inside the parentheses first.

$25 \times 1 + 1$ ← Simplify the exponent.

$25 + 1$ ← Next, multiply.

26 ← Then add.

Evaluate each expression.

1. $2^3 + 4 \times (-5)$ **2.** $(-9 + 5) \div 2$ **3.** $(-3)^2 - 4 + (-4)$ **4.** $(-6 - 4) \times 5^2$

For **5** through **8**, evaluate each expression for $a = -3$.

5. $a + 5 \times 2$ **6.** $-2 \times a^2$ **7.** $(9 \div a) \times 5$ **8.** $(a + 11) \times 5$

Use the table for **9** and **10**.

Data

Movie-rental Stores	
Store A	2 DVDs for $3 each
Store B	3 DVDs for $2 each

9. **Writing to Explain** Two movie-rental stores have different prices. Store A offers 2 DVDs for $3 each. Store B offers 3 DVDs for $2 each. Which price is better? Explain.

10. Rodney wants to rent 4 DVDs from Store A. Use the Distributive Property of Multiplication to write an equation that shows how much it will cost.

11. The steps Lynne took to evaluate the expression $4y - 8 \div 2$ when $y = -3$ are shown at the right.

$4y - 8 \div 2$ when $y = -3$

$4 \times (-3) = -12$

$-12 - 8 = -20$

$-20 \div 2 = -10$

What should Lynne have done differently in order to evaluate the expression?

A subtracted 8 from $(-12 \div 2)$

B subtracted $(8 \div 2)$ from -12

C divided $(-12 - 8)$ by (-12×2)

D divided $(-12 - 8)$ by $(-12 - 8)$

Lesson
10-9

Understand It!
The coordinate plane can be thought of as two intersecting number lines.

Graphing Points on a Coordinate Plane

Hands-On
grid paper

How can you graph a point on a coordinate plane?

A coordinate plane is a grid containing two number lines that intersect in a right angle at zero. The number lines, called the *x*- and *y*-axes, divide the plane into four quadrants.

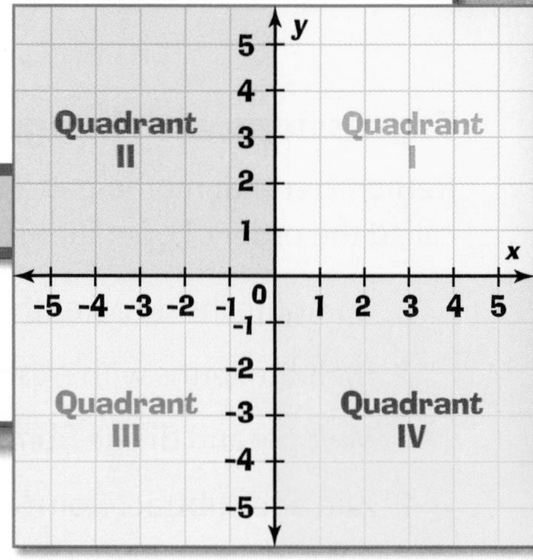

Another Example **How can you use a coordinate plane to locate points on a map?**

A grid map of Washington, D.C., is shown at the right. Give the coordinates of the Lincoln Memorial.

- Find the Lincoln Memorial on the map.
- Follow the grid line directly to the *x*-axis to find the *x*-coordinate, –5.
- Follow the grid line directly to the *y*-axis to find the *y*-coordinate, –3.

The coordinates of the Lincoln Memorial are (–5, –3).

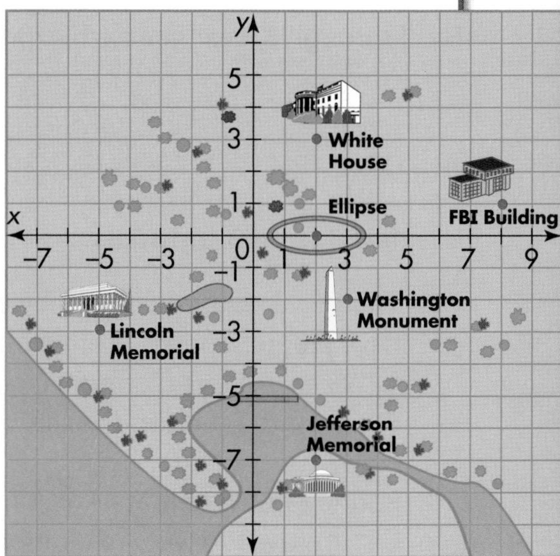

Explain It

1. If a point is to the left of the *y*-axis, what do you know about its *x*-coordinate?

2. What are the coordinates of the Washington Monument?

Guided Practice*

Do you know HOW?

For **1** through **3**, draw a coordinate plane. Graph and label the points given.

1. *W* (–5, 1) **2.** *X* (4, 3) **3.** *Z* (–2, 0)

Do you UNDERSTAND?

4. In which quadrant does a point lie if its *x*- and *y*- coordinates are negative?

5. Do (4, 5) and (5, 4) locate the same point? Explain.

*For another example, see Set H on page 259.

An ordered pair (*x*, *y*) of numbers gives the coordinates that locate a point relative to each axis. Graph the points *Q* (2, –3), *R* (–1, 1), and *S* (0, 2) on a coordinate plane.

To graph any point *P* with coordinates (*x*, *y*):

- Start at the origin, (0, 0).
- Use the *x*-coordinate to move right (if positive) or left (if negative) along the *x*-axis.
- Then use the *y*-coordinate of the point to move up (if positive) or down (if negative) following the *y*-axis.
- Draw a point on the coordinate grid and label the point.

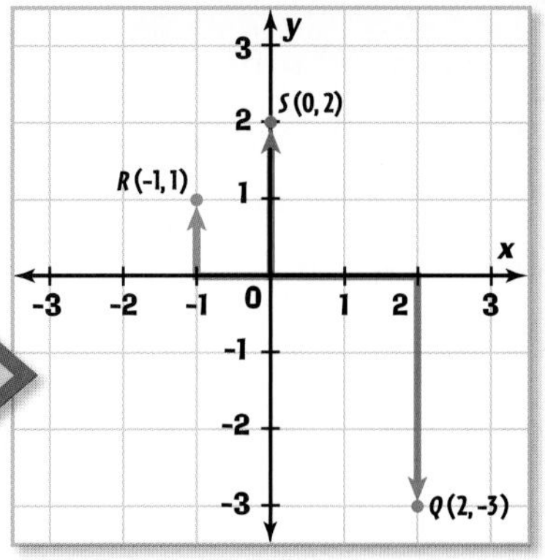

Independent Practice

For **6** through **13**, draw a coordinate grid and label the *x*- and *y*-axes between –10 and 10. Graph and label these points on the graph.

6. *A* (1, –1) **7.** *B* (5, 7) **8.** *C* (–9, 2) **9.** *D* (5, –2)

10. *E* (–4, –8) **11.** *F* (0, 3) **12.** *G* (–5, 0) **13.** *H* (–4, –10)

For **14** through **21**, give the ordered pair of each point.

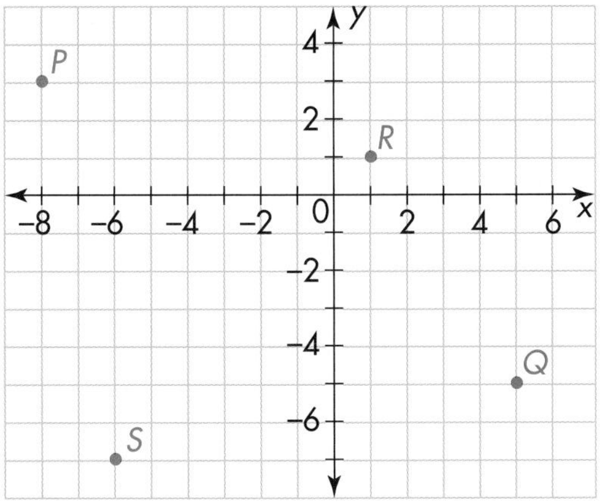

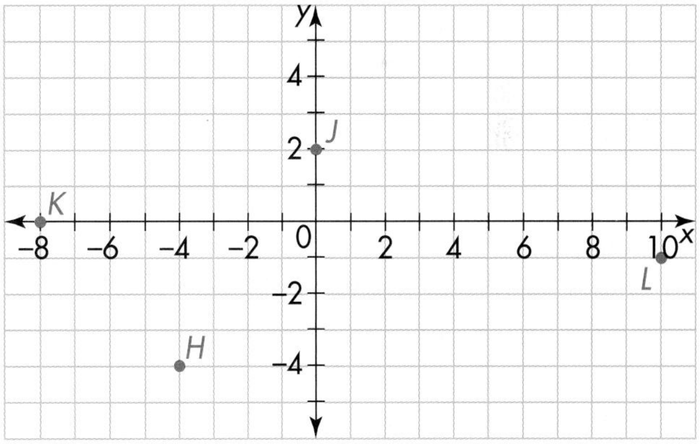

14. *P* **15.** *Q* **18.** *H* **19.** *J*

16. *R* **17.** *S* **20.** *K* **21.** *L*

For **22** and **23**, draw a coordinate plane and graph the ordered pairs. Connect the points in order and describe the figure you drew.

22. (–5, 2), (–10, 2), (–10, –3), (–5, –3) **23.** (8, –2), (10, –2), (10, 4), (8, 4)

DIGITAL Animated Glossary, eTools **www.pearsonsuccessnet.com**

Problem Solving

For **24** through **27**, use the map of the town of Descartes at the right. The Market Square is at the origin.

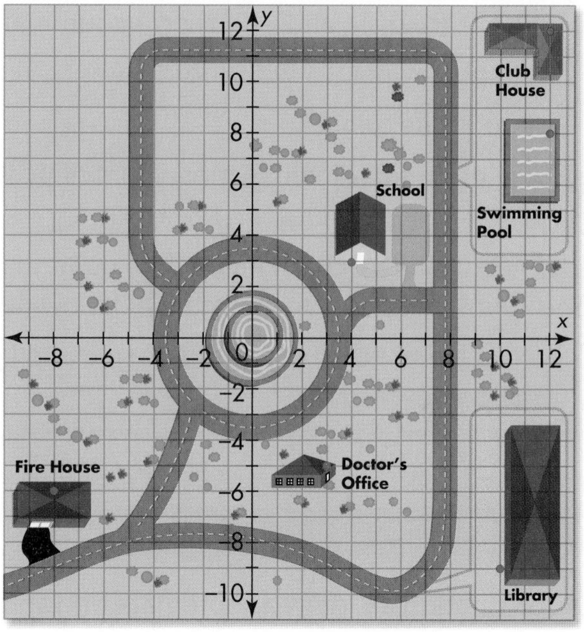

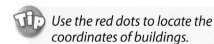

Tip *Use the red dots to locate the coordinates of buildings.*

24. Give the coordinates of the Library.

25. What building is located in Quadrant III?

26. What building is located at (12, 12)?

27. **Writing to Explain** If you were at the Market Square and you wanted to get to the Doctor's Office, according to the map, how would you get there?

Draw a coordinate grid like the one at the right, with the *x*- and *y*-axes between –6 and 6. Use the grid for **28** through **30**.

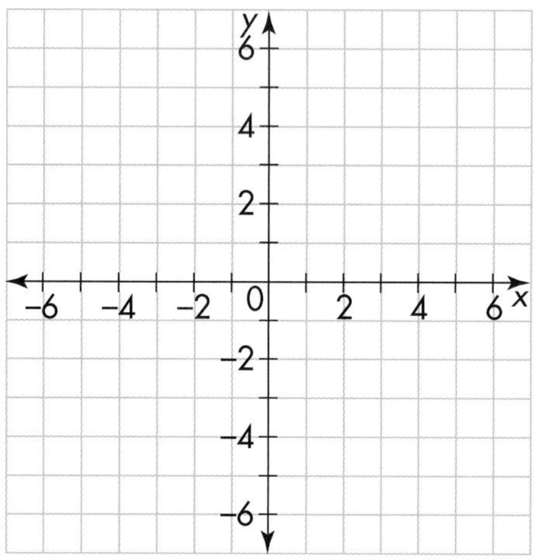

28. Graph and label points *A*(–2, 2), *B*(2, 2), *C*(2, –2), and *D*(–2, –2). Connect the points to form figure *ABCD*. What figure is formed?

29. Move point *B* two units up and label the new point *M*. Move point *C* two units up and label the new point *N*. What are the coordinates of point *M* and *N*? What figure does *AMND* form?

30. Multiply the *x*-coordinates of points *A* and *B* by 3 and graph the new points. Label them *R* and *S*. What are the coordinates of points *R* and *S*? What figure does *RSCD* form?

31. Which ordered pair locates point *P* on the coordinate plane on the right?

A (–4, –4) **C** (4, 3)

B (–4, 4) **D** (–3, 4)

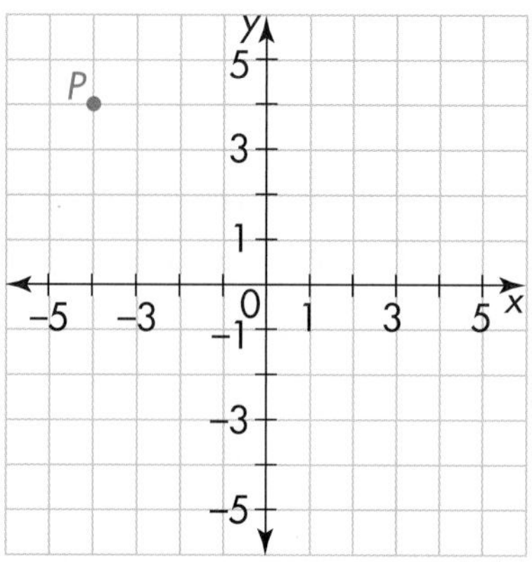

Mixed Problem Solving

Math and Science

Some astronomers use a star map to help them find constellations in the sky. You can use a coordinate grid over the star map to help you locate stars. The section of the sky map at the right shows the Big Dipper. The main stars in the constellation are named with letters from the alphabet.

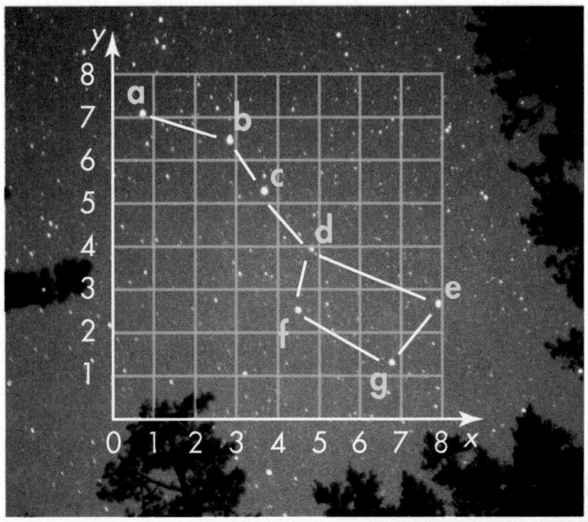

For **1** through **6**, match letters on the map to the coordinate pair.

1. What star is located nearest (3, 6)?
2. What are the nearest coordinates of *c*?
3. What are the nearest coordinates of *e*?
4. What star is located nearest (1, 7)?
5. What star is located nearest (5, 4)?
6. **Writing to Explain** Why would using a coordinate grid help you look at the sky?

Tom stood in his backyard to draw his own sky map. Draw a coordinate grid like the one at the right and mark the positive *y*-axis as North. Map the following stars, planets, and objects using the coordinate grid.

7. Sirius (–7, –6)
8. Betelgeuse (4, 4)
9. North Star (0, 3)
10. Orion (3, 3)
11. Moon (8, –4)
12. Vega (6, 6)

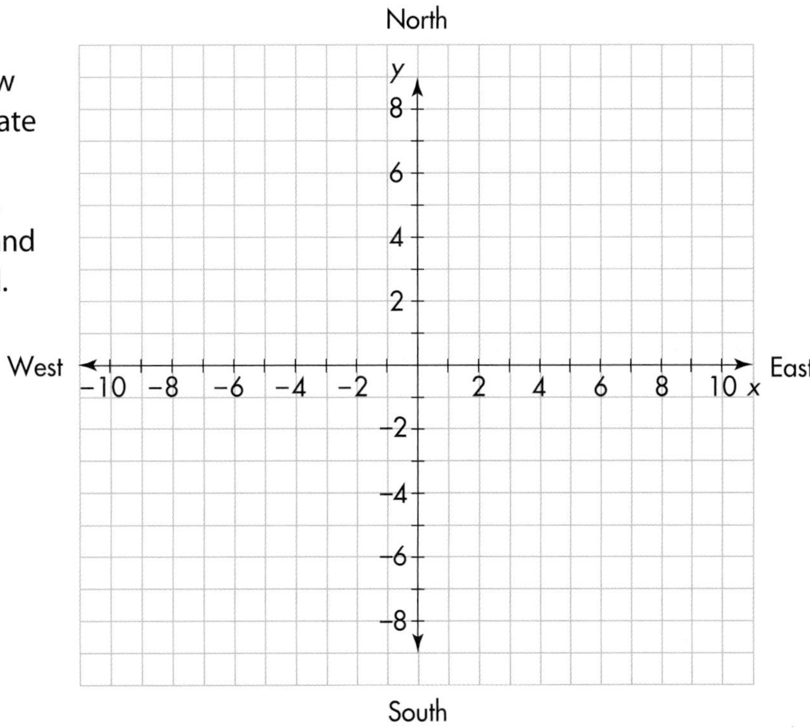

Lesson
10-10

Understand It!
Some problems having a series of steps and a known end result can be solved by starting with the end result and then reversing the steps.

Problem Solving

Work Backward

Sanjay and Nathaniel are riding the elevator in their building. They rode up 10 floors, down 16, and up 25. If the elevator ended up on the floor shown in the picture, on which floor did they start?

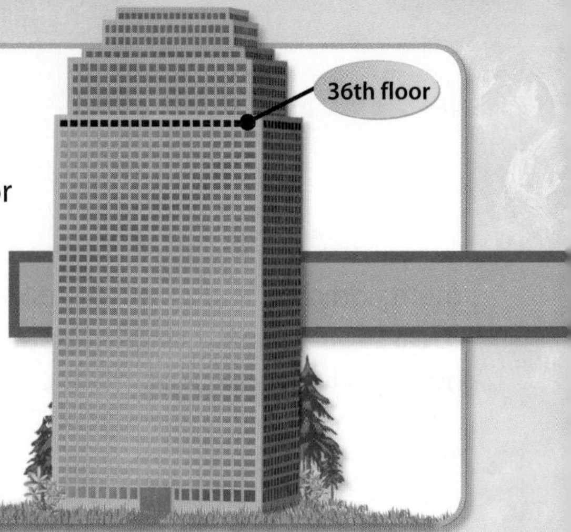

Another Example When do you work backward to solve a problem?

One summer night, the temperature dropped 17°F between 8 P.M. and 6 A.M. By 10 A.M., the temperature had increased 6°F. By noon, the temperature increased another 12°F from 10 A.M. to noon, making the temperature 92°F. What was the temperature at 8 P.M. the previous night?

Read and Understand

What do I know? The temperature changed after 8 P.M., and the temperature at noon the next day was 92°F.

What am I being asked to find? The temperature at 8 P.M. the previous night

Plan and Solve

Think: Work backward when there is an end result after a series of steps, and you are asked to find the information in the first step.

8 P.M.		6 A.M.		10 A.M.		Noon
☐°F	→ −17°	☐°F	→ +6°	☐°F	→ +12°	92°F

Work backward from the temperature at noon.

91°F	← +17°	74°F	← −6°	80°F	← −12°	92°F

The temperature was 91°F.

Explain It

1. Why can you work backward to solve the problem?
2. What can you do to check your answer?

Read and Understand

What do I know?

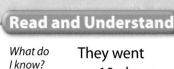

They went up 10, down 16, up 25, and ended on the 36th floor.

What am I being asked to find?

On which floor did they start riding the elevator?

Plan and Solve

If you know the ending position and each change made, then you can use the inverse of each change to work backward.

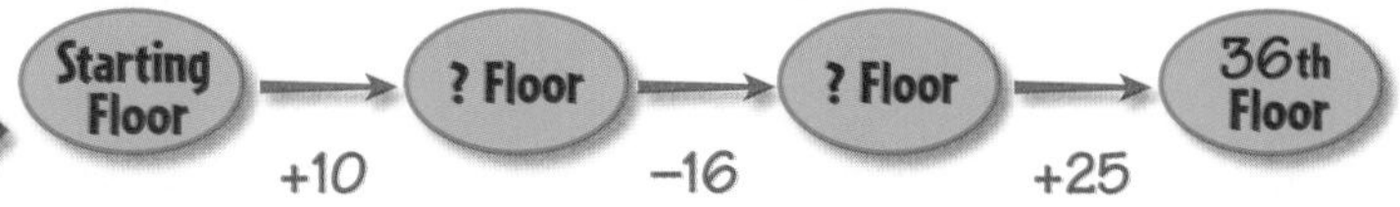

Work backward from the 36th floor.

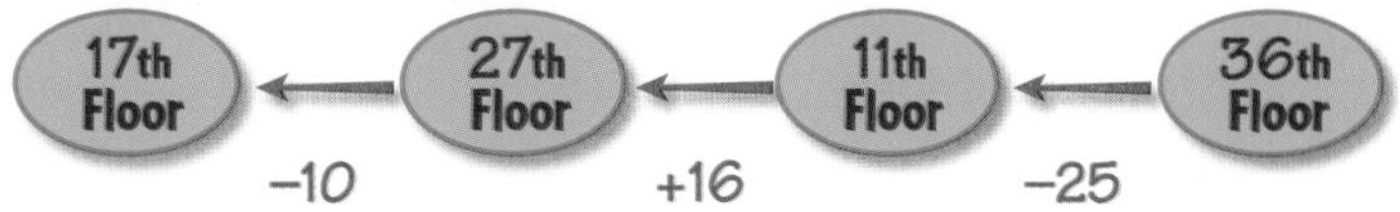

They started on the 17th floor.

Guided Practice*

Do you know HOW?

Solve. Check your answer.

1. Gustavo chose a number, added 3 to it, divided the sum by 2, and subtracted 1. The result was 4. What was Gustavo's number?

Do you UNDERSTAND?

2. In the elevator problem, what operation undoes adding 25?
3. **Write a Problem** Write a word problem that can be solved by working backward.

Independent Practice

Solve. Check your answers.

4. Jessie's mom had a bowl of apples. Liz took three to a picnic, Jessie packed one in her lunch, and Jessie's dad ate one. There were only three left. How many apples were in the bowl to start with?
5. Amy spent $9 at the movies, earned $18 for babysitting, and bought a book for $7. She had $13 left. How much money did she have at the start?
6. Arnie rode 14 miles on his bike. He started from his house and rode to Nick's house. They rode 4.6 miles to the park, 2.4 miles to the store, and 3 miles back to Arnie's house. What is the distance from Arnie's house to Nick's house?

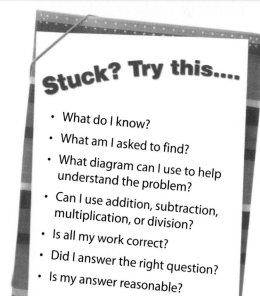

Stuck? Try this....

- What do I know?
- What am I asked to find?
- What diagram can I use to help understand the problem?
- Can I use addition, subtraction, multiplication, or division?
- Is all my work correct?
- Did I answer the right question?
- Is my answer reasonable?

*For another example, see Set I on page 259.

Problem Solving

7. Scott, Adrian, and Juan are jumping at the skate park. Scott jumped twice as high as Juan. Adrian jumped 4 ft, which was 2 ft less than Scott. How high did Juan jump?

8. Tyler paid \$6.93 for 5.5 pounds of grapes for the class picnic. Find the price per pound of grapes. Write an equation that describes the situation and then solve it.

9. **Algebra** Solve each equation to find the missing integer.

   A $-7 + \square = 2$

   B $3 - \square = -4$

   C $-6 \times \square = 36$

   D $\frac{\square}{-2} = -4$

10. Allie is saving for new computer equipment that costs \$110. She started saving in week one. She saved \$26 in week two, spent \$14 in week three, and saved \$47 in week four. She now has \$91. How much did she save during week one?

11. **Geometry** The area of a rectangle is 18 square ft. If one side is 3 ft long, what are the lengths of each side?

12. **Strategy Focus** Mike has a rain gauge in his backyard. He empties it every night before he goes to bed. There was rain in the gauge when Mike took his first measurement before breakfast. At 10 A.M., Mike measured an increase of 0.3 inch. At lunch, he measured an increase of 0.6 inch. Before dinner, Mike noted an increase of 0.1 inch, and before he emptied it that night there was an increase of 0.4 inch. There was a total of 2.7 inches of rain in the gauge. How much did it rain during the previous night before breakfast?

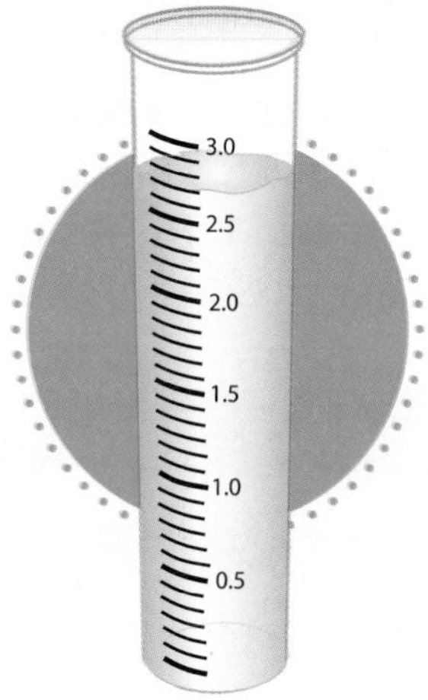

Think About the Process

13. Jordan is thinking of a number. If you triple the number, add 9, and divide by 10, you end up with 3. What order of operations would you do to work backward to find the number?

    A addition, multiplication, subtraction

    B multiplication, subtraction, division

    C division, addition, multiplication

    D multiplication, addition, division

14. For softball training, Ursula runs $\frac{1}{4}$ mile, walks $\frac{1}{8}$ mile, and runs $\frac{1}{2}$ mile. She wants to increase her total distance to a whole mile. What expression would you use to find how much more distance she needs to reach her goal?

    A $\frac{1}{4} + \frac{1}{8} + \frac{1}{2} - 1$

    B $1 - (\frac{1}{4} + \frac{1}{8} + \frac{1}{2})$

    C $1 + \frac{1}{4} + \frac{1}{8} + \frac{1}{2}$

    D $\frac{1}{4} + \frac{1}{8} + (1 - \frac{1}{2})$

Stop and Practice

Skills Review Use <, >, or = to compare.

1. -3 ○ 4
2. -9 ○ -10
3. 5 ○ 6
4. -5 ○ -6

Order the following integers from least to greatest.

5. 3, −3, −9, 5
6. −11, 10, 0, −1
7. 14, −7, 2, −5

Find the sum or difference.

8. $-6 + 2$
9. $3 - 6$
10. $6 + -5$
11. $8 - 2$

Find the product or quotient.

12. $-9 \div 3$
13. 6×-5
14. $-8 \div 2$
15. -7×-3

Solve and check each equation.

16. $e \div 3 = -15$
17. $-6 \times k = -36$
18. $16 + p = -4$
19. $G - 6 = -2$

Error Search Find each solution that is not correct. Write it correctly and explain the error.

20. $8 \times -2 = 16$
21. $5 - 3 = 2$
22. $-15 \div -3 = -5$
23. $-36 + -6 = 42$

Number Sense

Estimating and Reasoning Choose the correct answer.

24. The product of a negative integer and a negative integer is (always/sometimes/never) positive.

25. The sum of a positive integer and a negative integer is (always/sometimes/never) negative.

26. The quotient of a negative integer and a positive integer is (always/sometimes/never) positive.

27. The difference of a negative integer and a negative integer is (always/sometimes/never) negative.

Topic 10

Test

1. Which point on the number line represents –4? (10-1)

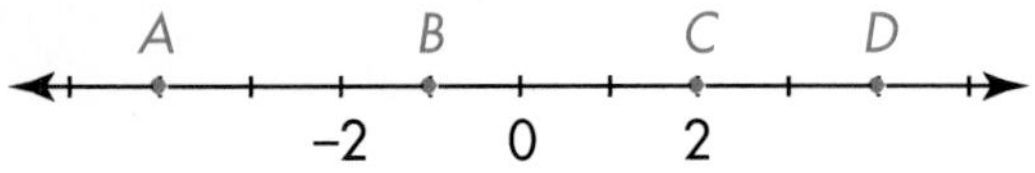

A Point *A*

B Point *B*

C Point *C*

D Point *D*

2. If the temperature outside is 10°F and the wind is blowing at 15 miles per hour, the wind chill index is –7°F. What is the difference between the actual temperature and the wind chill index? (10-5)

A 3°F

B 7°F

C 17°F

D 22°F

3. The table shows the resulting golf scores as compared with par after 6 rounds of golf. What is Emma's average score compared to par for one round? (10-7)

Data

Name	Score
Cassie	–4
Emma	–12
Juanita	6

A 2

B –2

C –6

D –18

4. What is $-3 + 7$? (10-4)

A –10

B –4

C 4

D 10

5. What is $-5n$ when $n = 4$? (10-6)

A –1

B –9

C –15

D –20

6. Which point represents –1.4 on the number line? (10-3)

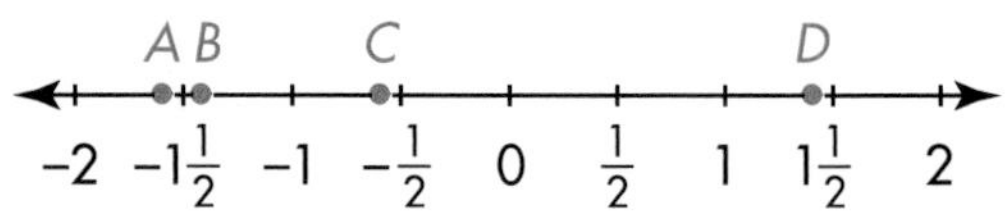

A Point *A*

B Point *B*

C Point *C*

D Point *D*

7. Amelia had some money saved before she started saving $2 each week. After 3 weeks, her total savings were $16. How much money had Amelia saved at the beginning of the 3 weeks? (10-10)

A $2

B $8

C $10

D $14

8. What is the product of $-8(-20)$? (10-6)

A 160

B 28

C –28

D –160

9. At the end of a football game, Emilio had a loss of 3 yards, Carson had a loss of 7 yards and Tracy had a loss of 6 yards. Which of the following comparisons is true? (10-2)

A $-3 > -7$

B $-7 > -6$

C $-3 < -7$

D $-3 < -6$

10. A company had losses over a 4-year period of 16 million dollars. What is the solution to the equation $4x = -16$ where x is the company's average loss each year in millions of dollars? (10-8)

A $x = 4$

B $x = -4$

C $x = -12$

D $x = -64$

11. The grid map shows the location of some places in Amy's town. What are the coordinates of the library? (10-9)

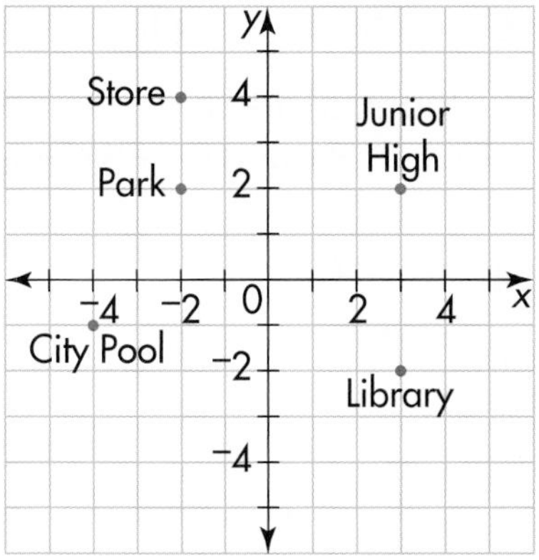

A (−3, 2)

B (−2, 3)

C (3, −2)

D (2, −3)

12. What is $18 \div -6$? (10-7)

A −12

B −3

C 3

D 12

13. The table gives some elevations, compared to sea level, of places in the United States. Which of the following lists the places in order from the one with the least elevation to the one with the greatest? (10-2)

Data

Place	Elevation
Potomac River	1
New Orleans	−8
Lake Champlain	95
Death Valley	−282

A New Orleans, Death Valley, Potomac River, Lake Champlain

B Death Valley, New Orleans, Potomac River, Lake Champlain

C Death Valley, New Orleans, Lake Champlain, Potomac River

D Potomac River, New Orleans, Lake Champlain, Death Valley

14. What is $-16 + a$ when $a = -5$? (10-4)

A 21

B 11

C −11

D −21

Set A, pages 222–225

For each point on the number line, write the integer, its opposite, and its absolute value.

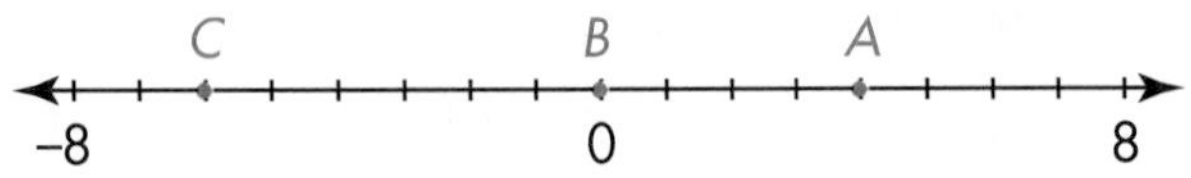

A: 4, –4, 4 *B*: 0, 0, 0 *C*: –6, 6, 6

Compare 4 and –6. Which is less?

–6 is farther to the left on the number line than 4, so –6 is less. $-6 < 4$

Use the number line to help you write 0, 4, and –6 in order from greatest to least.

The order from greatest to least is 4, 0, –6.

Remember that opposites have the same absolute value, which is their distance from zero.

For each point on the number line, write the integer, its opposite, and its absolute value.

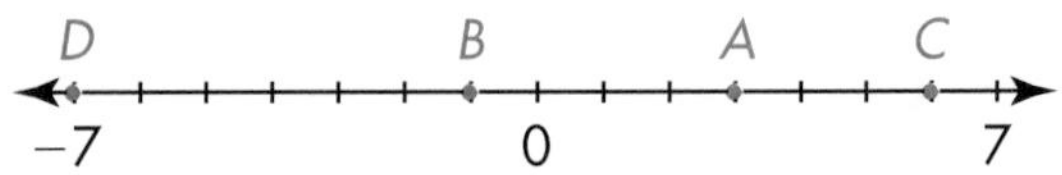

1. *A* **2.** *B* **3.** *C* **4.** *D*

Use $<$, $>$, or $=$ to compare.

5. 7 ◯ –3 **6.** $|-23|$ ◯ 23

7. –50 ◯ –54 **8.** $|-4|$ ◯ 0

Order from greatest to least.

9. –13, 14, 0, 8, –6, –23

Set B, pages 226–228

Rational numbers are numbers that can be written as a quotient $\frac{a}{b}$, where *a* and *b* are integers and *b* does not equal 0.

Order the numbers –0.1, 0.75, and $-\frac{1}{4}$ from least to greatest by graphing them on a number line.

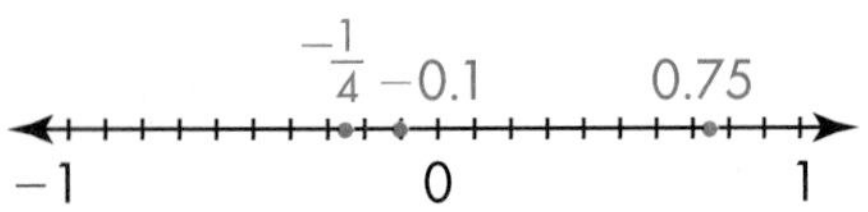

Write the order: $-\frac{1}{4}$, –0.1, 0.75

Compare 0.55 and $\frac{3}{5}$.

Convert $\frac{3}{5}$ to a decimal. $5\overline{)3.0}$ = 0.6

0.6 is to the right of 0.55 on a number line.

So, $0.6 > 0.55$ or $0.55 < 0.6$.

Remember that all positive decimals, mixed numbers, and fractions have opposites that are located to the left of the zero on the number line.

For **1** through **3**, graph each rational number on the same number line.

1. $\frac{3}{4}$ **2.** $-\frac{2}{5}$ **3.** 0.5

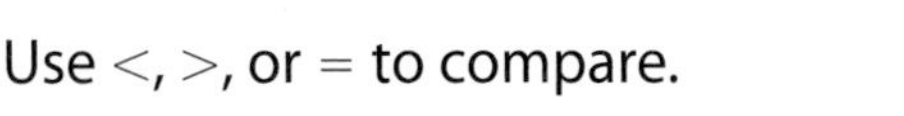

Use $<$, $>$, or $=$ to compare.

4. 0.25 ◯ $\frac{1}{4}$ **5.** $1\frac{5}{8}$ ◯ 1.6

6. 3.65 ◯ $3\frac{3}{4}$ **7.** $-\frac{2}{3}$ ◯ $-\frac{3}{4}$

Set C, pages 230–232

Use the rules for adding integers with different signs to find 4 + (–8).

Step 1 Find the absolute value of the addends. $|4| = 4$ $|-8| = 8$

Step 2 Subtract the lesser absolute value. $8 - 4 = 4$

Step 3 Use the sign of the addend with the greater absolute value. –4

So, the sum is –4.

To add intergers with the same signs, use the steps above, but the sum will always have the same sign as both addends.

Remember that you can think about walking a number line to add integers, walking backward for negative addends and forward for positive addends.

Find each sum.

1. 8 + (–7)
2. –16 + (–2)
3. –12 + 4
4. 9 + 29
5. 1 + (–14)
6. –5 + (–15)
7. 15 + (–32)
8. –11 + (–12)
9. –22 + 35
10. 29 + (–17)
11. –54 + 4
12. –27 + (–5)

Set D, pages 234–236

Find 7 – (–2).

7 + (–(–2)) ← **Subtracting –2 is like adding the opposite of –2.**

7 + 2 ← **The opposite of –2 is 2.**

So, the difference is 9.

Use a number line to find 7 – (–2).

Start at 0, facing the positive integers. Walk forward 7 steps for 7.

Since subtracting –2 is like adding 2, walk forward 2 steps for –2. Stop at 9.

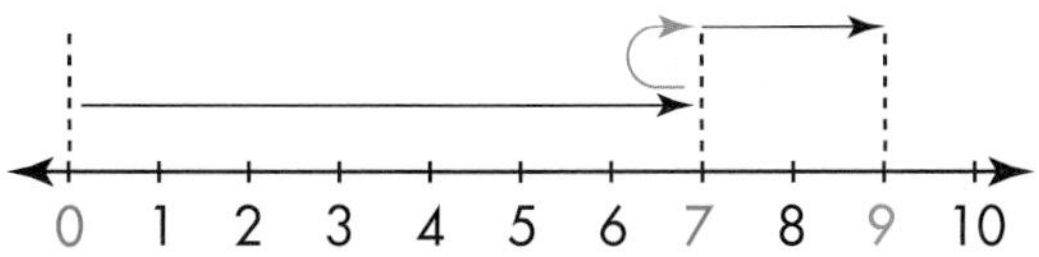

So, 7 – (–2) is 9.

Remember that subtracting an integer is the same as adding its opposite. So the rules for adding integers can also help you subtract integers.

Find each difference.

1. 5 – (–9)
2. –8 – (–6)
3. –11 – (–11)
4. 7 – 18
5. 3 – (–5)
6. 4 – (–13)
7. 7 – 19
8. 5 – (–4)
9. –2 – (–7)
10. 4 – (–4)
11. –15 – 15
12. 50 – 57

Set E, pages 238–239

Find the product $18 \times (-5)$.

Rules for Multiplying Integers

- The product of two integers with the same sign is positive.
- The product of two integers with different signs is negative.

One factor is positive and the other factor is negative, so the product is negative.

$18 \times (-5) = -90$

Remember that the product of two integers with different signs is negative. The product of two integers with the same signs is positive.

Find each product.

1. -12×3 **2.** $-8 \times (-5)$

3. $-4 \times (-41)$ **4.** -18×6

5. $-47 \times (-10)$ **6.** $2 \times (-39)$

7. $-60 \times (-15)$ **8.** $72 \times (-20)$

Set F, pages 240–241

Find the quotient $-51 \div (-17)$.

Use the relationship between multiplication and division to identify the sign of the quotient.

Both of the integers are negative, so the quotient is positive.

$-51 \div (-17) = 3$

Remember that the quotient of two integers with different signs is negative. The quotient of two integers with the same sign is positive.

Find each quotient.

1. $-32 \div 4$ **2.** $-81 \div (-3)$

3. $121 \div -11$ **4.** $-96 \div (12)$

5. $1{,}500 \div -15$ **6.** $320 \div (-16)$

7. $-525 \div 10$ **8.** $-2.5 \div (-5)$

Set G, pages 242–244

Solve the equation $r + (-12) = 5$.

$r + (-12) = 5$

$r - 12 = 5$

$r - 12 + 12 = 5 + 12$

$r = 5 + 12$

$r = 17$

Solve the equation $\frac{a}{-4} = -8$.

$\frac{a}{-4} = -8$

$\frac{a}{-4} \times (-4) = -8 \times (-4)$

$a = 32$

Remember to use the properties of equality when solving equations with integers.

Solve each equation.

1. $x - (-10) = -8$ **2.** $y + 22 = 15$

3. $m \times 7 = -84$ **4.** $n \div (-4) = 15$

5. $a + (-16) = -15$ **6.** $b - 18 = 23$

7. $s \div 17 = 102$ **8.** $t \times (-11) = 132$

9. $\frac{s}{-6} = -7$ **10.** $\frac{p}{-11} = -13$

Set H, pages 246–248

An ordered pair (x, y) of numbers gives the coordinates that locate a point on a coordinate plane.

To graph any point P with coordinates (x, y):

Step 1 Start at the origin, (0, 0).

Step 2 Use the x-coordinate to move right (if positive) or left (if negative) along the x-axis.

Step 3 Then use the y-coordinate of the point to move up (if positive) or down (if negative) following the y-axis.

Step 4 Draw a point on the coordinate grid and label the point.

Remember that the number lines called x- and y-axes divide the coordinate plane into four quadrants.

For **1** through **6**, give the ordered pair for each point.

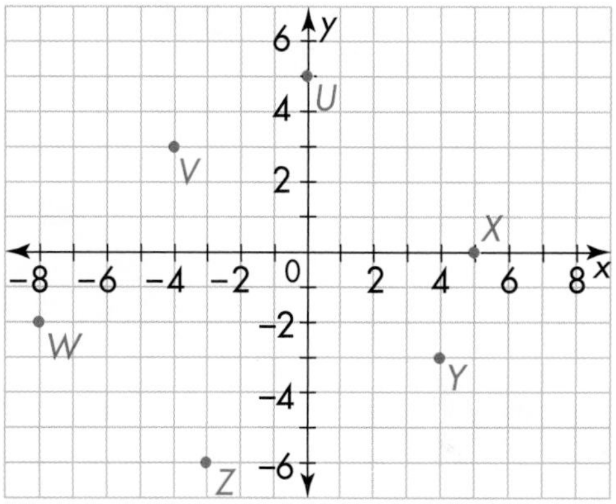

1. U **2.** V

3. W **4.** X

5. Y **6.** Z

Set I, pages 250–252

Alec's class went to 2 one-act plays. The evening lasted 3 hr, with a 0.25 hr intermission. The second play was 1.25 hr. How long was the first play?

Work backward by subtracting the hours you know from the total time of the evening.

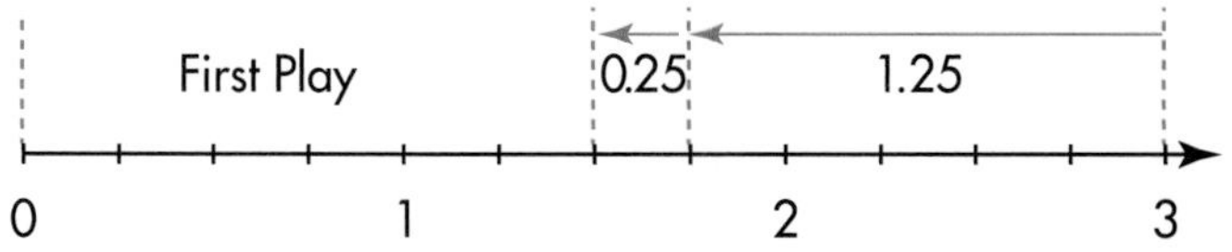

The first play lasted 1.5 hr.

You can work backward when there is an end result after a series of steps, and you are asked to find the information in the first step.

Remember that if you know the ending position and each change made, then you can use the inverse of each change to work backward.

1. This week Sam talked on the phone for 2 hours, which is half the time he talked last week. How long did he talk on the phone last week?

2. Joanna has 9 yards of plastic. This is 3 times the amount she needs to cover a picnic table. How much plastic does she need to cover one table?

Topic 11

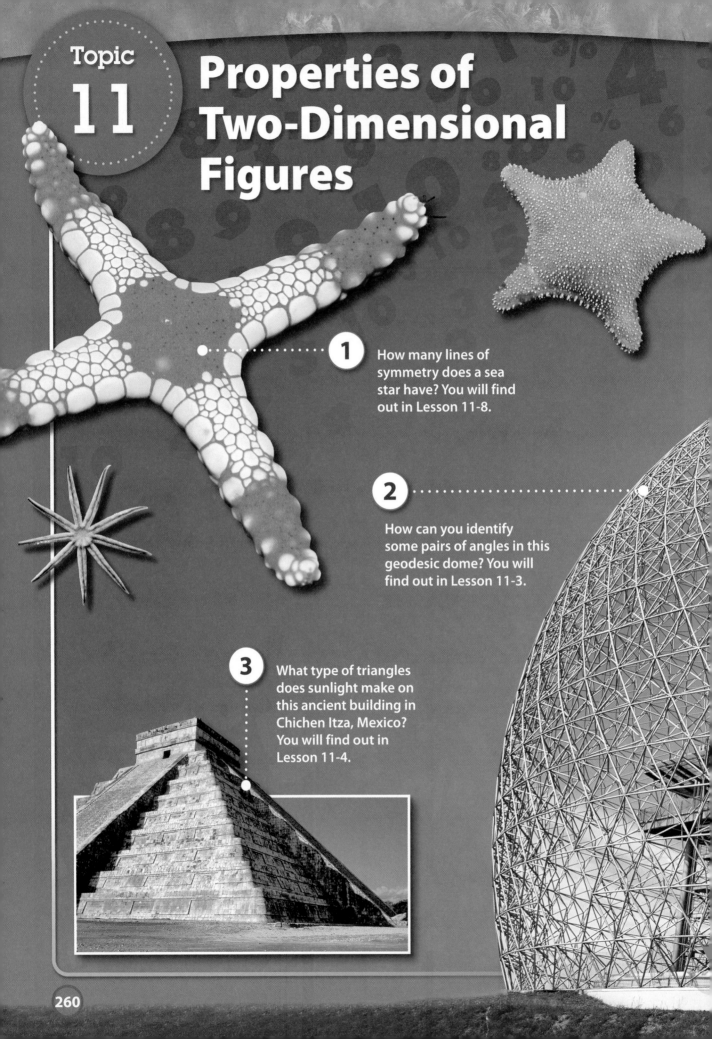

Properties of Two-Dimensional Figures

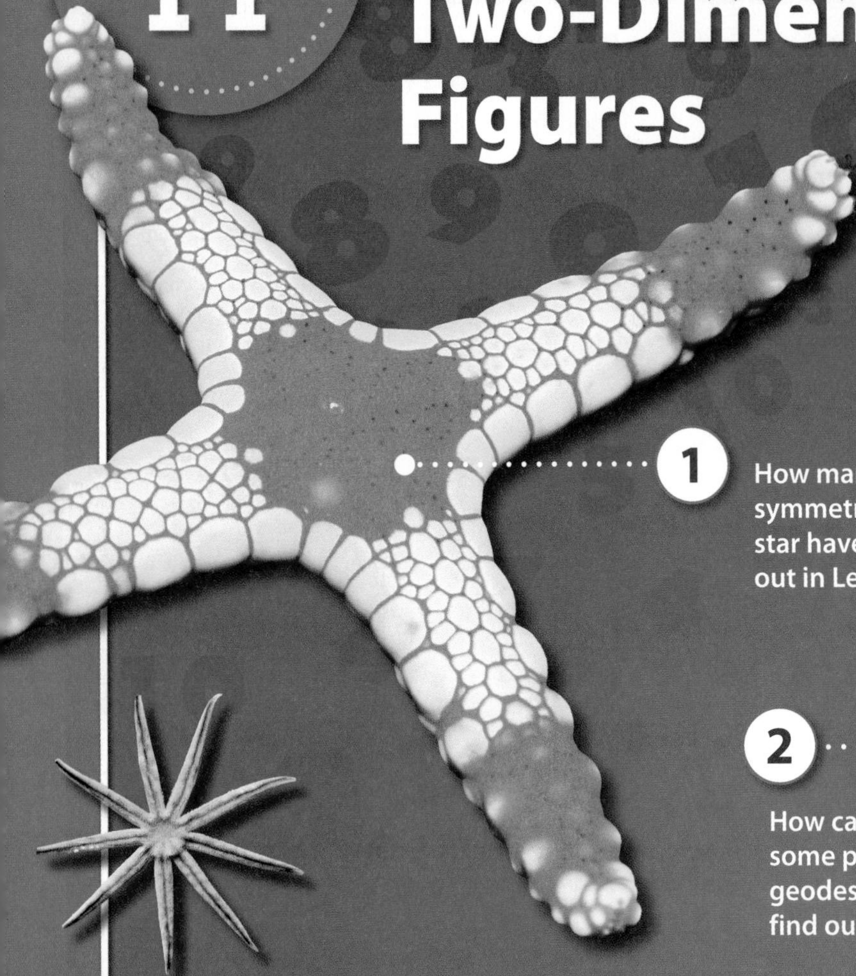

1. How many lines of symmetry does a sea star have? You will find out in Lesson 11-8.

2. How can you identify some pairs of angles in this geodesic dome? You will find out in Lesson 11-3.

3. What type of triangles does sunlight make on this ancient building in Chichen Itza, Mexico? You will find out in Lesson 11-4.

Review What You Know!

Vocabulary

Choose the best term from the box.

- perpendicular
- congruent
- angle

1. Two line segments are __?__ if they are the same length.
2. Two rays that have the same endpoint form a(n) __?__.
3. Two lines that meet to form right angles are called __?__.

Lines and Segments

Identify these pairs of line segments.

4. 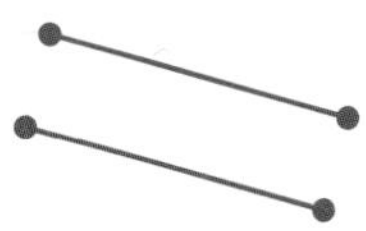

5. 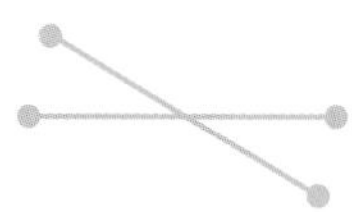

6. 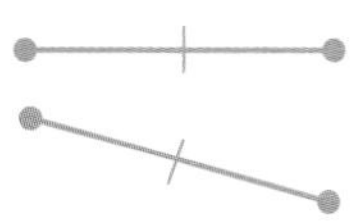

7. 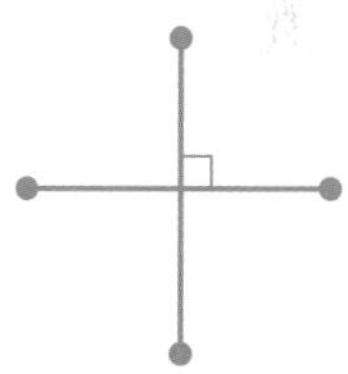

Properties

Writing to Explain Write an answer for each question.

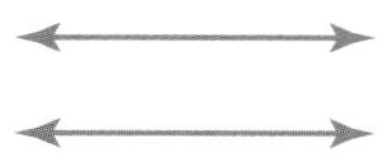

8. How are the two lines above different from perpendicular lines? Explain.
9. Are the two lines above the same length? Explain.

Lesson
11-1

Understand It!
Words, pictures, and symbols can describe properties of two-dimensional figures.

Basic Geometric Ideas

What words can describe two-dimensional figures?

	What You Show	What You Write
A point is an exact location in space.		P or point P
A line is a straight path of points that goes on forever in two directions.		$\overleftrightarrow{CD}$ or $\overleftrightarrow{DC}$
A ray is part of a line, with one endpoint, extending forever in only one direction.		$\overrightarrow{MN}$

Other Examples

What You Show | **What You Write**

Intersecting lines pass through the same point.

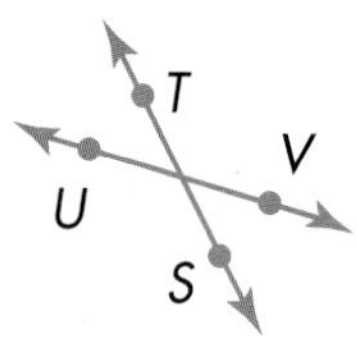

$\overleftrightarrow{ST}$ intersects $\overleftrightarrow{UV}$

A plane is a flat surface that extends forever in all directions.

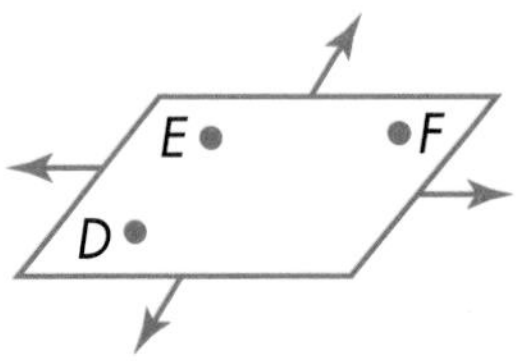

▱DEF

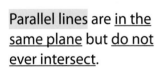

Parallel lines are in the same plane but do not ever intersect.

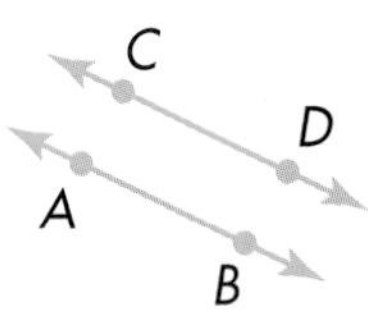

$\overleftrightarrow{CD} \parallel \overleftrightarrow{AB}$

Perpendicular lines are intersecting lines that form a right angle.

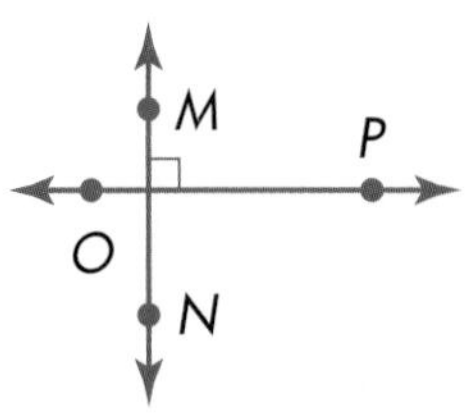

$\overleftrightarrow{MN} \perp \overleftrightarrow{OP}$

Explain It

1. Explain the relationship between parallel lines and a plane.

2. Look around your classroom and identify examples of intersecting line segments, perpendicular line segments, and parallel line segments.

	What You Show	What You Write
A line segment is part of a line with two endpoints.	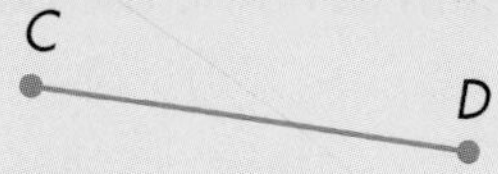	$\overline{CD}$ or $\overline{DC}$
Line segments that are the same length are congruent line segments.	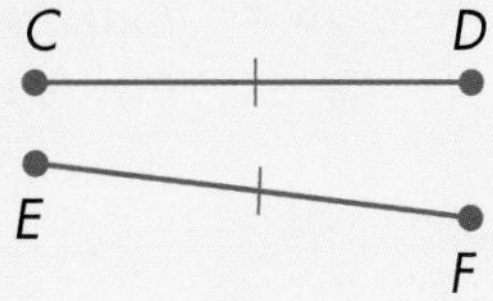	$\overline{CD} \cong \overline{EF}$
The midpoint of a line segment is halfway between the two endpoints. It forms two new congruent segments.		G or midpoint G

Guided Practice*

Do you know HOW?

Use symbols to identify each figure.

1. 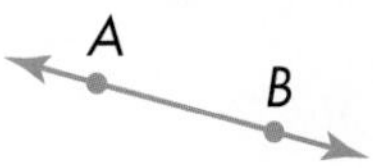

2. 

3. 

4. 

Do you UNDERSTAND?

5. What is formed where two lines intersect?

6. If $\overline{CD}$ above is 2 inches long, how long is $\overline{EF}$? Explain.

7. In Exercises 1 and 4, why can you say $\overleftrightarrow{AB}$ two ways but $\overrightarrow{NP}$ only one way?

Independent Practice

In **8** though **13**, use symbols to name each figure.

8. 

9. 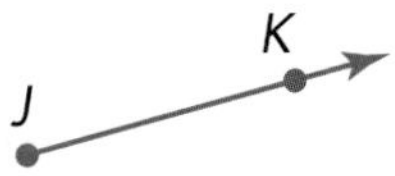

10. 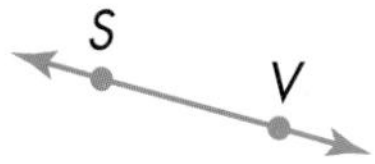

11. 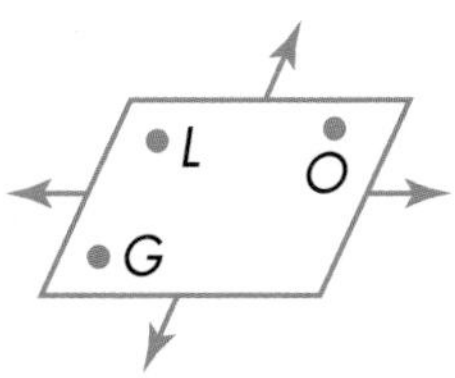

12. 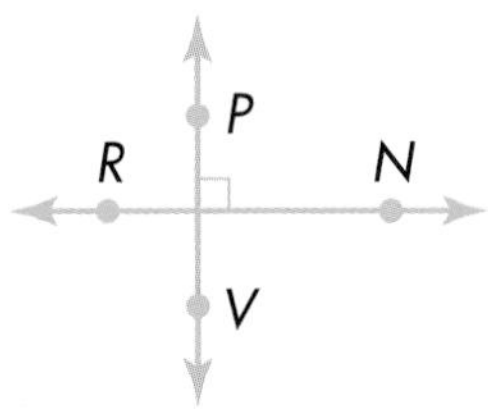

13. 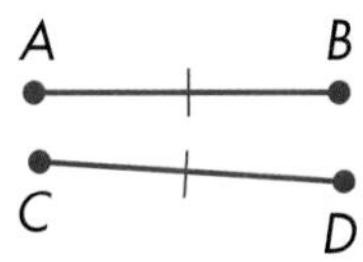

In **14** and **15,** draw each figure.

14. $\overleftrightarrow{EM} \parallel \overleftrightarrow{AW}$

15. Point B is the midpoint of $\overline{DG}$.

DIGITAL Animated Glossary
www.pearsonsuccessnet.com

For another example, see Set A on page 294.

Independent Practice

In **16** through **21**, use the diagram to name the figures.

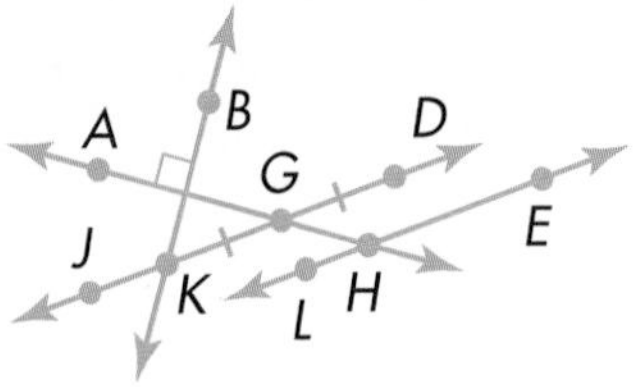

Tip *A small square inside an angle is a sign that the angle is a right angle (the two rays of the angle are perpendicular).*

16. two lines that intersect

17. three rays

18. two perpendicular lines

19. three line segments

20. two parallel lines

21. a midpoint

Problem Solving

22. First St., Second St., and Third St. intersect Lansing St. and Farmers St. forming 90° angles.

a Name two streets that are parallel.

b Name two streets that are perpendicular.

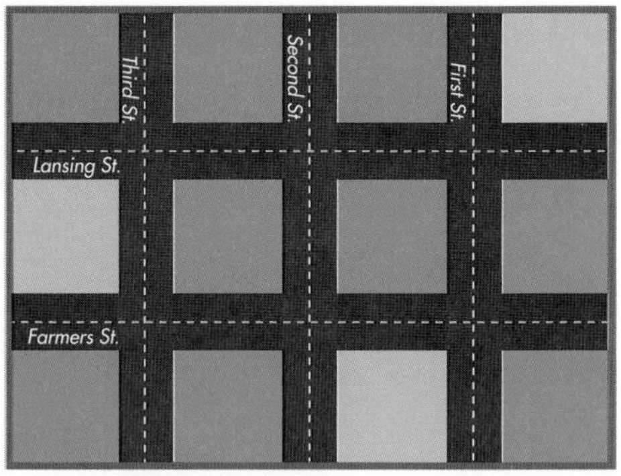

23. **Think About the Process** Greg earned $935 last month. After he paid his rent, he had $515 left. Which equation would you use to find how much Greg paid as rent?

A $935 - x = 515$ **C** $x - 515 = 935$

B $515 - x = 935$ **D** $x - 935 = 515$

24. **Reasoning** Which describes the lines formed by the mirrors in this periscope?

A perpendicular **C** rays

B intersecting **D** parallel

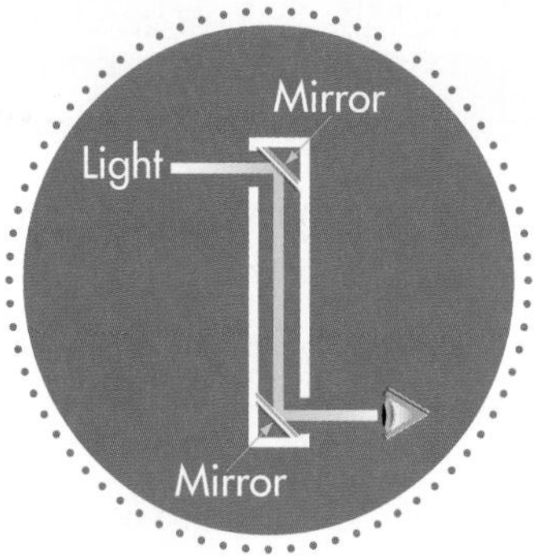

25. If 386 students at Central Middle School are involved in a school sport, how many students are not involved in a school sport?

Data

Central Middle School	
Grade 6	263 students
Grade 7	301 students
Grade 8	278 students

26. How many different lines can you draw through one point? How many different lines can you draw through a set of two points?

27. **Writing to Explain** Two bike trails, *AC* and *FH*, are congruent. Trail *AC* is 2.3 miles long and uphill. Which is the longer trail? Explain.

Enrichment

Perpendicular Bisectors

A **perpendicular bisector** is a line that divides a line segment into two equal parts and is perpendicular to the segment. The perpendicular bisector contains the segment's midpoint.

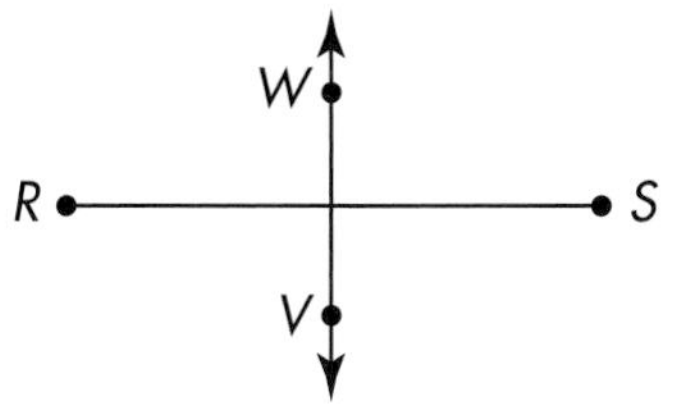

A geometric construction is a step-by-step process to build and draw a geometric shape. To construct the perpendicular bisector of a line segment, use a straightedge and a compass.

Example: To construct the perpendicular bisector of $\overline{AB}$, follow the steps below.

1. Trace $\overline{AB}$.

2. Place your compass center on point *A* and set the opening more than halfway to point *B*. Draw a large arc that goes both below and above $\overline{AB}$.

3. With the same compass setting, place the compass center on *B* and draw another large arc.

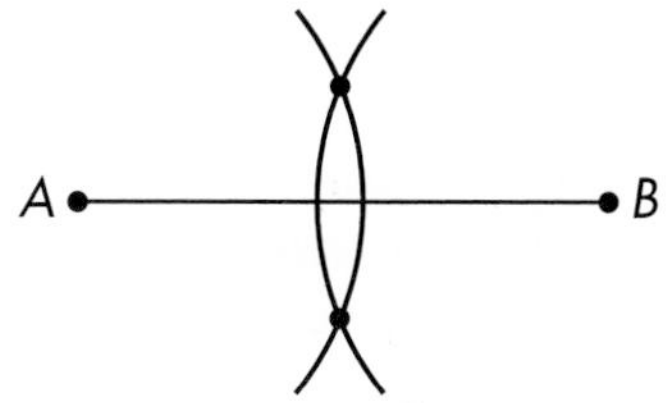

4. Label the points of intersection *C* and *D*. Draw $\overleftrightarrow{CD}$. $\overleftrightarrow{CD}$ is the perpendicular bisector of $\overline{AB}$.

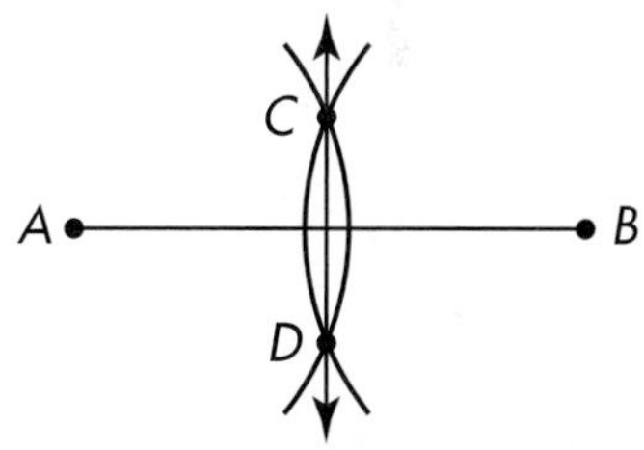

Practice

1. Trace $\overline{MN}$ at right. Construct a perpendicular bisector to $\overline{MN}$.

2. Perpendicular lines cross each other at right angles. In the illustration at the right, $\overleftrightarrow{CD}$ is the perpendicular bisector of $\overline{AB}$. How could you check to see if $\overleftrightarrow{CD}$ is the perpendicular bisector of $\overline{AB}$?

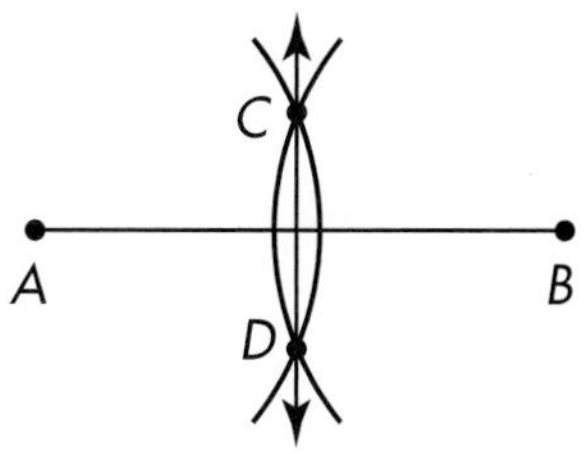

3. **Draw a Picture** Create and color your own geometric construction using a straightedge and a compass. Include at least one perpendicular bisector.

4. **Reasoning** Kayla tried to construct a perpendicular bisector. Her results are shown at the right. What do you think she did wrong?

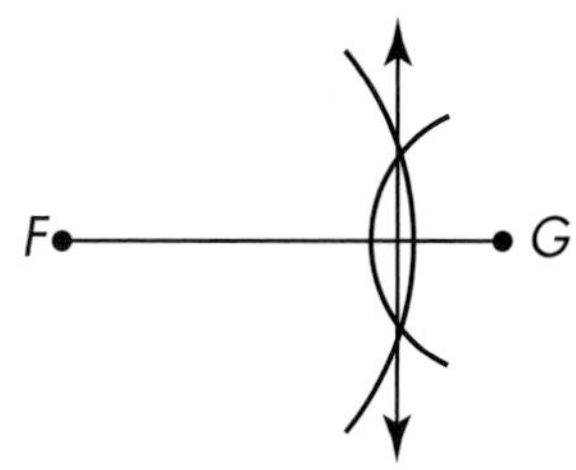

5. Use a compass and straightedge. Draw a line segment and its perpendicular bisector. Place the compass center at the midpoint and draw a circle. Extend the segment and perpendicular bisector so as to intersect the circle at four points. Draw a 4-sided shape connecting the four points. What is this shape?

Lesson
11-2 Measuring and Drawing Angles

Hands-On
protractor

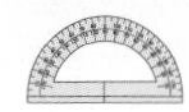

Understand It!
Angles can be described and classified by their measures.

How can you measure angles?

Angle *FGH* is written ∠*FGH*. An angle is formed when two different rays have the same endpoint, called the vertex. The two rays form the sides of the angle.

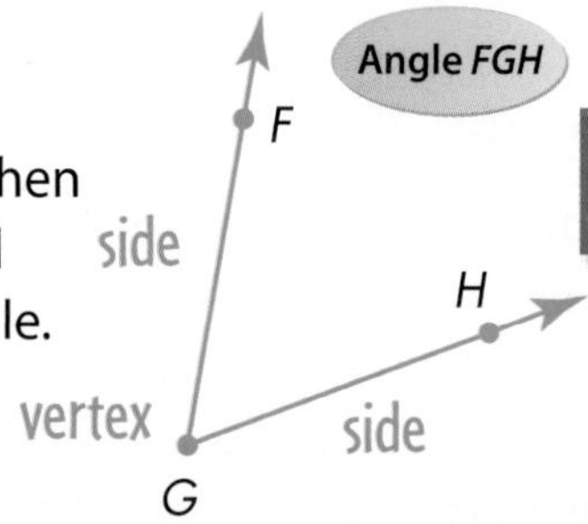

What is the measure of ∠*FGH*?

You can use a protractor to measure the size of an angle. An angle is measured in degrees (°).

Another Example **What are some different types of angles?**

Angles can be classified by their measures.

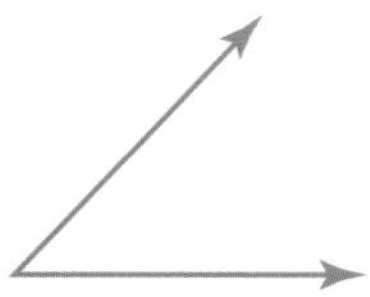

Acute angle: angle between 0° and 90°

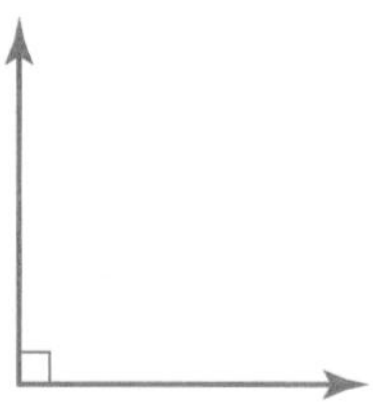

Right angle: angle of exactly 90°

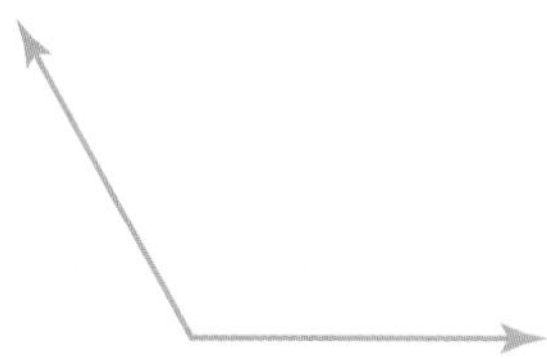

Obtuse angle: angle between 90° and 180°

Straight angle: angle of exactly 180°

How can you draw an angle with a given measure?

Draw an obtuse angle with the measure 100°.

Step 1

Draw $\overrightarrow{DW}$ and mark a point *W* on the ray.

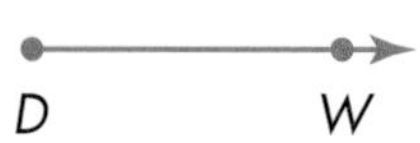

Step 2

Place the protractor's center on endpoint *D* and line up the ray with the 0° mark. Use the same scale to place a point at 100°.

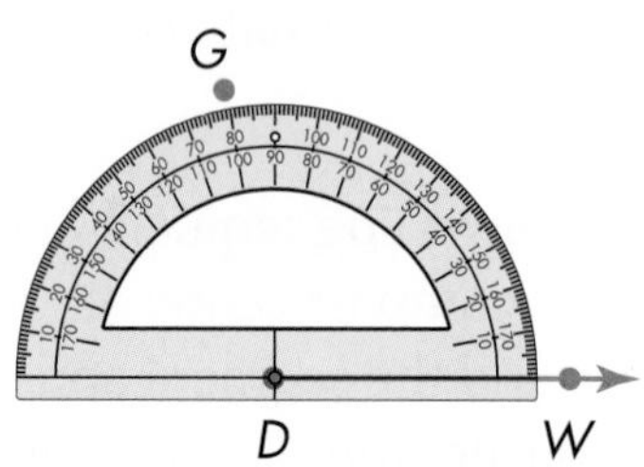

Step 3

Use a straightedge to draw $\overrightarrow{DG}$.

m∠GDW = 100°

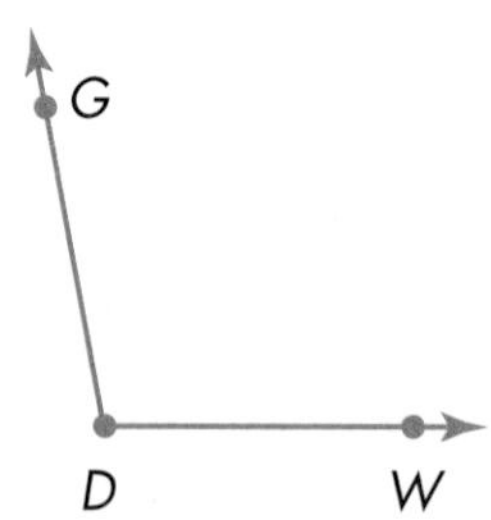

Place the protractor's center on the angle's vertex, *G*. Then line up the 0° mark on the protractor with one side of the angle.

Find where the other side of the angle crosses the protractor.

Read the angle measure. There are two measures on the protractor. Use the same scale of measures that was used to line up the angle at zero.

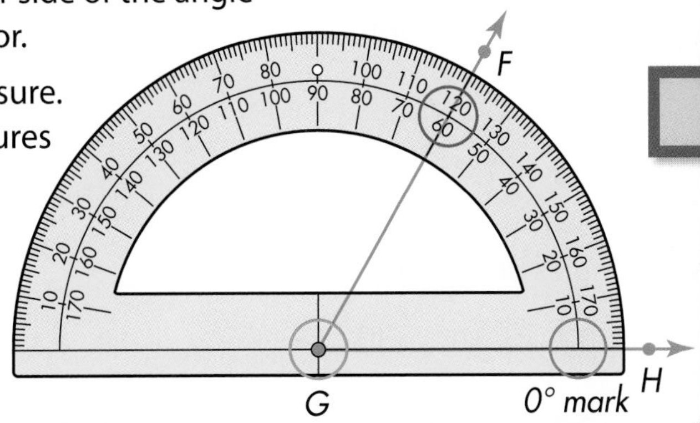

The measure of angle *FGH* is 60°.

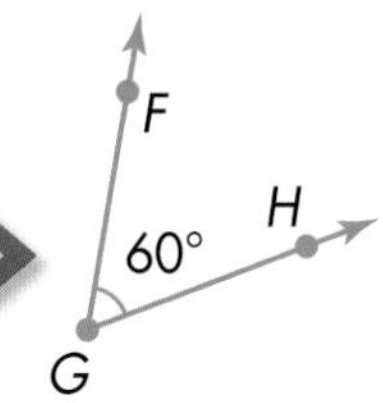

Write:

m∠*FGH* = 60°

Guided Practice*

Do you know HOW?

Measure the angle, then classify each angle as acute, right, obtuse, or straight.

1.

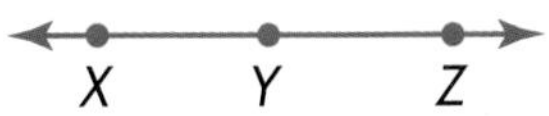

2.

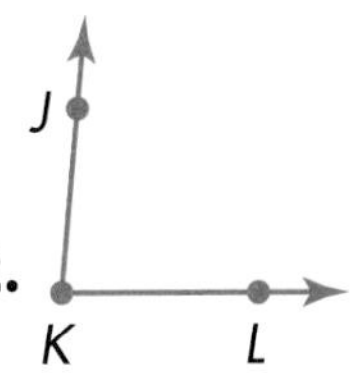

Draw the angles. Classify each angle as acute, right, obtuse, or straight.

3. 153° **4.** 30°

Do you UNDERSTAND?

5. Why would obtuse angles always use the larger numbers on a protractor and acute angles always use the smaller numbers?

6. If $\overrightarrow{GJ}$ is added to endpoint *G* to make a straight angle *JGH* in the example at the top of the page, what is the measure of the new ∠*JGF*?

Independent Practice

In **7** through **12**, measure the angle, then classify each angle as acute, right, obtuse, or straight.

7.

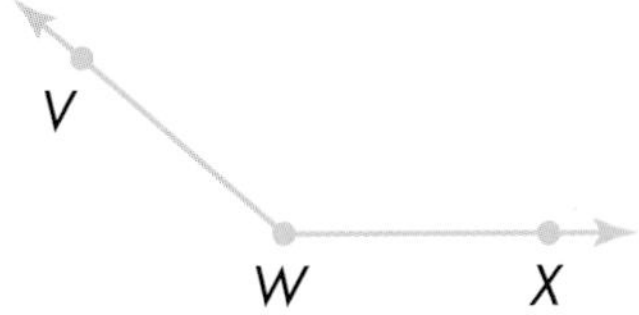

8.

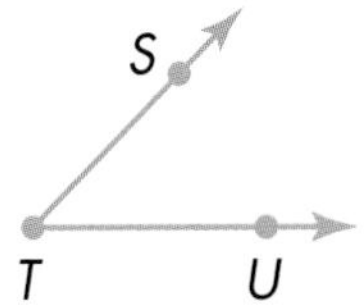

9.

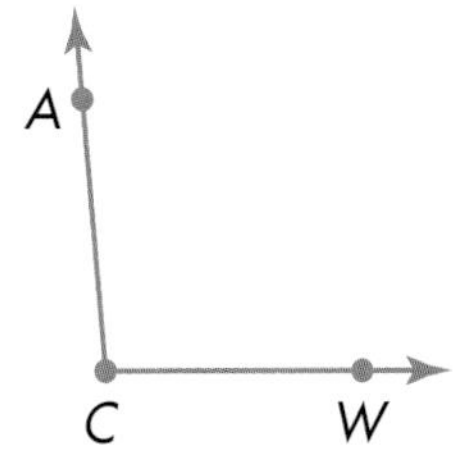

10.

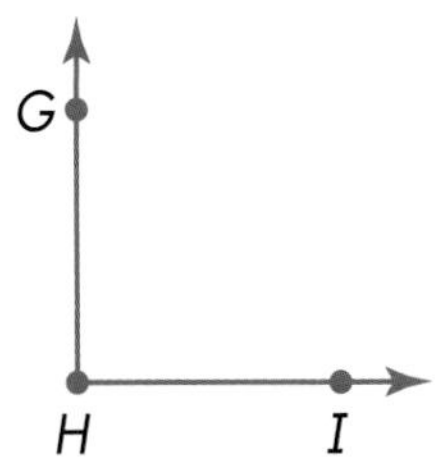

11.

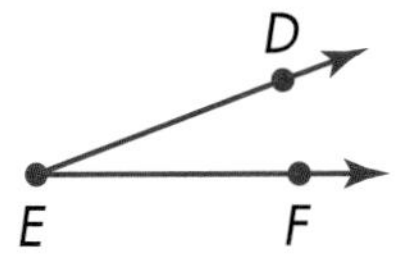

12.

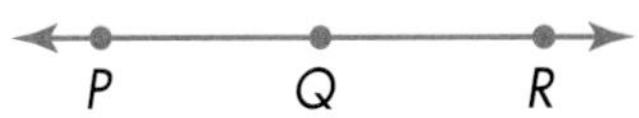

DIGITAL Animated Glossary, eTools
www.pearsonsuccessnet.com

****For another example, see Set B on page 294.***

Independent Practice

In **13** through **15**, give the measurement of each angle. Classify each angle as acute, obtuse, or straight.

13. 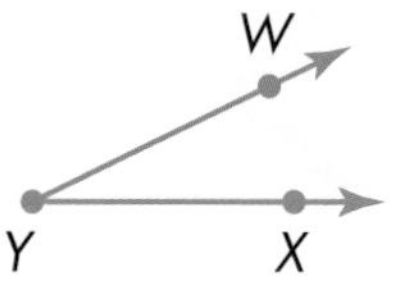

14. 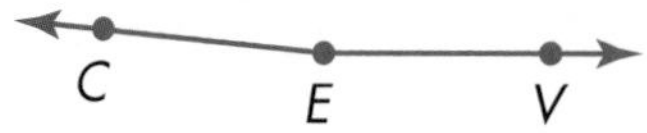

15. 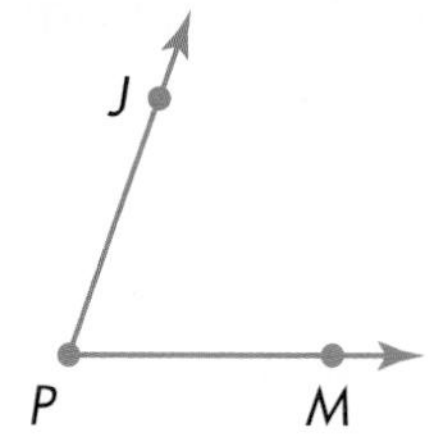

For **16** through **21**, draw the angles described.

16. a right angle

17. an 80° angle

18. a 55° angle

19. a 117° angle

20. a 22° angle

21. a 148° angle

Problem Solving

Without using a protractor, draw estimated angles of measures given in **22** through **24**. Then use a protractor to check your work.

22. 15°

23. 83°

24. 155°

Use the drawing of Mr. Patel's class garden at the right for **25** through **27**.

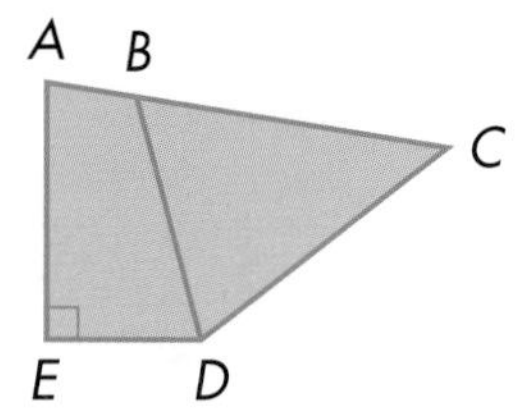

25. Which angle in the garden is a right angle?

26. Which angle in the garden is obtuse?

27. If $\angle ABC$ in the garden is a straight angle, what is the sum of $\angle ABD$ and $\angle CBD$?

28. **Writing to Explain** Describe how these angles are alike and different.

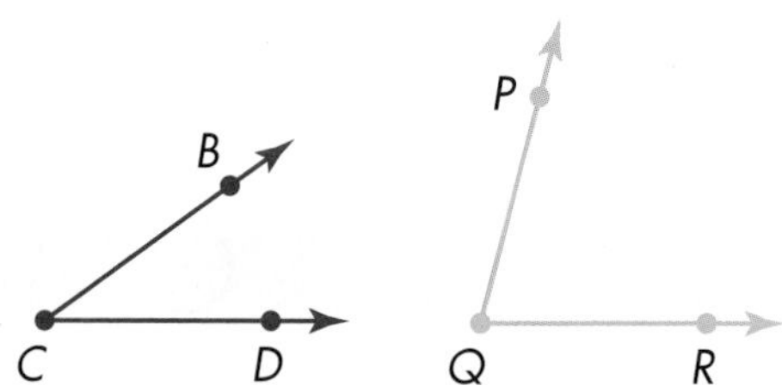

29. A page is separated into x number of columns, each $2\frac{1}{2}$ inches wide. If the width of the page is 10 inches, which equation can be used to solve for x?

A $2\frac{1}{2} \times 10 = x$

B $10x = 2\frac{1}{2}$

C $2\frac{1}{2}x = 10$

D $2\frac{1}{2} \div 10 = x$

30. Which kind of angle is angle S?

A obtuse

B acute

C right

D straight

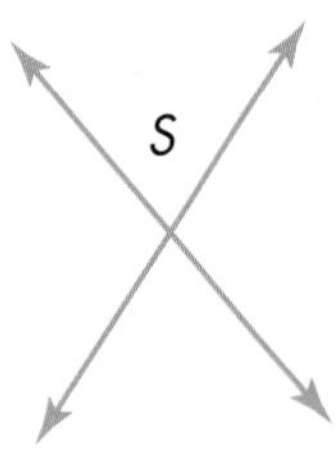

Enrichment

Construct an Angle Bisector

An **angle bisector** is a ray that splits an angle into two congruent angles. The endpoint of the angle bisector is the vertex of the angle.

Tip *When tracing an angle to construct a bisector, extend the rays of the angle. This makes it easier to draw the arcs.*

Example: Trace ∠*ABC*. Then follow the steps to construct the bisector of ∠*ABC*.

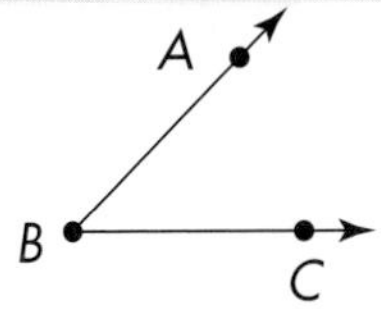

Step 1 Place your compass point on point *B* and draw an arc intersecting the sides of ∠*ABC*. Label the points of intersection *Q* and *P*.

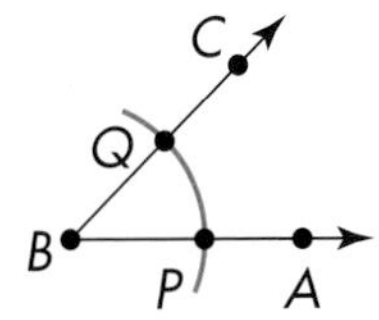

Step 2 Adjust the compass to any setting greater than $\frac{1}{2}$ the length of *QP*. Place the compass center on *Q* and draw an arc.

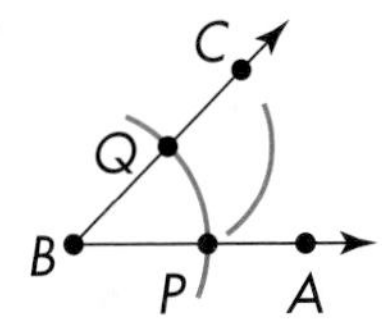

Step 3 With the same compass setting, place the compass point on *P* and draw another arc. Label the point of intersection *R*. With a straightedge, draw $\overrightarrow{BR}$. $\overrightarrow{BR}$ is the bisector of ∠*ABC*.

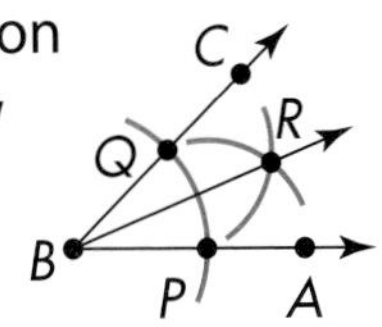

Practice

Trace ∠*QRS* at the right.

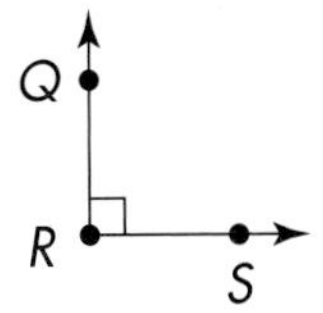

1. Construct the bisector of ∠*QRS*. Label the bisector $\overrightarrow{RZ}$.

2. What is the measure of ∠*QRZ*?

3. Trace ∠*LMN*. Then construct the bisector $\overrightarrow{MO}$ of ∠*LMN*.

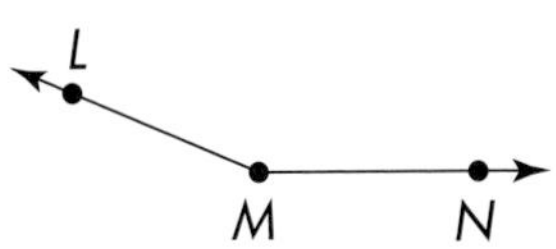

4. Trace ∠*DEF*. Then construct the bisector $\overrightarrow{EG}$ of ∠*DEF*.

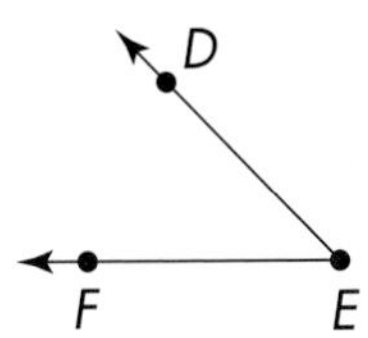

5. Trace the compass map design at the right. Use what you know about constructing angle bisectors to draw in 45° NE, 135° SE, 225° SW, and 315° NW.

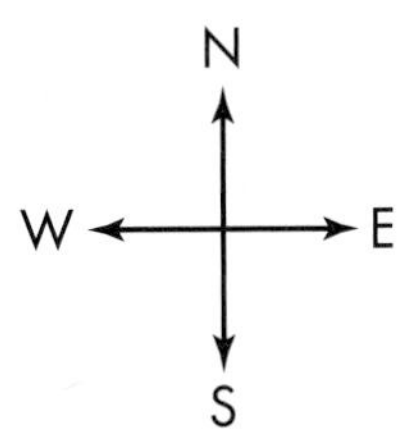

6. **Reasoning** How could you use a protractor and straight edge to draw an angle bisector?

Lesson
11-3

Understand It!
Some pairs of angles are related by their positions or their measures.

Angle Pairs

What are some special pairs of angles?

Look at the scissors. Can you tell by looking at the angle between the blades what the angle between the handles measures?

Vertical angles are a pair of angles that are formed by intersecting lines and have no side in common. The blades and handles of the scissors form vertical angles.

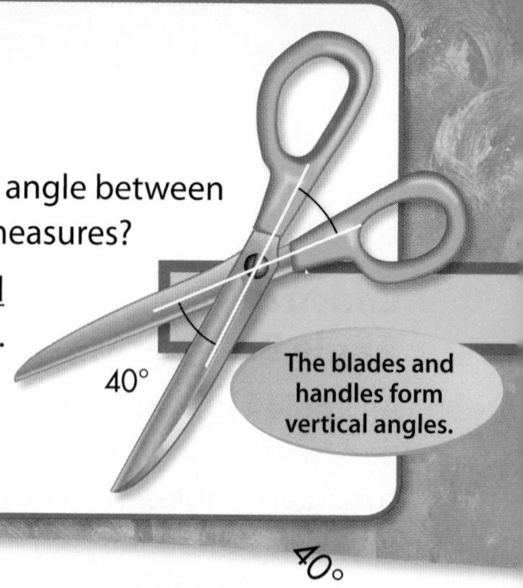

Other Examples

Other special pairs of angles:

Adjacent angles are a pair of angles with a common vertex and a common side but no common interior points. For example, $\angle EFG$ and $\angle GFH$ are adjacent angles.

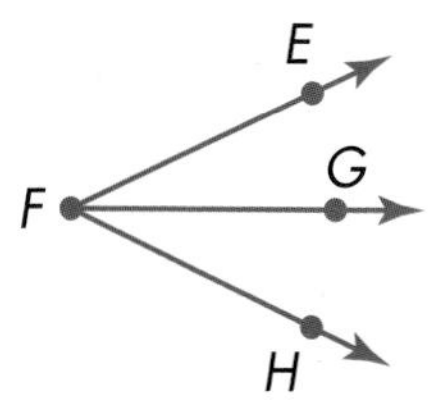

Complementary angles are two angles whose measures add up to 90°. $\angle QRS$ and $\angle TUV$ are complementary angles.

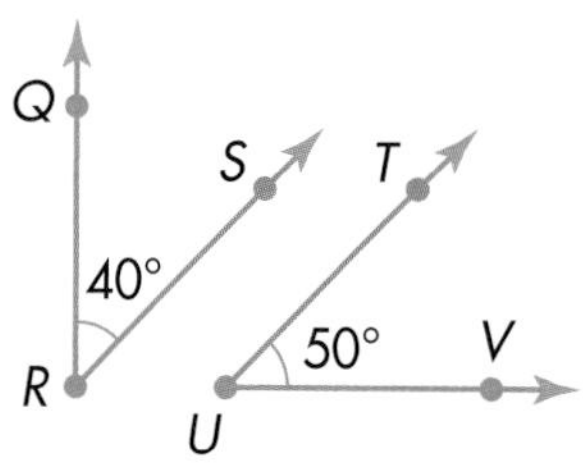

$m\angle QRS + m\angle TUV = 90°$

Supplementary angles are two angles whose measures add up to 180°. $\angle WXY$ and $\angle ABC$ are supplementary angles.

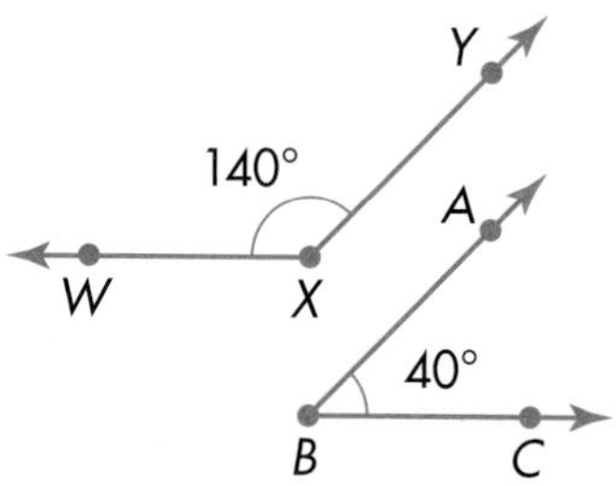

$m\angle WXY + m\angle ABC = 180°$

Explain It

1. Why aren't the angles *WXY* and *ABC* complementary angles?
2. If $\angle QRS$ and $\angle ABC$ are congruent angles, what kind of angles are $\angle QRS$ and $\angle WXY$?

Congruent angles have the same measure. Vertical angles are congruent angles. $\angle LPK$ and $\angle MPN$ are vertical angles.

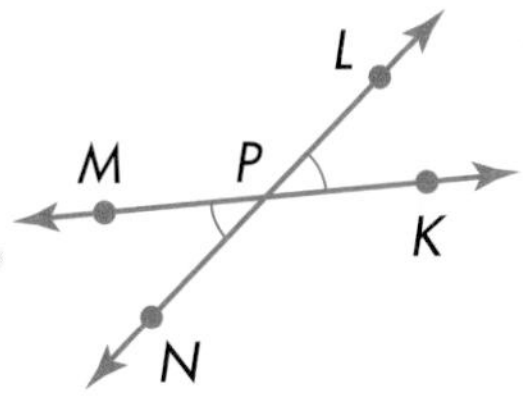

The arcs inside the angles show that they are congruent.

$\angle LPK$ is congruent to $\angle MPN$.

You can write $\angle LPK \cong \angle MPN$.

The angle between the blades and the angle between the handles are congruent.

$\angle LPK \cong \angle MPN$

If $m\angle LPK = 40°$, then $m\angle MPN = 40°$.

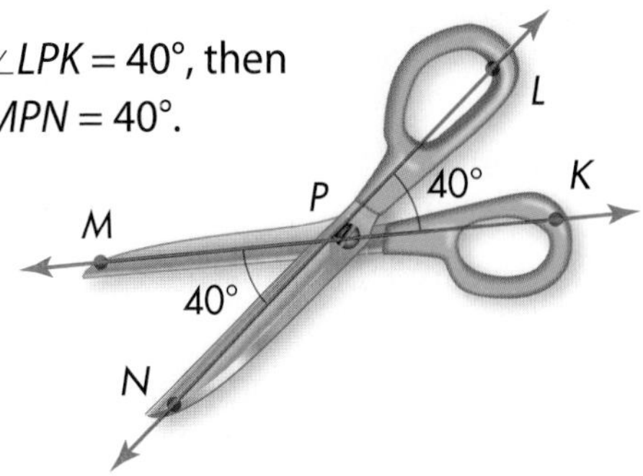

Guided Practice*

Do you know HOW?

In **1** through **3**, find the values of the variables.

Tip *Remember that the measure of a straight angle is 180°.*

1. x

2. y

3. z

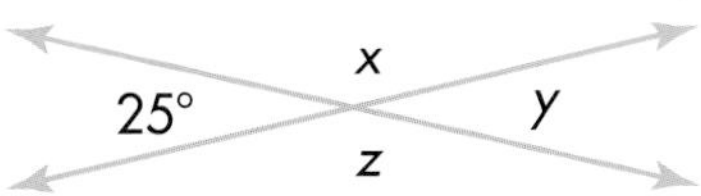

Do you UNDERSTAND?

4. When two lines intersect, how many pairs of vertical angles are formed?

5. Which angle above is supplementary to $\angle MPN$?

6. Look at the angles formed by the scissors at the top of the page. What are the measures of $\angle LPM$ and $\angle KPN$?

Independent Practice

In **7** through **10**, find x.

7.

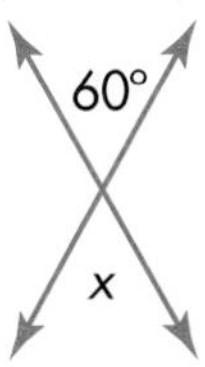

8.

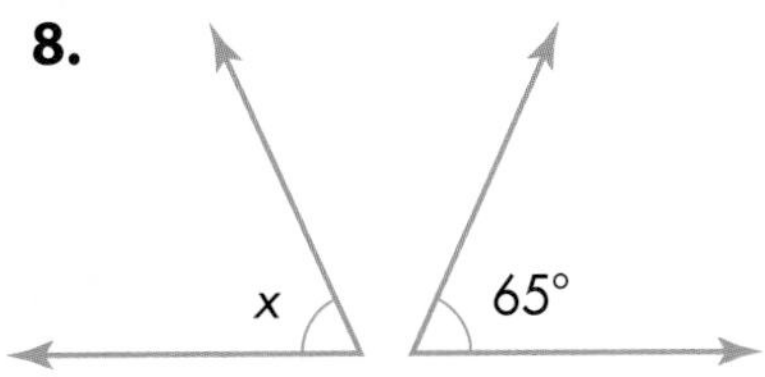

9.

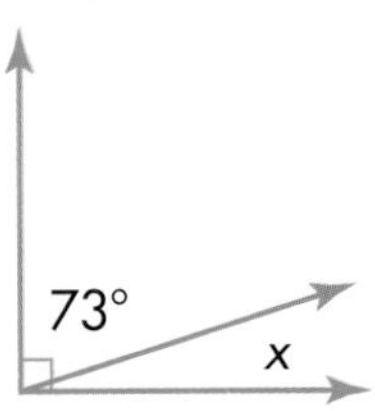

10.

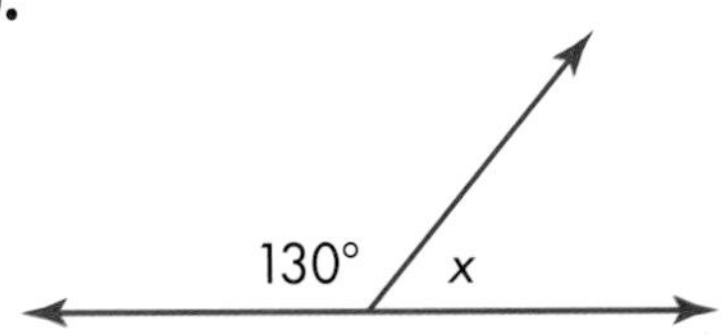

Find the measures of the angles that are complementary to the angles in **11** and **12**.

11. 63°

12. 20°

Find the measures of the angles that are supplementary to the angles in **13** and **14**.

13. 63°

14. 20°

DIGITAL Animated glossary **www.pearsonsuccessnet.com**

**For another example, see Set B on page 294.*

Independent Practice

Use the diagram at the right for **15** through **19**.

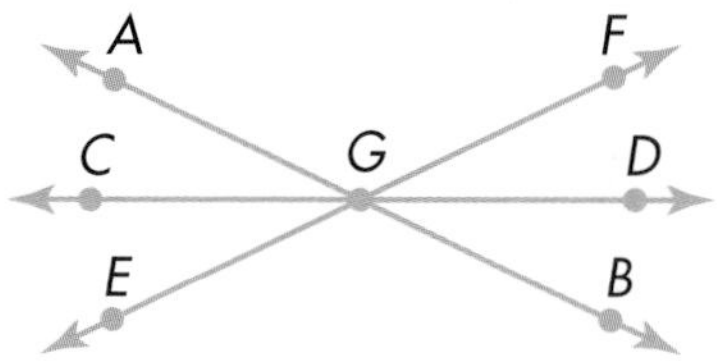

15. Identify six obtuse angles.

16. Identify a pair of vertical angles.

17. Identify a pair of adjacent angles.

18. Are there any complementary angles in the diagram? If so, identify them.

19. Identify three different pairs of supplementary angles.

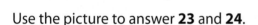

Problem Solving

Use this map to answer **20** and **21**.

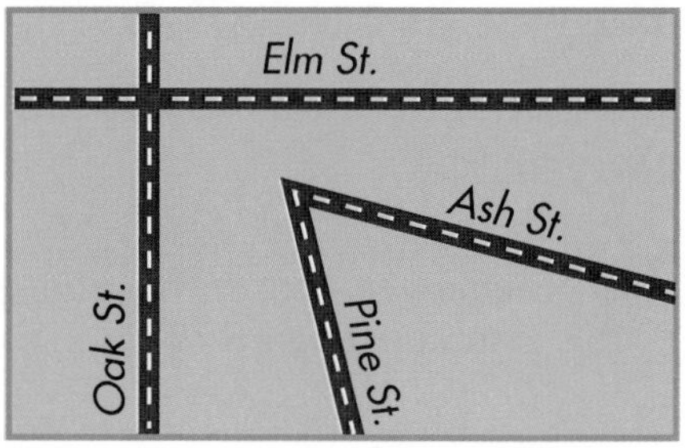

20. What kind of angle does Oak Street make with Elm Street?

21. What kind of angle describes the turn from Pine Street to Ash Street?

22. **Writing to Explain** Can two acute angles be supplementary? Can two obtuse angles be supplementary? Explain.

Use the picture to answer **23** and **24**.

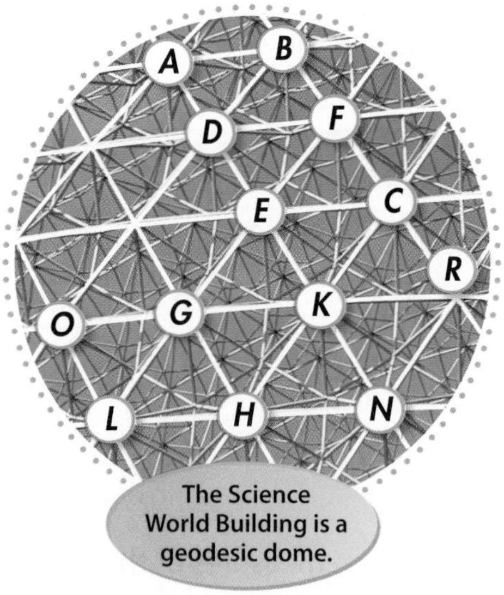

The Science World Building is a geodesic dome.

23. Which angles on the dome are vertical angles?

A ∠*ABD* and ∠*DEF*

B ∠*DEF* and ∠*GEK*

C ∠*GHK* and ∠*LHN*

D ∠*LHG* and ∠*GHN*

24. **Think About the Process** Why are angles *EKH* and *CKN* vertical angles?

A They are formed by intersecting lines and have a common side.

B They are formed by intersecting lines and have no common side.

C They have a common vertex and a common side.

D They are formed by parallel lines and have no common side.

Going Digital

Supplementary and Complementary Angles

Use eTools

Geometry Drawing

Name the measures of two pairs of supplementary angles.

Step 1 Go to the Geometry Drawing eTool. Click on the Draw a line segment tool.

Click in the workspace, drag, and click again to draw line segment *AB*. Click on point *A* and then drag in another direction to create angle *CAB*. Finally, click on point *A* again and drag to point *D* so *D*, *A*, and *B* are all on the same line.

Step 2 Measure the angles. Click on the distance measurement tool palette. Expand to show the triangle. Click on the Angle Measurement tool. To measure angle *DAC*, click on point *D*, then *A*, and then *C*. See the lower right corner. Measure angle *CAB* similarly. The sum of the measures should be 180 degrees.

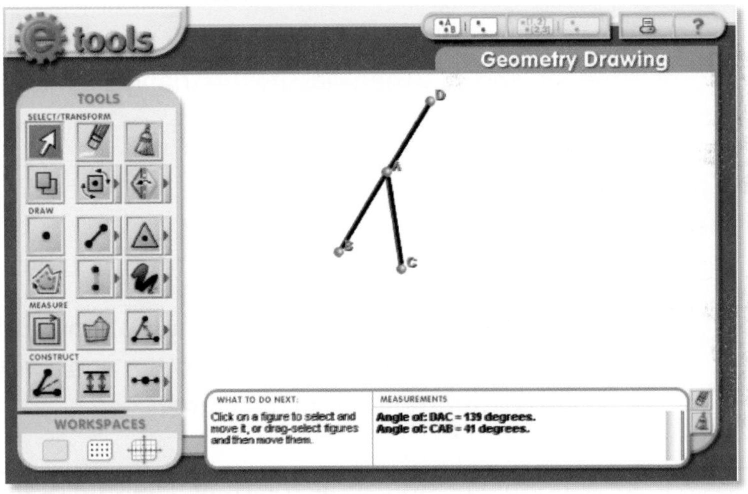

If it isn't, click on the Arrow tool and use it to move point *D* until the sum is 180 degrees, which will mean that *D*, *A*, and *B* are all on the same line. Angles *DAC* and *CAB* are supplementary. Write down their measures.

Step 3 Use the Arrow tool to move point *C* and watch how the measures change.

Practice

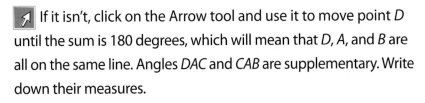

1. Move point *C* so angle *CAB* is acute. Move point *D* until angle *DAC* plus angle *CAB* is 90 degrees, a right angle. Move point *C* again to find the measure of two pairs of complementary angles. Write down their measures.

Lesson
11-4 Triangles

Hands-On
protractor

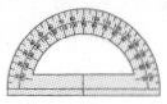

Understand It!
Triangles can be classified and described by the measures of their angles and their sides.

How can you classify triangles?

The angle measures within a triangle are related. The sum of the measures of the three angles of a triangle is 180°.

When the three angles of a triangle are joined together as three adjacent angles, they make a straight angle.

$m\angle A + m\angle B + m\angle C = 180°$

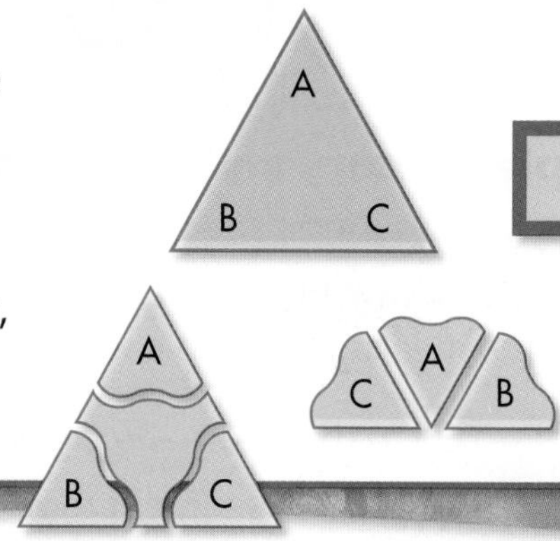

Another Example

How can you draw a triangle from given information?

Draw a triangle with a 4 cm side between two angles that measure 35° and 55°. Then classify the triangle by its angles and by its sides.

Step 1 Draw a 4 cm line segment.

Step 2 Use a protractor to draw a 35° angle at one end of the segment and a 55° angle at the other end. Extend the sides of the angles until they meet.

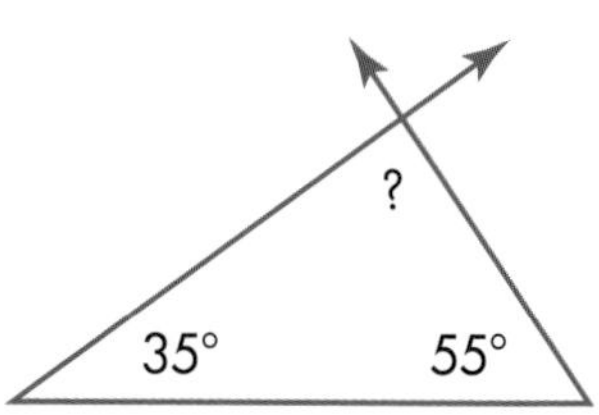

Step 3 Find the missing angle measure. The sum of the measures of the angles of a triangle is 180°.

$35 + 55 + \square = 180$ $\qquad$ $35 + 55 + 90 = 180$

The missing angle measure is 90°.

Step 4 Classify the triangle by its angles and by its sides. Use a protractor and ruler to check the measurements. The triangle has one right angle and two acute angles, so it is a right triangle. The three sides are different lengths, so it is a scalene triangle. The triangle is a right scalene triangle.

Explain It

1. Explain how to find the missing angle measure.
2. **Reasoning** How would you draw a right isosceles triangle?

Triangles can be classified by their angles.

Acute triangle

All angles are acute angles.

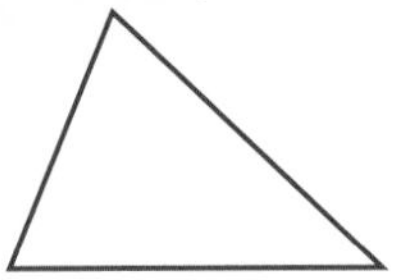

Right triangle

One angle is a right (90°) angle.

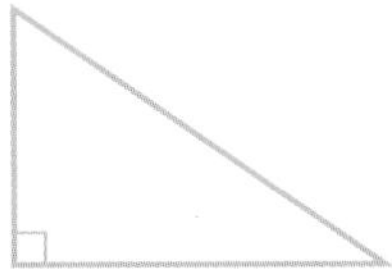

Obtuse triangle

One angle is an obtuse angle.

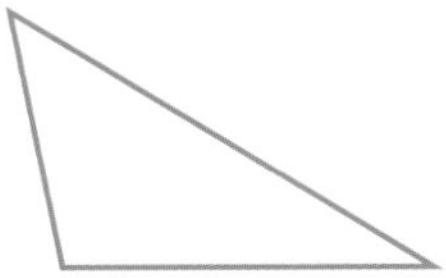

Triangles can be classified by their sides.

Equilateral triangle

All sides are congruent.

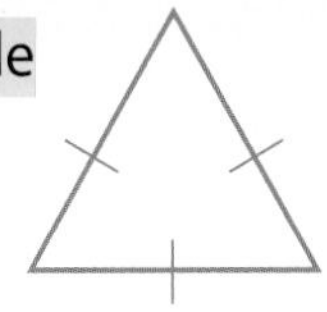

Isosceles triangle

At least two sides are congruent.

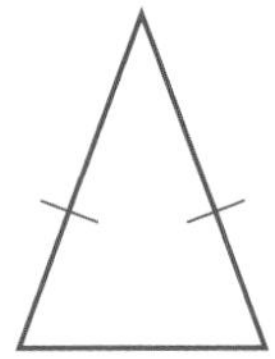

Scalene triangle

No sides are congruent.

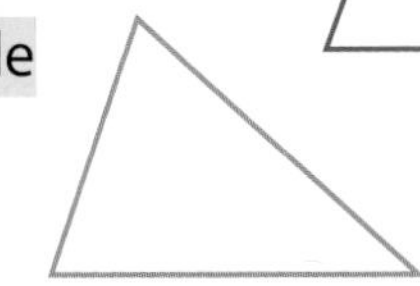

Guided Practice*

Do you know HOW?

Find the missing angle measure. Then classify each by its angles and its sides.

Tip *Remember that the three angles of a triangle always add up to 180°.*

1.

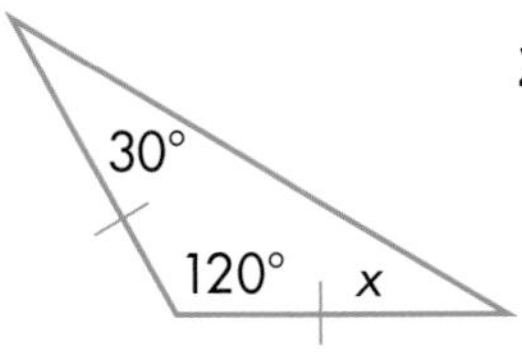

2.

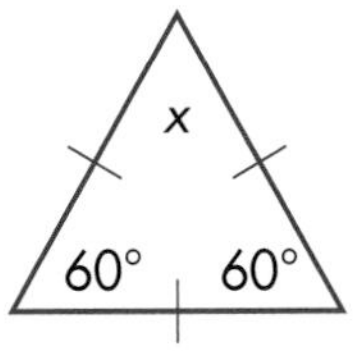

Do you UNDERSTAND?

3. How do you know that the two acute angles in a right triangle are complementary?

4. Suppose that a right triangle has a 30° angle. What are the measurements of the other angles?

5. Can an isosceles triangle be an obtuse triangle? Explain.

Independent Practice

In **6** through **11**, find the missing angle measures and classify the triangles by their angles and sides.

6.

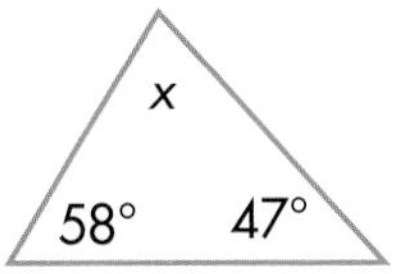

7.

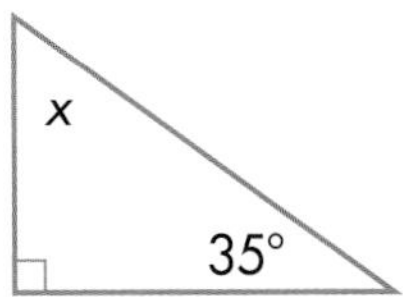

8.

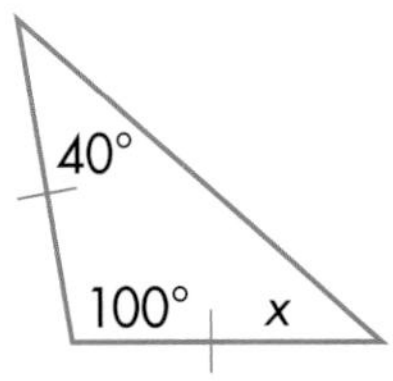

9.

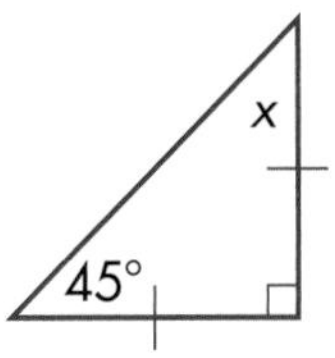

10.

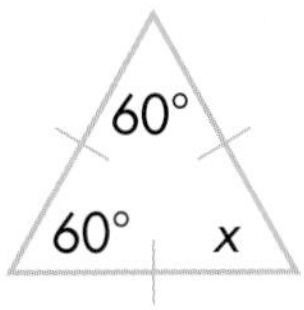

11.

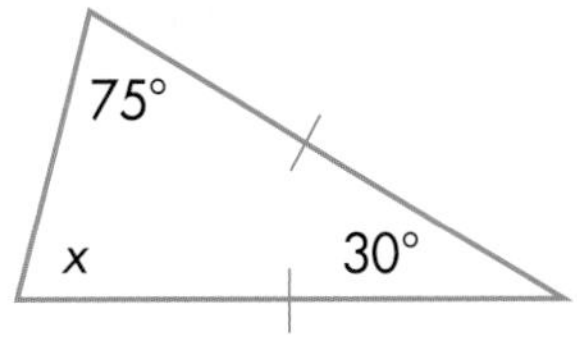

DIGITAL Animated Glossary, eTools **www.pearsonsuccessnet.com**

**For another example, see Set C on page 295.*

Independent Practice

For **12** through **16**, draw the described triangle.

Tip *Start with the angle.*

12. a right isosceles triangle

13. a triangle with two acute angles

14. an obtuse scalene triangle

15. Draw a triangle with a 2-inch side between two 35° angles. Then classify the triangle by its angles and sides.

16. Draw a triangle with a 125° angle between sides of 3 inches and 4 inches.

Problem Solving

17. **Reasoning** What type of angle is the largest angle in an equilateral triangle?

18. **Writing to Explain** What type of angle is the largest angle in a right triangle? Explain.

19. Haleh earned $108 painting 12 shutters. How much would she earn for painting 15 shutters?

20. A triangle has 42° and 29° angles. What is the measure of the third angle? Is it acute, right, or obtuse?

21. The 13-member choir attended a concert. Tickets cost $25 each. The bus ride cost $2.25 per member each way. How much did the choir spend on the trip?

Use the picture to the right to answer **22** and **23**.

22. Isosceles triangles are formed by the light on this pyramid. How would you describe these triangles by their angles?

A scalene **C** obtuse

B acute **D** right

23. Four stairways, each having 91 steps, extend from the base to the top of El Castillo. Which operation would you use to find how many stair steps there are in the pyramid?

A squaring **C** subtraction

B multiplication **D** division

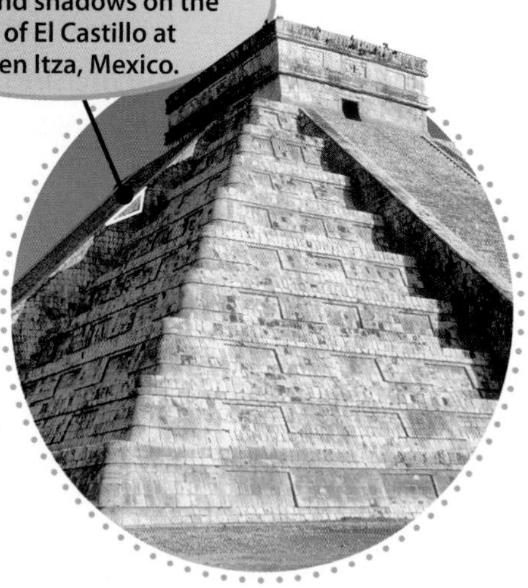

At 3 P.M. on an equinox, the sun makes triangles of light and shadows on the stairs of El Castillo at Chichen Itza, Mexico.

Mixed Problem Solving

Tangrams are ancient Chinese puzzles made up of geometric shapes. All tangrams have the same seven pieces, which fit together to form a square. The objective is to create a design using all seven pieces, called tans. The tans must all be touching, but they may not overlap.

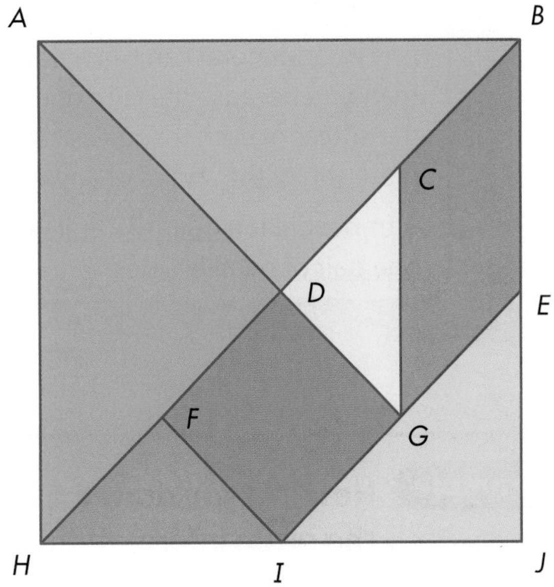

Use the square tangram for **1** through **7**.

1. What shape do the 7 pieces of the tangram make?

2. What shape is formed by points *A*, *D*, and *H*?

3. Identify three pairs of parallel lines.

4. Identify a pair of perpendicular lines.

5. What shape is formed by points *C*, *B*, *E*, and *G*?

6. What shape is formed by points *H*, *B*, and *J*?

7. How many triangles do you see in the tangram?

On a separate sheet of paper, use the above design to create your own tangram. Using the tans from your tangram, try to make the design at the right, using all seven tans. Make sure none of them overlap. Use the puzzle for **8** through **10**.

8. Describe the shape the tangram puzzle forms.

9. **Make a Design** Make your own tangram puzzle from the pieces. Name your design and describe what shape your design makes.

10. **Writing to Explain** Explain how you created your own shape in Exercise 9.

Lesson

11-5

Understand It!
Quadrilaterals can be classified by the special properties of their sides and angles.

Quadrilaterals

Hands-On
protractor

What are the properties of different quadrilaterals?

Any quadrilateral can be divided into two triangles. Because the sum of the measures of the angles of each triangle is 180°, the sum of the measures of the angles of any quadrilateral is 360°.

A trapezoid is a quadrilateral with only one pair of parallel sides.

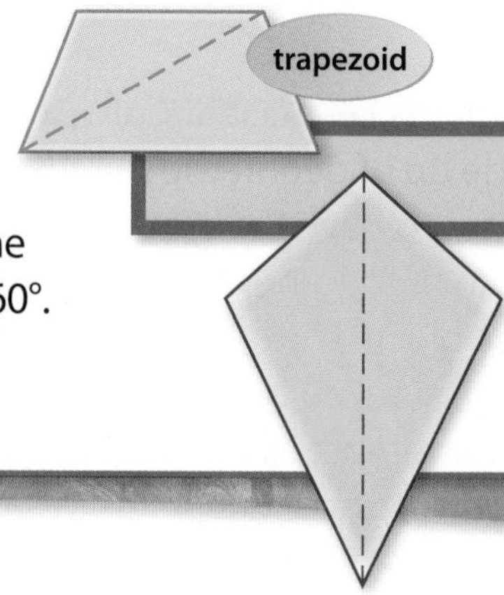

Another Example **How can you draw a quadrilateral from the given information?**

Suppose you want to draw a parallelogram with 5 cm and 2 cm sides. The measures of the opposite angles are 135° and 45°. Using a protractor, follow these steps to draw this parallelogram.

Step 1 Draw a 5 cm line segment.

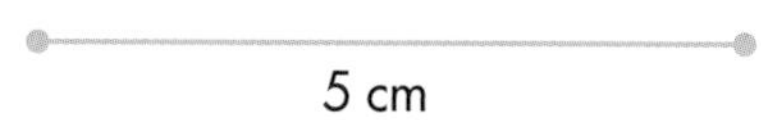

Step 2 Draw a 45° angle at one end of the segment and a 135° angle at the other end. Mark off 2 cm on each side.

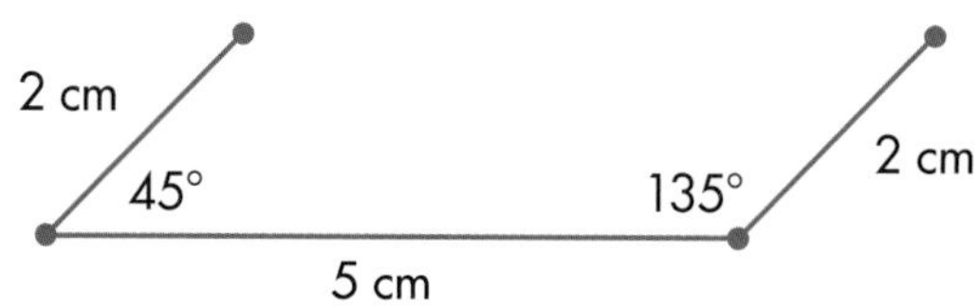

Step 3 Connect the two sides with a line segment. Check that the last side measures 5 cm.

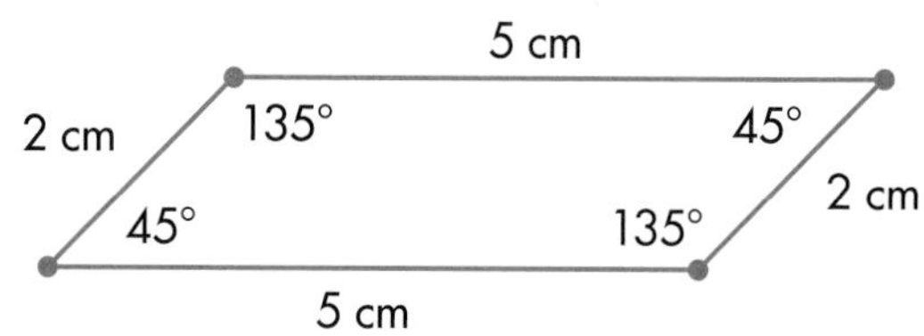

The sum of the measures of the angles of the parallelogram is 45° + 135° + 45° + 135° = 360°.

Explain It

1. How would the parallelogram change if the opposite angles given were both 90°?
2. How could you draw a quadrilateral with congruent sides but no right angles?

A parallelogram is a quadrilateral with both pairs of opposite sides parallel. Opposite sides are congruent, and opposite angles are congruent.

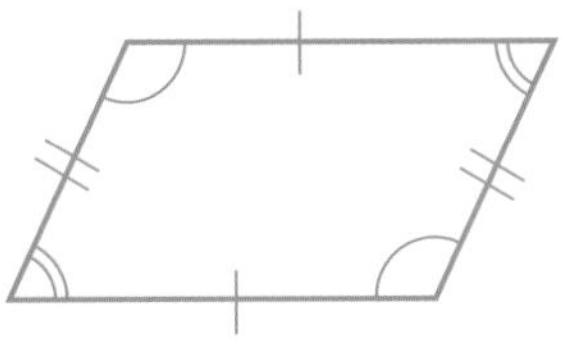

A rhombus is a parallelogram with all sides congruent.

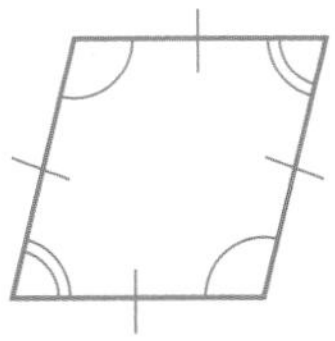

A rectangle is a parallelogram with four right angles.

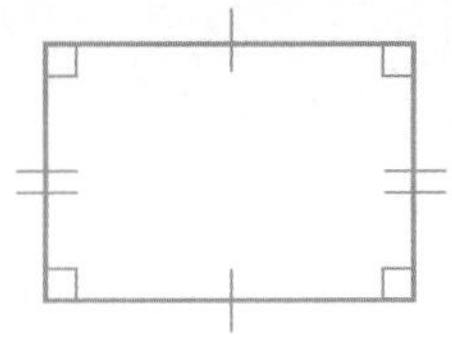

A square is a rectangle with all sides congruent. A square is also a rhombus.

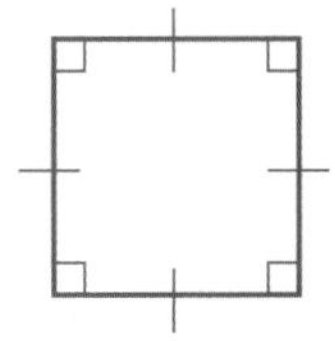

Guided Practice*

Do you know HOW?

Classify each polygon in as many ways as possible. Find the missing angle measurement.

1.

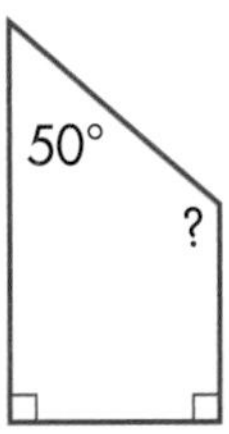

2.

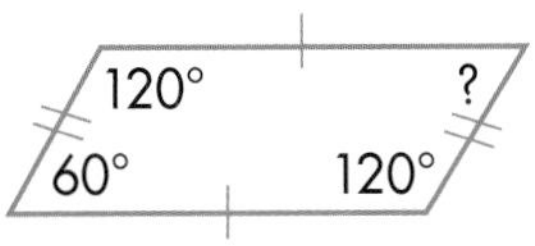

3.

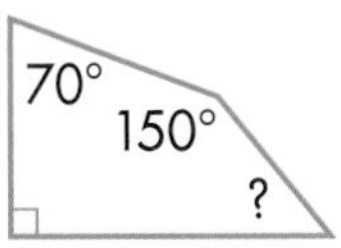

4.

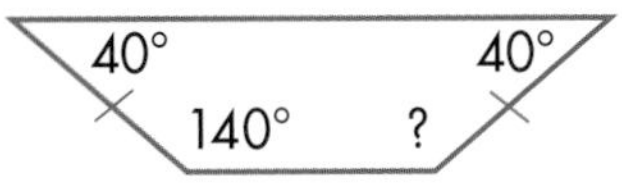

Do you UNDERSTAND?

5. Can all rhombuses be classified as squares? Explain.

6. What is the measure of the missing angle in the diagram? Explain how you found the answer.

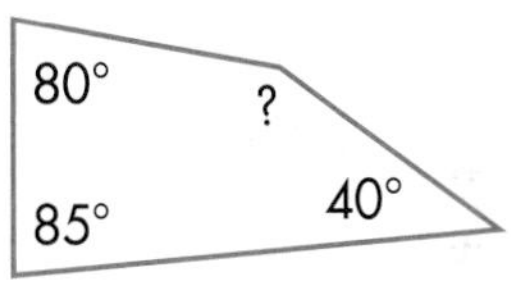

Independent Practice

In **7** through **10**, classify each polygon in as many ways as possible.

7.

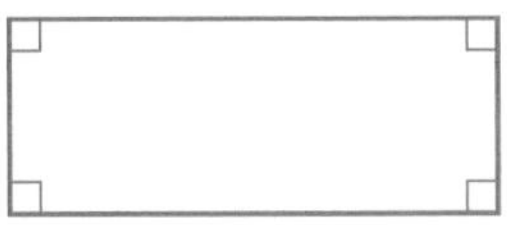

8.

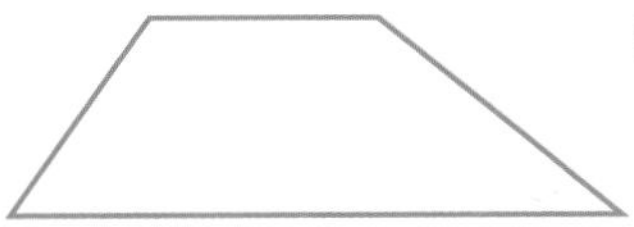

9.

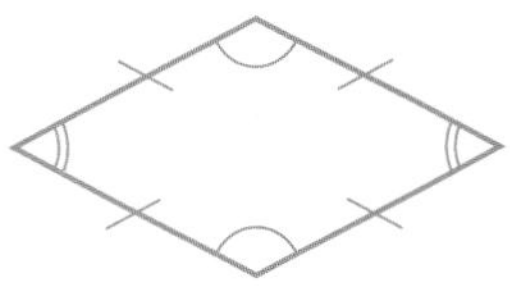

10.

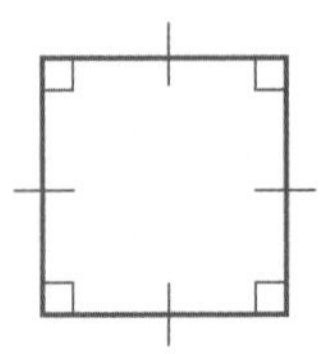

DIGITAL Animated Glossary, eTools **www.pearsonsuccessnet.com**

For another example, see Set C on page 295.

Independent Practice

For **11** through **13**, three angles of a quadrilateral are given. Find the measure of the fourth angle and classify each quadrilateral according to its angles.

11. 62°, 130°, 110° **12.** 65°, 115°, 65° **13.** 90°, 90°, 90°

For **14** and **15,** use the figure at the right to determine whether there is enough information to solve the problem. Solve if possible.

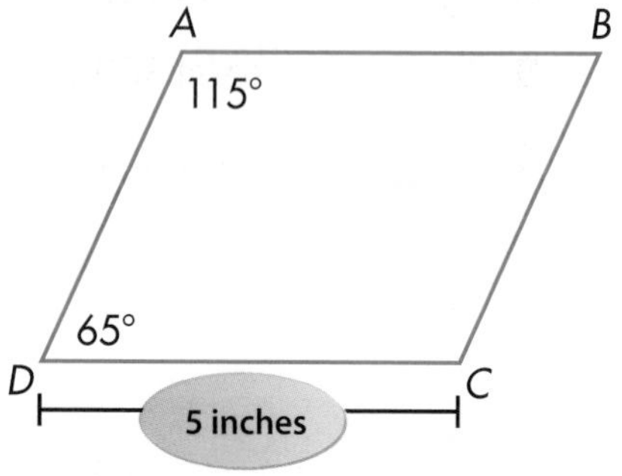

14. The quadrilateral has two pairs of parallel sides, and one side that measures 5 in. What are the measurements of the other three sides?

15. Find the m$\angle B$ and m$\angle C$ for the figure at the right.

For **16** and **17**, draw quadrilaterals with the given information. Label all side and angle measurements.

16. All four sides of the quadrilateral measure 5 cm. Two of the opposite angles are 130°.

17. A quadrilateral has congruent opposite sides and angles. One side measures 8 cm, and another side measures 2 cm. The top right angle measures 45°.

Problem Solving

For **18** and **19**, write each word phrase as an algebraic expression.

18. twice *n* increased by 12 **19.** *m* squared divided by 3

20. The computer club raised $105.75 for new software. A math program costs $49.50. A reading program costs $65.39. About how much more money does the club need to pay for the software?

21. What quadrilaterals and other polygons can you see in the drawing at the right?

22. Writing to Explain All parallelograms have opposite sides parallel. Are squares and other rectangles parallelograms? Explain.

Problem Solving

23. If you divide a square into two congruent triangles, what type of triangles are they?

24. Draw a 5 cm side between a 100° and a 40° angle. Then classify the triangle by its angles and sides.

25. What is true about every quadrilateral?

A The angles total 180°.

B The angles total 360°.

C There are two sets of congruent sides.

D There are two sets of congruent angles.

26. What kind of triangle is a yield sign? Classify it in as many ways as possible.

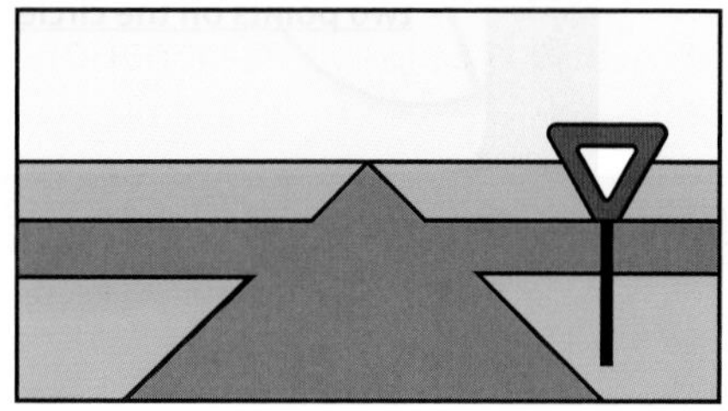

27. Writing to Explain What characteristics help you classify a quadrilateral as a rhombus but not a square? Explain.

28. Reasoning A quadrilateral has four congruent sides. One of its angles measures 75°. What are the measures of its other three angles?

29. Think About the Process Which set of angles could be the measures of angle pairs in a parallelogram?

A 95°, 120° **B** 70°, 110° **C** 25°, 49° **D** 80°, 90°

30. If you cut off one vertex of a triangle, as shown in the figure, how many sides does the new polygon have? Classify the new polygon in as many ways as possible.

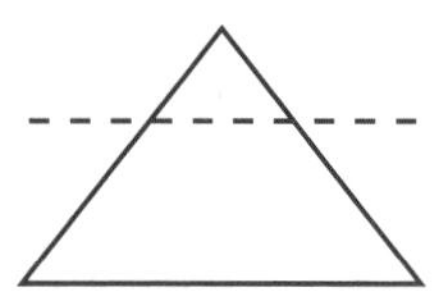

31. In its first week, a new movie had box-office sales of eight million, five hundred sixty-five thousand, four hundred three. Write the number in standard form.

For **32** and **33**, use the table. Tyler's family is planning a trip during a school break. At their destination, some months are rainier than others. They want to go when there is less chance of rain.

Data

Month	Rainfall (inches)
March	3.6
June	1.4
July	0.7
August	1.3
November	2.0
December	6.3

32. Write the rainfall per month in order from least to greatest.

33. Which month would be best for a visit? Explain.

Lesson
11-8

Understand It!
Some figures can be reflected or rotated, and the result is the original figure.

Symmetry

What are symmetric figures?

Aria is creating a square mosaic tile design in art class. The art teacher said to create a design that has at least two lines of symmetry.

Does Aria's tile design have at least two lines of symmetry?

Another Example What is rotational symmetry?

When a figure rotates onto itself in less than a full turn, the figure has rotational symmetry. The shapes below have rotational symmetry.

$180°$ ($\frac{1}{2}$ turn) rotational symmetry

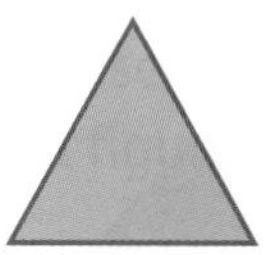

$120°$ ($\frac{1}{3}$ turn) rotational symmetry

$90°$ ($\frac{1}{4}$ turn) rotational symmetry

$45°$ ($\frac{1}{8}$ turn) rotational symmetry

Guided Practice*

Do you know HOW?

For **1** and **2**, identify the type(s) of symmetry; tell the number of lines of symmetry or smallest turn needed for rotational symmetry.

1. 

2. 

3. How many lines of symmetry, if any, do each of the figures in Another Example have?

Do you UNDERSTAND?

4. How could you check to see if a paper shape has reflection symmetry?

5. Describe the symmetry of a regular hexagon.

6. Does Aria's mosaic tile design have rotational symmetry? Explain.

DIGITAL Animated Glossary **www.pearsonsuccessnet.com**

*For another example, see Set F on page 297.

A figure has reflection symmetry if it can be reflected onto itself. The line of reflection is a line of symmetry. Some figures have more than one line of symmetry.

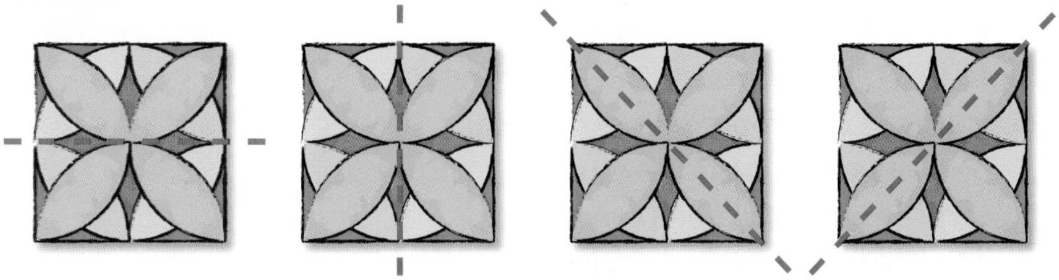

Aria's design has four lines of symmetry. Her design meets her art teacher's directions.

Independent Practice

In **7** through **10**, tell if each figure has reflection symmetry, rotational symmetry, or both. If it has reflection symmetry, how many lines of symmetry are there? If it has rotational symmetry, what is the smallest turn that will rotate the figure onto itself?

7. 

8. 

9. 

10. 

Problem Solving

11. **Draw a Picture** Draw a picture of a scalene triangle and its reflection over a vertical line.

12. **Reasoning** Why does a rotation have to be less than 360° to show rotational symmetry?

13. How many times does Caleb have to turn this figure 90° to get it back to its original position?

14. **Writing to Explain** How many lines of symmetry does a circle have? Explain.

15. Elli wants to draw a figure that has reflection symmetry but not rotation symmetry. What shape might Elli draw?

16. This sea star has 5 arms. How many lines of symmetry does it have?

17. Which shape has exactly 2 lines of symmetry?

A T **B** E **C** N **D** I

Lesson
11-9

Understand It!
Some problems can be solved by finding a pattern and making a table to extend the pattern.

Problem Solving

Make a Table and Look for a Pattern

Polygons with four or more sides can be divided into triangles by connecting vertices. A quadrilateral can be divided into 2 triangles. From a single vertex, how many triangles can a regular polygon with 20 sides be divided into?

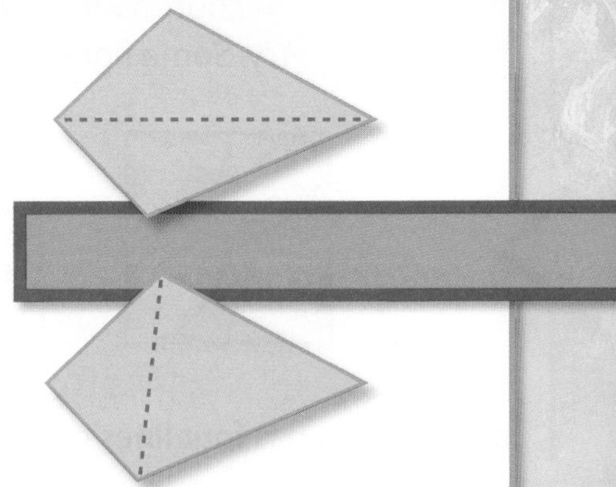

Guided Practice*

Do you know HOW?

1. Complete the table to show the number of dots needed for the 4th triangle shape in this series.

Triangle shape	1st	2nd	3rd	4th
Number of dots	1	3	6	

Do you UNDERSTAND?

2. Explain the pattern for the table in Exercise 1.

3. Explain how a table can make it easier to see a pattern.

4. **Write a Problem** Write a problem that can be solved by making a table and looking for a pattern.

Independent Practice

5. A diagonal is a line that connects two vertices of a figure that are not already connected by a side. For example, a 5-sided figure can have 5 diagonals. How many diagonals can an 8-sided figure have? Use the simple figures below to help you make a table to solve this problem. State the pattern that you find.

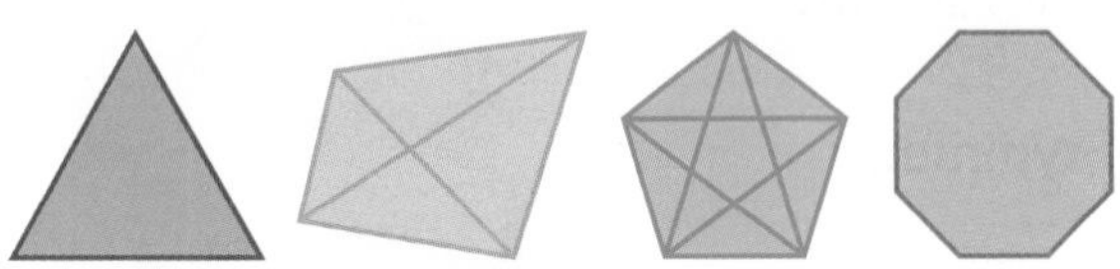

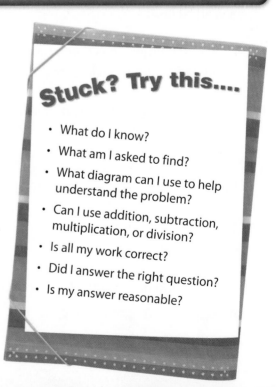

Stuck? Try this....

- What do I know?
- What am I asked to find?
- What diagram can I use to help understand the problem?
- Can I use addition, subtraction, multiplication, or division?
- Is all my work correct?
- Did I answer the right question?
- Is my answer reasonable?

*For another example, see Set G on page 297.

Plan and Solve

Look at some simple figures.

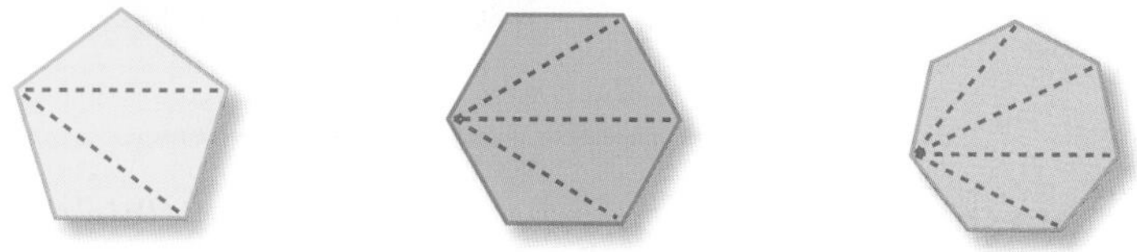

Notice how many sides are in each polygon and how many triangles are formed by connecting a single vertex to other vertices. Make a table and look for a pattern.

Number of sides	4	5	6	7
Number of triangles	2	3	4	5

The pattern is that the number of triangles is 2 less than the number of sides.

From a single vertex, a 20-sided polygon can be divided into 18 triangles.

6. A bell is ringing. Each ring lasts 4 seconds. There are 2 seconds between rings. Copy and complete the table for the first 4 rings. Find the pattern to tell how long the ringing lasts if it rings 10 times.

Rings	1	2	3	4
Total time	4 s	10 s	16 s	

7. The three rectangles at right are labeled with their measurements and areas. Create a table to find a pattern for the rectangles. Use the pattern to find the area of a rectangle that is 5 ft × 20 ft.

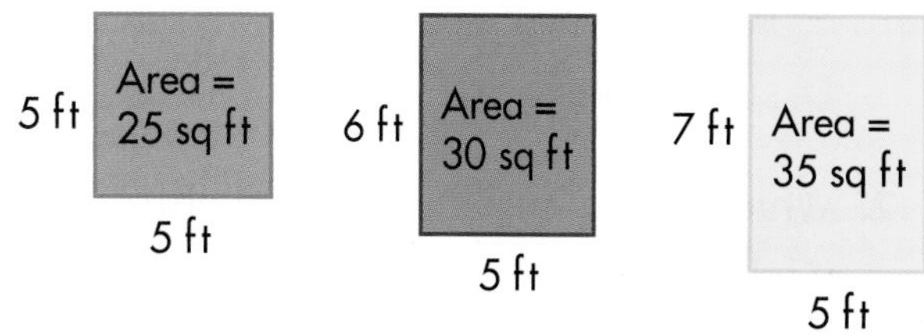

8. These connected triangles form linked sides of three dots each. Use a table to find out how many such triangles you would have to connect to create 20 linked sides of 3 dots each.

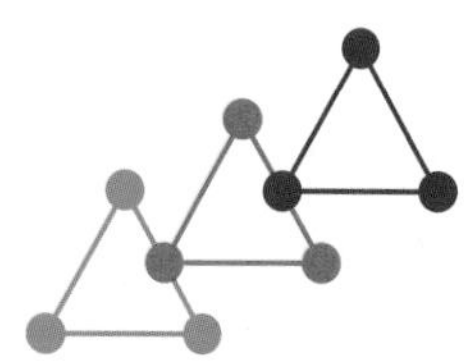

9. What is the pattern for the numbers in the chart on the right? Copy and complete the table.

a	2	3	4	5	10	100
b	6	9	12			

10. XYZ Company is giving a 25¢ discount on the second widget bought and an additional 25¢ discount on each additional widget bought, for up to 5 widgets. Use the pattern in the table to find the total cost of 5 widgets.

Number of widgets	1	2	3	4	5
Total cost	$2.75	$5.25	$7.50	$9.50	

1. The picture shows a diagram of a garden. What is the best description of the relationship between the row of tulips and the row of periwinkles? (11-1)

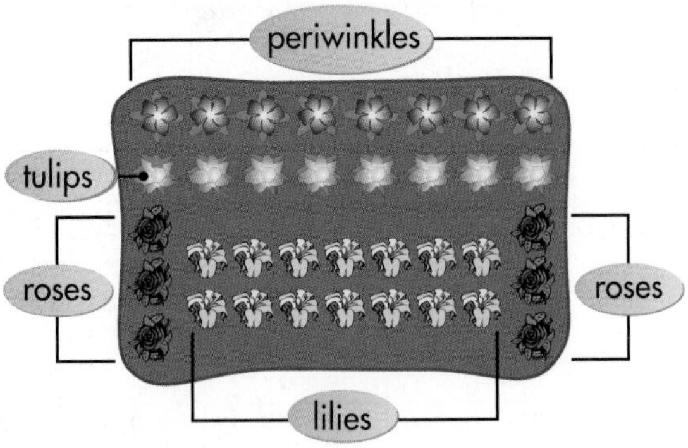

A intersecting

B parallel

C perpendicular

D supplementary

2. Which triangle is isosceles and obtuse? (11-4)

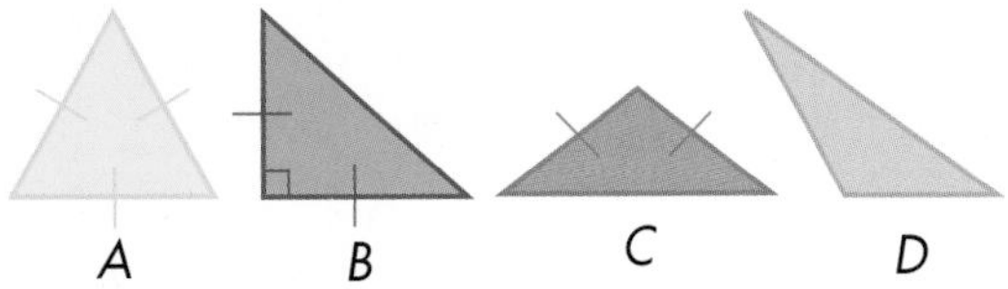

A Triangle *A*

B Triangle *B*

C Triangle *C*

D Triangle *D*

3. Travis drew a quadrilateral with opposite sides that were not congruent. Which of the following could he have drawn? (11-5)

A rhombus

B trapezoid

C parallelogram

D rectangle

4. Which of the following statements correctly describes the diagram? (11-3)

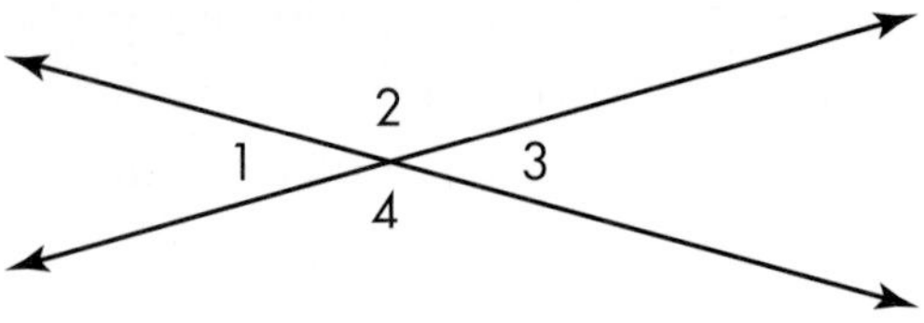

A $\angle 1$ is congruent to $\angle 3$.

B $\angle 1$ is supplementary to $\angle 3$.

C $\angle 1$ is obtuse.

D $\angle 1$ is complementary to $\angle 4$.

5. The shape has been moved. Which best describes the movement? (11-7)

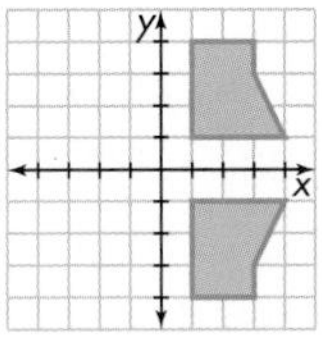

A reflection

B translation

C rotation

D magnified

6. What is the smallest turn that will make this figure rotate onto itself? (11-8)

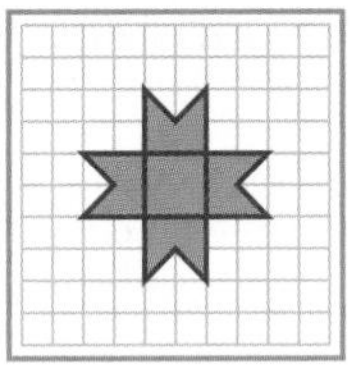

A 90°

B 60°

C 45°

D 30°

7. Ashley's trampoline has a design as shown in the diagram. If each sector in the diagram is the same size, what is the measure of $\angle HIJ$? (11-6)

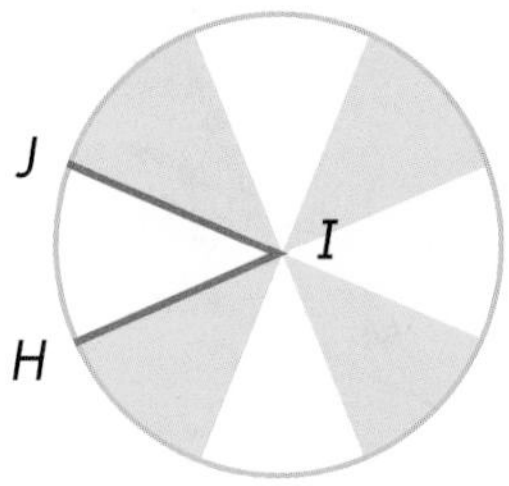

A 15°

B 30°

C 45°

D 90°

8. Katie drew a 150° angle. Which angle could be the one she drew? (11-2)

A 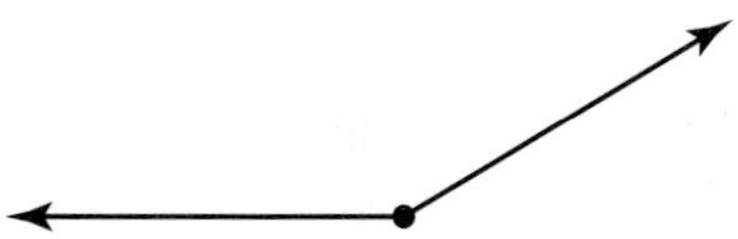

B 

C 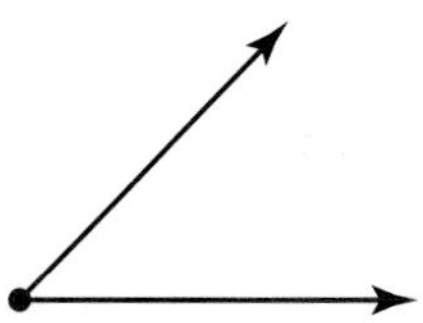

D 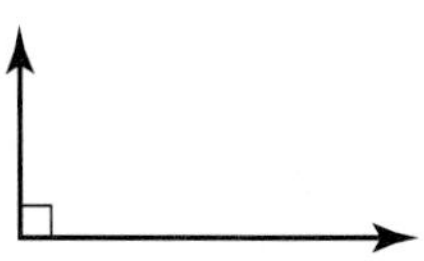

9. Which of the following best describes the edge of a long straight road? (11-1)

A point

B line

C obtuse angle

D plane

10. Tiles can be used to frame a square tile pattern of any size as shown in the diagram. How many tiles would be used to frame 25 green tiles arranged in a square? (11-9)

Number of center tiles	1	4	9	16	25
Number of frame tiles	8	12	16		

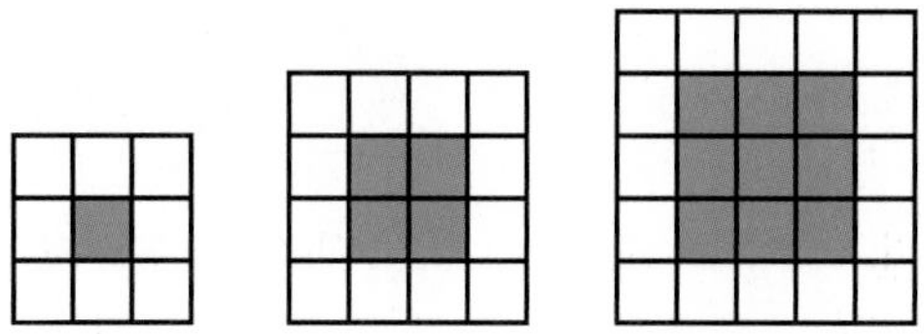

A 20

B 22

C 24

D 36

11. Some farmers irrigate crops with a system where a sprinkler arm rotates about a point as shown in the diagram. Which of the following can be used to describe the sprinkler arm? (11-6)

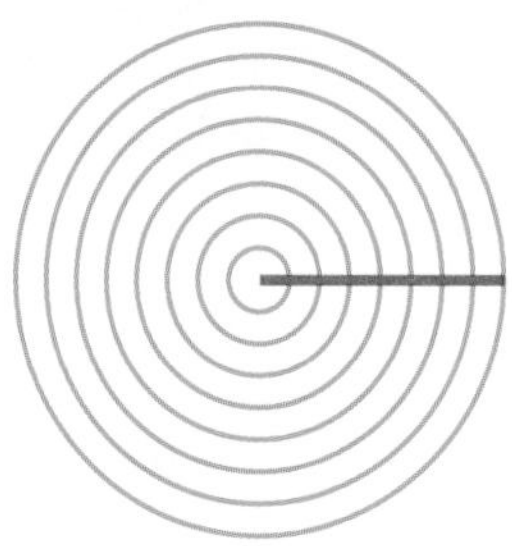

A diameter

B chord

C arc

D radius

Topic 11

Reteaching

Set A, pages 262–264

The terms in the table relate to the figure on the right.

Part	Description	Explanation
$\overrightarrow{GA}$	ray	endpoint at *G* and extends forever through *A*
$\overleftrightarrow{AD}$	line	extends forever in both directions
$\overline{GL}$	line segment	part of a line having two endpoints
L	point	midpoint for $\overline{GJ}$
$\overleftrightarrow{FC}$ and $\overleftrightarrow{KN}$	parallel lines	never intersect
$\overleftrightarrow{AD}$ and $\overleftrightarrow{EB}$	perpendicular lines	meet at a right angle
$\overline{GL}$ and $\overline{LJ}$	congruent	are the same length
$\overleftrightarrow{KN}$ and $\overleftrightarrow{BE}$	intersecting lines	pass through the same point, *M*

Remember that the letters in the diagram above show the location of points, and these points are used to identify rays, lines, line segments, and angles.

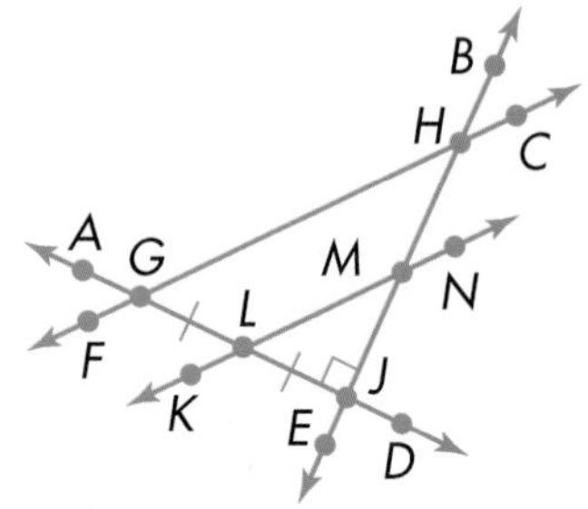

Use the diagram above to answer **1** through **5**.

1. Identify two lines that intersect.
2. Identify two lines that are perpendicular.
3. Identify two lines that are parallel.
4. What is the measure of $\angle BJL$?
5. If you drew a line through points *A* and *B*, how would it relate to $\overleftrightarrow{GH}$?

Set B, pages 266–268, 270–272

The figure below shows a protractor's center placed on the vertex at point *K*. Use this diagram to complete the exercises.

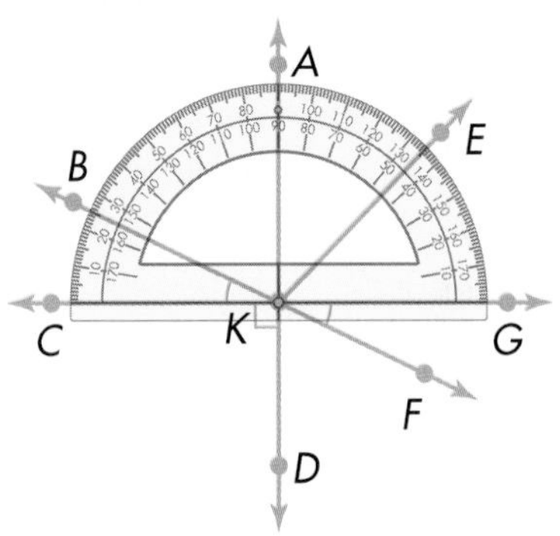

Remember to use the scale on the protractor that lines an angle side with 0°. Vertical angles are congruent. Adjacent angles share a common vertex and a common side. The measures of complementary angles total 90°, and the measures of supplementary angles total 180°.

1. Find the measures for $\angle GKE$ and $\angle GKB$.
2. What are two complementary angles to $\angle BKC$?
3. Is $\angle FKD$ an acute, right, obtuse, or straight angle?
4. What type of angle is $\angle AKF$?
5. What angle is adjacent to $\angle GKF$?

Set C, pages 274–276, 278–281

Triangles

Shape	Angles	Sides	Sample
acute triangle	all acute	need not be congruent	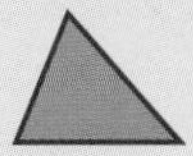
right triangle	one right	need not be congruent	
obtuse triangle	one obtuse	need not be congruent	
equilateral triangle	all congruent	all congruent	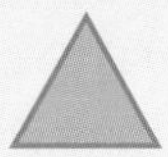
isosceles triangle	at least two congruent	at least two congruent	
scalene triangle	none congruent	none congruent	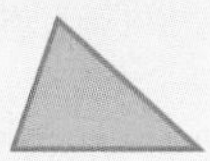

Quadrilaterals

Shape	Angles	Sides	Sample
trapezoid	need not be congruent	only one pair parallel	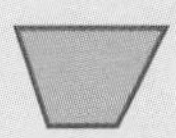
parallelogram	opposites are congruent	opposites parallel and congruent	
rhombus	opposites are congruent	opposites parallel; all congruent	
rectangle	4 right angles	opposites parallel and congruent	
square	4 right angles	opposites parallel; all congruent	

Remember that the sum of the angles of any triangle is 180°. The sum of the angles of any quadrilateral is 360°. You can use a protractor to draw a triangle or quadrilateral from given information.

Draw the described shapes in **1** through **4**.

1. An obtuse triangle
2. A rhombus with a 55° angle
3. A scalene triangle
4. An equilateral acute triangle
5. What types of triangles do you get if you cut an equilateral triangle in half from a vertex to the opposite side?
6. What types of triangles do you get if you cut a square diagonally?
7. If one angle in a right isosceles triangle is 45°, what are the measures of the other two angles?
8. How are a rhombus and a parallelogram that's not a rhombus alike and different?
9. How are a square and a rhombus that's not a square alike and different?
10. One angle in a parallelogram is 75°. What are the measures of the other three angles?
11. One angle in a trapezoid is 35°. Why can't you use that angle to find the other three angles?

Set D, pages 282–283

A circle is a closed plane figure made up of all points the same distance from a point called the center. Review these parts of a circle.

center: *M*
radius: $\overline{MA}$
diameter: $\overline{SZ}$
chord: $\overline{JK}$
central angle: $\angle AMZ$

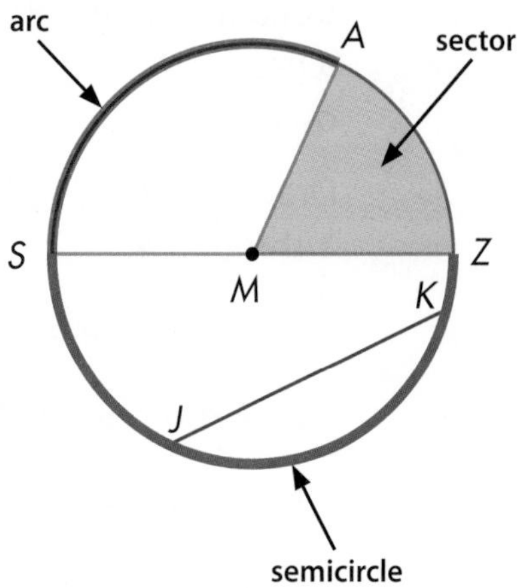

Remember that the sum of the adjacent central angles of any circle equals 360°.

In **1** and **2**, identify the part of the circle shown in red.

1.

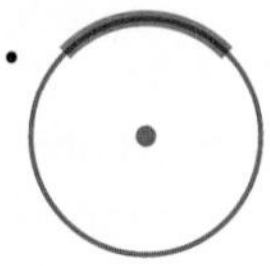

2.

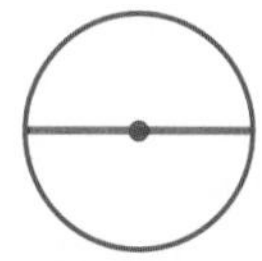

3. What is the length of the diameter of a circle with a 2-inch radius?

4. What are the measures of $\angle CBD$ and $\angle ABC$?

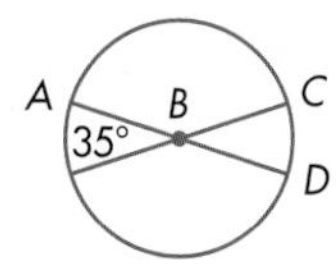

Set E, pages 284–286

These triangles are congruent. Corresponding sides and angles of congruent polygons are congruent.

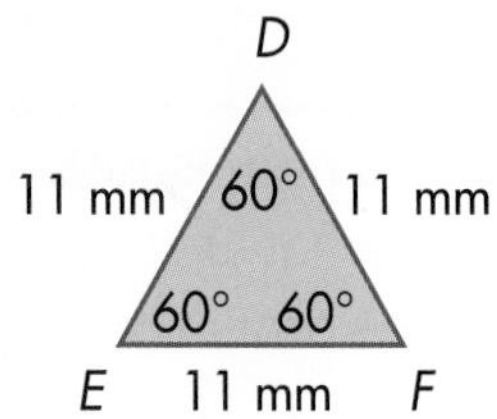

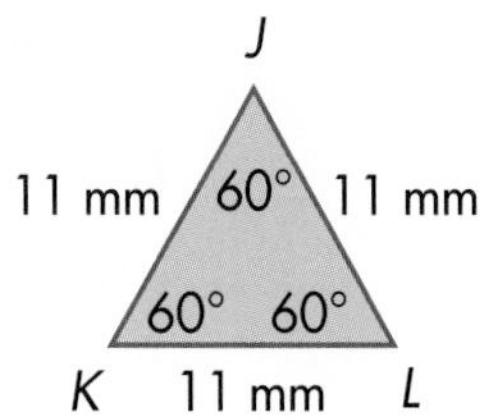

A transformation can be used to move a figure to a new position without changing its size or shape.

A **translation** moves a figure in a straight direction.

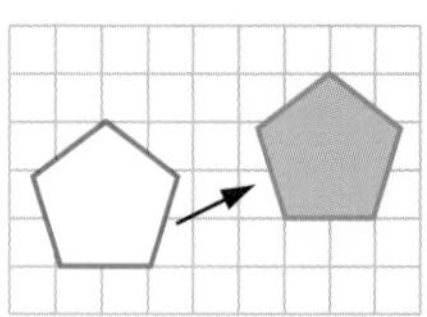

A **reflection** of a figure gives its mirror image over a line.

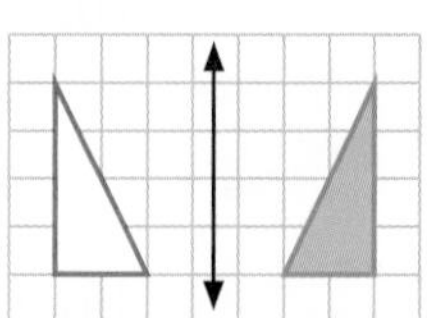

Remember that two figures are congruent if the corresponding sides and angles have the same measures.

1. These quadrilaterals are congruent. Find the measure of $\angle T$, $\overline{TU}$, and $\angle U$.

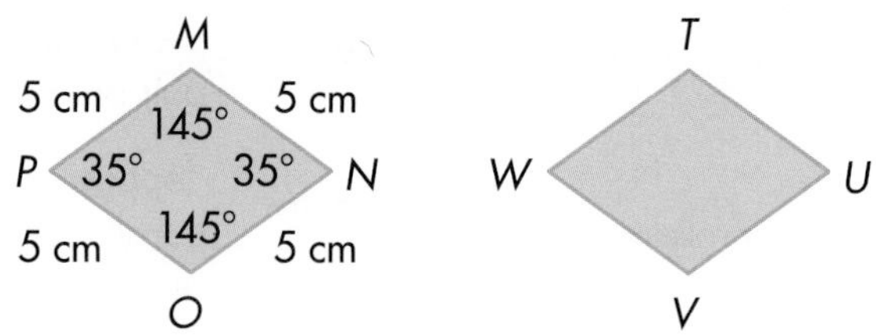

2. Tell whether these figures are related by a translation, a reflection, a glide reflection, or a rotation.

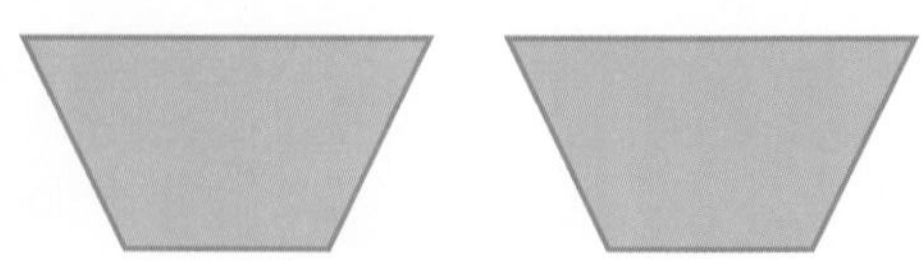

Set F, pages 288–289

The figure to the right has four lines of reflection symmetry.

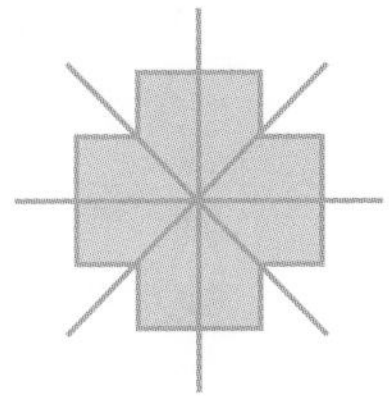

The star figure can rotate onto itself in less than a full turn. It has 72° ($\frac{1}{5}$-turn) rotational symmetry.

Remember that a figure has reflection symmetry if it can be reflected onto itself.

For **1** and **2**, tell whether each figure has reflection symmetry, rotational symmetry, or both.

1. 

2. 

Set G, pages 290–291

Figure 1 has 3 rows and 3 columns of squares. For each successive figure, another row and column of squares are added.

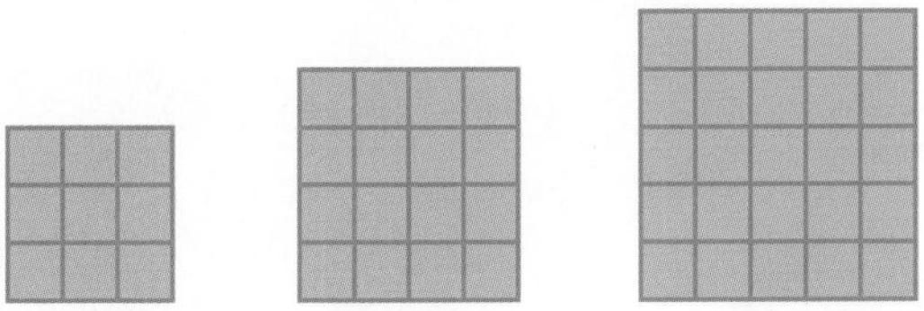

Figure 1 **Figure 2** **Figure 3**

If this pattern continues for 3 more figures, how many squares will be in Figure 6?

Make a table and find the pattern.

Figure	Rows	Columns	Total Squares
1	3	3	9
2	4	4	16
3	5	5	25
4	6	6	36
5	7	7	49
6	8	8	64

There will be 64 squares in Figure 6.

Remember that some problems can be solved by finding a pattern and making a table to extend the pattern.

1. Find the pattern and draw the next three figures.

2. Find the pattern and complete the table.

# of Pounds	Total Cost
2	\$3.50
3	\$5.25
4	\$7.00
5	
6	

Topic 12
Ratios, Rates, and Proportions

1 The *SR-71 Blackbird* is the fastest plane in the world. At top speed, how many miles can it travel in one minute? You will find out in Lesson 12-3.

2 How much water flows over Niagara Falls in one second? You will find out in Lesson 12-1.

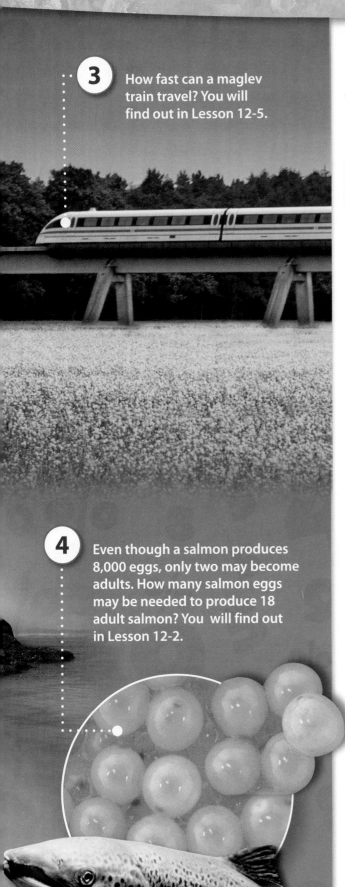

3 How fast can a maglev train travel? You will find out in Lesson 12-5.

4 Even though a salmon produces 8,000 eggs, only two may become adults. How many salmon eggs may be needed to produce 18 adult salmon? You will find out in Lesson 12-2.

Review What You Know!

Vocabulary

Choose the best term from the box.

- fraction
- equivalent fractions
- divisible

1. Fractions that name the same amount are called __?__.

2. A number that can be used to describe a part of a set or a part of a whole is a(n) __?__.

3. A number is __?__ by another number when the quotient is a whole number and the remainder is 0.

Equivalent Fractions

Write two equivalent fractions.

4. $\frac{3}{4}$ **5.** $\frac{7}{8}$ **6.** $\frac{12}{5}$

7. $\frac{1}{2}$ **8.** $\frac{9}{57}$ **9.** $\frac{1}{3}$

Equations

Solve each equation and check your answer.

10. $3n = 24$ **11.** $8c = 0$

12. $y \div 48 = 2$ **13.** $d \div 5 = 7$

Inverse Operations

14. Writing to Explain In the equation $6b = 24$, which operation must you perform to get the variable alone on one side of the equation?

Lesson
12-1

Understand It!
Comparisons between two quantities can be expressed as ratios.

Understanding Ratios

What is a mathematical way to compare quantities?

Tom's Pet Service takes care of cats and dogs. Currently, there are more dogs than cats. Compare the number of cats to the number of dogs. Then compare the number of cats to the total number of pets at Tom's Pet Service.

Guided Practice*

Do you know HOW?

A sixth-grade basketball team has 3 centers, 5 forwards, and 6 guards. Write a ratio for each comparison in three different ways.

1. Forwards to guards
2. Centers to total
3. Centers to guards

Do you UNDERSTAND?

4. What are two different types of comparisons a ratio can be used to make? How is this different from a fraction?

5. In the example at the top, compare the number of dogs to the total number of pets.

Independent Practice

A person's blood type is denoted with the letters A, B, and O, and the symbols + and –. The blood type A+ is read as *A positive.* The blood type B– is read as *B negative.*

In **6** through **14**, use the data file to write a ratio for each comparison in three different ways.

Data

Blood Donors

Type	Donors
A+	45
B+	20
AB+	6
O+	90
A–	21
B–	0
AB–	4
O–	9
Total	195

6. O+ donors to A+ donors
7. AB– donors to AB+ donors
8. B+ donors to total donors
9. O– donors to A– donors
10. B– donors to B+ donors
11. O– donors to total donors
12. A+ and B+ donors to AB+ donors
13. A– and B– donors to AB– donors
14. Which comparison does the ratio $\frac{90}{9}$ represent?

DIGITAL
Animated Glossary
www.pearsonsuccessnet.com

For another example, see Set A on page 318.

A ratio is a relationship where for every x units of one quantity there are y units of another quantity. A ratio can be written three ways:

x to y,

$x:y$, or

$\frac{x}{y}$

The quantities x and y in a ratio are called terms.

Use a ratio to compare the number of cats to the number of dogs:

14 to 17,

14:17, or

$\frac{14}{17}$

This ratio compares one part to another part.

Use a ratio to compare the number of cats to the total number of pets:

14 to 31,

14:31, or

$\frac{14}{31}$

This ratio compares one part to the whole.

Problem Solving

15. Look for patterns in the table. Copy and complete the table.

Number of students with pets	1	3	9	■	81
Total number of students	3	9	■	81	■

16. On average, about 45,000,000 gallons of water flow over the Niagara Falls in 60 seconds. About how much water flows over the Niagara Falls in one second?

17. **Think About the Process** Martine's quilt is made of 6 red squares and 18 blue squares. Which ratio compares the number of blue squares to the total number of squares in the quilt?

A 6:18 **C** 6:24

B 18:6 **D** 18:24

18. **Writing to Explain** Rita's class has 14 girls and 16 boys. How do the ratios 14:16 and 14:30 describe Rita's class?

19. Gil has $128 in his savings account. He saves n dollars each week. Write an expression for the amount of money in his account in 10 weeks.

20. A math class surveyed the musical preferences of 42 students. Use their data file to write a ratio for each comparison in three different ways for **a**, **b**, and **c**.

a Students who prefer punk to students who prefer hip-hop

b Students who prefer classic rock to the total number of students surveyed

c Students who prefer rock or classic rock to students who prefer all other types of music

Data

Favorite Music Type	Number of Students
Rock	12
Classic rock	4
Hip-hop	18
Punk	2
Heavy metal	6

Lesson
12-2

Understand It!
You can use multiplication or division to find equal ratios. Two equal ratios form a proportion.

Equal Ratios and Proportions

How can you find equal ratios?

The ratio of the number of basketball players to the number of baseball players at Grove School is 16 to 48. One way to write the terms of this ratio is $\frac{16}{48}$. You can use what you know about fractions to find equal ratios and to write a ratio in simplest form.

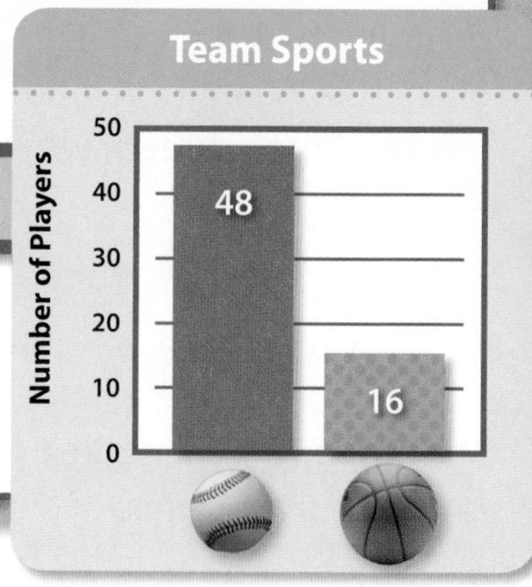

Another Example **How can you decide whether two ratios form a proportion?**

Use the steps below to decide whether each pair of ratios shown form a proportion.

Ratios to Compare	$\frac{7 \text{ laps}}{14 \text{ min}}, \frac{12 \text{ laps}}{24 \text{ min}}$	$\frac{16 \text{ shots}}{12 \text{ baskets}}, \frac{6 \text{ shots}}{4 \text{ baskets}}$
a Compare the units to see if they are the same across the top and bottom.	$\frac{\text{Top units}}{\text{Bottom units}} \rightarrow \frac{\text{laps}}{\text{min}}$ The units are the same.	$\frac{\text{Top units}}{\text{Bottom units}} \rightarrow \frac{\text{shots}}{\text{baskets}}$ The units are the same.
b Write each ratio in simplest form. Divide by the GCF.	$\frac{7 \div 7}{14 \div 7} = \frac{1}{2}$ $\frac{12 \div 12}{24 \div 12} = \frac{1}{2}$	$\frac{16 \div 4}{12 \div 4} = \frac{4}{3}$ $\frac{6 \div 2}{4 \div 2} = \frac{3}{2}$
c Compare the simplest forms to see if they are the same.	Both equal $\frac{1}{2}$, so the ratios are proportional.	$\frac{4}{3} \neq \frac{3}{2}$ so the ratios are not proportional.

Explain It

1. What is always true about the simplest forms of two ratios that are proportional?

2. If the ratio of girls to boys in a class is 4 to 5, does that mean there are exactly 4 girls and 5 boys in the class? Explain.

One Way

Use multiplication. Multiply both terms by the same nonzero number. For example:

$$\frac{16 \times 3}{48 \times 3} = \frac{48}{144}$$

So, $\frac{16}{48}$, and $\frac{48}{144}$ are equal ratios.

A mathematical statement that two ratios are equal is called a proportion.

So, $\frac{16}{48} = \frac{48}{144}$ is a proportion.

Another Way

Use division. Divide both terms by the same nonzero number. For example:

$$\frac{16 \div 2}{48 \div 2} = \frac{8}{24}$$

You can divide the terms by their GCF (greatest common factor) to write the ratio in simplest form.

$$\frac{16 \div 16}{48 \div 16} = \frac{1}{3}$$

So, $\frac{16}{48}$, $\frac{8}{24}$, and $\frac{1}{3}$ are all equal ratios.

Guided Practice*

Do you know HOW?

In **1** through **3**, write three ratios that are equal to the given ratio.

1. $\frac{12}{21}$ **2.** 1:3 **3.** 6 to 8

Tell if each pair of ratios is proportional.

4. $\frac{3 \text{ hits}}{27 \text{ at bats}}$, $\frac{4 \text{ hits}}{32 \text{ at bats}}$

5. $\frac{7 \text{ hours}}{56 \text{ times}}$, $\frac{3 \text{ hours}}{24 \text{ times}}$

Do you UNDERSTAND?

6. How can you write a ratio in simplest form?

7. Use the ratios in Another Way above to form a proportion.

8. Do the ratios $\frac{16}{48}$ and $\frac{12}{32}$ form a proportion?

Independent Practice

In **9** through **16**, write three ratios that are equal to the given ratio.

9. $\frac{6}{7}$ **10.** $\frac{4}{5}$ **11.** 13:15 **12.** 4 to 9

13. 5 to 5 **14.** 12:60 **15.** $\frac{25}{15}$ **16.** 1 to 7

Leveled Practice In **17** through **19**, write = if the ratios are proportional. If they are not proportional, write ≠.

17. 1:3 ◯ 3:1 **18.** $\frac{6}{7}$ ◯ $\frac{36}{42}$ **19.** 5 to 8 ◯ 15 to 32

DIGITAL Animated Glossary **www.pearsonsuccessnet.com**

For another example, see Set B on page 318.

Independent Practice

In **20** through **22**, tell if each pair of ratios is proportional.

20. $\frac{\text{9 blue}}{\text{17 red}}, \frac{\text{36 blue}}{\text{68 red}}$ **21.** $\frac{\text{20 balls}}{\text{12 bats}}, \frac{\text{15 balls}}{\text{9 bats}}$ **22.** $\frac{\text{14 dogs}}{\text{20 cats}}, \frac{\text{7 birds}}{\text{10 cats}}$

In **23** through **30**, write the ratios in simplest form.

23. $\frac{6}{9}$ **24.** 2:30 **25.** 21 to 36 **26.** $\frac{8}{64}$

27. 4:20 **28.** $\frac{28}{36}$ **29.** 28 to 4 **30.** 16:48

Problem Solving

31. Equal ratios can be found by extending pairs of rows or columns in the multiplication table. Write three equal ratios for $\frac{2}{5}$ using the multiplication table.

X	0	1	2	3	4	5	6
0	0	0	0	0	0	0	0
1	0	1	2	3	4	5	6
2	0	2	4	6	8	10	12
3	0	3	6	9	12	15	18
4	0	4	8	12	16	20	24
5	0	5	10	15	20	25	30
6	0	6	12	18	24	30	36

32. Writing to Explain The ratio of the maximum speed of Car A to the maximum speed of Car B is 2:3. Explain whether Car A or Car B is faster.

33. Number Sense The table below shows the time in seconds it takes to burn songs of different lengths on a CD. Write a ratio showing the approximate "length of song in seconds" to "seconds to burn a song."

Data

Length of Song	Seconds to Burn Song
61s	12s
137s	28s
171s	35s
237s	47s
294s	60s

34. Wildlife officials want to increase the population of wild salmon. Use the information in the picture below to determine which ratio shows how many salmon eggs may be needed to produce 18 adult salmon.

A 444 eggs to 9 adults

B 16,000 eggs to 9 adults

C 72,000 eggs to 18 adults

D 144,000 eggs to 18 adults

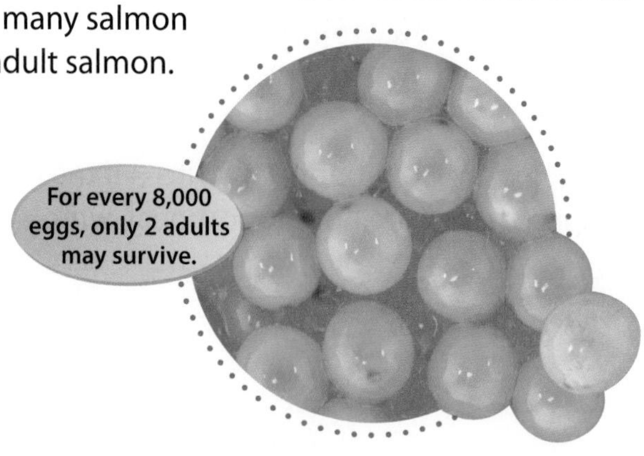

For every 8,000 eggs, only 2 adults may survive.

Mixed Problem Solving

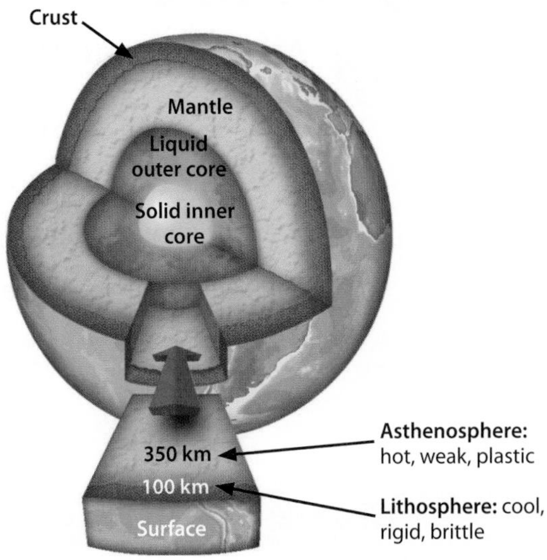

1. What is the ratio of the width of Earth's lithosphere to the width of Earth's asthenosphere shown in the diagram?

2. Earth's diameter is about 12,000 km. The diameter of its inner core is about 2,400 km. The diameter of Planet X is about 6,100 km. If Planet X and Earth are proportional, estimate the diameter of Planet X's inner core.

3. Jupiter's diameter is about 142,900 km. What is the approximate ratio of Earth's diameter to Jupiter's diameter?

4. Because Jupiter's mass is much larger than Earth's mass, gravity is much stronger on Jupiter. The table uses a ratio to approximate what people weigh on Earth compared to what they might weigh on Jupiter.

   a Look for a pattern in the weights. What ratio shows the pattern?

   b What does that ratio mean?

   c Use the ratio you found to determine how much a person weighing 187 lb on Jupiter weighs on Earth.

Data

Weight on Earth	Weight on Jupiter
70 lb	154 lb
80 lb	176 lb
90 lb	198 lb
100 lb	220 lb
110 lb	242 lb
120 lb	264 lb
130 lb	286 lb

5. One year on Mars equals 1.88 years on Earth. What would your age be if you were born on Mars?

6. **Strategy Practice** You can multiply the density and volume of a substance to find its mass. The density of ocean water at the surface is about 1,025 kg per m^3. Write an equation to calculate the mass of 12 m^3 of ocean water.

Lesson
12-3 Understanding Rates and Unit Rates

Understand It!
Rates are a special type of ratio where quantities with different units of measure are being compared.

Are there special types of ratios?

A rate is a special type of ratio that compares quantities with unlike units of measure, such as $\frac{150 \text{ miles}}{3 \text{ hours}}$. If the comparison is to 1 unit, the rate is called a unit rate, such as $\frac{50 \text{ miles}}{1 \text{ hour}}$. Find how far the car travels in 1 minute.

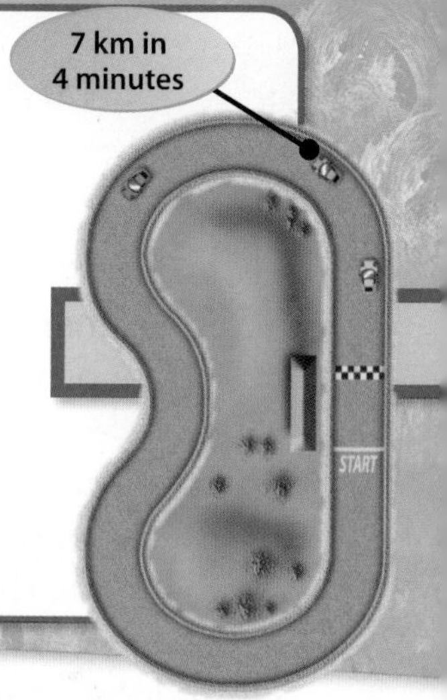

Guided Practice*

Do you know HOW?

Write each as a rate and as a unit rate.

1. 60 km in 12 hours
2. 26 cm in 13 s
3. 230 miles on 10 gallons
4. $12.50 for 5 lb

Do you UNDERSTAND?

5. What makes a unit rate different from another rate?
6. Explain the difference in meaning between these two rates: $\frac{5 \text{ trees}}{1 \text{ chimpanzee}}$ and $\frac{1 \text{ tree}}{5 \text{ chimpanzees}}$.

Independent Practice

In **7** through **18**, write each as a rate and a unit rate.

7. 38 minutes to run 5 laps
8. 36 butterflies on 12 flowers
9. 252 days for 9 full moons
10. 18 eggs laid in 3 days
11. 56 points scored in 8 games
12. 216 apples growing on 9 trees
13. 125 giraffes on 50 hectares
14. 84 mm in 4 seconds
15. 123 miles driven in 3 hours
16. 210 miles in 7 hours
17. 250 calories in 10 crackers
18. 15 countries visited in 12 days

DIGITAL Animated Glossary
www.pearsonsuccessnet.com

For another example, see Set C on page 318.

First, write how fast the car travels as a rate.

7 km in 4 minutes

$\frac{7 \text{ km}}{4 \text{ min}}$

To find the unit rate, divide the first term by the second term.

Divide 7 kilometers by 4 minutes.

```
   1.75
4)7.00
 -4
  30
 -28
   20
 - 20
    0
```

To understand why it works, remember that you can divide the terms of any ratio by the same number to find an equal ratio.

$$\frac{7 \div 4}{4 \div 4} = \frac{1.75}{1}$$

The unit rate is $\frac{1.75 \text{ km}}{1 \text{ min}}$.

The car can go 1.75 kilometers in 1 minute.

Problem Solving

Use the bar graph about the top speeds that different ocean animals can swim for **19** through **21**.

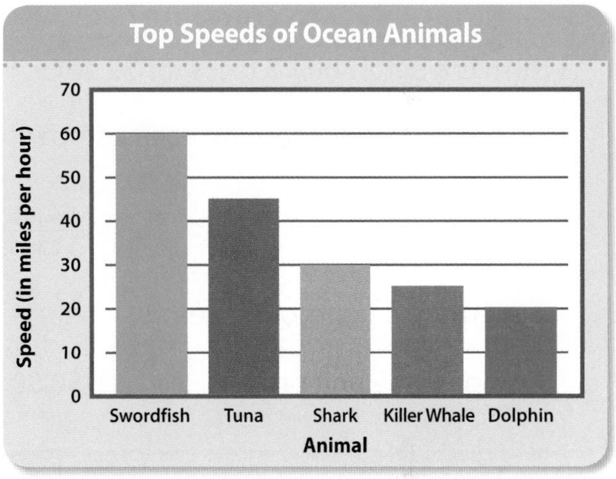

19. Give three equivalent rates that describe the top speed of a tuna.

20. At top speeds how much faster can a swordfish swim than a killer whale?

21. Which animal swims at a top speed of about 0.33 mile per minute? Explain how you found your answer.

22. The *SR-71 Blackbird* is the fastest plane in the world. It can reach a maximum speed of 2,512 mph. What is its maximum rate of speed in miles per minute?

23. **Think About the Process** Mischa buys 4 tickets to a soccer game. The total cost before taxes is $90. Which equation would you use to determine the price, *p*, of each ticket?

A $4p = 90$

B $90p = 4$

C $4 + p = 90$

D $p \div 4 = 90$

24. **Writing to Explain** Make a list of three rates that describe what you do. For example, you could describe how many classes you attend in a day. For each example, explain why it is a rate.

Lesson
12-4

Understand It!
Unit rates or unit prices allow for easy comparisons.

Comparing Rates

How can you use unit rates to compare?

Ethan swam 11 laps in the pool in 8 minutes. Austin swam 7 laps in the same pool in 5 minutes. Which boy swam at a faster rate?

Find the unit rates to compare who swam faster.

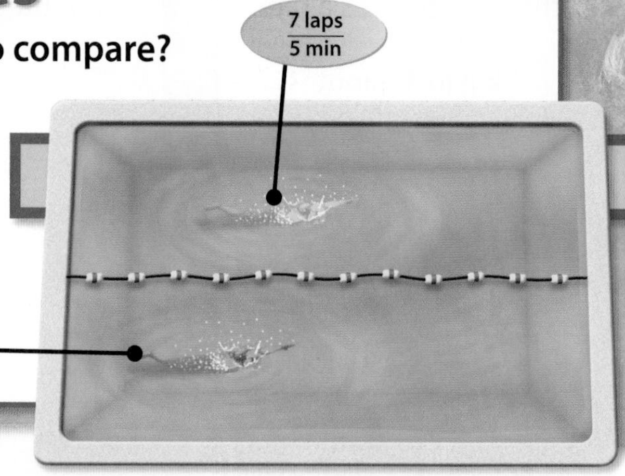

Another Example How can you use unit prices to compare?

Which is a better buy, 3 tacos for $2.40 or 4 tacos for $3.40?

Find the cost of one taco for each comparison:

- Write each cost as a rate. $\frac{\$2.40}{3 \text{ tacos}}$ $\frac{\$3.40}{4 \text{ tacos}}$
- Find the quotients of the terms. $\frac{\$2.40}{3} = \$0.80$ $\frac{\$3.40}{4} = \$0.85$
- Compare the unit prices. $\$0.80 < \$0.85$, so 3 tacos for $2.40 is a better buy.

Guided Practice*

Do you know HOW?

Find the unit rates to answer the question.

1. Which has a faster average speed: a car that travels 600 feet in 20 seconds or a motorcycle that travels 300 feet in 12 seconds?

a Write each speed as a rate.

b Find the unit rate of the car.

c Find the unit rate of the motorcycle.

d Compare the unit rates.

Do you UNDERSTAND?

2. How does finding the unit rates allow you to compare two rates?

3. Why is a unit price a kind of unit rate?

4. Explain how to decide which is a better buy, an 8-pack of pencils on sale for $0.99, or a 10-pack of pencils at the regular price of $1.09.

*For another example, see Set D on page 319.

Find Ethan's unit rate.

- Write his rate. $\frac{11 \text{ laps}}{8 \text{ minutes}}$
- Divide the first term by the second term.

$$\frac{11}{8} = 1\frac{3}{8} = 1.375$$

- Ethan swam 1.375 laps per minute.

Find Austin's unit rate.

- Write his rate. $\frac{7 \text{ laps}}{5 \text{ minutes}}$
- Find the quotient of the terms.

$$\frac{7}{5} = 1\frac{2}{5} = 1.4$$

- Austin swam 1.4 laps per minute.

$1.4 > 1.375$, so Austin swam at a faster rate.

Independent Practice

In **5** through **7**, find each unit rate and determine which rate is greater.

5. 217 miles in 7 hours or 396 miles in 12 hours

6. 12 laps in 8 minutes or 15 laps in 9 minutes

7. 45 strikeouts in 36 innings or 96 strikeouts in 80 innings

In **8** through **10**, determine which is a better buy.

8. 2 books for \$15 or 6 books for \$45

9. 2 gallons for \$5.98 or $\frac{1}{2}$ gallon for \$1.69

10. 6 boxes for \$3.90 or 24 boxes for \$16.80

Problem Solving

11. Writing to Explain How can you find which container is the better value?

12. On some days, the temperature quickly changes. On Monday the temperature changed 30°F in 6 hours. On Saturday the temperature changed 44°F in 10 hours. On which day did the temperature change at a quicker rate?

13. Katrina and her friends sent 270 instant messages in the span of 45 minutes. What is the unit rate of the messages they sent?

A 270 messages: 45 min

B 60 messages: 1 min

C 6 messages: 1 min

D 270 messages: 1 min

14. Estimation The school district requires a 15:1 ratio of students to adults on a field trip. About how many adults will be needed for a field trip with 72 students?

15. Algebra Amil and Abe rode in a bike-a-thon. Amil rode 15 miles in 55 minutes. Abe rode for 77 minutes. Their rates were proportional. How many miles did Abe ride?

Lesson
12-5

Understand It!
Distance, rate, and time can be related to each other by a mathematical formula.

Distance, Rate, and Time

How are distance, rate, and time related?

Leilani is flying from Los Angeles to Honolulu. If the flight takes 6 hours and the distance is 2,574 miles, what is the average speed of the airplane?

A formula is a rule that uses symbols to relate quantities. The formula $d = r \times t$ relates distance (d), rate (r), and time (t). Rate in this formula means average speed.

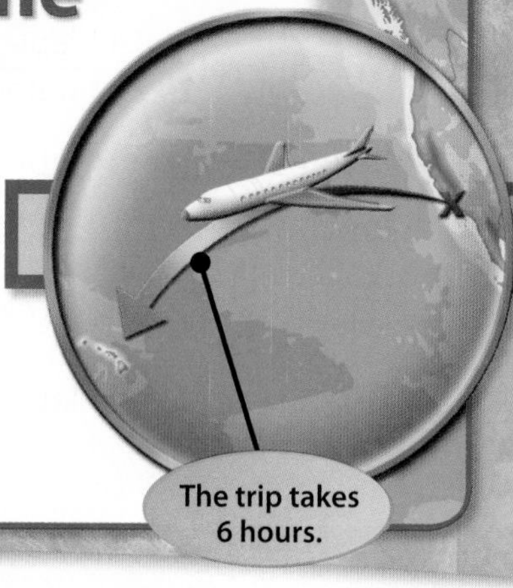

Another Example How can you used the average speed to find the distance or time?

Finding Distance

distance = d; rate = 55 mph; time = $\frac{1}{2}$ hr

$$d = r \times t$$

$$d = 55 \times \frac{1}{2}$$

$$d = 27.5$$

The distance is 27.5 miles.

Finding Time

distance = 96 ft; rate = 32 ft per s; time = t

$$d = r \times t$$

$$96 = 32t$$

$$\frac{96}{32} = \frac{32t}{32}$$

$$3 = t$$

The time is 3 seconds.

Explain It

1. In the first example in Another Example, suppose the time had been given as 30 minutes. Why should you convert the 30 minutes to $\frac{1}{2}$ hour before using the formula?

2. How can you use properties of equality and inverse relationships to change the formula $d = r \times t$ to $\frac{d}{r} = t$?

3. How can you use properties of equality and inverse relationships to change the formula $d = r \times t$ to $\frac{d}{t} = r$?

Step 1

Use the formula.

$$d = r \times t$$

Substitute values for the two variables you know. The average speed is the rate.

$2{,}574 \text{ miles} = r \times 6 \text{ hours}$

Step 2

Use properties of equality and inverse relationships to get the unknown variable alone on one side of the equation:

- Divide both sides by 6 hours. $\frac{2{,}574 \text{ miles}}{6 \text{ hours}} = \frac{r \times 6 \text{ hours}}{6 \text{ hours}}$
- Simplify each side. $\frac{429 \text{ miles}}{1 \text{ hour}} = r$

The average speed of the plane is 429 miles per hour (mph).

Guided Practice*

Do you know HOW?

In **1** through **3**, use the following table to find the missing variables.

Data

Trip	time	rate	distance
A	18 hours	r mph	7,794 miles
B	t hours	80 mph	576 miles
C	12 hours	8 mph	d miles

1. Rate of the vehicle in Trip A

2. Time traveled in Trip B

3. Distance traveled in Trip C

Do you UNDERSTAND?

4. When using a formula to find a missing variable, why is it important to apply the same operation to both sides of the equation?

5. In the above example, while coming back from Hawaii, the plane enters a jet stream. Traveling in the jet stream shortens the return trip by 1 hour. What is the average rate of the plane during the return trip?

Independent Practice

In **6** through **11**, find the missing variable.

6. distance = 12 mi; time= 2 h; rate = ▢

7. distance = 568 mi; time= 8 h; rate = ▢

8. distance = 120 cm; rate = 3 cm per s; time = ▢

9. rate = 56 mi per day; time = 47 days; distance = ▢

10. distance = 349 mi; rate = 3 mi per s; time = ▢

11. time = 12 h; rate = 32 km per h; distance = ▢

DIGITAL Animated Glossary **www.pearsonsuccessnet.com**

For another example, see Set E on page 319.

Problem Solving

12. Writing to Explain Explain how you can find how far a boat has traveled if you know the boat's average rate of speed and the time it has been traveling.

13. Estimation A plane travels at a rate of 470 miles per hour for 6 hours. Use estimation to determine whether the plane has flown more than 3,000 miles.

14. Number Sense Which rate is faster: a bird traveling at 2 kilometers per hour or an insect traveling at 1,000 meters per hour?

15. Number Sense A car traveled from Indianapolis, Indiana, to Miami, Florida, at an average rate of 50 miles an hour. The distance was 1,203 miles. Approximately how much time did the trip take?

A About 12 hours
B About 22 hours
C About 24 hours
D About 32 hours

16. Marcus took a train to visit his aunt. The train traveled at an average speed of 60 mph. The trip took 45 minutes. How far was the distance traveled?

A 45 miles
B 60 miles
C 15 miles
D 2,700 miles

17. A leatherback turtle swims at an average rate of 2.5 kilometers per hour.

a At its average rate of speed, how long will it take a leatherback turtle to swim 10 kilometers?

b At its average rate of speed, how far can a leatherback turtle swim in 30 minutes?

In **18** and **19**, determine the time or distance that the maglev train traveled.

18. If the maglev train traveled at 480 kilometers per hour for $\frac{1}{4}$ hour, what distance would the train travel?

19. If the maglev train traveled at 500 kilometers per hour for 10 km, what is the approximate amount of time the train would have traveled?

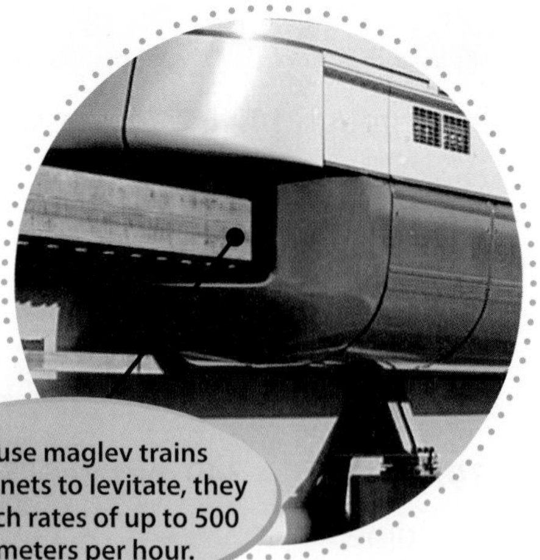

Because maglev trains use magnets to levitate, they can reach rates of up to 500 kilometers per hour.

Going Digital

Finding Rate, Time, or Distance

Ostriches can run at a top speed of about 40 miles per hour. If an ostrich maintains an average speed of 32 miles per hour, how many minutes would it take the ostrich to run 16 miles?

Step 1 Use the formula $d = rt$ and substitute for the two variables you know; $d = 16$ miles and $r = 32$ mph.

$$d = rt$$

$$16 = 32t$$

Step 2 Use properties of equality and inverse relationships to get the unknown variable alone on one side of the equation.

$\frac{16}{32} = t$ Press: 16 [÷] 32 [ENTER =] Display: 0.5

It would take the ostrich 0.5 hours to run 16 miles at 32 mph.

$$0.5 = t$$

Step 3 Change 0.5 hours to minutes: 1 hour = 60 minutes.

Press: [×] 60 [ENTER =] Display: 0.30

It would take the ostrich 30 minutes to run 16 miles at 32 mph.

Practice

1. If an ostrich runs 6 miles in 12 minutes, what is its average speed, in miles per hour?

2. If an ostrich maintains an average speed of 25 miles an hour, how many minutes would it take the ostrich to run 10 miles?

3. An ostrich runs at 40 miles per hour for 10 minutes. How far does it travel?

4. A jet flies 12.5 miles in 4 minutes. What is its average speed in miles per hour?

Lesson
12-6

Understand It!
Drawing a picture to represent a problem can help solve the problem.

Problem Solving

Draw a Picture

Gillian is making jewelry using gold beads and colored beads. The ratio of the number of gold beads to the number of colored beads used in a piece of jewelry is 4:5. What fraction of the beads are colored beads?

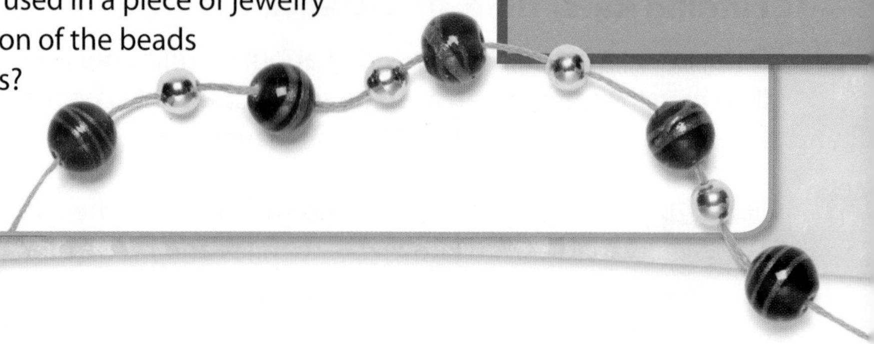

Guided Practice*

Do you know HOW?

Use the picture to solve the problem.

1. Figure A is 3 times as long as Figure B.

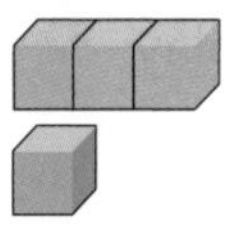

a What is the ratio of the length of Figure A to the length of Figure B?

b What fraction of the length of Figure A is the length of Figure B?

Do you UNDERSTAND?

2. In the example above, how does drawing a picture help solve the problem?

3. **Write a Problem** Write a real-world problem that you can solve by drawing a picture.

Independent Practice

Draw a picture to solve the problem.

4. Tomas and Isaac shared a sum of money in the ratio of 3:5.

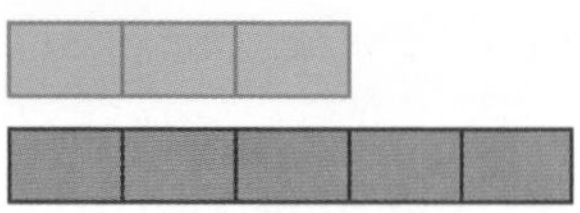

a Express Isaac's share as a fraction of Tomas's share.

b What fraction of the whole sum of money is Tomas's share?

c What fraction of the whole sum of money is Issac's share?

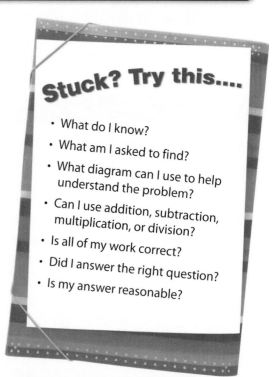

Stuck? Try this....

- What do I know?
- What am I asked to find?
- What diagram can I use to help understand the problem?
- Can I use addition, subtraction, multiplication, or division?
- Is all of my work correct?
- Did I answer the right question?
- Is my answer reasonable?

*For another example, see Set F on page 319.

Plan and Solve

Draw a Picture to show the relationship. The ratio of the number of gold beads to the number of colored beads is 4:5.

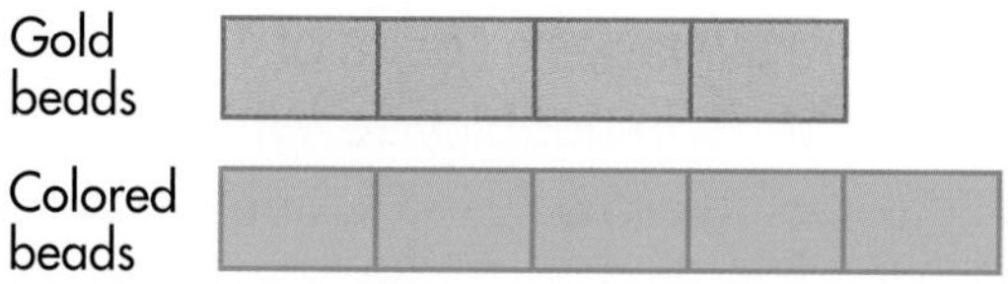

If there were 4 gold beads and 5 colored beads, there would be 9 beads in all. The fraction of colored beads would be $\frac{5}{9}$.

Look Back and Check

Is your answer reasonable?

Yes, there could be 12 gold and 15 colored beads or 8 gold and 10 colored beads, but the ratio is always 4:5.

$$\frac{12}{15} = \frac{8}{10} = \frac{4}{5}$$

The fraction of colored beads in the jewelry is always $\frac{5}{9}$.

Problem Solving

5. Write to Explain Yvette did 30 sit-ups and 18 push-ups. She wrote the ratio 3:5 to compare the number of sit-ups to the number of push-ups. Is this correct? Explain how you know.

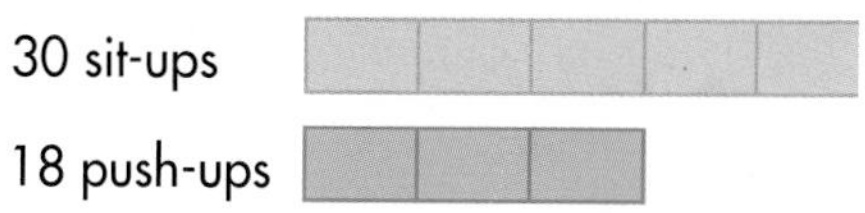

6. Arely is making a necklace of beads. For every 3 silver beads, there is 1 crystal bead and 2 purple beads. If there are 36 beads in the necklace, how many silver, crystal, and purple beads are there?

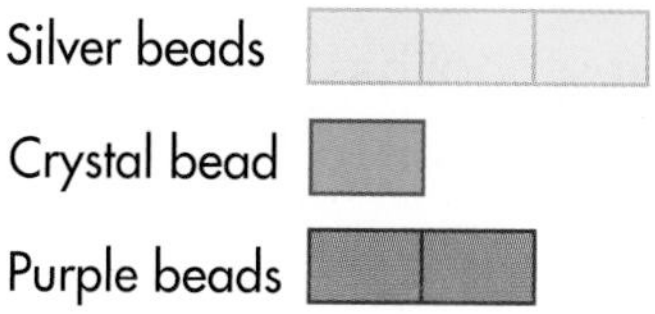

7. Make a Table Hanna wants to take her friends to a movie. If the ticket price is $8, how much will it cost her if 3 or more friends come? Make a table.

8. The picture shows the ratio of Ali's weight to Minghua's weight. What is the ratio of Ali's weight to Minghua's?

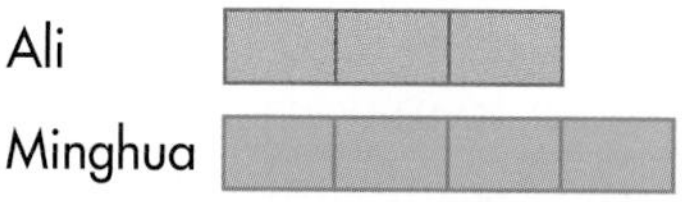

9. Write an Equation Kendall rides his bike at a speed of 15 miles per hour. How far does he ride in 20 minutes?

10. There are 24 players on a team. Two of every three players were on the team last year. How many players were on the team last year? Draw a picture to solve.

11. Work Backward A band played 20 songs. They took 3 breaks. After the last break, they played 3 songs. They played twice as many songs after the previous break. They played 5 songs before their first break. How many songs did they play between their first break and their second break?

12. Think About the Process For a 48-ft fence, Horatio used 1 post at the beginning and then 1 post every 6 ft. Which expression will find how many posts he used?

A $(48 - 6) + 1$ **C** $(48 \div 6) + 1$

B $(48 + 6) + 1$ **D** $(48 \times 6) + 1$

Test

1. The table shows the party affiliations of Senate members of the 109th Congress. What is the ratio of Republicans to Democrats? (12-1)

Party Affiliation	Number of Senators
Republican	55
Democrat	44
Independent	1

A 4:9

B 5:9

C 4:5

D 5:4

2. A preschool has a student-teacher ratio of 5 to 2. Which of the following ratios is equal to this ratio? (12-2)

A 45 teachers to 18 students

B 45 students to 18 teachers

C 35 students to 10 teachers

D 10 students to 7 teachers

3. In order to make a special color of purple, Sydney mixed 12 pints of red paint and 10 pints of blue. Which of the following is the simplest form of the ratio of red paint to blue paint? (12-2)

A $\frac{6}{11}$

B $\frac{10}{12}$

C $\frac{12}{10}$

D $\frac{6}{5}$

4. Claire averages a speed of 15 miles per hour on her bicycle. Which of the following can be used to find the distance she will travel in 2.5 hours? (12-5)

A $d = \frac{15 \text{ miles}}{1 \text{ hour}} \div 2.5 \text{ hours}$

B $d \times \frac{15 \text{ miles}}{1 \text{ hour}} = 2.5 \text{ hours}$

C $d = \frac{15 \text{ miles}}{1 \text{ hour}} \times 2.5 \text{ hours}$

D $\frac{15 \text{ miles}}{1 \text{ hour}} = d \times 2.5 \text{ hours}$

5. The table shows the results of typing tests administered to 4 job applicants. Which applicant typed the most words per minute? (12-4)

Applicant	Words Typed	Time (in minutes)
Smith	84	2
Johnson	102	3
Ramirez	144	4
Yates	153	3

A Smith

B Johnson

C Ramirez

D Yates

6. Doug caught 10 fish over a period of 4 hours. Which of the following is a unit rate per hour for this situation? (12-3)

A 5 fish per 2 hours

B 2.5 fish per hour

C 4 hours per 10 fish

D 2.5 hours per fish

7. Some elephants drink 350 gallons of water in a week. What step can be used to find the unit rate for water per day? (12-3)

A Divide 7 by 350.

B Multiply 7 by 50.

C Divide 350 by 7.

D Multiply 350 by 7.

8. April can buy a package of 10 folders for $1.20 or a package of 8 folders for $1.12. Which is the better buy? (12-4)

A The 10-pack is cheaper at $0.12 than the 8-pack at $0.14 each.

B The 8-pack is cheaper at $0.12 each than the 10-pack at $0.14 each.

C The 10-pack is cheaper at $0.12 each than the 8-pack at $0.15 each.

D The 8-pack is cheaper at $0.12 each than the 10-pack at $0.15 each.

9. The table shows the number of units that are rented and owned in a building. What is the ratio of the rented units to the total number of units in the building? (12-1)

Data

Type of Occupancy	Number of Units
Rented	24
Owned	52

A 6 to 19

B 6 to 13

C 19 to 6

D 13 to 6

10. Which number makes the two ratios form a proportion? (12-2)

$\frac{6}{9} = \frac{\square}{36}$

A 3

B 10

C 15

D 24

11. An accountant wrote 52 checks in 4 days. Which of the following is the rate for this situation? (12-3)

A $\frac{\text{52 days}}{\text{check}}$

B $\frac{\text{52 checks}}{\text{4 days}}$

C $\frac{\text{26 checks}}{\text{day}}$

D $\frac{\text{52 checks}}{\text{day}}$

12. An animal shelter has a ratio of cats to dogs that is 9:7. What fraction of these animals are dogs? (12-6)

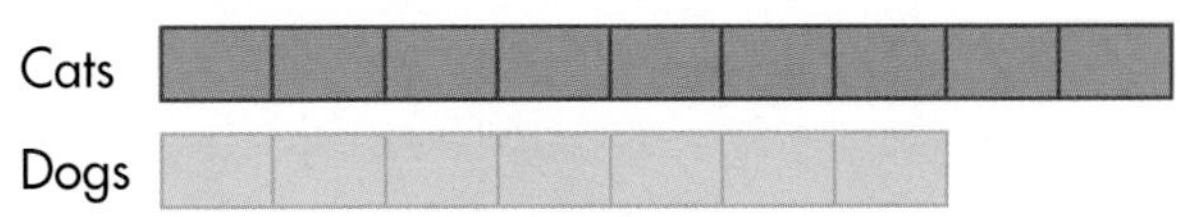

A $\frac{7}{16}$

B $\frac{9}{16}$

C $\frac{7}{9}$

D $\frac{16}{7}$

Topic 12

Reteaching

Set A, pages 300–301

Write a ratio comparing the number of rectangles to the number of circles in three ways.

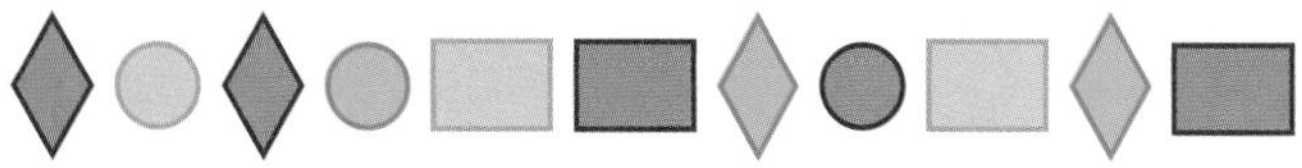

There are 4 rectangles and 3 circles.

4 to 3   4:3 $\frac{4}{3}$

Remember that a ratio compares two quantities and it can be written in three ways.

Write a ratio for each comparison in three ways.

1. green figures to purple figures
2. rectangles to diamonds
3. purple figures to all figures

Set B, pages 302–304

Find two ratios equal to $\frac{21}{126}$.

One Way

Multiply.

$$\frac{21 \times 2}{126 \times 2} = \frac{42}{252}$$

Another Way

Divide.

$$\frac{21 \div 3}{126 \div 3} = \frac{7}{42}$$

Write the ratio $\frac{64}{88}$ in simplest form.

Divide both terms by the GCF of 64 and 88, which is 8.

$$\frac{64}{88} = \frac{64 \div 8}{88 \div 8} = \frac{8}{11}$$

Remember that to find equal ratios, you must multiply or divide both terms by the same value.

Give two ratios that are equal to each.

1. $\frac{5}{12}$ **2.** 14:32

3. 3 to 4   **4.** $\frac{7}{8}$

Write each ratio in simplest form.

5. 30 to 42   **6.** $\frac{56}{72}$

Set C, pages 306–307

Write 20 meters in 4 minutes as a rate and as a unit rate.

Think of the expression "20 meters in 4 minutes" as a rate, a special type of ratio that compares quantities with unlike units of measure.

$$\frac{20 \text{ meters}}{4 \text{ min}}$$

To find the unit rate, divide the first term by the second term.

$20 \div 4 = 5$ The unit rate is 5 meters per minute.

Remember that a unit rate is a comparison to 1 unit.

Write each example as a unit rate.

1. 78 miles on 3 gallons
2. 18 laps in 6 minutes
3. 48 sandwiches for 16 people
4. 49 houses in 7 blocks
5. 500 pounds of fish caught in 2 days

Topic 12

Reteaching

Set D, pages 308–309

On Pet Day, Meg's turtle crawled 30 feet in 6 minutes, and Pat's turtle crawled 25 feet in 5 minutes. Whose turtle crawled at a faster rate?

Find each unit rate and determine which rate is greater.

Write each rate: $\frac{30 \text{ ft}}{6 \text{ min}}, \frac{25 \text{ ft}}{5 \text{ min}}$

Find each unit rate: $\frac{5 \text{ ft}}{1 \text{ min}}, \frac{5 \text{ ft}}{1 \text{ min}}$

Both turtles crawled at the same rate.

Remember that converting rates to unit rates or unit prices makes them easy to compare.

Find each unit rate to answer the question.

1. Which is the better buy?
   $5.00 for 4 mangoes
   $6.00 for 5 mangoes
2. Who earned more each month?
   Atif: $84 over 3 months
   Jafar: $100 over 4 months

Set E, pages 310–312

Julia flies a plane at a rate of 390 miles per hour. How far will she fly in 3.5 hours?

Use the formula $d = r \times t$ to relate distance (d), rate (r), and time (t). You can substitute values for any two variables you know and use properties of equality and inverse relationships to find the unknown variable.

d = 390 miles per hour × 3.5 hours

= 1,365 miles

Remember that rate is the average speed.

In **1** through **3**, copy and complete the table.

Data

Race	Rate	Distance	Time
1	56 mph	4,480 mi	▢ h
2	70 mph	▢ mi	9 h
3	▢ mph	111 mi	2 h

Set F, pages 314–315

Haley is making a beaded bracelet. The ratio of turquoise beads to crystal beads is 6:4. What fraction of the beads are crystal beads?

Draw a picture to show the relationship. The ratio of turquoise beads to crystal beads is 6:4.

Turquoise beads
Crystal beads

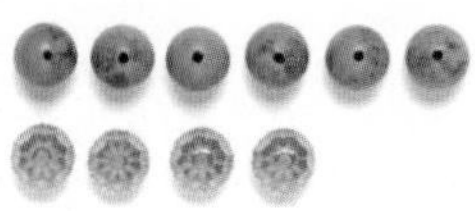

If there are 6 turquoise beads and 4 crystal beads in a bracelet, there would be 10 beads in all. The fraction of crystal beads is $\frac{4}{10} = \frac{2}{5}$.

Remember to look back and check the question that was asked.

Draw a picture to solve each problem.

1. A wall is made up of green tiles and yellow tiles. If $\frac{1}{3}$ of the tiles are green, what is the ratio of green tiles to yellow tiles?
2. Raevan jogs two blocks and walks one block intervals for 12 blocks. How many blocks did she jog?

Topic 13 Solving Proportions

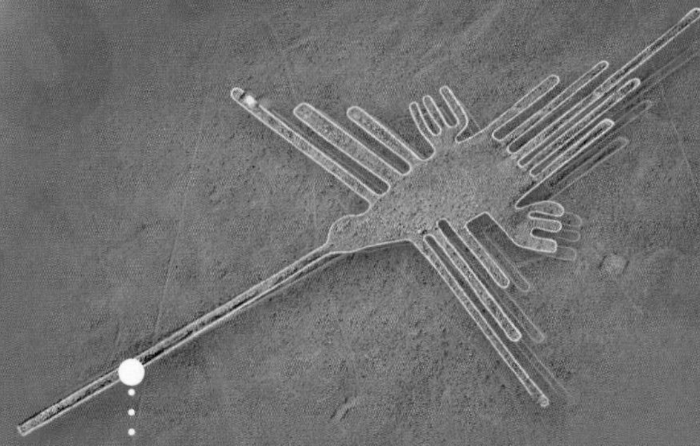

1 Similar figures have the same shape but not necessarily the same size. How could you use the idea of proportional lengths to determine if the figure of this Nazca ground drawing is similar to a real hummingbird? You will find out in Lesson 13-5.

2 The Statue of Liberty is about 46 meters tall. How many times taller is the world's tallest tree? You will find out in Lesson 13-3.

3 This model of the Empire State Building in New York was made using interlocking blocks. How can you find the scale to make models and drawings? You will find out in Lesson 13-6.

4 Cheetahs can run very fast. How can proportions help you find out about how far a cheetah can run per minute? You will find out in Lesson 13-2.

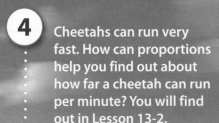

Review What You Know!

Vocabulary

Choose the best term from the box.

- common factor
- ratio
- unit rate

1. A __?__ is a ratio in which one of the terms is 1 unit.

2. A __?__ is used to compare unlike quantities.

3. A factor that is the same for two or more numbers is a __?__.

Simplifying Fractions

Simplify each fraction.

4. $\frac{12}{18}$ **5.** $\frac{21}{36}$ **6.** $\frac{55}{11}$

Multiplication and Division

Find each product.

7. 9×13 **8.** 7×15

Find each quotient.

9. $134 \div 5$ **10.** $434 \div 2$

Ratios and Proportions

Writing to Explain Write an answer for each question.

11. If *rate* × *time* = *distance*, what equation expresses time?

12. What is the difference between a ratio and a proportion?

Lesson
13-1 Using Ratio Tables

Understand It!
Tables can be used to represent equal ratios and solve proportions.

How can you use ratio tables to solve a proportion?

For every 7 cans of tennis balls sold at a sports store, 3 tennis rackets are sold. At this rate, how many cans of tennis balls would be sold if 15 tennis rackets were sold?

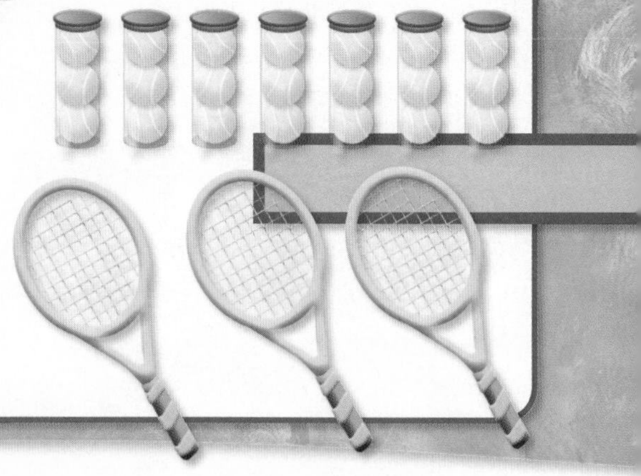

Guided Practice*

Do you know HOW?

1. To make plaster, Kevin mixes 3 cups of water with 4 pounds of plaster powder. Complete this ratio table. How much water will he mix with 20 pounds of powder?

Cups of water	3				
Pounds of powder	4	8	12		

2. **Writing to Explain** How would you find the number of cups of water Kevin would mix with 40 pounds of powder?

Do you UNDERSTAND?

3. In the example above, what equivalent ratio would you use to find how many tennis rackets would be sold if a total of 49 cans of tennis balls were sold?

4. Suppose 2 out of 3 campers on the trip were boys. How many of the 15 campers were boys? Make a ratio table to show how you solved this proportion.

$$\frac{2 \text{ boys}}{3 \text{ campers}} = \frac{n \text{ boys}}{15 \text{ campers}}$$

Independent Practice

The local radio station schedules 2 minutes of news for every 20 minutes of music. Complete the ratio table. Then use the table for **5** through **7**.

Minutes of music	20	30	40	50	60
Minutes of news	2	3			

5. What is the ratio of minutes of music to minutes of news?

6. If there were only one minute of news, how many minutes of music would there be? Write a proportion.

7. How many minutes of news would the disc jockey have to play for every 60 minutes of music?

*For another example, see Set A on page 340.

Write a proportion. Use x for the number of cans of tennis balls that would be sold if 15 rackets were sold.

$$\frac{7 \text{ cans}}{3 \text{ rackets}} = \frac{x}{15 \text{ rackets}}$$

Make a ratio table to solve the proportion. Find ratios equivalent to $\frac{7}{3}$. Multiply both terms of the ratio by 2, 3, 4, and so on, until you find 15 tennis rackets sold.

Total cans sold	7	14	21	28	$\square$
Total rackets sold	3	6	9	12	15

$$\frac{7}{3} = \frac{35}{15}$$

If 15 rackets were sold, then 35 cans of tennis balls would be sold.

In **8** through **13**, answer the question and draw a ratio table to show how you solved each proportion.

8. $\frac{3 \text{ yellow balls}}{7 \text{ green balls}} = \frac{\square \text{ yellow balls}}{21 \text{ green balls}}$

9. $\frac{\$200}{8 \text{ hours}} = \frac{\$50}{\square \text{ hours}}$

10. $\frac{110 \text{ mi}}{2 \text{ h}} = \frac{\square \text{ mi}}{6 \text{ h}}$

11. $\frac{2 \text{ girls}}{3 \text{ boys}} = \frac{\square \text{ girls}}{24 \text{ boys}}$

12. $\frac{6 \text{ ft}}{\square \text{ sec}} = \frac{180 \text{ ft}}{60 \text{ sec}}$

13. $\frac{\$3}{2 \text{ oz}} = \frac{\square}{16 \text{ oz}}$

Problem Solving

14. Alberta found that 6 cars passed her house in 5 minutes. At this rate, how many cars would you expect to pass her house in 2 hours?

15. Writing to Explain Explain the difference between a data table and a ratio table.

16. Anya rode 4 miles on her bicycle in 20 minutes. At this rate, how long will it take her to ride 24 miles?

17. Carol needs $\frac{1}{3}$ yard of ribbon for each bow she makes. If she has $5\frac{1}{2}$ yards of ribbon, how many complete bows can she make?

18. Lauren drove her car 240 miles on 10 gallons of gasoline. At this rate, about how many gallons will she use on a 1,200 mile trip?

A 2,400 gallons

B 120 gallons

C 50 gallons

D 24 gallons

19. Ramon read 12 pages in 20 minutes. At this rate, how many pages can he read in 30 minutes?

20. Geometry Giyo wants to divide her $10\frac{1}{2}$-foot by $7\frac{1}{4}$-foot garden into 3 sections. What is the area of each section? Find $10\frac{1}{2} \times 7\frac{1}{4} \div 3$.

Lesson
13-2 Using Unit Rates

Understand It!
Unit rates can be used to solve proportions involving rates.

How can you use a unit rate to solve a proportion?

A bicycle tour group travels 320 miles in 5 days. How far could they travel in 8 days if they maintained the same average speed?

Find a unit rate to solve the problem.

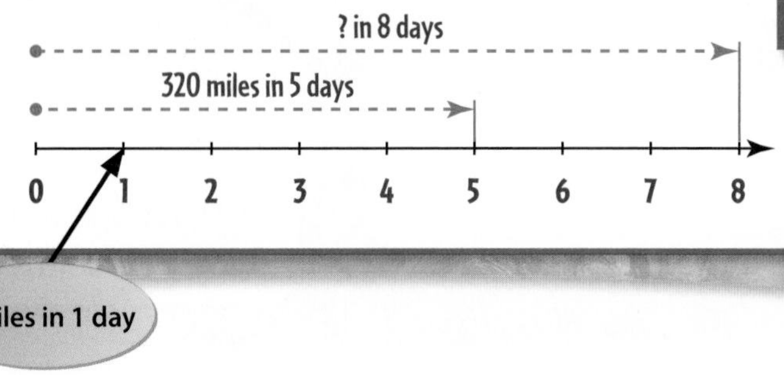

Guided Practice*

Do you know HOW?

In **1** and **2**, compute the unit rate.

1. Another bicycle tour group travels 245 miles in 5 days. How far do they travel in 1 day, if they traveled the same amount each day?

2. A construction crew can spread 2 tons of gravel in 90 minutes. How long does it take them to spread 1 ton?

Do you UNDERSTAND?

Use the information in the example above to answer **3** and **4**.

3. **Reasonableness** How do you know that 512 miles in 8 days is a reasonable answer?

4. Write another proportion to represent the situation in the example above. What is the solution to your new proportion?

Independent Practice

Leveled Practice In **5** through **12**, find the unit rate.

5. $\frac{\text{320 mi}}{\text{16 gal}}$ **6.** $\frac{\text{75 cm}}{\text{3 h}}$ **7.** $\frac{\text{150 snacks}}{\text{50 students}}$ **8.** $\frac{\text{54 songs}}{\text{3 h}}$

9. $\frac{\text{60 min}}{\text{20 calls}}$ **10.** $\frac{\text{33 books}}{\text{11 weeks}}$ **11.** $\frac{\text{1,275 ants}}{\text{5 anthills}}$ **12.** $\frac{\text{\$60}}{\text{5 days}}$

In **13** through **18**, use unit rates to solve the proportions. Estimate to check reasonableness.

13. $\frac{\text{2 in.}}{\text{1 yr}} = \frac{x\text{ in.}}{\text{13 yr}}$ **14.** $\frac{\text{8 h}}{\text{1 day}} = \frac{\text{56 h}}{x\text{ days}}$ **15.** $\frac{x\text{ sales}}{\text{1 h}} = \frac{\text{45 sales}}{\text{5 h}}$

16. $\frac{\text{39 chairs}}{\text{1 row}} = \frac{x\text{ chairs}}{\text{6 rows}}$ **17.** $\frac{\text{3 hikes}}{\text{week}} = \frac{\text{48 hikes}}{x\text{ weeks}}$ **18.** $\frac{\text{3 strikeouts}}{\text{1 inning}} = \frac{x\text{ strikeouts}}{\text{3 innings}}$

For another example, see Set B on page 340.

Step 1

Find the unit rate.

The group traveled 320 miles in 5 days. The unit rate tells how many average miles they traveled per day.

Divide 320 by 5. $320 \div 5 = 64$

The unit rate is $\frac{64}{1}$. The group traveled an average of 64 miles a day.

Step 2

Use the unit rate to find how far the group could travel in 8 days.

1 unit = 64 mi

Multiply 64 mi by 8.

$8 \times 64 = 512$

The group could travel 512 miles in 8 days.

Problem Solving

19. Elephants can charge at speeds of 0.7 kilometers a minute. Use a proportion to find this speed in kilometers per hour.

20. A cheetah can chase after its prey at about 80 kilometers per hour. Use a proportion to calculate about how many kilometers a cheetah could run in 1 minute.

Tip *Use the number of minutes in an hour to help you find a unit rate.*

21. **Estimation** If a machine takes 1 minute to fill 6 cartons of eggs, how long will it take to fill 418 cartons?

22. **Writing to Explain** How are the ratios 4 laps : 1 h and 32 laps : 8 h alike and how are they different?

Use the table for **23** through **25**.

23. What is Martha's unit rate?

24. What is Allison's unit rate?

Data

	Number of Laps	Time
Martha	20	82 min
Allison	16	64 min

25. About how many hours would it take Martha to run 44 laps?

26. **Think About the Process** Suppose the unit rate for people passing through a turnstile is 7 people per minute. How would you express the number of people passing through the turnstile in 5.5 minutes?

A Use multiplication, and then division.

B Use multiplication, and then round.

C The problem cannot be answered.

D Change the unit rate so the answer is a whole number.

Lesson

13-3

Understand It!
Cross products of equal ratios can be used to solve proportions.

Ways to Solve Proportions

How can you use cross multiplication to solve proportions?

Alex makes granola to take for a healthy snack at school. If he wants to make only 5 cups of granola, how many cups of rolled oats should he use?

$$\frac{6 \text{ cups oats}}{9 \text{ cups granola}} = \frac{n \text{ cups oats}}{5 \text{ cups granola}}$$

6 c of rolled oats are needed to make 9 c of granola.
Rolled Oats

When a number is multiplied by its reciprocal or multiplicative inverse, the product is 1. Cross multiplication is like multiplying both sides of the equation by a multiplicative inverse.

$$\frac{6}{9} = \frac{n}{5} \rightarrow \frac{6}{9}\left(\frac{9}{6}\right) = \frac{n}{5}\left(\frac{9}{6}\right) \rightarrow 1 = \frac{9n}{30} \rightarrow 30 = 9n \rightarrow 3\frac{1}{3} = n$$

Guided Practice*

Do you know HOW?

Solve each proportion by using cross multiplication.

1. $\frac{6}{8} = \frac{p}{12}$

2. $\frac{g}{12} = \frac{5}{15}$

3. $\frac{4}{m} = \frac{5}{36}$

4. $\frac{1.4}{1.2} = \frac{n}{2.6}$

Do you UNDERSTAND?

5. In the example above, the ratio of oats to granola is 6:9. Use cross multiplication to show that the ratio 2:3 is equivalent to the ratio 6:9.

Independent Practice

Use cross multiplication to solve **6** through **14**.

6. $\frac{22 \text{ students}}{1 \text{ bus}} = \frac{x \text{ students}}{5 \text{ buses}}$

7. $\frac{8 \text{ points}}{1 \text{ game}} = \frac{96 \text{ points}}{g \text{ games}}$

8. $\frac{\$34}{3 \text{ days}} = \frac{\$204}{m \text{ days}}$

9. $\frac{0.5 \text{ gal paint}}{1 \text{ wall}} = \frac{s \text{ gal paint}}{4 \text{ walls}}$

10. $\frac{h \text{ flowers}}{1 \text{ vase}} = \frac{72 \text{ flowers}}{8 \text{ vases}}$

11. $\frac{\$2.99}{2 \text{ gal}} = \frac{n}{10 \text{ gal}}$

12. $\frac{28 \text{ pages read}}{2 \text{ hours}} = \frac{x \text{ pages}}{5 \text{ hours}}$

13. $\frac{y \text{ cm}}{3 \text{ min}} = \frac{56 \text{ cm}}{8 \text{ min}}$

14. $\frac{8 \text{ ft}}{t \text{ sec}} = \frac{40 \text{ ft}}{25 \text{ sec}}$

*For another example, see Set C on page 340.

Solve the proportion by using cross multiplication. The products of the cross multiplication are equal.

$\frac{6}{9} = \frac{n}{5}$ ← **Multiply on the diagonals.**

$6 \times 5 = 9n$ ← **The products of cross multiplication.**

$30 = 9n$

$n = 3\frac{1}{3}$

Alex needs $3\frac{1}{3}$ cups of oats to make 5 cups of granola.

To see why it works, multiply both sides by 5 and 9.

$\frac{6}{9} = \frac{n}{5}$

$5 \times \cancel{9} \times \frac{6}{\cancel{9}} = \frac{n}{\cancel{5}} \times \cancel{5} \times 9$

$5 \times 6 = n \times 9$

The result is the same as the cross products.

Problem Solving

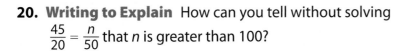

Use the graph for **15** through **17**.

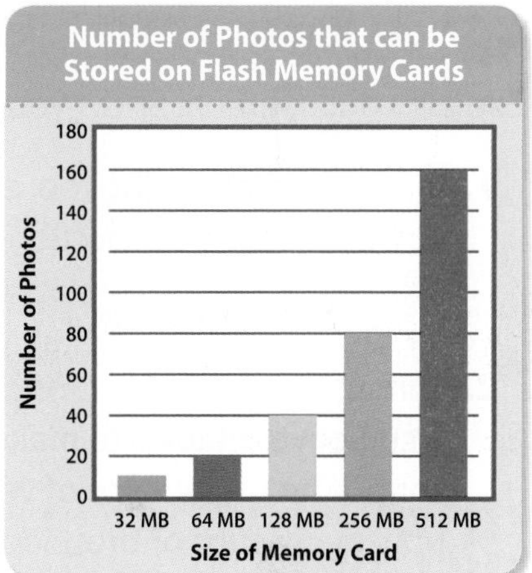

15. According to the graph, a 256 MB card holds 80 photos. Write a proportion and solve it to find how many photos are on a 32 MB card.

16. How many photos per megabyte (the unit rate) can be stored?

17. How many photos can be stored on a card with 1,024 MB?

18. **Estimation** If a car travels 48 miles per hour, about how many miles does it travel in 5 hours?

19. **Number Sense** Francine can read 24 pages in 30 minutes. How can you mentally calculate the number of pages she can read in 45 minutes?

20. **Writing to Explain** How can you tell without solving $\frac{45}{20} = \frac{n}{50}$ that n is greater than 100?

21. The world's tallest reported living tree, called Hyperion, measures 115.2 meters tall. About how many times taller is the tree than the Statue of Liberty?

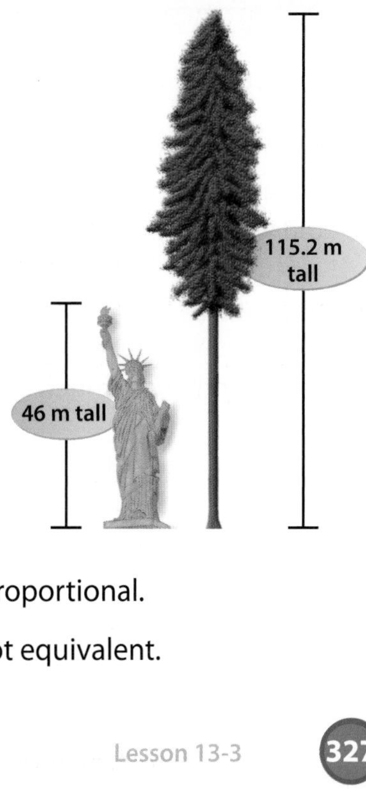

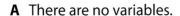

22. Think About the Process Why is the following problem not answerable? $\frac{x \text{ mi}}{\text{h}} = \frac{7 \text{ mi}}{\text{gal}}$

A There are no variables.

B The value for miles is not given.

C The ratios are proportional.

D The units are not equivalent.

Lesson
13-4

Understand It! Mathematical explanations can be given using words, pictures, numbers, or symbols. A good explanation should be correct, simple, complete, and easy to understand.

Problem Solving

Writing to Explain

The steepness of a ramp is the ratio of the height to the length of the base. The ramp at the right has a steepness of 3:4. What would be the length of another ramp with the same steepness if the height were 9 feet?

Jim's answer: 9 is 6 more than 3. If I add 6 to 4, the sum is 10. The new length is 10 feet.

Is Jim's answer correct? Explain.

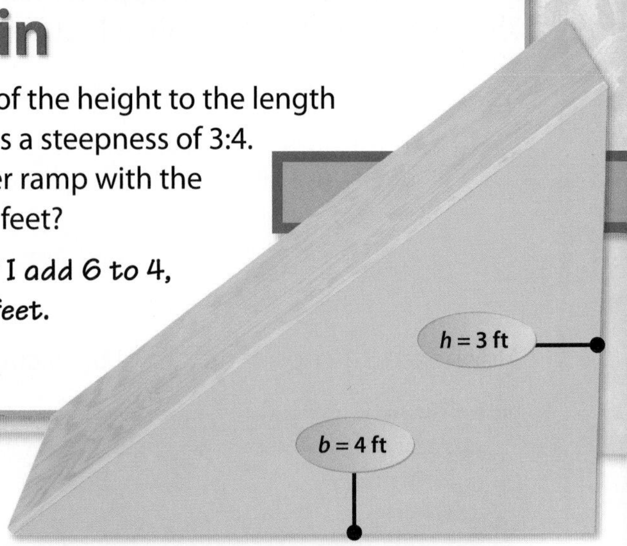

Guided Practice*

Do you know HOW?

Explain your solution. Show your work.

1. In the example at the top, explain how you could use a proportion to solve the problem.

2. Tom uses a ratio of 2 cups of broth to 1 cup of vegetables to make his famous soup. If he uses 4 cups of vegetables, how many cups of broth does he need?

Do you UNDERSTAND?

3. In the example above, how does the picture help in writing the explanation?

4. **Write a Problem** Write a problem that includes a picture to use to help solve the problem. Then solve the problem.

Independent Practice

Explain your solution. Show your work.

5. Jackie goes for a 1-mile run every morning. Today she ran the mile in less time than she did yesterday. On which day did she run faster?

6. Bob earns $5 each day delivering newspapers. He saves $3 and spends the rest. If he saved $27 in a month, how much money did he spend?

7. Ursula's car travels 160 miles on 4 gallons of gas. How far will the car travel on 3 gallons of gas? Explain.

Stuck? Try this....

- What do I know?
- What am I asked to find?
- What diagram can I use to help understand the problem?
- Can I use addition, subtraction, multiplication, or division?
- Is all of my work correct?
- Did I answer the right question?
- Is my answer reasonable?

*For another example, see Set D on page 341.

Read and Understand

Show the information you know.

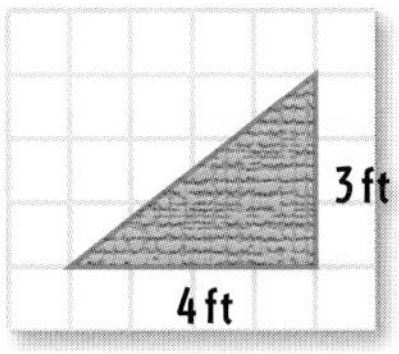

Use words, pictures, numbers, and symbols to write good math explanations.

Plan and Solve

Build a bigger ramp using the smaller ramp several times.

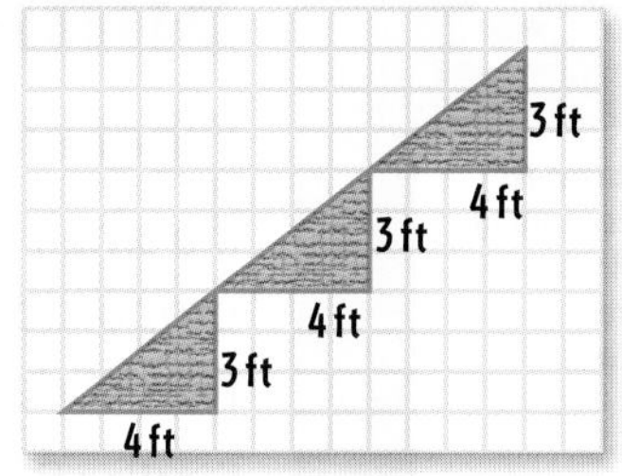

Height: $3 + 3 + 3 = 9$

Length of the base: $4 + 4 + 4 = 12$

The ratio 9:12 is equal to 3:4. The correct length of the new ramp is 12 feet.

Jim's answer is not correct.

8. Dionne read 40 pages in 20 minutes. How many pages did she read per minute?

9. The Picnic Basket sells 60 soups for every 96 sandwiches. At this rate, how many soups will be sold for every 32 sandwiches? Explain.

10. A truck driver started the year making \$0.35 per mile. Halfway through the year, she received a raise and began earning \$0.43 per mile. She drove 48,000 miles the first 6 months and 45,000 miles the second 6 months. How much did she earn for the year?

11. The Chinese calendar has years named after animals. The animals are named in this order: Rat, Ox, Tiger, Rabbit, Dragon, Snake, Horse, Sheep, Monkey, Rooster, Dog, and Pig. If 2007 is the Year of the Pig, how would you find the name of the year you were born? What is the name of the year you were born?

12. Indonesia has more than 13,000 islands, and over 250 languages are spoken there. What is the ratio of islands to languages spoken? Reduce your answer.

13. October 31 is National Knock-Knock Joke Day. To honor the day, Annika wants to give 3 different knock-knock jokes to each friend. Make a table that shows how many jokes she will need to collect for 1 to 5 friends. Write an expression that describes the relationship.

14. Children in the United States go to school about 180 days per year. Children in Japan go to school about 240 days per year. Which ratio describes the correct relationship of U.S. school days to Japanese school days?

A 240:180 **B** 3:4 **C** 4:3 **D** 12:9

Independent Practice

The triangles shown below are similar. Use proportions to find the missing values in **9** through **11**.

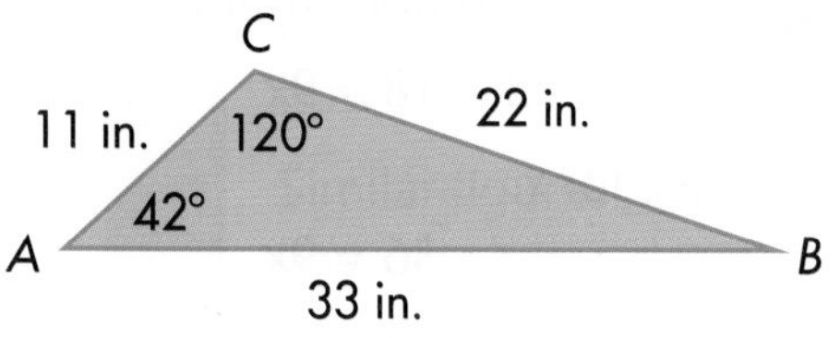

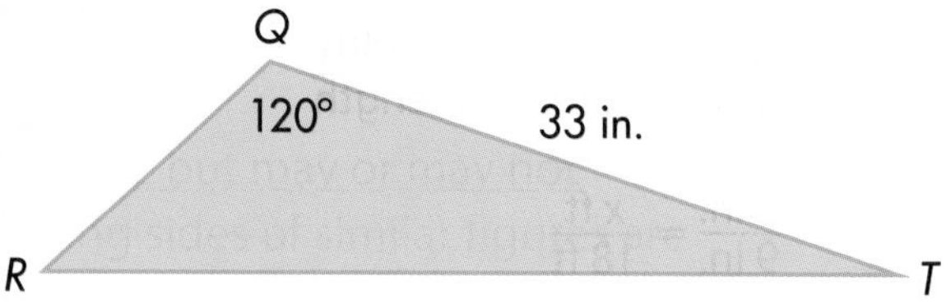

9. Find *QR*.

10. Find *RT*.

11. In triangle *ABC* above, what is the measure of $\angle B$?

12. Draw a triangle that is similar to the triangles shown above. Write the measurement of all of the angles and the lengths of all the sides.

Problem Solving

13. In the diagram below, the tree and its shadow and the meterstick and its shadow form similar triangles. Estimate the height of the tree.

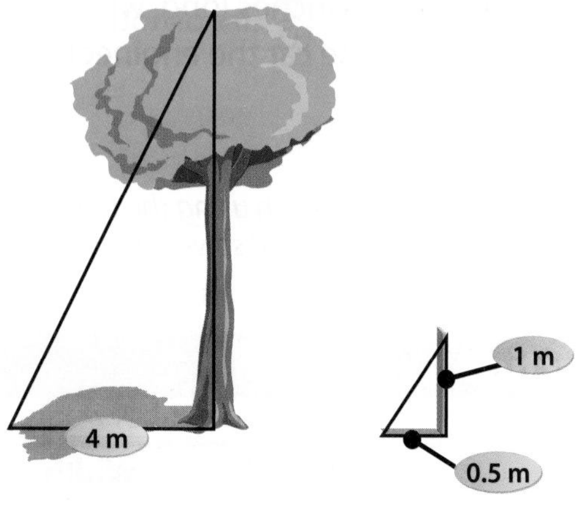

A 4 m

B 8 m

C 0.5 m

D 20 m

14. **Writing to Explain** One of the Nazca grand drawings in Peru is a hummingbird with a reported length and wingspan shown below. A real hummingbird can be 8 cm long and have a wingspan of 10 cm. Explain why the Nazca drawing and a real hummingbird are not similar figures.

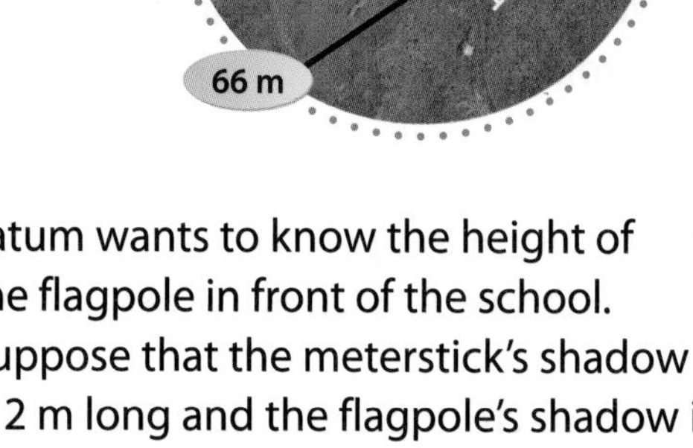

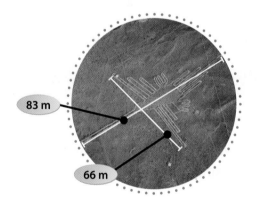

15. **Estimation** Two rectangles are similar figures. One rectangle is 98.5 feet long and 50 feet wide. If the other rectangle is 25 feet wide, estimate its length.

16. Tatum wants to know the height of the flagpole in front of the school. Suppose that the meterstick's shadow is 2 m long and the flagpole's shadow is 20.2 m long. Using the method shown in Exercise 13, what is the height of the flagpole?

Going Digital

Similar Triangles

Use e tools
Geometry Drawing
Draw a right triangle with side lengths of 5 units and 3 units. Draw another one with side lengths of 10 units and 6 units. The triangles are similar. Compare the lengths of the third sides and the measures of the corresponding angles.

Step 1 Draw the triangles.

Go to the Geometry Drawing eTool. Click on the Geoboard workspace icon. Then click on the Draw a line segment icon. Click on one dot in the geoboard, drag straight down 5 units, then click again. Click on point *B*, drag right 3 units and click again. To complete the triangle, click on point *A*, drag to point *C*, and click on *C*. Draw triangle *DEF* similarly. Make $\overline{DE}$ 10 units vertically and $\overline{EF}$ 6 units horizontally.

Step 2 Measure.

Click on the icon for measuring the distance between two points. Click on point *A* and then on point *B*. The lower right corner should show that side $\overline{AB}$ is 5 units. Measure $\overline{BC}$, $\overline{AC}$, $\overline{DE}$, $\overline{EF}$, and $\overline{DF}$ similarly. Notice how the length of each side in *DEF* is twice the length of the corresponding side in *ABC*. Click on the little triangle next to the icon for measuring the distance between two points to expand the tool palette. Then click on the Angle measurement icon. Click on point *B*, then *A*, and then *C*. The measure of angle *BAC* is 31 degrees. Measure the other angles in both triangles. Notice that corresponding angles have the same measure.

Practice

Use the Broom tool to clear the workspace. Draw each pair of triangles and compare the lengths of the third sides and the measures of the corresponding angles.

1. **Triangle *ABC*:** $\overline{AB}$ is 6 units, $\overline{BC}$ is 4 units, and angle *ABC* is a right angle. **Triangle *DEF*:** $\overline{DE}$ is 3 units, $\overline{EF}$ is 2 units, and angle *DEF* is a right angle.

2. **Triangle *ABC*:** $\overline{AB}$ is 3 units, $\overline{BC}$ is 4 units, and angle *ABC* is a right angle. **Triangle *DEF*:** $\overline{DE}$ is 9 units, $\overline{EF}$ is 12 units, and angle *DEF* is a right angle.

Lesson
13-6

Understand It!
Maps and scale drawings are proportional to real places or things.

Maps and Scale Drawings

What is a scale drawing?

For the school yearbook, Mikayla needs to reduce a photo to fit a spot that is 2 inches high.

How wide would the yearbook photo be if the smaller photo was the same scale as the original photo?

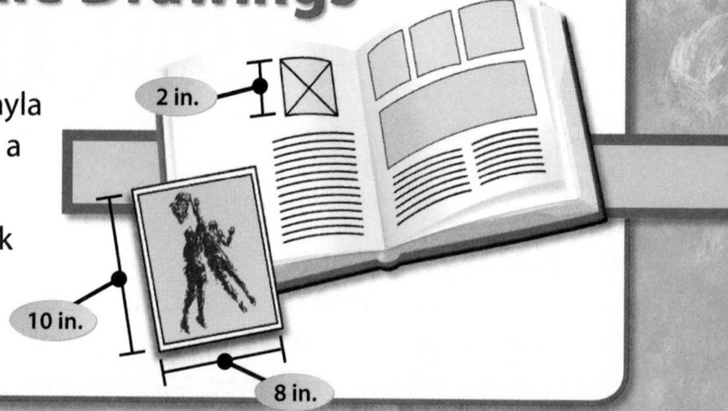

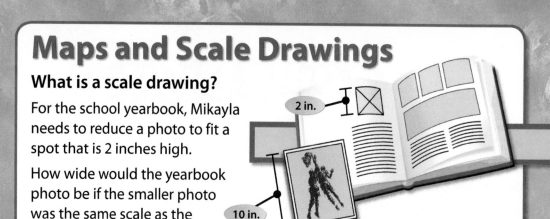

Another Example How can you use the scale on a map?

What You Think

A map is also a scale drawing.

The scale on the map is 1 inch = 112 miles.

On the map, the distance from Brandonsville to New Patterson is 2 inches. What is the actual distance?

Use a proportion to find the actual distance.

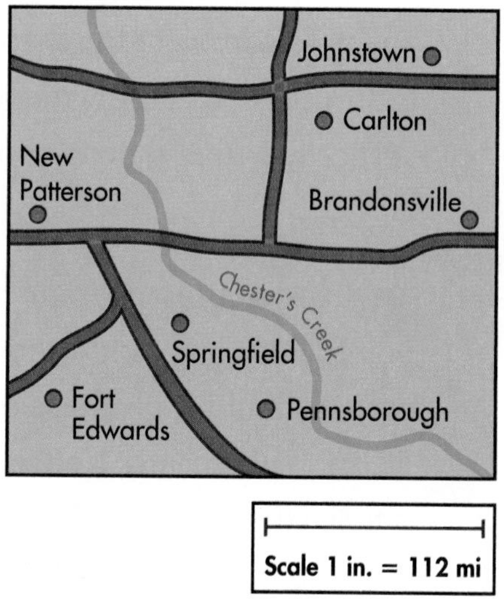

What You Write

Let *d* be the actual distance between Brandonsville and New Patterson.

$\frac{1 \text{ inch}}{112 \text{ miles}} = \frac{2 \text{ inches}}{d \text{ miles}}$ ← map distance ← actual distance

$1(d) = 2(112)$ Use cross multiplication to solve.

$d = 224$

The actual distance from Brandonsville to New Patterson is 224 miles.

Explain It

1. **Estimation** About how many miles does $3\frac{1}{8}$ inches represent on the map?
2. **Reasonableness** If the map were enlarged, is it reasonable to assume that the scale would remain the same? Explain.

In a scale drawing, the dimensions of an object are reduced or enlarged by the same ratio or scale.

The dimensions of the scale drawing and the original figure are proportional. They are similar figures.

To find the scale, compare the heights of the figures.

The scale is 10 in. : 2 in.

Write and solve a proportion to find the width of the reduced photo. Use y for the reduced width.

Height   Width

$$\frac{10 \text{ in.}}{2 \text{ in.}} = \frac{8 \text{ in.}}{y \text{ in.}}$$ ← actual measurements / ← reduced measurements

$10y = 16$

$y = 1.6$

The width of the yearbook photo will be 1.6 in.

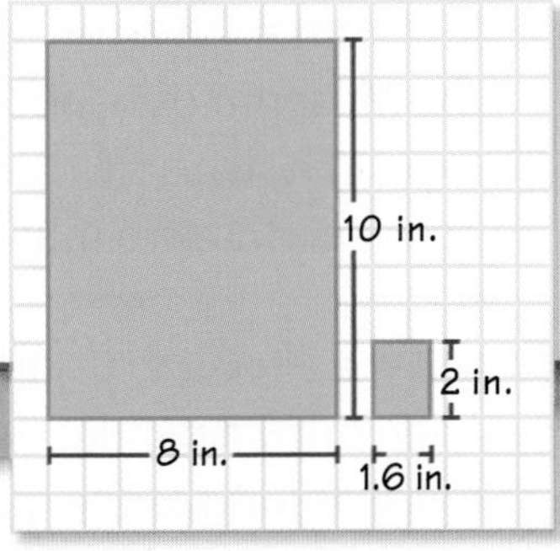

Guided Practice*

Do you know HOW?

Determine the actual distance based on the scale.

1. If the scale on a map is 1 cm: 15 km, how many km would 6.5 cm represent?
2. If the map scale is 1 in. : 550 mi, what is the actual distance if the map distance is 7 in.?

Do you UNDERSTAND?

3. If the height of a space in the yearbook above is 4 in., what strategy would you use to find the width? What is the width?
4. **Write a Problem** Write a real-world problem using the following information: a map has a scale of 1 inch: 2 miles.

Independent Practice

Use the scale drawing to answer **5** through **7**.

5. Caleb walked from his house to the water park. What was the actual distance he walked?
6. It took Caleb 30 minutes to walk from his house to the water park. If he walks at the same pace, how long will it take him to walk from the water park to the theater?
7. If Caleb walked from his house to the theater, from the theater to the water park, and from the water park to his house, what would be the total actual distance he walked?

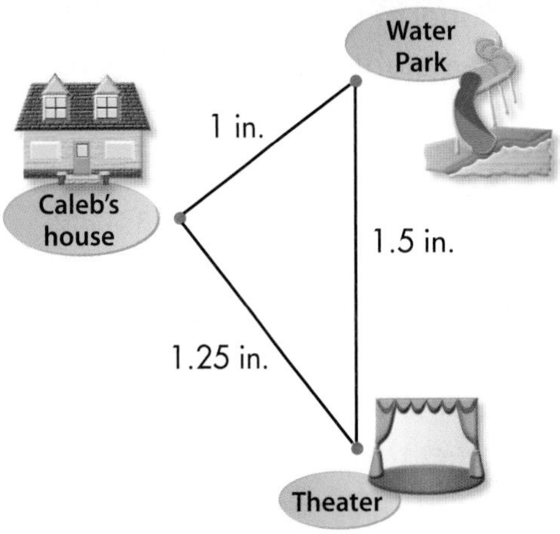

DIGITAL Animated Glossary **www.pearsonsuccessnet.com**

For another example, see Set F on page 341.

Problem Solving

8. Geometry Rectangles *A* and *B* are proportional figures. Find the height of rectangle *B*.

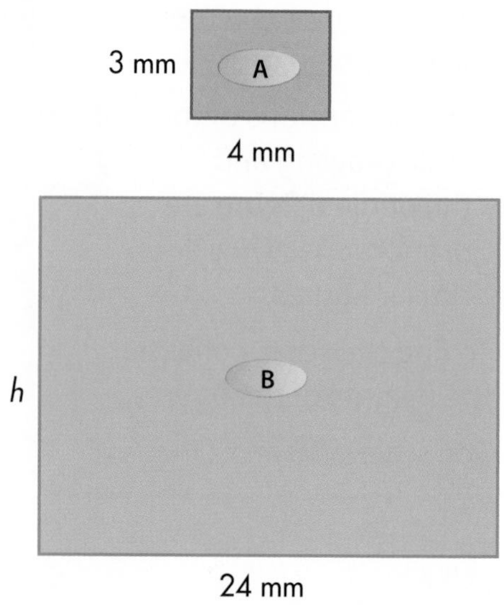

9. Writing to Explain The scale on a map of Chicago's lakefront is 2.5 cm = 4 km. Both the Field Museum and the Museum of Science and Industry are on the map. Explain how Sadie could calculate the actual distance between the two museums.

10. Draw a Picture Using grid paper, draw a pencil. Then draw a picture of a proportional pencil that is twice as long as the first pencil. Include a scale on your drawing.

Algebra Use the formula $d = r \times t$ to solve **11** and **12**.

11. Jorge drives at a rate of 30 miles per hour. How long will it take him to drive 150 miles?

12. Ileana runs at a rate of 6 miles per hour. If she ran for 7 hours last week, how many miles did she run?

13. Reasoning If the actual distance between Charlotte, North Carolina and Charleston, South Carolina is about 200 miles, what would be the distance on a map with a scale of 0.5 inch = 50 miles?

14. The Empire State Building in New York is about 1,450 feet tall. Suppose you used the scale 1 in. = 50 ft to make a model of the Empire State Building. Use a proportion to find the height of your model of the Empire State Building.

15. **Think About the Process** On a scale drawing of a computer chip, 100 mm on the drawing represents an actual size of 1 mm. Which of the following expressions gives the actual length of an object that is 3 mm long in the drawing?

A 3×100

B $3 - 100$

C $3 \div 100$

D $100 \div 3$

16. **Think About the Process** A recipe that feeds 2 people calls for 4 tomatoes, 2 onions, and 5 oz of cheese. What operation will help you change the recipe to feed 6 people?

A Add 3 to each item.

B Multiply each item by 3.

C Divide each item by 3.

D Multiply each item by itself.

Mixed Problem Solving

Math and Social Studies

The Great Pyramid of Giza, Egypt, is one of the seven wonders of the ancient world. It was built more than 4,000 years ago and remained the tallest building in the world until the 20th century. Use proportions and similar figures in **1** through **6**.

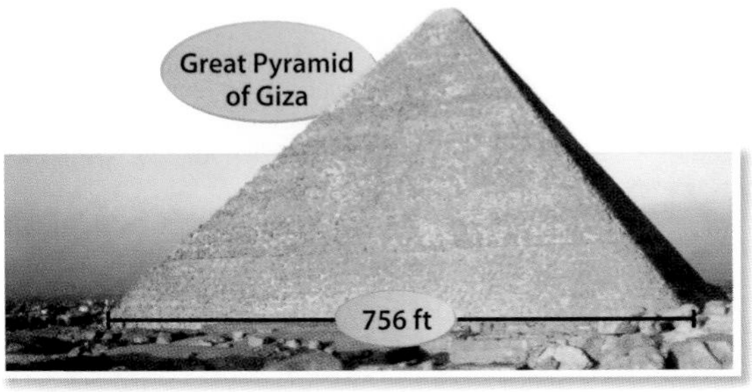

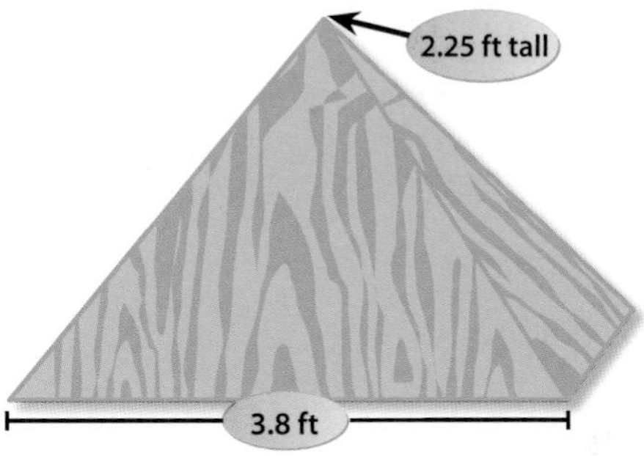

1. A model proportional to the Great Pyramid is shown above. Use the dimensions of the model to find the height of the Great Pyramid. Round your answer to the nearest whole number.

2. The pyramid at Menkaure, Egypt, was 215 ft tall, and its base is 345.5 ft wide. If a model proportional to the pyramid at Menkaure is 4.3 ft tall, what is the width of the base of the model? Round your answer to the nearest tenth.

3. The illustration below shows one side of the Great Pyramid and a triangle that is similar. Find the measure of $\angle D$.

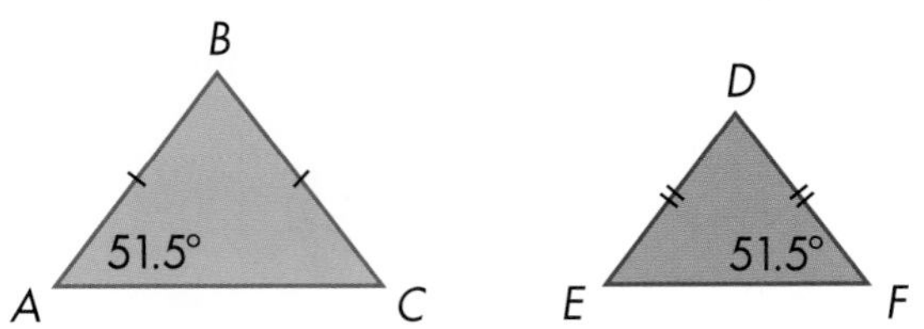

4. **Strategy Focus** Solve using the strategy: Write an equation. The base of the Great Pyramid is made of large limestone blocks. The upper block in the drawing below shows the length and width of one block. The lower block is a similar figure. What is the height, *x*, of the pyramid's base block?

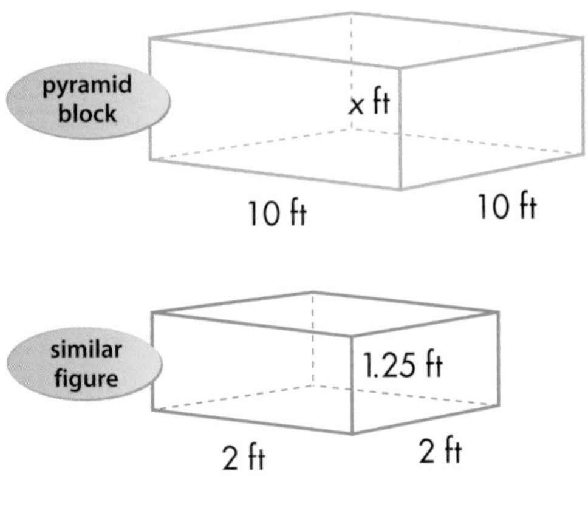

5. The base of the Great Pyramid is a square with an area of 571,536 ft^2. If one of the sides of a similar figure is 5 cm, what is the area of this figure?

6. Write a problem that compares the dimensions of the Great Pyramid with a similar figure.

Test

1. The ratio of width to height is 4 to 3. What is the width if the height is 18 inches? (13-1)

Width inches	4	8	12	16		
Height inches	3	6	9	12	15	18

A 21 inches

B 23 inches

C 24 inches

D 26 inches

2. In one hour, 32 cars pass through a particular intersection. At the same rate, how long would it take for 96 cars to pass through the intersection? (13-2)

A 2 hours

B 3 hours

C 8 hours

D 16 hours

3. A standard tennis court is 120 feet long and 60 feet wide. On a model of a new park, the court is 4 inches wide. How long is the court on the model? (13-6)

A 2 inches

B 3 inches

C 6 inches

D 8 inches

4. If the scale on a map is 2 cm = 9 km, how many kilometers would 3 centimeters equal on the map? (13-6)

A 6 km

B 12.5 km

C 13.5 km

D 18 km

5. What is the first step when using cross multiplication to solve the proportion $\frac{2}{12} = \frac{m}{18}$? (13-3)

A $2 \times 18 = 12m$

B $2 \times 12 = 18m$

C $12 \times 18 = 2m$

D $2 \times 12 = 18m$

6. Most showers use 5 gallons of water each minute. Which of the following can be used to find *x*, the number of gallons of water used during an 8-minute shower? (13-2)

A $\frac{5 \text{ gal}}{1 \text{ m}} = \frac{x \text{ gal}}{8 \text{ m}}$

B $\frac{5 \text{ gal}}{1 \text{ m}} = \frac{8 \text{ m}}{x \text{ gal}}$

C $\frac{5 \text{ gal}}{x \text{ m}} = \frac{1 \text{ gal}}{8 \text{ m}}$

D $\frac{5 \text{ gal}}{8 \text{ m}} = \frac{x \text{ gal}}{1 \text{ m}}$

7. The triangles shown are similar. What is the length of *x*? (13-5)

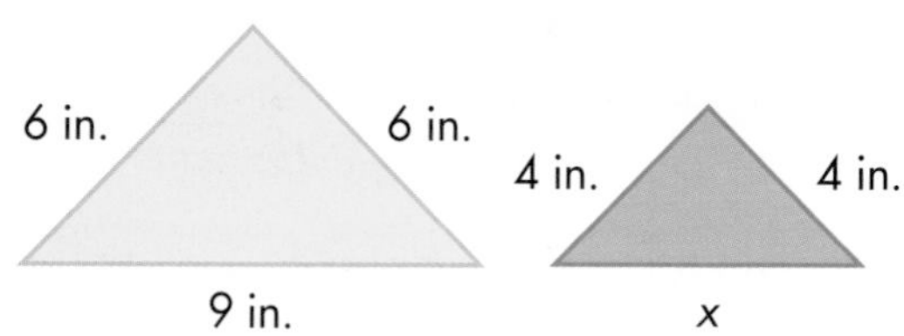

A 3 inches

B 4 inches

C 4.5 inches

D 6 inches

8. Bruce planted a 24-inch tall tree that grows at a rate of 18 inches each year. How many years will it take the tree to grow to 69 inches? (13-3)

A 1.5 years

B 2.5 years

C 5 years

D 9 years

9. The table shows the relationship in note value between half notes and eighth notes. What is the missing value in the table? (13-1)

Half notes	2	4	6		10
Eighth notes	8	16	24	32	40

A 4

B 8

C 16

D 20

10. Claudio is fertilizing his lawn. Four pounds of fertilizer are to be applied to every 1,000 square feet of lawn. How many pounds should Claudio apply if his lawn is 8,750 square feet? (13-2)

A 2.2 pounds

B 32 pounds

C 35 pounds

D 70 pounds

11. CDs are on sale at 4 for $38. Which explains correctly how much 6 CDs cost? (13-4)

A Divide $38 by 4 to get a unit price of $9.50. Then multiply 6 by $9.50 to get $63.

B Divide $38 by 6 to get a unit price of $6.33. Then multiply 4 by $6.33 to get $25.33.

C Use the proportion $\frac{\$38}{6} = \frac{x}{4}$. Solve $6x = 152$ to get $27.33.

D Use the proportion $\frac{\$38}{4} = \frac{x}{6}$. Solve $4x = 228$ to get $57.

12. Which proportion can be used to find the width, *w* of the large rectangle? (13-5)

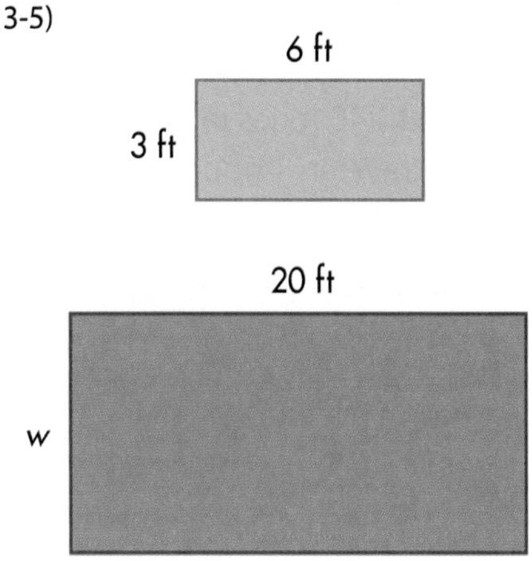

A $\frac{w}{3} = \frac{20}{6}$

B $\frac{w}{3} = \frac{6}{20}$

C $\frac{w}{20} = \frac{6}{3}$

D $\frac{w}{6} = \frac{20}{3}$

Reteaching

Set A, pages 322–323

About how many songs could a 1 GB (gigabyte) music player hold?

File size	256 MB	512 MB	1 GB
Songs	60 songs	120 songs	■

Tip *1 GB = about 1,024 MB (megabytes).*

Write a proportion.

$\frac{512}{120} = \frac{1{,}024}{x}$

$512x = 122{,}880$

$x = 240$

A 1 GB music player can hold about 240 songs.

Remember that the values in a ratio table are proportional.

The ratio table below shows the relationship between the amount Toby earns and the amount he saves. Extend the table to answer **1** and **2**.

Earnings	\$10	\$20	\$30
Savings	\$7	\$14	\$21

1. How much would Toby save if he earned \$40?
2. If Toby saved \$35, how much did he earn?

Set B, pages 324–325

If a car travels 240 miles in 5 hours, how many miles will it travel in 1 hour?

Find the unit rate.

$240 \div 5 = 48$

The unit rate is $\frac{48}{1}$.

$\frac{240}{5} = \frac{48}{1}$

The car will travel 48 miles in 1 hour.

Remember to make sure your proportion contains equivalent units.

Solve each proportion using the unit rate given.

1. $\frac{17 \text{ applicants}}{\text{week}} = \frac{x \text{ applicants}}{14 \text{ weeks}}$
2. $\frac{\$12.29}{\text{ticket}} = \frac{x}{4 \text{ tickets}}$
3. $\frac{4 \text{ tsp flour}}{\text{serving}} = \frac{x \text{ tsp flour}}{13 \text{ servings}}$

Set C, pages 326–327

Use cross multiplication to solve the following proportion.

$\frac{80}{200} = \frac{x}{25}$ ← Multiply on the diagonals.

$200x = 80 \times 25$ ← The products of cross multiplication.

$200x = 2000; x = 10$

Remember that you use cross multiplication to solve the following proportions.

1. $\frac{7}{8} = \frac{x}{72}$
2. $\frac{5}{11} = \frac{25}{x}$
3. $\frac{15}{12} = \frac{x}{60}$
4. $\frac{2}{5} = \frac{x}{100}$

Topic 13

Reteaching

Set D, pages 328–329

Brand A shampoo is \$7.68 for a 24 oz bottle.
Brand B shampoo is \$12.60 for 36 oz.
Which is a better buy?

Compare the unit price for each shampoo.

\$7.68 for 24 oz → unit price is \$0.32 per oz

\$12.60 for 36 oz → unit price is \$0.35 per oz

The 24 oz bottle is a better buy.

Remember that you can use words, pictures, numbers, symbols, graphs, tables, diagrams, and models to explain your reasoning.

1. Which is the better buy, 2 boxes of Hearty Bran cereal at \$4.86 or 4 boxes for \$10? Explain.

Set E, pages 330–332

The rectangles below are similar. Solve for *y*.

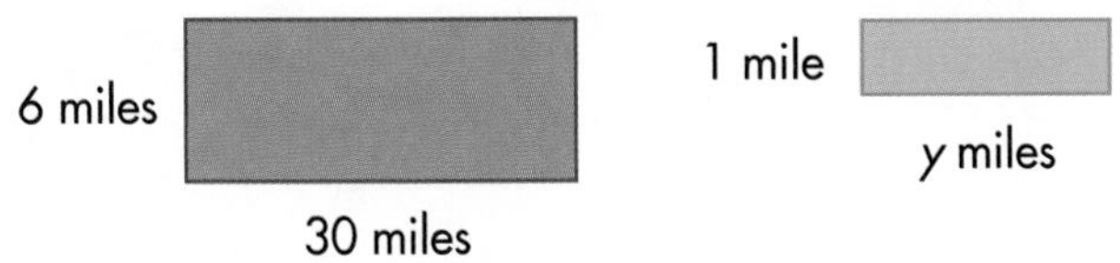

$\frac{6}{30} = \frac{1}{y}$ ← **Write a proportion. Use cross multiplication.**

$6y = 30$ ← **Solve for *y*.**

$y = 5$

The length of *y* is 5 miles.

Remember that the corresponding sides of similar figures are proportional.

Compare similar figures. Solve for *x*.

1. △ *ABC*: 5 cm, 6 cm, 10 cm
   △ *DEF*: 15 cm, 18 cm, *x* cm

2. ▭ *A*: 4 in. long, 18 in. wide
   ▭ *B*: *x* in. long, 90 in. wide

Set F, pages 334–336

The scale on a map is 1 inch: 240 miles. If two cities are 5 inches apart, what is the actual distance in miles?

Write a proportion to find the data.

$\frac{1 \text{ inch}}{240 \text{ miles}} = \frac{5 \text{ inches}}{x \text{ miles}}$

$x = 240 \times 5$

$x = 1200$

The map distance between the two cities is 5 inches, so the actual distance between the two cities is 1,200 miles.

Remember that maps and scale drawings are reduced or enlarged by the same ratio.

1. The map scale is 1 in. : 5 mi. If the map distance between Sean's home and the state park is 3 inches, what is the actual distance?

2. The drawing of the new school has a scale of 1 in. : 8 ft. In the drawing, the school is 6 inches tall. What is the actual height of the school?

Topic 14

Understanding Percent

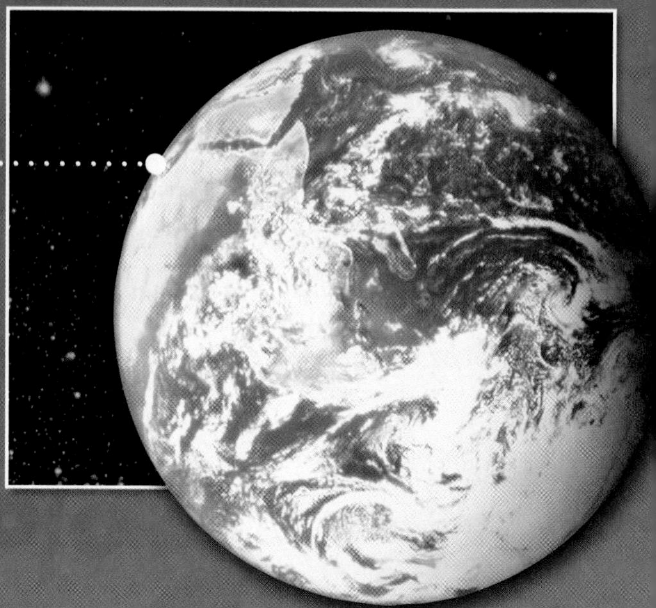

1 Many chemical elements can be found in Earth's atmosphere. What percent is nitrogen? You will find out in Lesson 14-2.

2 The *Queen Mary 2* is the largest cruise ship in the world. How does the length of the *Queen Mary 2* compare in size to the height of the Washington Monument? You will find out in Lesson 14-3.

3

Easton the Great won Best in Show in 60% of his shows. In how many shows was Easton entered? You will find out in Lesson 14-1.

4

What percent of an adult's weight is water? You will find out in Lesson 14-5.

Review What You Know!

Vocabulary

Choose the best term from the box.

• proportion	• fraction
• ratio	• decimal

1. A __?__ can be written as x to y, $x : y$, or $\frac{x}{y}$.
2. A __?__ is a mathematical statement that two ratios are equal.
3. A number with one or more numbers to the right of the decimal point is a __?__.
4. A number that can be used to describe a part of a whole is a __?__.

Proportions

Solve each proportion.

5. $\frac{60 \text{ mi}}{1 \text{ h}} = \frac{x \text{ mi}}{5 \text{ h}}$
6. $\frac{8 \text{ h}}{2 \text{ days}} = \frac{x \text{ h}}{7 \text{ days}}$
7. $\frac{12 \text{ ft}}{2 \text{ sec}} = \frac{x \text{ ft}}{11 \text{ sec}}$
8. $\frac{68 \text{ beats}}{1 \text{ min}} = \frac{x \text{ beats}}{10 \text{ min}}$

Decimal Computation

Simplify.

9. 679.53×100
10. $4.75 \times 1{,}000$
11. $12{,}359 \div 1{,}000$
12. $4 \div 100$
13. $1 \div 1{,}000$
14. 0.25×0.1

Decimals and Fractions

15. **Writing to Explain** Explain how to convert $\frac{3}{8}$ to a decimal.

Lesson
14-1

Understand It!
A percent is relative to the size of the whole. The whole is 100%.

Understanding Percent

What is a percent?

A percent is a special kind of ratio in which the first term is compared to 100. The percent is the number of hundredths that represents the part of the whole.

What percent of people prefer Bright White Toothpaste?

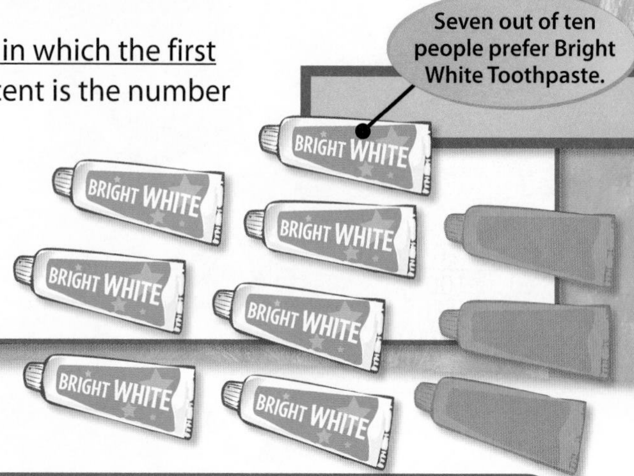

Another Example How do percents relate to the whole?

Each line segment below represents 100%, but the line segments are different lengths. Points *A*, *B*, and *E* are the same distance from zero on each line segment. Use a proportion to find what percent or part of each line segment points *A*, *B*, and *E* represent. The length from zero to each point is relative to the length of each line segment.

Point *A*	**Point *B***	**Point *E***
$\frac{1}{2} = \frac{A}{100}$	$\frac{1}{4} = \frac{B}{100}$	$\frac{1}{5} = \frac{E}{100}$
$100 = 2A$	$100 = 4B$	$100 = 5E$
$50 = A$	$25 = B$	$20 = E$
Point $A = 50\%$	Point $B = 25\%$	Point $E = 20\%$

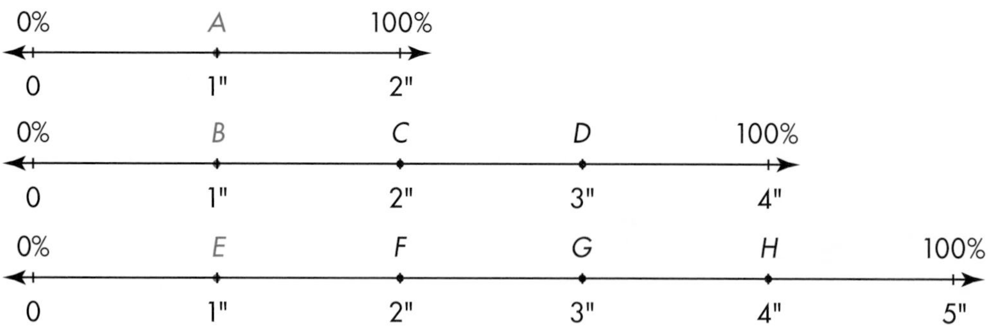

Explain It

1. **Number Sense** Use mental math to find the percents associated with the points *C*, *D*, *F*, *G*, and *H*.

One Way

Use a grid to model the percent.

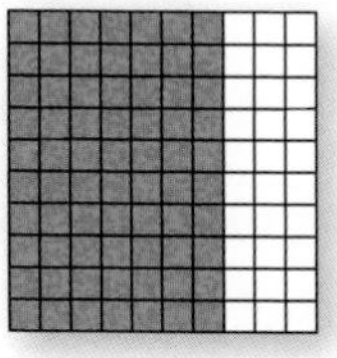

$\frac{7}{10} = \frac{70}{100} = 70\%$

Another Way

Use number lines to model the percent.

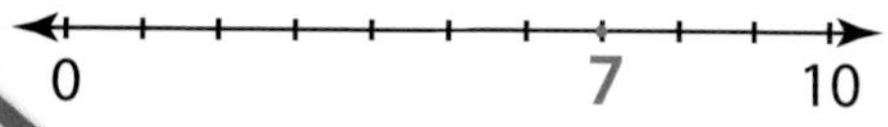

$\frac{7}{10} = \frac{70}{100} = 70\%$

Another Way

Use a proportion to find the percent.

$\frac{7}{10} = \frac{x}{100}$

$700 = 10x$

$70 = x$

70% of people prefer Bright White Toothpaste.

Guided Practice*

Do you know HOW?

In **1** through **3**, write the percent of each figure that is shaded.

1. 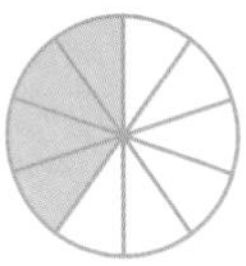

2. 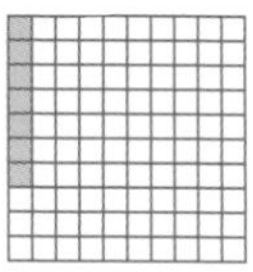

3. 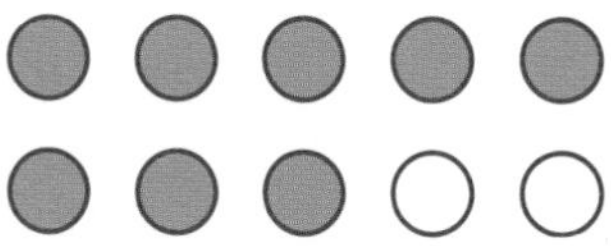

Do you UNDERSTAND?

4. What is the whole to which a percent is compared?

5. Why are tenths, fifths, and fourths easy to convert to percents?

6. Suppose that 4 out of 5 people prefer Bright White Toothpaste. What percent of people prefer that toothpaste?

Independent Practice

In **7** through **13**, write the percent of each figure that is shaded.

7. 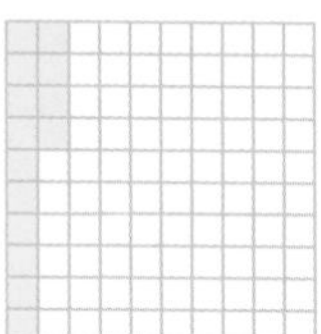

8. 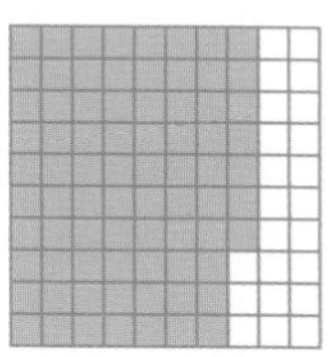

9. 

10. 

11. 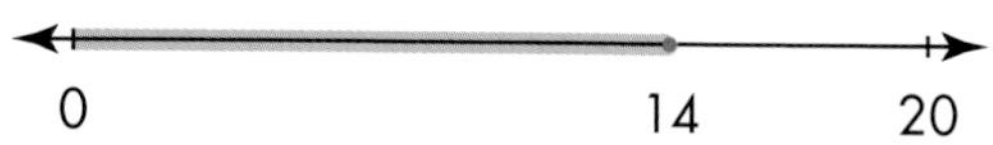

12. 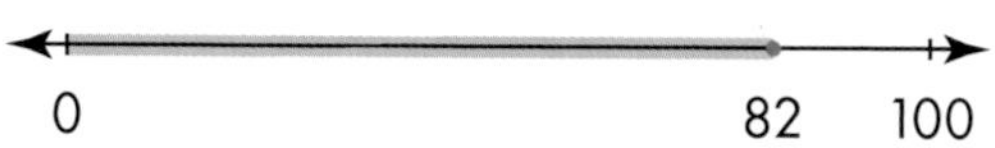

13. 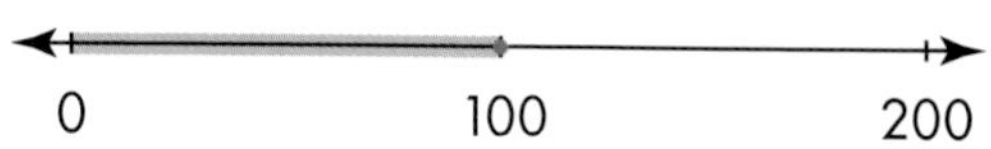

DIGITAL Animated Glossary **www.pearsonsuccessnet.com**

**For another example, see Set A on page 366.*

Problem Solving

Geometry Use line segment *AB* to find the answers to **14** and **15**.

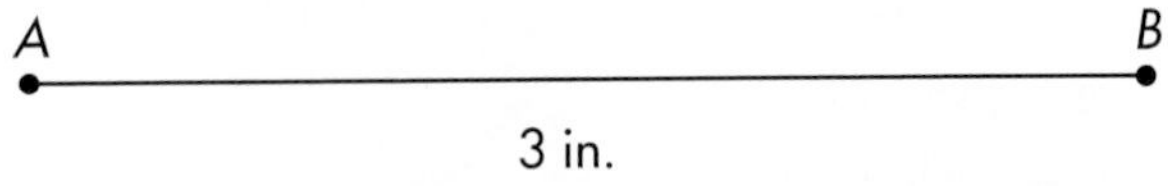

14. If line segment *AB* represents 50%, what is the length of a line segment that is 100%?

15. If line segment AB is 300%, what is the length of a line segment that is 100%?

16. **Strategy Focus** Draw a picture or use a proportion to find each percent.

a $\frac{3}{4}$ **b** $\frac{4}{5}$ **c** $\frac{13}{20}$

17. Suppose that a diamond weighs 0.0182 carat. What is that number in expanded form?

18. **Writing to Explain** Is 25% always the same amount? Explain your answer and provide examples.

19. Easton won Best in Show in 60% of the shows he entered. In how many shows was Easton entered if he won Best in Show 15 times last year?

20. **Estimation** Each line segment below represents 100%. Estimate the percents that points *A*, *B*, and *C* represent.

a

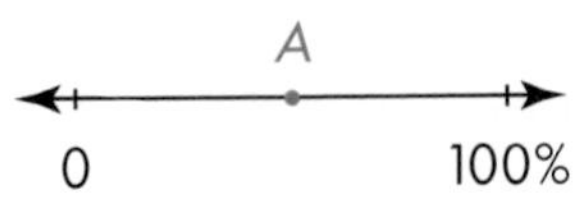

b

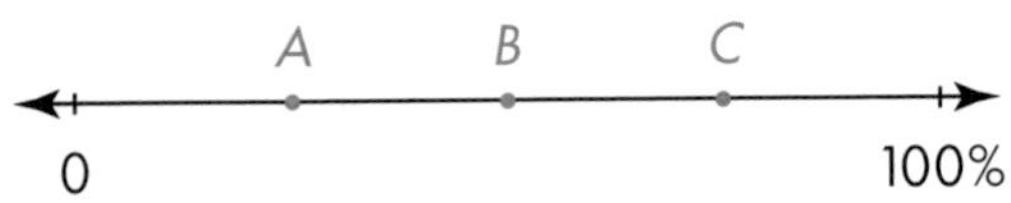

21. Sixteen lizards have white stripes on their tails. The ratio of lizards with white tail stripes to those with yellow tail stripes is 1:2. How many lizards have yellow tail stripes?

22. **Think About the Process** Fifty runners started the race. Nineteen runners finished in under 30 minutes. Which of the following proportions shows how to find what percent 19 is of 50?

A $\frac{19}{50} = \frac{x}{100}$ **B** $\frac{19}{100} = \frac{x}{50}$ **C** $\frac{19}{x} = \frac{50}{100}$ **D** $\frac{50}{19} = \frac{x}{100}$

23. One side of a school building has 10 windows. Four windows have the blinds down. Which model represents the percent of windows with the blinds down?

A

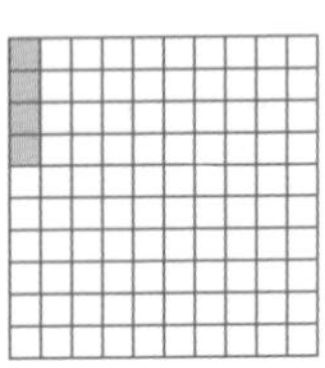

B

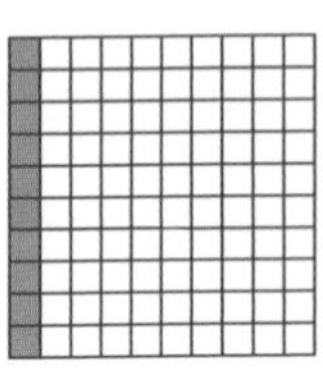

C

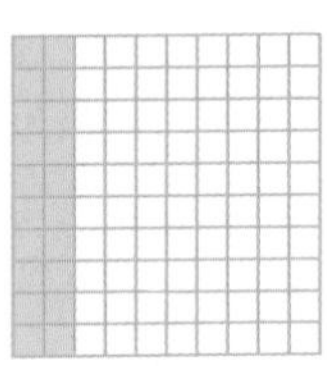

D

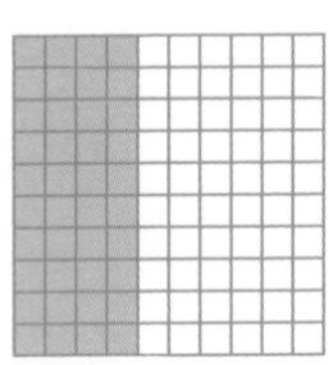

Mixed Problem Solving

The After School Center took a survey of its members to find out which types of music are most popular among boys and girls. They displayed the data in two circle graphs. Use the graphs to answer the questions.

Boys' Favorite Music

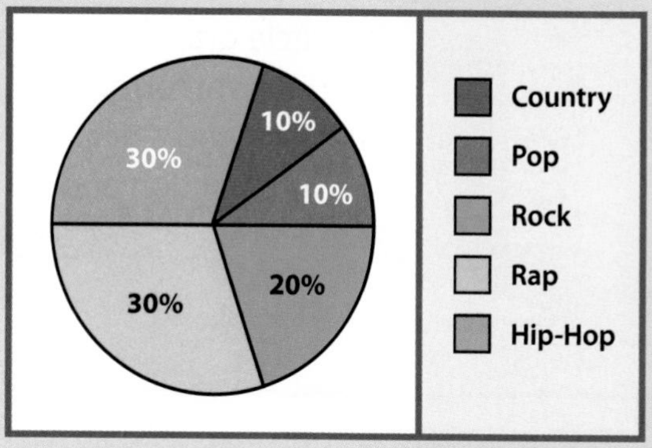

Girls' Favorite Music

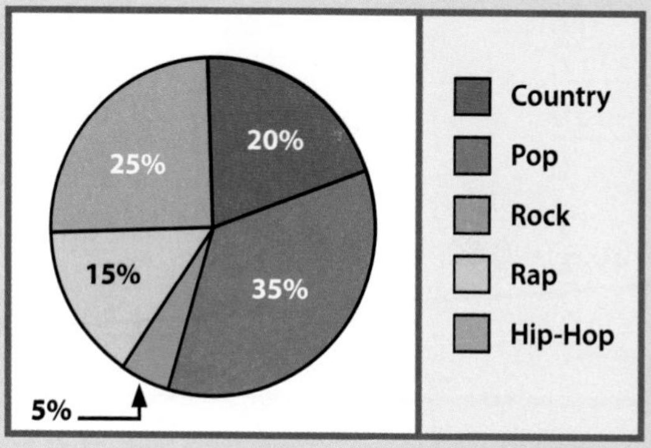

1. What percentage of boys like hip-hop the most?

2. Which type of music do girls like most?

3. Which two types of music do the boys like the most?

4. Which type of music was chosen by $\frac{1}{5}$ of the boys?

5. Which type of music did $\frac{1}{4}$ of the girls choose as their favorite?

6. Twenty girls were surveyed. Which type of music did three girls choose? (Hint: Use a proportion.)

7. Twenty boys were surveyed. Which two types of music were chosen by 2 boys each?

8. Which type of music do the girls like least?

9. If fifteen boys chose hip-hop as their favorite, how many boys were surveyed?

10. If fourteen girls chose pop music, how many girls were surveyed?

11. If 200 boys were surveyed, which type of music did 60 boys choose?

Lesson
14-2

Understand It!
A part of a whole can be represented by a fraction, decimal, or percent.

Fractions, Decimals, and Percents

How are fractions, decimals, and percents related to one another?

Fractions, decimals, and percents are three ways to show portions of a whole.

The circle graph shows each part in a different form. Write 30% as a fraction and a decimal. Write 0.10 as a fraction and a percent.

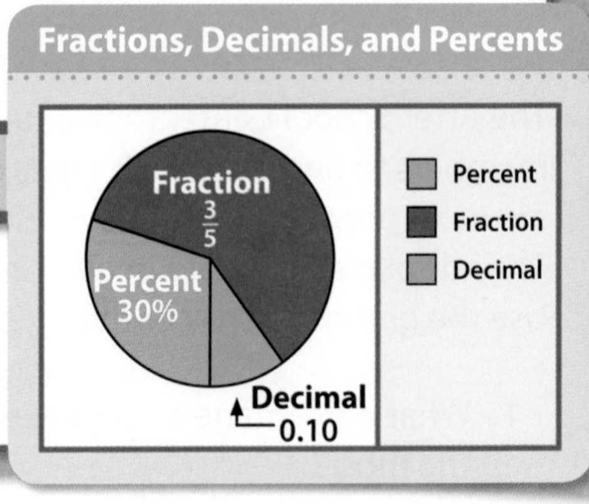

Another Example How can you change a fraction to a decimal and percent?

Write $\frac{3}{5}$ as a decimal and a percent.

Use division.

$$5\overline{)3.0}\quad \text{quotient } 0.6$$
$$-\,3\,0$$
$$0$$

So, $\frac{3}{5} = 0.60$.

Use a proportion.

$$\frac{3}{5} = \frac{x}{100}$$
$$3(100) = 5x$$
$$300 = 5x$$
$$60 = x$$

So, $\frac{3}{5} = \frac{60}{100} = 60\%$.

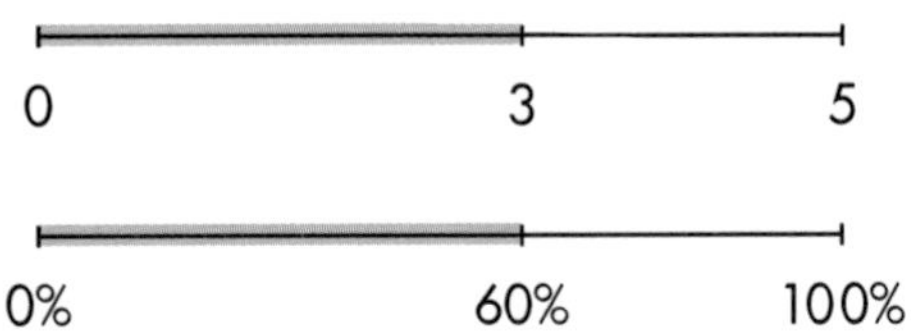

Guided Practice*

Do you know HOW?

In **1** through **6**, write each number in two other ways.

1. 27% **2.** 0.91 **3.** $\frac{6}{100}$

4. 0.465 **5.** 49% **6.** $\frac{5}{8}$

Do you UNDERSTAND?

7. Why are you able to change between fractions, decimals, and percents?

8. How is the decimal point moved when changing from a decimal to a percent?

Independent Practice

In **9** through **11**, express the value in two other ways.

9. 0.25 **10.** $\frac{2}{2}$ **11.** 7%

*For another example, see Set B on page 366.

A percent compares a number to 100, so you can write 30% as a fraction and a decimal.

$$30\% = \frac{30}{100}$$

Simplify the fraction:

$$\frac{30 \div 10}{100 \div 10} = \frac{3}{10}$$

30% can also be written as $\frac{3}{10}$ or 0.30.

Use decimal place value to write the decimal 0.10 as a fraction and a percent.

Fraction:

$$0.10 = \frac{10}{100} = \frac{1}{10}$$

Percent:

$$0.10 = \frac{10}{100} = 10\%$$

0.10 can also be written as $\frac{1}{10}$ or 10%.

In **12** through **20**, express the value in two other ways.

12. 38%

13. $\frac{7}{8}$

14. 0.04

15. $\frac{1}{3}$

16. 65%

17. 0.46

18. 29%

19. 0.01

20. $\frac{5}{12}$

Problem Solving

21. Many chemical elements can be found in Earth's atmosphere. Use the circle graph to answer the following questions.

a What fraction of Earth's atmosphere is made up of nitrogen?

b What part of Earth's atmosphere is made up of oxygen? Write the part as a decimal.

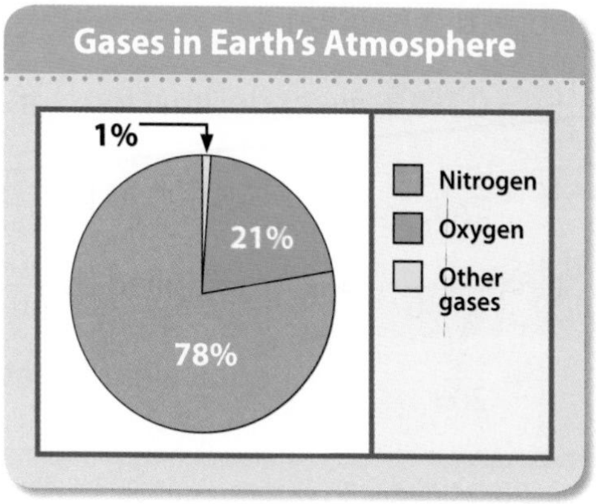

22. Estimation Mrs. Nellon's class sold 18 rolls of wrapping paper. Altogether, the school sold 82 rolls. About what percent of the sales came from Mrs. Nellon's class?

23. Writing to Explain Explain how you would use mental math to express $\frac{16}{25}$ as a percent.

24. Number Sense Choose the answer that shows the following values in order from least to greatest: $\frac{1}{3}$, 0.25, 16%.

A $\frac{1}{3}$, 0.25, 16%

B 0.25, 16%, $\frac{1}{3}$

C 16%, 0.25, $\frac{1}{3}$

D 16%, $\frac{1}{3}$, 0.25

25. In a stock market game, Sergio bought 150 shares of stock at a price of $\frac{5}{8}$ a game dollar per share. How much game money did 150 shares cost?

Lesson

14-3

Understand It!
Percents greater than 100% describe a value greater than one whole. Percents less than 1% describe a value less than one hundredth of the whole.

Percents Greater Than 100 and Less Than 1

How can you express percents greater than 100?

Jan and Kim built model cars for a science project. Kim's car traveled 140% as far as Jan's car. How can you write 140% as a fraction and as a decimal?

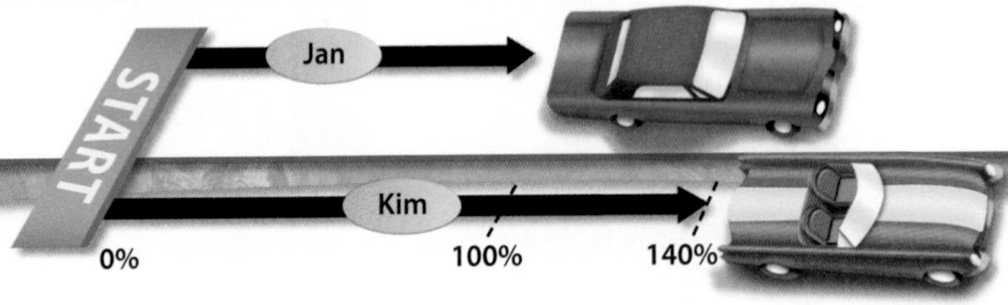

Another Example

How can you express percents less than 1?

Write $\frac{1}{2}$% as a fraction and as a decimal.

Use what you know about the relationships among fractions, decimals, and percents.

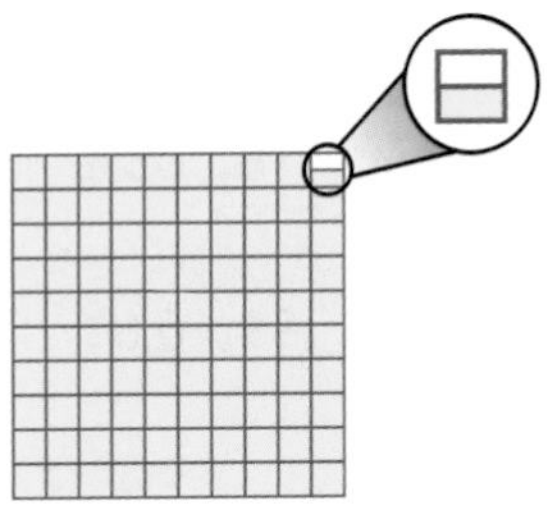

Change to a fraction.		Change to a decimal.
$\frac{1}{2}\% = 0.5\%$ ←	decimal form of $\frac{1}{2}$%	→ $\frac{1}{2}\% = 0.5\%$
$0.5\% = \frac{0.5}{100}$ ←	fraction as part of 100	→ $0.5\% = \frac{0.5}{100}$
$\frac{0.5}{100} = \frac{5}{1{,}000}$ ←	multiplied by $\frac{10}{10}$	→ $\frac{0.5}{100} = \frac{5}{1{,}000}$
$= \frac{1}{200}$	equivalent forms	$= 0.005$

Guided Practice*

Do you know HOW?

In **1** through **4**, write each percent as a fraction and as a decimal. Write fractions in simplest form.

1. 150%

2. 0.2%

3. 325%

4. $\frac{3}{10}$%

Do you UNDERSTAND?

5. Why is 140% greater than 1?

6. Explain the difference between $\frac{1}{2}$ and $\frac{1}{2}$%.

7. Why was $\frac{0.5}{100}$ multiplied by $\frac{10}{10}$?

*For another example, see Set C on page 367.

A percent compares a number to 100. The distance Jan's car traveled represents the whole or 100%.

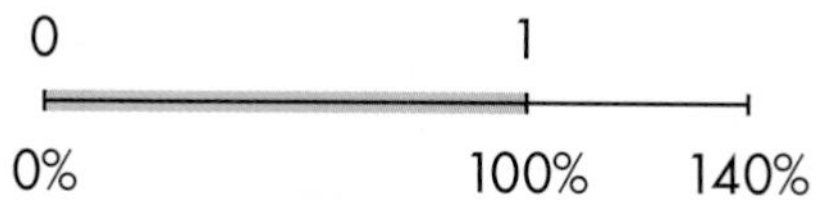

Kim's car traveled 140% as far. Expressed as a fraction, a percent greater than 100 will always be an improper fraction.

$$140\% = \frac{140}{100} = \frac{7}{5}$$

Similarly, percents greater than 100% will always have a decimal value greater than 1.

$$140\% = \frac{140}{100} = 1.40 = 1.4$$

So, $140\% = \frac{7}{5} = 1.4$.

Independent Practice

In **8** through **19,** write each percent as a fraction and as a decimal. Write fractions in simplest form.

8. 28% **9.** 322% **10.** 54% **11.** 210%

12. 72% **13.** 555% **14.** 90% **15.** 300%

16. 0.75% **17.** 160% **18.** 120% **19.** $\frac{1}{5}$%

Problem Solving

20. **Number Sense** Use the information about the *Queen Mary 2* to answer the following questions.

a How do you express 200% as a fraction and a decimal?

b Three-quarters of the staterooms on the *Queen Mary 2* have balconies. How would you express this number as a fraction, a decimal, and a percent?

The Queen Mary 2 is more than 200% longer than the Washington Monument is high.

21. **Writing to Explain** Nathan set his computer to print at 50% of the 8.5 in. × 11 in. page he normally uses. Ahmad thinks a document 50% its size will look huge. Is Ahmad correct about Nathan's printed report? Explain.

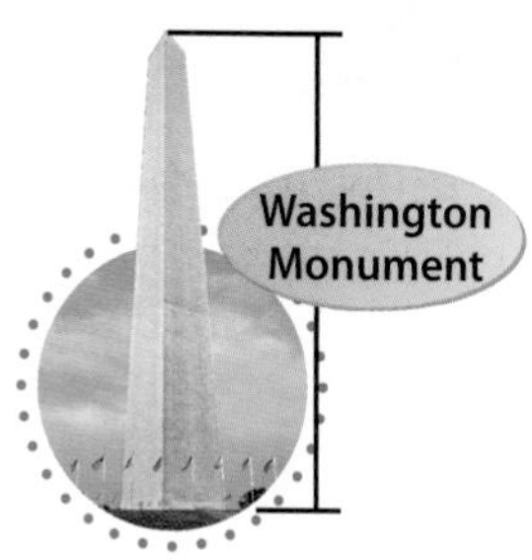

22. **Number Sense** Which is NOT equivalent to the others?

A 0.56% **B** 0.056 **C** 0.0056 **D** $\frac{0.56}{100}$

Lesson
14-4

Understand It!
You can use benchmark fractions as compatible numbers to estimate percents.

Estimating Percent

How can you use fractions to estimate percents?

This graph shows the eye colors among students at Lake Mark School. You can use fraction equivalents and compatible numbers to estimate the percent of a number.

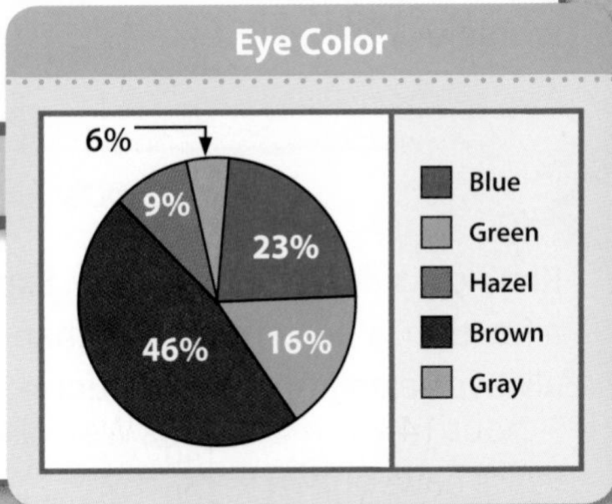

Use these benchmark percents and their fraction equivalents to help you estimate.

Percent	10%	20%	25%	$33\frac{1}{3}$%	50%	$66\frac{2}{3}$%	75%
Fraction	$\frac{1}{10}$	$\frac{1}{5}$	$\frac{1}{4}$	$\frac{1}{3}$	$\frac{1}{2}$	$\frac{2}{3}$	$\frac{3}{4}$

Guided Practice*

Do you know HOW?

In **1** and **2**, estimate the percent of each number.

Tip *Use benchmark fractions and compatible numbers.*

1. 47% of 77; 47% ≈ 50% and 77 ≈ 80
So, 50% of 80 = ▭.

2. 18% of 48; 18% ≈ 20 and 48 ≈ 50
So, 20% of 50 = ▭.

Do you UNDERSTAND?

3. Explain how to estimate 32% of 212.

4. In the graph at the top, suppose that there are 195 students in the fifth grade. How can you estimate the number of fifth graders who have hazel eyes?

Independent Practice

In **5** through **16**, estimate the percent of each number.

5. 74% of 63
6. 18% of 96
7. 47% of 183
8. 8% of 576
9. 34% of 55
10. 27% of 284
11. 67% of 866
12. 4% of 802
13. 47% of 78
14. 33% of 238
15. 65% of 89
16. 6% of 489

*For another example, see Set D on page 367.

Mr. Weinstein's class has 28 students. Use the graph to estimate how many students in his class have brown eyes.

Think $46\% \approx 50\%$ and $50\% = \frac{1}{2}$

So, 46% of $28 \approx \frac{1}{2}$ of 28.

$$\frac{1}{2} \times 28 = 14$$

About 14 students in Mr. Weinstein's class have brown eyes.

The total number of fifth-grade students is 118. Use the graph to estimate how many fifth-grade students have blue eyes.

Think $23\% \approx 25\%$ and $118 \approx 120$

$25\% = \frac{1}{4}$. So, 23% of $118 \approx \frac{1}{4}$ of 120.

$$\frac{1}{4} \times 120 = 30$$

About 30 fifth-grade students have blue eyes.

Problem Solving

17. **Number Sense** If 10% of 60 is 6, what is 5% of 60? Explain how you found your answer.

18. Granola bars cost 24 cents each. Estimate how much money Heather needs to buy 19 granola bars.

19. Use estimation to complete the following sentences:

a 49% of ☐ is about 8.

b 26% of ☐ is about 20.

c 198% of ☐ is about 99.

20. **Writing to Explain** A winter jacket is marked down 50% from $80. A sign says to take an additional 50% off the sale price. Does that mean the jacket is free? Explain.

21. Explain how you use prime factors to find the GCF of 45 and 75.

22. **Algebra** Estimate to find x if 25% of x is about 30.

23. Roland has 180 coins in his collection. Approximately 67% of the coins are quarters. About how many quarters does he have?

24. There are about 300 million residents in the U.S. If 36% of them live in the South, estimate how many live in this area of the U.S.

25. **Think About the Process** Vanessa scored 78% on a test with 120 questions on it. Which benchmark fraction could you use to best **estimate** the number of questions that Vanessa answered correctly?

A $\frac{1}{2}$ **B** $\frac{3}{4}$ **C** $\frac{2}{3}$ **D** $\frac{78}{100}$

26. **Number Sense** What do the decimal forms of $\frac{2}{3}$, $\frac{1}{6}$, and $\frac{2}{9}$ have in common?

Lesson

14-5

Understand It!
Finding a percent of a number is like finding a part of a whole. The number is the whole.

Finding the Percent of a Number

How can you calculate percentages?

The fourth, fifth, and sixth graders at Green Oaks School are taking a field trip to the museum. The circle graph shows what percent of the students are in each grade. Of the 575 students attending the field trip, how many are sixth graders?

Students Attending Field Trip

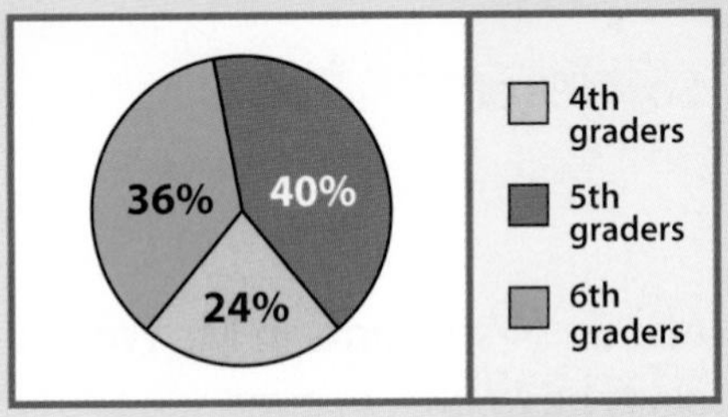

Another Example

How can you find what percent one number is of another number?

Kevin had \$180 in savings. He used his savings to buy a new bicycle that cost \$108. What percent of his total savings did the bicycle cost?

Estimate.

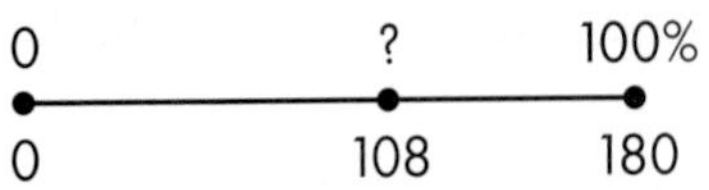

Think of compatible numbers to 180.

$108 \approx 120$

$\frac{108}{180} \approx \frac{120}{180} = \frac{12}{18} = \frac{2}{3}$

$\frac{2}{3} = 66\frac{2}{3}\%$

My estimate is $66\frac{2}{3}\%$.

Write a proportion. $\frac{\text{part}}{\text{whole}} = \frac{\text{percent value}}{100}$

Let p = the percent value.

$\frac{108}{180} = \frac{p}{100}$

$10{,}800 = 180p$

$60 = p$

60% is close to $66\frac{2}{3}\%$. The bicycle cost 60% of Kevin's savings.

How can you use a calculator to find the percent of a number?

Find 24% of 47.

Enter: 24 [%] [×] 47 [ENTER =] Display: 11.28

Or use the decimal form of the percent.

Enter: 0.24 [×] 47 [ENTER =] Display: 11.28

Estimate.

Think $36\% \approx 33\frac{1}{3}\% = \frac{1}{3}$ and $575 \approx 600$.

So, 36% of 575 is about $\frac{1}{3}$ of 600.

$\frac{1}{3} \times 600 = 200$

About 200 sixth graders are attending.

Write a decimal to find 36% of 575.

$36\% = 0.36$

$0.36 \times 575 = 207$

207 is close to 200. The answer is reasonable.

Write a proportion.

$\frac{\text{part}}{\text{whole}} = \frac{\text{percent value}}{100}$

Let x = unknown part.

$\frac{x}{575} = \frac{36}{100}$

$100x = 20{,}700$

$x = 207$

207 sixth graders are attending the field trip.

Guided Practice*

Do you know HOW?

In **1** and **2**, estimate and then find the percent of each number.

1. 26% of 50

2. 47% of 300

In **3** and **4**, write what percent the first number is of the second number.

3. 18 of 62

4. 14 of 42

Do you UNDERSTAND?

5. In math, what operation does the word "of" mean?

6. In the example at the top, how could you use a decimal to find the number of 4th graders attending the field trip?

7. In Another Example, how could you use a calculator to find what percent 108 is of 180?

Independent Practice

Leveled Practice In **8** through **13**, estimate the percent of each number.

Tip *Convert the percent to a benchmark fraction and use compatible numbers.*

8. 52% of 38

$52\% \approx \square\%$

$38 \approx \square$

9. 47% of 79

$47\% \approx \square\%$

$79 \approx \square$

10. 23% of 117

$23\% \approx \square\%$

$117 \approx \square$

11. 18% of 74

$18\% \approx \square\%$

$74 \approx \square$

12. 72% of 98

$72\% \approx \square\%$

$98 \approx \square$

13. 8% of 832

$8\% \approx \square\%$

$832 \approx \square$

*For another example, see Set E on page 368.

Independent Practice

In **14** through **21**, find the percent of each number.

14. 2.5% of 16 **15.** 24% of 17 **16.** 42% of 12 **17.** 5.2% of 12

18. 125% of 80 **19.** 52% of 117 **20.** 250% of 20 **21.** 38% of 1,500

In **22** through **29**, write what percent the first number is of the second number.

22. 32 of 72 **23.** 9 of 45 **24.** 85 of 65 **25** 63 of 70

26. 20 of 33 **27.** 48 of 64 **28.** 16 of 16 **29.** 10 of 7.5

Problem Solving

30. A medium artichoke contains about 2 g of dietary fiber. It also contains about 12% of the recommended dietary fiber an average adult should eat each day. About how many artichokes would an average adult have to eat to get the recommended amount of dietary fiber?

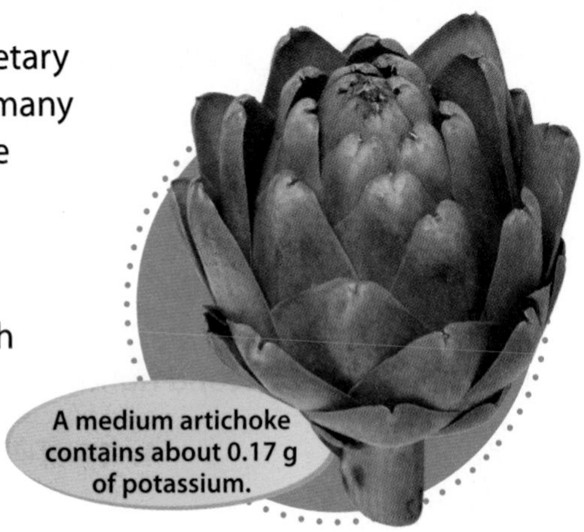
A medium artichoke contains about 0.17 g of potassium.

31. A medium artichoke contains 5% of the recommended amount of potassium an average adult should have each day. How many grams of potassium should the average adult have each day?

32. **Think About the Process** Liam is walking 15 miles in a walkathon. His goal is to raise \$214. He has already raised \$97. Which of the following equations could be used to determine what percent of his goal he has reached so far?

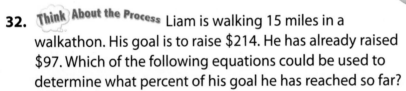

A $97x = \frac{214}{100}$ **B** $\frac{97}{214} = \frac{x}{100}$ **C** $\frac{214}{97} = \frac{x}{100}$ **D** $97 \times 214 = 100x$

33. **Writing to Explain** An art museum received a collection of 92 African American paintings. The museum can display 40 of the paintings on the first floor. Explain how you could find the percent of paintings displayed on the first floor.

34. In a 135-pound adult, about 94 pounds of the adult's weight is water. What percent of the weight is water, rounded to the nearest whole percent?

35. There are 5,280 feet in a mile. If a cloud is 5.3 miles above the ground, about how many feet above the ground is it?

36. Which of the following is a good **estimate** for 24% of 1,224?

A 300 **B** 293.76 **C** 50 **D** 28,000

Algebra Connections

Equations with Percents

Remember to use fraction or decimal equivalents to solve equations using percents. Then get the variable alone by using operations that have inverse relationships.

Adding w undoes subtracting w.

Subtracting x undoes adding x.

Multiplying by y undoes dividing by y.

Dividing by z undoes multiplying by z.

Example: 20% of w is 3.5.

Write an equation and solve:

$$20\% \times w = 3.5$$

$$0.20w = 3.5$$

$$0.20w \div 0.20 = 3.5 \div 0.20$$

$$w = 17.5$$

To check, substitute 17.5 for w.

$$0.20w = 3.5$$

$$0.20\,(17.5) = 3.5$$

$$3.5 = 3.5 \quad \text{It checks.}$$

Solve and check.

1. $20\% \times 45 = m$

2. $60\% \times g = 3$

3. $t \times 40\% = 120$

4. $(j\% \times 60) - 5 = 25$

5. 22% of $m = 55$

6. 15% of R is \$3.15

7. 16% of C is \$12

8. 35% of D is –26.25

9. 50% of $3h$ is –30

10. 25% of S is $\frac{1}{8}$

11. $66\frac{2}{3}\%$ of n is 8

12. 60% more than B is –1,200

13. 20% less than c is 32

14. 10% more than z is 22

15. $33\frac{1}{3}\%$ more than p is 16

16. 100% more than k is 110

17. 80% less than q is 16

18. Marni wants to give a 15% tip for her \$18 haircut. Find the amount of tip Marni should give. Write an equation.

19. 80% of Greg's class went on the field trip with 4 chaperones. If a total of 28 students and chaperones went, how many students are in Greg's class? Write an equation to solve the problem.

20. Nigel increased his book collection in the first month by 10%, to 55 books. Then he increased his collection by 20% in the second month. How many books were in his collection before the increase in the first month? How many books did he have at the end of the two months?

Lesson

14-6

Understand It!
Tips, taxes, discounts, and simple interest rates are often given as a percent. To find the tip, tax, discount, or simple interest earned, find the percent of a given amount.

Tips, Taxes, Discount, and Simple Interest

How do you calculate discounts or tax using percentages?

Geri's family ate dinner at a restaurant. The total cost of their dinner before tax is \$45.60. They have a coupon for 15% off the cost of their meal. If the rate of sales tax is 6.5%, how much did Geri's family pay for dinner?

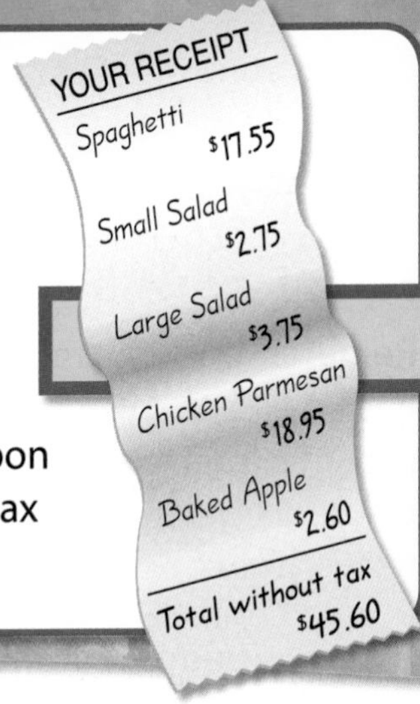

YOUR RECEIPT
Spaghetti
$17.55
Small Salad
$2.75
Large Salad
$3.75
Chicken Parmesan
$18.95
Baked Apple
$2.60
Total without tax
$45.60

Another Example How do you calculate a tip?

A tip is calculated on the total cost before the discount is taken. Suppose Geri's family wants to leave a tip of 20%. Let T = Tip.

$T = 20\% \times \$45.60$

$T = 0.20 \times 45.60$

$T = 9.12$

Geri's family should leave a tip of \$9.12.

How do you calculate simple interest?

Find how much simple interest is earned on a savings deposit of \$850, earning 5% simple interest for 6 years.

When you deposit money into a savings account, the amount of money you deposit is called the principal. The bank holds your money and pays you interest, a percentage of your deposit, based on the current interest rate. When the interest is paid only on the amount originally invested, it is called simple interest. The formula for simple interest is $\boldsymbol{I = prt}$.

Find the Simple Interest

Interest = *principal* × *rate* × *time*

$I = 850 \times 0.05 \times 6$

$I = \$255$ The deposit earns \$255 in interest over 6 years.

Find the total balance after 6 years.

Find the Total Principal and Interest

Total = *principal* + *interest*

Total = \$850 + \$255

Total = \$1,105 After 6 years, the balance will be \$1,105.

Explain It

1. In the example above, what will the total balance be after 10 years of earning interest?

The discount, d, is 15% of the cost of the dinner.

$d = 15\% \times \$45.60$

$d = 0.15 \times 45.60$

$d = \$6.84$

Find the price, p, of the dinner after the discount is taken.

$p = \$45.60 - \$6.84$

$p = \$38.76$

After the discount, the dinner cost $38.76.

The sales tax, t, is 6.5% of the discounted cost of the dinner.

$t = 6.5\% \times \$38.76$

$t = 0.065 \times 38.76$

$t = 2.5194$, or $t = 2.52$ ← **Round to the nearest cent.**

Find the total cost of the dinner.

$\$38.76 + \$2.52 = \$41.28$

The total cost of dinner with tax is $41.28.

Guided Practice*

Do you know HOW?

Find the sale price or total cost.

1. Regular Price: $25.50
Discount: 30%
Sale Price: ▢

2. Restaurant Bill: $60.79
Tip: 15%
Amount of Tip: ▢

Do you UNDERSTAND?

3. In the example above, if Geri's family received a 10% discount, how much would their total dinner cost?

4. In the example above, why would Geri's dad calculate a tip based on $45.60 and not on $38.76?

5. **Estimation** Explain how to estimate a 15% tip on a $29.95 restaurant bill.

Independent Practice

6. Regular Price: $250
Discount: 10%
Sale Price: ▢

7. Subtotal: $120.63
Sales Tax: 4%
Total Cost: ▢

8. Subtotal: $89.99
Tip: 13%
Total Cost: ▢

9. Principal: $720
Rate: 4%
Time: 2 years
Interest: ▢

10. Regular Price: $25.50
Discount: 25%
Sale Price: ▢

11. Subtotal: $52.50
Tip: 15%
Total: ▢

DIGITAL Animated Glossary
www.pearsonsuccessnet.com

For another example, see Set F on page 369.

Problem Solving

12. Shauna deposited \$76 in a simple interest account. If the simple interest rate is 4.5%, what will the total value of her account be after 3 years?

13. **Geometry** The area of Billy's garden plot is 20% smaller this year. What is the area of his new garden plot?

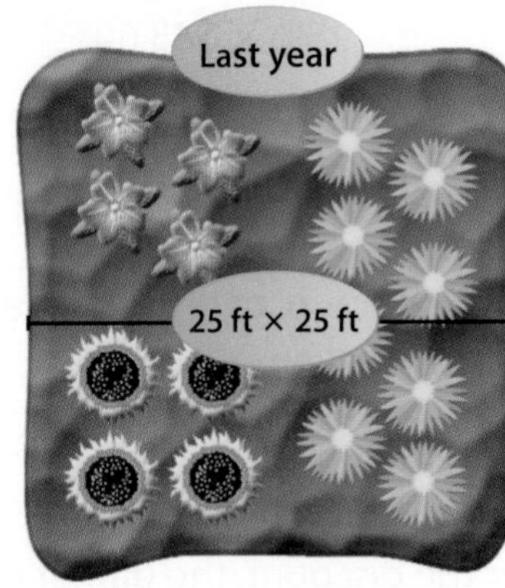

14. **Algebra** Gus saved \$350 during the summer working odd jobs. He put his savings into an account with a simple interest rate of 5.5%. How much did Gus have in the account after 2 years?

15. **Estimation** The total bill for lunch was \$12.72, of which \$0.72 was sales tax. What was the sales tax rate rounded to the nearest whole percent?

16. **Writing to Explain** Donna read this advertisement in the newspaper. Can she buy the game if she has only \$20? Explain.

17. A computer originally priced at \$240 is discounted 25%. What is the sale price?

A \$60 **B** \$180 **C** \$215 **D** \$300

18. **Writing to Explain** Les wants to borrow \$1,000. He saw the two bank advertisements at right. From which bank should he borrow? Explain your answer.

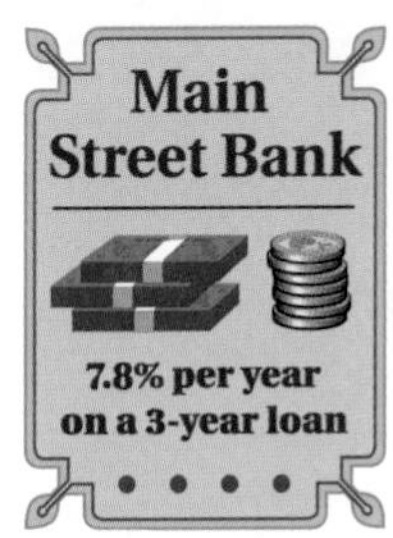

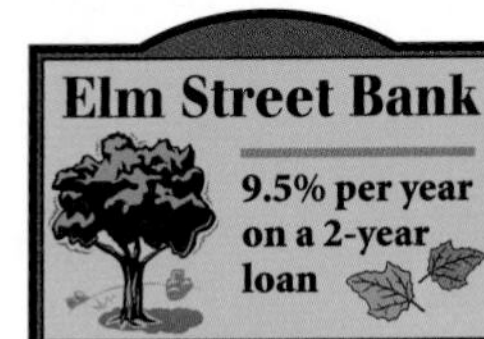

Elm Street Bank
9.5% per year on a 2-year loan

19. Reena increased the distance she runs each morning from 2 miles to 2.5 miles. By what percent did she increase her running distance?

A 0.5% **B** 20% **C** 80% **D** 25%

Use the store sign information for **20** and **21**.

Jeans: \$35
T-Shirts: \$12.99
Sweat Shirts: \$20.50
Shorts: \$17.50

20. Lea bought 3 T-shirts that were discounted 25%, and a pair of jeans at regular price. The sales tax was 6.25%. How much did Lea have to pay in all?

21. Julio bought two pairs of jeans. One pair of jeans was discounted 15%, and the other was discounted 20%. The sales tax was 4.5%. How much did Julio spend in all?

Going Digital

Solving Percent Problems

Use a calculator.

Travis bought a puppy that normally sells for $125. The pet store had a sale with all animals 15% off the original prices. What was the sale price of the puppy?

One Way

Find 15% of 125 or 0.15×125.

Press: 0.15 [×] 125 [ENTER =]

Display: 18.75

The discount is $18.75.
Subtract $125 - 18.75$.

Press: 125 [–] 18.75 [ENTER =]

Display: 106.25

Another Way

Find what percent the sale price is of the original price. 15% from 100%.

Press: 100 [–] 15 [ENTER =]

Display: 85

Find 85% of 125 or 0.85×125.

Press: 0.85 [×] 125 [ENTER =]

Display: 106.25

The sale price of the puppy was $106.25.

Practice

1. In addition to the $106.25, Travis had to pay 4.5% sales tax. How much was the sales tax to the nearest penny? How much did Travis pay for the puppy in all?

2. At El Tapatio, Josie spent $5.75 for the burritos and Miranda spent $6.25 for the fajitas. How much were their meals together? If tax is 5%, how much tax did they pay? How much did they spend for their meals, with tax? If they left a 20% tip on the total check (not including tax), how much tip did they leave? How much did they spend in all, including taxes and tip?

3. Tracy bought a jar of peanut butter that was 50% off. She had a coupon for an additional 10% off. How much did Tracy pay if the peanut butter originally cost $3.69?

Test

1. What percent of the line segment is shaded? (14-1)

   A 8%

   B 18%

   C 20%

   D 80%

2. What is 0.4% written as a decimal? (14-3)

   A 0.0004

   B 0.004

   C 0.04

   D 0.4

3. Most U.S. households spend about 5% of their income on entertainment. Which of the following is equal to 5%? (14-2)

   A $\frac{1}{20}$

   B $\frac{1}{5}$

   C $\frac{5}{10}$

   D $\frac{1}{2}$

4. The population of Gilbert, Arizona, increased 275% from 1990 to 2000. Which of the following is equal to 275%? (14-3)

   A 275

   B $27\frac{1}{2}$

   C $2\frac{3}{4}$

   D $\frac{11}{40}$

5. A study found that 9% of dog owners brush their dog's teeth. Of 578 dog owners, about how many would be expected to brush their dog's teeth? (14-4)

   A 60

   B 80

   C 100

   D 300

6. Richard bought a car for 15% off the list price. If the list price is $18,900, how much did Richard spend? (14-6)

   A $18,750

   B $17,010

   C $16,065

   D $2,835

7. The circle graph shows the distribution of children at an elementary school. If there are 205 children in the school, about how many are in the 5th grade? (14-4)

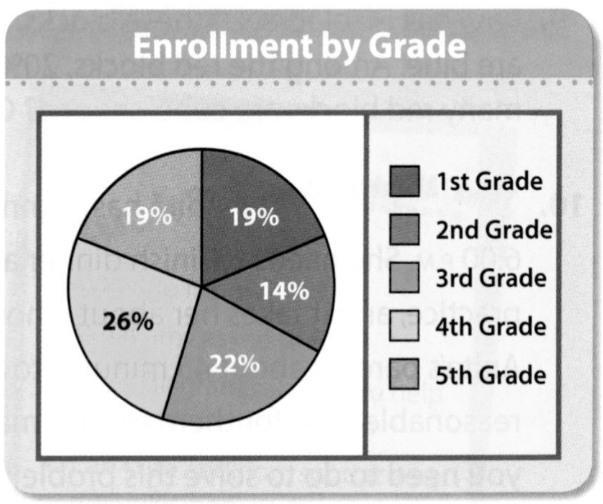

   A 20

   B 40

   C 50

   D 100

Topic 14

Test

8. All but 5 state capitals have an interstate highway serving them. What percent of 50 is 5? (14-5)

A 1%

B 5%

C 10%

D 20%

9. What percent of the grid is shaded? (14-1)

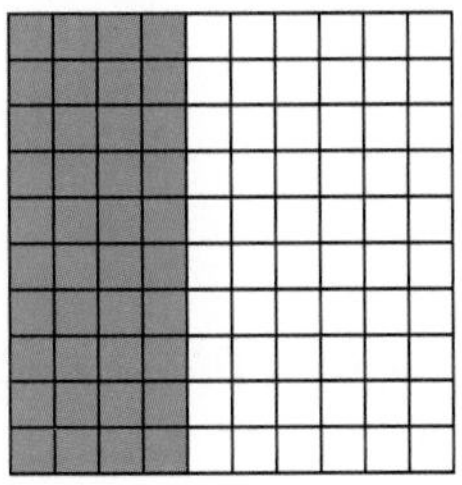

A 20%

B 40%

C 50%

D 250%

10. Which of the following can be used to find 65% of 28? (14-5)

A $\frac{n}{28} = \frac{65}{100}$

B $\frac{n}{28} = \frac{100}{65}$

C $\frac{n}{100} = \frac{28}{65}$

D $\frac{28}{n} = \frac{65}{100}$

11. If 20% of a number is 30, what is 50% of the number? (14-5)

A 150

B 100

C 90

D 75

12. What is $\frac{7}{25}$ written as a percent? (14-2)

A 70%

B 28%

C 7%

D 2.8%

13. What is the total cost for a $54 bill with a 10% tip? (14-6)

A $5.40

B $48.60

C $54.54

D $59.40

14. About 25% of the students at a college are freshmen. Of those, about 50% are women. Does that mean that 75% of the students at the college are freshman women? (14-7)

A No, because only $\frac{1}{4}$ of the students are freshmen; so 75%, or $\frac{3}{4}$, could not be freshman women.

B No, because 50% – 25% is only 25%. Therefore, about 25% are freshman women.

C Yes, because 25% + 50% = 75%.

D Yes, because 25% × 50% = 75%.

15. How much tax is charged on $18, if the tax rate is 4.5%? (14-6)

A $8.10

B $1.80

C $0.90

D $0.81

Set A, pages 344–346

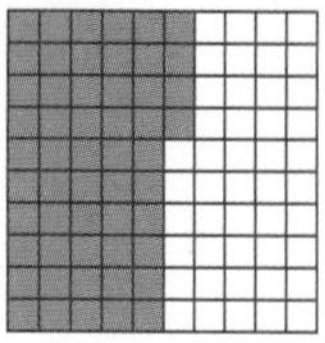

This figure has 54 out of 100, or $\frac{54}{100}$ parts shaded. So, 54% of the figure is shaded.

Use a proportion to find what percent each of the points *Q* and *R* represent in relation to the line segment on which they are located.

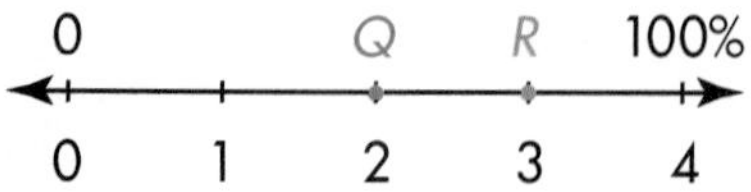

Point *Q*:

$$\frac{2}{4} = \frac{Q}{100}$$

$$200 = 4Q$$

$$50 = Q$$

Point $Q = 50\%$

Point *R*:

$$\frac{3}{4} = \frac{R}{100}$$

$$300 = 4R$$

$$75 = R$$

Point $R = 75\%$

Remember that *percent* means "of a hundred."

Find the percent shaded in each diagram.

1. 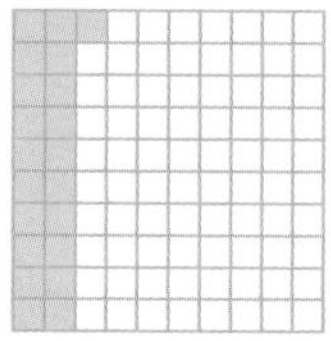

2. 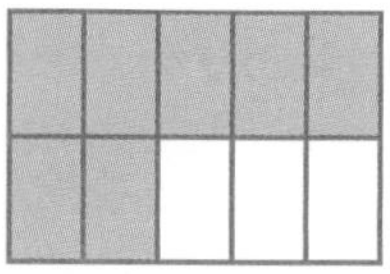

3. 

Find the percent represented by each point on the line segment. The line segment represents 100%.

4. 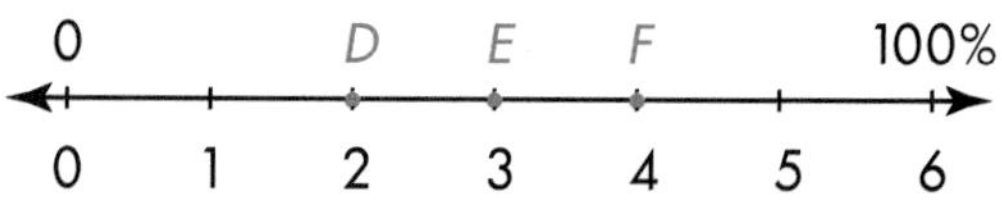

Set B, pages 348–349

Write 37% as a fraction and a decimal.

To find the fraction:

37% means 37 "of a hundred," or $\frac{37}{100}$.

To find the decimal:

$\frac{37}{100}$ can be read as "37 divided by 100."

To divide by 100, move the decimal point 2 places to the left.

37% = 0.37

Remember that you can also set up a proportion to change a fraction to a percent.

Write each value in two other ways.

1. 0.16

2. $\frac{63}{100}$

3. 27%

4. $\frac{7}{8}$

5. 0.55

6. 7%

7. 42%

8. $\frac{3}{5}$

9. 0.125

10. $\frac{47}{100}$

11. $\frac{3}{8}$

12. $33\frac{1}{3}\%$

13. 1

14. $\frac{2}{5}$

Topic 14

Reteaching

Set C, pages 350–351

Percents Greater Than 100

Express the shaded area in 3 ways.

Fraction as part of 100: $\frac{221}{100}$ or $2\frac{21}{100}$

Percent: $\frac{221}{100} = 221\%$

Decimal: $\frac{221}{100} = 2.21$

Percents Smaller Than 1

Express the shaded area of the circled part in 3 ways.

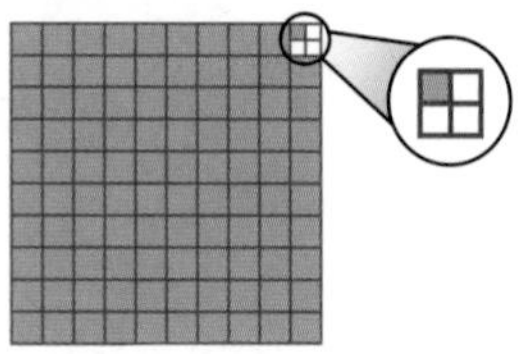

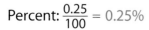

Fractions as part of 100: $\frac{0.25}{100}$

Percent: $\frac{0.25}{100} = 0.25\%$

Decimal: $\frac{0.25}{100} = 0.0025$

Remember that percents less than 1 are less than $\frac{1}{100}$, and that percents greater than 100 are more than one whole.

Express each as a fraction, a decimal, and a percent.

1.

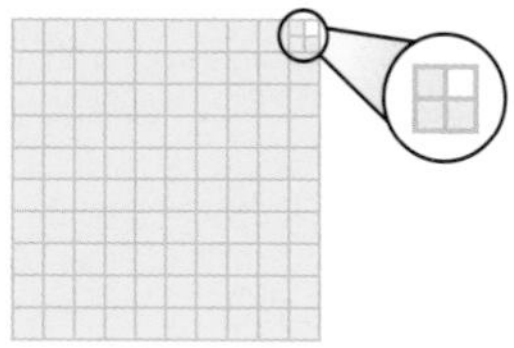

2.

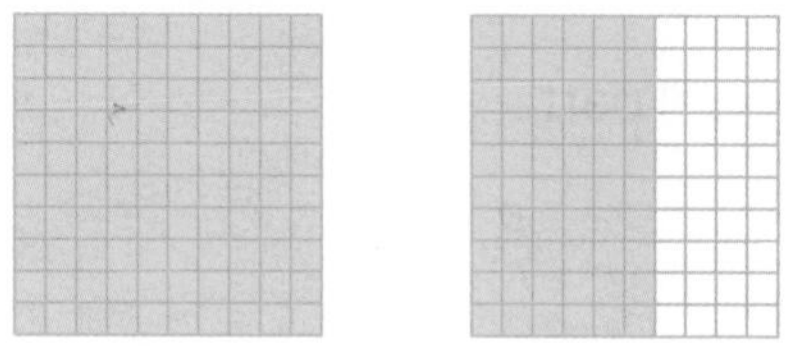

Write each as a percent.

3. 0.0025

4. $2\frac{1}{2}$

5. $\frac{7}{5}$

6. 0.0033

7. $\frac{8}{3}$

8. $\frac{1}{200}$

9. 0.00125

10. $\frac{12}{5}$

Set D, pages 352–353

You can use benchmark fractions and compatible numbers to estimate percents.

Find 24% of 83.

$24\% \approx 25\% = \frac{1}{4}$ and $83 \approx 80$

So, 24% of 83 $\approx \frac{1}{4}$ of 80.

$\frac{1}{4} \times 80 = 20$

24% of 83 is about 20.

Remember that it is easy to multiply a fraction and a number when the denominator of the fraction is a factor of the number.

Estimate the following values.

1. 22% of 96

2. 38% of 58

3. 47% of 88

4. 33% of 99

5. 12% of 358

6. 55% of 138

7. 68% of 72

8. 6% of 501

Set E, pages 354–356

Find 16% of 73.

Write a Decimal

Change the percent to a decimal and multiply.

$16\% = 0.16$

$0.16 \times 73 = 11.68$

16% of 73 is 11.68

Write a Proportion

Write a proportion:

$$\frac{\text{part}}{\text{whole}} = \frac{\text{percent value}}{100}$$

Let p equal part.

$$\frac{p}{73} = \frac{16}{100}$$

$$100p = 1{,}168$$

$$p = 11.68$$

16% of 73 is 11.68.

Use a Calculator

Find 54% of 80.

Enter: 0.54 [×] 80 [ENTER =]

Display: 43.2

or

Enter: 54 [%] [×] 80 [ENTER =]

Display: 43.2

54% of 80 is 43.2.

Remember that you can write a proportion to find the percent of a number.

$$\frac{\text{Part}}{\text{Whole}} = \frac{\text{Percent Value}}{100}$$

Find each value.

1. 9% of 124

2. 43% of 82

3. 90% of 40

4. 120% of 45

5. 0.5% of 150

6. 1% of 13

7. 45% of 55

8. 10% of 75

Tell what percent the first number is of the second number.

9. 3 of 20

10. 50 of 22

11. 24 of 30

12. 63 of 90

13. 52 of 30

14. 78 of 94

15. 65 of 73

16. 32 of 12

17. 8 of 20

18. 35 of 7

Set F, pages 358–360

Find the Discount and Sale Price

Discount: 20% off of \$75

$20\% \times \$75 = 0.20 \times 75 = \$15$

Sale Price: $\$75 - \$15 = \$60$

Find the Price with the Sales Tax

5.5% tax on \$128

Sales Tax: $0.055 \times 128 = \$7.04$

Price with Tax: $\$128 + \$7.04 = \$135.04$

Find the Tip:

15% of \$62.37

$0.15 \times 62.37 = 9.3555$ or \$9.36

Find the Simple Interest ($I = prt$):

Interest = principal × rate × time

Principal: \$750 Rate: 7.5%

Time: 2 years

$I = 750 \times 0.075 \times 2$; $I = \$112.50$

Remember discounts, sales tax, tips, and simple interest are all computed using a percent of a whole.

Find the sales price, total cost, or interest earned.

1. Regular Price \$18
   Discount 25%
   Sale Price ▢
2. Bill Subtotal \$32.76
   Tip (before tax) 15%
   Tax 4%
   Total Owed ▢
3. Principal \$15,000
   Rate 8.5%
   Time 5 years
   Interest ▢
4. Regular Price \$69.99
   Discount 20%
   Tax 7.0%
   Total Paid ▢

Set G, pages 362–363

The scuba equipment Carey wants was originally \$180 and is on sale for 20% off. Carey calculated the sale price is \$36.

Is Carey's answer reasonable?

Look Back and Check

20% of \$180 is \$36

The discount is \$36.

The sale price is $\$180 - \$36 = \$144$.

Carey's estimate is not reasonable because the sales price should not be less than half the original price.

Remember to look back and check to make sure your answer is reasonable and that you answered the right question.

Look back and check. Tell if the answer given is reasonable.

1. Ben is in charge of calculating the tip. The bill is \$46.82. He wants to leave a 15% tip. He calculated that the tip should be about \$7.00. Is Ben's answer reasonable?

Topic 15

Equations and Graphs

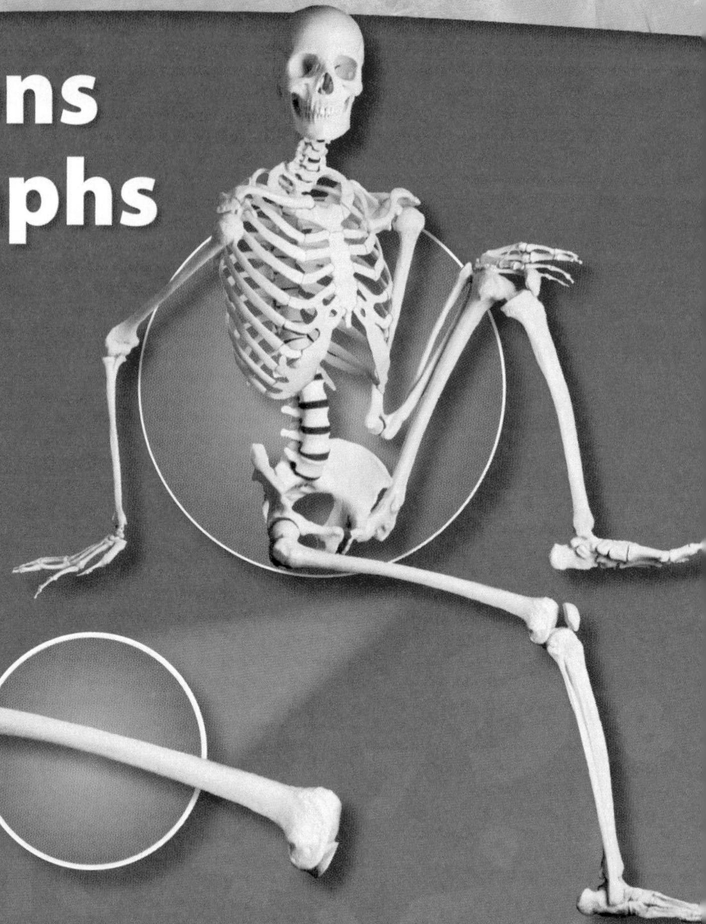

1. How do forensic scientists use the length of a femur bone to estimate a person's height? You will find out in Lesson 15-5.

2. How much does a hammerhead shark eat? You will find out in Lesson 15-4.

3 These tiles form an interesting design. How can you use an equation to express a pattern in a row of tiles? You will find out in Lesson 15-3.

4 How much does one of the most expensive teddy bears in the world cost? You will find out in Lesson 15-2.

Review What You Know!

Vocabulary

Choose the best term from the box.

- variable
- solution
- data

1. A __?__ is the value of the variable that makes an equation true.
2. A __?__ is a quantity that can change, often represented by a letter.
3. Information that is gathered is __?__.

Using Variables

Calculate y for the given value of x.

4. $y = -3x, x = 13$
5. $y = 10x, x = 0$
6. $y = -7x + 7, x = 5$
7. $y = 4x - 5, x = 14$

Understanding Rates

For each of the following, convert the rates given into unit rates.

8. 3 gallons of juice per 20 children
9. 63 strokes per 18 holes of golf

Writing Equations

10. **Writing to Explain** For every inch of necklace Ting is making, she uses 5 beads. If B equals the number of beads, and L equals the length of the necklace, write an equation that shows the relationship. Then explain how to solve this equation for B if the necklace is 24 inches long.

Lesson
15-1

Understand It!
Some equations must be solved by undoing two or more operations to find the value of the variable.

Equations with More Than One Operation

What steps can you use to solve some equations?

The hiking club has hiked 5 miles of the trail shown. How many miles must they hike each hour to finish the trail in 4 hours? Let x equal the number of miles to hike each hour.

miles left to hike	+	miles already hiked	=	total number of miles
$4x$	+	5	=	17

Another Example What inverse relationships and properties can you use?

Charles rented rock-climbing equipment for $20 per day. The store refunded $15 when he returned the equipment in good condition. After the refund, Charles spent $65 in all. For how many days did Charles rent the equipment? Let d represent the number of days Charles rented the equipment.

total rental fee	–	refund	=	amount Charles paid
$20d$	–	15	=	65

Step 1

First undo the subtraction using the Addition Property of Equality.

$$20d - 15 = 65$$
$$20d - 15 + 15 = 65 + 15$$
$$20d = 80$$

Step 2

Then undo the multiplication using the Division Property of Equality.

$$20d = 80$$
$$\frac{20d}{20} = \frac{80}{20}$$
$$d = 4$$

Step 3

Check.

$$20d - 15 = 65$$
$$20(4) - 15 = 65$$
$$80 - 15 = 65$$
$$65 = 65$$

It checks.

Charles rented the rock climbing equipment for 4 days.

Explain It

1. In the example above, how many steps did it take to solve the equation for d?

2. In the example above, what simpler equation do you have after adding 15 to both sides of the equation?

Step 1

When an equation has more than one operation, first undo addition or subtraction.

$4x + 5 = 17$

Subtract 5 from both sides.

$4x + 5 - 5 = 17 - 5$

$4x = 12$

Step 2

Then undo multiplication or division.

$4x = 12$

Divide both sides by 4.

$\frac{4x}{4} = \frac{12}{4}$

$x = 3$

They must hike 3 miles each hour.

Step 3

Check.

$4x + 5 = 17$

$4(3) + 5 = 17$

$12 + 5 = 17$

$17 = 17$

It checks.

Guided Practice*

Do you know HOW?

Copy and solve by filling in the blanks.

1. $\frac{x}{4} - 5 = 19$

$\frac{x}{4} - 5 + \square = 19 + \square$

$\frac{x}{4} = \square$

$\frac{x}{4} \times \square = 24 \times \square$

$x = \square$

Do you UNDERSTAND?

2. In the example at the top, why do you subtract 5 from both sides of the equation?

3. Suppose the hiking club members in the example had to complete their hike in 3 hours. How many miles would they have to hike each hour?

Independent Practice

Leveled Practice For **4** through **7**, tell which operation you would undo first and which operation you would undo next.

4. $15t - 15 = 45$ **5.** $62 = 3c + 8$ **6.** $25 = 5q - 50$ **7.** $\frac{d}{30} + 1 = 4$

For **8** through **19**, solve each equation and check your answer.

8. $\frac{x}{7} - 3 = 4$ **9.** $5b - 7 = 13$ **10.** $\frac{s}{4} + 3 = 9$ **11.** $24 + 12n = 60$

12. $12 + 5y = 92$ **13.** $-11n - 1 = 10$ **14.** $81 = 45 + \frac{r}{5}$ **15.** $\frac{m}{11} - 8 = 12$

16. $25 = 11g + 3$ **17.** $18 = \frac{z}{3} + 3$ **18.** $2m + 5 = 6$ **19.** $n + 2.5 = 6.5$

For another example, see Set A on page 394.

Problem Solving

20. Janine's family bought 5 box lunches and some bottled water for their hike. The bottled water cost \$4. The total cost of the water and lunches was \$19. How much did each box lunch cost? Let x represent the cost of a box lunch. Use the equation $5x + 4 = 19$ to solve.

21. Alejandro bought 4 T-shirts to give to his friends. After using a \$10-off coupon, he paid \$18 for the shirts. How much did each shirt cost? Let s represent the cost of each shirt. Use the equation $4s - 10 = 18$ to solve.

22. Writing to Explain Marty solved the equation below. Is Marty's solution correct? Why or why not?

Marty's work: $\frac{x}{3} - 5 = 6$

$3(\frac{x}{3}) - 5 = 3(6)$

$x - 5 = 18$

$x - 5 + 5 = 18 + 5$

$x = 23$

23. Think About the Process After you add 3 to both sides of the equation $27 = \frac{m}{6} - 3$, what should you do next?

A Multiply both sides by 6.

B Divide both sides by 6.

C Add 6 to both sides.

D Subtract 6 from both sides.

24. Think About the Process After you subtract 3 from both sides of the equation $42x + 3 = 87$, which operation should you *use* next to undo the multiplication?

A addition

B subtraction

C multiplication

D division

25. Think About the Process Which operation would you *undo* first to solve the equation $12n + 23 = 83$?

A addition

B multiplication

C division

D subtraction

26. Reasoning Without solving, how can you tell that $x = 7$ is not a solution of $3x + 10 = 20$?

27. The month of April has 30 days. Corey's iguana eats $2\frac{1}{2}$ ounces of peas a day. How many ounces of peas will Corey's iguana eat during the month of April?

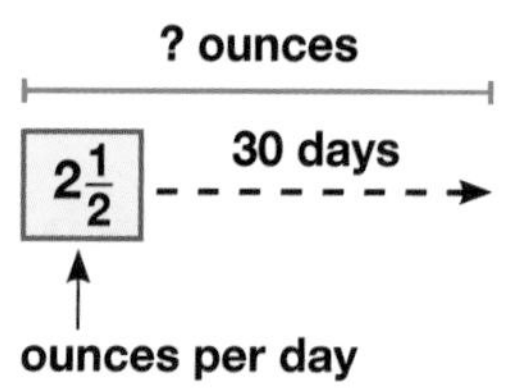

28. Vladimir exercises for at least 30 minutes each evening. One evening he jogged for $\frac{3}{4}$ hour and biked for $\frac{1}{8}$ hour. How much time did Vladimir spend that evening on his two exercises?

Algebra Connections

Equation Sense: Estimate the Solution to the Equation

Remember that you can estimate the solution to an equation by using number sense and rounding.

Use number sense and rounding to estimate a solution for each equation. For **1** through **12**, estimate the value of the variable in each equation.

1. $x + 56 = 93$

2. $x - 34 = 121$

3. $254 = 75 + x$

4. $24 - J = 5$

5. $62 + k = 108$

6. $f - 81 = 38$

7. $y + 78 = 91$

8. $96 - b = 26$

9. $15a = 120$

10. $\frac{180}{t} = 45$

11. $7r = 112$

12. $\frac{h}{6} = 18$

Example: Find $x + 12 = -37$.

Use number sense and rounding to estimate the solution to the equation.

$x + 12 = -37$ ← **Will x be negative or positive?**

Think *negative + positive = negative for this equation.*

So, x is negative.

Then, use rounding to estimate the solution. Round 12 to 10 and −37 to −40.

$x + 10 = -40$ ← **What number added to 10 equals −40?**

$-50 + 10 = -40$

So, $x \approx -50$.

For **13** through **16**, solve each problem.

13. Estimate the value of one-third of 1,612 feet.

14. **Reasoning** Ronna is estimating the amount of a 15% tip for a \$20.36 bill. Her friend Suri said that \$2 is a good estimate. Do you agree? Explain.

15. **Writing to Explain** Why would you estimate to solve an equation?

16. Rob charges \$0.01 per square yard to mow a lawn. He estimates that each of his steps is about a yard. Before he gave Mrs. Rodriguez an estimate to mow her lawn, he paced the width of the yard in 33 steps and the length of her yard in 68 steps. What would be a good cost estimate for Rob to give to Mrs. Rodriguez? Estimate the area of the yard and then estimate the cost. Explain.

Lesson

15-2

Understand It!
Equations can be used to represent a pattern or rule.

Patterns and Equations

How can you find a pattern to write and solve an equation?

The table shows the cost of weekend tickets to the Slide and Splash Water Park. Find a pattern between the number of tickets, *n*, and the cost, *c*, of the tickets. How much would 6 tickets cost?

Write a rule and an equation that tells a pattern.

Number, *n*	Cost, *c*
3	$16.50
4	$22.00
5	$27.50
6	

Guided Practice*

Do you know HOW?

1. The table shows Brenda's age, *b*, when Talia, *t*, is age 7, 9, and 10. Write a rule and an equation that describes a pattern. Then find Brenda's age when Talia is 12.

Talia's age, *t*	Brenda's age, *b*
7	2
9	4
10	5
12	

Do you UNDERSTAND?

2. How can you find a pattern in a table to write a rule and an equation that describes a pattern?

3. In the example at the top, how much will 12 tickets cost?

4. **Writing to Explain** What should be done if the pattern does not check for other values in the table?

Independent Practice

Leveled Practice In **5** through **8**, write a rule and an equation to fit a pattern in each table.

5.

x	−2	−1	0	1	2
y	30	31	32	33	34

6.

m	0	1	2	3	4
n	0	−3	−6	−9	−12

7.

a	−3	−2	−1	0	1
b	11	12	13	14	15

8.

x	0	6	12	18	24
y	0	1	2	3	4

For another example, see Set B on page 395.

Find the price of one ticket, p, when 3 tickets cost $16.50.

$$3p = \$16.50$$
$$\frac{3p}{3} = \frac{\$16.50}{3}$$
$$p = \$5.50$$

One ticket costs $5.50. Check the cost for 4 and 5 tickets.

$$4 \times \$5.50 = \$22.00$$
$$5 \times \$5.50 = \$27.50$$

$5.50 checks for 4 and 5 tickets.

State the rule:

The total cost, c, is $5.50 times the number of tickets, n.

Write an equation:

$c = \$5.50 \times n$, or $c = 5.5n$

Find the cost of 6 tickets:

$c = 5.5(6)$

$c = 33$

The cost of 6 tickets is $33.00.

Write a rule and an equation to fit a pattern in each table for **9** and **10**. Then use the rule to complete the table.

9.

u	0	1	2	3	4
v	25	24	23		

10.

x	0	9	18	27	36
y	0	1	2		

Problem Solving

11. To celebrate their 125th anniversary, a company in Germany produced 125 very expensive teddy bears. The bears, known as the "125 Karat Teddy Bears," are made of mohair, silk, and gold thread and have diamonds and sapphires for eyes.

The chart at the right shows the approximate cost of different numbers of these bears. Based on the pattern, how much does one bear cost?

Data

Cost of "125 Karat Teddy Bears"

Number, n	Cost, c
4	$188,000
7	$329,000
11	$517,000
15	$705,000

12. Writing to Explain Explain how you can find a pattern in the chart showing the cost of "125 Karat Teddy Bears." Use the pattern to write a rule and an equation.

Think About the Process For **13** and **14**, which equation best describes the pattern in each table?

13.

r	−2	0	2	4	6	8
s	−4	−2	0	2	4	6

A $s = -2r$

B $s = r - 2$

C $s = \frac{r}{2}$

D $s = r + 2$

14.

x	−1	−0.5	0	0.5	1	1.5
y	−2	−1	0	1	2	3

A $y = -x$

B $y = -2x$

C $y = 2x$

D $y = 0.5x$

Lesson

15-3

Understand It!
Tables and patterns can be used to represent situations and solve problems.

More Patterns and Equations

How can you use patterns to solve an equation that has more than one operation?

Ethan owes his mother \$75. He is repaying her \$5 each week. How much will Ethan still owe after 12 weeks?

Guided Practice*

Do you know HOW?

In **1**, use the equation given to complete the table.

1. $y = 2x - 7$

x	−1	0	1	2	3
y	−9	−7	−5		

2. State the rule for the pattern in the table in words.

Do you UNDERSTAND?

3. In the example at the top, look for a pattern. What happens to the value of y when the value of x is increased by 1?

4. Find the value for y when $x = 10$. What does this mean in relation to the example?

Independent Practice

Leveled Practice In **5** and **6**, use the pattern and equation to complete each table.

5. $t = -5d + 5$

d	−3	−2	−1	0	1
t	20	15	10		

6. $y = \frac{1}{2}x - 1$

x	0	2	4	6	8
y	−1	0	1		

In **7** and **8**, use the equation to complete each table.

7. $y = 2x + 1$

x	−1	0	1	2
y		1		

8. $p = -q + 6$

q	−3	−2	−1	0
p	9			

*For another example, see Set C on page 395.

Step 1

Make a table to show the amount Ethan still owed after 0, 1, 2, and 7 weeks.

Week, x	Amount still owed, y
0	$75
1	$70
2	$65
7	$40

Step 2

Use the pattern to write an equation.

Let x = the number of weeks

Let y = the amount still owed

Amount still owed		Loan amount		Amount paid after x weeks
y	=	$75	−	$5x$

Step 3

Find how much Ethan will still owe after 12 weeks.

$y = 75 - 5x$

$y = 75 - 5(12)$

$y = 75 - 60$

$y = 15$

Ethan will still owe $15 after 12 weeks.

In **9** and **10**, use the equation to complete each table.

9. $b = \frac{a}{2} - 2$

a	8	5	2	0	−2
b	■	■	■	■	■

10. $y = -3x + 10$

x	−2	0	2	4	6
y	■	■	■	■	■

Problem Solving

11. **Think About the Process** Which equation describes this pattern?

x	−2	−1	0	1
y	−16	−10	−4	2

A $y = 4x - 6$

B $y = -6x + 4$

C $y = 4x + 6$

D $y = 6x - 4$

12. A parking garage charges $2.50 for parking up to 1 hour and $1.25 for each additional hour. If a car is parked for h hours, what is the parking charge? How much would it cost to park 6 hours? Use the equation $c = \$2.50 + \$1.25\,(h - 1)$ to make a table for 2, 3, 4, 5, and 6 hours.

13. Elizabeth is using 1-inch square tiles to decorate a wall. Use the equation $p = 2t + 2$ to make a table to show the perimeter, p, of t tiles in a single row when t is 1, 2, 3, and 6.

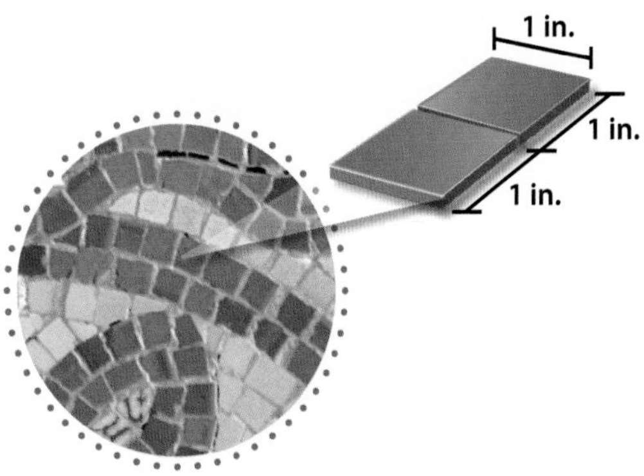

14. **Writing to Explain** Explain the rule for the pattern given by the equation $p = 2t + 2$ in Exercise 13.

Lesson

15-4

Understand It!
Linear equations can be graphed on a coordinate plane by using three values for each variable.

Graphing Equations

Hands-On
grid paper

How can you graph a linear equation?

The booster club members are making school pompoms. Their supplies cost \$4, and they plan to sell the pompoms for \$1 apiece.

Let x = the number of pompoms sold.
Let y = the profit.

Graph the equation $y = x - 4$ to show the relationship between x and y.

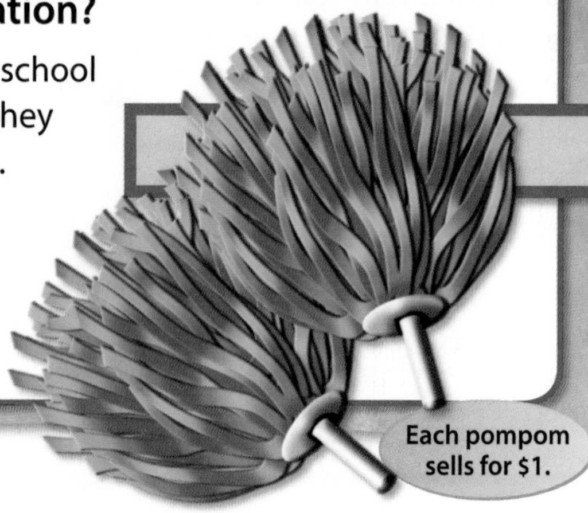

Another Example When does the graph of a linear equation go through the origin?

Make a T-table and graph of $y = 4x$.

Step 1

Make a T-table, using at least three x-values.

$y = 4x$	
x	y
−1	−4
0	0
1	4

$4(-1) = -4$
$4(0) = 0$
$4(1) = 4$

Step 2

Graph each ordered pair. Draw a line through the points and extend the line in both directions. The line shows all the values that make the equation true.

The graph of a linear equation will go through the origin if the equation is $y = ax$, where a can be any nonzero number.

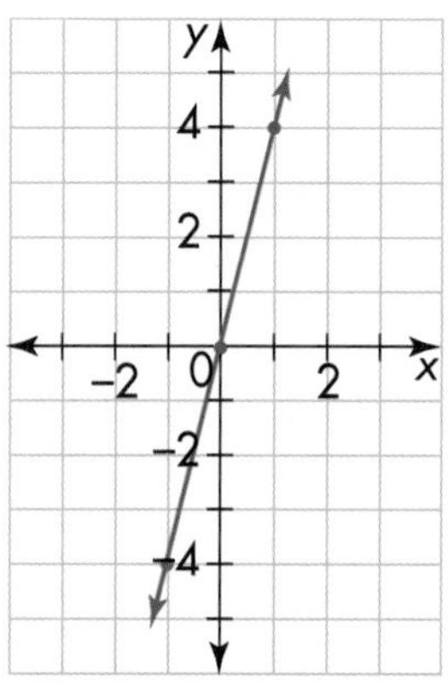

Guided Practice*

Do you know HOW?

1. Copy the T-table and fill in the values using the equation $y = 3x$. Draw a coordinate plane and graph the equation.

$y = 3x$	
x	y
−2	▢
0	▢
2	▢

Do you UNDERSTAND?

2. In the Another Example, what is true about the x-value and y-value of any point on the line of the graph?

3. In the example at the top, explain why points with negative x-values do not relate to the problem.

DIGITAL Animated Glossary, eTools
www.pearsonsuccessnet.com

*For another example, see Set D on page 396.

Step 1

Make a T-table for $y = x - 4$.

x	y
0	−4
2	−2
6	2

Always choose at least three x-values; then find the corresponding y-values.

Step 2

Graph each ordered pair in the T-table on a coordinate plane.

Use a straight edge to draw a line through the points.

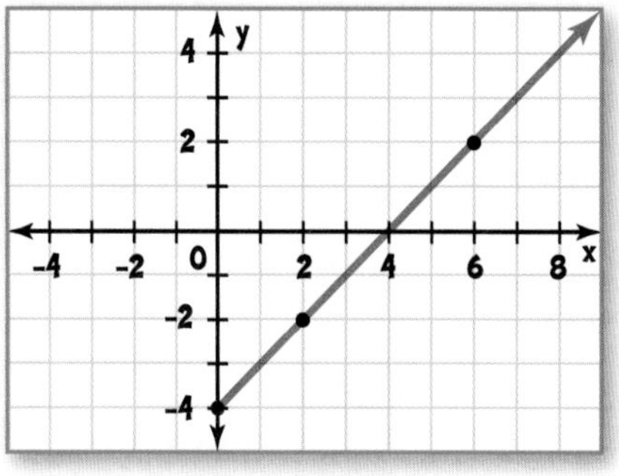

Since the graph of $y = x - 4$ is a straight line, the equation is a linear equation.

Independent Practice

In **4** through **11**, make a T-table using the values −2, 4, and 6 for x. Draw a coordinate plane and graph the equations.

4. $y = x$ **5.** $y = 3 + x$ **6.** $y = x + 8$ **7.** $y = x - 3$

8. $y = 2x$ **9.** $y = x + 1$ **10.** $y = -x$ **11.** $y = \frac{x}{2}$

Problem Solving

During a movie matinee, the film broke, so the manager refunded the ticket price to everyone attending.

Data

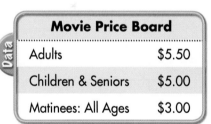

Movie Price Board	
Adults	\$5.50
Children & Seniors	\$5.00
Matinees: All Ages	\$3.00

12. If the manager had to refund \$33.00, how many people were at the theater?

13. Suppose you do not know how many people were in the theater. Draw a graph of $y = 3x$ to show how much the manager would have to refund the customers. Label the axes by 5s.

14. Which equation was used to make the graph on the right?

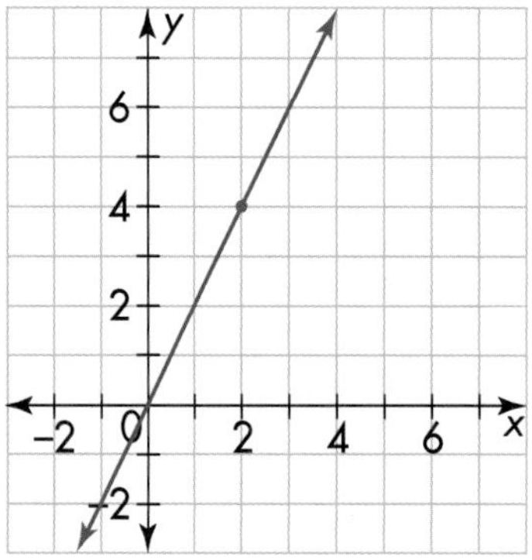

A $y = 4x$ **C** $y = 2x$

B $y = x + 2$ **D** $y = x + 2$

15. A hammerhead shark may eat about 4% of its body weight in food each day. If one shark eats about 7.5 pounds of food a day, make a T-table of $y = 7.5x$ to show how many pounds of food this shark eats in x days. Use x-values of 0, 6, and 8.

Lesson
15-5

Understand It! Equations with two or more operations can be graphed similarly to equations with one operation.

Graphing Equations with More Than One Operation

Hands-On
grid paper

How can you graph a linear relationship involving two operations?

The temperature was –6°C and increased 2°C each hour for 6 hours. The equation $y = -6 + 2x$ shows the relationship between x, the number of hours, and y, the temperature. After how many hours was the temperature 0°C?

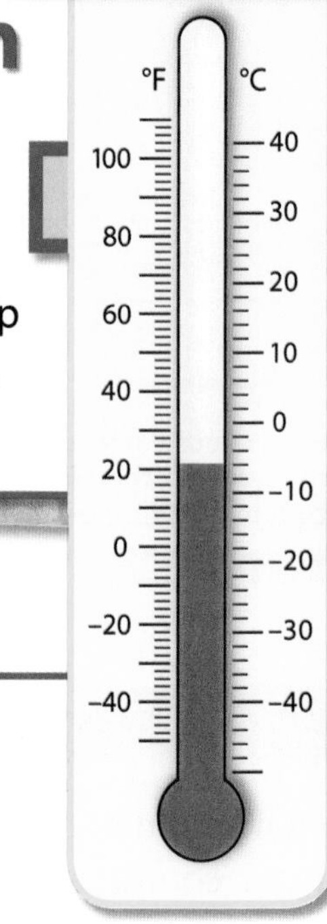

Another Example How can you use a linear relationship to convert measures of temperature?

Temperatures in most of the world are given in degrees Celsius. The equation $F = 1.8C + 32$ shows the relationship between the Fahrenheit (F) and Celsius (C) temperature scales. Graph the equation and use the graph to estimate what –5° Celsius is in degrees Fahrenheit.

Step 1 $F = 1.8C + 32$

Make a T-table for $C = -10, 0,$ and 10.

°C	–10	0	10
°F	14	32	50

Step 2 Graph the ordered pairs. Draw a line showing all the values for which the equation is true.

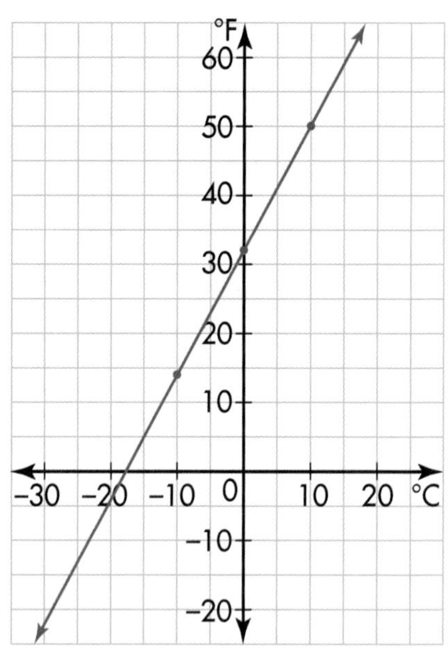

Step 3 Use the graph to estimate the Fahrenheit temperature for –5°C.

–5°C equals about 23°F.

Explain It

1. In the example above, why do you think the C-values of –10, 0, and 10 were used?

2. How can you convert –5°C to degrees Fahrenheit? Convert –5°C to degrees Fahrenheit.

Step 1

Make a T-table for $y = -6 + 2x$.

x	y
0	−6
2	−2
4	2

Step 2

Graph each ordered pair on a coordinate plane. Draw a line through the points.

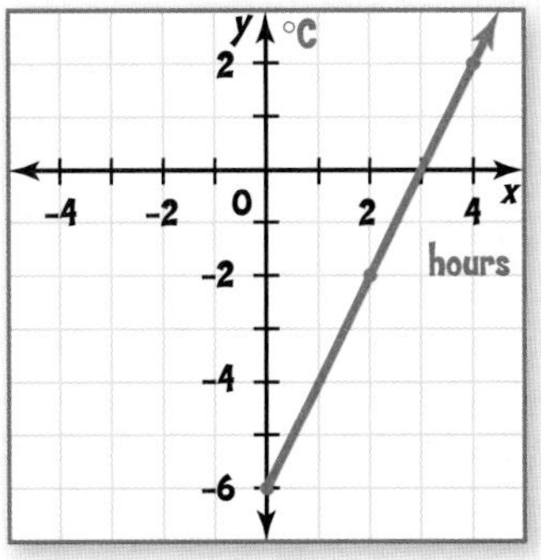

Step 3

Use the graph to find the point with a y-value of 0.

Point (3, 0) is on the graph of $y = -6 + 2x$.

The temperature was 0°C after 3 hours.

Guided Practice*

Do you know HOW?

1. Copy and complete the T-table below for $y = 5x - 5$. Then graph the equation.

x	y
−1	−10
0	
1	

$y = 5x - 5$

← $y = 5(-1) - 5$

$y = -5 - 5$

$y = -10$

Do you UNDERSTAND?

2. Is the equation $y = 5x - 5$ a linear equation? Explain.

3. At what point does the equation $y = 5x - 5$ cross the y-axis?

4. Is the point (1, 0) a solution of $y = 5x - 5$? Explain.

Independent Practice

Leveled Practice Copy and complete the T-tables for each of the equations below. Then graph each equation.

5. $y = -3x + 1$

x	y
−1	
0	
1	

6. $y = 2x + 3$

x	y
−1	
0	
1	

7. $y = 3 - 2x$

x	y
−1	
0	
1	

For **8** through **11**, make a T-table and graph each equation.

8. $y = 4x + 5$ **9.** $y = -2x + 2$ **10.** $y = -x + 10$ **11.** $y = -2x - 1$

DIGITAL eTools **www.pearsonsuccessnet.com**

For another example, see Set E on page 396.

Problem Solving

A zookeeper uses the chart at right to figure out how much food to put in the pens of different herbivores. The zookeeper adds a fixed amount of extra food per pen.

For **12** through **14**, use the equation given to make a T-table and draw a graph in the first quadrant showing the relationship between the amount of food and number of animals. Let x = the number of animals, and let y = the total amount of food.

Data

animal	feed per animal (lb)	extra feed per pen (lb)
deer	2.5	3
sheep	4	3
goats	1	5
antelope	1.5	3
elk	7	3

12. antelope $y = 1.5x + 3$ **13.** deer $y = 2.5x + 3$ **14.** sheep $y = 4x + 3$

Use the graphs made in 12 through 14 to answer **15** and **16**.

15. If there are 2 antelope in a pen, how much feed should the zookeeper give them?

16. Writing to Explain The zookeeper brings 15 pounds of food to the sheep pen. How can you determine how many animals there are?

17. Think About the Process Which equation is shown in the graph at right?

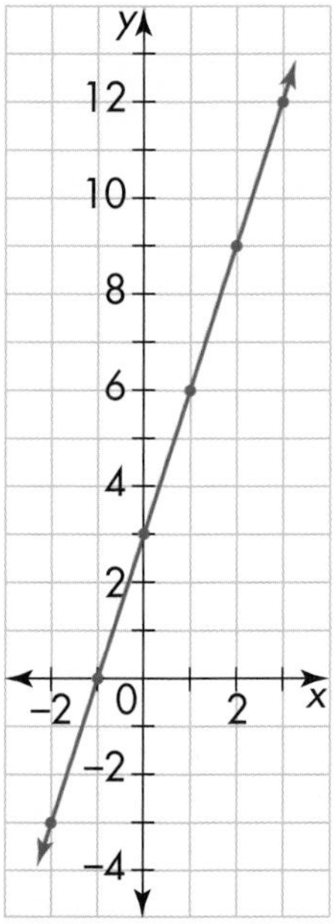

A $y = 0.5x + 3$ **C** $y = 3x + 3$

B $y = 3x - 7$ **D** $y = -3x + 3$

18. Which of the following ordered pairs is found on the line $y = 5 - 6x$?

A (1, 11) **B** (0, 6) **C** (5, 6) **D** (1, −1)

19. At what point does the line $y = -8x + 7$ cross the y-axis?

A (0, −7) **B** (0, 7) **C** (−8, 7) **D** (15, 0)

20. Terry received 44 points out of a possible 50 points on the math test. What was his score as a percent?

21. Forensic scientists can use the length of the thighbone or femur in centimeters to help estimate the height of a skeleton. One equation they may use is $h = 2.6f + 65$, where h represents height and f represents the length of the femur in centimeters. About how tall was this person?

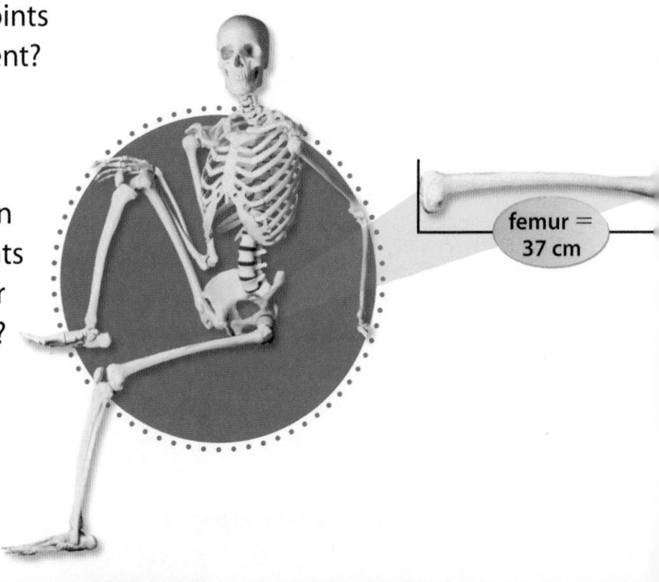

Going Digital

Graphing Equations

Use eTools
Spreadsheet/Data/Grapher

Graph $y = x + 5$, $y = 3x$, and $y = \frac{1}{2}x - 4$.
Compare each graph to $y = x$.

Step 1 Go to the Spreadsheet/Data/Grapher eTool. Click on the Equation Grapher workspace icon.

The graph of $y = x$ is shown. Note that $y = x$ is the same as $y = 1.00x + 0.00$. Click on the dot and drag the line up until the equation shows $y = 1.00x + 5.00$. So $y = x + 5$ is up 5 units from $y = x$.

Step 2 Move the line back to $y = 1.00x + 0.00$. Choose another place on the line and drag until the equation shows $y = 3.00x + 0.00$. Notice how the equation goes through the points (0, 0) and (3, 1). From (0, 0) you can find another point by going up 3 units and right 1 unit.

Step 3 Since $\frac{1}{2} = 0.5$, move the line until the equation shows $y = 0.50x - 4.00$. Notice, from (0, –4) you go up 1 unit and right 2 units to get to another point.

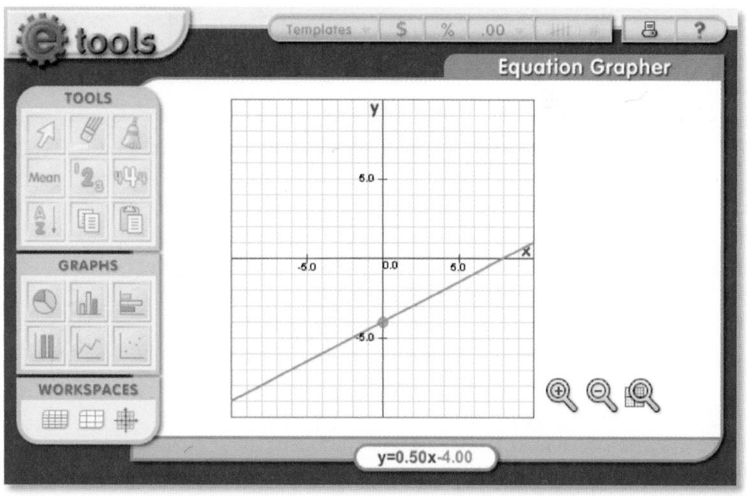

Practice

Predict what each graph will look like and then graph to check.

1. $y = x + 7$ **2.** $y = x - 6$ **3.** $y = 2x$ **4.** $y = \frac{1}{3}x$

5. $y = -4x$ **6.** $y = 3x - 1$ **7.** $y = 2x - 5$ **8.** $y = \frac{1}{4}x + 2$

Lesson

15-6

Understand It!
Functions are special relations that can be represented in tables or graphs.

Functions

What is a function?

Any set of ordered pairs (x, y) is called a relation. Equations, tables, and graphs can represent relations.

A function is a special relation in which there is only one y-value (output) for each x-value (input).

The table shows the hours and miles that Lara biked. Is the set of ordered pairs in the table a function?

Data

Lara's Bike Ride

Total Hours (x)	Total Miles (y)
1	6
2	12
3	18
4	24

Other Examples

Function

The equation $y = -3$ is a function.

x	y
2	−3
0	−3
−3	−3

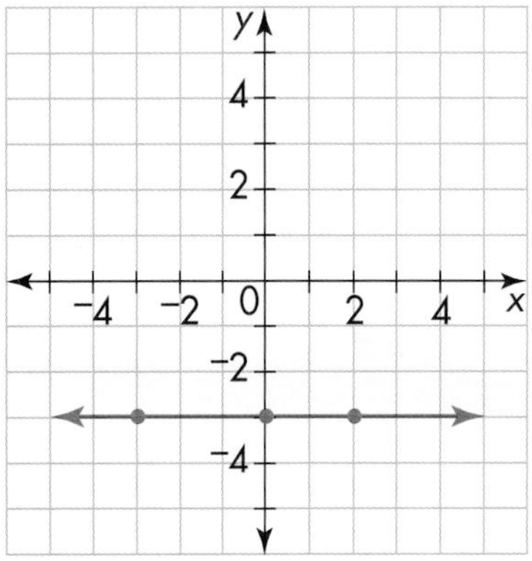

Not a Function

The relation in this table is not a function.

x	y
4	−3
2	2
4	3
−2	1
0	0

There are two y-values for the x-value, 4.

Function

This graph represents a function.

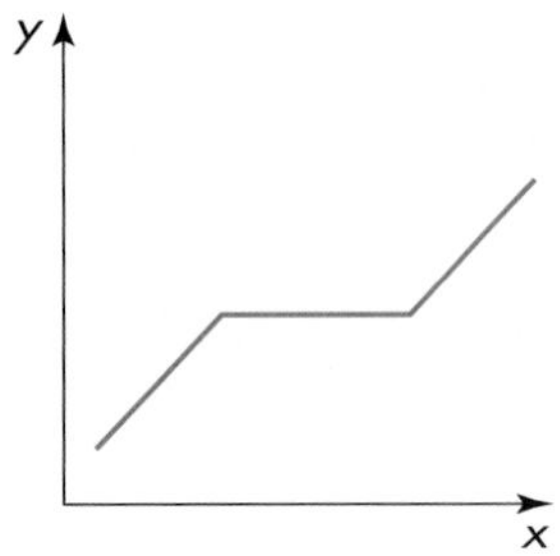

Each x-value has only one y-value.

Not a Function

This graph does not represent a function.

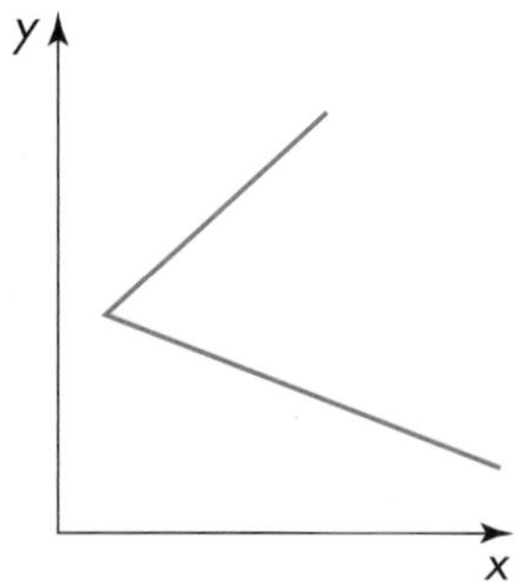

Some x-values have more than one y-value.

Function

Each x-value in Lara's table has only one y-value, so it is a function. The equation, $y = 6x$, describes this function.

Lara's Bike Ride

Not a Function

Not all relations are functions. A table and graph of the equation $x = 3$ is shown below.

It is not a function.

x	y
3	2
3	0
3	-3

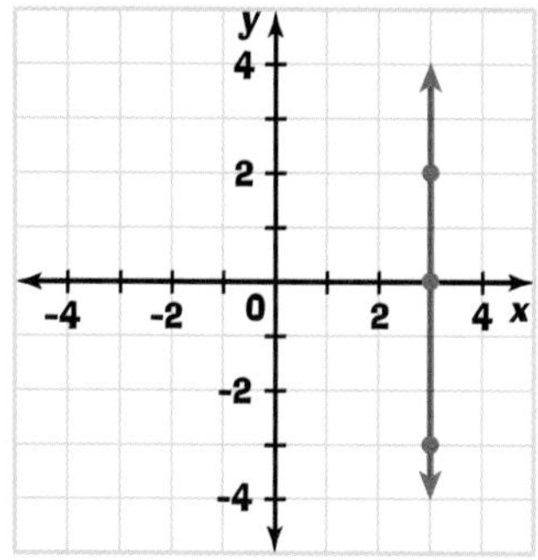

Guided Practice*

Do you know HOW?

In **1** and **2**, tell whether each relation is a function.

1.

x	y
2	8
3	12
4	16
5	20

2.

x	y
1	1
0	0
1	−1
4	2

Do you UNDERSTAND?

3. Explain why this graph represents a function.

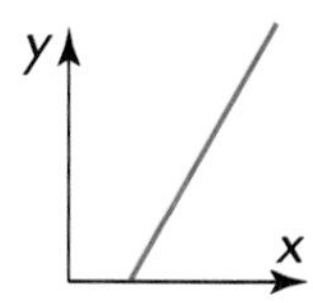

4. Explain why this graph does not represent a function.

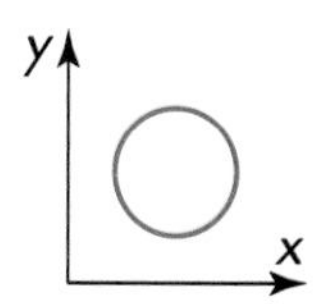

Independent Practice

In **5** through **8**, tell whether each relation shown in the table is a function.

5.

x	y
−3	9
−4	16
3	9
4	16

6.

x	y
2	5
3	7
4	7
5	9

7.

x	y
−1	2
0	3
−1	−2
0	−3

8.

x	y
−3	−2
−2	−1
2	3
−3	4

9. Which graph below represents a function?

a

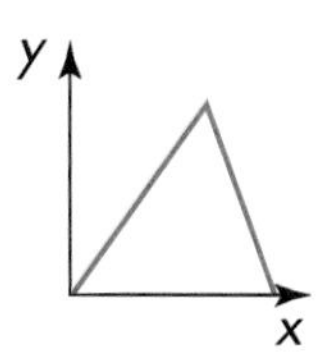

b

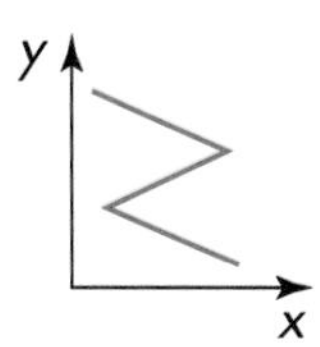

c

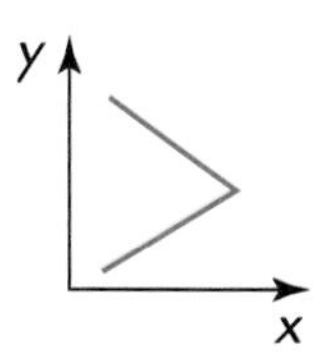

DIGITAL Animated Glossary **www.pearsonsuccessnet.com**

For another example, see Set F on page 397.

Problem Solving

Zach made a graph to show the hours and miles that he rode his bike on Saturday. Use Zach's graph for **10** through **12**.

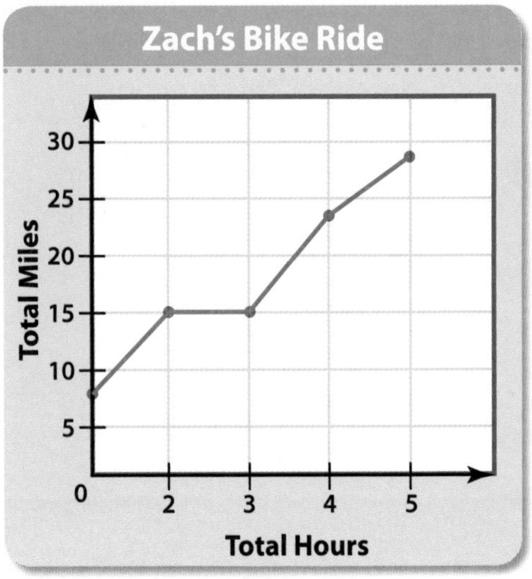

10. Why do you think Zach's total mileage did not increase between 2 and 3 hours?

11. How do you know that Zach did not ride at the same speed for the whole trip?

12. **Writing to Explain** Does Zach's graph represent a function? Explain why or why not.

13. Wholesome O's cereal contains 10 grams of carbohydrates per ounce. Draw a graph to represent the number of carbohydrates in 2, 4, 6, and 10 ounces of cereal.

14. Some states require a \$0.05 deposit when you buy drinks in glass bottles.

a Write an equation to show the relationship between *b*, bottles bought, and *d*, deposit paid.

b Use your equation to copy and complete the table at the right.

Data

Number of Bottles Bought (b)	Deposit Paid (d)
5	
8	
10	
12	
24	

15. A plumber charges \$79.50 an hour plus a \$50 fee for each visit.

a Make a table to show the cost for a 1-hour, 2-hour, 3-hour, and 4-hour visit.

b Does the table represent a function? Explain.

16. **Think About the Process** Sally exercises 4 times per week. On the days she exercises, she drinks $2\frac{1}{2}$ cups of water during her excercise. Which shows how many cups of water Sally drinks during her exercise in two weeks?

A $2\frac{1}{2} \div 2 + (4 \times 8)$

B $4 \times 2\frac{1}{2}$

C $4 + 2\frac{1}{2} \times 2$

D $4(2\frac{1}{2}) \times 2$

17. **Algebra** Evaluate the expression $y(3x + 23)$ for $x = -2$ and $y = 2$.

Enrichment

Solving Inequalities

An inequality is a mathematical sentence that contains $>$, $<$, $\geq$, or $\leq$. You know that any value that makes an inequality true is a solution. To solve inequalities, use inverse relationships and the following rules describing properties of inequalities.

You may add or subtract any positive or negative number to both sides of an inequality without changing the inequality.

	Add	Subtract
You know:	$3 < 7$	$3 < 7$
So:	$3 + 2 < 7 + 2$	$3 - 2 < 7 - 2$
Check:	$5 < 9$	$1 < 5$

You may multiply or divide both sides of an inequality by any **positive** number without changing the inequality.

	Multiply	Divide
You know:	$6 < 8$	$6 < 8$
So:	$6 \times 2 < 8 \times 2$	$6 \div 2 < 8 \div 2$
Check:	$12 < 16$	$3 < 4$

Example: Solve $2x - 6 < 2$. Then graph the solution.

1. Add 6 to both sides. $2x - 6 + 6 < 2 + 6$; $2x < 8$
2. Divide both sides by 2. $2x \div 2 < 8 \div 2$; $x < 4$
3. Graph the solution on a number line.

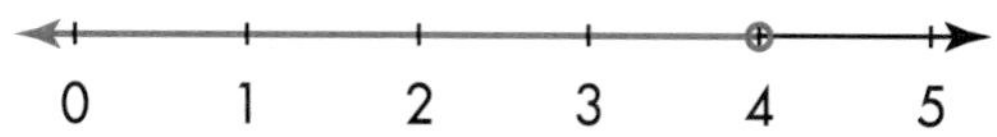

Because x is not equal to 4 and x is also less than 4, the arrow points to the left. The open circle means that 4 is *not* a solution.

Use a point on the graph to check the solution, such as $x = 3$.

$(2 \times 3) - 6 < 2$

$6 - 6 < 2$

$0 < 2$ The inequality is true, so 3 is a solution.

Practice

Solve **1** through **6** for x. Then graph each solution.

1. $3x - 7 < 2$

2. $2x - 5 \geq x - 3$

3. $2 + 5x \geq 2x - 13$

4. $(x \times 3) + 7 < 4$

5. $\frac{x}{5} - 4 > 1$

6. $4x - 9 < 23$

7. a What inequality is shown at the right?

b Solve the inequality for x.

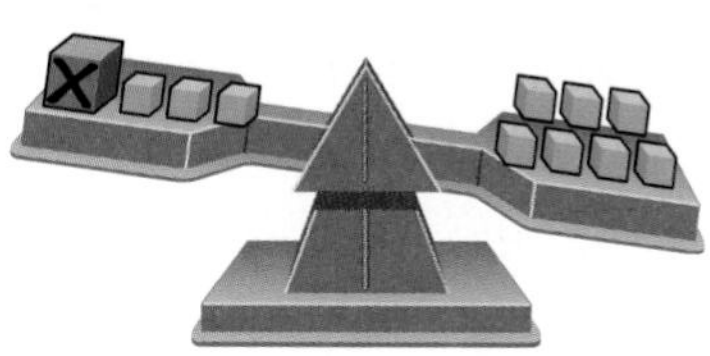

Lesson
15-7

Understand It!
Some problems can be solved by acting out the situation and using reasoning.

Problem Solving

Act It Out and Use Reasoning

Ernie is packing 6 boxes and 6 bags of food for hurricane disaster relief.
The food distribution rules are:

1. **Each bag must have the same number of oranges.**
2. **Each box must have the same number of oranges.**
3. **Each bag or box must have at least 1 orange.**

How many different ways can Ernie pack the oranges?

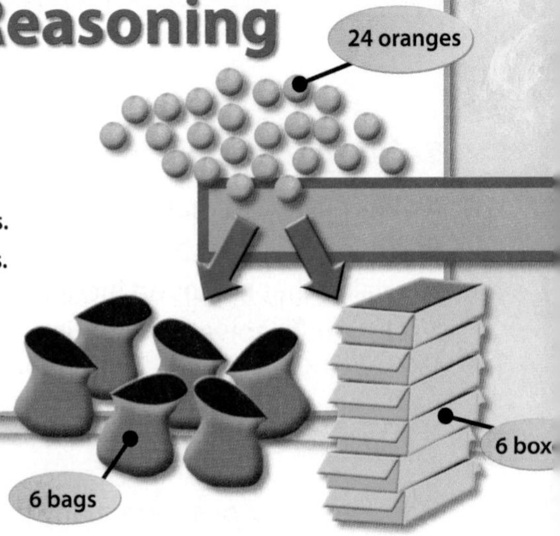

Guided Practice*

Do you know HOW?

For **1**, make a table and use counters to solve.

1. Geri has two fish tanks and 20 fish. She wants each tank to contain an even number of fish. How many different ways can Geri arrange the fish in the tanks?

Tank 1				
Tank 2				

Do you UNDERSTAND?

2. In the hurricane relief example above, how do you know when you have found all of the possible solutions?

3. **Write a Problem** Write a real-world problem that you can solve by using logical reasoning and acting it out.

Independent Practice

In **4** and **5**, act out the problem and use reasoning to solve.

4. Ramon has 20 gift cards to give to his mom, dad, and twin sisters. He wants to give each of them at least 1 card, and he wants to give each sister the same number and each parent the same number. How many different ways can he give out the cards?

Make a table to show your reasoning. Show all the possible combinations that reach this goal.

5. Eileen is giving 12 of her old toys to 2 different charities. She wants to give a minimum of 2 toys to each charity. How many different ways are possible for Ellen to distribute the toys?

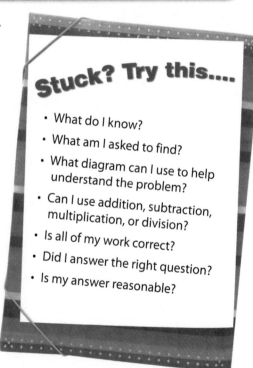

Stuck? Try this....

- What do I know?
- What am I asked to find?
- What diagram can I use to help understand the problem?
- Can I use addition, subtraction, multiplication, or division?
- Is all of my work correct?
- Did I answer the right question?
- Is my answer reasonable?

*For another example, see Set G on page 397.

Plan and Solve

Make a table to show the possibilities.

Oranges per Bag		
Oranges per Box		

Think If there is 1 orange in each bag, is it possible to put the remaining oranges evenly in 6 boxes?

Plan and Solve

Use 24 counters to find all possibilities.

Oranges per Bag	1	2	3
Oranges per Box	3	2	1

There are 3 different ways Ernie can pack the oranges.

In **6** through **14**, solve each problem.

6. Parker jogged 2 more miles than half the distance that Mackie jogged. The equation $P = \frac{M}{2} + 2$ shows the relationship. Make a table and a graph that show the relationship.

7. Sari washes cars. She charges $7 per minivan and $4 per car. She earned $41 last weekend. How many vehicles of each type did she wash?

8. Geometry Write an equation for the area of a rectangle that is three times as long as it is wide. Use only one variable.

9. Reasoning The water in the birdbath is frozen today. Is the outside temperature 20°F or 20°C? Explain.

10. Number Sense Alicia bought a soccer ball for 25% off the regular price of $29.95. What was the sale price?

11. Jolie needs an average score of 75 on three tests. She has a 73 and a 70. What score must she get on the third test?

12. Tanya needs 19 bottles of juice for the field trip. The store sells the bottles of juice in packs of 6. If she already has 1 bottle of juice, complete the table to find how many packs she should buy.

Packs of Juice			
Bottles per Pack			

13. Writing to Explain Ross bought classic comic books for $10 each. When the price increased to $17 per book, he sold all of his comic books except one. His profit was $49. How many comic books did Ross buy? Explain how you found the answer.

14. Sara needs a total of 90 points to get an A in class. She already has 6 points. If each book report is worth 7 points, what is the least number of book reports Sara can do and still get her A?

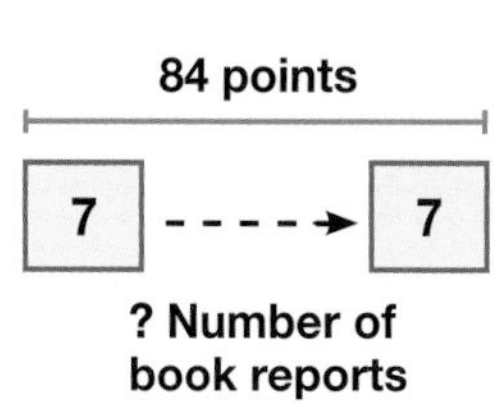

A 12 **B** 13 **C** 15 **D** 16

1. What is the first step in solving the equation $\frac{z}{2} - 5 = 4$? (15-1)

   A Add 5 to each side of the equation.

   B Add 4 to each side of the equation.

   C Multiply both sides of the equation by 2.

   D Divide both sides of the equation by 2.

2. Which equation can be used to describe the pattern in the table? (15-2)

a	0	1	2	3	4
b	−5	−4	−3	−2	−1

   A $b + a = -5$

   B $b = a + 5$

   C $b = a - 5$

   D $a = b - 5$

3. Which of the following equations can be used to graph the line shown? (15-5)

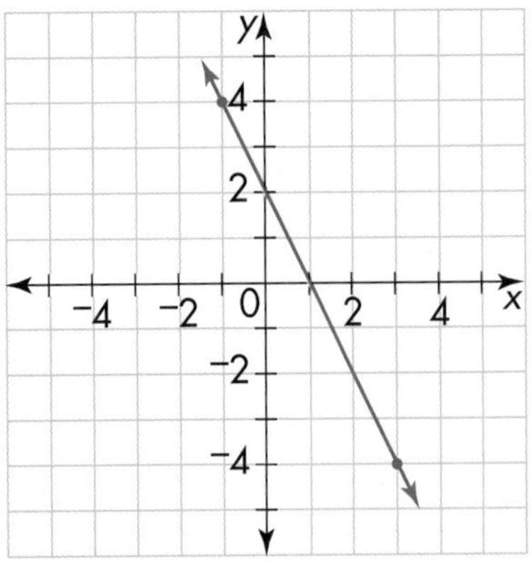

   A $y = 2x + 2$

   B $y = -2x + 2$

   C $y = x + 2$

   D $y = x - 2$

4. Jorge has 16 quarters to spend on arcade games. He only wants to play pinball and the racing game. If each game takes 2 quarters to play and he plays both games at least one time, how many different combinations of times can Jorge play the two games? (15-7)

   A 16 combinations of times

   B 8 combinations of times

   C 7 combinations of times

   D 6 combinations of times

5. April has a total of 56 points on homework in her math class. There are 4 assignments remaining. The equation $p = 4g + 56$ can be used to find April's points, p, after a grade of g on each assignment. Which table could be used to represent the equation? (15-3)

A

g	2	4	6	8	10
p	62	64	66	68	70

B

g	2	4	6	8	10
p	64	72	80	88	96

C

g	2	4	6	8	10
p	64	68	72	76	80

D

g	2	4	6	8	10
p	56	60	64	68	72

6. The school cafeteria seats 8 people at each small table. There is an additional large table that seats 12 people. The equation $8n + 12 = 60$ can be used to find n, the number of tables needed to seat 60 people. Which value of n makes the equation true? (15-1)

A 3

B 6

C 8

D 9

7. Which relation is a function? (15-6)

A

x	−3	1	3	1
y	2	6	8	12

B

x	−4	−2	1	−2
y	0	2	4	6

C

x	−2	0	2	4
y	−3	2	3	6

D

x	2	3	4	3
y	4	9	16	27

8. Which point is on the graph of the equation $y = -2x$? (15-4)

A (3, −6)

B (3, 1)

C (−6, 3)

D (0, −2)

9. The table shows the number of cups of coffee that can be made from coffee beans. Which equation describes the pattern in the table? (15-2)

Pounds of beans, p	1	2	3	4
Cups of coffee, c	32	64	96	128

A $c = p - 31$

B $c = p + 31$

C $p = 32c$

D $c = 32p$

10. Which equation can be used to graph the line shown? (15-4)

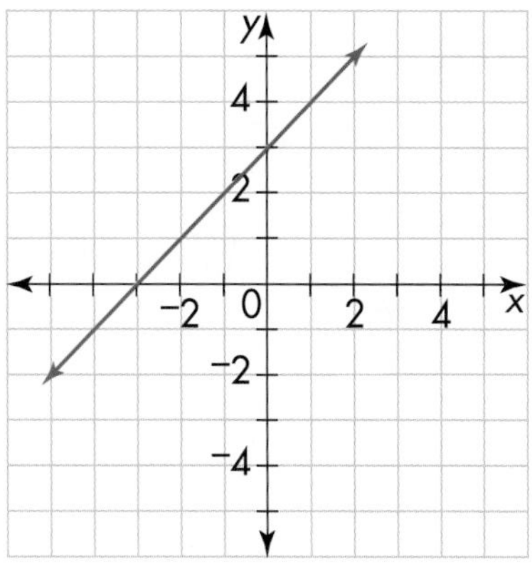

A $y = -3x$

B $y = 3x$

C $y = x - 3$

D $y = x + 3$

11. What is the value of y when $x = -5$ in the equation $y = -4x + 3$? (15-5)

A $y = -17$

B $y = 5$

C $y = 17$

D $y = 23$

Set A, pages 372–374

Use inverse relationships to undo the operations in an equation. Multiplication undoes division. Addition undoes subtraction.

When solving equations with more than one operation, undo addition and subtraction first. Then undo multiplication and division next.

Georgia owes $15 dollars to her brother. She earns $6 an hour babysitting. How many hours does she have to baby-sit to have $27 after she repays her brother?

Solve the equation and check the answer.

$$6x - 15 = 27$$

Step 1 Undo the subtraction by using addition.

$$6x - 15 + 15 = 27 + 15$$
$$6x = 42$$

Step 2 Undo the multiplication by using division.

$$\frac{6x}{6} = \frac{42}{6}$$
$$x = 7$$

Georgia needs to baby-sit 7 hours to have $27 after repaying her brother.

Check.

$$6x - 15 = 27$$
$$6(7) - 15 = 27$$
$$42 - 15 = 27$$
$$27 = 27$$

It checks.

Remember to keep the equation balanced when undoing operations. When you perform an operation on one side of an equation, you must perform the same operation on the other side of the equation.

Tell which operation you would undo first and which operation you would undo next to solve.

1. $8H + 2 = 18$
2. $5 + 3J = 26$
3. $\frac{m}{3} - 5 = 35$
4. $\frac{s}{4} + 2 = 26$
5. $\frac{C}{9} - 3 = 0$
6. $4 + 11d = 48$

Solve each equation and check your answer.

7. $4k - 8 = 16$
8. $-5p - 4 = 26$
9. $\frac{t}{9} - 80 = -81$
10. $9 + 2w = 33$
11. $\frac{s}{2} - 13 = 3$
12. $11d + 1 = 100$
13. $42 - 5r = 2$
14. $6 + 9C = 33$
15. $12F - 15 = 81$
16. $\frac{W}{6} + 7 = 29$

Set B, pages 376–377

Find the rule that shows the pattern. Then use the rule to complete the table.

x	3	4	6	7	8
y	12	16	24		

Step 1 Find the rule.

What operation and relation can be used to get:

- From 3 to get 12
- From 4 to get to 16
- From 6 to get to 24?

Rule: The y-value is 4 times the x-value.

Equation: $y = 4x$.

Step 2 Evaluate the rule for $x = 7$ and $x = 8$.

$y = 4(7) = 28$
$y = 4(8) = 32$

Remember that you may can use multiplication, division, addition, or subtraction to find the rule.

Find a rule and use the rule to write an equation to fit the pattern in each table. Then complete the table.

1.

x	−10	−8	0	2	10
y	−5	−4	0		

2.

x	−5	0	5	7	10
y	0	5	10		

3.

x	−8	−4	0	16	20
y	−16	−12	−8		

Set C, pages 378–379

Alex has $10 saved. He earns $8 per week doing household chores. If he saves half of his earnings each week, how many weeks will it take him to save enough money to buy a $30 game?

Make a table to show Alex's total savings each week. Use the table and the equation $s = 10 + \frac{8}{2}(w)$ to answer the question.

w	1	2	3	4	5	6
s	14	18	22	26	30	34

Alex will have enough money to buy a $30 game from his savings after 5 weeks.

Remember to substitute a value for one of the variables in the equation to complete the table.

Use the equation to copy and complete each table.

1. $y = 2x - 2$

x	−2	−1	0	1	2
y	−6	−4	−2		

2. $y = -5x + 1$

x	−1	0	1	2	3
y					

Set D, pages 380–381

Draw a graph of the equation $y = x + 1$.

Step 1 Make a T-table. Always include at least 3 x-values.

x	y
0	1
2	3
–2	–1

Step 2 Graph each ordered pair on a coordinate plane. Then draw a line through the points. Extend the line to show more values that make the equation true.

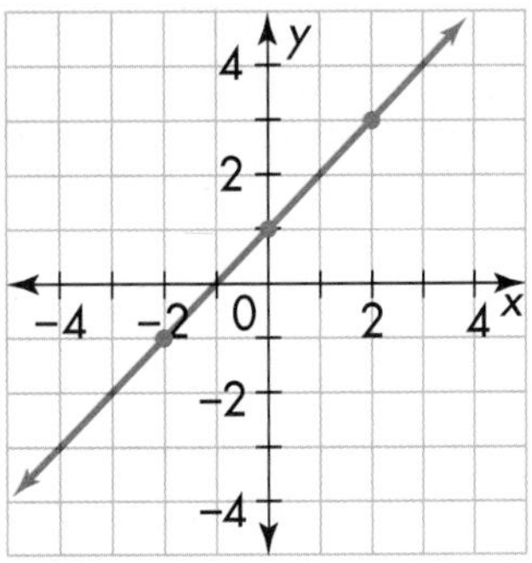

Remember that ordered pairs that make an equation true can be used to graph the equation.

Copy the coordinate plane below and use it to graph **1** and **2**.

1. $y = x + 3$

2. $y = -x$

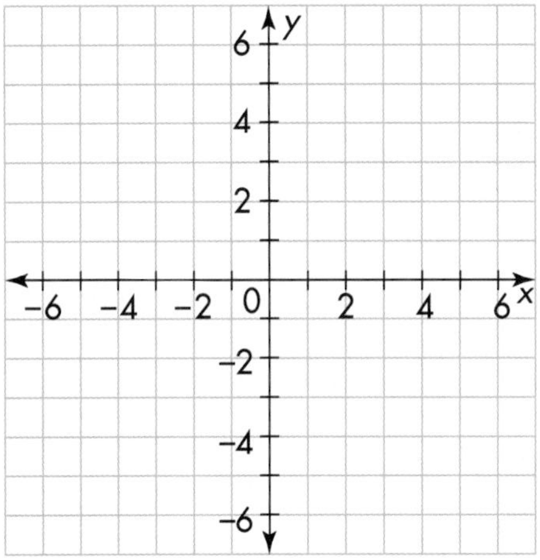

Set E, pages 382–384

The temperature on the mountain was 15°F. During the night it decreased 2°F each hour. How many hours will it take for the temperature to drop to 0°? Graph the equation $T = -2H + 15$ to find out.

Step 1 Make a T-table. List at least three values for H.

H	T
0	15
5	5
10	–5

Step 2 Graph each ordered pair and draw a line through the points.

Step 3 Use the graph to find the point with a T-value of 0. It will take $7\frac{1}{2}$ hours for the temperature to drop to 0°.

Remember to include both positive and negative x-values in your T-table.

Make a T-table and graph each equation.

1. $y = 6 + 3x$

2. $y = -5x + 1$

3. $y = 10 - x$

4. $y = 4x + 4$

5. $y = x$

6. At what value does the graph of the equation $y = 6 + 3x$ cross the y-axis?

7. Does the graph of $y = 2x - 2$ pass through the origin?

8. Does the ordered pair (7, 6) lie on the line $y = -7x + 55$?

Topic 15

Reteaching

Set F, pages 386–388

A function is a special relation in which there is only one *y*-value (output) for each *x*-value (input).

Function

The table below represents the equation $y = 2x + 3$. It shows a function.

x	1	2	3	4
y	5	7	9	11

Not a Function

The table below shows a relation that is not a function.

x	−2	0	2	−2
y	0	2	2	3

There are 2 *y*-values for the *x*-value − 2.

Remember that in a function, each *x*-value has only one *y*-value.

In **1** through **4**, tell whether each relation shown in the table is a function.

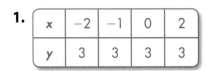

1.

x	−2	−1	0	2
y	3	3	3	3

2.

x	−1	0	−1	2
y	−1	0	1	8

3.

x	−1	0	1	2
y	0	0	0	0

4.

x	0.5	2	2	0.5
y	−1	−2	2	1

Set G, pages 390–391

Linda has 12 puppets that she keeps in two different boxes. She wants to keep a non-zero multiple of 3 puppets in each box. In how many ways can she store all of the puppets in the two different boxes?

Make a table to show the possibilities. Then use 12 counters to find all of the possibilities.

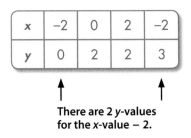

Box 1	3	6	9
Box 2	9	6	3

There are 3 ways to store the puppets.

Remember, acting out a problem can help you use logical reasoning to find a solution.

1. Maria has 10 goldfish that she keeps in two different aquariums. She always keeps a prime number of goldfish in each aquarium.

In how many ways can she divide up the goldfish among the two different aquariums?

Topic 16

Measurement

1 How fast did the winning wheelchair athlete complete the New York marathon? You will find out in Lesson 16-5.

2 How fast is the fastest pickup truck? You will find out in Lesson 16-4.

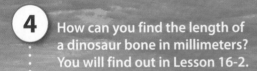

3 How can you make green slime? You will find out in Lesson 16-1.

4 How can you find the length of a dinosaur bone in millimeters? You will find out in Lesson 16-2.

Review What You Know!

Vocabulary

Choose the best terms from the box.

- length
- capacity
- weight
- mass

1. The _?_ of an object can be measured in inches and centimeters.

2. The _?_ of an object can be measured in pints and liters.

3. The _?_ of an object can be measured in pounds, and the _?_ of an object can be measured in kilograms.

Units of Measurement

What is the best unit of measurement for each? Choose inch, foot, yard, ounce, pound, ton, cup, quart, or gallon.

4. length of a soccer field
5. height of a person
6. weight of a newborn kitten
7. weight of a truck trailer
8. gasoline
9. serving of trail mix

Number Sense

Writing to Explain Write an answer for each question.

10. Explain how to find the value of a number with an exponent.

11. Explain why the value 1,000,000 is written as 10^6.

Lesson
16-1 Converting Customary Measures

Understand It!
Multiply to convert larger units of measure to smaller units of measure; divide to convert smaller units of measure to larger units of measure.

How can you change between units of customary measurement?

The sidewalk in front of a store is 54 feet long and 4.5 feet wide. What is the length of the sidewalk in yards? What is the width of the sidewalk in inches?

A table of customary units can help you convert from one unit of measurement to another.

Customary Units of Length

foot (ft)	1 ft = 12 in.
yard (yd)	1 yd = 3 ft 1 yd = 36 in.
mile (mi)	1 (mi) = 5, 280 ft 1 (mi) = 1, 760 yd

Another Example How can you convert units of weight?

56 oz = ☐ lb ← An ounce is smaller than a pound, so divide.

$$16\overline{)56.0} = 3.5$$
$-\ 48$
80
$-\ 80$
0

56 oz = 3.5 lb

Customary Units of Weight (Data)

pound (lb)	1 lb = 16 ounces (oz)
ton (T)	1T = 2,000 lb

How can you convert units of capacity?

Capacity is the volume of a container measured in liquid units.

2 gal = ☐ pt ← A gallon is larger than a pint, so multiply.

Customary Units of Capacity (Data)

cup (c)	1 c = 8 fluid ounces (fl oz)
pint (pt)	1 pt = 2 c
quart (qt)	1 qt = 2 pt
gallon (gal)	1 gal = 4 qt

First, change gallons to quarts: 2 gal = (2 × 4)qt = 8 qt

Then, change quarts to pints: 8 qt = (8 × 2)pt = 16 pt

Write your answer: 2 gal = 16 pt

Explain It

1. If you were changing tons to pounds, which operation would you use?

54 ft = ___ yards

To change from smaller units to larger units, divide.

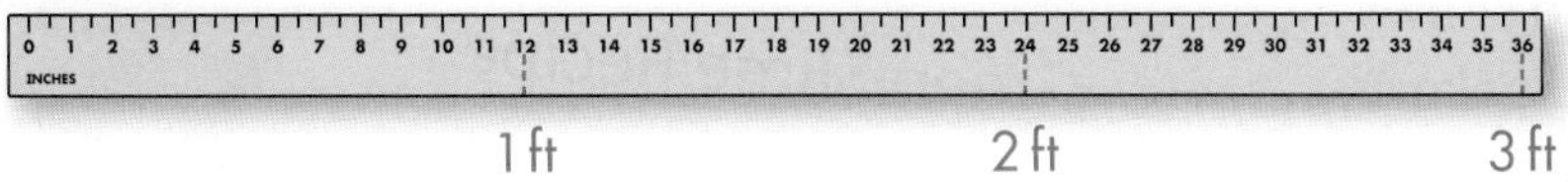

Think 3 feet = 1 yard

$54 \div 3 = 18$

54 ft = 18 yd

The sidewalk is 18 yards long.

4.5 ft = ___ inches

To change from larger units to smaller units, multiply.

12 inches = 1 foot

$4.5 \times 12 = 54$

4.5 ft = 54 in.

The sidewalk is 54 in. wide.

Guided Practice*

Do you know HOW?

In **1** through **4**, copy and complete.

1. 3 gal = ___ qt

2. 36 in. = ___ ft

3. 2 mi = ___ ft

4. 5 pt = ___ c

Do you UNDERSTAND?

5. When do you divide to convert units?

6. Using the information about capacity in the Another Example, find how many cups are in 2 gallons.

Independent Practice

Copy and complete.

Tip: You may need to solve a simpler problem in order to convert some amounts.

7. 4 yd = ___ ft

8. 32 oz = ___ lb

9. 2 pt = ___ c

10. 4 qt = ___ gal

11. 2,000 lb = ___ T

12. 450 in. = ___ yd

13. 4 pt = ___ qt

14. 6,000 lb = ___ T

15. 21 pt = ___ c

16. 6 pt = ___ qt

17. 96 in. = ___ ft

18. 2 qt = ___ fl oz

19. 16 c = ___ pt

20. 9 T = ___ lb

21. 1.5 mi = ___ ft

22. 2,640 yd = ___ mi

23. 4 lb = ___ oz

24. 360 ft = ___ yd

25. **Number Sense** How many one-cup servings are in 1 gallon?

26. How many inches are in $6\frac{1}{2}$ ft?

27. How many ounces are in 2 lb 8 oz?

DIGITAL Animated Glossary **www.pearsonsuccessnet.com**

For another example, see Set A on page 422.

Problem Solving

28. Number Sense The note card shows one recipe for green slime. To make 2 recipes of slime for a class project, Cheryl needs 2 pints of water. She has 3 cups of water. Is this enough water for 2 recipes?

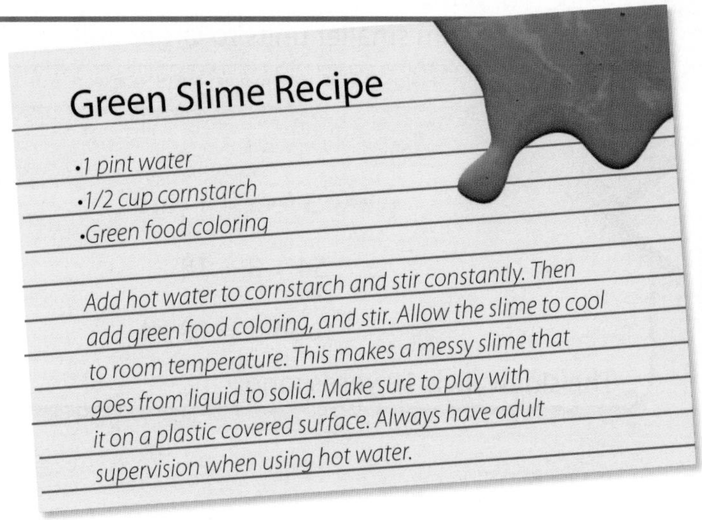

Green Slime Recipe
•1 pint water
•1/2 cup cornstarch
•Green food coloring
Add hot water to cornstarch and stir constantly. Then add green food coloring, and stir. Allow the slime to cool to room temperature. This makes a messy slime that goes from liquid to solid. Make sure to play with it on a plastic covered surface. Always have adult supervision when using hot water.

29. Writing to Explain Len needs to run at least 3 miles a day to get ready for a cross-country race. One lap of the school track is 400 yards. If Len runs 10 laps a day will he cover at least 3 miles? Explain.

30. Suppose that a space shuttle weighs 4.5 million pounds at liftoff. What is the space shuttle's weight in tons?

31. Reasoning How is converting from cups to pints similar to converting from ounces to pounds?

32. A door is $3\frac{1}{2}$ feet wide. How many inches are in $3\frac{1}{2}$ feet?

A 36 inches **C** 40 inches

B 38 inches **D** 42 inches

33. The pilot of an airplane announced the plane was at a cruising altitude of $6\frac{1}{2}$ miles. How many feet is this?

34. Bill is making smoothies for his friends. If 4 ounces of fruit is needed for each smoothie, how many pounds of fruit does he need to make 10 smoothies?

35. Chrissy is buying a yard of felt for an art project. Two stores at the right have the felt she needs. Which felt is a better buy?

36. Think About the Process To convert from feet to inches, which operation do you need to perform?

A Addition **C** Multiplication

B Subtraction **D** Division

37. Think About the Process To convert from pints to gallons, which operation do you need to perform?

A Addition **C** Multiplication

B Subtraction **D** Division

Mixed Problem Solving

The values of musical notes can be written as fractions. Each note is twice as long as the one below it in the table. For instance, a half note equals 2 quarter notes.

Musical Note	Standard Symbol
Whole note	𝅝
Half note	𝅗𝅥
Quarter note	♩
Eighth note	♪
Sixteenth note	𝅘𝅥𝅯
Thirty-Second note	𝅘𝅥𝅰

Use this table for **1** through **3**.

1. If you convert a whole note to half notes, how many half notes will you have?

2. If you convert a quarter note to sixteenth notes, how many sixteenth notes will you have?

3. If you convert a sixteenth note to thirty-second notes, how many thirty-second notes will you have?

In music, rests are an important part of the rhythm. A rest has the same value as its corresponding note. For instance, a whole rest has the same value as a whole note.

Like notes, each rest is twice as long as the one below it in the table. For instance, a whole rest equals 2 half rests.

Musical Rest	Standard Symbol
Whole rest	𝄻
Half rest	𝄼
Quarter rest	𝄽
Eighth rest	𝄾
Sixteenth rest	𝄿
Thirty-Second rest	𝅀

Use this table for **4** through **6**.

4. What type of rest has the same value as a sixteenth note?

5. If you convert a quarter rest to eighth rests, how many eighth rests will you have?

6. If you convert a quarter rest to sixteenth rests, how many sixteenth rests will you have?

7. If a quarter note has 1 beat, what is the value of the rests in the 2nd measure of the music to the right?

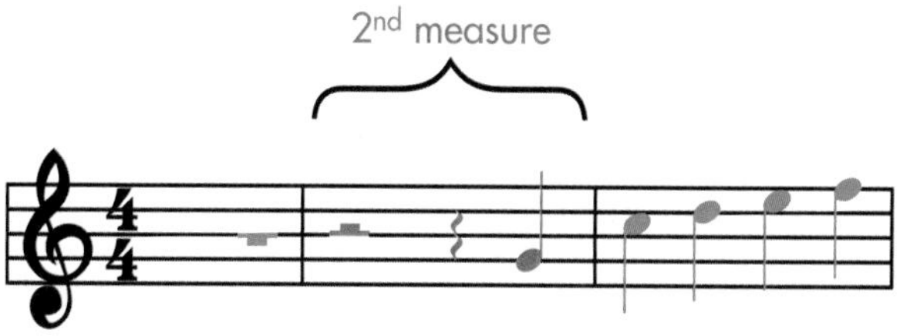

Lesson
16-3

Understand It!
The smaller the unit of measure used, the more precise the measurement.

Units of Measure and Precision

Hands-On
metric ruler

Which metric measurement is the most precise?

Don and Stacy are building a model boat that is 100 cm long. They need to measure accurately. Which measurement is more precise, centimeters or millimeters?

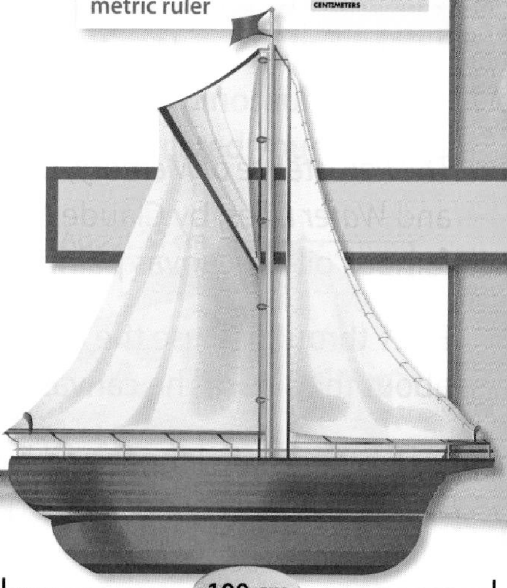

Another Example Which customary measurement is the most precise?

The pencil at the right measures about 4 inches. What is its length to the nearest whole, half, quarter, eighth, and sixteenth of an inch? Which of these measurements is the most precise?

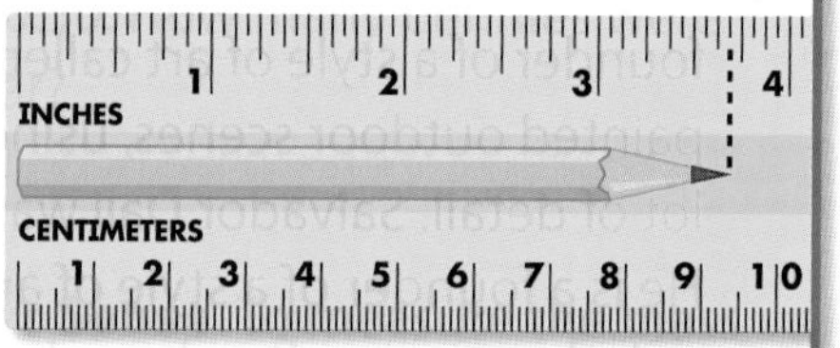

Measure the length to the nearest units and record your findings.

Data

Whole inch	4 in.
Half inch	$3\frac{1}{2}$ in.
Quarter inch	$3\frac{3}{4}$ in.
Eighth inch	$3\frac{5}{8}$ in.
Sixteenth inch	$3\frac{11}{16}$ in.

As with metric measurements, the smaller the customary units used for measuring, the more precise the measurement. A sixteenth of an inch is the smallest unit used for inches.

$3\frac{11}{16}$ is the most precise measurement.

Explain It

1. How do you measure the pencil to the nearest quarter inch?

2. Which measurement is more precise, sixteenth inch or millimeter? Explain.

All measurements are approximations. Don measured the model plank below to the nearest centimeter. It measured about 5 cm long.

Stacy measured the plank to the nearest millimeter. It measured about 52 mm long.

A millimeter is a smaller unit than a centimeter.

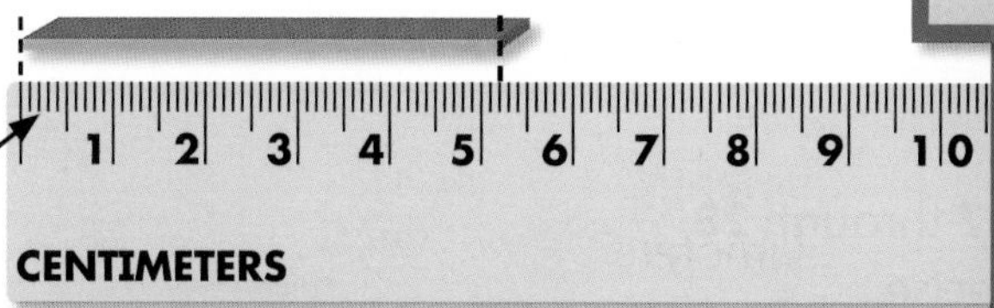

The smaller the units used for measuring, the more precise the measurement.

52 mm is more precise than 5 cm.

Don and Stacy should measure the pieces of the boat in millimeters.

Guided Practice*

Do you know HOW?

For **1** and **2**, measure each segment to the nearest eighth inch and nearest centimeter.

1.

2.

For **3** and **4**, measure each segment to the nearest sixteenth inch and nearest millimeter.

3.

4.

Do you UNDERSTAND?

5. How do you know which unit of measurement is more precise?

6. **Writing to Explain** Manuel and Ava each measured the perimeter of the garden. Their measurements were 6 yards and 17 feet. Which measurement is more precise?

Independent Practice

For **7** through **12**, measure each segment to the nearest eighth inch and nearest centimeter.

7.

8.

9.

10.

11.

12.

DIGITAL eTools **www.pearsonsuccessnet.com**

*For another example, see Set C on page 422.

Independent Practice

For **13** through **16**, measure each segment to the nearest sixteenth inch and nearest millimeter.

13.

14.

15.

16.

For each pair of measurements in **17** through **28**, tell which measurement is more precise.

17. 12 cm or 123 mm

18. 634 mm or 63 cm

19. 21 mm or 2 cm

20. 3 m or 302 cm

21. 6.1 m or 612 mm

22. 1,100 mm or 1 m

23. 4 ft or 1 yd

24. 3 L or 3,100 mL

25. 50 g or 1 kg

26. $2\frac{1}{2}$ ft or 25 in.

27. 4 yd or 13 ft

28. 1.5 mi or 7,600 ft

Problem Solving

29. **Writing to Explain** Wendy measured a shoelace and said it was 1 foot long. Bill measured the same shoelace and said it was 12 inches long. Even though 12 inches = 1 foot, explain why Bill's measurement is more precise.

30. Kristen wants to rent a bicycle. The table at the right shows how much two shops charge to rent bicycles. Which bicycle shop would be less expensive if Kristen rents a bicycle for 5 hours?

Data

Rental Cost

Bicycle Shop	Cost for 1st Hour	Each Additional Hour
Cycle Pro Shop	$10	$6
Bev's Bicycles	$12	$5

31. Three students measured the height of the door to the classroom. The measurements were 7 feet, 2 yards, and 6 feet 10 inches. Which of these measurements is the most precise?

32. The height of Mt. Everest is 8,848 m. Express this height in kilometers.

33. Suppose you want to measure the length of a small paper clip. Which unit would you use to get the most precise measurement?

A Meters

B Millimeters

C Inches

D Centimeters

Enrichment

Exact Answer or Estimate

Some problems require exact answers, while others need only an estimate. How can you tell if an exact answer or an estimate is needed to answer a word problem?

Phrases, such as "about how many," "more than," or "less than," mean that an estimate may give you enough information to answer the problem. If an estimate is all that is needed, you can often estimate using mental math.

If the problem asks, "What is the total?," "how many," or "how much," calculate the exact amount.

Example: Susan wants to put a wallpaper border in the hallway. The hallway is a rectangle with a length of 9 feet and a width of $4\frac{1}{3}$ feet. If one roll of wallpaper border is 16 feet long, will 2 rolls be enough for Susan to complete the hallway?

Step 1 What do you know?

The dimensions of the hall are 9 feet by $4\frac{1}{3}$ feet and one roll is 16 feet.

Step 2 What are you trying to find?

Whether 2 rolls of wallpaper border are enough to complete the hallway
An estimate is all that is needed;
2 rolls are enough.

Practice

Tell whether an exact answer or an estimate is needed. Then solve.
For **1** through **3**, use the information on the map.

Forest Preserve

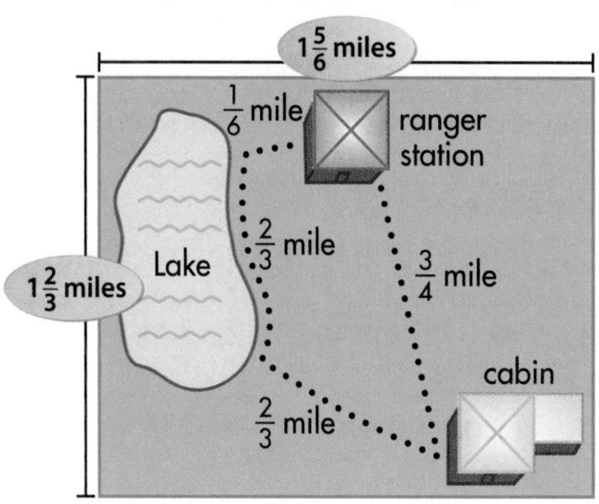

1. How much greater is the length of the forest preserve than the width?

2. If Jack can walk $\frac{1}{2}$ mile every 10 minutes, would he be able to walk from the cabin to the ranger's station in less than 20 minutes?

3. Jack takes a daily walk from his cabin to the ranger station, to the lake, then along the lake and back to his cabin. How far will he have walked in three days?

4. Mara is making three recipes that each require milk. One recipe calls for $\frac{5}{6}$ cup of milk, another calls for $\frac{2}{3}$ cup, and the third requires $1\frac{1}{3}$ cup. How much milk will Mara need?

5. A truck is built to haul up to 2 tons of cargo. If the truck is loaded with 54 barrels, and each barrel weighs 190 pounds, is the truck over or under its limit?

Lesson
16-4

Understand It!
Division and multiplication can be used to change between customary units of measurement and metric units of measurement. Conversions are usually based on approximate equivalents.

Relating Customary and Metric Measures

How can you convert between measurement systems?

Tim is building a scarecrow to keep birds out of his garden. The directions use metric units and suggest that the scarecrow be at least 2 meters tall. Rounded to the nearest tenth, how many inches is 2 meters?

Other Examples

Converting Customary Units and Metric Units for Weight/Mass and Capacity

$12 \text{ kg} \approx \square \text{ lb}$

$1 \text{ kg} \approx 2.2 \text{ lb}$

Multiply.

$12 \times 2.2 = 26.4$

$12 \text{ kg} \approx 26.4 \text{ lb}$

$5 \text{ gal} \approx \square \text{ L}$

$1 \text{ gal} \approx 3.79 \text{ L}$

Multiply.

$5 \times 3.79 = 18.95$

Round to the nearest tenth.
$5 \text{ gal} \approx 19.0 \text{ L}$

$3 \text{ qt} \approx \square \text{ L}$

$1 \text{ L} \approx 1.06 \text{ qt}$

Divide.

$3 \div 1.06 = 2.83$

Round to the nearest tenth.
$3 \text{ qt} \approx 2.8 \text{ L}$

Guided Practice*

Do you know HOW?

Complete. Round to the nearest tenth.

1. $5 \text{ in.} = \square \text{ cm}$

2. $2 \text{ mi} \approx \square \text{ km}$

3. $113 \text{ g} \approx \square \text{ oz}$

4. $13.2 \text{ kg} \approx \square \text{ lb}$

Do you UNDERSTAND?

5. When converting centimeters to inches, do you multiply or divide by 2.54?

6. How would you find the number of liters in 1 pint?

Independent Practice

Copy and complete. Round to the nearest tenth.

7. $9.1 \text{ qt} \approx \square \text{ L}$

8. $1.0 \text{ gal} \approx \square \text{ L}$

9. $2 \text{ in.} = \square \text{ cm}$

10. $4 \text{ gal} \approx \square \text{ L}$

*For another example, see D on page 423.

The table shows the relationships between customary and metric measurements. Only the equivalent for inches and centimeters is exact. All other equivalents are approximate.

Customary and Metric Unit Equivalents

Length	Weight/Mass	Capacity
1 in. = 2.54 cm	1 oz ≈ 28.35 g	1 L ≈ 1.06 qt
1 m ≈ 39.37 in.	1 kg ≈ 2.2 lb	1 gal ≈ 3.79 L
1 mi ≈ 1.61 km	1 metric ton (t) ≈ 1.102 T	

Use 1 m ≈ 39.37 in.

To change from a larger unit to a smaller unit, multiply.

2m ≈ ▢ in.

$2 \times 39.37 = 78.74$

Round to the nearest tenth.

2 meters is about 78.7 inches.

Copy and complete. Round to the nearest tenth.

11. 5 km ≈ ▢ mi **12.** 85 g ≈ ▢ oz **13.** 196 in. ≈ ▢ m **14.** 10 L ≈ ▢ qt

15. 5.5 t ≈ ▢ T **16.** 50 lb ≈ ▢ kg **17.** 25 in. ≈ ▢ cm **18.** 30.2 kg ≈ ▢ lb

19. 51.6 gal ≈ ▢ L **20.** 10 oz ≈ ▢ g **21.** 3 pt ≈ ▢ L **22.** 3.5 m ≈ ▢ in.

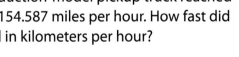

Problem Solving

23. Writing to Explain Suppose that 1 British pound (£) has a value of $1.80. In London, a magazine costs £ 2. In Chicago, the same magazine costs $3.50. In which city is the magazine cheaper?

24. Temperature can be measured in degrees Fahrenheit (*F*) and in degrees Celsius (*C*). Use this formula to convert 50° Fahrenheit to Celsius: $9 \times C = (F - 32) \times 5$

25. Reasoning Francesca wants to convert 1 meter to feet. Use what you know about customary measures to explain how she could do this.

26. Estimation How could you use estimation to convert 15 oz into grams?

27. The fastest production-model pickup truck reached a top speed of 154.587 miles per hour. How fast did this truck travel in kilometers per hour?

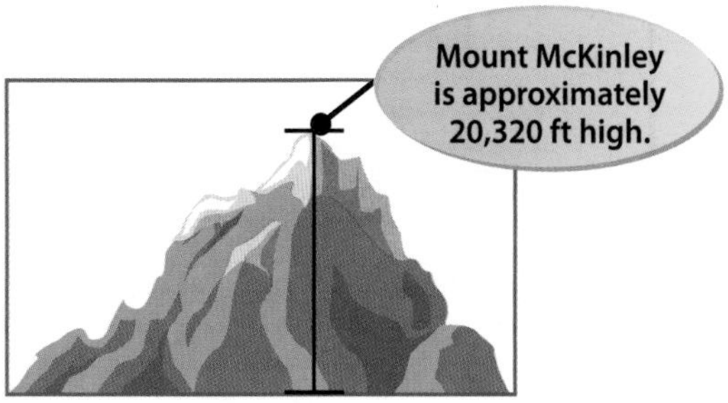
Mount McKinley is approximately 20,320 ft high.

28. How high is Mount McKinley in meters? Round to the nearest whole number.

29. Think About the Process To convert pounds to kilograms, which operation do you need to perform?

A Addition
B Subtraction
C Multiplication
D Division

Lesson
16-5

Understand It!
If you know two of the values among starting time, ending time, and elapsed time, you can calculate the missing value.

Elapsed Time

How can you find how much time passes between two events?

Yul biked along a part of the Lewis and Clark Trail. He started at 8:05 A.M. and finished biking at 1:25 P.M. How long did Yul bike?

The difference in time between 8:05 A.M. and 1:25 P.M. is the elapsed time.

Another Example How can renaming help you find elapsed time?

Find the elapsed time from 4:25:55 P.M. to 6:15:20 P.M.

6 h 15 min 20 s	→	5 h 74 min 80 s
− 4 h 25 min 55 s	→	− 4 h 25 min 55 s
		1 h 49 min 25 s

Think Since 15 min < 25 min and 20 s < 55 s, I need to rename to subtract. 1 h = 60 min and 1 min = 60 s

Elapsed Time: 1 h 49 min 25 s

How do you find the starting time or ending time using elapsed time?

End Time: 11:20 A.M.
Elapsed Time: 3 h 40 min

Subtract the elapsed time from the ending time to find the start time.

11 h 20 min	→	10 h 80 min
− 3 h 40 min	→	− 3 h 40 min
		7 h 40 min

Start Time: 7:40 A.M.

Start Time: 6:20 P.M.
Elapsed Time: 6 h 15 min

Add the elapsed time to the starting time to find the end time.

6 h 20 min
+ 6 h 15 min
12 h 35 min

End Time: 12:35 A.M. ← **12 midnight is 12:00 A.M.**

Explain It

1. When adding or subtracting units of time, when do you need to rename?

One Way

Break the elapsed time into parts.

$$
\begin{array}{rl}
 & 12 \text{ h } 00 \text{ min} \\
- & 8 \text{ h } 05 \text{ min} \\
\hline
 & 3 \text{ h } 55 \text{ min} \\
+ & 1 \text{ h } 25 \text{ min} \\
\hline
 & 4 \text{ h } 80 \text{ min} \\
 & \text{or} \\
 & 5 \text{ h } 20 \text{ min}
\end{array}
$$

- 3 h 55 min ← **Elapsed time before noon**
- + 1 h 25 min ← **Elapsed time from noon to 1:25 P.M.**
- 5 h 20 min ← **Total elapsed time**

Yul biked for 5 hours 20 minutes.

Another Way

Use mental math to find the elapsed time. Count forward from the starting time for each unit.

Count the number of hours from 8:05 A.M. to 1:25 P.M.: 5 hours.

Count the number of minutes from 1:05 to 1:25 20 minutes.

Yul biked for 5 hours 20 minutes.

Guided Practice*

Do you know HOW?

In **1** through **3**, find each elapsed time.

1. 6:02 P.M. to 9:17 P.M.

2. 2:13 A.M. to 10:09 P.M.

3. 10:09 P.M. to 2:13 A.M.

In **4** and **5**, add or subtract.

4. 1 h 13 min 42 s + 20 min 29 s = ▢

5. 1 h 13 min 42 s − 20 min 29 s = ▢

Do you UNDERSTAND?

6. When should you break a problem into parts to find elapsed time?

7. **Writing to Explain** In the example at the top, if Yul started at 8:30 A.M., how would you use mental math to find the elapsed time?

8. If Yul made a stop 2 hours 35 minutes after starting the ride, what time did he stop?

Independent Practice

For **9** through **14**, find each elapsed time.

9. 3:05 P.M. to 9:27 P.M.

10. 4:11 A.M. to 8:09 A.M.

11. 4:15 P.M. to 6:33 P.M.

12. 1:39 P.M. to 7:17 P.M.

13. 9:29 A.M. to 2:14 P.M.

14. 9:05 A.M. to 9:05 P.M.

In **15** through **20**, find each starting time or ending time.

15. Start Time: 3:24 A.M.
Elapsed Time: 7 h 4 min

16. End Time: 7:48 P.M
Elapsed Time: 5 h 5 min

17. Start Time: 11:21 P.M.
Elapsed Time: 8 h 6 min

18. End Time: 12:16 P.M.
Elapsed Time: 3 h 5 min

19. Start Time: 5:18 P.M.
Elapsed Time: 5 h 50 min

20. End Time: 10:39 P.M.
Elapsed Time: 8 h 45 min

For another example, see Set E on page 423.

Independent Practice

For **21** through **26**, add or subtract.

21. 29 min 17 s + 7 min 21 s

22. 14 h 4 min 14 s − 6 h 24 min

23. 3 h 24 min 49 s + 2 h 36 min 13 s

24. 1 h 15 min 42 s − 20 min 29 s

25. 6 h 18 min 32 s + 56 min 39 s

26. 5 h 39 min 44 s − 2 h 42 min 51 s

Problem Solving

27. Jill is preparing Thanksgiving dinner. She wants the turkey to be done by 5:30 P.M. The turkey will take approximately 3 hours 20 minutes to cook. What is the latest time that she should put the turkey into the oven?

28. It took Mark a total of 4 hours 40 minutes to clean the garage and cut the grass. If it took 1 hour 45 minutes to cut the grass, how long did it take him to clean the garage?

29. **Algebra** A homing pigeon flew a distance of 120 miles in 4 days. If it flew *x* miles in the first 3 days, write an expression to tell how many miles it flew on the last day.

30. Every morning Tyler jogs 2.85 kilometers. Every evening before dinner he jogs 1.5 kilometers. How many kilometers does he jog each week?

31. In a recent year, the winner in the wheelchair race of the New York Marathon finished in 1:31:11 (1 hour, 31 minutes, 11 seconds). In the following year, the winning wheelchair athlete's time was 1:29:22. How much faster was the winning time in the following year?

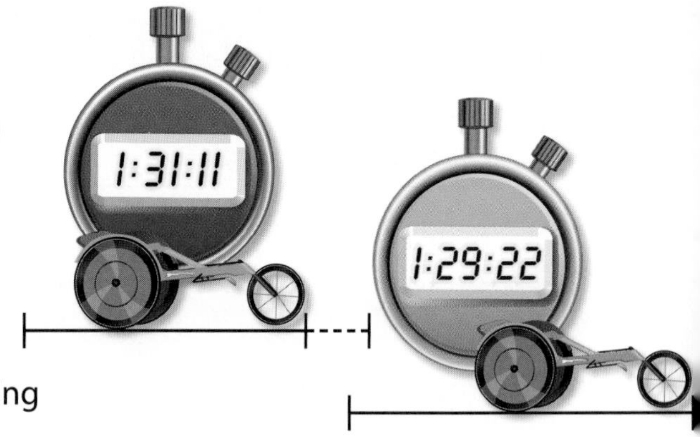

32. **Writing to Explain** Explain how to find the ending time of a concert that begins at 8:05 P.M. and lasts 2 hours 14 minutes.

33. Ross had been driving for 3 hours 15 minutes. He arrived at his destination at 11:40 A.M. What time did he leave?

A 8:55 a.m **C** 2:55 pm

B 8:25 a.m **D** 8:40 pm

34. Which number is a composite number?

A 13 **C** 57

B 7 **D** 29

Enrichment

Temperature Conversion

Temperatures in degrees Fahrenheit (°F), or in degrees Celsius (°C), can be measured with a thermometer. To convert between Fahrenheit and Celsius temperature scales, use the following equations.

Conversion Formulas

Celsius (C) to Fahrenheit (F)

$$F = \frac{9}{5}C + 32$$

Fahrenheit (F) to Celsius (C)

$$C = (\frac{5}{9})(F - 32)$$

Temperatures should be to the nearest whole degree.

Example:
Pure water boils at 100°C. What is 100°C in degrees Fahrenheit?

Step 1 Choose the correct conversion formula.

Use $F = \frac{9}{5}C + 32$.

Step 2 Substitute the value of the temperature you know and solve.

$$F = (\frac{9}{5})(100) + 32$$

$$F = 180 + 32$$

$$F = 212$$

Pure water boils at 212°F.

Practice

For **1** through **8**, find each temperature in degrees Fahrenheit to the nearest whole degree.

1. 25°C **2.** 10°C **3.** 45°C **4.** 0°C

5. 16°C **6.** 29°C **7.** –2°C **8.** –25°C

For **9** through **16**, find each temperature in degrees Celsius to the nearest whole degree.

9. 65°F **10.** 85°F **11.** 63°F **12.** 72°F

13. 45°F **14.** 102°F **15.** 6°F **16.** 5°F

17. African violets grow best in a temperature warmer than 60°F and cooler than 80°F. Will they grow well if they are kept in an area that is 30°C? Explain.

18. If the temperature is 5°C, is 15°F or 45°F a better estimate for the temperature? Explain.

Lesson
16-6

Understand It! Some problems can be solved by identifying relationships and using reasoning to draw conclusions.

Problem Solving

Use Reasoning

Jane's game has three sizes of jumps: small, medium, and large. How can you find the size of the small, medium, and large jumps?

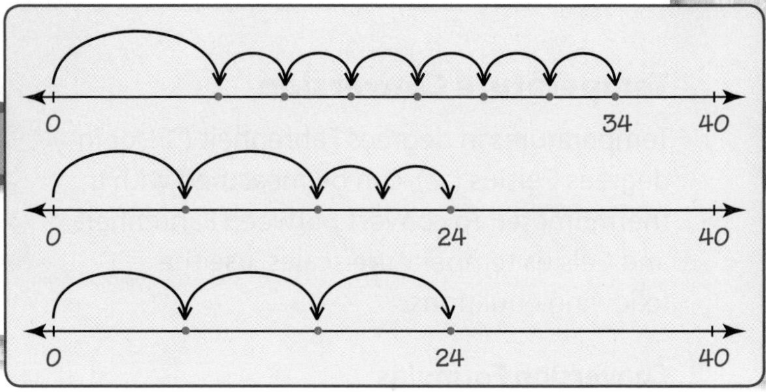

Guided Practice*

Do you know HOW?

1. If Jane takes two large jumps, how many small jumps will it take her to reach 40?

2. Jane is on 11 and wants to get as close as she can to 40 in the fewest jumps possible without going over. How many jumps can she take?

Do you UNDERSTAND?

3. If there are 2 small jumps in a medium jump, which operation should you use to convert from small jumps to medium jumps?

4. **Write a Problem** Use the jump diagram above to create and solve a problem.

Independent Practice

A fruit market sells fruit based on equivalent amounts. Use the table for **5** through **7**.

Data

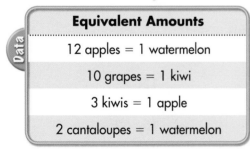

Equivalent Amounts
12 apples = 1 watermelon
10 grapes = 1 kiwi
3 kiwis = 1 apple
2 cantaloupes = 1 watermelon

5. How many kiwis are equivalent to 5 apples?

6. How many apples are equivalent to 1 cantaloupe?

7. How many grapes are equivalent to 1 watermelon?

Stuck? Try this....

- What do I know?
- What am I asked to find?
- What diagram can I use to help understand the problem?
- Can I use addition, subtraction, multiplication, or division?
- Is all of my work correct?
- Did I answer the right question?
- Is my answer reasonable?

*For another example, see Set E on page 423.

Plan and Solve

Use reasoning to make conclusions and find the size of each jump.

Begin with medium jumps. 3 medium jumps end at 24.
$3 \times \square = 24$

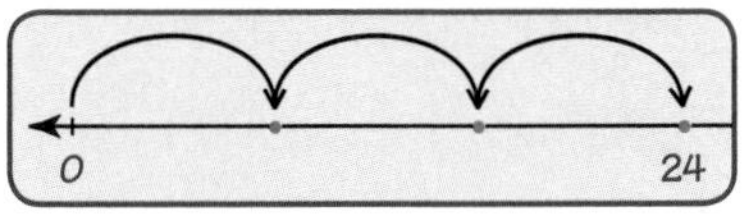

$3 \times 8 = 24$

So, a medium jump is 8 units.

Use the size of the medium jumps to find the size of a small jump. Since 2 medium jumps is 16, $24 - 16 = 8$.
$2 \times \square = 8$

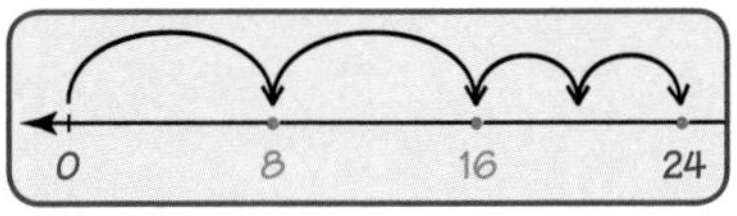

$2 \times 4 = 8$

So, a small jump is 4 units.

Use the size of the small jumps to find a large jump. 6 small jumps of 4 units each make 24.
$34 - 24 = \square$

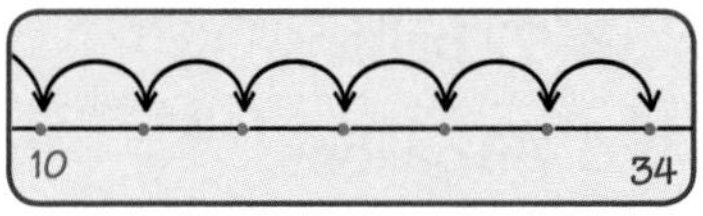

$34 - 24 = 10$

So, a large jump is 10 units.

8. **Think About the Process** Rebecca runs 12 laps on a track. There are 400 meters per lap. What is the best first step to find how many yards she ran?

A Find the total number of meters.

B Find the total number of yards.

C Find the number of yards in a meter.

D Find the number of meters in a kilometer.

9. **Think About the Process** What operation would you use to convert Pacific Standard Time to Eastern Standard Time?

A Addition

B Subtraction

C Multiplication

D Division

10. If the Moon orbits Earth once in about a month, about how many times does the Moon orbit Earth in five years?

11. Katie, Brian, Jessica, Callie, and Dave are all wearing different-colored shirts (red, blue, green, white, and orange). Katie and Brian never wear primary colors. The boys are not wearing white. None of the girls are wearing green. Only Dave is wearing a color that has the letter *O* in it. Callie is not wearing red. Find the color of shirt that each person is wearing.

Use the clocks for **12** and **13.**

12. If it is 4:00 A.M. in Tokyo, what time is it in London?

13. New York is five hours behind London. If it is 2:00 P.M. in New York, what time is it in Tokyo?

14. When it is 10:00 A.M. in Los Angeles, it is 1:00 P.M. in New York. If it is 3:00 A.M. in New York, what time is it in Los Angeles?

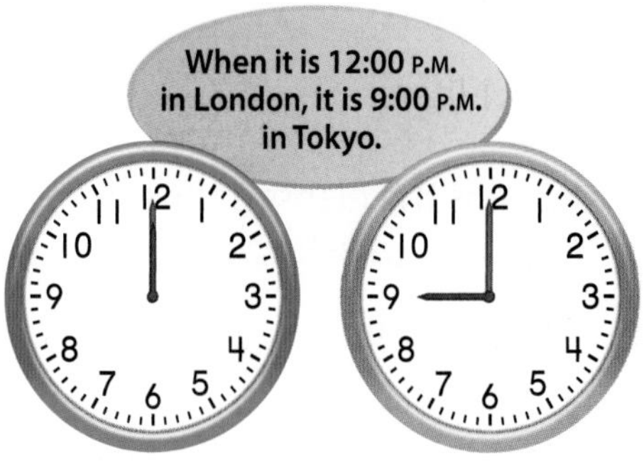

Test

1. If Mrs. Banks made 44 quarts of jelly, how many gallons did she make? (16-1)

   A 11 gallons

   B 22 gallons

   C 88 gallons

   D 176 gallons

2. How many milliliters are in the container shown? (16-2)

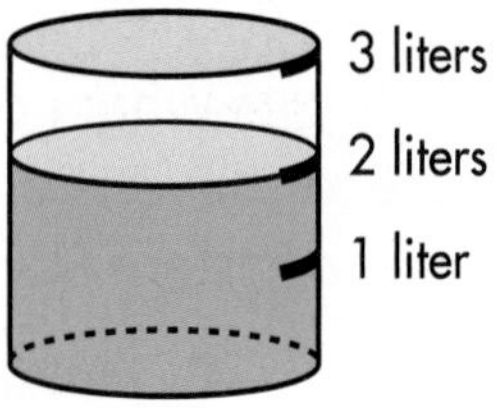

   A 2 milliliters

   B 20 milliliters

   C 200 milliliters

   D 2,000 milliliters

3. An average adult has about 6 quarts of blood in his or her body. How many liters are equal to 6 quarts? Use 1 L ≈ 1.06 qt to convert. Round to the nearest tenth. (16-4)

   A 4.9 liters

   B 5.7 liters

   C 6.4 liters

   D 7.1 liters

4. What is the elapsed time from 10:14 P.M. to 3:30 A.M.? (16-5)

   A 5 h 16 min

   B 5 h 26 min

   C 6 h 16 min

   D 6 h 44 min

5. The Willamette meteorite found near Portland, Oregon, weighs 14 tons. How many pounds does the meteorite weigh? (16-1)

   A 7 pounds

   B 28 pounds

   C 7,000 pounds

   D 28,000 pounds

6. Debbie's pet bird has a mass of 125 grams. How many kilograms is the mass of the bird? (16-2)

   A 0.125 kilograms

   B 1.25 kilograms

   C 1,250 kilograms

   D 125,000 kilograms

7. The table shows some of the world's tallest towers. How many inches high is the Milad Tower? Use 1 m ≈ 39.37 in. to convert. Round to the nearest tenth. (16-4)

Data

Tower	Height in Meters
Canadian National Tower, Toronto	553
Ostankino Tower, Moscow	537
Oriental Pearl Tower, Shanghai	468
Milad Tower, Tehran	435

   A 11 inches

   B 17,126.0 inches

   C 5,708.7 inches

   D 43,500 inches

8. A football game started at 11:50 A.M. and lasted for 3 hours and 48 minutes. At what time did the football game end? (16-5)

A 4:02 P.M.

B 3:38 P.M.

C 2:38 P.M.

D 3:02 A.M.

9. Which of the following measurements is the most precise? (16-3)

A 1 meter

B 125 centimeters

C 1,253 millimeters

D 1.2 meters

10. Which step can be taken to convert 6 inches to centimeters? (16-4)

A Multiply 6 by 2.54.

B Divide 6 by 2.54.

C Multiply $\frac{1}{2}$ by 2.54.

D Divide $\frac{1}{2}$ by 2.54.

11. The table shows the relationship among the points for markers in a game. How many purple markers are equal to a green marker? (16-6)

5 red = 1 green
15 purple = 1 yellow
10 yellow = 1 red

A 50

B 75

C 150

D 750

12. The deepest lake in the world is Lake Baikal in Siberia, Russia. It is a natural lake that is 5,712 feet deep. Which step can be taken to find the depth of the lake in yards? (16-1)

A Divide 5,712 feet by 12.

B Multiply 5,712 feet by 12.

C Divide 5,712 feet by 3.

D Multiply 5,712 feet by 3.

13. Mount Everest is 8,850 meters tall. How many kilometers high is Mount Everest? (16-2)

A 0.885 kilometers

B 8.85 kilometers

C 88.5 kilometers

D 88,850 kilometers

14. A designer measured the width of a window to the nearest whole, quarter, eighth, and sixteenth of an inch. The measurements are shown in the table. Which measurement is the most precise? (16-3)

Data

Unit	Width
Whole inch	36 in.
Quarter inch	$35\frac{3}{4}$ in.
Eighth inch	$35\frac{7}{8}$ in.
Sixteenth inch	$35\frac{13}{16}$ in.

A Whole inch

B Quarter inch

C Eighth inch

D Sixteenth inch

Set A, pages 400–402

How many feet is 5 miles?

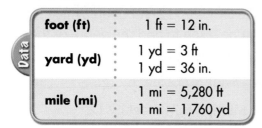

Data		
	foot (ft)	1 ft = 12 in.
	yard (yd)	1 yd = 3 ft 1 yd = 36 in.
	mile (mi)	1 mi = 5,280 ft 1 mi = 1,760 yd

1 mi = 5,280 ft

5 × 5,280 = 26,400

5 mi = 26,400 ft

To change from larger units to smaller units,multiply.

Remember to divide when changing from smaller units to larger units.

Copy and complete.

1. 1 mi = ___ ft **2.** 36 in. = ___ yd

3. 3 yd = ___ ft **4.** 3,520 yd = ___ mi

5. 2 yd = ___ in. **6.** 264 ft = ___ yd

7. Tony's bedroom is 12 feet long. How many yards long is his bedroom?

Set B, pages 404–406

How many meters is 7.01 km?

Data	Name	Abbreviation	Number of Base Units
Length	**kilo**meter	km	1,000
	meter	m	1
	centimeter	cm	$\frac{1}{100}$
	millimeter	mm	$\frac{1}{1,000}$

1,000 m = 1 km; 7.01 km, × 1,000 = 7,010 m

Remember that to convert within the metric system, you always multiply or divide by a multiple of 10.

Copy and complete.

1. 5 km = ___ m **2.** 900 cm = ___ m

3. 83 mm = ___ cm **4.** 3.7 m = ___ mm

5. Jessie wants to swim 1.5 km. How many meters is this?

Set C, pages 408–410

Measure the paper clip to the nearest sixteenth inch and nearest millimeter.

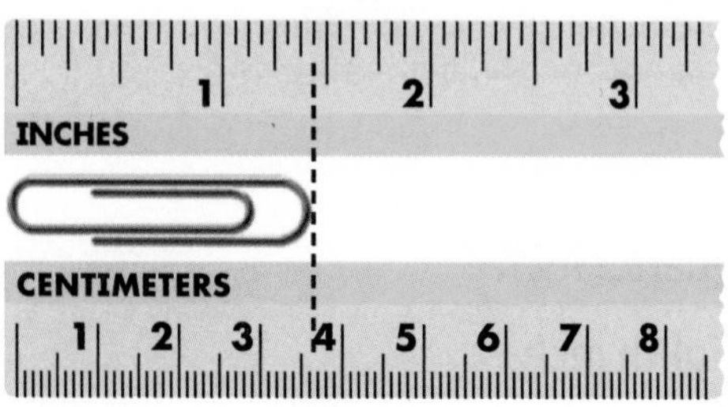

Nearest sixteenth inch: $1\frac{7}{16}$ inches

Nearest millimeter: 36 millimeters

Remember to line up the zero mark of your ruler with one end of the object being measured. The smaller the units used for measuring, the more precise the measurement.

Measure each segment to the nearest sixteenth inch and nearest millimeter.

1.

2.

Reteaching

Set D, pages 412–413

Round to the nearest tenth. 5 km ≈ □ mi

Customary and Metric Unit Equivalents (Data)

Length	Weight/Mass	Capacity
1 in. = 2.54 cm	1 oz. ≈ 28.35 g	1 L ≈ 1.06 qt
1 m ≈ 39.37 in.	1 kg ≈ 2.2 lb	1 gal ≈ 3.79 L
1 mi ≈ 1.61 km	1 metric ton (t) ≈ 1.102 T	

1 mi ≈ 1.61 km

5 ÷ 1.61 = 3.106

5 km ≈ 3.11 mi

To change from a smaller unit to a larger unit, divide.

Remember to use the table to tell how to change between customary and metric units.

Round to the nearest tenth.

1. 2 in. ≈ □ cm
2. 5 mi ≈ □ km
3. 3 oz ≈ □ g
4. 7 lb ≈ □ kg
5. 10 L ≈ □ qt
6. 5.5 t ≈ □ T
7. Frank's cat weighs 8 pounds. How many kilograms is this?
8. A marathon is 26.2 miles. How many kilometers is this?

Set E, pages 414–416

Find the elapsed time from 8:20 A.M. to 11:12 A.M.

Subtract the starting time from the ending time.

11 h 12 min	→	10 h 72 min
− 8 h 20 min	→	− 8 h 20 min
Elasped time	→	2 h 52 min

Remember to break the problem into parts when the elapsed time extends past noon or midnight.

1. 1:43 P.M. to 6:21 P.M.
2. 7:13 A.M. to 10:42 A.M.
3. 10:15 A.M. to 3:02 P.M.

Set F, pages 418–419

What is the size of the small and large jumps? Use reasoning to find the size of each jump.

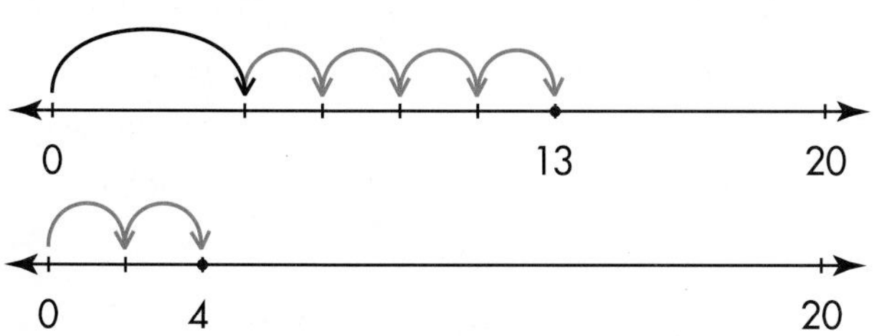

Two small jumps end at 4: 2 × □ = 4.
Since 2 × 2 = 4, a small jump must be 2.
Use the size of the small jumps to find the size of the large jump: □ + (4 × 2) = 13.
The large jump must be 5: 5 + 8 = 13.

Large jump: 5 units Small jump: 2 units

Remember that you can use reasoning to solve some problems.

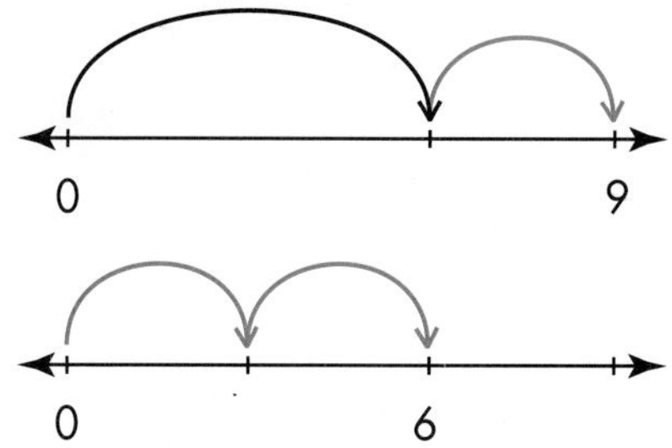

1. Use the number lines to find the sizes of the large and small jumps.

Topic 17 Perimeter and Area

1 What is the area covered by this giant lily pad? You will find out in Lesson 17-5.

2 Look at the shapes in these origami figures. How can you find the area of them? You will find out in Lesson 17-3.

3 How can you find the circumferences of Saturn's rings? You will find out in Lesson 17-4.

4 How much area is needed to create a living chessboard? You will find out in Lesson 17-2.

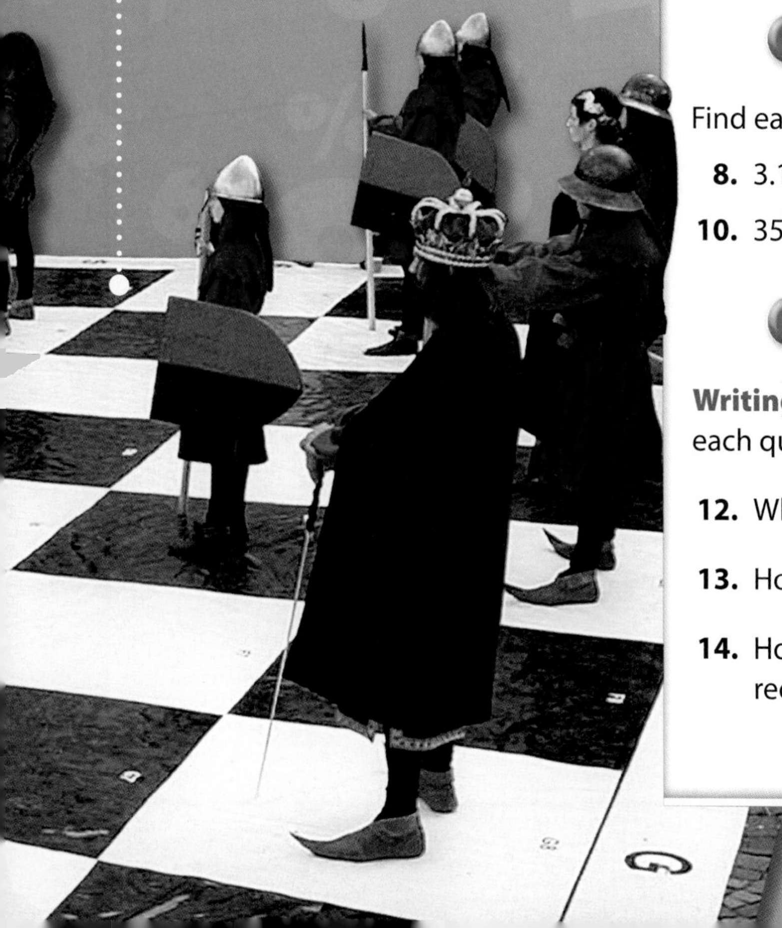

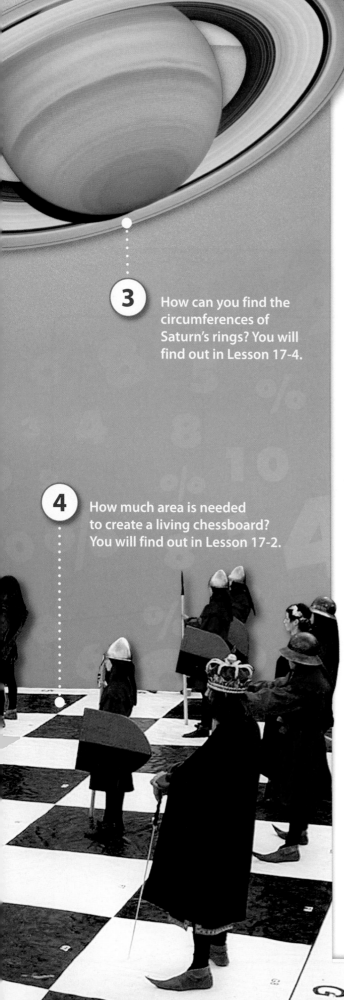

Review What You Know!

Vocabulary

Choose the best term from the box.

- polygon
- perpendicular
- parallelogram

1. A rectangle is an example of a __?__, but a circle is not.

2. __?__ lines form a right angle.

3. A __?__ has opposite sides that are parallel and the same length.

Evaluating Expressions

Find the value of each expression when $\ell = 7$ and $w = 9$.

4. $\ell \times w$

5. $\ell + \ell + w + w$

6. $2\ell + 2w$

7. $w \times \ell$

Multiplying Decimals

Find each answer.

8. 3.14×12

9. 45.8×5^2

10. 35×12.8

11. 64.9×5.8

Geometry

Writing to Explain Write an answer for each question.

12. Why is a circle not considered a polygon?

13. How is a parallelogram like a rectangle?

14. How is a parallelogram different from a rectangle?

Lesson
17-1

Understand It!
The distance around a polygon can be measured by combining the lengths of each side.

Perimeter

How can you find the distance around a polygon?

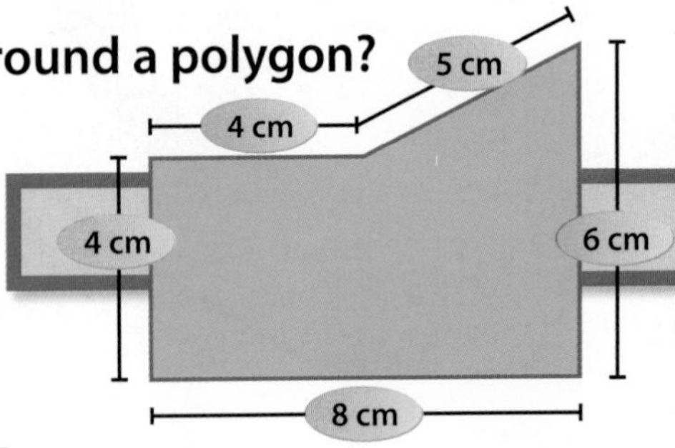

The distance around a polygon is called the perimeter of a polygon.

The perimeter (P) of a polygon is the sum of the lengths of its sides.

For the figure at the right:
$P = 4 + 4 + 5 + 6 + 8$. Its perimeter is 27 cm.

Another Example How can you find the perimeter of a polygon that has unknown sides?

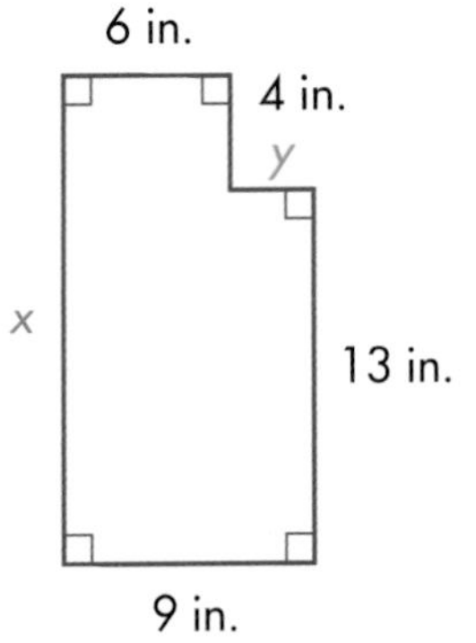

Find the perimeter of the figure.

The length of side x is 17 inches because it equals the sum of the lengths of two parallel sides, 13 in. and 4 in.

The length of side y is 3 inches because it equals the difference between the lengths labeled 9 in. and 6 in.

The lengths of all the sides are known. So, the perimeter can be found.

$$P = 17 + 6 + 4 + 3 + 13 + 9 = 52$$

The perimeter is 52 inches.

Explain It

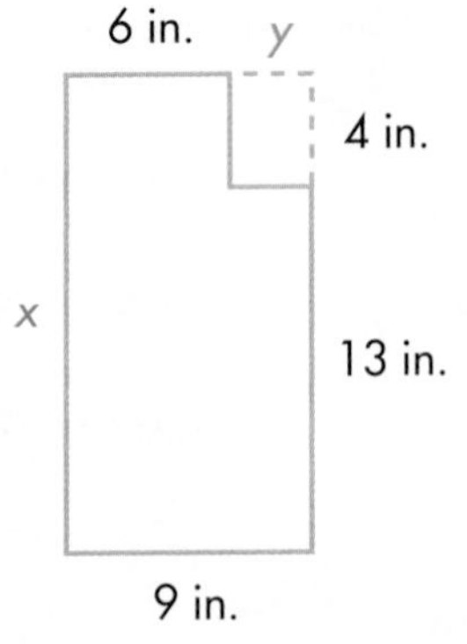

1. Diane extended two sides to make a rectangle. Explain what she did and how it helps to find the measures of x and y.

2. Write a formula for finding the perimeter of an equilateral triangle. Let s equal the length of one side.

Perimeter of a Square

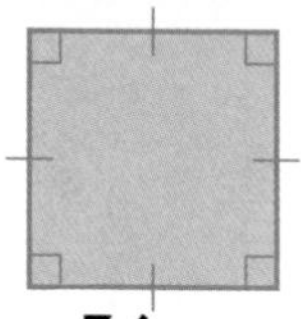
7.6 cm

Since a square has 4 sides (s) that have equal lengths, you can use the formula $P = 4s$.

$P = 4s$
$P = 4(7.6)$
$P = 30.4$

4s means $4 \times s$

The perimeter of the square is 30.4 cm.

Perimeter of a Rectangle

7 in.
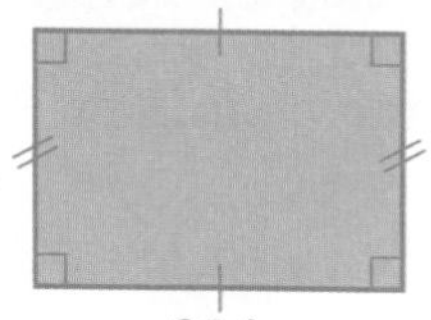
21 in.

Since a rectangle has two equal lengths (ℓ) and two equal widths (w), you can use the formula $P = 2\ell + 2w$.

$P = 2\ell + 2w$
$P = 2(21) + 2(7)$
$P = 42 + 14$
$P = 56$

The perimeter of the rectangle is 56 in.

Guided Practice*

Do you know HOW?

In **1** through **4**, find the perimeter of each shape.

1. square with 5-inch sides

2. rectangle with length 12 cm and width 8 cm

3.
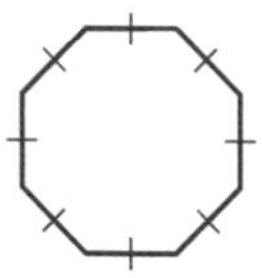
23 mm

4.
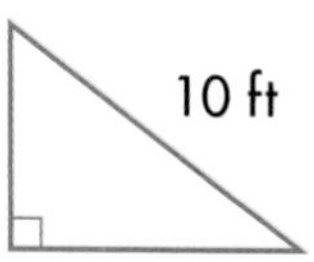

Do you UNDERSTAND?

5. If you do not remember the formula for finding the perimeter of a rectangle, how could you find its perimeter?

6. A carpenter is putting wood molding around a room that is 10 feet by 10 feet. How many feet of molding does he need?

Independent Practice

In **7** through **14**, find the perimeter of each shape.

Tip *A regular polygon has sides of equal length.*

7. regular hexagon, sides 5 in. long

8. rectangular rug, 5 ft long, 3 ft wide

9. equilateral triangle, sides 12 in.

10. octagonal stop sign, sides 12 in.

11. plywood piece, 3 ft wide, 4 ft long

12. rectangular room, 20 m long, 9 m wide

13. square tile, side 30 cm long

14. regular decagon, sides 8 mm long

DIGITAL Animated Glossary **www.pearsonsuccessnet.com**

For another example, see Set A on page 450.

Independent Practice

In **15** through **17**, find the perimeter.

15.

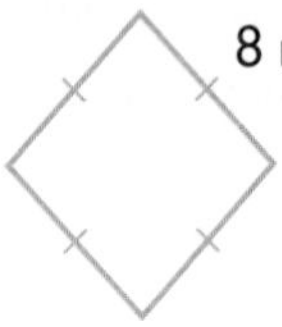

16.

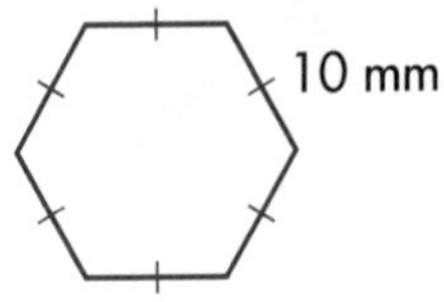

17.

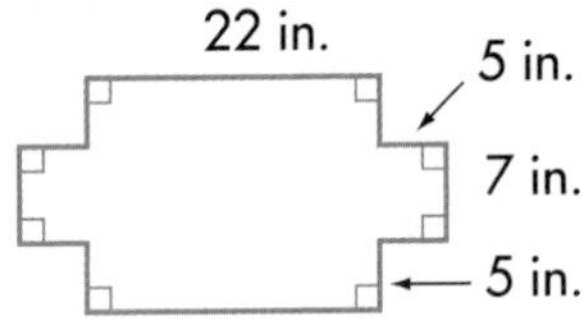

In **18** through **20**, find the length of each unknown side, and then find the perimeter.

18.

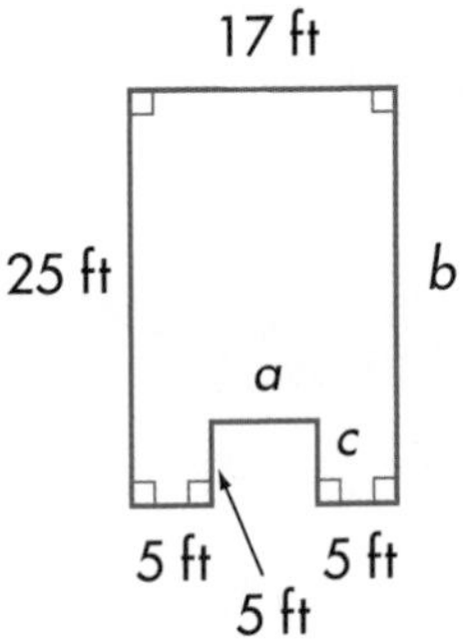

19.

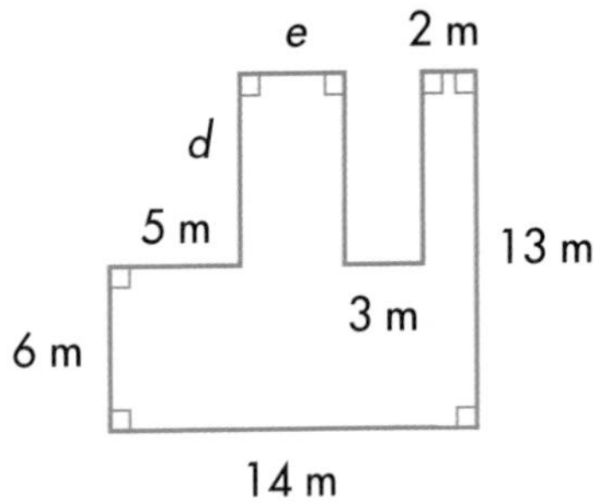

20.

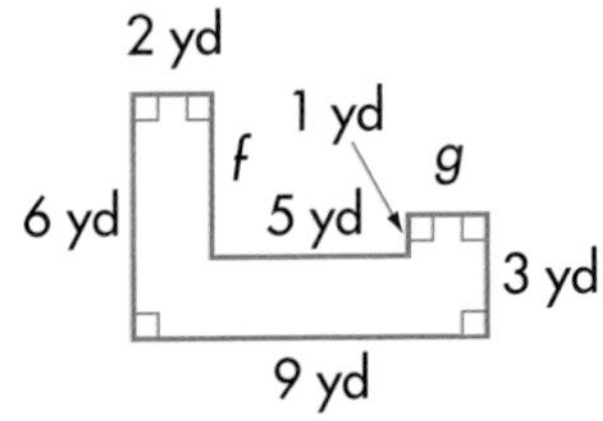

Problem Solving

21. Greta bought 3 lb 4 oz of peanuts and shared 1 lb 12 oz with the class. What is the weight of the remaining peanuts?

22. **Number Sense** The perimeter of a regular octagon is 26 ft. What is the length of each side?

23. **Writing to Explain** Name two units that could be used to measure perimeter and two that could not be used. Explain the difference.

24. Manuel wanted some film for a field trip. Film costs \$4.50 a roll. How much will 5 rolls cost?

25. Fort Ross was built by Russian settlers in 1812 as a farming and trading outpost. Approximately, what was the total length of the fort's walls?

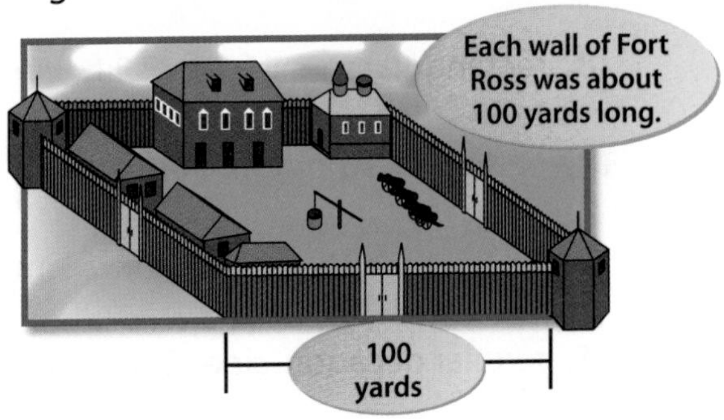

A About 100 yards **C** About 400 yards

B About 200 yards **D** About 10,000 yards

26. Jack and Rina are putting a wallpaper border around the walls of a game room. A floor plan of the game room is shown below. If the border comes in 15-foot rolls, about how many rolls will they need?

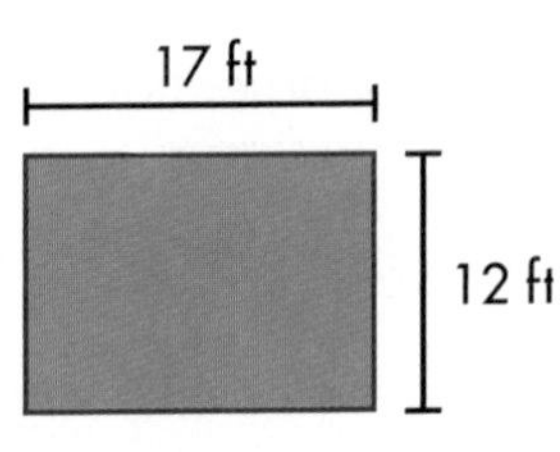

A 2 **C** 29

B 4 **D** 41

Algebra Connections

Perimeters of Similar Figures

Remember that when polygons are similar, their corresponding sides are proportional.

Rectangles **A** and **B** shown below are similar figures.

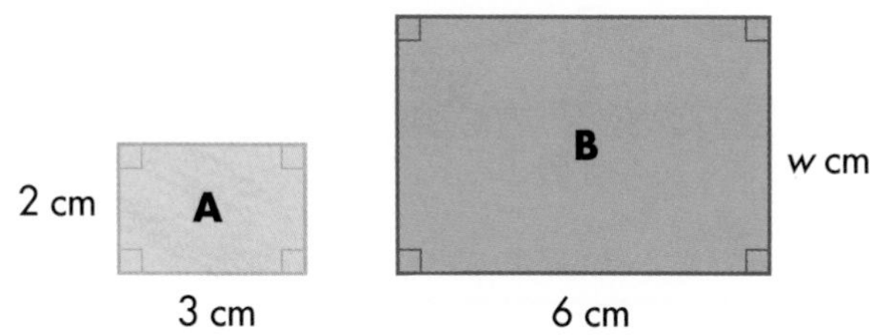

Example: Use what you know about similar figures to find the perimeter of Rectangle **B**.

Step 1 Write and solve a proportion to find w, the width of Rectangle **B**.

$$\frac{w}{2} = \frac{6}{3}$$

$$3w = 12$$

$$w = 4$$

Step 2 Find the perimeter of Rectangle **B**.

$$P = 2\ell + 2w$$

$$= 2(6) + 2(4)$$

$$= 12 + 8$$

$$= 20$$

The perimeter of Rectangle **B** is 20 cm.

For **1**, the parallelograms are similar. Use what you know about similar figures to solve for x; then find the perimeter of Parallelogram **N**.

1.

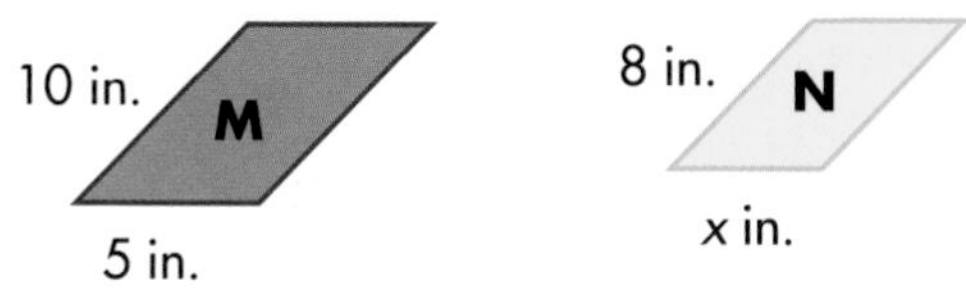

For **2** and **3**, write and solve a proportion to find the missing values for the similar figures shown.

2.

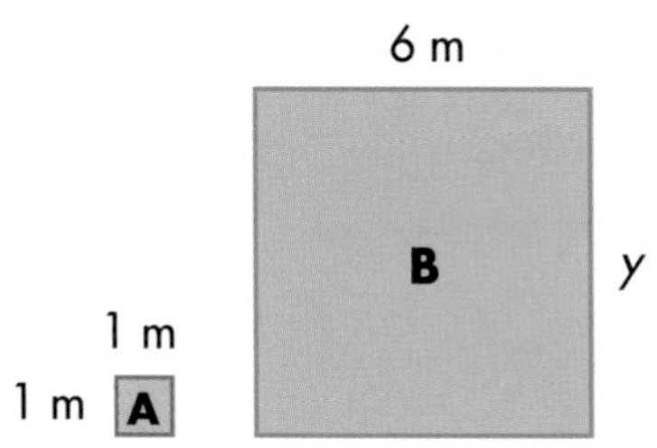

3.

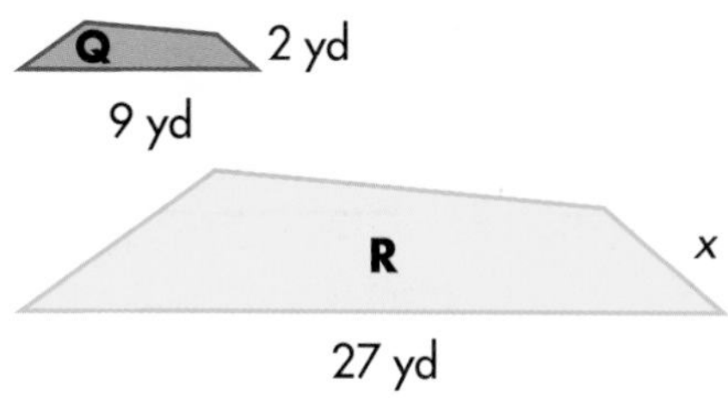

For **4** and **5**, use the figure at the right.

4. Write and solve an equation for the perimeter of Polygon **P**.

5. If a shape similar to Polygon **P** has a perimeter of 64 cm, what would the length of each side be? Explain how you found your answer.

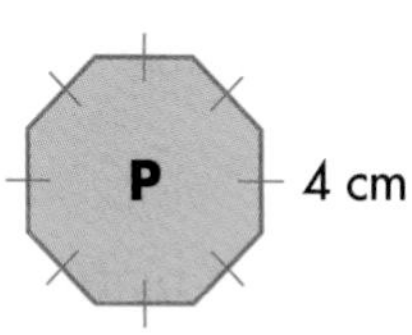

Lesson
17-2

Understand It!
The area of a shape is measured by the number of square units it takes to cover the shape.

Area of Rectangles and Irregular Figures

How can you measure the area of a rectangle?

The area of a figure is the amount of surface it covers. Tessa is covering a bulletin board with fabric. The board is 4 feet high and 5 feet long. How much fabric does she need?

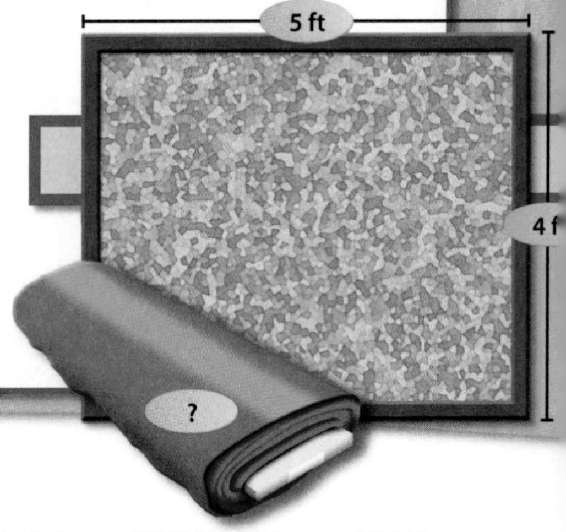

Another Example **How can you measure the area of an irregular figure?**

Richard is helping his father put sod in a portion of the yard. The yard is rectangular, 12 feet long and 8 feet wide, with a 5-foot-by-5-foot flower garden in one corner. How much sod will they need?

One Way

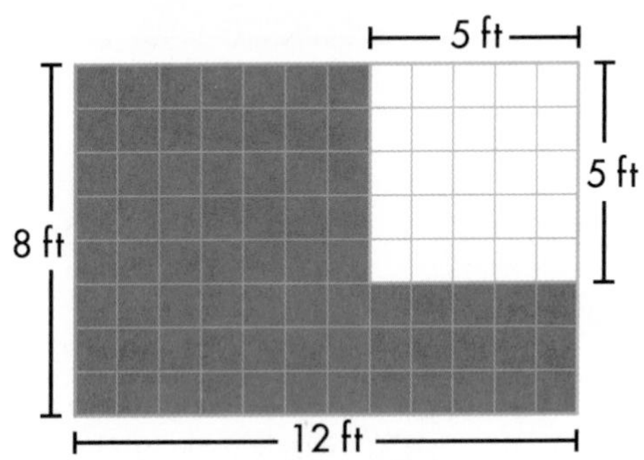

Draw a picture of the yard on graph paper. Let each square represent 1 square foot of sod. Count the squares in the picture, excluding the squares for the garden.

They will need 71 square feet of sod.

Another Way

Use a formula to find the total area of the yard and subtract the area of the garden.

Area of the yard:

$A = \ell \times w = 12 \times 8 = 96$

Area of the garden:

$A = \ell \times w = 5 \times 5 = 25$

Area to be sodded:

$A = 96 - 25 = 71$

They will need 71 ft^2 of sod.

Explain It

1. Look at the picture above. How could you use a formula to calculate the amount of sod needed without finding the area of the garden?

One Way

Draw a picture on graph paper. Then count the squares covered by the drawing.

There are 20 squares.

$A = 20 \text{ ft}^2$

"ft^2" is read "square feet."

Tessa needs 20 square feet of fabric.

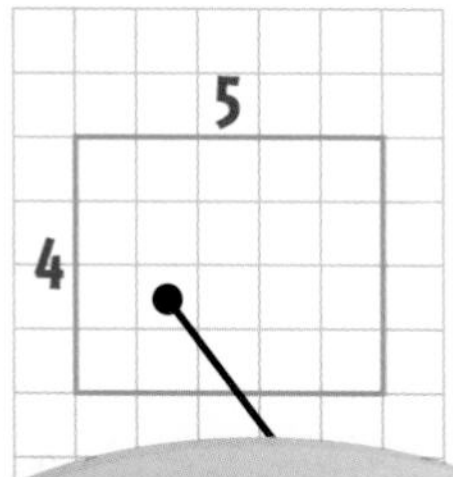

Area is always given in square units. A square foot, for example, is one foot high and one foot wide.

Another Way

Use a formula. The formula for finding the area of a rectangle is $A = \ell \times w$.

$A = \ell \times w$ ← **Think** ℓ is the length and w is the width.

$A = 5 \times 4$

$A = 20 \text{ ft}^2$

Tessa needs 20 square feet of fabric.

Other Examples

Use the formula for the area of a rectangle to find an unknown measurement when you know the area and the length of one side. Find the length, ℓ, of the rectangle.

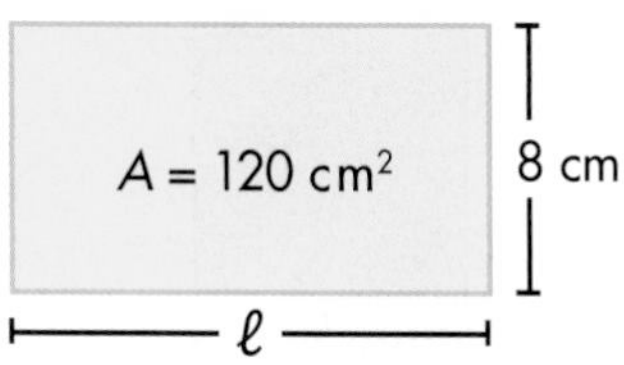

$$A = \ell \times w$$
$$120 = \ell \times 8$$
$$120 \div 8 = \ell \times 8 \div 8$$
$$15 = \ell$$

The length of the rectangle is 15 cm.

Guided Practice*

Do you know HOW?

Find the area of the figures in **1** and **2**.

1.

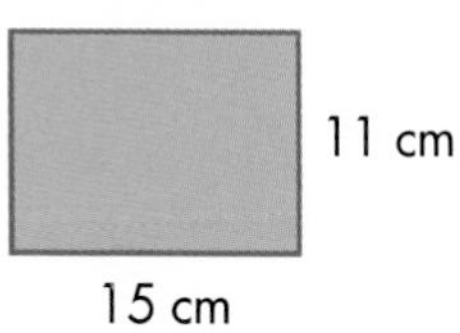

2.

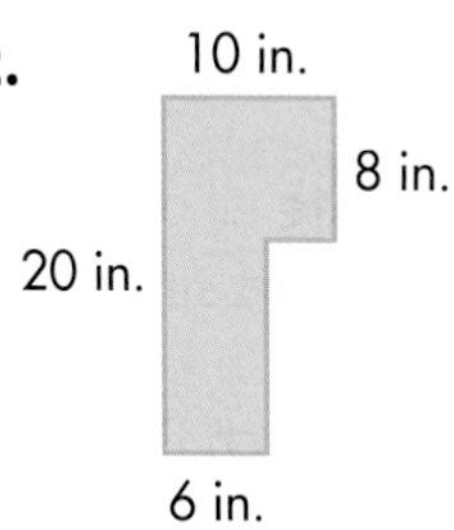

3. Find the missing length.

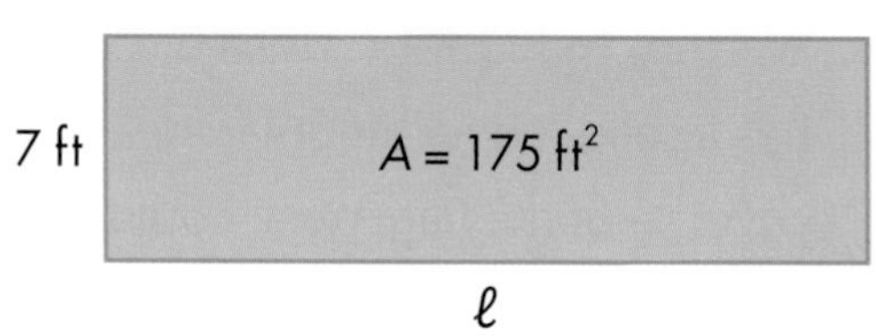

Do you UNDERSTAND?

4. Find the area and perimeter of a square measuring 4 inches on each side. Compare the answers. What is the same? What is different?

5. In the example at the top, suppose Tessa used 24 ft^2 of fabric to cover a bulletin board that is 3 ft wide. How long is the bulletin board? Explain how you found the answer.

DIGITAL Animated Glossary **www.pearsonsuccessnet.com**

For another example, see Set B on page 450.

Independent Practice

In **6** through **11**, find the area of each figure.

6.

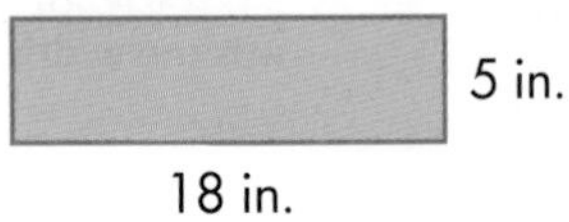

7.

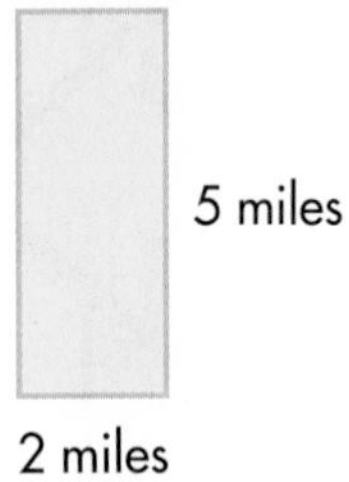

8.

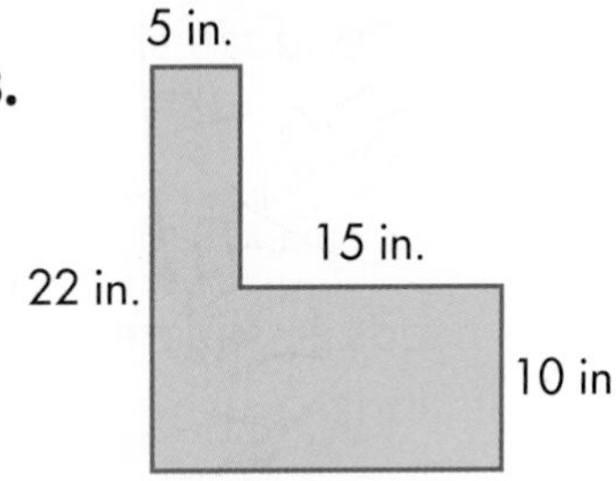

9.

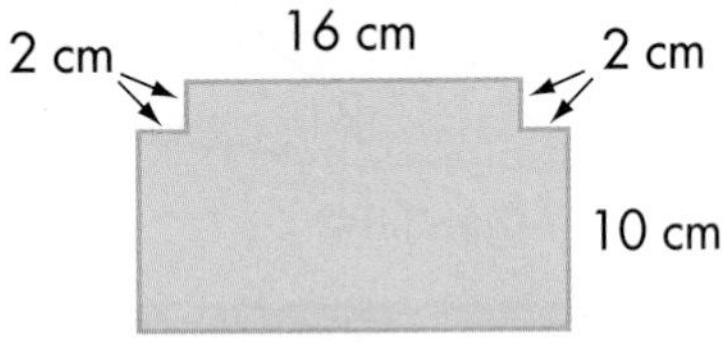

10.

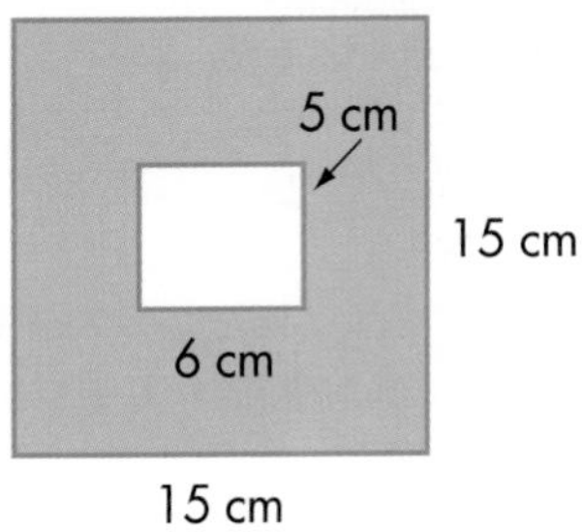

11.

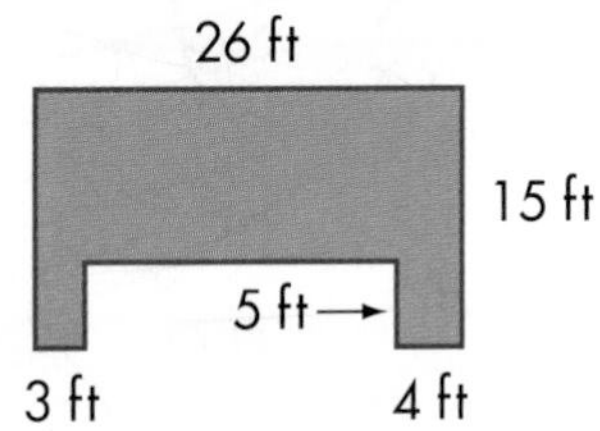

In **12** through **14**, find the missing lengths.

12.

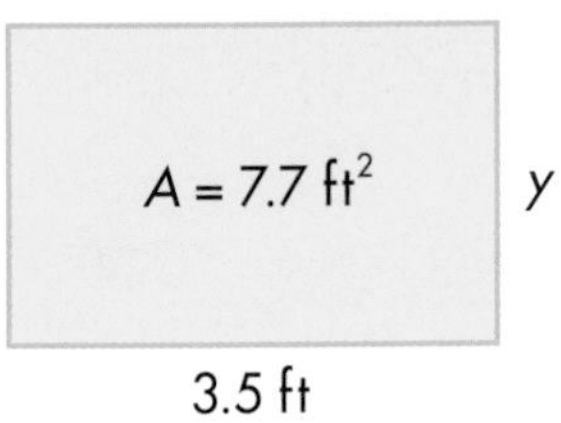

13.

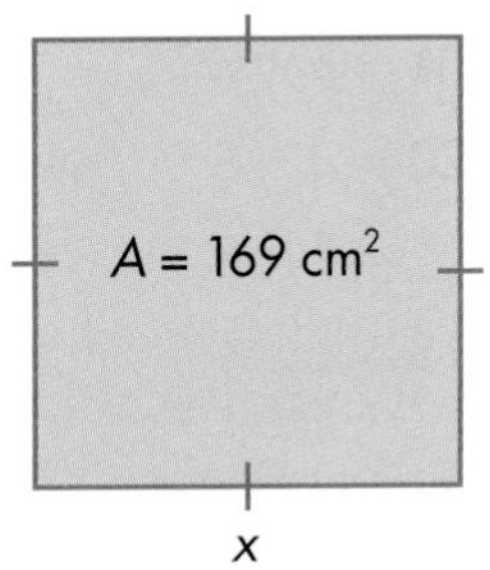

14.

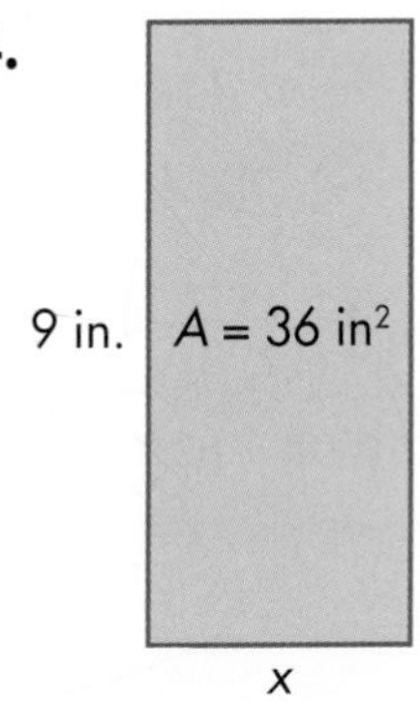

Problem Solving

15. Tito is painting a wall that measures 8 ft by 16 ft. There is a window that is 5 ft by 4 ft in the wall. What is the area that Tito will paint?

16. Flags can come in many sizes. Copy the chart below and fill in the areas for the rectangular flags. Then use your completed chart for **17** through **19**.

Data

Flag Size	Flag Area
4 in. × 6 in.	
12 in. × 18 in.	
2 ft × 3 ft	
3 ft × 5 ft	
4 ft × 6 ft	

17. Are all of the different-sized flags in the chart similar figures? Explain.

18. Which flag is larger, the one with an area of 216 in^2 or the one with an area of 6 ft^2?

19. **Writing to Explain** The 4 ft × 6 ft flag has a solid red rectangular area that covers $\frac{1}{3}$ of the flag. What could be the dimensions of this red area? Explain.

Problem Solving

20. **Reasoning** Can the distance from your house to your school be measured in square miles? Explain.

21. Marcy rode her bike around a $\frac{1}{4}$-mile track 16 times in 30 minutes. What was her speed in miles per hour?

22. Janelle purchased a bathing suit on sale for $25.00, with sales tax of 6%. What was the total cost for her suit?

23. Suppose the length of a side of a square is *s*. Write a formula to find the area of a square.

24. **Writing to Explain** If you know the perimeter of a rectangle and the length of one side, can you calculate the width? Explain.

25. Marcus wants to put a $6\frac{1}{2}$-foot bookcase against a $12\frac{1}{4}$-foot wall. If he centers the bookcase, how far will it be from each end of the wall?

26. Hayley wants to plant ivy in her back yard in a shady part that is 24 feet long and 6 feet wide. Ivy to cover 1 square foot will cost $2.50. How much will it cost to plant enough ivy to cover the shaded area?

27. Mr. Scott's workshop is a rectangle that measures 25 feet by 27 feet. His new woodworking equipment will take up an area of 300 ft^2. Will the new equipment fit into the workroom?

28. **Reasoning** On a chessboard, the squares alternate betweeen light and dark. Which best describes the area of the light squares?

    A Half as much as the dark squares

    B Twice as much as the dark squares

    C Equal to the dark squares

    D One-fourth less than the dark squares

29. Suppose that a square on a living chessboard measures 4 ft $\times$ 4 ft. How much area does the whole board cover?

    A 72 ft^2

    B 256 ft^2

    C 512 ft^2

    D 1,024 ft^2

A living chess board has 64 squares.

Lesson
17-3

Understand It!
The formula for the area of a rectangle can help you find the formula for the area of a parallelogram and the area of a triangle.

Area of Parallelograms and Triangles

How can you use the formula for the area of a rectangle to find the area of a parallelogram?

Look at the parallelogram below. If you move the triangle to the opposite side, you form a rectangle with the same area as the parallelogram.

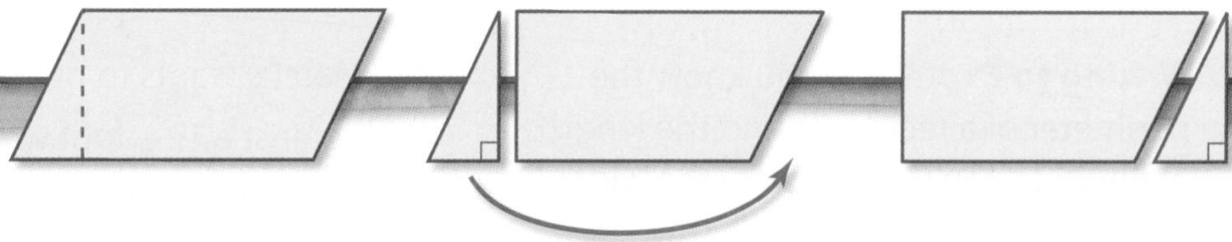

Another Example

How can you use the formula for the area of a parallelogram to find the area of a triangle?

Since two congruent triangles can form a parallelogram, the area of one triangle must be half the area of the parallelogram that has the same base and height.

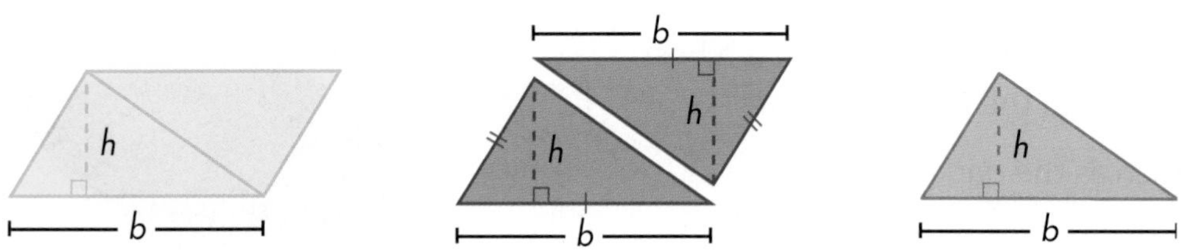

Area of a Parallelogram

$A = bh$

Area of a Triangle

$A = \frac{1}{2}bh$

Tip *Remember to write area in square units (units²).*

Explain It

1. A rectangle and a parallelogram have the same base and height. How are their areas related?
2. A parallelogram and a triangle have the same base and height. How are their areas related?

The base of the parallelogram (b) equals the length of the rectangle (ℓ).

The height of the parallelogram (h), which is perpendicular to the base, equals the width of the rectangle (w).

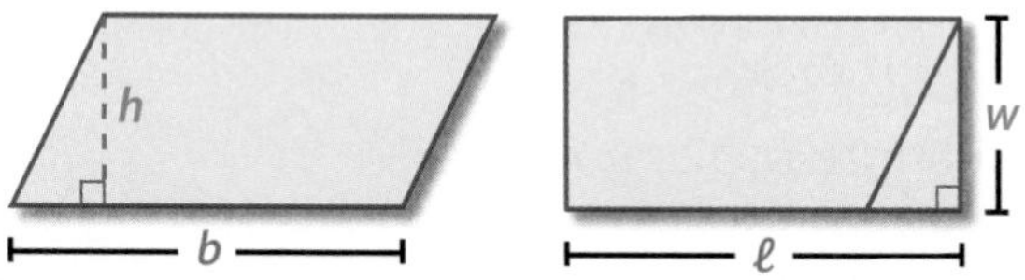

The area of the parallelogram equals the area of the rectangle.

Area of a Rectangle → $A = \ell \times w$

Area of a Parallelogram → $A = b \times h$

$A = bh$

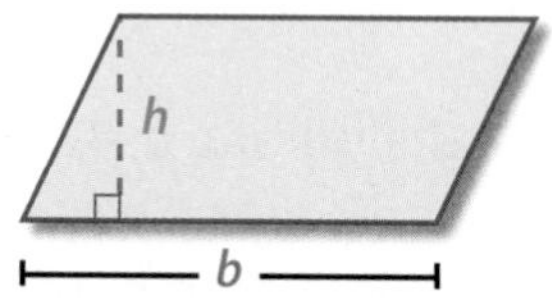

Other Examples

Find the area of the parallelogram.

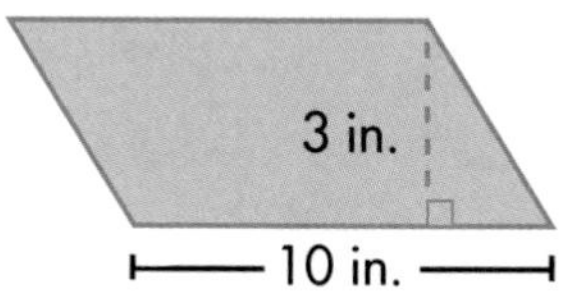

$A = b \times h$

$A = 10 \times 3$

$A = 30$

The area of the parallelogram is 30 in^2.

Find the area of the triangle.

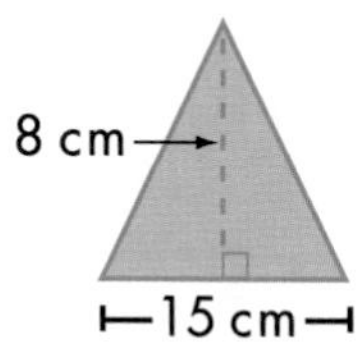

$A = \frac{1}{2}bh$

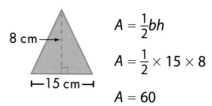

$A = \frac{1}{2} \times 15 \times 8$

$A = 60$

The area of the triangle is 60 cm^2.

Guided Practice*

Do you know HOW?

Use a formula to find the area of each parallelogram or triangle.

1.

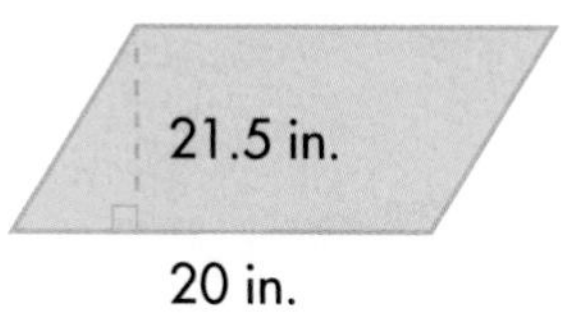

2.

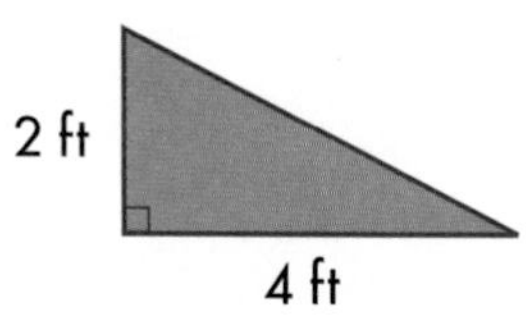

3. Triangle: b: 14 cm; h: 23 cm

4. Parallelogram: b: 27 ft; h: 32 ft

Do you UNDERSTAND?

5. **Writing to Explain** Explain how two parallelograms can have the same area but not be congruent to each other.

6. Find the height of a triangle if its area is 24 square meters and its base is 8 meters. Explain how you got your answer.

7. **Writing to Explain** A parallelogram is 5 yards long and 9 feet high. Lori said that the area is 45 square feet. Is she correct? Explain why or why not.

***For another example, see Set B on page 450.**

Independent Practice

Find the area of each parallelogram or triangle.

8.

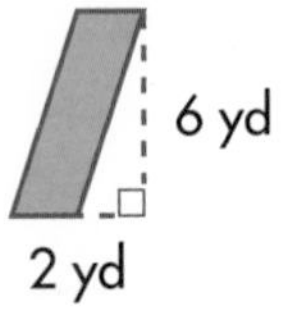

9.

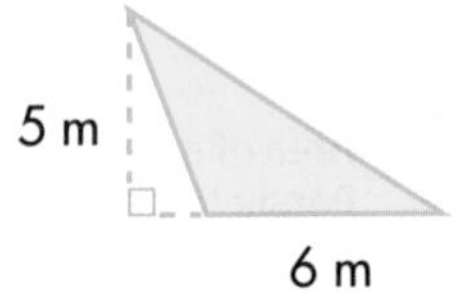

10.

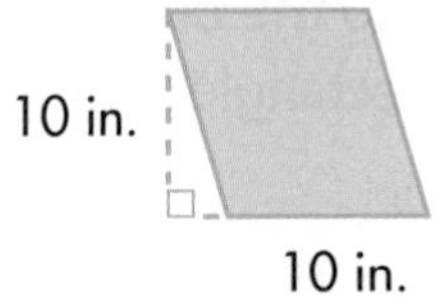

11.

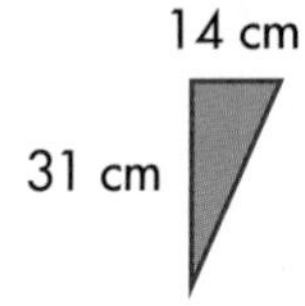

12. Parallelogram: *b*: 42 m; *h*: 33 m

13. Triangle: *b*: 32 in.; *h*: 2 yd

14. Triangle: *b*: 8 ft; *h*: 14 ft

15. Triangle: *b*: 12 ft; *h*: 6 in.

16. Parallelogram: *b*: 22 in.; *h*: 22 in.

17. Parallelogram: *b*: 30 cm; *h*: 10 mm

18. Triangle: *b*: 5 yd; *h*: 3 yd

19. Parallelogram: *b*: 24 in.; *h*: 2 ft

20. Triangle: *b*: 32 cm; *h*: 2 m

21. **Estimation** Estimate the area of a triangle with a base of 19.64 cm and a height of 30.23 cm.

22. Parallelogram: *b*: 8 ft; *h*: 2 yd

Problem Solving

23. **Writing to Explain** If you know both the area and height of a triangle, how can you find the base?

24. When can the leg of an isosceles triangle be used as the height of the triangle?

25. Fawzia wanted to make an origami fish for each of her 22 classmates. It takes 30 minutes to make one fish. How long will it take Fawzia to make all the fish?

A 320 minutes **C** 600 minutes

B 11 hours **D** 660 hours

26. **Number Sense** Ms. Lopez drew parallelogram *M* with $h = 6$ in. and $b = 6$ in., and parallelogram *N* with $h = 4$ in. and $b = 8$ in. Which parallelogram has the greater area, *M* or *N*?

Use the origami figure for **27** and **28**.

27. What is the area in centimeters of the triangle outlined on the figure?

28. What is the area of the parallelogram outlined on the figure?

A 4.44 cm^2

B 10.44 cm^2

C 9.44 cm^2

D Need more information

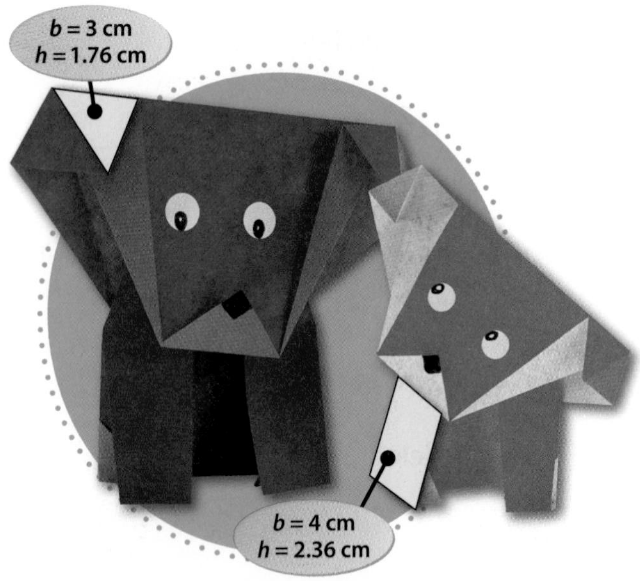

Enrichment

Area of Trapezoids

A trapezoid is a quadrilateral that has only one pair of opposite sides that are parallel. These parallel sides are called bases. They are labeled b_1 and b_2.

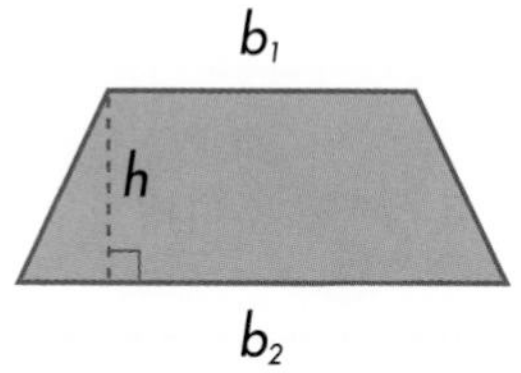

If a congruent trapezoid is joined with the trapezoid as shown, the two figures form a parallelogram. The area of a parallelogram is $A = bh$.

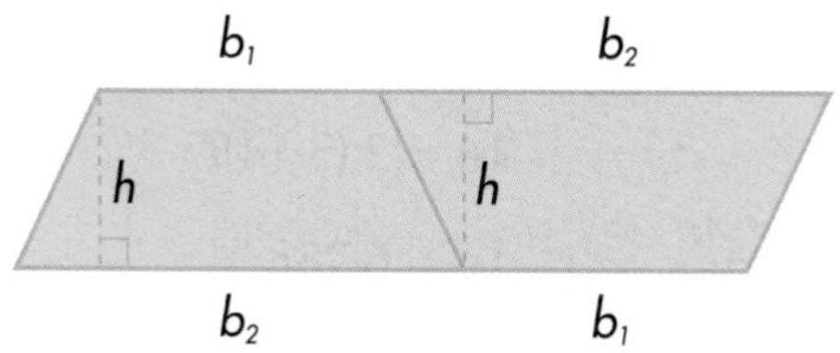

The base of this parallelogram is $b_1 + b_2$.

Half the area of this parallelogram is the area of one trapezoid. So, the formula for the area of a trapezoid is $A = \frac{1}{2}h(b_1 + b_2)$.

Example:

Find the area of the trapezoid.

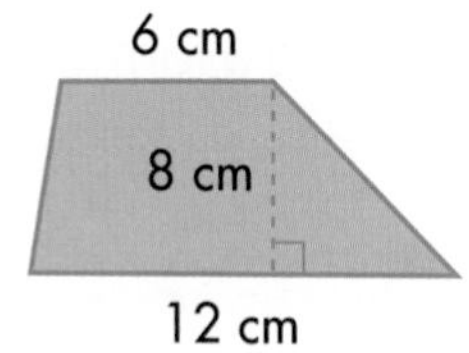

Tip *Area should be expressed in square units.*

$A = \frac{1}{2}h(b_1 + b_2)$

$A = \frac{1}{2} \times 8(6 + 12)$

$= \frac{1}{2} \times 8(18)$

$= \frac{1}{2} \times 144$

$= 72$

The area of the trapezoid is 72 cm^2.

Practice

For **1** through **4**, find the area of each trapezoid.

1.

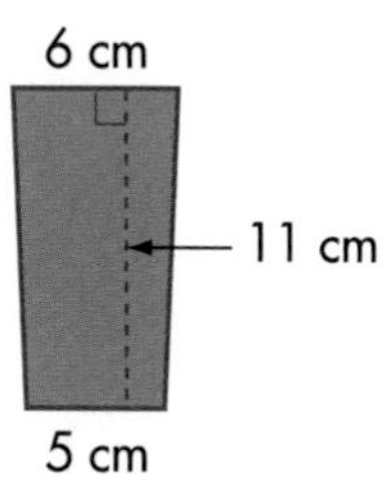

2.

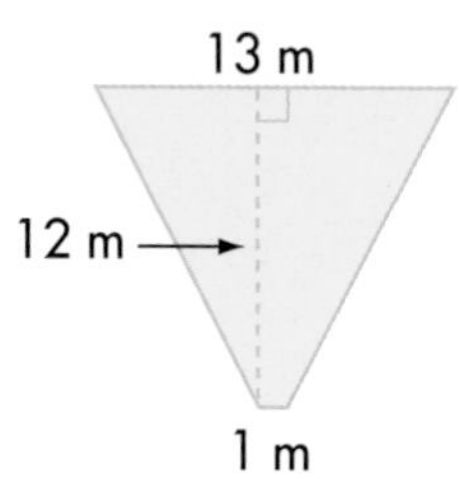

3.

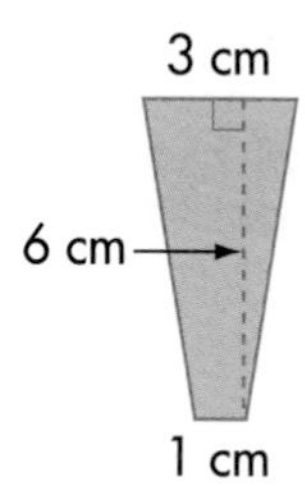

4.

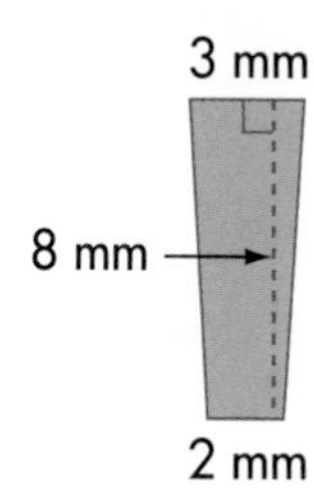

For **5** and **6**, find the missing measurement for each trapezoid.

5. Base $b_1 = 5$ ft Base $b_2 = $ ▢
Height $h = 17$ ft Area $= 255\ ft^2$

6. Base $b_1 = 9$ cm Base $b_2 = 13$ cm
Height $h = $ ▢ Area $= 88\ cm^2$

Lesson

17-4

Understand It!
The distance around a circle is related to the diameter of the circle. Knowing one of them helps you find the other.

Circumference

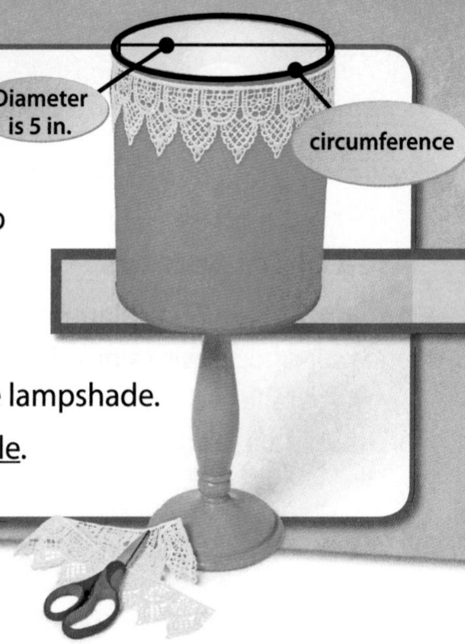

How can you find circumference?

Ana is going to glue some lace around the top edge of a lampshade whose circular opening has a diameter of 5 in. and a radius of 2.5 in. How much lace does she need?

Use a formula to find the circumference of the lampshade.

Circumference (C) is the distance around a circle.

Another Example

How can you find the diameter or radius if you know the circumference of a circle?

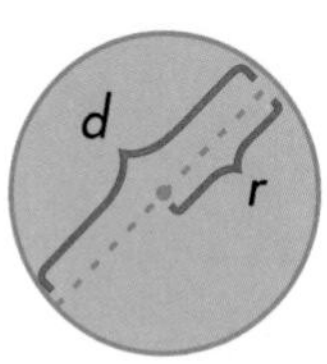

$C = 14$ in.

$d = $ ▢

$r = $ ▢

Substitute the value of C and π. Solve the equation for d.

$$C = \pi d$$

$$14 = 3.14d$$

$$\frac{14}{3.14} = \frac{3.14d}{3.14}$$

$$4.46 = d$$

The diameter is approximately 4.46 inches.

Substitute the value of C and π. Solve the equation for r.

$$C = 2\pi r$$

$$14 = 2\,(3.14)r$$

$$14 = 6.28r$$

$$\frac{14}{6.28} = \frac{6.28r}{6.28}$$

$$2.23 = r$$

The radius is approximately 2.23 inches.

How can you find circumference using a calculator?

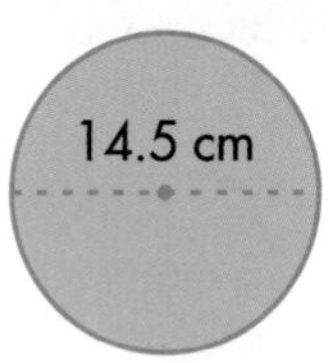

$C = \pi d$

Press: 

Display: 45.55309

The circumference is about 45.55 cm.

Explain It

1. Explain when you would use $\frac{22}{7}$ for π instead of 3.14.

2. How would you find the radius of a circle whose circumference is 10 cm?

One Way

Use the formula, $C = \pi d$.

C is the circumference of the circle and d is the diameter. The Greek letter π (read pi) represents the ratio of the circumference to the diameter for every circle.

π is approximately 3.14, or $\frac{22}{7}$. The digits do not repeat and never end. All calculations involving π are approximations.

$C = \pi d$

$C = (3.14)(5)$

$C = 15.70$

In the book, equal signs are used for calculations involving π.

Anna needs about 16 inches of lace.

Another Way

Use the formula, $C = 2\pi r$.

Since the diameter of a circle is twice the radius, $2r$ can be used to replace d in the formula.

$C = 2\pi r$

$C = 2(3.14)(2.5)$

$C = 15.70$

The answer is the same. Anna needs about 16 inches of lace.

Guided Practice*

Do you know HOW?

Use the diameter or radius shown for each circle to find its circumference. Use 3.14 or $\frac{22}{7}$ for π.

1. 

2. 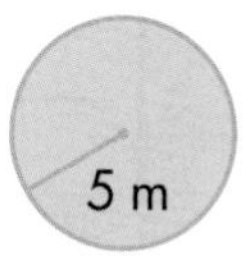

Do you UNDERSTAND?

3. **Number Sense** Why should you change the equal sign to an approximate equal symbol when you compute the circumference of a circle?

4. In the problem above, how would you estimate the circumference?

Independent Practice

In **5** through **8**, find the circumference. Use 3.14 for π.

5. 

6. 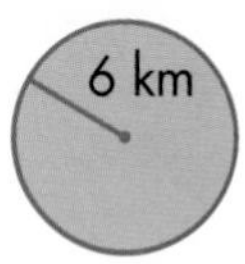

7. 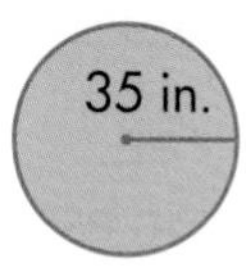

8. 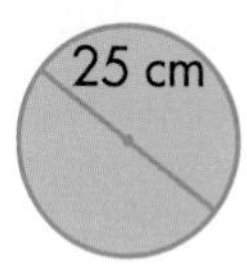

Find the missing measurement. Use 3.14 for π. Round to the nearest hundredth.

9. $r = 21$ ft
$C = $ ▢

10. $d = 9$ yd
$C = $ ▢

11. $C = 35$ mm
$r = $ ▢

12. $C = 32$ m
$d = $ ▢

13. $d = 21$ in.
$C = $ ▢

14. $r = $ ▢
$C = 9$ mm

15. $d = $ ▢
$r = 15$ in.
$C = $ ▢

16. $d = $ ▢
$r = $ ▢
$C = 109.9$ cm

DIGITAL Animated Glossary **www.pearsonsuccessnet.com**

For another example, see Set C on page 451.

Independent Practice

For **17** through **20**, find each circumference using 3.14 for π. Then find each circumference using $\pi = \frac{22}{7}$.

17.

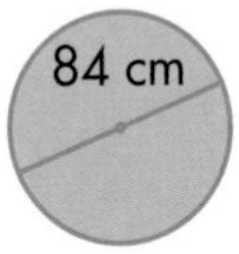

18.

19.

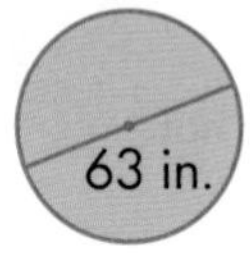

20.

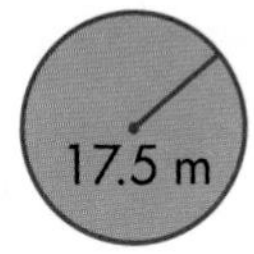

Problem Solving

21. If a clock face has a radius of 5.5 centimeters, what is the circumference of the clock face?

22. How is this graph incorrect?

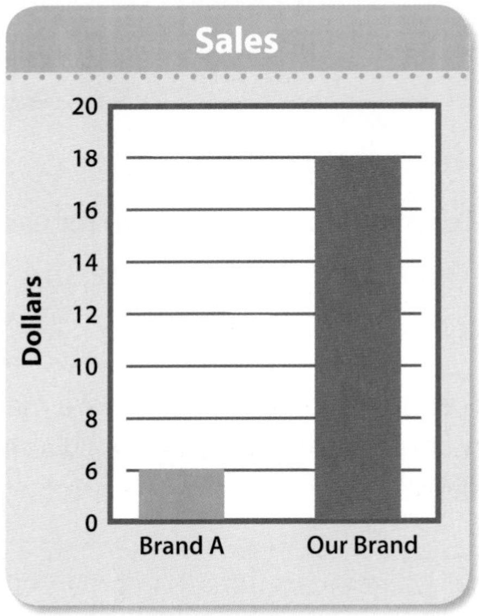

23. **Writing to Explain** Explain how finding the circumference using both 3.14 and $\frac{22}{7}$ can help you check an answer.

24. **Estimation** The minute hand of a clock is 4.2 inches long. Does the point of the hand move more or less than 24 inches in one hour?

25. The number π to four decimal places is 3.1416. How do you read this number?

This table shows the diameter and circumference for some of Saturn's rings. Use the information for **26** and **27**.

Data

Ring	Diameter	Circumference
C	184,000 km	
B	235,000 km	737,900 km
A	273,600 km	859,104 km
G		1,091,464 km

26. **Estimation** Explain how you can estimate the diameter of Ring G.

27. What is the circumference of Ring C?

A about 860,000 km

B about 254,000 km

C about 577,760 km

D about 225,000 km

28. **Think About the Process** If the circumference of a circle is known, how would you find the missing diameter?

A Multiply the circumference by 2π.

B Divide the circumference by π.

C Multiply the circumference by $\frac{\pi}{2}$.

D Divide the circumference by 2π.

Mixed Problem Solving

Math and Social Studies

The earliest known use of a wheel was in Mesopotamia in 3500 B.C. It was used as a tool to help people make pots and dishes out of clay. Wheels made it possible to turn pots and dishes as they were made.

Use this potter's wheel for **1** through **3**.

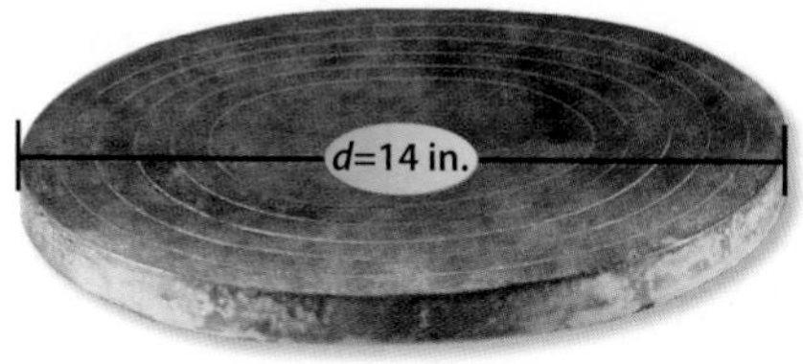

1. Suppose you wanted to make a circular dish with a circumference of 50 in. Would it fit on this potter's wheel?

2. Would a circular pot with a diameter of 11 inches fit on the wheel? How can you tell without doing a calculation?

3. **Reasoning** Why would a circular dish that has a radius of 13 inches not fit on the wheel in the picture?

Use the ancient bowl and plate for **4** and **5**. Round your answers to the nearest tenth.

4. This ancient bowl and plate were made by hand before the potter's wheel was invented. What is the circumference of this ancient bowl?

5. What is the circumference of the plate?

Cylinder seals were often used in Mesopotamia as a way for people to initial clay tablets. As the seal was rolled along a piece of clay, the pictures on the cylinder pressed into the clay. Use the cylinder seal below for **6** through **8**.

6. What is the circumference of the cylinder seal above?

7. How is the length of the marking made by one complete rotation of the seal related to the circumference of the cylinder seal?

8. Approximately how many complete rotations of the cylinder were needed to create an image that was 25 cm long?

Lesson
17-5

Understand It!
The formula for finding the area of a parallelogram can help you understand how to find the area of a circle.

Area of a Circle

How do you find the area of a circle?

A circular garden has a radius of 21 feet. What is the area of the garden?

Rearrange the sections of a circle to approximate a parallelogram. The area of a parallelogram, $A = bh$, may be used to find the formula for the area of a circle.

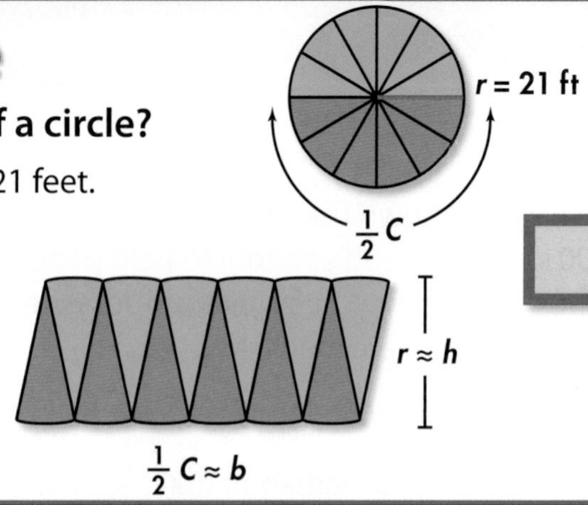

Guided Practice*

Do you know HOW?

Find the area of each circle to the nearest whole number. Use 3.14 or $\frac{22}{7}$ for π.

1. 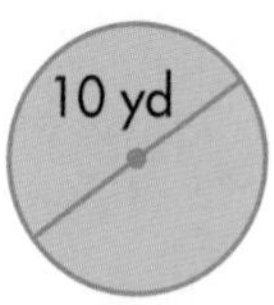

2. 

3. $d = 54$ in.

4. $r = 10$ mi

Do you UNDERSTAND?

5. In the comparison at the top of the page, how do the triangular shapes in the parallelogram relate to the circle?

6. Find the area of the garden above using 3.14 for π. Why is the value of the area slightly different than the values calculated using $\frac{22}{7}$ or the calculator?

Independent Practice

For **7** through **10**, find the area of each circle to the nearest whole number. Use 3.14 or $\frac{22}{7}$ for π.

7. 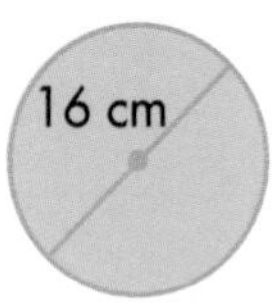

8. 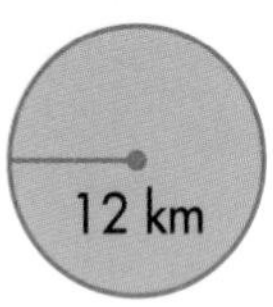

9. 

10. 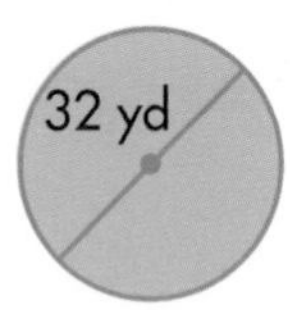

Find the missing measurements for each figure. Round to the nearest whole number. Use 3.14 or $\frac{22}{7}$ for π.

11. $d = 8$ in.
$r =$
$C =$
$A =$

12. $d =$
$r = 32$ mm
$C =$
$A =$

13. $d =$
$r =$
$C = 371$ mm
$A =$

14. $d =$
$r =$
$C =$
$A = 113$ sq in.

*For another example, see Set C on page 451.

Find the formula for area of a circle.

$A = b \times h$	**Area of a parallelogram**
$A = \frac{1}{2}C \times r$	**Equivalent measures**
$A = \frac{1}{2}(2\pi r) \times r$	**$C = 2\pi r$**
$A = \pi r \times r$	**Simplified**
$A = \pi r^2$	**Area of a circle**

Use the formula for a circle to find the area of the garden.

$A = \pi r^2$ ← **Use $\frac{22}{7}$ for π.**

$A = \frac{22}{7}(21)(21)$

$A = 1{,}386\ \text{ft}^2$

Use a calculator to find the area.

Press: π × 21 ^ 2 ENTER = F↔D

Display: 1385.442

Problem Solving

15. Find the approximate area and circumference of each coin. Round your answer to the nearest whole number.

a Dime

b Nickel

c Quarter

16. When you use both 3.14 and $\frac{22}{7}$ for π, why don't you get exactly the same answer?

17. Writing to Explain Explain how to find the area of a semicircle with a radius of 5 feet.

18. A small radio station broadcasts in all directions to a distance of 40 miles. About how many square miles are in the station's broadcast area?

A About 1,256 sq mi

B About 2,512 sq mi

C About 5,024 sq mi

D About 20,096 sq mi

19. Giant lily pads found in Brazil can have a diameter of 4 feet. What is the area of the top of the lily pad?

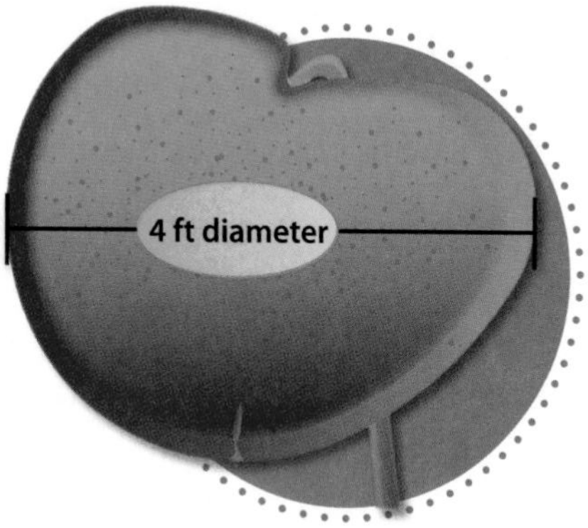

20. A dartboard has a radius of 25 cm. What is the area of the board at which you would throw darts?

Lesson
17-6

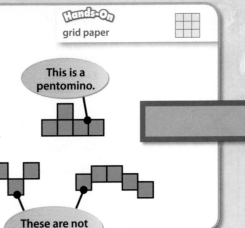

Understand It!
Some problems can be solved by using objects to model possible solutions.

Problem Solving

Use Objects

Hands-On
grid paper

A pentomino is an arrangement of 5 identical squares, each having a common side with at least one other square. There are 12 possible pentominoes.

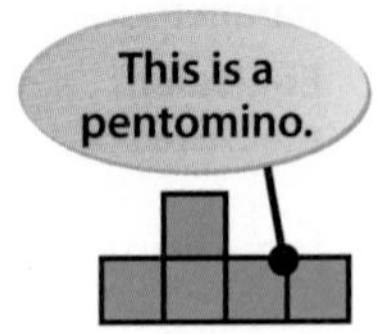
This is a pentomino.

Find a pentomino that can be folded along the lines to make an open-top box.

These are not pentominoes.

Guided Practice*

Do you know HOW?

1. Which figure is a pentomino?

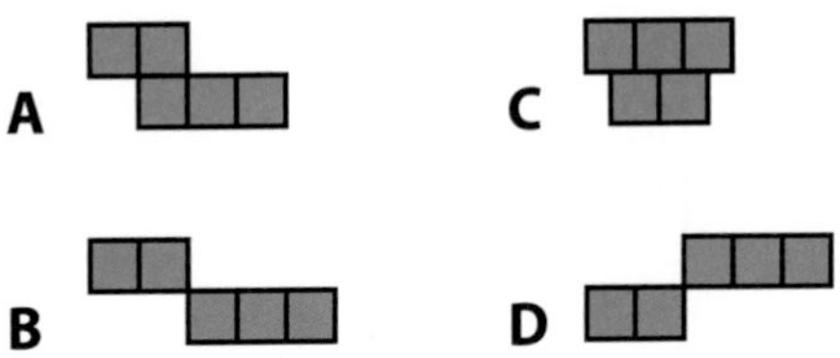
A
C
B
D

2. Can Pentomino P fold into an open-top box?

Do you UNDERSTAND?

3. Besides T, find two more pentominoes that can be folded to create an open-top box.

4. **Write a Problem** Write a problem that you can solve by using objects.

Independent Practice

Fit two pentominoes together to create the shapes for **5** and **6**.

5. 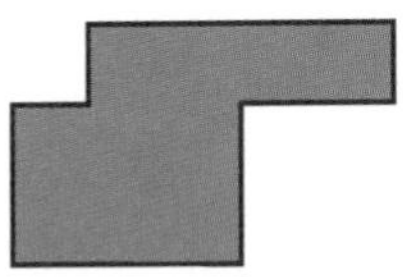

6. 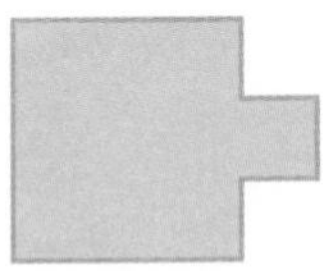

7. Which pentominoes have line symmetry?

8. Which pentominoes have line symmetry with more than one line?

9. Which pentominoes have rotational symmetry?

10. Arrange pentominoes U, F, and P to create a rectangle.

Stuck? Try this....

- What do I know?
- What am I asked to find?
- What diagram can I use to help understand the problem?
- Can I use addition, subtraction, multiplication, or division?
- Is all of my work correct?
- Did I answer the right question?
- Is my answer reasonable?

*For another example, see Set D on page 451.

Read and Understand

There are 12 possible pentominoes.

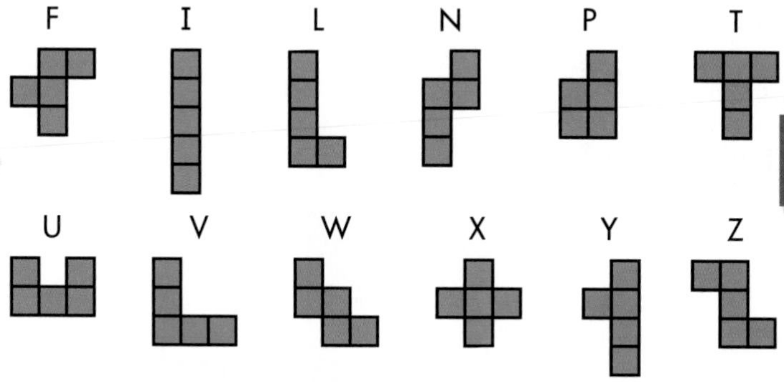

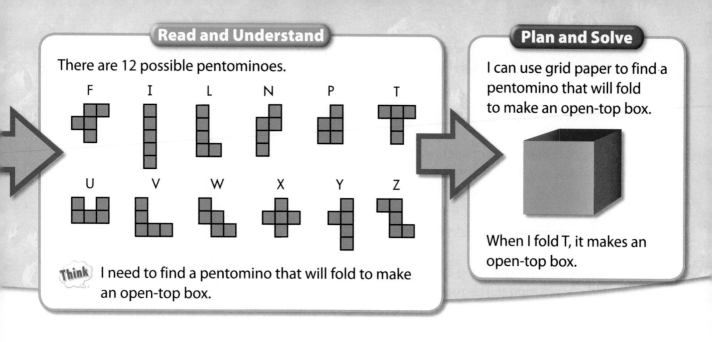

Think I need to find a pentomino that will fold to make an open-top box.

Plan and Solve

I can use grid paper to find a pentomino that will fold to make an open-top box.

When I fold T, it makes an open-top box.

11. If 1 square in a pentomino is equal to 1 unit, how many square units are there in a pentomino?

12. If you combine two pentominoes, how many square units is the figure that they form?

13. Use pentominoes to create a rectangle with 20 square units.

14. Use pentominoes to create a rectangle with 15 square units.

15. If you used all 12 pentominoes to create a figure, how many square units would the figure have?

16. Use pentominoes to create a rectangle with 20 square units that is different from the rectangle you created for Exercise 13.

17. How many square units are in this figure using 5 pentominoes?

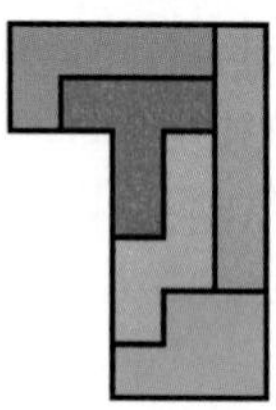

18. Use exactly 4 pentominoes to create this shape.

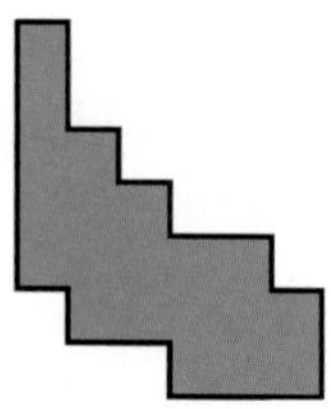

19. How many square units are in this figure using 4 pentominoes?

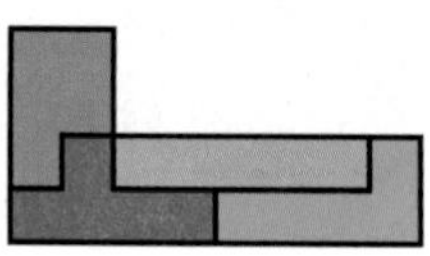

20. Can you make this shape with exactly 2 pentominoes? Explain.

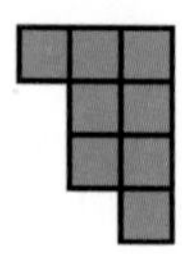

Independent Practice

21. If you remove one square from a pentomino, you have a *tetromino*. How many different tetrominoes are there?

22 Harris has a comic book collection that is worth $600. If it increases in value by 10% each year, how much will it be worth after three years?

23. What 6 pentominoes are used to create this animal?

24. Theo and Elena are planning a rectangular garden and want to build a scale model. The real garden will be 10 times as wide and 10 times as long as the model. How many times larger will the area of the real garden be than the model?

25. It is possible to form a 3 × 20 rectangle with all 12 pentominoes. Here is a start, using 8 of the pentominoes. Can you add the last 4 pentominoes to complete the rectangle?

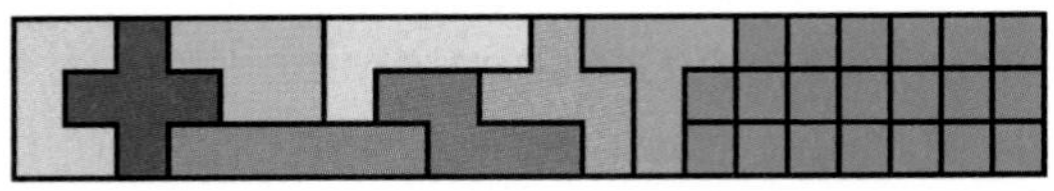

26. Which pentomino has the greatest perimeter? Which has the least?

27. **Writing to Explain** Kyle says that for a rectangle, the larger the perimeter is, the larger the area will be. Is he right? If not, explain why he is wrong.

Think About the Process

28. The Outdoor Club is taking a 6-mile hike. They hike at a rate of 3 miles per hour. Which expression will find how long the whole hike will take?

A 6 miles × 3 miles per hour

B $\frac{\text{6 miles}}{\text{3 miles per hour}}$

C $\frac{\text{3 miles per hour}}{\text{6 miles}}$

D (2 miles × 3 miles per hour) + (4 miles × 2 miles per hour)

29. Juli is planning a bulletin board by making a model. She wants a square with a side of *p* units inside a square with a side of 8 units. Which expression will find the area of the shaded dark blue square?

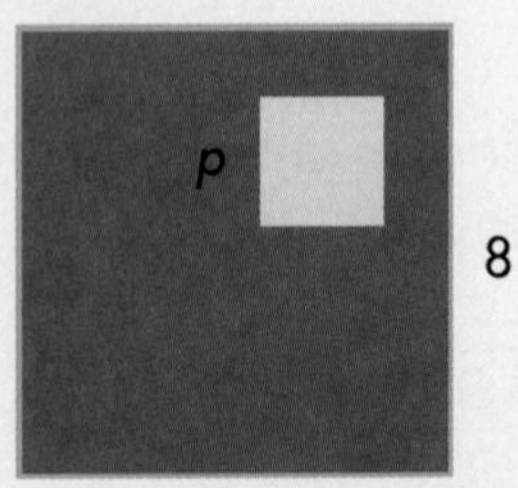

A $64 + 4p$

B $64 - 2p$

C $64 - p^2$

D $64 + p^2$

Going Digital

Circumference and Area of a Circle

Use **e tools**

Geometry Drawing

A sprinkler for watering a lawn sprays water 6 feet from the sprinkler head. What is the circumference of the circle the sprinkler waters? What is the area of the lawn the sprinkler waters?

Step 1 Go to the Geometry Drawing eTool. On the Draw tool palette, click on the button next to the triangle polygon to expand this tool palette. Click on the Circle tool. Click near the center of the workspace to set the center of the circle. Then click on another point.

Step 2 Click on the Distance Measurement tool. Click on point *A*, the center of the circle. Then click on point *B* on the circle. The distance between points *A* and *B* (the radius) should appear in the lower right corner of the workspace. Click on the Arrow tool icon. Then click on point *B* and drag until the radius is close to 6 units. If the circle does not fit in the workspace, use the Arrow tool to drag the center to the middle until it does fit.

Step 3 Click on the Perimeter Measurement tool and then on the circle.

Click on the Area Measurement tool and then on the circle. Are the measures that appear reasonable? A formula for circumference of a circle is $C = \pi(2r)$, so the circumference should be a little more than $3 \times 2 \times 6 = 36$ units. The formula for the area of a circle is πr^2, so the area should be a little more than $3 \times 6^2 = 108$ square units. Use the eTool to answer the questions in the problem above.

Practice

Find the circumference and area of a circle with each radius.

1. $r = 5$ units **2.** $r = 3$ units **3.** $r = 4.5$ units **4.** $r = 1$ units

Topic 17 Test

1. Caroline is framing a rectangular picture that measures 8 inches by 10 inches. Which of the following can be used to find the perimeter of the picture? (17-1)

A $P = 2(8) \times 2(10)$

B $P = 2(8) + 2(10)$

C $P = 2(8) - 2(10)$

D $P = 8 \times 10$

2. Two squares are arranged as shown. Which of the following can be used to find the area of the yellow square? (17-2)

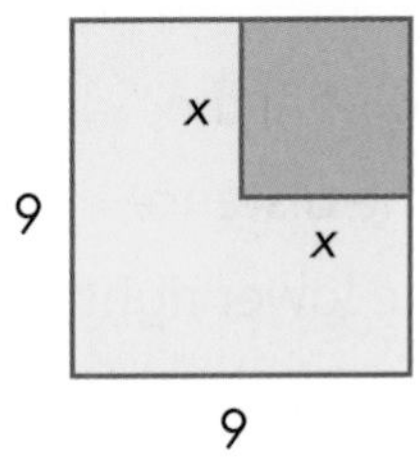

A $9^2 - x^2$

B $(9 - x)^2$

C $2(9) + 2(9 - x)$

D $9^2 + x^2$

3. What is the perimeter of the figure shown? (17-1)

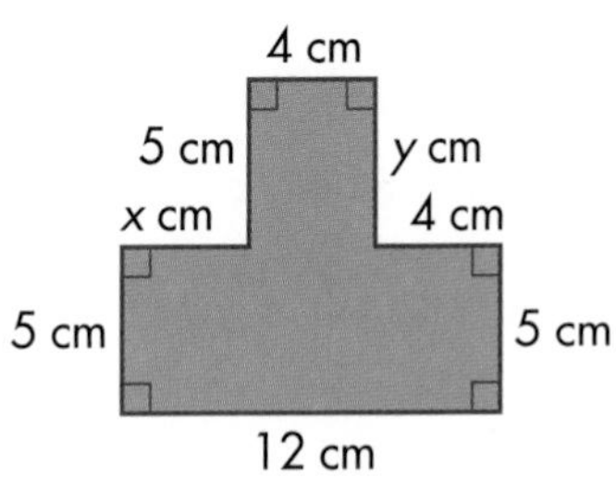

A 35 cm

B 40 cm

C 44 cm

D 120 cm

4. Which equation can be used to find A, the area of the parallelogram shown, in square meters? (17-3)

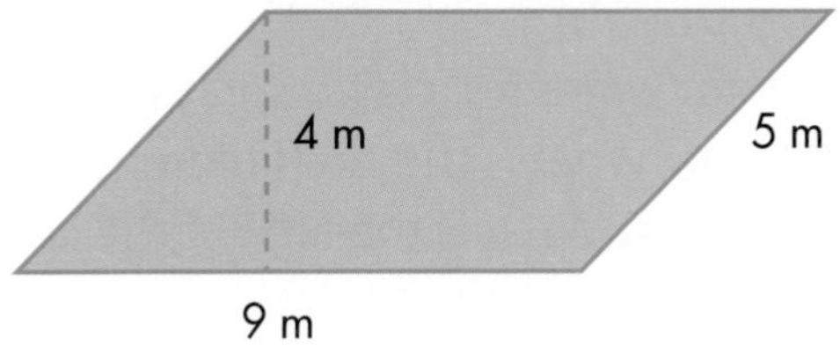

A $A = 5 \times 9$

B $A = 4 \times 9$

C $A = \frac{1}{2} \times 5 \times 9$

D $A = \frac{1}{2} \times 4 \times 9$

5. Which of the following can be used to find the area of the clock? (17-5)

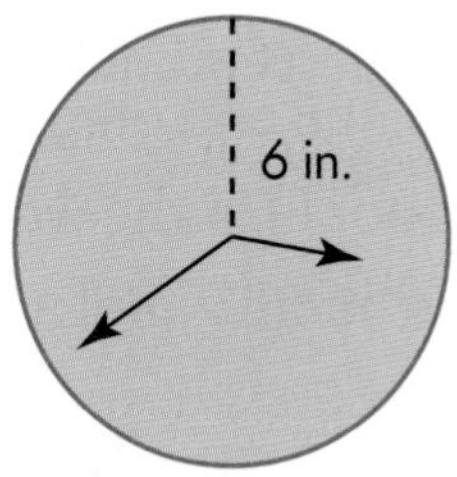

A $A = 3.14 \times 3$

B $A = 3.14 \times 6$

C $A = 3.14 \times 12$

D $A = 3.14 \times 36$

6. What is the area of a square flower bed if one side has a length of 8 feet? (17-2)

A 16 square feet

B 24 square feet

C 32 square feet

D 64 square feet

7. A community painted a stripe around the tank on the water tower in their town as shown. Which is closest to the length of the stripe? (17-4)

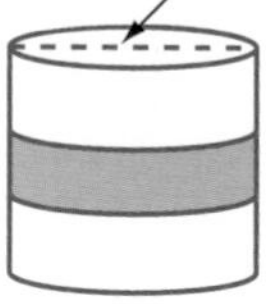

A 18.86 yards

B 37.68 yards

C 113.14 yards

D 452.57 yards

8. What is the approximate area of a circle whose radius is 2 cm? (17-5)

A 6.28 square centimeters

B 12.14 centimeters

C 12.56 square centimeters

D 39.44 square centimeters

9. Which of the following can be used to find the circumference of the dinner plate shown? (17-4)

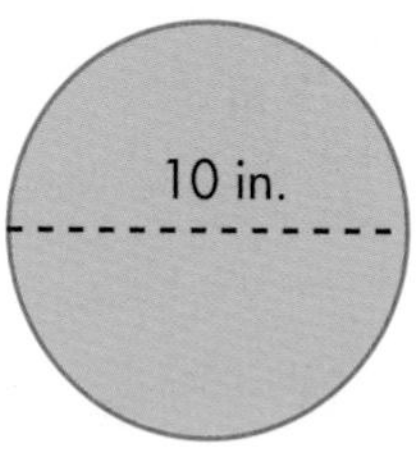

A $C = 100 \times \pi$

B $C = 25 \times \pi$

C $C = 10 \times \pi$

D $C = 5 \times \pi$

10. If the perimeter of the rectangle shown is 18 millimeters, which equation can be used to find n? (17-1)

A $18 = 6 + 2n$

B $18 = 6 + n$

C $18 = 12 - 2n$

D $18 = 12 + 2n$

11. Mr. Aufleger is painting the gable of his house which is triangular shaped. If the base of the triangle is 16 feet and the height is 6 feet, what is the area of the gable? (17-3)

A 24 square feet

B 44 square feet

C 48 square feet

D 96 square feet

12. If each square of a pentomino represents a table that seats one person on each side, which of the following will NOT seat 12 people? (17-6)

A 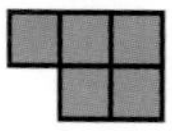

B 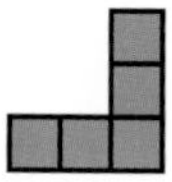

C 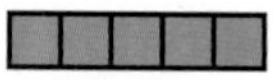

D 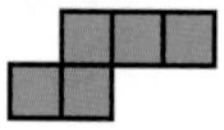

Reteaching

Set A, pages 426–428

Find the perimeter of the shapes below.

The perimeter is the distance around a polygon.

For a regular hexagon:
$6 \times 13 = 78$ cm

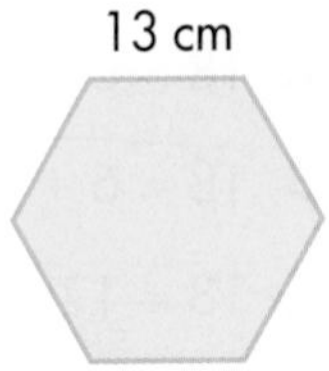

For a parallelogram:
$(2 \times 20) + (2 \times 12) = 64$ in.

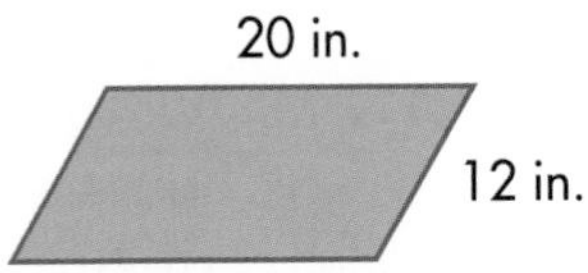

For an irregular polygon:
$5 + 3 + 1 + 10 + 6 +$
$4 + 10 + 17 = 56$ yd

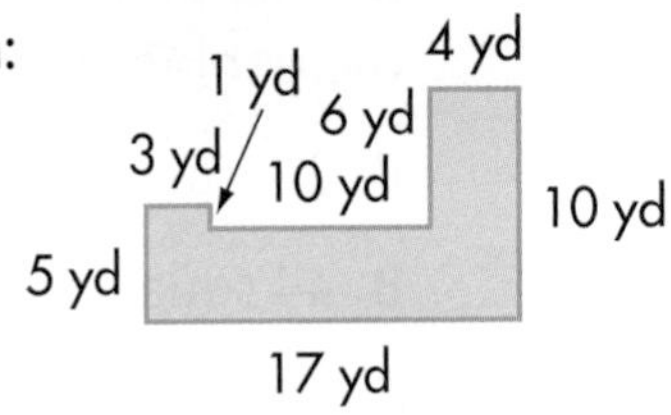

Remember that you can use what you know about geometric shapes to find unknown sides.

Find the perimeter.

1.

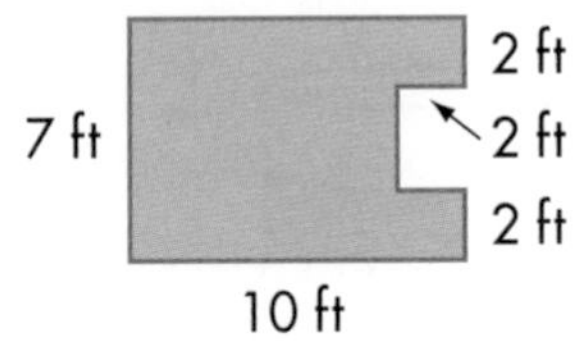

2.

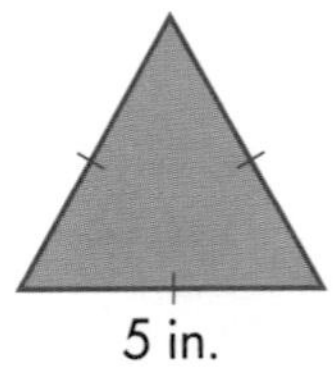

3. A rhombus with side lengths of 14 cm

4. A rectangle with width 8 in. and length 2 in.

Set B, pages 430–436

Use these formulas to find the area of each figure.

Rectangles: $A = \ell \times w$

Parallelograms: $A = b \times h$

Triangles: $A = \frac{1}{2} b \times h$

$A = \ell \times w$
$A = 18 \times 12$
$A = 216 \text{ m}^2$

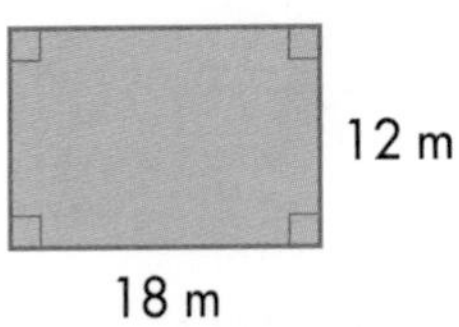

$A = b \times h$
$A = 12 \times 8$
$A = 96 \text{ ft}^2$

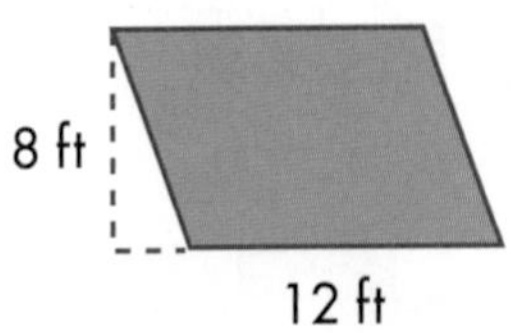

$A = \frac{1}{2} b \times h$

$A = \frac{1}{2}(26) \times 20$

$A = 260 \text{ cm}^2$

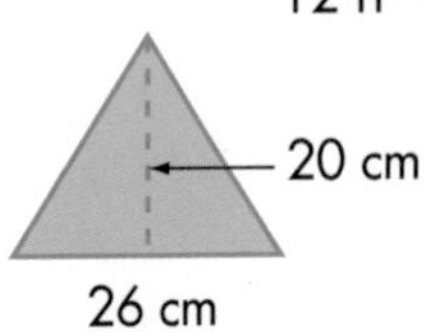

Remember that areas are measured in square units.

Find the area.

1.

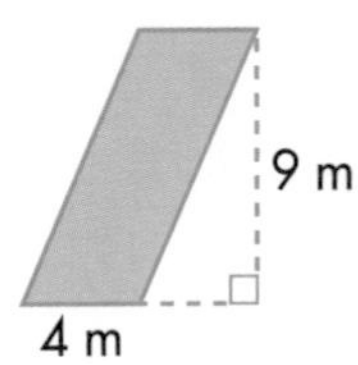

2.

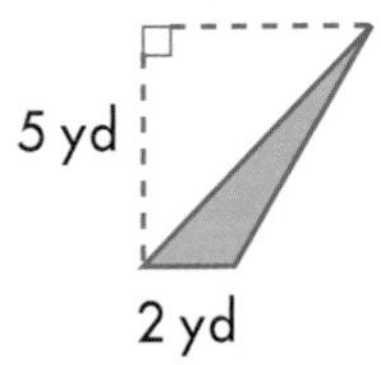

3.

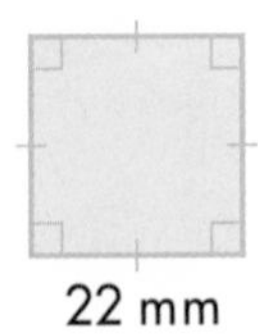

4.

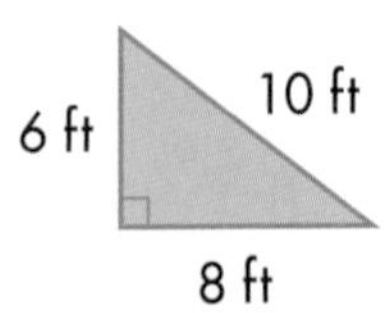

5. If the square in Exercise 3 were divided diagonally into two triangles, what would be the heights of the triangles?

Set C, pages 438–440, 442–443

Use a formula to find the circumference and area. Use both 3.14 and $\frac{22}{7}$ for π.

Circumference

$C = \pi d$ or $C = 2\pi r$

Since the radius is shown, use the second formula.

$C = 2 \times 4 \times 3.14 = 25.12$ ft

$C = 2 \times 4 \times \frac{22}{7} = 25\frac{1}{7}$ ft

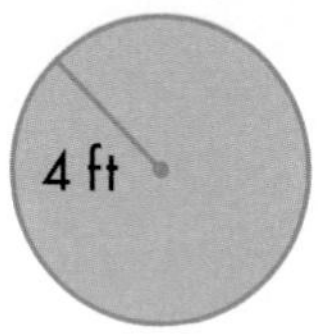

Area

$A = \pi r^2$

$A = 3.14 \times 4 \times 4 = 50.24\ \text{ft}^2$

$A = \frac{22}{7} \times 4 \times 4 = 50\frac{2}{7}\ \text{ft}^2$

Remember that the units for area are square units.

Find the missing measurements. Use 3.14 or $\frac{22}{7}$. Round to the nearest whole number.

1. $d =$ □
   $r = 5$ m
   $C =$ □
   $A =$ □

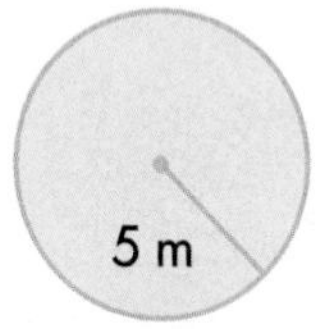

2. $d = 3$ in.
   $r =$ □
   $C =$ □
   $A =$ □

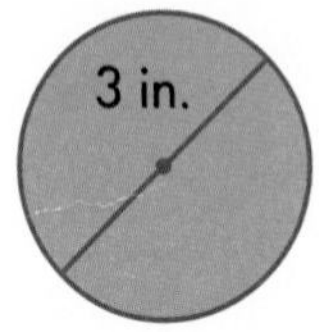

Set D, pages 444–446

A pentomino is a shape made of 5 squares. Each square in a pentomino shares at least one side with another square.

The figure above is made up of 5 squares. Each square shares at least one side with another square. This figure is a pentomino.

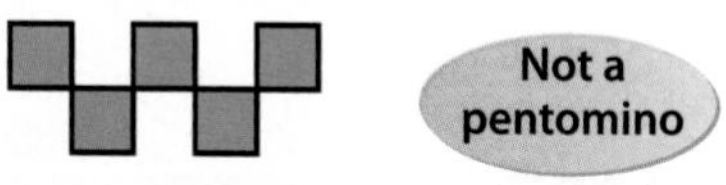

The figure above is made up of 5 squares, but each square does not share at least one side with another square. This figure is not a pentomino.

Remember that a pentomino has an area of 5 square units.

1. Which of these figures is <u>not</u> a pentomino?

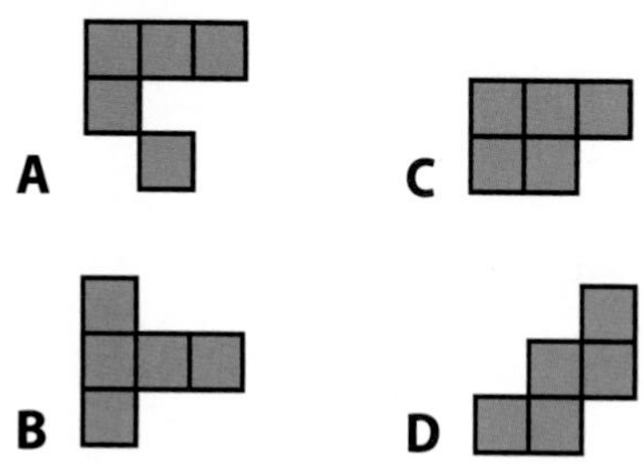

2. How many pentominoes would make this figure?

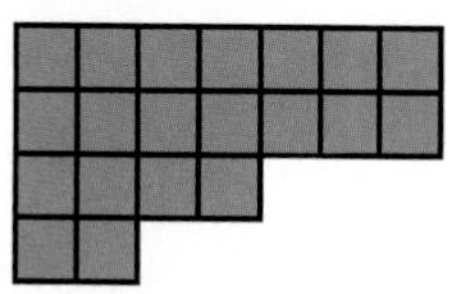

3. Can this shape be made using exactly 3 pentominoes? Explain.

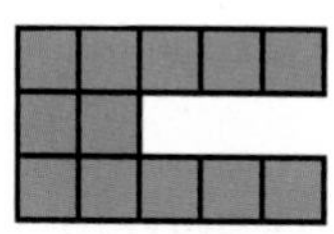

Topic 18

Volume and Surface Area

1

This Ice Hotel is built entirely out of ice and snow. What is the volume of the blocks that are used to build this temporary hotel? You will find out in Lesson 18-3.

How could you classify the shape of this bar of solid gold? You will find out in Lesson 18-1.

2

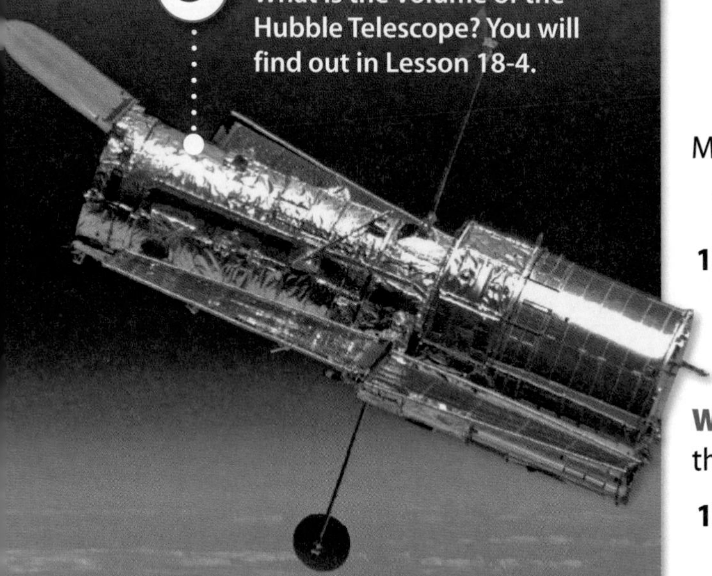

3

What is the volume of the Hubble Telescope? You will find out in Lesson 18-4.

Review What You Know!

Vocabulary

Choose the best term from the box.

- area
- perimeter
- radius

1. The surface of a figure covers the figure's __?__.
2. The distance around the outside of a polygon is its __?__.
3. One-half of the diameter of a circle is the circle's __?__.

Area

Find the area of each figure.

4. A rectangle with dimensions 4 ft × 7 ft
5. A triangle with a base 14 in. long and a height of 9 in.
6. A square with a side 3 m long

Operations

Multiply or divide.

7. 16×6 **8.** 3×42 **9.** $216 \div 3$

10. $364 \div 14$ **11.** 4.75×2.5 **12.** $128 \div 4$

Formulas

Writing to Explain Write an answer for the question.

13. How is finding the area of a triangle different from finding the area of a rectangle?

Lesson

18-1

Understand It!
Solids can be described and classified by their properties.

Solid Figures

How are polyhedrons classified?

A polyhedron is a three-dimensional figure made of flat polygon-shaped surfaces called faces. The line segment where two faces intersect is called an edge. The point where several edges meet is called a vertex.

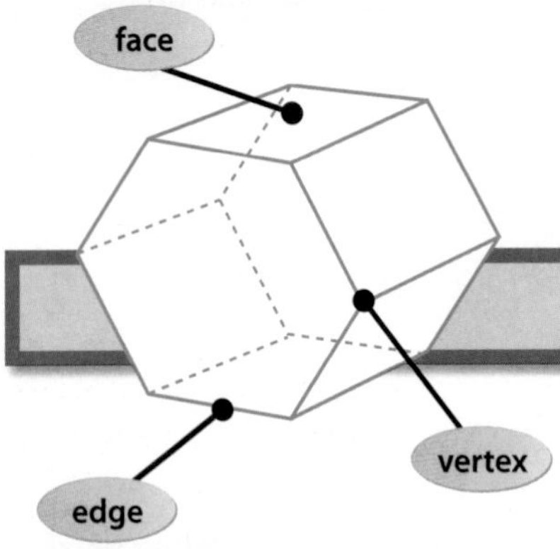

Another Example How are three-dimensional figures with curved surfaces classified?

Some three-dimensional figures are not polyhedrons.

Cylinder

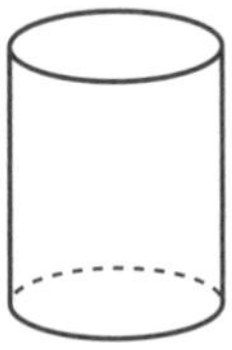

A cylinder has two circular bases that are parallel and congruent.

Sphere

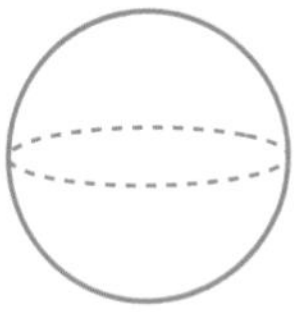

A sphere has no base. Every point on a sphere is the same distance from the center.

Cone

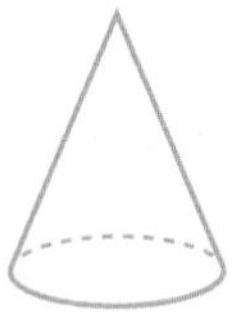

A cone has one circular base. The points on this circle are joined to one point outside the base.

Explain It

1. Why is a cylinder NOT a polyhedron?
2. What is the shape of the face of a cylinder that connects to the two bases?
3. How are a cylinder, a sphere, and a cone alike and different?

Prisms

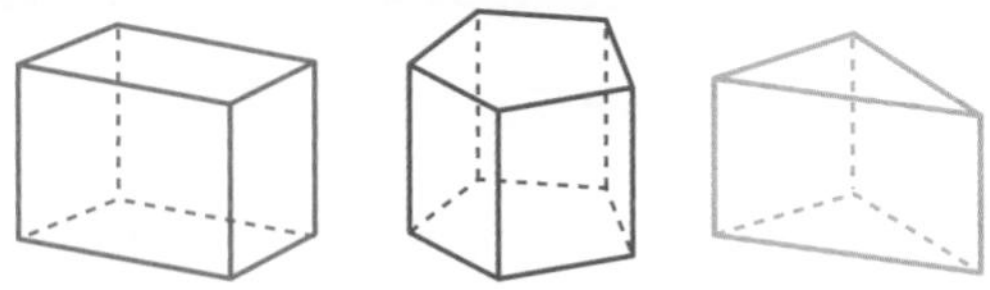

Rectangular prism | Pentagonal prism | Triangular prism

A prism is a polyhedron with two congruent, parallel, polygon-shaped bases. A prism is named by the shape of its bases. The other faces are parallelograms.

Pyramids

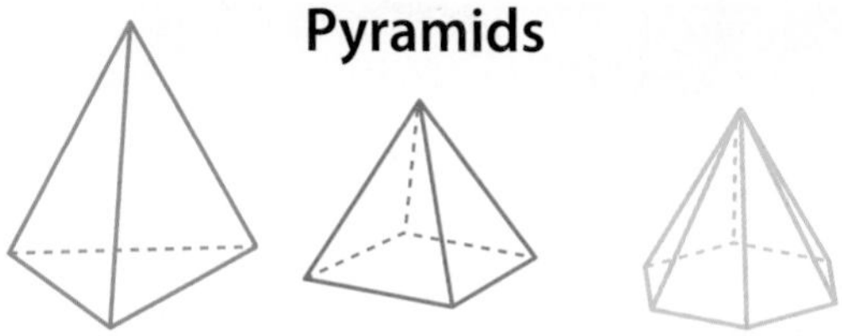

Triangular pyramid | Rectangular pyramid | Hexagonal pyramid

A pyramid is a polyhedron that has one base. A pyramid is named by the shape of its base. Triangular faces join the edges of the base to a point outside the base, which is called a vertex.

Another Example

How can you identify a solid from its net?

A net is a plane figure pattern which, when folded, makes a solid.

Think about unfolding a box to make a net for a rectangular prism.

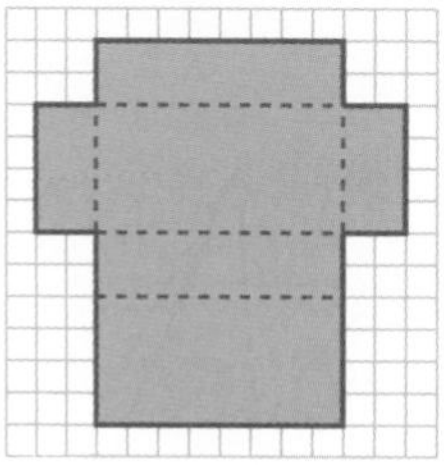

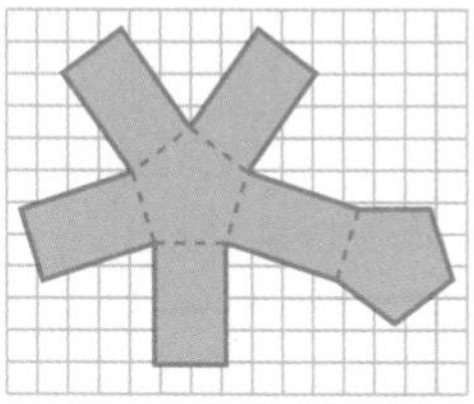

The net shows 2 congruent pentagonal bases and 5 rectangular sides, so it represents a pentagonal prism.

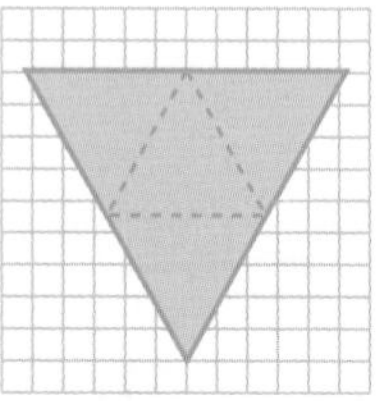

The net shows a triangular base and 3 triangular faces, so it represents a triangular pyramid.

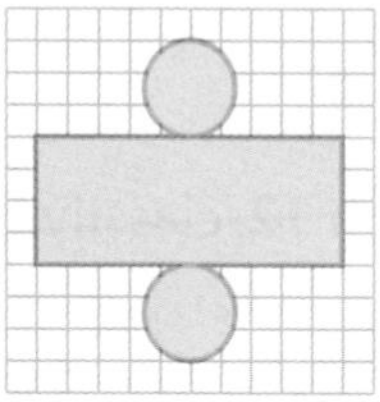

The net shows a rectangle and 2 circular faces that appear to be parallel and congruent, so it represents a cylinder.

Explain It

1. What solid figures are represented by the two nets shown below?

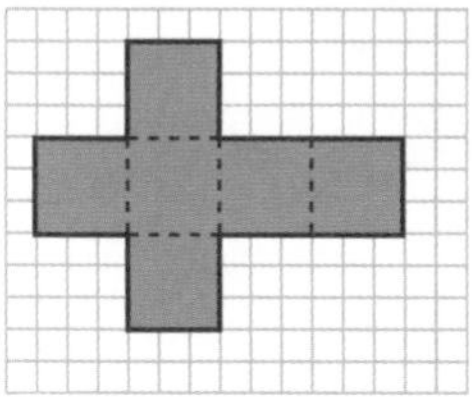

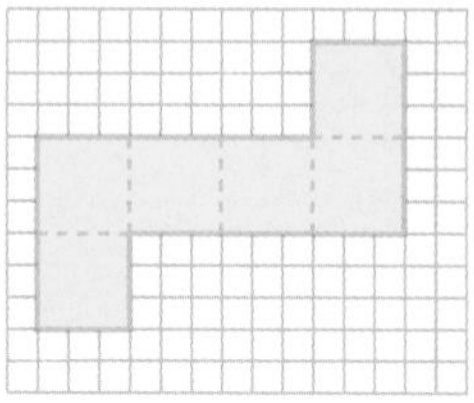

DIGITAL Animated Glossary **www.pearsonsuccessnet.com**

Guided Practice*

Do you know HOW?

Classify each polyhedron. Name all faces (including bases), edges, and vertices.

1.

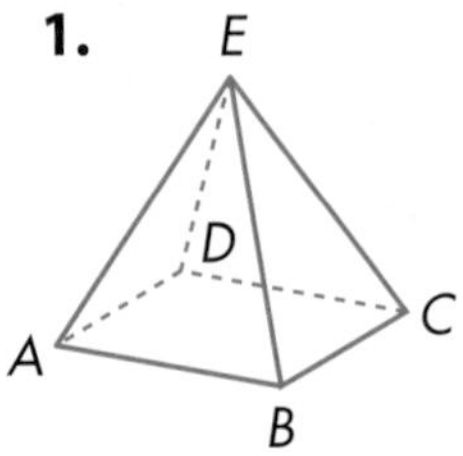

2.

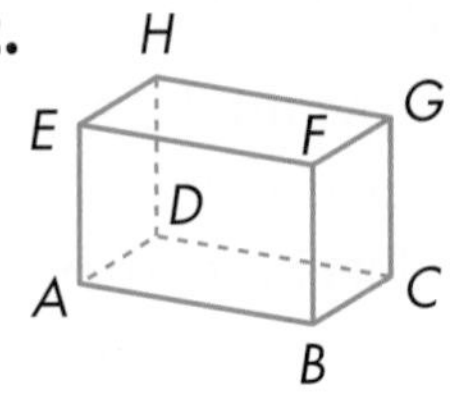

Do you UNDERSTAND?

3. Explain the difference between a vertex and an edge.

4. Explain the difference between a pyramid and a prism.

5. What would you look for if you were classifying polyhedrons?

Independent Practice

For **6** through **8**, classify each polyhedron. Name all vertices, edges, faces, and bases.

6.

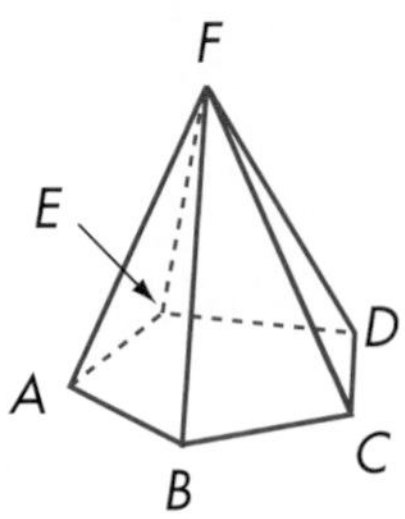

7.

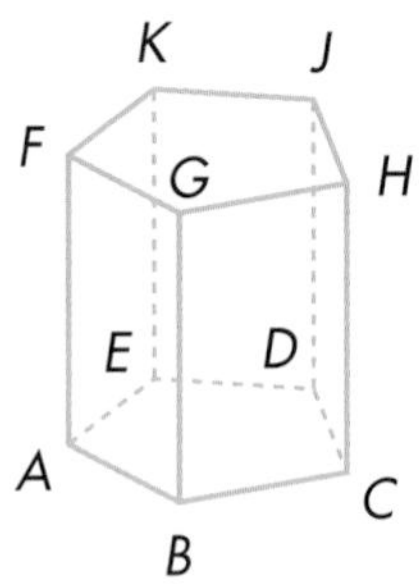

8.

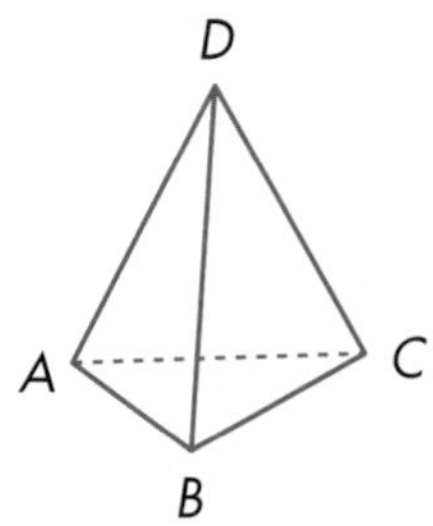

For **9** through **12**, classify each figure.

9.

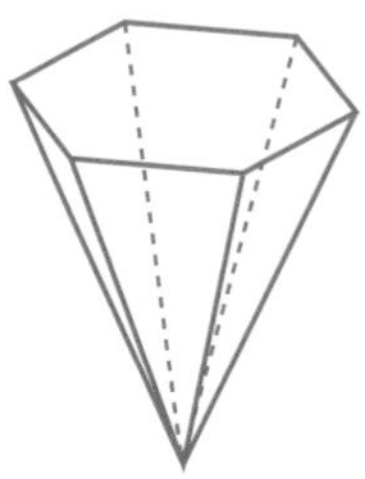

10.

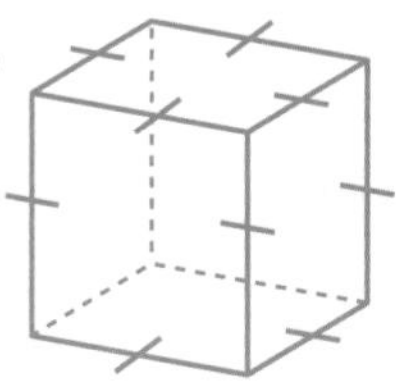

11.

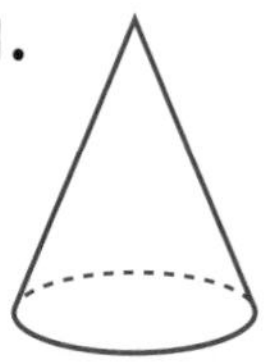

12.

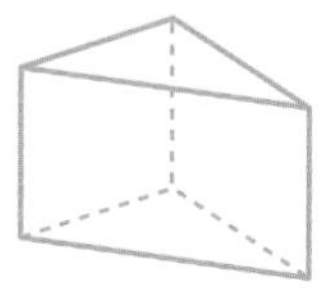

For **13** through **15**, identify each solid from its net.

13.

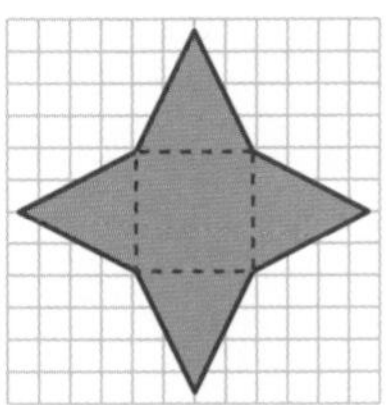

14.

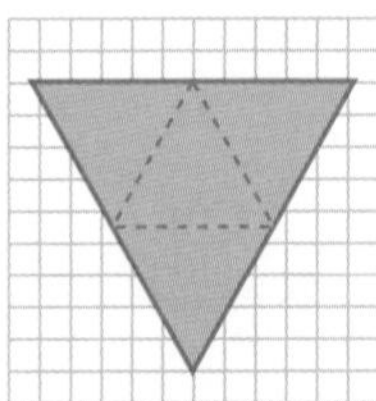

15.

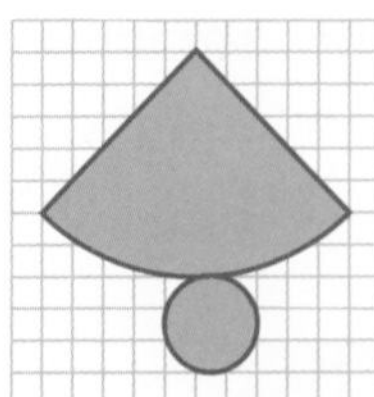

*For another example, see Set A on page 472.

Problem Solving

Use the information in the chart for **16** through **18**.

Data

	Price for 1	Price for 5	Price for 1 dozen
Pencils	$0.10	$0.45	$0.80
Pens	$0.25	$1.00	$2.25
Paper	$0.05	$0.20	$0.50
Folder	$0.50	$2.00	$5.00

16. Mrs. Stanford wants to buy supplies for the classroom. She would like to purchase 2 dozen pencils, 4 dozen pieces of paper, 24 pens, and 17 folders. What is her total cost?

17. If a student wants to buy 21 pencils, how much would they cost?

A $2.10 **B** $1.65 **C** $1.90 **D** $1.50

18. Suzette wants to buy 15 folders. Find the price if she buys them individually, in groups of 5, or as a dozen with 3 singles. Which way does she save the most money?

Use the table at right for **19** through **22**.

Polyhedron	Faces (*F*)	Vertices (*V*)	*F* + *V*	Edges (*E*)
Trianglar Pyramid				
Cube				
Pentagonal Prism				

19. The Swiss mathematician Leonhard Euler (OY-ler) and the French mathematician Rene Descartes (dā KART) both discovered a pattern in the numbers of edges, vertices, and faces of polyhedrons. Complete the table to look for a pattern.

20. **Number Sense** Describe any pattern you see in the table that relates the number of edges to the number of faces and vertices.

21. **Algebra** Write a formula to describe your pattern. Does the pattern work for a hexagonal prism?

22. **Writing to Explain** If a rectangular prism has 12 edges and 6 faces, how could you use a formula to find the number of vertices the figure has?

23. Classify the shape of this bar of gold. How many faces does it have? How many vertices? How many edges?

24. **Writing to Explain** Why are the faces on a pyramid triangular, regardless of the shape of its base?

25. An octagonal pyramid has 9 faces and 9 vertices. How many edges does it have?

A 9 **B** 16 **C** 18 **D** 20

Independent Practice

For **9** through **11**, find the surface area of each figure.

9.

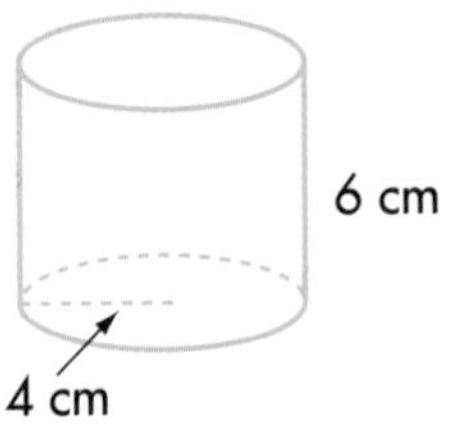

10.

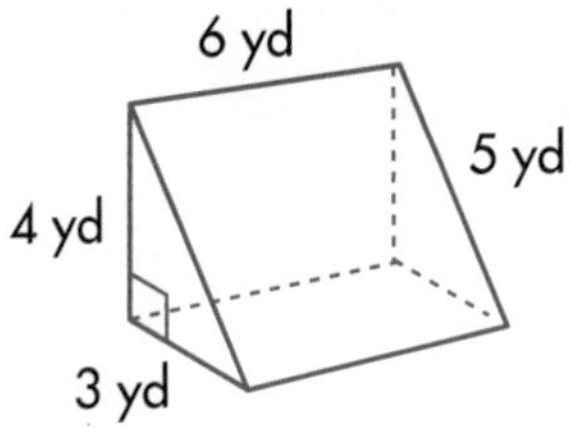

11.

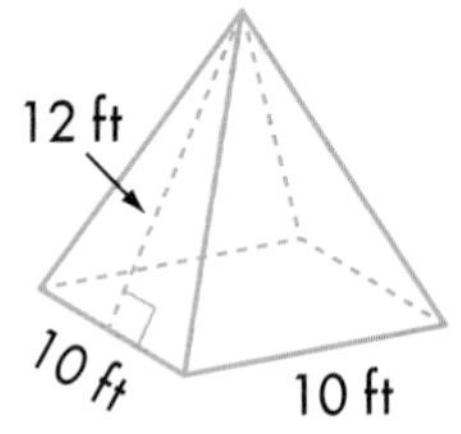

Problem Solving

12. Mr. and Mrs. Hernandez have a pool in their backyard with a length of 32 feet and a width of 16 feet. They want to purchase a cover for the pool. If the cover needs to be 2 feet longer and 2 feet wider than the pool, what will be the perimeter of the cover?

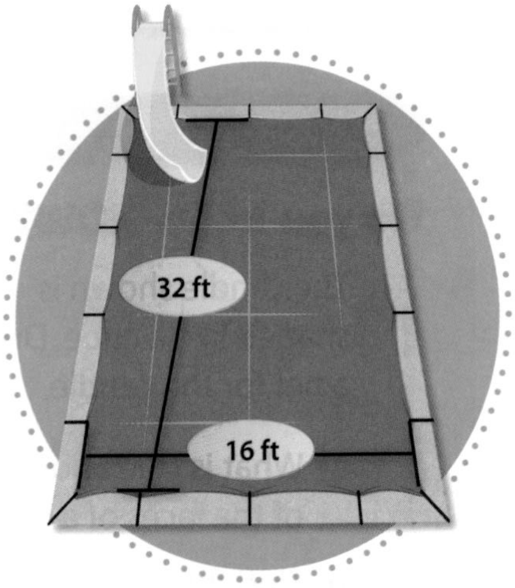

13. What is the area of Mr. and Mrs. Hernandez's pool cover?

14. Fred listened to the weather report in the afternoon. The meteorologist said that the temperature had risen 25°F from the early morning temperature of −12°F. What was the afternoon temperature?

A 37°F **B** 13°F **C** −37°F **D** −13°F

15. Mia wants to use brown paper to cover a ballot box for the student council election. The box is 18 inches long, 15 inches wide, and 12 inches tall. How many square inches of paper will Mia need?

The table shows the dimensions of three colors of tiles. Use the table for **16** through **19**.

Data

Color	Tile Size	Area
Black	4 in. × 4 in.	
Red	2 in. × 2 in.	
Green	8 in. × 8 in.	

16. Fill in the area of each color tile.

17. Miriam wants to tile the surface of a rectangular storage case that is 24 inches long, 16 inches wide, and 8 inches tall. If she uses all green tiles, how many tiles will she need?

18. If Miriam uses all black tiles, how many tiles will she need?

19. How many red tiles have the same area as 6 green tiles?

A 24 **B** 96 **C** 16 **D** 32

Algebra Connections

Is It a Function?

A function is a special relationship in which there is only one *y*-value for each *x*-value.

Tell whether each set of ordered pairs is a function.

Example:

Think *x-values −2, −1, and 2 only have one y-value.*

Function

x	−2	−1	2
y	0	1	4

Not a function

The *x*-value −2 has more than one *y*-value.

x	−2	−1	−2
y	−4	−2	4

1.

x	−4	−2	0	3
y	4	6	8	11

2.

x	−1	0	−1	0
y	2	3	−2	−3

3.

x	2	2	2	2
y	−1	1	−4	4

4.

x	−3	−2	2	4
y	−2	1	13	19

For **5** and **6**, copy and complete the tables to solve the problems.

5. Jess is going bowling with his friends. He is making a table showing how much they will pay for the games. Find the missing values in the table and write a rule that fits the pattern.

6. Janice is planning a trip. She is making a table to show how many miles she can travel. Complete the table and write a rule that fits the pattern.

Data

Games	Price
1	$0.75
2	
3	$2.25
4	
5	$3.75
6	

Data

Gallons of Gas	Miles
1	28
4	112
5.5	154
6.5	
7	
8.5	
10	

7. The drama club is going to see a play. If the club has $110 for the trip and tickets cost $13.50 each, how many members can attend the play? Make a function table to find the group cost for 1 to 10 members.

Lesson
18-3

Understand It!
What you know about area can help you find the volume of some figures.

Volume of Rectangular Prisms

How can you determine the volume of a rectangular prism?

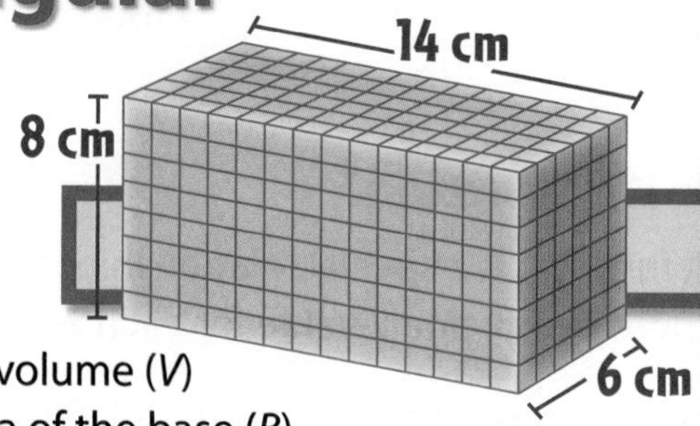

Volume is the number of cubic units needed to fill a solid figure. To find the volume (V) of a rectangular prism, multiply the area of the base (B) by the height (h) of the figure. Use the formula $V = B \times h$.

Guided Practice*

Do you know HOW?

Find the volume of each rectangular prism.

1. 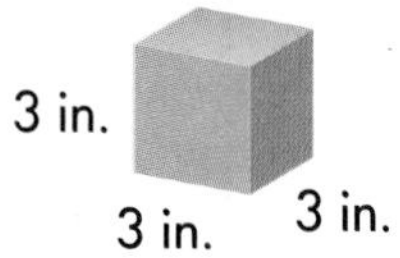

2. 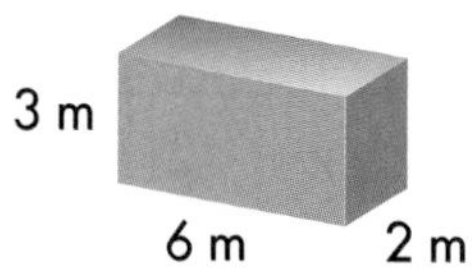

3. 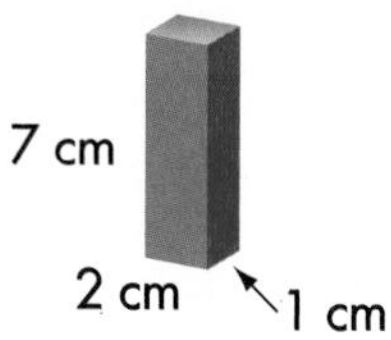

4. 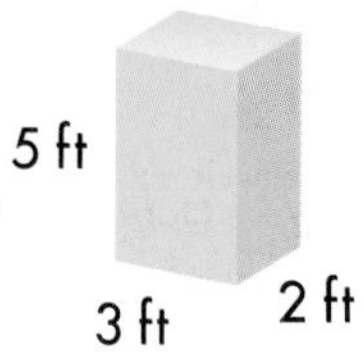

Do you UNDERSTAND?

5. If you know the area of the base and the volume of a rectangular prism, how can you find the height?

6. If you turned the rectangular prism from the example above on one side, how would your formula change? Would the volume change?

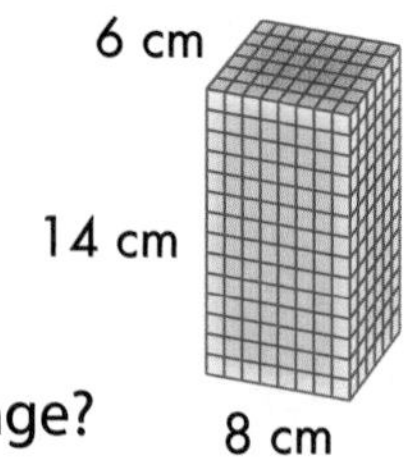

Independent Practice

Leveled Practice In **7** through **10**, find the volume of each rectangular prism.

7. 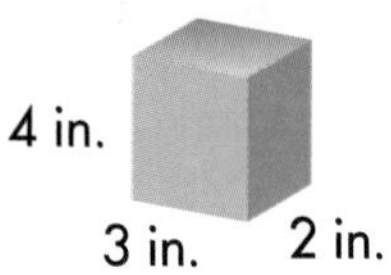

$V = B \times h$
$V = 6\text{ in}^2 \times$ ☐
$V =$ ☐

8. 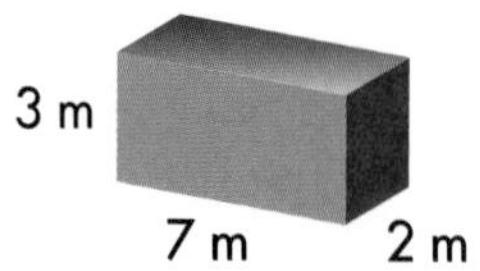

$V = B \times h$

9. 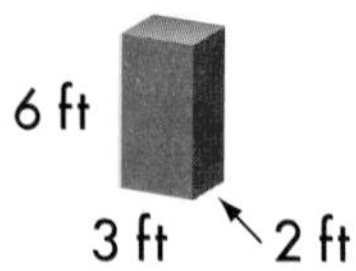

10. 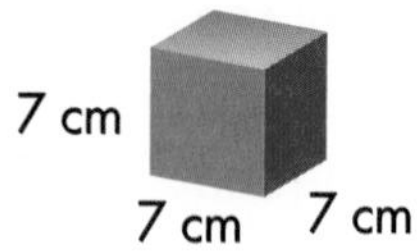

DIGITAL
Animated Glossary
www.pearsonsuccessnet.com

For another example, see Set C on page 473.

Step 1

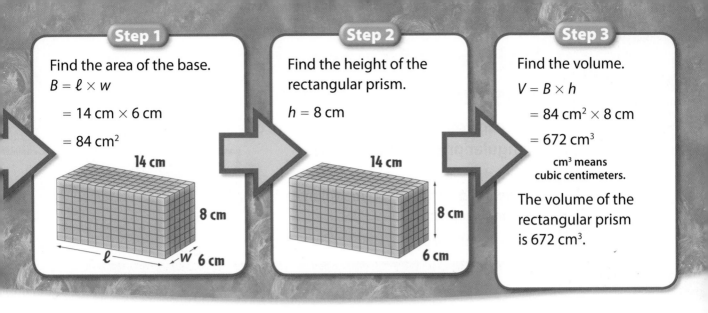

Find the area of the base.

$B = \ell \times w$

$= 14 \text{ cm} \times 6 \text{ cm}$

$= 84 \text{ cm}^2$

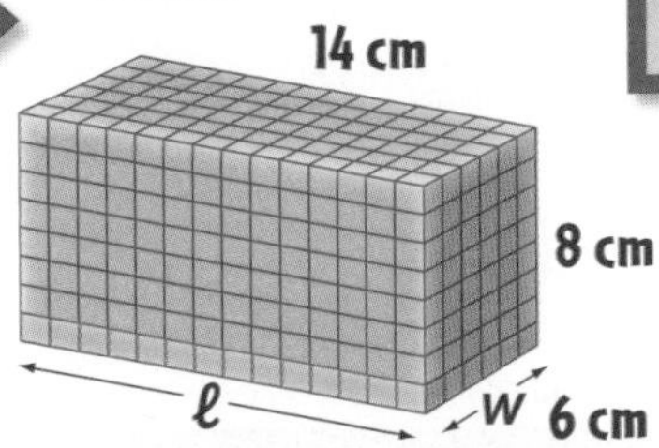

Step 2

Find the height of the rectangular prism.

$h = 8 \text{ cm}$

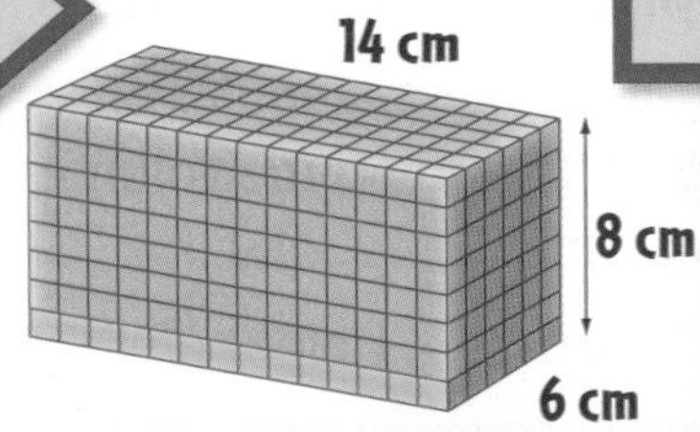

Step 3

Find the volume.

$V = B \times h$

$= 84 \text{ cm}^2 \times 8 \text{ cm}$

$= 672 \text{ cm}^3$

cm^3 means cubic centimeters.

The volume of the rectangular prism is 672 cm^3.

In **11** through **13**, find the missing value for each rectangular prism.

11. Volume: 56 in^3
Length: 4 in.
Width: 7 in.
Height:

12. Volume: 144 ft^3
Length:
Width: 9 ft
Height: 4 ft

13. Volume: 240 ft^3
Length: 8 ft
Width:
Height: 6 ft

Problem Solving

14. How many cubic inches are in one cubic foot?

15. Would 150 cm^3 of sand fit inside a $4 \text{ cm} \times 3 \text{ cm} \times 10 \text{ cm}$ rectangular prism?

16. **Writing to Explain** Why can the formula for the volume of a rectangular prism also be written as $V = \ell \times w \times h$?

17. **Think About the Process** Which of these equations gives the volume of a cube?

A $V = 16 \times 4$ **C** $V = 9 \times 4$

B $V = 8 \times 2$ **D** $V = 12 \times 6$

18. Suppose the blocks of ice used to build the rooms of the Ice Hotel are $4 \text{ ft} \times 4 \text{ ft} \times 5 \text{ ft}$. What is the volume of a block of ice?

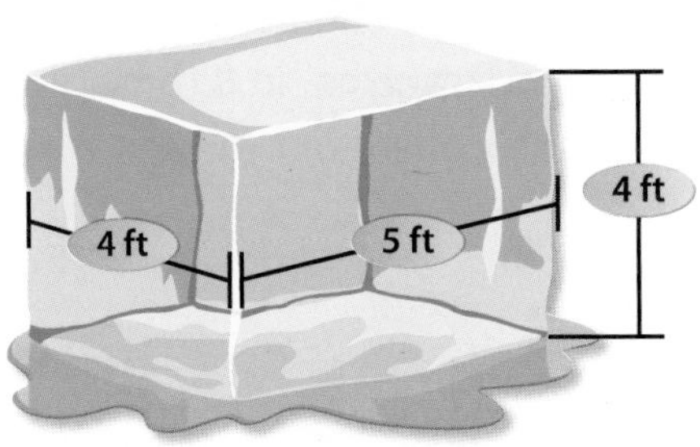

19. **Number Sense** Consider a rectangular prism that measures $3 \text{ cm} \times 2 \text{ cm} \times 6 \text{ cm}$.

a Will the actual volume of the rectangular prism change if you measure the sides in inches rather than centimeters? Explain.

b Does the numerical volume change if you measure the sides in inches? Explain.

Lesson
18-4

Understand It!
What you know about area can help you find the volume of some figures.

Volume of Triangular Prisms and Cylinders

How can you determine the volume of triangular prisms and cylinders?

Finding the volume of a triangular prism or cylinder is similar to finding the volume of a rectangular prism.

Volume = Area of Base × Height or $V = B \times h$

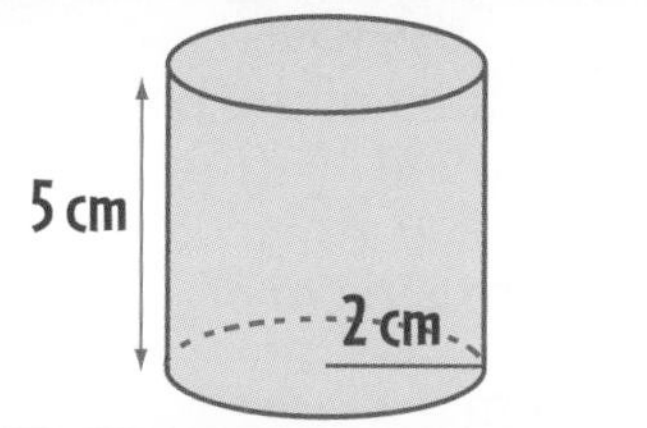

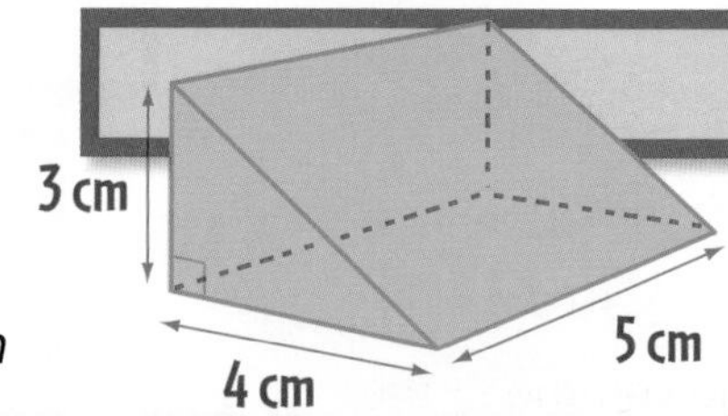

Guided Practice*

Do you know HOW?

Find the volume of each triangular prism.

1. 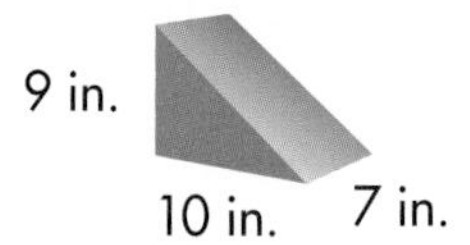

2. 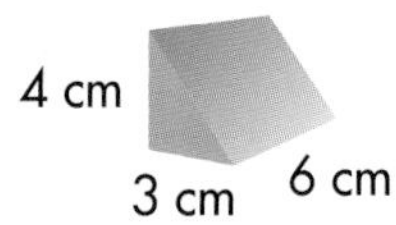

Find the volume of each cylinder. Use 3.14 as an approximation for π.

3. 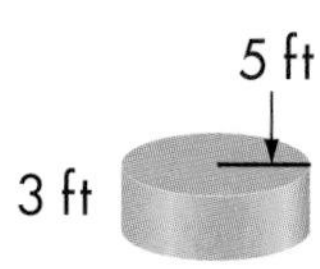

4. 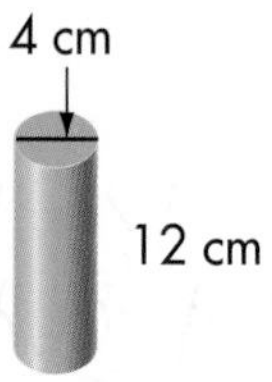

Do you UNDERSTAND?

5. How is finding the volume of a triangular prism similar to finding the volume of a rectangular prism?

6. Compare the volume of the triangular prism shown above to the volume of a rectangle prism that is 4 cm long, 3 cm wide, and 5 cm tall.

7. When computing volume, how is the formula for finding the area of the base for a cylinder different from finding the area of the base of a rectangular prism?

Independent Practice

Leveled Practice In **8** through **11**, find the volume of each triangular prism or cylinder.

8. 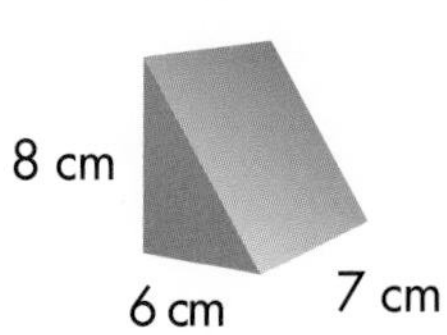

$V = B \times h$

$V = 24 \times$ ▢

9. 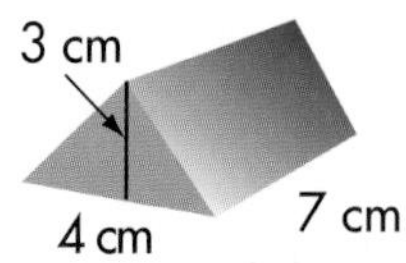

$V = B \times h$

10. 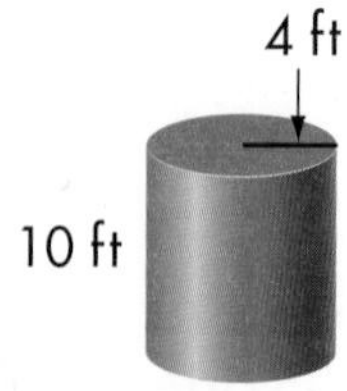

11. 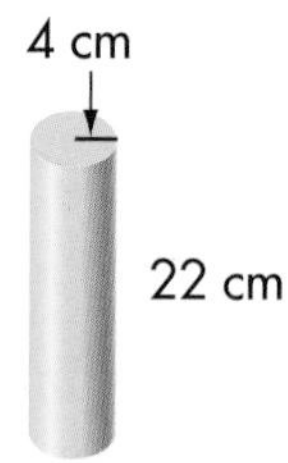

*For another example, see Set C on page 473.

Triangular Prism

The base is a triangle. Use the area of the triangle (B) to find the volume.

$$V = B \times h$$

$$V = (\tfrac{1}{2} \times 3 \text{ cm} \times 4 \text{ cm}) \times 5 \text{ cm}$$

$$V = 6 \text{ cm}^2 \times 5 \text{ cm}$$

$$V = 30 \text{ cm}^3$$

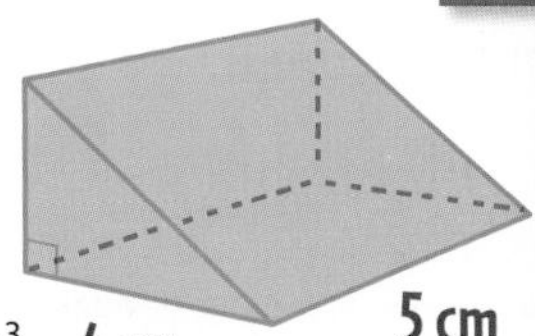

The volume of the triangular prism is 30 cm^3.

Cylinder

The base is a circle. Use the area of the circle (B) to find the volume.

$$V = B \times h$$

$$V = [3.14 \times (2 \text{ cm})^2] \times 5$$ **Use 3.14 for π.**

$$V = (3.14 \times 4 \text{ cm}^2) \times 5$$

$$V = 12.56 \text{ cm}^2 \times 5$$

$$V = 62.8 \text{ cm}^3$$

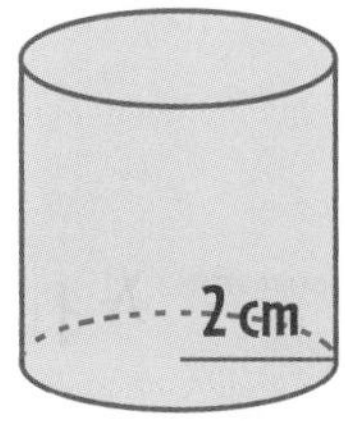

The volume of this cylinder is 62.8 cm^3.

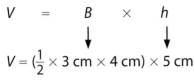

In **12** and **13**, find the missing value.

12. Volume of triangular prism: 56 in^3
Length of base: 4 in.
Height of base: 7 in.
Height of the prism: ☐

13. Volume of a cylinder: 113.04 ft^3
Radius of base: ☐
Height of the cylinder: 4 ft

Problem Solving

14. The Hubble Telescope was launched in 1990. The telescope is shaped like a cylinder and measures 15.9 m long with a diameter of 4.2 m. To the nearest cubic meter, what is the volume of the Hubble Telescope?

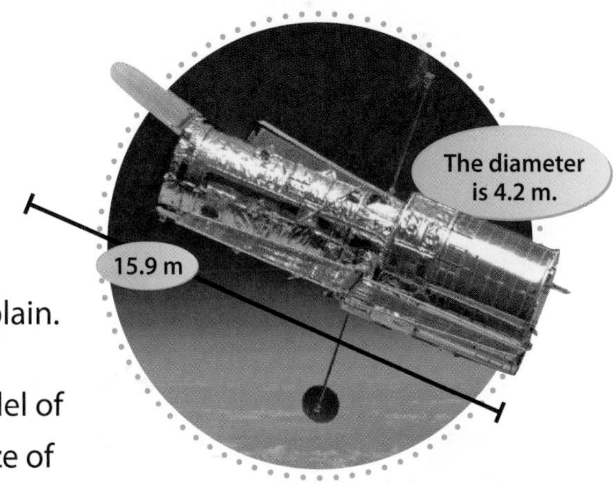

15. Writing to Explain If you double the radius of a cylinder, will the volume also double? Explain.

16. Number Sense Kesuki is making a scale model of the Hubble Telescope that is $\frac{1}{100}$ the actual size of the telescope.

a What is the length in centimeters of Kesuki's model?

b What is the radius in centimeters of the model?

17. A triangular prism is 5 inches tall. The triangular bases are 6 inches long and 6 inches high. What is the volume of the prism?

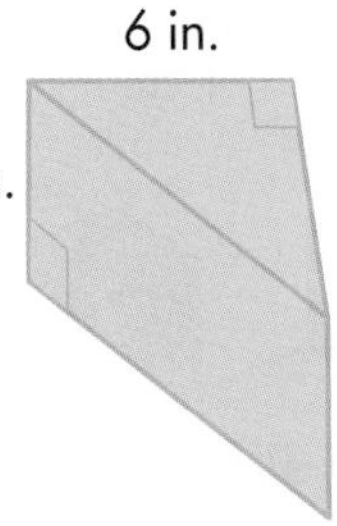

A 90 in^2 **B** 180 in^2 **C** 90 in^3 **D** 180 in^3

Lesson

18-5

Understand It! Some problems can be solved by using objects to model the problem and by using reasoning in the problem.

Problem Solving

Hands-On
unit cubes

Use Objects and Reasoning

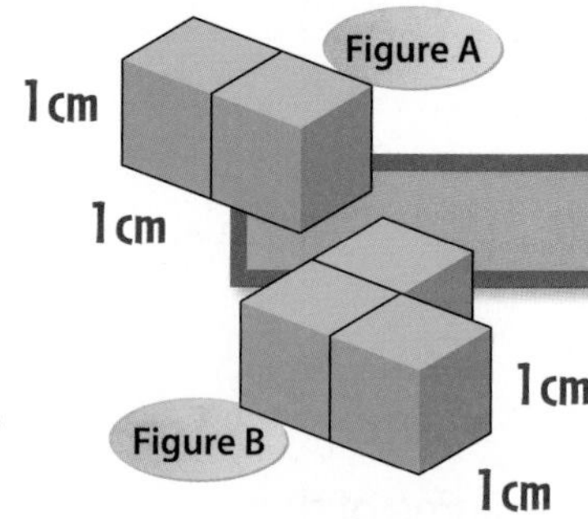

Figure A has a volume of 2 cubic centimeters (cm^3). It has a surface area of 10 square centimeters (cm^2).

Find the volume and surface area of Figure B.

Then use cubes to make a figure with a volume of 4 cm^3 and a surface area of 18 cm^2.

Guided Practice*

Do you know HOW?

1.

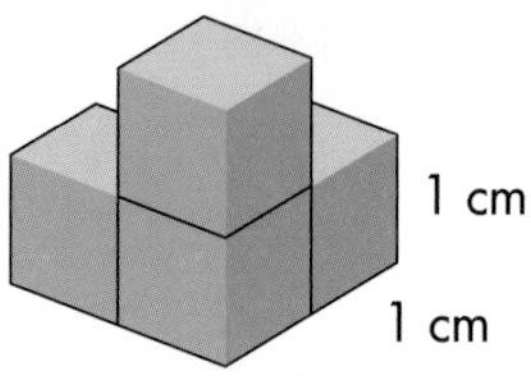

a What is the volume of this solid?

b What is the surface area of this solid?

Do you UNDERSTAND?

2. How can using cubes help you answer questions about volume and surface area?

3. **Write a Problem** Arrange 5 cubes, each measuring 1 centimeter on each edge, to form a solid figure. Draw the solid. Write questions about the volume and surface area for a partner to answer. Include the answer.

Independent Practice

Find the volume and surface area of each solid.

4.

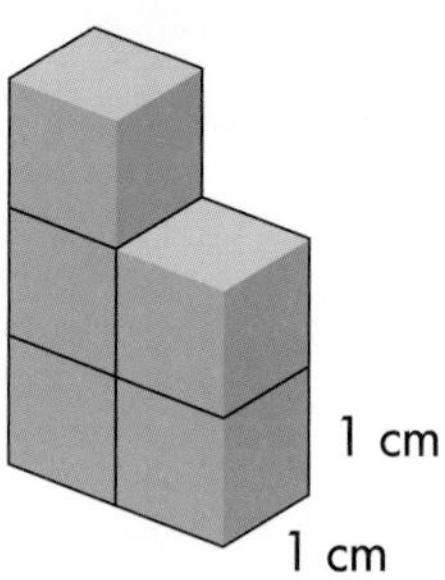

5.

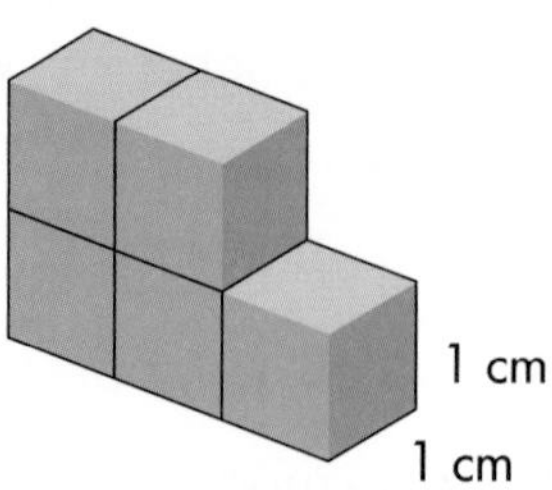

6.

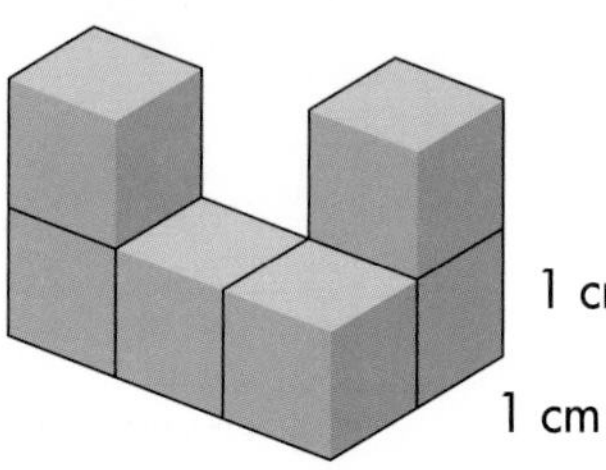

7.

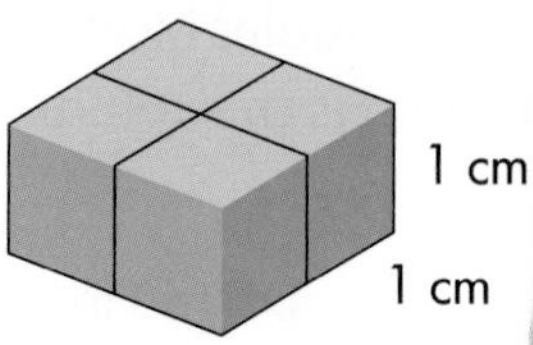

Stuck? Try this....

- What do I know?
- What am I asked to find?
- What diagram can I use to help understand the problem?
- Can I use addition, subtraction, multiplication, or division?
- Is all my work correct?
- Did I answer the right question?
- Is my answer reasonable?

*For another example, see Set D on page 473.

Plan and Solve

Count the cubes to find the volume.

I see 3 cubes. None are hidden.

The volume is 3 cm^3.

Count all the outside faces of the cubes in the figure to find the surface area.

I see 7 faces, and 7 more faces on the bottom and the back of the figure are hidden.

The surface area is 14 cm^2.

Plan and Solve

Use centimeter cubes to make a figure with 4 cubes that has 18 outside faces.

Think I counted the number of cubes to find the volume and the outside faces to find the surface area.

It has a volume of 4 cm^3 and a surface area of 18 cm^2.

For **8** through **11**, use centimeter cubes to make a shape with the given volume and surface area. Draw your answers.

8. Matt used centimeter cubes to make a solid that had a volume of 5 cubic centimeters and a surface area of 22 square centimeters. What might his solid have looked like?

9. April and Julie each made differently shaped solids with a volume of 4 cubic centimeters and a surface area of 18 square centimeters or less. What might their 2 solids have looked like?

10. Sebastian made a solid shape with a volume of 6 cubic centimeters and a surface area greater than 21 square centimeters. What might his solid have looked like?

11. Alberto made a solid shape with a volume of 8 cubic centimeters and a surface area of 24 square centimeters. What might his solid have looked like?

Use the solid shape to the right for **12** and **13**. Draw your answers.

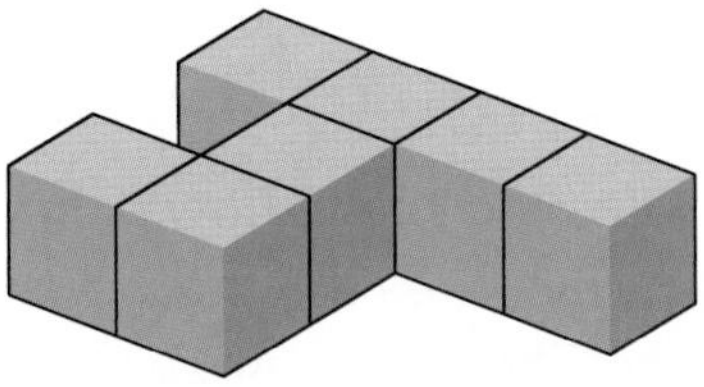

12. Use 7 centimeter cube blocks to make a different shape with the same surface area.

13. Use centimeter cube blocks to make a shape that has the same volume as the illustration but a smaller surface area.

DIGITAL eTools **www.pearsonsuccessnet.com**

Independent Practice

14. You can use a formula to find the surface area of a tower of centimeter cube blocks.

a Using your blocks, make a stack x blocks tall. Fill in the table with the surface area of your tower.

Blocks, x	2	3	5	7	10
Surface area, y					

b Find a pattern and make a conjecture. Look at your table. What pattern do you see? Write an equation for the pattern.

c Test your conjecture. Substitute the value 6 for x in the formula. What is the value of y? Build a tower 6 blocks tall. Count the faces to determine the surface area. Is your conjecture correct?

15. How does the sum of the volume of 4 individual cubes compare to the volume of a stack of 4 cubes?

For **16** and **17**, use centimeter cube blocks to help draw your pictures.

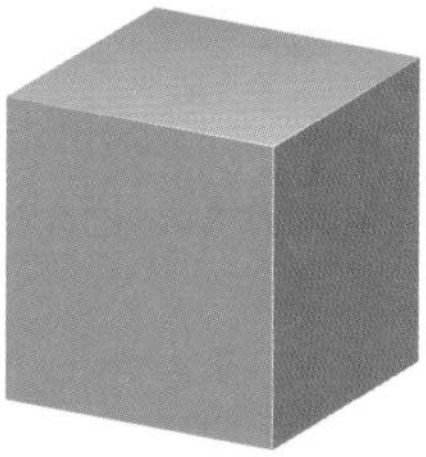

volume = 1 cubic centimeter
surface area = 6 square centimeters

16. Draw a cube that has twice the length, width, and height of the 1 cm cube. What is the volume and surface area of the new solid?

17. Draw a cube that has triple the length, width, and height of the 1 cm cube. What is the volume and surface area of the new solid?

18. **Writing to Explain** Why can two solids with the same volume have different surface areas?

Think About the Process

19. Which expression shows how to find the total surface area of 4 individual 1 cm blocks? The blocks are not touching each other.

A 4(4)

B 4(1) + 2

C 4(4) + 2

D $4 \times (4 + 2)$

20. How can you find the surface area of the figure on the right?

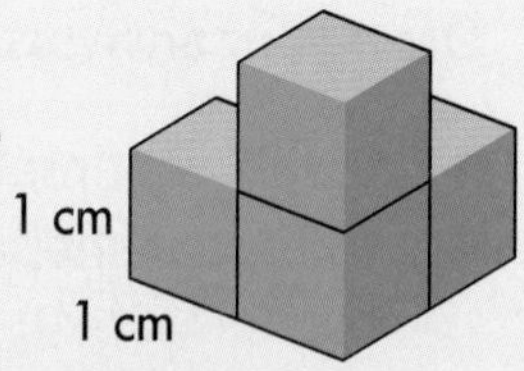

A Count the number of faces.

B Count the number of cubes.

C Count the number of cubes and subtract by 2.

D Count the number of cubes and multiply by 6.

Stop and Practice

Classify each figure. Identify whether or not the figure is a polyhedron.

1. 
2. 
3. 
4. 

For **5** through **7**, complete the following table.

		Number of Faces	Number of Vertices	Number of Edges
5.				
6.				
7.				

For **8** through **10**, find the volume of each figure.

8. 

9. 

10. 

Error Search Determine if the volume is correct. If the volume is incorrect, write it correctly and explain the error.

11. 

radius: 3 cm
height: 18 cm
volume: 162 cm^3

12. 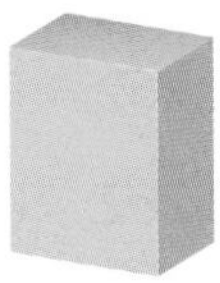

length: 12 in.
width: 3 in.
height: 15 in.
volume: 540 in^3

13. 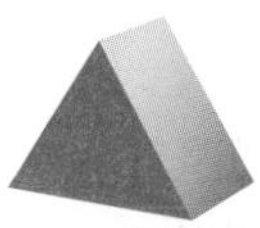

length of base: 0.5 ft
height of base: 1.5 ft
height of prism: 3 ft
volume: 2.25 ft^3

14. 

radius: 2 in.
height: 3 in.
volume: 37.68 in.

Number Sense

Estimating and Reasoning Write whether each statement is true or false. Explain your answer.

15. A cylinder and rectangular prism with the same height and width will have equal volumes.

16. The volume of an 8 cm cube will be less than 100 cm^3.

Test

1. Which of the following can be used to find the volume of a rectangular prism whose base area is 15 square inches and height is 4 inches? (18-3)

   A $V = 15 + 4$

   B $V = 15 \times 4 \times 4$

   C $V = 15 \times 4$

   D $V = \pi \times 15 \times 4$

2. What is the surface area of the triangular prism shown? (18-2)

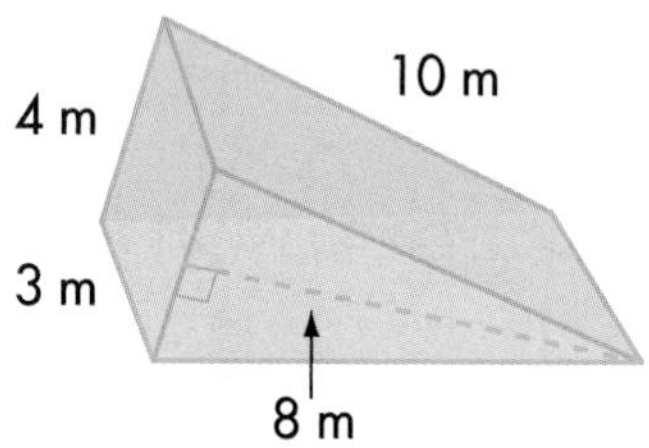

   A 48 m^2

   B 104 m^2

   C 116 m^2

   D 136 m^2

3. A rectangular prism has a volume of 400 cubic feet. The length and width of the base are 5 feet and 10 feet. Which equation can be used to find *h*, the height of the prism, in feet? (18-3)

   A $400 = 50h$

   B $400 = 30h$

   C $400 = 25h$

   D $400 = 15h$

4. A speaker is shown below. How many faces does it have? (18-1)

   A 4

   B 6

   C 8

   D 12

5. The volume of wax in the candle shown is 2,262 cm^3. Which equation can be used to find *h*, the height of the candle, in centimeters? (18-4)

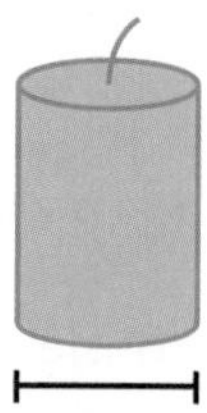

   A $2{,}262 = (\pi \times 6)h$

   B $2{,}262 = (\pi \times 6^2)h$

   C $2{,}262 = (\pi \times 12)h$

   D $2{,}262 = 1(\pi \times 12^2)h$

6. What is the volume of the play oven shown? (18-3)

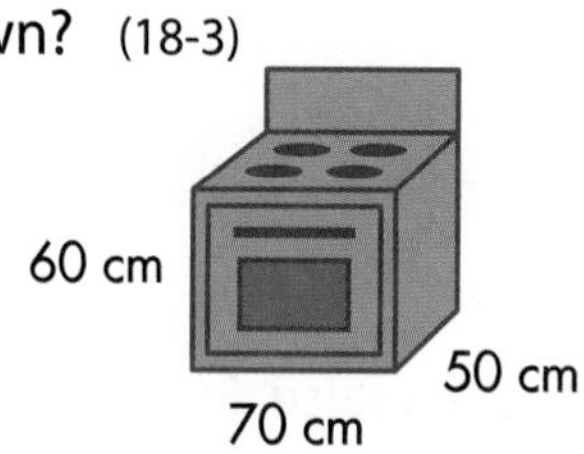

   A 3,500 cm^3

   B 4,200 cm^3

   C 7,200 cm^3

   D 210,000 cm^3

7. How much water can 4 feet, or 48 inches, of the pipe shown hold? (18-4)

A 1,356.48 in^3

B 1,492.68 in^3

C 5,425.92 in^3

D 5,568.48 in^3

8. A soup can has a circular base with a radius of 2 inches. If the height of the can is 5 inches, which of the following can be used to find the surface area of the soup can? (18-2)

A $2(3.14 \times 2^2) + (2 \times 3.14 \times 2 \times 5)$

B $3.14 \times 2^2 + 2 \times 3.14 \times 2 \times 5$

C $3.14 \times 2^2 \times 5$

D $2(3.14 \times 4^2) + (2 \times 3.14 \times 4 \times 4)$

9. Some shipping boxes are stacked as shown. If the face of each box is a square and each box represents one cubic unit, what is the surface area of the figure formed by the shipping boxes? (18-5)

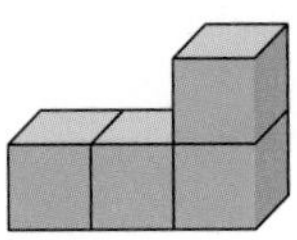

A 14 square units

B 17 square units

C 18 square units

D 24 square units

10. If the volume of the triangular prism shown below is 18 cubic inches, what is the area of one triangular base? (18-4)

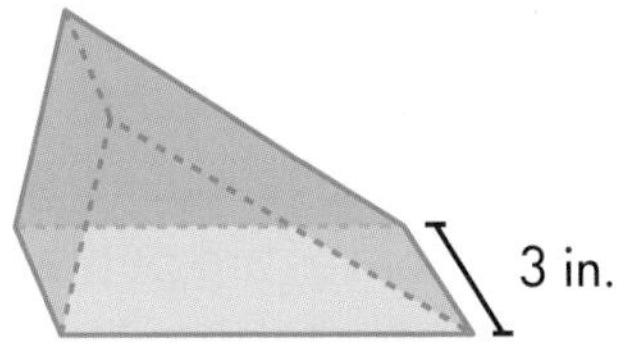

A 3 in^2

B 6 in^2

C 12 in^2

D 18 in^2

11. Which of the following does NOT represent a polyhedron? (18-1)

A

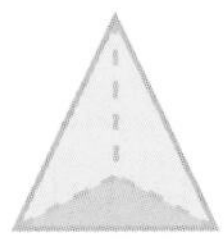

B

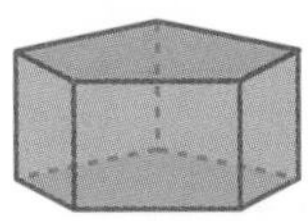

C

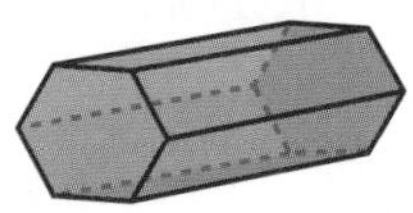

D

12. Which of the following best describes a baseball? (18-1)

A cylinder

B cone

C prism

D sphere

Set A, pages 454–457

To classify a polyhedron, first determine whether it is a prism or a pyramid. Then use the shape of its base to name it.

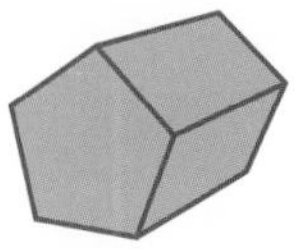

This figure has two congruent parallel bases, so it is a prism. The bases are pentagons, so it is a **pentagonal prism**.

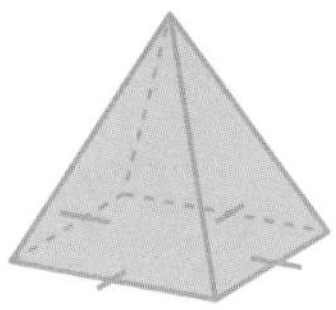

This figure has one base, and the edges are joined at a point outside the base, so it is a pyramid. The base is a square and the faces are triangles, so it is a **square pyramid**.

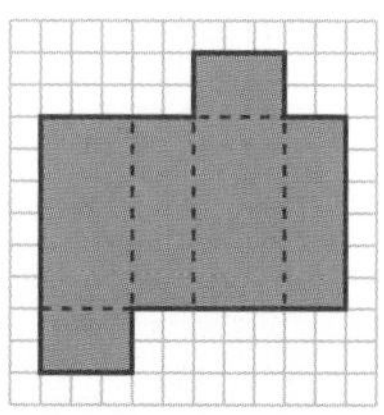

A **net** shows what a polyhedron would look like "unfolded," with all surfaces on the plane. This is a net of a rectangular prism.

Remember that not all solids are polyhedrons. Cylinders, spheres, and cones have curved surfaces and are not polyhedrons.

Identify each solid figure in **1** through **3**, and state whether the solid figure is a polyhedron.

1. 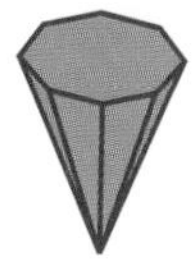 **2.** 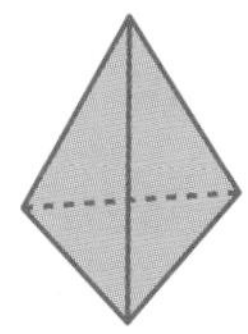 **3.** 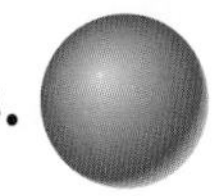

4. What figure can be made from this net?

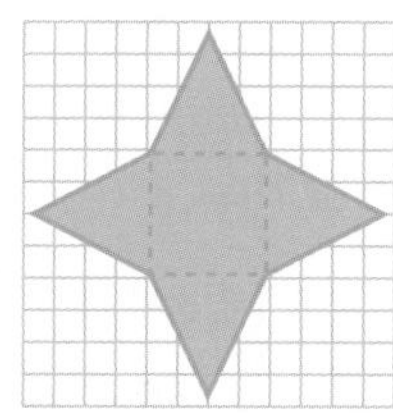

Set B, pages 458–460

To find the total surface area (SA) of a polyhedron, add the areas of each face. Find the SA of the rectangular prism below.

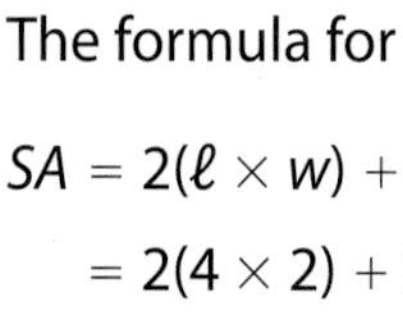

All faces are rectangles. The opposite faces of a rectangular prism have the same area. The prism has a length (ℓ) of 4 feet, a width (w) of 2 feet, and a height (h) of 6 feet.

The formula for the area of a rectangle is $\ell \times w$.

$$\begin{aligned} SA &= 2(\ell \times w) + 2(w \times h) + 2(\ell \times h) \\ &= 2(4 \times 2) + 2(2 \times 6) + 2(4 \times 6) \\ &= 2(8) + 2(12) + 2(24) \\ &= 16 + 24 + 48 \\ &= 88 \text{ ft}^2 \end{aligned}$$

The surface area of the rectangular prism is 88 ft^2.

Remember that surface area is always measured in square units, such as in^2, ft^2, and m^2.

Find the surface area of each solid.

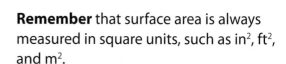

1. 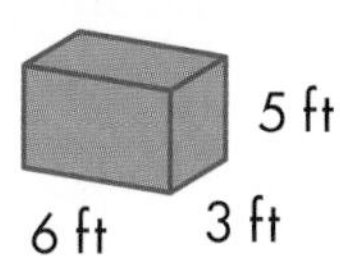

2. 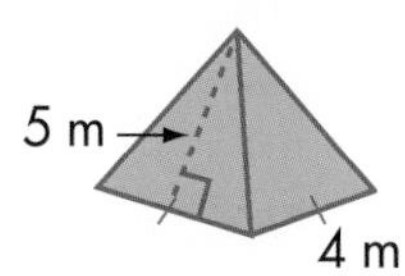

3. Use the net to find the surface area of the cylinder.

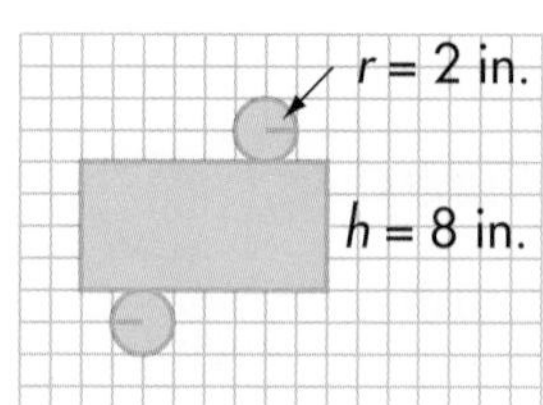

Set C, pages 462–465

To find the volume (V) of a rectangular prism, triangular prism, or cylinder, multiply the area of the base (B) by the height (h) of the figure:

Volume (V) = area of base × height = $B \times h$

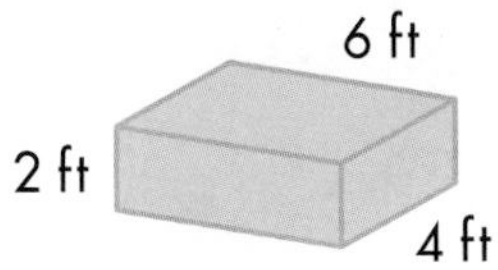

Volume of a rectangular prism:

$B = \ell \times w = 4 \text{ ft} \times 6 \text{ ft} = 24 \text{ ft}^2$

$V = 24 \text{ ft}^2 \times 2 \text{ ft} = 48 \text{ ft}^3$

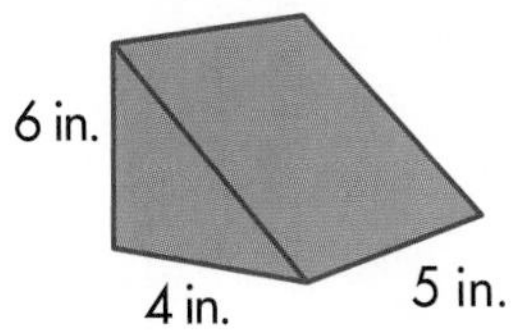

Volume of a triangular prism:

$B = \frac{1}{2} b \times h = 2 \text{ in.} \times 6 \text{ in.} = 12 \text{ in}^2$

$V = 12 \text{ in}^2 \times 5 \text{ in.} = 60 \text{ in}^3$

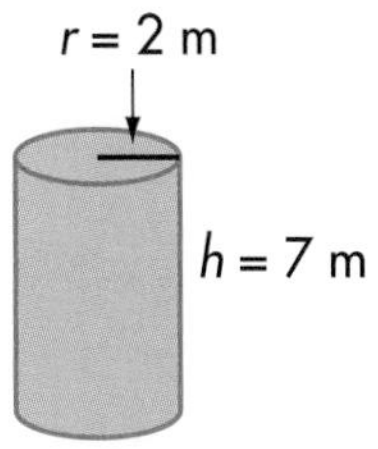

Volume of a cylinder:
Use 3.14 for π.

$B = \pi r^2 \approx 3.14 \times 2 \text{ m} \times 2 \text{ m} = 12.56 \text{ m}^2$

$V \approx 12.56 \text{ m}^2 \times 7 \text{ m} = 87.92 \text{ m}^3$

Remember that volume is always measured in cubic units, such as in^3, ft^3, and m^3.

Find the volume of each solid.

1.

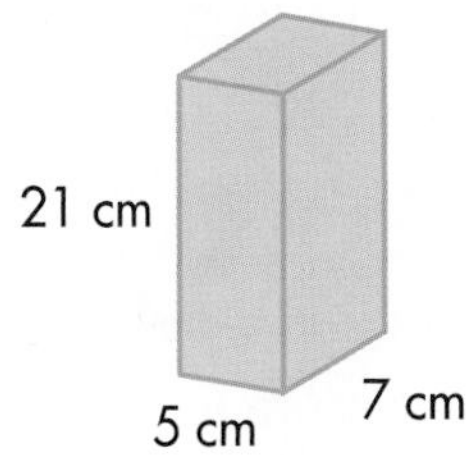

2.

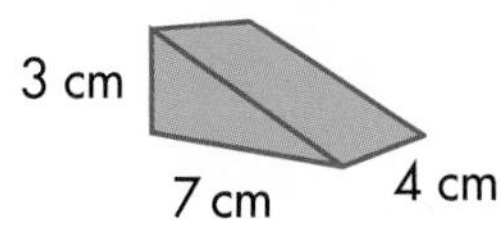

3.

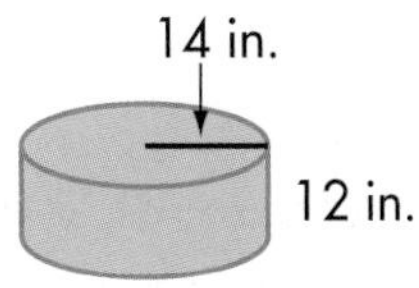

Set D, pages 466–468

You can use objects and reasoning to find patterns and solve problems.

The blocks in the figure are 1-centimeter cubes. Find the volume and surface area of the figure.

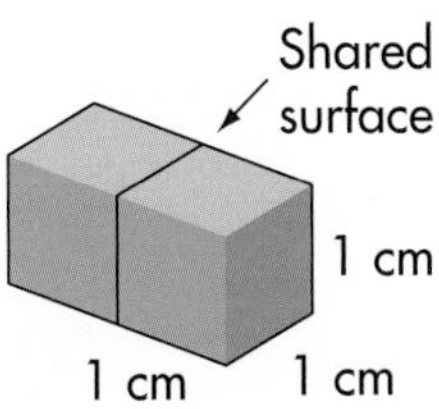

Volume

1 cube is 1 cubic centimeter

2 cubes are 2 cubic centimeters

Surface Area

Area of 1 face: 1 square centimeter

Faces on 1 cube: 6

Shared faces on 2 cubes together: 2

Number of faces you can see: 10

Area of 2 cubes together: 10 square centimeters

Remember that figures made up of the same number of one-unit cubes (same volume) may have different surface areas. When finding the surface area of figures made of the same kind of cubes, do not count surfaces that face each other.

Find the volume and surface area of each figure below. The figures are made of 1-centimeter cubes.

1.

2.

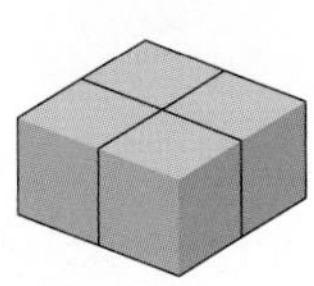

Topic 19

Data and Graphs

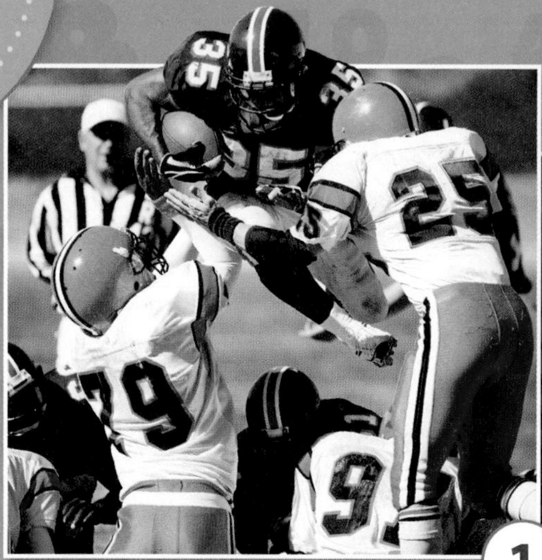

1

Who makes more money at the start of their professional careers, basketball players or football players? You will find out in Lesson 19-1.

2

This ball of rubber bands set a world's record. How much did it weigh? You will find out in Lesson 19-7.

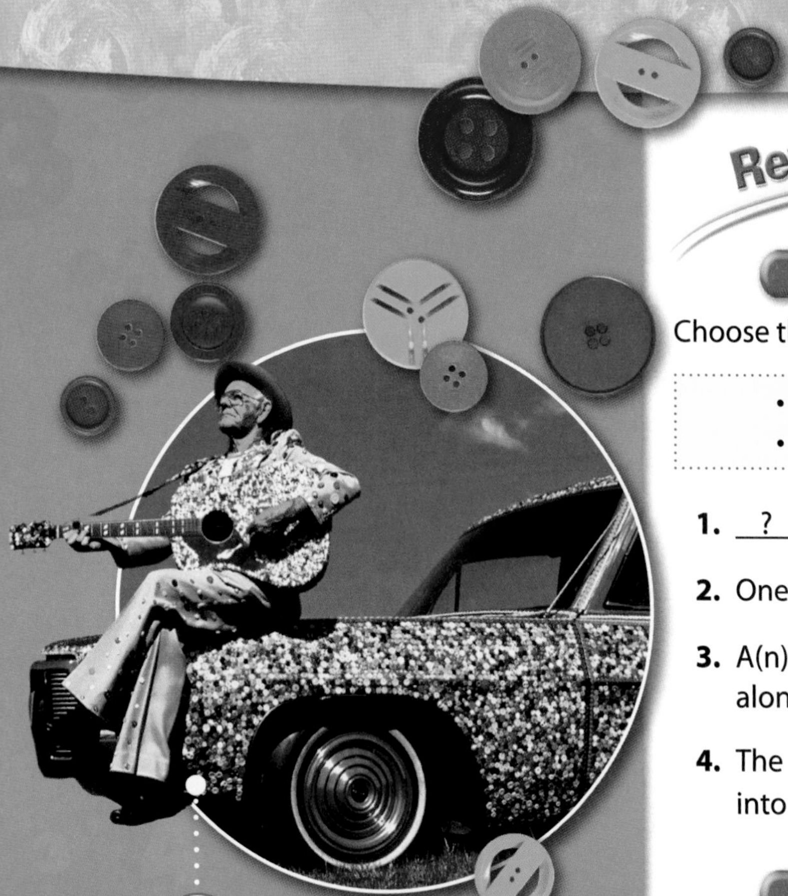

3

This button collection is one of the top 20 largest collections. What is the average number of items in five of the largest collections? You will find out in Lesson 19-5.

Review What You Know!

Vocabulary

Choose the best terms from the box.

- axes
- data
- percent
- interval

1. __?__ are the values represented by graphs.
2. One-quarter can also be named as 25 __?__.
3. A(n) __?__ is the distance between values along the side or bottom of a graph.
4. The lines that divide a coordinate plane into quadrants are the *x*- and *y*- __?__.

Finding Percents

Find the percent of each number.

5. 12% of 1,600
6. 50% of 9,452
7. 67% of 33
8. 87.5% of 5,900
9. 1% of 990
10. 5% of 20

Angles

Measure the following angles.

11. 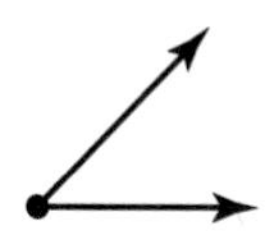

12. 

Averages

13. **Writing to Explain** Matt scored an 85 on the first math test, an 82 on the second math test, and an 89 on the third math test. How can you find the average score? Explain.

Lesson
19-1 Reading and Making Graphs

Understand It!
Line graphs and bar graphs can be used to compare two related sets of data. The data in a graph can be used to answer a question.

How are data represented in a double-line graph?

Line graphs are often used to represent data over time. This double-line graph shows two similar sets of data points, with connecting line segments.

Between what years did participation in college sports decrease for both men and women? Look for trends in the data.

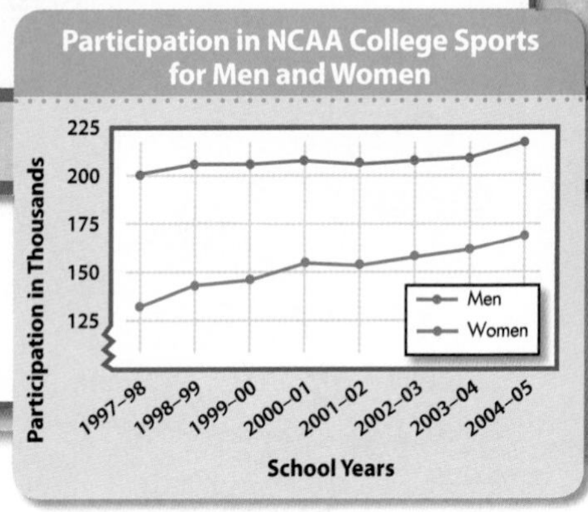

Another Example How are data represented in a double-bar graph?

Bar graphs are often used to compare data. A double-bar graph compares two similar sets of data, represented as bars, on one graph. Use the table at the right to make a double-bar graph showing the number of Winter Olympic medals won by each country in 2002 and in 2006.

Data

Country	2002	2006
Germany	36	29
Norway	25	19
Russia	13	22
United States	34	25

Step 1 Write a title and label the horizontal and vertical axes.

Step 2 On the vertical axis, mark and label equal intervals beginning with zero. Draw a line across the graph at each interval.

Step 3 On the horizontal axis, write the categories at equal intervals.

Step 4 Choose colors and make a key to show what each color represents.

Step 5 Draw a bar for each data value and color the bar with the appropriate color.

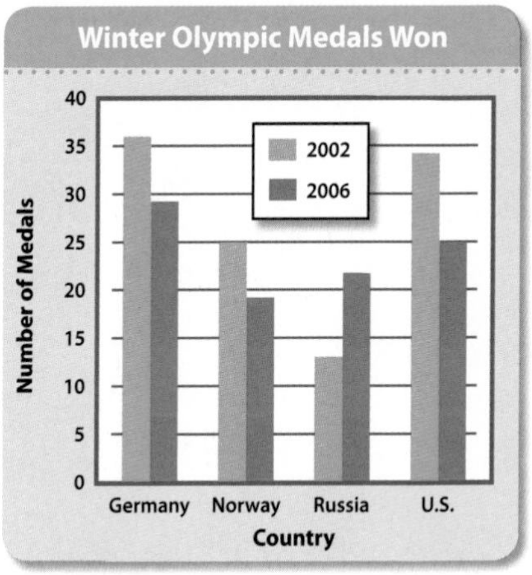

Explain It

1. Which country earned more Winter Olympic medals in 2006 than in 2002?
2. Is it quicker to make a comparison of Winter Olympic medals won in 2002 and 2006 using the data in the table or in the double-bar graph?

Find the years between which both line segments go down.

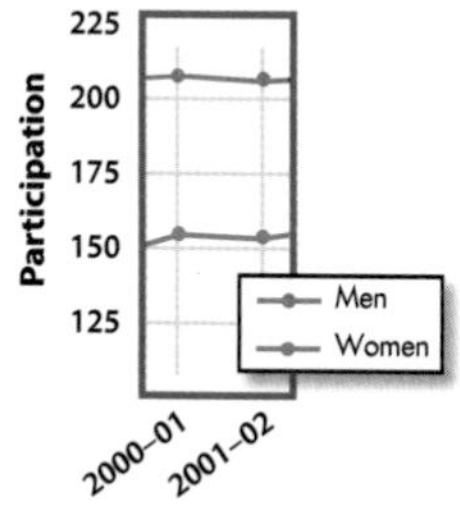

Participation decreased between the 2000–01 and the 2001–02 school years.

Line graphs may show a trend or general direction in the data that can help you predict what the data might be in the future. Look for a trend in women's participation.

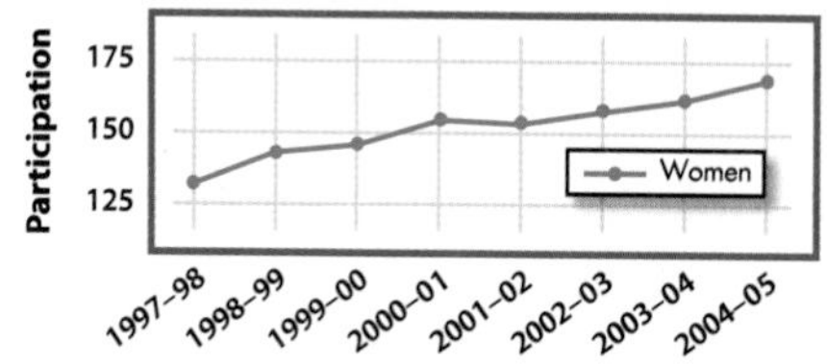

The general direction of the line graph is going up, so it is reasonable to predict that women's participation in college sports will continue to increase.

Guided Practice*

Do you know HOW?

1. Bill and Renee are keeping track of the types of books they read. Make a double-bar graph to compare their data.

Data

Book Type	Bill	Renee
Fiction	6	4
Biography	3	7
Other	2	1

Do you UNDERSTAND?

2. In the example at the top, predict what will happen to men's participation in NCAA sports. Explain.

3. How can line graphs help you estimate unknown quantities?

4. Why is a key necessary in a graph?

Independent Practice

Use the graph at the right for **5** and **6**.

5. Why is a line graph used to show the data?

6. Describe any trends you see in the graph.

7. Jimmy has sorted the school's band uniforms into small, medium, and large sizes. He wants to make a graph to show how many new and used uniforms are in each group. What kind of graph should he make?

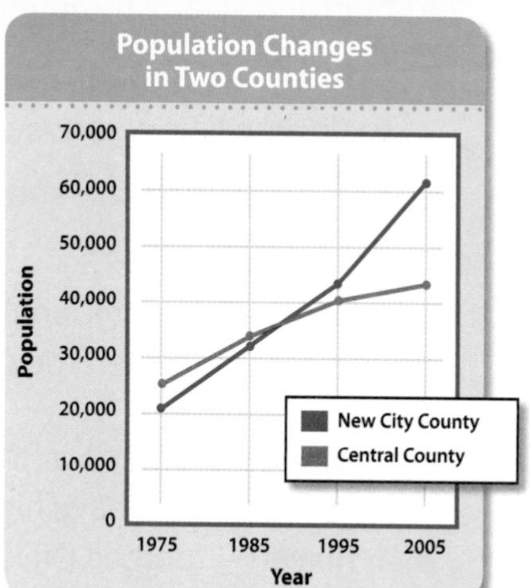

DIGITAL
Animated Glossary
www.pearsonsuccessnet.com

For another example, see Set A on page 514.

Independent Practice

The table at the right shows the number of people registered for four summer classes during June and July. Use the table to complete **8** and **9**.

8. Make a double-bar graph using the information in the table at the right.

9. Use the graph you made to answer this question: Which class had the largest increase in students from June to July?

Data

Summer Classes (people registered)

Class Name	June	July
Jujitsu	45	38
Yoga	67	72
Painting	34	36
Orchestra	89	91

Problem Solving

10. The table at the right gives monthly bank balances for Kelly and Jess. Which kind of graph is most appropriate to show the data? Use paper or a computer program to make a graph for the data.

Data

	Jan.	Feb.	Mar.	Apr.	May	June
Jess	$14	$45	$27	$34	$44	$10
Kelly	$23	$35	$41	$45	$51	$60

11. Writing to Explain Explain what trends you can see in the ways that Kelly and Jess handle their money.

Al Aziziyah, near the Libyan capital of Tripoli, had the highest temperature ever recorded on Earth: 136°F. Death Valley, CA, had the highest temperature ever recorded in North America: 134°F. Use the graph at the right for **12**.

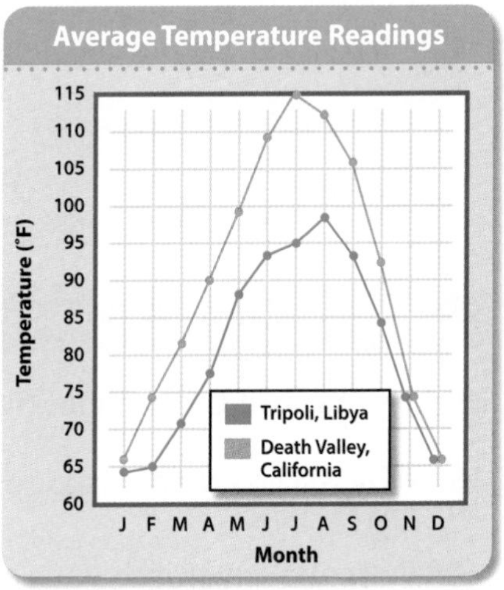

12. Which best describes the temperature trends throughout the year in Tripoli, Libya?

A high and steady throughout the year

B a steady rise through August and then they start to decline

C start high in January and then decline until July, when they rise again

D remain steady until June and then rise dramatically until October when they start to fall

13. According to the graph at the right, which professional sport is reported to have higher minimum salaries for their players—football (NFL) or basketball (NBA)?

14. How do years of experience affect salaries in both leagues?

Algebra Connections

Related Variables

Remember that a set of ordered pairs (x, y) may be related by a linear equation. A graph can show the relation between variables in a linear equation.

For **1** and **2**, use the following graph.

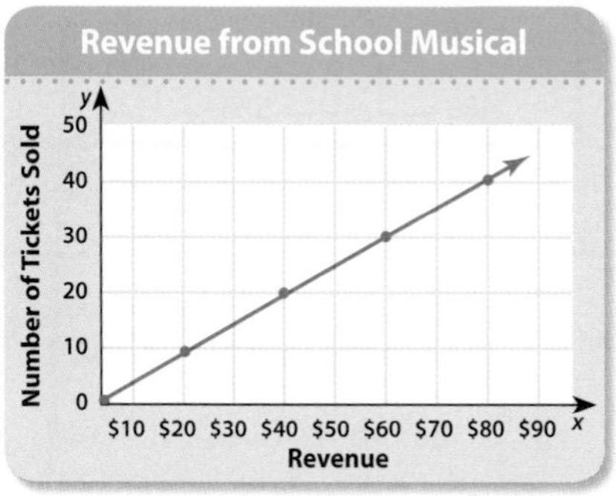

Example: Suppose the Lee family went on vacation. They started with \$2,000. They spent at a rate of \$150 each day. The graph below shows how much money they had left after x days. The linear equation shown is $y = 2{,}000 - 150x$.

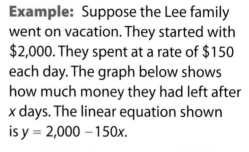

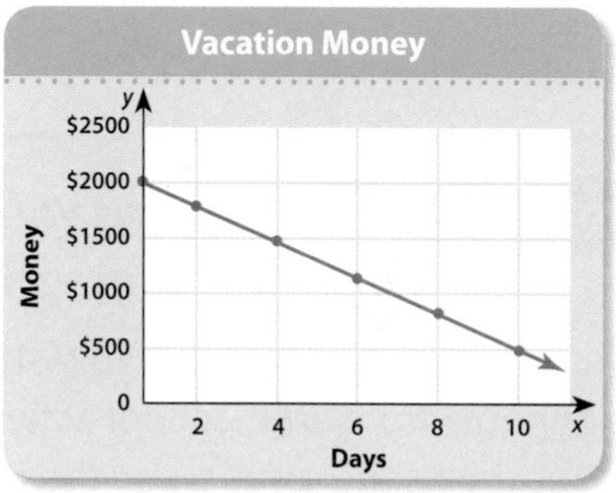

1. Grant School is putting on a school musical and charging \$2 per ticket. The graph shows the total revenue the school will earn with different numbers of tickets sold. Which algebraic equation best describes the total revenue earned, R, based on the number of tickets sold, t?

A $R = 2 + t$ **B** $R = \frac{t}{2}$ **C** $R = 2t$ **D** $R = \frac{2}{t}$

2. Make a graph that shows revenue for the musical if the ticket price is increased to \$3.

For **3** through **5**, use the graph at the right.

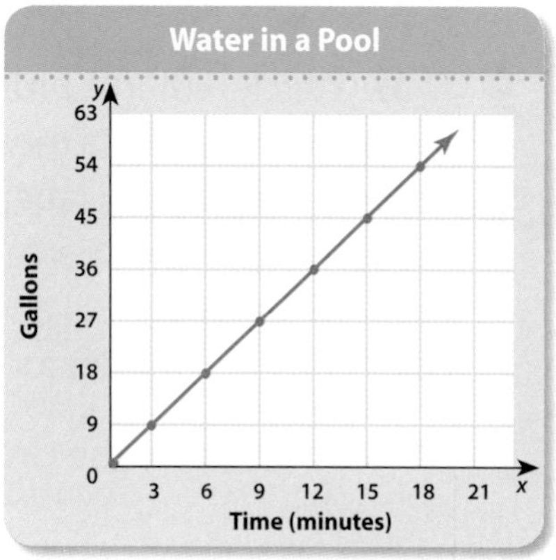

3. Kent added water to a swimming pool. The graph shows the amount of water in the pool over time. Estimate how much water was in the pool after 10 minutes.

4. What was the rate of water added to the pool in gallons per minute?

5. Which algebraic equation best describes the total gallons, G, of water in the swimming pool after m minutes?

A $G = 3m$ **B** $G = 9m$ **C** $G = 3m + 9$ **D** $G = 9m \div 1$

Lesson
19-2 Circle Graphs

Understand It!
A circle graph shows how portions of a set of data compare with the whole.

Hands-On: protractor

How are data represented in a circle graph?

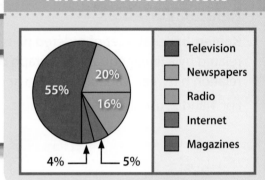

A survey asked 500 people for their favorite source of news. The results are shown on the circle graph. How many people said their favorite source of news is television?

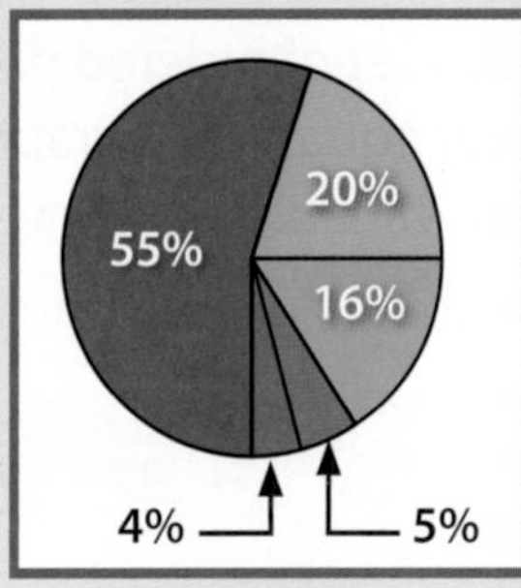

Another Example How do you construct a circle graph?

Jeremy asked 200 of his fellow students what time they get home from after-school activities. The table at the right shows the results. Use the following table and the steps listed below to make a circle graph.

Data

Home Arrival Times	
Before 4:00 P.M.	40
4:00 P.M.–5:00 P.M.	95
After 5:00 P.M.	65

Home Arrival Times	**Step 1** Find the percent for each category. Round to the nearest tenth of a percent.	**Step 2** Use the percents to calculate the measure of each **central angle.** Round to the nearest whole degree. Remember, there are 360° in a circle.
Before 4:00 P.M.	$\frac{40}{200} = 0.20 = 20\%$	20% of $360 = 0.20 \times 360 = 72°$
4:00 P.M.–5:00 P.M.	$\frac{95}{200} = 0.475 = 47.5\%$	47.5% of $360 = 0.475 \times 360 = 171°$
After 5:00 P.M.	$\frac{65}{200} = 0.325 = 32.5\%$	32.5% of $360 = 0.325 \times 360 = 117°$

Step 3 Draw a circle. Using a protractor, draw a central angle with a measure of 72°. Color the sector and label it with the category name and percent. Then draw the other central angles and color and label the sectors.

Step 4 Write a title above the circle.

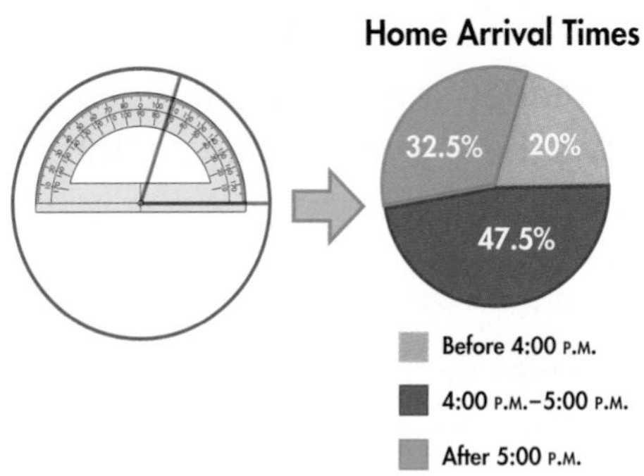

Explain It

1. How could you verify that your calculations were reasonable in Step 2?

What You Think

A circle graph shows how different parts of a set of data compare to the whole set. Circle graphs often display the percent that corresponds to each part of the whole.

The graph shows that 55% of the 500 people surveyed chose television.

What You Write

Find 55% of 500.

$55\% \times 500 = \square$

$0.55 \times 500 = 275$

Of the people surveyed, 275 chose television as their favorite source of news.

Guided Practice*

Do you know HOW?

Use the example at the top for **1** and **2**.

1. How many people chose radio as their favorite choice for news?

2. Which source of news was the least popular in the survey?

3. Look at the circle graph in Another Example. In a sample of 1,000 students, about how many would you expect to get home between 4:00 P.M. and 4:30 P.M.?

Do you UNDERSTAND?

4. In the example at the top, explain why you could use the proportion $\frac{55}{100} = \frac{x}{500}$ to find out how many people surveyed chose television.

5. Can all the percents of the sectors in a circle graph add up to 120%? Explain.

Independent Practice

Penny and her family created a monthly budget of $2,300 for expenses. Use the circle graph at the right for **6** through **8**.

Penny's Family Budget

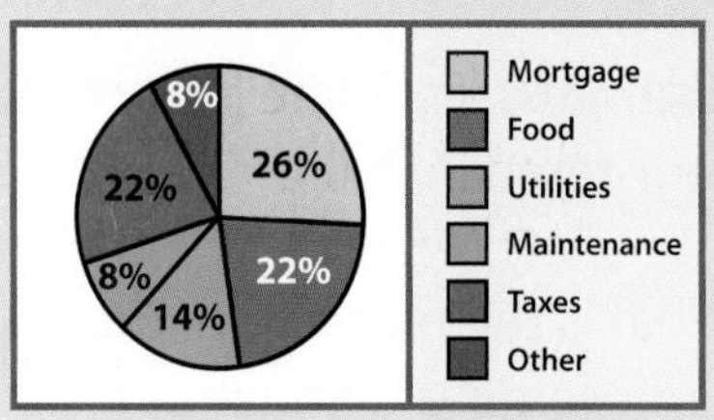

6. How much money was budgeted for food each month?

7. Estimate the amount of money the family spends on other expenses.

8. What is the measure of the central angle that represents taxes?

DIGITAL Animated Glossary, eTools **www.pearsonsuccessnet.com**

For another example, see Set B on page 514.

Independent Practice

Jenna is learning how paper is recycled in the United States. She finds out that about 10 million tons of writing paper were recycled in a recent year into other paper products. Use the circle graph at the right for **9** through **11**.

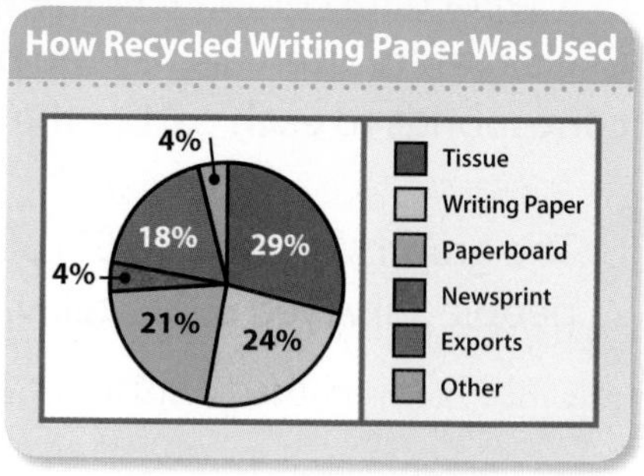

9. About how much writing paper was recycled to make tissue?

10. Estimate the amount of paper that was recycled to make newsprint.

11. Which two materials together made up 50% of the recycled paper products?

Problem Solving

12. Writing to Explain Explain how you would draw a sector that represented more than 50% of the circle without drawing an angle greater than 180°. Look at the diagram at the right for a hint.

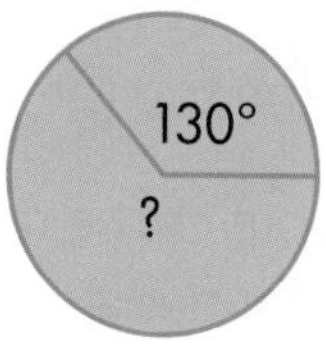

13. Number Sense Archimedes was a mathematician in ancient Greece. By investigating the perimeter of regular polygons inside and outside of a circle, he estimated the value of π to be between $3\frac{1}{7}$ and $3\frac{10}{71}$. Compare $3\frac{1}{7}$ to $3\frac{10}{71}$. Explain your reasoning.

Use the circle graph at the right and the following information for **14** through **16**.

The Labrador Retriever was the top registered purebred dog in the United States among about 498,000 people registering their dogs in a recent year.

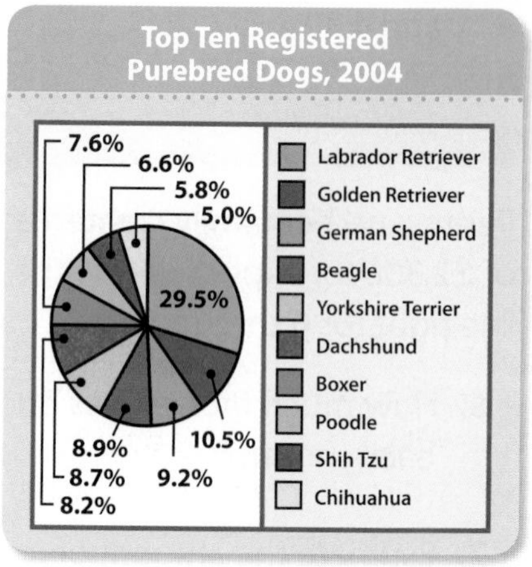

14. Estimate Estimate how many Labrador Retrievers were registered in 2004.

15. What is the measure of the angle sector representing Chihuahuas?

16. About how many Golden Retrievers were registered?

A 5,229,000 **B** 522,900 **C** 52,290 **D** 5,290

Going Digital

Drawing Circle Graphs

Use eTools

Spreadsheet/Data/Grapher

The table shows the number of students enrolled in U.S. schools in a recent year. Make a circle graph of the data.

Enrollment in U.S. Schools	
Level	**Students Enrolled**
Pre-K to 8	38,540,000
9 to 12	15,914,000
College	16,468,000

Step 1 Go to the Spreadsheet/Data/ Grapher eTool. Type the information from the table into the spreadsheet. Do not use commas in the numbers.

Step 2 Select the 3 rows and 2 columns with the data.

Step 3 Click on the circle graph icon. Type in the title for the graph. Make sure percent is selected.

Then click OK.

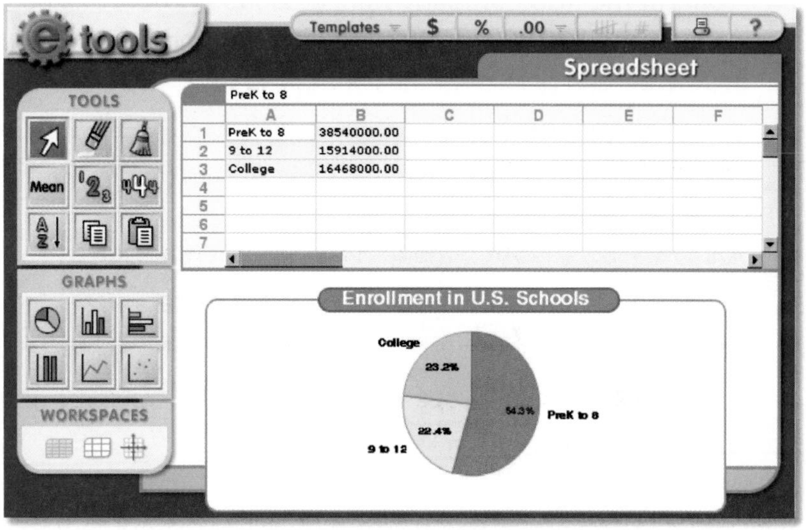

Practice

1. In a recent year, U.S. colleges and universities awarded 595,133 two-year degrees, 1,291,900 four-year degrees, 482,118 master's degrees, and 124,858 degrees beyond a master's, which includes doctorate and professional degrees.

   Create a circle graph to show the percent of degrees awarded in each of these categories.

Lesson

19-3

Understand It!
The purpose of the data display determines the most appropriate type of graph to use. Some graphs can be misleading.

Comparing Graphs

How do different types of graphs represent data differently?

A survey asked 500 people which type of transportation they most often use to get to work. The results are shown in the table. Compare how a bar graph and a circle graph represent the data.

Data

Transportation to Work

Type	Number	Percent
Car	275	55%
Train	100	20%
Bus	80	16%
Walk	25	5%
Other	20	4%

Another Example How can graphs be misleading?

Profits at the RGB Company were $22,000 in 2006, $29,000 in 2007, and $39,000 in 2008. Which graph more fairly shows the increase in profits for the RGB Company?

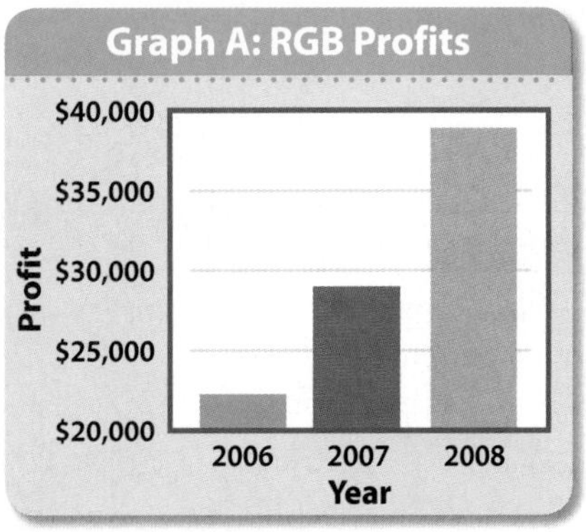

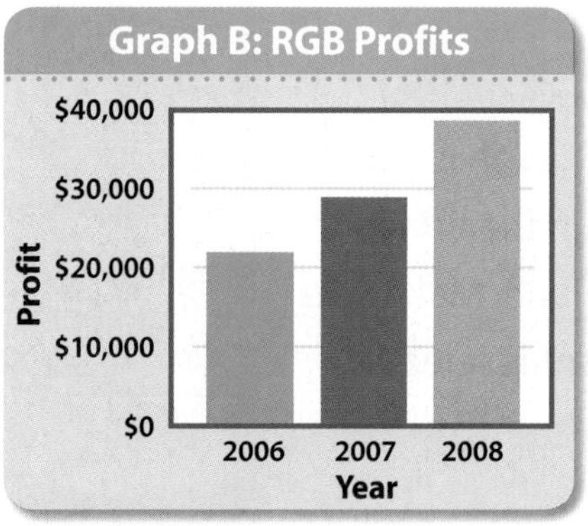

Graph A starts at $20,000 and uses intervals of $5,000.

The length of the bars make it look like profits quadrupled from 2006 to 2007 and doubled between 2007 and 2008. This graph can be misleading.

Graph B starts at zero and uses intervals of $10,000.

The lengths of the bars reflect the amounts of the profits in proportion to one another.

So, Graph B more fairly shows the RGB Company's growth in profits.

Explain It

1. How are Graph B and Graph A different?

2. How do smaller intervals between numbers on the *y*-axis of Graph A affect the length of the bars?

Bar Graph

A bar graph makes it easy to compare numerical data to one another.

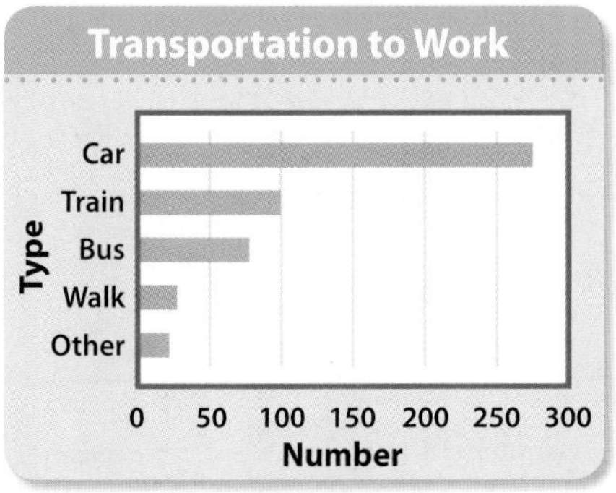

Circle Graph

A circle graph shows how different parts of a set of data compare to the whole set. Each part is a percent of the whole.

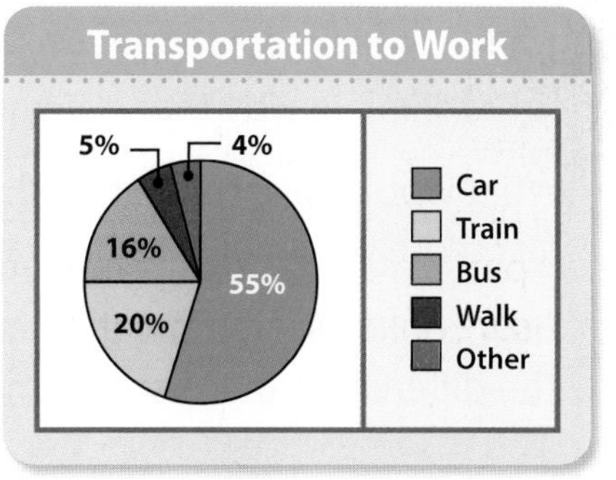

Guided Practice*

Do you know HOW?

Use the table for **1** and **2**.

Number in Marching Band

Year	Horns	Flutes	Drums
2006	14	4	6
2007	18	6	10
2008	20	8	12

1. Which type of graph would best compare each part to the whole marching band in 2008?

2. Which type of graph would best compare the number of horns in 2006 to the number of horns in 2008?

Do you UNDERSTAND?

3. In the transportation survey, if the number of people surveyed were 1,000 and the number of each type of transportation doubled, how would the circle and bar graphs change?

4. Is the bar graph at the top fair or misleading? Explain.

5. Using the marching band table, suppose you wanted to compare the numbers in each part of the band in 2007 and 2008. Which type of graph would best represent the data?

Independent Practice

There are 120 hours in a school week. Jason wanted to know exactly how he was spending his time. Use the table for **6** and **7**.

Jason's Activities

Type	Hours	Percent
Sleep	42	35%
School	44	37%
Family	18	15%
Sports	6	5%
Other	10	8%

6. Which type of graph should Jason make to compare the number of hours for each activity?

7. Which type of graph should Jason make to represent his activities as parts of a whole school week?

For another example, see Set B on page 514.

Independent Practice

8. Jake graphed his science test scores on the bar graph at the right.

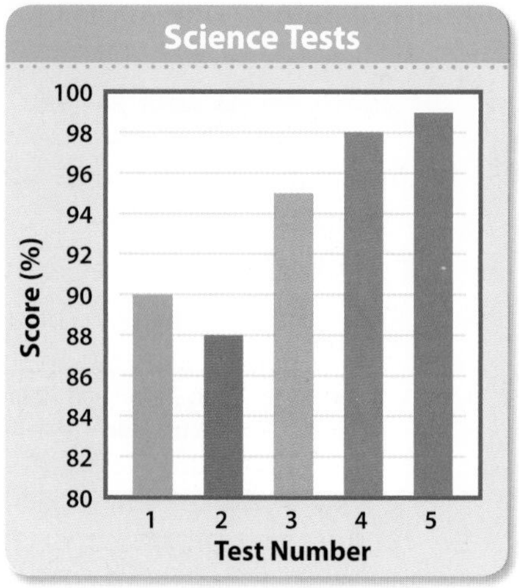

   a Jake says that his last score was double his first score. Explain why that claim is misleading.

   b What would Jake have scored on his first test if his last score were twice as high as his first score?

   c How could Jake redraw the graph so that it shows the differences in his scores more accurately?

Problem Solving

Use the bar graph at the right to answer **9** and **10**.

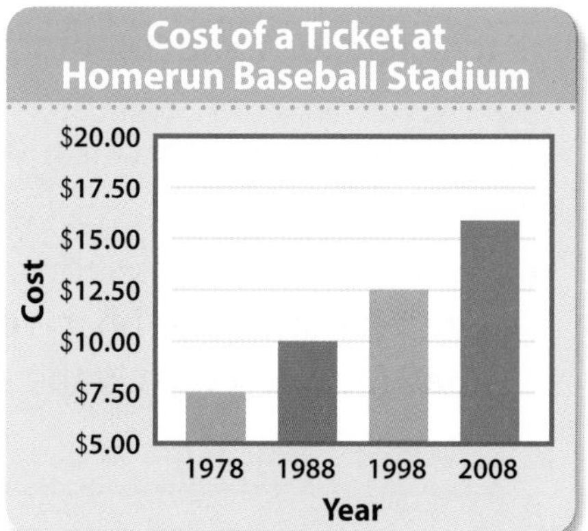

9. **Writing to Explain** Why is this claim misleading? "Prices for baseball tickets tripled over the last thirty years."

10. How much would tickets have to cost in 2008 for the claim to be true?

    A \$7.50 **B** \$16.00 **C** \$22.50 **D** \$30.00

11. Candace polled 25 students about their favorite type of book: 12 chose *fiction*, 7 chose *biographies*, 3 chose *poetry*, and 3 chose *other*. Make a graph that compares each type of book as a part of the whole group surveyed.

Use the circle and bar graphs at the right to answer **12** and **13**.

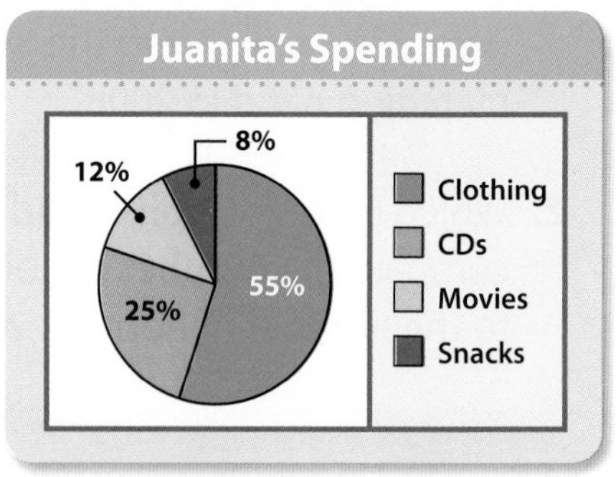

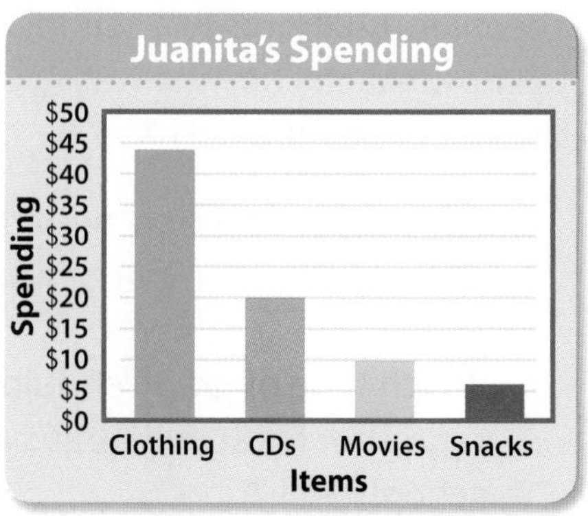

12. Which graph best shows that Juanita spent more than half of her money on clothes?

13. Which graph best shows that Juanita spent twice as much money for CDs as she did for movies?

14. About how much money did Juanita spend on CDs? Which graph best shows you that?

    A \$20; the bar graph **C** \$20; the circle graph

    B \$25; the bar graph **D** \$25; the circle graph

Algebra Connections

Comparing Line Graphs

Remember that a line graph often represents data collected over time. The double-line graph, below on the right, compares the rates of two boats. Use what you know about rates to describe the trends and compare their speeds.

Example: What is the speed, as a unit rate, of the houseboat in the double-line graph below? If the houseboat continues at this speed, how far will it travel in 6 hours?

The speed is the distance that the houseboat travels in 1 hour. It travels 10 miles per hour (mph).

$$\frac{10 \text{ mi}}{1 \text{ hr}} = \frac{x}{6 \text{ hrs}}$$

$$\frac{10}{1} = \frac{x}{6}$$

$$x = 60 \text{ mi}$$

The houseboat can travel 60 miles in 6 hours.

Use the graph to answer **1** through **4**.

1. What is the unit rate of speed of the ski boat? At this rate, how far will it travel in 6 hours?

2. How much farther does the ski boat travel than the houseboat travels in 2 hours?

3. Let x = the number of times faster the ski boat travels than the houseboat travels. Solve $30 = 10x$.

4. Based on the trends shown, is it reasonable to predict that the ski boat will always travel farther than the houseboat in the same amount of time?

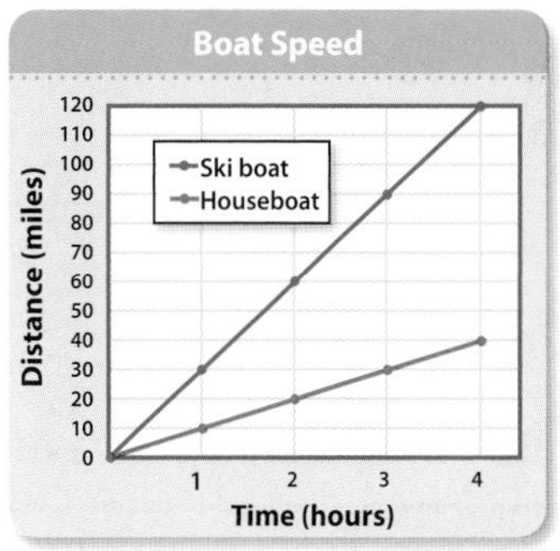

Use the data in the line graphs for **5** and **6**.

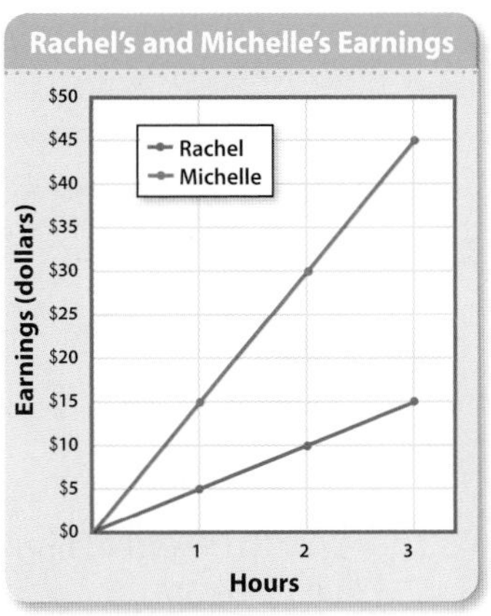

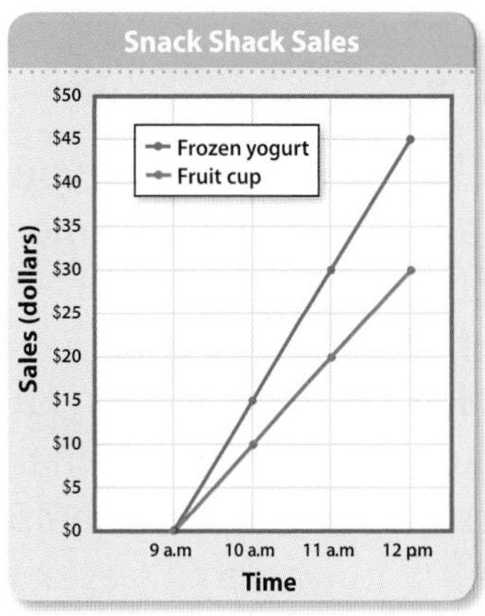

5. Rachel and Michelle work at a different rate per hour. How much will each of them earn in 5 hours? Describe the trend you see in their earnings.

6. The Snack Shack tracked the sales for frozen yogurt and fruit cups for each hour of the morning. Compare the sales of each snack. Predict how much the sales will be at 3 P.M.

Lesson
19-4

Understand It!
Some problems can be solved by making, reading, and analyzing a graph.

Problem Solving

Make a Graph

This graph, called a scattergram, compares data points for two variables. Every point on this scattergram represents a hoofed animal and was plotted by comparing the height and neck length of the animals. Study the graph. Which point represents which animal?

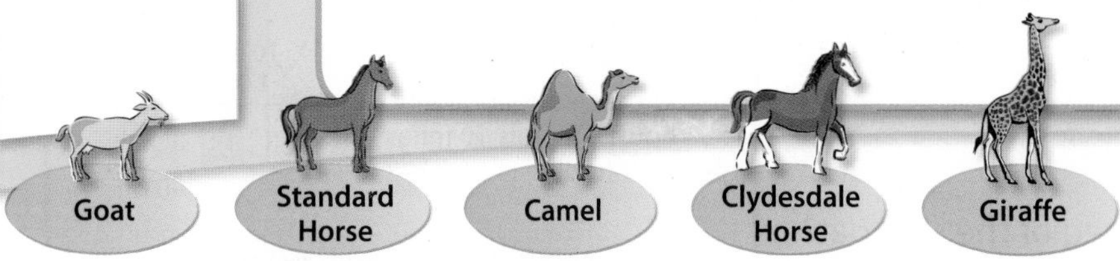

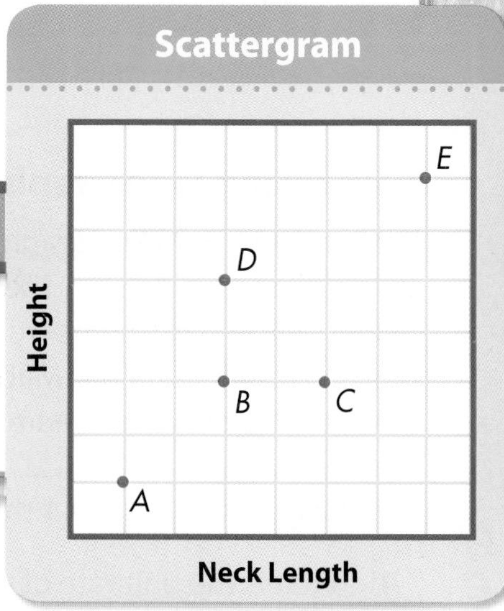

Guided Practice*

Do you know HOW?

Use the diagram for **1**.

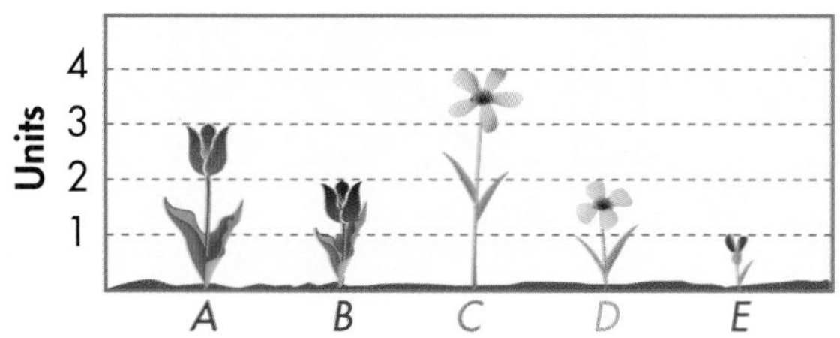

1. Make a scattergram comparing the heights and numbers of petals of the flowers.

Do you UNDERSTAND?

2. How does a scattergram help compare the relationship between two variables?

3. **Write a problem** Write a problem that can be solved by making a graph.

Independent Practice

4. What kind of graph would you make to show how a family spends their money each month? Explain your answer.

5. What kind of graph would you make to compare the number of books sold in three different bookstores in June and July? Explain your answer.

6. What kind of graph would you make to compare high and low temperatures among five cities?

7. What kind of graph would you make to show the cost of electricity and gas for a family over one year?

Stuck? Try this....

- What do I know?
- What am I asked to find?
- What diagram can I use to help understand the problem?
- Can I use addition, subtraction, multiplication, or division?
- Is all of my work correct?
- Did I answer the right question?
- Is my answer reasonable?

*For another example, see Set B on page 514.

Plan and Solve

The goat and giraffe are easy to find. The giraffe is the tallest and has the longest neck (*E*). The goat is the shortest and has the shortest neck (*A*).

The standard horse and the camel are the same height. Their points are aligned horizontally (*B* and *C*). The camel has a longer neck (*C*). The Clydesdale has to be the last point (*D*).

The Clydesdale and the standard horse have the same size neck. Their points are aligned vertically (*D* and *B*). The Clydesdale is taller.

Scattergram

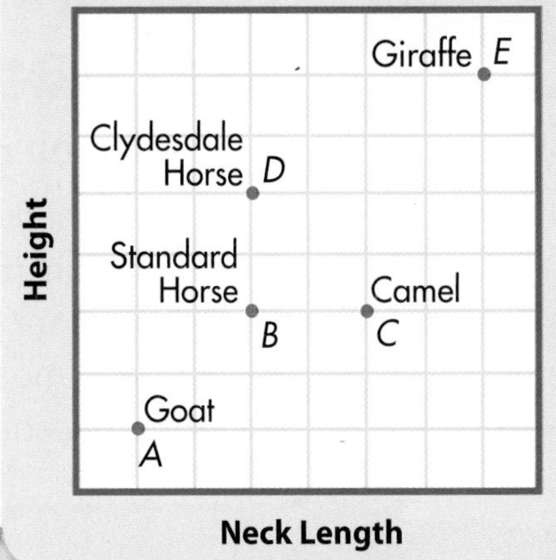

8. Lola conducted a survey of 240 students to find out their favorite vegetables. The results are in the table at right.

a Make a circle graph using Lola's data.

b What is the measure of the central angle that represents corn?

c How many students in Lola's survey liked beans best?

Data

Type of Vegetable	Identified as Favorite
Carrots	43%
Lettuce	13%
Corn	17%
Beans	22%
Broccoli	5%

9. Why is a line graph useful for showing trends in data?

10. The double-bar graph at the right shows high and low temperatures one August day. Which city had a difference of 15°F between its high and low temperatures?

11. Which two cities have the most similar high and low temperatures?

High and Low Temperatures (°F)

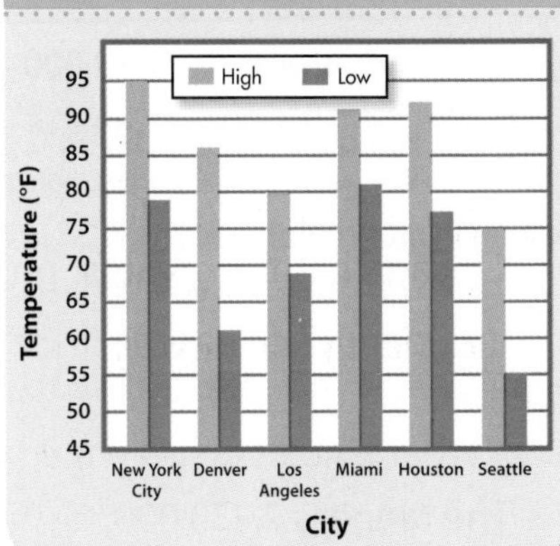

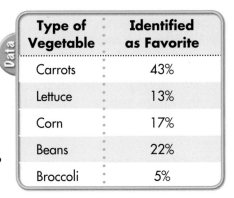

12. Think About the Process Which type of graph would be best for comparing the engine power and acceleration speed of a group of race cars?

A circle graph **C** pictograph

B scattergram **D** bar graph

13. Which type of graph would be best for comparing the annual precipitation in San Bernadino and Lake Tahoe?

A circle graph **C** line graph

B scattergram **D** bar graph

DIGITAL Animated Glossary **www.pearsonsuccessnet.com**

Lesson
19-5

Understand It!
The mean, median, and mode describe the central tendency of a data set. The range describes how spread out the data set is.

Mean, Median, Mode, and Range

How can you describe a set of data?

The lengths of five boa constrictors are shown. Find the mean, median, and mode to describe this set of data. The mean, median, and mode are known as measures of central tendency.

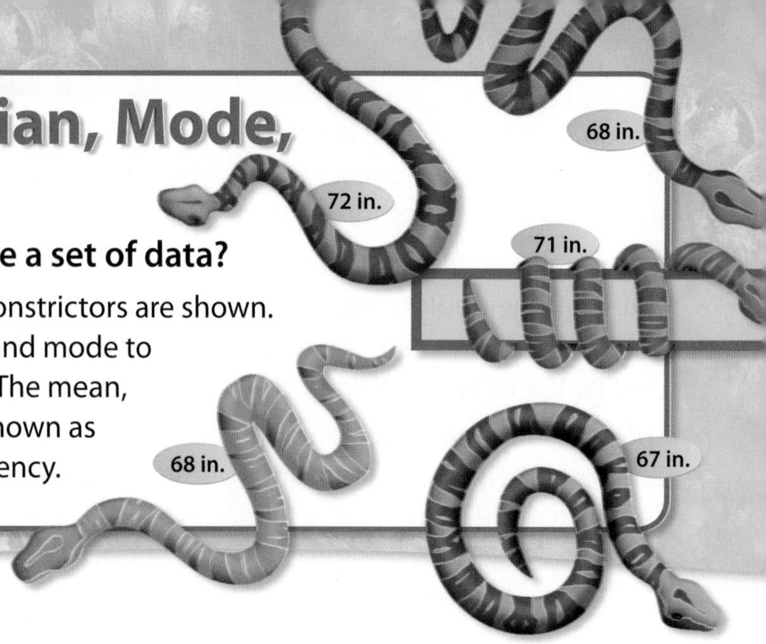

Another Example What does the range of a data set describe?

The range describes how spread out a data set is. To find the range, subtract the least number in the set from the greatest number in the set.

Find the range of populations for the eight cities shown in the table below.

Data

City	Population	City	Population
Chicago	2,843,000	Savannah	128,000
Indianapolis	784,000	Elizabeth	126,000
Jacksonville	783,000	Lafayette	112,000
Honolulu	377,000	Independence	110,000

Chicago has the greatest population: 2,843,000
Independence has the least population: − 110,000
2,733,000

The range is 2,733,000.

Explain It

1. Is the population data in the example above spread out or clustered? Explain.

2. What are the median and mode of the populations shown in the table?

The mean is the sum of all the data in a set divided by the total number of data values in the set. The mean is often called the average.

There are 5 snakes. Add their lengths, then divide.

$71 + 68 + 67 + 72 + 68 = 346$

$346 \div 5 = 69.2$

The mean is 69.2.

The median is the middle number in a data set that is arranged in numerical order.

67, 68, 68, 71, 72

The median is 68.

If there is an even number of values, the median is the average of the two middle values.

The mode is the number or value that occurs most often in the data set.

71, 68, 67, 72, 68

The mode is 68.

A data set can have more than one mode or no mode.

Guided Practice*

Do you know HOW?

Use this data set for **1** through **4**. Round decimal answers to hundredths.

Tip: Check that the mean, median, and mode are not greater than the largest data value.

Data set: 11, 5, 8, 5, 6, 7, 5, 8, 8, 9, 9, 4

1. Find the mean.

2. Find the median.

3. Find the mode.

4. Find the range.

Do you UNDERSTAND?

5. Which measure of central tendency is always part of any data set?

6. In the example at the top, are the data widely spread out or clustered? Explain.

7. In Another Example, which measure of central tendency would change the most if Chicago were excluded?

Independent Practice

Find the mean, median, mode, and range of each data set. Round decimal answers to the nearest hundredth.

8. 74, 67, 54, 66, 80, 77, 70, 82, 79

9. 1.57, 1.62, 1.67, 1.72, 1.63, 1.75, 1.59

10. 5.3, 4.6, 4.6, 5.3, 5.3, 4.2, 3.9, 5.1, 5.2

11. 0.4, 0.5, 0.2, 0.4, 0.1, 0.8, 0.4, 0.4

12. 205, 207, 210, 208, 211, 215, 215

13. −2, 6, 7, 5, 4, −3, −11, 13, −2, −2, 5, 4

14. 0°C, 5°C, −8°C, −3°C, 1°C, 6°C, 2°C, −7°C

15. −11, 1, 11, −10, −10, 0

DIGITAL Animated Glossary **www.pearsonsuccessnet.com**

For another example, see Set C on page 515.

Independent Practice

For **16** through **21**, write a set of data that fits the description.

16. The mean is 8.

17. The median is 7.

18. The mode is 16.

19. The median and mean are equal.

20. The range is 0.

21. The mean is 1, and the range is 5.

Problem Solving

The table at the right shows the number of items in five of the 20 largest collections. Use the table for **22** and **23**.

Collections

Items	Number
Buttons	439,900
Golf balls	74,849
Four-leaf clovers	72,928
Refrigerator magnets	101,733
Fruit stickers	34,500

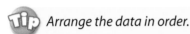

Tip *Arrange the data in order.*

22. What are the mean and median values?

23. Exclude the highest and lowest values. What are the mean and median values?

24. **Number Sense** Could a data set ever have the same mean, median, and mode, and a range of 0? Explain.

25. Yusef and Jaron bought a sandwich to share. It cost \$4.99 plus $5\frac{1}{2}$% tax. If they split the cost evenly, how much did each person spend?

26. **Writing to Explain** Could the range ever be greater than the largest number of a data set? Explain.

27. **Think About the Process** Ana wants to put a fence around a circular flowerbed. What expression can Ana use to find the circumference of the flowerbed?

A $\pi \times 4$ **B** $2\pi \div 4$ **C** $2\pi \times 4$ **D** $\pi \div 8$

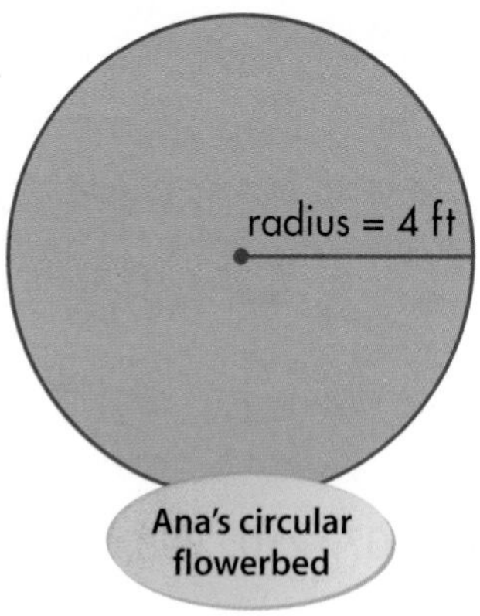

28. **Think About the Process** Adele scored 6 points in her first basketball game, 8 points in her second game, and 11 points in her third game. After 4 games, her mean score was 10. Which equation will help find how many points Adele scored in her fourth game?

A $\frac{(6 + 8 + 11 - p)}{4} = 10$

B $\frac{(6 + 8 + 11 + p)}{4} = 10$

C $(6 + 8 + 11 - p) \times 4 = 10$

D $(6 + 8 + 11 + p) \times 4 = 10$

Going Digital

Mean, Median, Mode, and Range

Use e tools

Spreadsheet/Data/Grapher eTool

The heights in inches of the 12 members of the sixth-grade boys' basketball team at Jefferson Middle School are listed below. Find the mean, median, mode, and range of the data.

70, 60, 63, 65, 62, 61, 65, 64, 68, 65, 59, 62

Step 1 Go to the Spreadsheet/Data/Grapher eTool. Type the data in a column. Use the arrow tool to select the data. Mean Click on the mean icon. The mean is 63.67. Click OK.

Step 2 Click on the median icon. The median is 63.5. Click OK.

Step 3 Click on the mode icon. The mode is 65. Click OK.

Step 4 Click on the sort data icon. The greatest number in the data is 70 and the least is 59. In column B, type = 70 − 59 and press Enter. The range is 11.

Practice

Find the mean, median, mode, and range of each set of data.

1. Heights in inches of the girls' basketball team:
   60, 63, 56, 64, 63, 65, 62, 62, 59, 62

2. Points Tammy scored in each game:
   5, 4, 0, 2, 8, 4, 5, 1

3. Points scored by the team in each game:
   39, 53, 44, 36, 38, 39, 49, 51

Lesson 19-6

Understand It!
The shape of data is easy to see when they are displayed in a frequency table or histogram.

Frequency Tables and Histograms

How can you make and use a frequency table?

Mr. Maxwell timed the cross country team in a 2-mile run. How can he represent the data? Make a frequency table to show the number of times a data value or range of values occurs in the data set.

Data

Times	
16:45	17:14
14:25	14:02
18:40	16:52
16:03	15:18
15:12	17:49
17:35	23:10
19:15	17:55

Another Example How can you make and use a histogram?

A histogram is a graph that uses bars to show the frequency of equal ranges or groups of data. Use the frequency table above to make a histogram displaying the cross-country team times.

Step 1 Title your graph.

Step 2 Use the frequency of the data to choose the scale for the vertical axis.

Step 3 List the time intervals along the horizontal axis.

Step 4 Graph the data by drawing a bar for each interval.

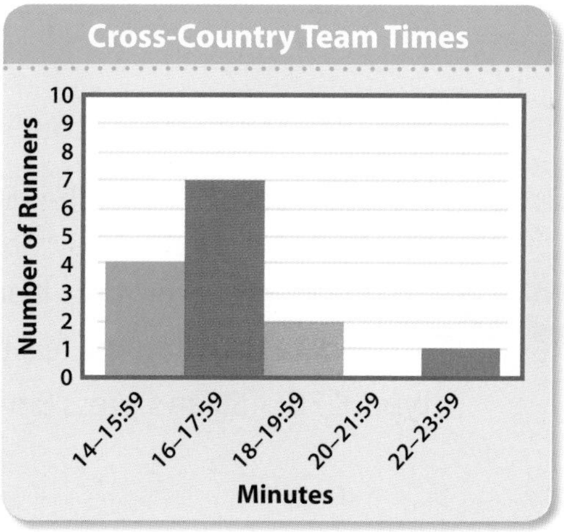

Most of the running times cluster between 14 and 18 minutes. There is a gap in the data between 20 and 22 minutes. The running time between 22 and 24 minutes may be considered an outlier, a data point that has a value much greater or much less than the other points in a data set.

Explain It

1. What does the tallest bar of the histogram represent?

2. How many running times were less than 18 minutes? How do you know?

DIGITAL Animated Glossary **www.pearsonsuccessnet.com**

Step 1

Choose a range that contains all of the data and divide that range into equal intervals or groups.

Step 2

Mark the data in the frequency table using a tally mark for each data value in the range.

Step 3

Count the tally marks and record the frequency.

Running Times	Tally	Frequency
14:00–15:59	IIII	4
16:00–17:59	~~IIII~~ II	7
18:00–19:59	II	2
20:00–21:59		0
22:00–23:59	I	1

Guided Practice*

Do you know HOW?

A toy-store owner asked the age of each child who came into his store one day. The ages of the children were 12, 8, 3, 5, 5, 10, 13, 11, 7, 6, 9, 6, 10, 12, 7, 6.

1. What is the range of ages?

2. Complete the frequency table below for the children shopping at the toy store.

Age Range	*Tallies*	*Frequency*
3–5	III	
6–8	~~IIII~~ I	
9–11	IIII	
12–14	III	

Do you UNDERSTAND?

3. Use the information from the frequency table in Exercise 2 to copy and complete the histogram.

4. **Writing to Explain** If you wanted to know how many 8-year-olds shopped at the toy store, would this histogram help you? Explain.

Independent Practice

Use the information on the right for **5** and **6**.

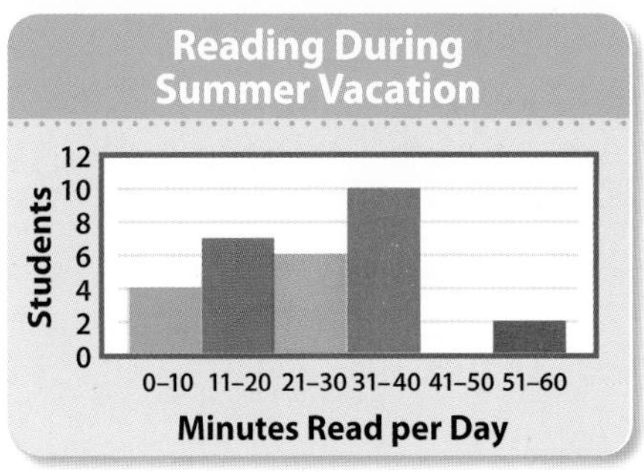

5. How long do the largest group of students spend reading each vacation day?

   A 0–10 minutes
   B 11–20 minutes
   C 21–30 minutes
   D 31–40 minutes

6. Which interval of minutes represents a gap in the data?

For another example, see Set D on page 515.

Independent Practice

Walter tracked the average daily temperature for two weeks. When he finished, he made a frequency table of his data. Use the table for **7** and **8**.

7. What size of interval did Walter choose to group the daily temperatures?

8. Which interval of temperatures contains outliers? Explain.

Average Daily Temperatures

Temp(°F)	*Tally*	*Frequency*
36–40	I	1
41–45	IIII	4
46–50	~~IIII~~ II	7
51–55		0
56–60		0
61–65	II	2

Problem Solving

Use the data at the right for **9** through **13**.

9. Make a frequency table to represent the data.

Tip *Use intervals of 10 years to represent the data: 1–10, 11–20, and so on.*

Data

Ages of Swimmers at Public Pool

12	74	13	20
12	7	19	11
9	7	10	12
6	10	21	24

10. Use your frequency table to represent the data as a histogram.

11. Where do most of the data cluster?

A 0–20 **C** 41–60

B 21–40 **D** Above 61

12. Where are the gaps in the data?

13. **Writing to Explain** Does the data have an outlier? Explain.

14. **Algebra** Matt's age is 14 less than three times Sarah's age. If Sarah is 10 years old, which expression can be used to find Matt's age?

A $14 - 3x$

B $3x - 14$

C $3(x - 14)$

D $14x - 3$

15. **Think About the Process** Which type of graph would be best to display the percentages of the sixth-grade students' favorite sports?

A Line graph

B Histogram

C Bar graph

D Circle graph

Enrichment

Box-and-Whisker Plots

A **box-and-whisker plot** uses a number line to summarize data. The data are organized from least to greatest and then divided into four equal parts, called **quartiles**.

Follow the steps to make a box-and-whisker plot of the test scores.

Example: Mr. Garcia's math class took a test. The scores for his 31 students were 74, 86, 94, 67, 79, 63, 83, 88, 78, 62, 70, 92, 98, 80, 68, 62, 90, 84, 94, 66, 65, 96, 76, 66, 80, 74, 87, 84, 69, 77, and 88.

Step 1 Write the data in order from least to greatest.

	62	63	65	66	66	67	68	69	70	74	74	76	77	78	79	80	80	83	84	84	86	87	88	88	90	92	94	94	96	

Step 2 Find the median of the data. It divides the data into halves. Then find the median for each of these halves. These are the quartile divisions. They divide the data into four quartiles.

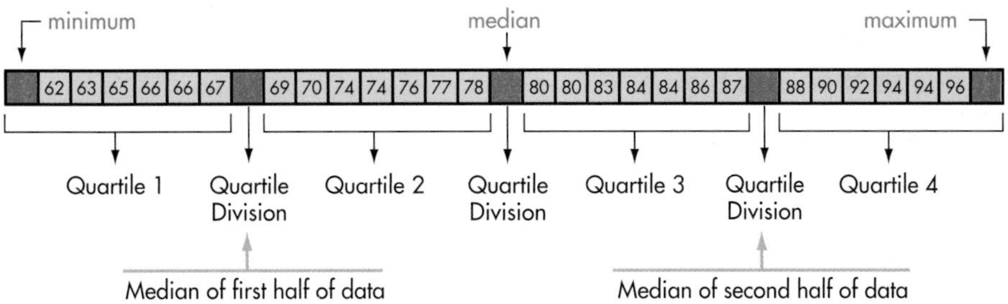

Step 3 Use the minimum, and maximum to draw a number line. Then draw a *box* using the middle two quartiles and label the median. The part of the number line showing the 1st and 4th quartiles are *whiskers*.

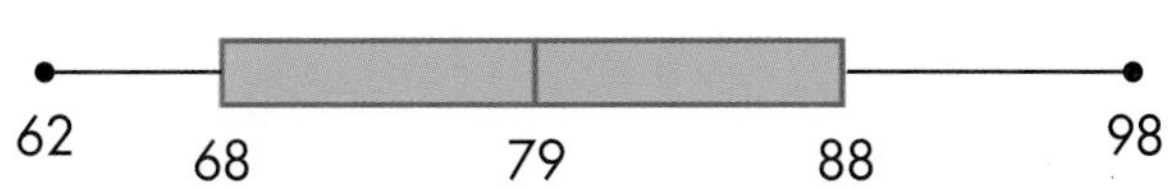

Practice

Make a box-and-whisker plot for each set of data.

1. Miss Hanson's students earned the following scores on their science tests:

73, 78, 66, 61, 85, 90, 99, 76, 64, 70, 72, 72, 93, 81, 71, 79, 85, 89, 84, 75, 79, 91, 82

2. Jamell is a runner on the track team. Here are his times in minutes for the last season:

9, 13, 12, 15, 9, 11, 10, 16, 13, 14, 10, 15, 14, 14, 13, 16, 10

Lesson
19-7 Stem-and-Leaf Plots

Understand It!
Because the data in a stem-and-leaf plot are organized by place value, it is easy to identify the median, mode, and range of the data.

How can you make and use a stem-and-leaf plot?

A stem-and-leaf plot is a chart that uses place value to organize and show individual values in a set of numerical data. The table shows a data set of the cost of a pair of jeans at 10 stores.

Cost of Jeans ($)

25	32	29	36	8
27	40	34	40	33

Make a stem-and-leaf plot of the data in the table. Then, use the plot to find the median and the mode.

Guided Practice*

Do you know HOW?

For **1** through **4**, make and use a stem-and-leaf plot.

1. Copy the stem-and-leaf plot in the example above and then add the cost of jeans at 3 more stores to the data set: $34, $28, and $39.

2. What is the mode of the new data?

3. What is the median of the new data?

4. What is the range of the new data?

Do you UNDERSTAND?

5. Suppose one store charged $51 for a pair of jeans. How would you add this data value to the stem-and-leaf plot in the example above?

6. Stem 3 has more leaves than the other stems. What does that tell you about the data set?

7. Does the data about the price of jeans have an outlier? If so, what is it?

Independent Practice

Use the stem-and-leaf plot for **8** through **10**. The stem-and-leaf plot shows pictures collected by students for an art project.

Number of Pictures Collected

Stem	Leaves
1	9
2	7 7 8
3	2 3 4 7
4	1

KEY: 1 | 9 means 19.

8. What numbers make up the data set?

9. How many data values are between 20 and 40?

10. What are the median, mode, and range of the data?

DIGITAL Animated Glossary **www.pearsonsuccessnet.com**

*For another example, see Set E on page 516.

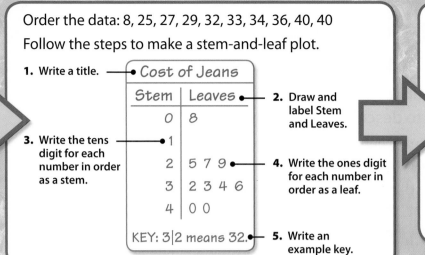

Order the data: 8, 25, 27, 29, 32, 33, 34, 36, 40, 40

Follow the steps to make a stem-and-leaf plot.

1. Write a title.

2. Draw and label Stem and Leaves.

3. Write the tens digit for each number in order as a stem.

4. Write the ones digit for each number in order as a leaf.

5. Write an example key.

Cost of Jeans

Stem	Leaves
0	8
1	
2	5 7 9
3	2 3 4 6
4	0 0

KEY: 3|2 means 32.

Find the median.

Count the leaves from top to bottom and from left to right. The median is half way between the 5th and 6th data values.

3|2 3 ← values 32 and 33

The median is $32.50.

Find the mode.

Identify the leaf value that is most often repeated in one stem.

4|0 0 ← The mode is $40.

11. In a timed race, 10 students took the following times to solve a math puzzle. Represent the data in a stem-and-leaf plot.

Data

Time to Solve (min)

20	14	18	23	15
16	17	16	18	19

Use your plot for **12** and **13**.

12. In your stem-and-leaf plot, how many stems are there? How many leaves are there?

13. What was the median time to solve the puzzle?

Problem Solving

14. Reasoning Shelby scored 85, 84, 77, and 87 on four math tests. She says that a stem-and-leaf plot of her scores would have 3 leaves. Is she correct? Explain.

15. A world record-setting rubber-band ball weighed 3,120 lb. How much did it weigh in kilograms?

Tip *1 kg equals about 2.2 lb.*

16. What is the median cost of the shoes in the following stem-and-leaf plot?

Cost of Shoes

Stem	Leaves
2	3 5 5 9
3	0 2 9
4	1 6

KEY: 2|9 means 29.

A $3 **B** $5 **C** $25 **D** $30

17. Geometry The stem-and-leaf plot shows the side lengths of an irregular pentagon. What is the perimeter of the pentagon?

Side Lengths

Stem	Leaves
0	8
1	1 5 9
2	2

KEY: 1|5 means 15.

18. Algebra The mean of the data is 36. What is the value of x in the stem-and-leaf plot?

Stem	Leaves
3	0 1 x
4	1 5

A 2 **B** 3 **C** 4 **D** 6

Lesson

19-8

Understand It!
The best measure of central tendency is determined by the data itself and the situation for using the data.

Appropriate Use of Statistical Measures

Which measure of central tendency is most useful to describe a given situation?

Gary says he usually gets 98 on his weekly quiz. Does his statement accurately describe his overall performance? Justify your answer using measures of central tendency.

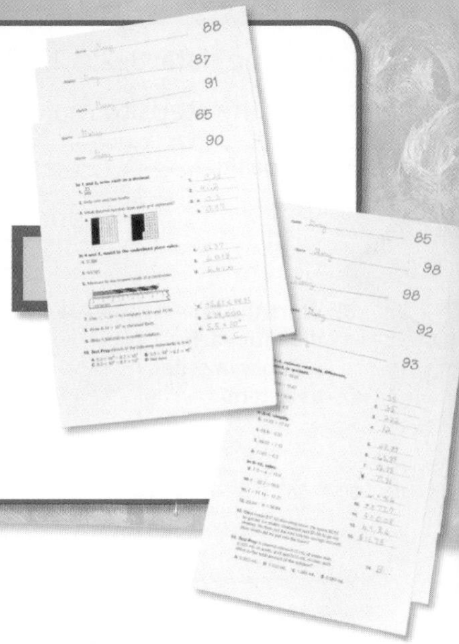

Guided Practice*

Do you know HOW?

Suppose that 5 different stores sell a quart of milk for one of the following prices:

$1.50, $1.50, $1.55, $1.70, $1.80

1. What is the median, mode, and mean?

2. Which measure of central tendency best describes the data set? Why?

Do you UNDERSTAND?

3. Could you have used a line plot to display the data at the top of the page? Why or why not?

4. In the example at the top, suppose the data set had only 3 values: 90, 98, and 90. Is the median the best measure of central tendency for this data set? Explain.

Independent Practice

Use the 9 game scores in the data set at the right for **5** through **12**:

Data

50	60	100
65	50	55
65	70	50

5. Make a stem-and-leaf plot to organize the data set.

6. What is the mode of the data set?

7. What is the median of the data set?

8. What is the mean of the data set?

9. Which measure of central tendency best describes the data set? Why?

10. Identify any outliers.

11. If the outlier 30 is added to the data set, what is the mean of the new data set?

12. Which measure of central tendency best describes the new data set, including 30?

*For another example, see Set F on page 516.

Step 1

Organize Gary's scores in a table or graph. Find the mean, median, mode, and outliers.

Stem	Leaves
6	5
7	
8	5 7 8
9	0 1 2 3 8 8

Mean: 88.7; median: 90.5; mode: 98; 65 is an outlier.

Step 2

Look for clusters, gaps, and outliers to help you reason what the measures of central tendency tell you about Gary's scores.

- **The mode, 98, makes his typical score seem better than it really is.**
- **The mean, 88.7, is affected by the outlier. It makes his typical score seem lower than it really is.**
- **The median, 90.5, is in the middle of the cluster of his typical scores.**

Step 3

Draw conclusions: Gary's statement is misleading.

The median, 90.5, best describes his performance.

It includes the outlier and falls within the cluster of his typical scores.

The data set described in the table has 5 values. Use the table for **13** through **17**.

Tip *Start with the median value.*

Data

Mean	Median	Mode
14,000	13,000	12,500

13. What is the middle number of the data set?

14. Which number occurs at least twice?

15. Why must the other two numbers in the data set be greater than 13,000?

16. What is a possible data set for these measures?

17. Which measure of central tendency best describes the data set you wrote in Exercise 16? Why?

Problem Solving

18. **Algebra** A data set containing 3 values has a median of 100 and a mean of 120. It has no mode. If x and y are the two values other than the median, which equation best represents their value?

A $(x + y) = 120$

B $(x + y + 100) = 120$

C $(x + y) = 120 + 100$

D $(x + y + 100) \div 3 = 120$

19. **Number Sense** Last month an automobile dealership sold 3,116 vehicles. Of these, 455 were trucks. Approximately what percent of the vehicles sold last month were trucks?

A approximately 0.15%

B approximately 4.55%

C approximately 15%

D approximately 455%

20. **Writing to Explain** For the data set x, 600, y, the *best* measure of central tendency is the mode. If the mode equals 600, explain why x and y do not both equal 600.

21. A data set contains the following values: 0, 1, 3, 5, 18. Is there an outlier? Explain.

Lesson

19-9

Understand It!
A sample of a population can help you learn about that population. How well a sample represents a population depends on how the sample is chosen.

Samples and Surveys

How can you select a sample?

A survey uses questions to collect data. Polling, or asking people questions, is one kind of survey.

Tiffany wants to survey students to find out how many plan to come to Math Night. It would be unreasonable to survey all of the 400 students at her school, so Tiffany selected 50 students to survey. How can Tiffany use the sample?

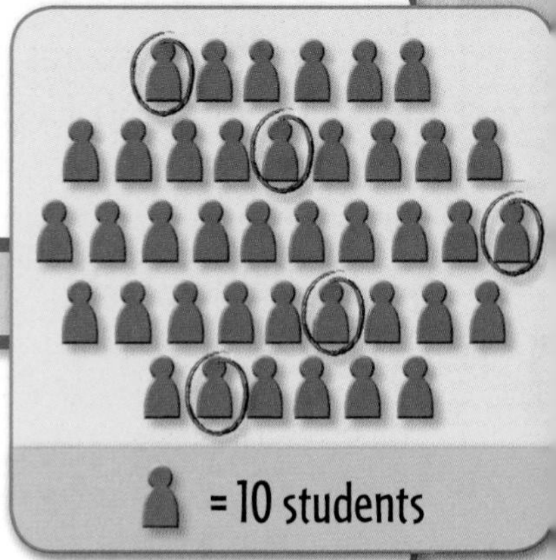

Another Example **Why might a sample be biased?**

John also surveyed 50 students to find how many students plan to come to Math Night. He chose the first 50 students he met.

This sample may be biased. A biased sample is one in which either the size of the sample, or the choice of sample members, is not a good match to the entire population.

John's sample may not represent all students at the school. The first 50 students he met might be a particular group, such as all fifth graders, or students on their way to a math club meeting. John's sample may be biased.

Explain It

1. How could John get a more representative sample?

Guided Practice*

Do you know HOW?

In **1** and **2**, identify the population studied and tell whether the data represent a sample or an entire population.

1. The mean test score on Ms. Zarifa's math test was 82.
2. Based on a poll of sixth graders, 45% of students in all grades at Anderson School ride bikes.

Do you UNDERSTAND?

3. Does the poll used in Exercise 2 provide a representative sample for the school? Explain.
4. If you wanted to know the average weight of puppies in a litter, would you need to use a sample? Explain.
5. In the example at the top, how would Tiffany's estimate change if 25 of the students she surveyed will attend?

*For another example, see Set G on page 517.

Data about a population, an entire group of people or things, may be collected and analyzed.

A sample, or part of the population, may be used when it is too difficult to study the entire population.

Tiffany selected a sample by putting the names of every student into a box and drawing out 50 names.

This is a random sampling, in which each member of the population has an equal chance of being chosen. A random sample is often a good way to obtain a representative sample, a sample that provides a good match for a population.

Results of survey: 30 of the 50 students will attend.

$$\frac{30}{50} = \frac{3}{5} = 60\%$$

So, Tiffany estimated that about 60% of 400 students, or 240 students, will come.

Independent Practice

In **6** through **9**, identify the population studied and tell whether the data represent a sample or an entire population.

6. At County Middle School, 47% of the students are enrolled in a home economics class.

7. Mr. Panos determined that 34% of the people served at his restaurant lived more than 10 miles away.

8. The soccer team averaged 3 goals a game last season.

9. The newspaper found that 40% of its 800,000 readers read the sports first.

Reggie wants to find the number of hours sixth graders play soccer each week. There are 250 students in sixth grade. In **10** through **15**, tell whether each sample might be biased and why.

10. Randomly survey 25 boys.

11. Randomly survey 25 girls.

12. Survey members of the boys' and girls' school soccer teams.

13. Randomly survey 20 girls and 20 boys.

14. Survey 10 of his friends that he sees at school.

15. Survey every fifth-grade student in the school.

16. Alana took a sample of 16 ounces of nut mix from a large barrel. She found that 4 ounces of the sample were cashews. About what percent of the mix in the barrel is cashews?

17. A company surveyed 500 voters from across the United States asking for which candidate they would vote; 215 chose Candidate A. About what percent of all voters prefer Candidate A?

DIGITAL Animated Glossary **www.pearsonsuccessnet.com**

Problem Solving

18. Writing to Explain A company wants to check its daily production of 250,000 newspapers to be sure each includes a sports section. Explain how the company could do this.

19. Using random sampling, a poll showed that 40 out of 50 students ride the bus to school. Carter says this means about 40% of all students ride the bus. Is Carter correct? Explain.

20. In Exercise 18, why wouldn't it make sense to use the entire population?

21. Emma spent $4\frac{1}{2}$ hours doing a social studies project. She finished at 4:45 P.M. When did she start?

22. Sacha bought 3 cans of apple juice, 4 cans of pomegranate juice, 3 cans of grapefruit juice, and 10 cans of orange juice. What fraction of the cans were pomegranate juice? What fraction of the cans were orange juice?

23. Alicia asked 100 people entering a shopping mall in Wilmington, Delaware, to name the first state to enter the Union. Forty-five of them correctly answered, "Delaware." Based on her survey, Alicia estimates that more than half of Americans know that Delaware was the first state to enter the Union. Do you agree? Explain.

24. Reasoning Why should the percentages of responses to a poll add up to 100%?

25. Algebra Warren has 160 soccer cards in a collection. He has 3 times as many national cards as international cards. How many international cards does Warren have? Write and solve an equation to find the answer. Use the diagram to help you write the equation.

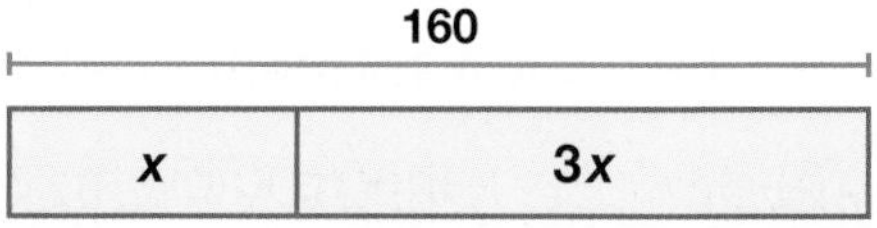

26. Number Sense About how many meters is the wingspan of an adult bald eagle?

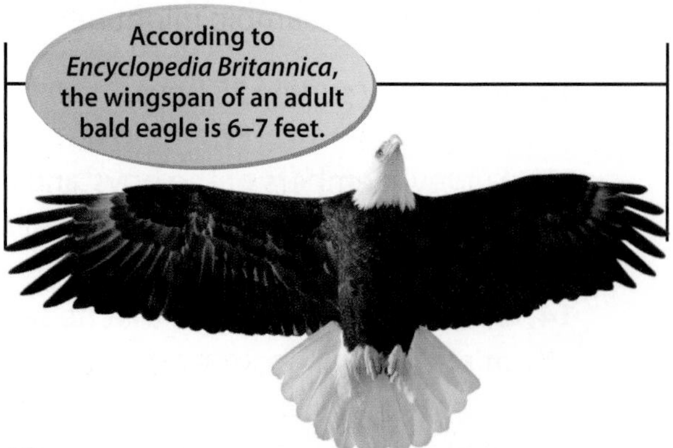

According to *Encyclopedia Britannica*, the wingspan of an adult bald eagle is 6–7 feet.

27. Gene asked 40 sixth graders, "What is the wingspan of an adult bald eagle?" Forty percent of the students knew the correct answer. How many students is this?

A 4 **B** 8 **C** 16 **D** 40

28. Think About the Process If Gene were to ask all 450 students in his school about the wingspan of a bald eagle, about how many could he expect to answer correctly?

A About 45 **B** About 90 **C** About 180 **D** About 300

Enrichment

Convenience and Systematic Sampling

Researchers do not always use random sampling to collect data about an entire population. Sometimes they may use convenience sampling or systematic sampling.

Convenience sampling uses any convenient method to choose the sample. Convenience sampling is usually biased and does not represent an entire population.

Systematic sampling uses a pattern to identify members of the sample. A systematic sampling is more likely to be representative of an entire population.

Example: Jana is taking a survey at the school Science Fair. Describe two ways that Jana could choose a sample and tell whether each way uses convenience sampling or systematic sampling.

1. Jana could survey the first 20 people who arrive at the Science Fair. This is a convenience sampling and would be biased because the first 20 people may be from a particular group.
2. Jana could survey every tenth person who arrives at the Science Fair. This is a systematic sampling and would be more likely to be representative of everyone coming to the fair.

Practice

Tell which sampling method is being used.

1. A mayor wants to know how residents feel about a tax increase to build a new soccer stadium. The first 100 people in line at a soccer game were polled.
2. Karim wants to determine if the players in the city soccer league want to have a longer season. He surveyed every tenth name on a list of the 430 players.
3. A principal wants to know how many sixth graders have siblings. The principal asks the first 10 students walking into one of the sixth grade classes.
4. A mayor wants to know how many teenagers have after-school jobs. He polls 5 teens working at the movie theater.
5. Juanita wants to know students' favorite school lunch. She surveys every fifth student in line to buy lunch.
6. An electronics store owner interviews every 20th customer about customer satisfaction.
7. Andan wants to know what percentage of his Social Studies book contains photographs. He checks every fifteenth page.
8. Jolie wants to know how many people are voting for the current mayor. She asks the first 25 people to go into one polling place.
9. Lin is conducting a survey to find out what movie is most popular with sixth graders. Lin surveyed every fifth student from a list of students in each sixth-grade class.

Lesson
19-10

Understand It!
The wording of questions can influence statistical results and the validity of claims.

Using Statistics to Draw Conclusions

How can you analyze and evaluate claims?

Use the results from a survey taken at Lee Middle School to explain why the way in which the questions are asked might influence the results obtained. Does the data support a claim that "Students say NO to bicycle helmets"?

Data

Sixth Grade Survey Results	Yes	No
1. Does wearing a helmet make bicycling safer?	88%	12%
2. Should bicyclists be forced to wear a helmet?	48%	52%

Another Example How can survey questions affect results?

Evie and Chad conducted surveys about whether students think skateboarding is dangerous. Compare their questions and the bar graphs showing their results.

Evie

Question 1: Don't you agree that skateboarding is dangerous?

Most Students Say Skateboarding Is Dangerous

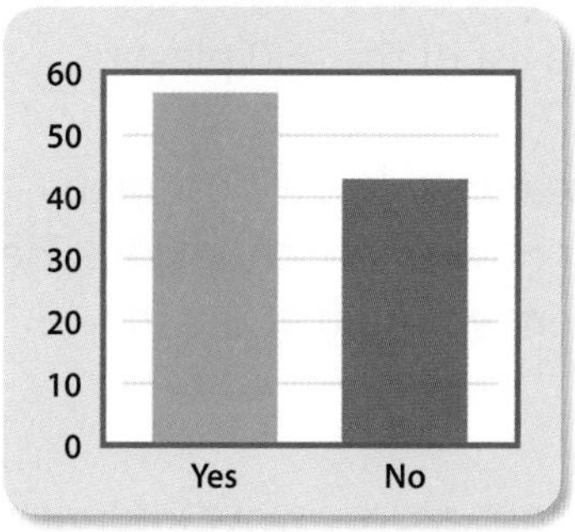

Chad

Question 2: Do you think that skateboarding is dangerous?

Most Students Say Skateboarding Is Not Dangerous

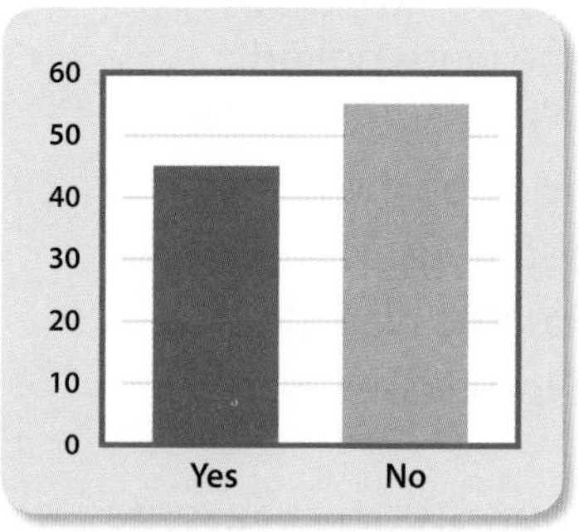

Evie's question is a leading question. It asked students to agree with a *yes* response. Chad's question is more fair.

Explain It

1. How did Evie's question influence the results of her survey?

How questions are asked can influence survey results.

Question 1 included the word *safer*, and people are likely to support safety.

Question 2 included with word *forced*, and people are likely to oppose being forced.

To get unbiased information, questions should avoid words that are likely to produce strong reactions in people.

Ask: Should bicyclists be *required* to wear a helmet?

Students Say NO to Bicycle Helmets

This claim was made based on the survey results for Question 2.

Even though Question 2 used the word *forced*, the results were almost equal.

The survey did not ask students if they usually wear a bicycle helmet.

The claim is misleading and is not justified by the results of the survey.

Guided Practice*

Do you know HOW?

Use the information below for **1** and **2**. Becca asked 25 students to name the vegetable they hate the least. The table shows her results.

Data

Peas	Corn	Broccoli	Carrots
32%	28%	16%	24%

So, Becca claimed that peas were the favorite vegetable of students at school.

1. Explain why the way the question was asked may have influenced the results.

2. Is the claim that Becca made justified? Explain.

Do you UNDERSTAND?

3. How can the way a question is asked influence the results obtained?

4. In the example at the top, suppose the heading read "Students Agree that Helmets Make Bicyling Safer." Does the data support that claim?

5. Is the question "Do you think gas-guzzling cars should be allowed on the highways?" a fair question?

Independent Practice

6. Which question do you think is most fair regarding littering? Explain.

a Should people who throw their garbage in our parks be arrested?

b Should littering be against the law?

c Should the government interfere with what people do?

7. Which question do you think is most fair regarding taxes for schools? Explain.

a Are you in favor of helping children learn?

b Are you in favor of throwing more tax dollars at schools?

c Are you in favor of a tax increase to pay for a new school?

For another example, see Set G on page 517.

Independent Practice

Use the stem-and-leaf plot at the right for **8** and **9**. Tell whether each claim is valid. Explain your answer.

Test Scores

Stem	Leaves
7	2 6 7
8	1 3 4 8
9	0 5

KEY: 8 | 4 means 84

8. It is very likely that a test taker will earn a score of 90 or higher.

9. It is likely that a random test taker will score higher than 80.

Problem Solving

10. Writing to Explain At Lakeview School, 20% of students are in band and 30% participate in sports. Dan says this means that exactly half of the students are not in band or in a sport. Is he correct? Explain.

11. On the graph, it looks like Lauren sold twice as many boxes as Teresa. Is this a reasonable conclusion to draw? Explain.

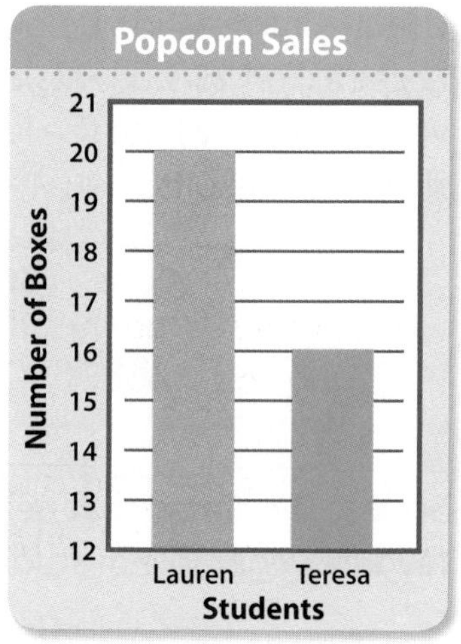

12. Kyle is surveying his class of 30 students to find out whether more students pack their lunch or buy a lunch. Should he survey a sample or the entire population? Explain.

13. A population contains 100,000 members. A random sample of 1,000 members is surveyed. Of the sample, 1% of the members replied "Other." Darby says this means 100% of the entire population would respond "Other." Is he correct? Explain.

14. Suppose you want to find about how many stitches are in 1 square foot of a knitted scarf. How would you find the answer? Explain why.

15. Think About the Process Gary is conducting a survey about favorite sports. He asked: *Don't you agree that basketball is your favorite sport?* Is his question fair? Explain.

16. Reasonableness The median age of the students at a college is 21.5 years. What is a reasonable conclusion?

A 50% of students are older than 21.5 years.

B No student is older than 21.5 years.

C No student is older than 43 years.

D The average age of a student is 21.5 years.

17. Number Sense A bucket of 500 coins contains quarters, dimes, and nickels. A random sample of 30 coins results in 5 nickels and 10 quarters. Based on the sample, about how many coins in the bucket are dimes?

A 15

B 100

C 150

D 250

Stop and Practice

Skills Review For **1** through **4**, choose the best graph to use for each situation. Match the letter of the types of graphs listed below.

a line graph **c** circle graph

b bar graph **d** histogram

1. Compare a whole to its parts.

2. Show changes over time.

3. Show the shape of the data.

4. Compare numerical data.

Error Search The stem-and-leaf plot to the right shows how long it takes some students to walk to school. Identify whether each statement is correct or incorrect based on the data. If a statement is incorrect, write it correctly.

Walking Times (in minutes)

Stem	Leaves
1	2 3 9
2	4 5 5
3	0 2 3

KEY: 3 | 2 means 32

5. The majority of students walk to school in under 30 minutes.

6. For these students, the median time is 25 minutes to walk to school.

7. The longest time it took the students to walk to school was 33 minutes, and the shortest time was 12 minutes.

Number Sense

Reasoning Students at Kelsey School had a car wash to raise money for a food pantry. Use the graph at right for **8** through **10**.

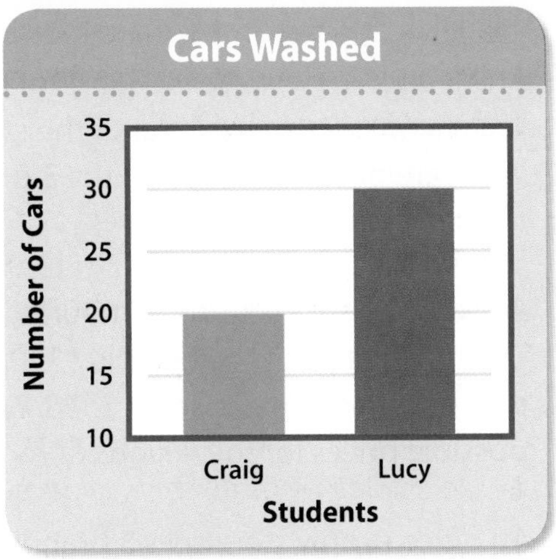

8. Why does the graph make it look as though Lucy washed twice as many cars as Craig?

9. Write a ratio in lowest terms comparing the number of cars Craig washed to the number of cars Lucy washed.

10. Write the number of cars Lucy washed as a percent of the number of cars Craig washed.

Lesson
19-11

Understand It!
Some problems can be solved by making a reasoned first try for what the answer might be and then checking and revising to find the correct answer.

Problem Solving

Try, Check, and Revise

A store sells 5 different kinds of milk in gallon jugs. The mean price of a gallon of milk is $3.29. No two prices are the same. List 5 possible prices for the gallons of milk. Make sure that each price is a reasonable price for a gallon of milk.

Guided Practice*

Do you know HOW?

In **1** through **3**, find possible prices for 4 kinds of yogurt sold at a store.

1. What are 4 possible prices, if the mean price is $0.73?

2. What are 4 possible prices, if the median price is $0.75?

3. What are 4 possible prices, if the mode for the prices is $0.80?

Do you UNDERSTAND?

4. In the example above, what are 5 possible prices for a gallon of milk if the median price is $3.29? if the mode is $3.29?

5. **Write a Problem** If 5 prices for a gallon of milk are *V*, *W*, *X*, *Y*, and *Z*, write an equation for the mean, $3.29.

Independent Practice

Solve.

6. An electronics store sells 3 kinds of printers. The mean price of a printer at the store is $150. What are possible prices for the 3 printers the store sells?

7. A bike shop sells 4 kinds of mountain bikes. The mean price of the bikes is $320, and the median price of the bikes is $325. What are possible prices for the 4 kinds of mountain bikes?

8. An office supply store sells 3 brands of paper. The mode and mean prices are both $2.29. What are possible prices for the 3 brands?

Stuck? Try this....

- What do I know?
- What am I asked to find?
- What diagram can I use to help understand the problem?
- Can I use addition, subtraction, multiplication, or division?
- Is all of my work correct?
- Did I answer the right question?
- Is my answer reasonable?

*For another example, see Set H on page 517.

Plan and Solve

Use reasoning. Find 5 possible prices having a mean of $3.29.

Try these possible prices: $2.89, $2.99, $3.09, $3.29, $3.49

Check to see if the mean is equal to $3.29.

$2.89 + 2.99 + 3.09 + 3.29 + 3.49 = 15.75$

$15.75 \div 5 = \$3.15$

The mean is too low, so you need to use higher prices.

Plan and Solve

Revise the prices using what you know. The mean was 14 cents too low.

Try adding 14 cents to each price: $3.03, $3.13, $3.23, $3.43, $3.63

Check to see if the mean equals $3.29.

$3.03 + 3.13 + 3.23 + 3.43 + 3.63 = 16.45$

$16.45 \div 5 = \$3.29$

5 possible prices for the milk are $3.03, $3.13, $3.23, $3.43, and $3.63.

A table at a yard sale has 7 miscellaneous items for sale. For **9** through **11**, find possible prices for the items.

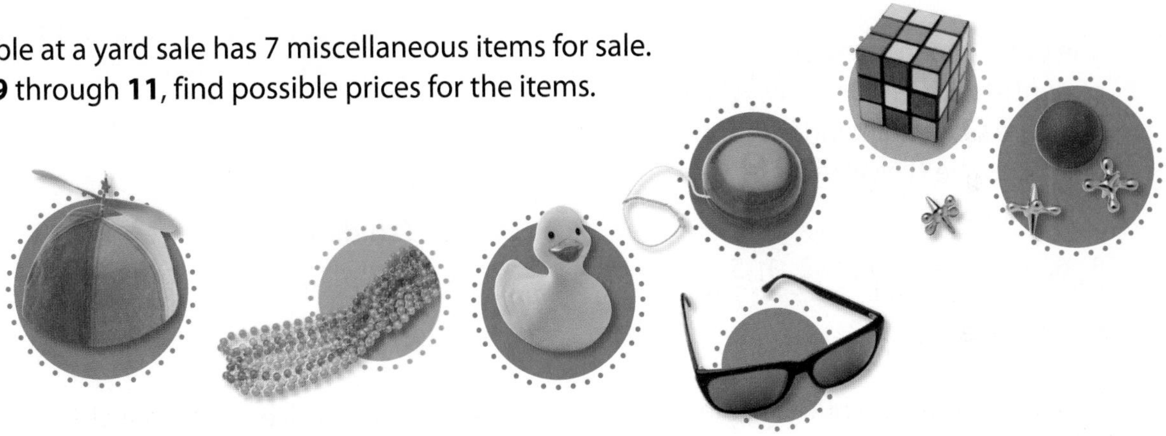

9. What are 7 possible prices of the items, assuming that each item has a different price, if the mean price is $0.28?

10. What are 7 possible prices of the items, assuming that each item has a different price, if the median price is $0.29?

11. What are 7 possible prices of the items, assuming that some of the items have the same price, if the mode of the prices is $0.27?

12. The mode of a set of 5 numbers is 57. What are 5 possible numbers in the set if the other numbers are less than the mode?

13. The mean of a set of 5 positive numbers is 29. The median is 28. The mode is 33. What are 5 possible numbers?

14. The mean of a set of 3 numbers is 39. One of the numbers is 35. What are possible values of the 2 other numbers, assuming that all 3 numbers are different?

15. The scores on Briana's first 4 science exams gave her an average (mean) of 88. What are 4 possible scores she might have received?

16. The mean of a set of 5 temperatures is positive and the median is negative. What are 5 possible temperatures of the data set?

Topic 19

Test

1. The numbers of pets per home for 8 friends are listed below. What is the mean of the data set? (19-5)

2, 4, 6, 3, 2, 1, 4, 2

A 2

B 3

C 5

D 6

2. The years of experience for a group of dentists are listed below. Which measure of central tendency best describes the typical years of experience? (19-8)

8, 6, 12, 7, 4, 4, 12, 32, 1, 5

A Mode

B Mean

C Median

D Outlier

3. The circle graph shows the cars sold at a dealership during November. If the dealership sold 400 cars that month, how many were SUVs? (19-2)

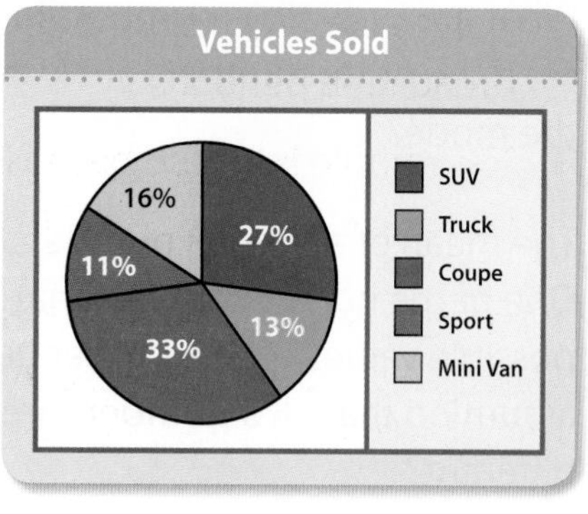

A 100

B 108

C 200

D 292

4. According to the histogram, how many students have between 8 and 15 absences? (19-6)

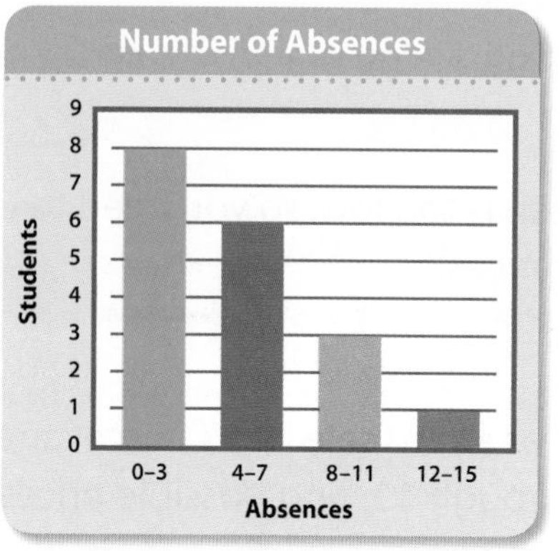

A 1 student

B 3 students

C 4 students

D 5 students

5. The mean price of a textbook is \$82 and the range of prices is \$16. What are possible prices for the textbook? (19-11)

A \$82, \$82, \$82, \$82, \$98

B \$90, \$90, \$74, \$74, \$74

C \$82, \$82, \$88, \$76, \$82

D \$82, \$84, \$90, \$80, \$74

6. Which of the following questions would be considered most fair for a survey of opinions on a school dress code? (19-10)

A Should students be told what they can wear to school?

B Should students be allowed to wear inappropriate clothing?

C Do teachers have the right to dictate student clothing?

D Are you in favor of a school dress code?

7. Which field of study shown in the graph had the greatest enrollment at four-year institutions? (19-1)

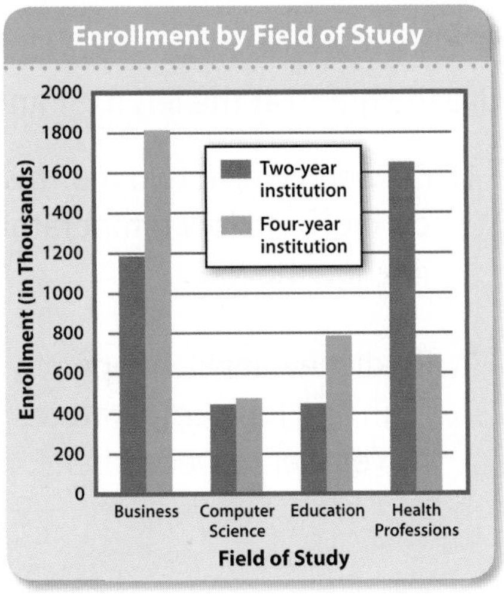

A Business

B Computer Science

C Education

D Health Professions

8. A company used the graph shown to advertise Brand B. What makes the graph misleading? (19-3)

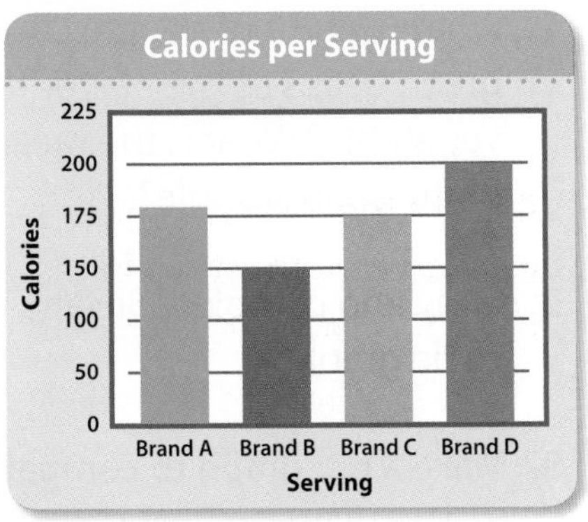

A The bars are the same width.

B The vertical axis starts at zero.

C The title is misleading.

D The intervals on the vertical axis are different sizes.

9. What is the mode of the data shown in the stem-and-leaf plot? (19-7)

Students per Class

Stem	Leaves
1	7 7 8 8
2	0 3 3 4 4 4 6
3	0

KEY: 2 | 6 means 26 Students

A 24

B 22

C 18

D 12

10. Peyton stood in front of a popular restaurant from 7:00 A.M. to 10:00 P.M. and asked people to name their favorite restaurant. Which of the following best describes the sample? (19-9)

A The sample is not biased.

B The sample is biased because many people will name the popular restaurant Peyton is standing near.

C The sample is biased because Peyton is not sampling customers from a broad time period.

D The sample is biased because children are not included in the poll.

11. What type of graph would be best to show temperature change over several hours? (19-4)

A Circle graph

B Line graph

C Double-bar graph

D Scatterplot

Set A, pages 476–478

High and low temperature data are shown in the double-line graph.

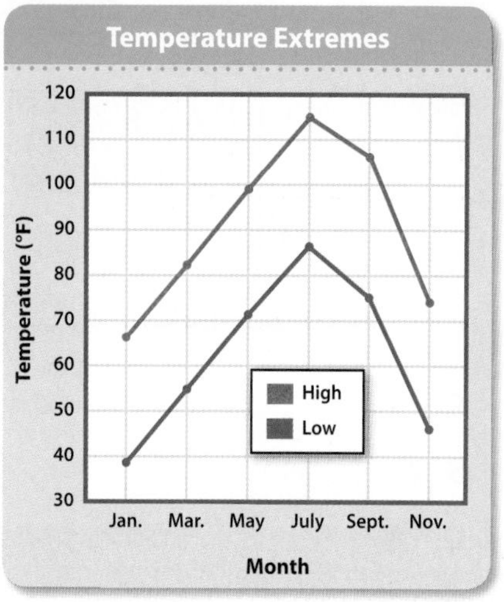

Remember that a double-line graph shows two sets of related data collected over time. A line graph can also show trends.

Use the graph at the left for **1** and **2**.

1. Between which two months do high and low temperatures change the most?

2. Predict what will happen to high and low temperatures from November to December. Explain.

Set B, pages 480–482, 484–486, 488–489

Susan polled 25 people about their favorite green vegetable. 12 chose broccoli, 8 chose green beans, and 5 chose peas. Susan started a circle graph.

Step 1 Find the percent of people who chose broccoli.

$$\frac{12}{25} = 0.48 = 48\%$$

Step 2 Use the percent to calculate the measure of the central angle.

$$48\% \times 360 = 172.8 \approx 173°$$

Step 3 Draw a circle and a 173° central angle. Color and label the sector.

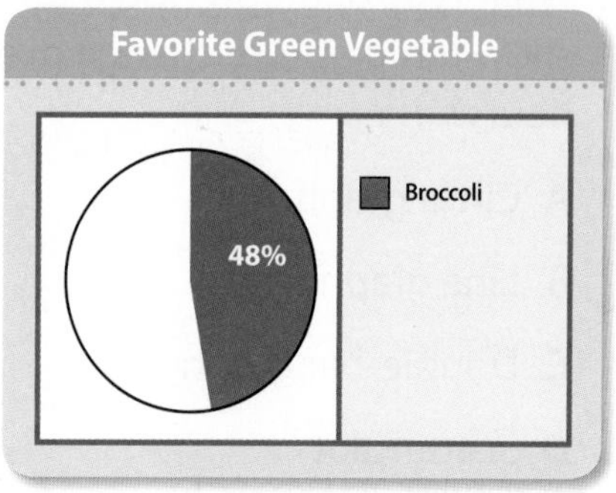

Remember that circle graphs show how parts of a set of data compare to the whole set. Bar graphs make it easy to compare numerical data.

Use the data at the left for **1** through **3**.

1. What percent of people chose green beans as their favorite vegetable? What is the measure of the central angle?

2. Copy and complete Susan's circle graph.

3. Make a bar graph to compare Susan's data.

4. Compare the graphs. Which graph makes it easier to compare how many people chose green beans, and how many people chose peas?

Set C, pages 490–492

Find the mean, median, mode, and range of the following set of data.

Total Game Points				
129	124	128	120	124

The mean is the sum of all the data in a set divided by the total number of data values in the set. The mean is 125.

$(129 + 124 + 128 + 120 + 124) \div 5 = 125$

The median is the middle number in a data set that is arranged in numerical order.

120, 124, 124, 128, 129

The mode is the number that occurs most often. The mode is 124.

120, 124, 124, 128, 129

The range is the difference between the greatest number and least number in the data set.

$129 - 120 = 9$

Remember to order the data values from least to greatest before you begin. The mean, median, and mode are measures of central tendency. A data set can have more than one mode or no mode. The range describe how spread out the data is.

What are the mean, median, mode, and range of each of the data sets?

1. 2, 5, 5
2. 11, 13, 11, 13
3. 27, 26, 25, 24
4. 100, 200, 500, 300, 500
5. 1.4, 1.3, 1.1, 1.4, 1.9, 1.8, 1.7, 1.4
6. Make up a data set of five numbers that have the same mean, median, and mode.

Set D, pages 494–496

At a summer camp, the ages of the campers are listed below.

12, 14, 12, 14, 10, 11, 15, 13, 13, 11, 12, 12, 7, 14, 12

The data can be organized in a frequency table.

Divide the range of data into equal intervals and mark the frequency of the data using tally marks.

Ages of Campers	6–8	9–11	12–14	15–17
Tally	|	|||	~~||||~~ ~~||||~~	|
Frequency	1	3	10	1

Remember that a histogram is a graph that uses bars to show the frequency of equal ranges or groups of data. It shows the shape of the data.

1. Represent the data in the frequency table on the left in a histogram.
2. Use your histogram in Exercise 1 to identify any clusters, gaps or outliers.

Set E, pages 498–499

Make a stem-and-leaf plot of the following data.

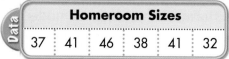

Homeroom Sizes					
37	41	46	38	41	32

Order the data from least to greatest. Write each tens digit as a stem. Write each ones digit as the leaves.

Homeroom Size

Stem	Leaves
3	2 7 8
4	1 1 6

KEY: 3 | 8 means 38

A stem-and-leaf plot makes it easy to find the median, mode, and range of the data.

Remember that a stem-and-leaf plot uses place value to organize a set of numerical data.

Math Scores							
77	83	87	72	94	90	81	96
74	88	75	80	95	87	68	89

1. Make a stem-and-leaf plot of the Math Scores in the table.
2. What is the median score?
3. What is the mode?
4. What is the range?

Set F, pages 500–501

A store manager says that he usually sells 90 games each week. Is the statement accurate? Which measure of central tendency best describes the data set?

Games Sold Each Week						
81	90	85	86	82	55	90

Find the mean, median, and mode with and without the outlier, 55.

	With Outliers	Without Outliers
Mean	81.3	85.6
Median	85	85.5
Mode	90	90

The manager's statement is not accurate. The medians or the mean without the outlier are the best measures of central tendency. He usually sells about 85 games each week.

Remember to consider the effect of outliers on mean, median, and mode when drawing conclusions and deciding which statistical measure to use with a data set.

Use this data set for **1** through **3**.

Home Runs Hit			
41	29	34	27
41	42	44	60

1. Find the mean, median, and mode of the number of home runs hit by 8 sluggers.
2. Which statistical measure best describes the data set?
3. Does the data set contain any outliers? Explain.

Set G, pages 502–504, 506–508

The sixth-grade class at Franklin School was surveyed.

Sixth Grade Survey Results	*Yes*	*No*
Should all students be forced to do an hour of homework every night?	21%	79%

Does the survey use a sample or an entire population?
Because only a portion of the school is surveyed, the survey uses a sample.

Was the sample a random sampling of the school?
It was not a random sample because only sixth graders were surveyed.

Is the sample biased?
The sample may be biased because sixth graders may not be a good match for the entire school.

What conclusions can you draw about the results based on the question asked?
The results may be biased because the question used the word *forced*. People are likely to oppose being forced to do things.

Remember that survey results are best if they are based on a representative sample.

In **1** and **2**, is the surveyed group a sample or the entire population?

1. 100 motorcycle owners about driving safety
2. All concert attendees on their favorite song performance

In **3** and **4**, is the sample biased? If it is, tell why it is biased.

3. Surveyed 500 randomly chosen people about their favorite brand of jeans
4. Surveyed 5 randomly chosen people about their favorite cereal
5. Tell whether this question is fair and explain why or why not. *Do you usually wear a helmet when you rollerblade?*

Set H, pages 510–511

Four people on an elevator have a mean weight of 115 pounds. No one weighs the same. What are 4 possible weights for the people?

Try: 103, 108, 114, 123

Check: $\frac{(103 + 108 + 114 + 123)}{4} = 112$

Revise:

Try adding 3 pounds to each weight.

4 possible weights for the people are 106, 111, 117, and 126.

$$\frac{(106 + 111 + 117 + 126)}{4} = 115$$

Remember, it may take many repetitions of Try, Check, and Revise to solve a problem.

1. Four friends drank a pitcher of lemonade. No person drank the same amount. If the mean amount the 4 friends drank is 2.5 cups, what are 4 possible amounts the four friends drank?
2. If the mode for the amount 4 friends drank is 2 cups and the mean amount is 2.5 cups, what are 4 possible amounts?

Topic 20 Probability

1 What is the probability of winning a prize by getting the ball in a certain colored cup? You will find out in Lesson 20-5.

2 Komodo dragons are the largest living lizards. If you were to see a Komodo dragon in the wild, what is the probability that it would be male? You will find out in Lesson 20-3.

3

One tree yielded five different fruits: plums, peaches, nectarines, apricots, and cherries. What are some fruit smoothie mixtures you could make? You will find out in Lesson 20-1.

Review What You Know!

Vocabulary

Choose the best term from the box.

- simplest form
- prime number
- set

1. The numbers 19 and 31 are two examples of a __?__.

2. A collection of numbers is an example of a __?__.

3. A fraction for which 1 is the only common factor for the numerator and denominator is in __?__.

Multiplication

Find each product.

4. $4 \times 1 \times 9$

5. $5 \times 8 \times 12 \times 10 \times 2$

6. $7 \times 21 \times 8 \times 3$

Equivalent Forms

Fill in the missing numbers.

7. $\frac{1}{4} = 0.\square = \square\%$

8. $\frac{\square}{\square} = 0.85 = \square\%$

9. $\frac{\square}{\square} = 0.\square = 32\%$

Statistics

Write an answer for the question.

10. **Writing to Explain** What is the difference between a sample and a population?

Lesson
20-1

Understand It!
Tables, tree diagrams, grids, and multiplication can be used to list all possible outcomes for compound events.

Counting Methods

How can you count all the possibilities?

The students on the school spirit committee are selling pennants. The table shows the different colors, sizes, and designs. How can you find the total number of possible choices of pennants they can sell?

School Pennants

Color	Size	Design
red	small	pole
green	large	rivets

Another Example

How can you find all possible outcomes for compound events?

Count all the possible outcomes for tossing a six-sided number cube two times.

Vocabulary	**Example**
An event is the result, or outcome, of a single experiment.	Tossing a 6 on the number cube is an event.
The set of all possible outcomes of an experiment is the sample space.	The sample space for one toss is 1, 2, 3, 4, 5, and 6.
A compound event is a combination of two or more single events.	Tossing the number cube two times is a compound event.

One Way

Make a grid.

First Toss (columns), *Second Toss* (rows)

	1	2	3	4	5	6
1	1,1	1,2	1,3	1,4	1,5	1,6
2	2,1	2,2	2,3	2,4	2,5	2,6
3	3,1	3,2	3,3	3,4	3,5	3,6
4	4,1	4,2	4,3	4,4	4,5	4,6
5	5,1	5,2	5,3	5,4	5,5	5,6
6	6,1	6,2	6,3	6,4	6,5	6,6

Another Way

Use the Counting Principle.

Outcomes for number cube on first toss		Outcomes for number cube on second toss		Total number of outcomes
6	×	6	=	36

Both the grid and the Counting Principle find 36 possible outcomes.

Explain It

1. Explain the relationship between "all possibilities" and the "sample space."

One Way

Draw a tree diagram to show all the possible choices.

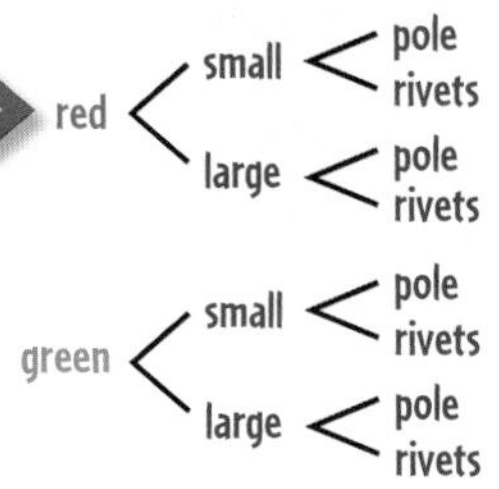

There are 8 choices.

Another Way

Make an organized list.

red, small, pole
red, small, rivets
red, large, pole
red, large, rivets
green, small, pole
green, small, rivets
green, large, pole
green, large, rivets

There are 8 choices.

Another Way

Use multiplication.

Choices for color		Choices for size		Choices for design		Total number of choices
2	$\times$	2	$\times$	2	=	8

There are 8 choices.

When you multiply to find the total number of choices, you are using the Counting Principle.

Guided Practice*

Do you know HOW?

1. Make an organized list of the possible outcomes when tossing a number cube (1–6) and a coin (heads or tails).

2. Draw a tree diagram to show all possibilities for tossing a coin (heads or tails) and a number cube (1–6).

3. Use the Counting Principle to find the total possible outcomes for spinning a spinner (with 5 equal sections) and tossing a number cube (1–6).

Do you UNDERSTAND?

4. Suppose three more colors—blue, yellow, and black—were added to the pennant options above. Which would be the quickest method to find the total number of possibilities: tree diagram, organized list, or counting principle? Explain.

5. If you toss a red number cube, a blue number cube, and a green number cube, each numbered 1–6, what is the number of possible outcomes?

Independent Practice

6. Think about 5 different colors of containers and 5 different colors of lids. How many container-and-lid outcomes are possible?

7. You have 8 flowers, each a different kind, and 3 different vases. How many possible outcomes are there for one flower in one vase?

8. Eli has 3 pairs of pants; blue, black, and brown. He has 5 different-colored shirts. How many possible outfits can Eli make?

DIGITAL Animated Glossary **www.pearsonsuccessnet.com**

**For another example, see Set A on page 540.*

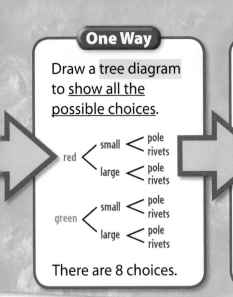

Independent Practice

Use the spinners at the right for **9** and **10**.

9. Suppose that you spin each spinner once. Make an organized list to show the sample space of letter and number pairs.

10. Suppose that you spin each spinner once. How many possible color outcomes could you have?

11. The cafeteria lunch menu has 5 entrées, 4 beverages, and 3 salads. How many outcomes for one entrée, one beverage, and one salad are possible using this menu?

12. Use these letters and numbers: A, E, I, O, U, and 2, 4, 6, 8. How many pairs of one letter and one number can you make?

Problem Solving

13. **Draw a Diagram** For a trip, Elyse packed a red, a green, and a pink shirt. She also packed a pair of jeans and a black skirt. Make a tree diagram to show all of Elyse's possible outfits.

14. **Algebra** Suppose that you have *h* hats, *c* coats, and *g* pairs of gloves. Write an algebraic expression that describes the possible number of hat and coat outcomes.

15. **Writing to Explain** What might be an advantage of using a tree diagram instead of the Counting Principle? Explain.

16. Alger received the following scores on his social studies quizzes: 73, 85, 71, 92, and 94. What is Alger's mean quiz score?

17. The computer lab teacher wants each student to create a 5-character password using the rules shown in the chart. The letters and digits may repeat. What is the total number of possible passwords?

Password Rules Chart
Use 3 digits followed by 2 letters.
Use any digit from 0 to 9.
Use any letter but *X* or *Z*.

By grafting the branches of other fruit trees onto one plum tree, an agronomist was able to grow all of the fruits shown in the picture at the right. Use the information to answer **18**.

18. How many possible fruit smoothie mixtures could you make using one type of fruit at a time and your choice of either plain or vanilla yogurt?

A 4 mixtures **C** 8 mixtures

B 10 mixtures **D** 12 mixtures

Mixed Problem Solving

Math and Social Studies

Spinning tops have been a favorite toy all over the world for centuries. Some tops are round. Some have flat sides that let them stop with one side facing up.

1. Suppose that you are using a 6-sided top. Three of the sides have pictures of animals, and three of the sides have pictures of plants. If the possible outcomes for a single spin are animal or plant, make a table that shows all possible outcomes for spinning the top twice.

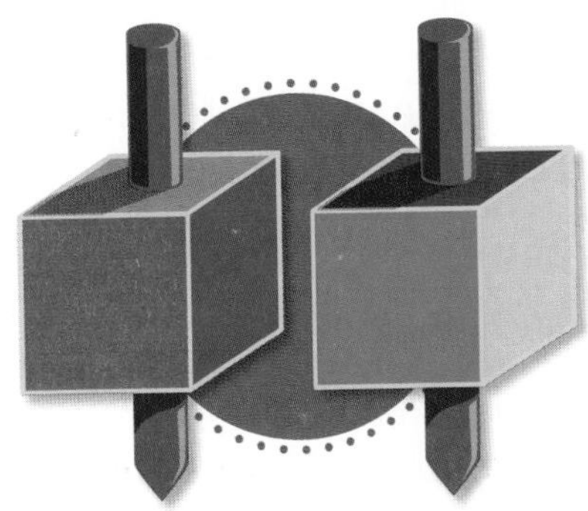

2. Suppose that you are using two 4-sided tops with flat faces and colors on the sides. If the first top has two red sides and two blue sides, and the second top has two green sides and two yellow sides, make a tree diagram to show all possible outcomes for the color of the tops when both tops are spun.

3. A Braille top has raised dots on each of its sides. Suppose that you are using a 4-sided Braille top with the letters *a*, *b*, *c*, and *d* on its sides. Copy and complete the grid to show the sample space for spinning the top twice.

		a	*b*	*c*	*d*
		⠁	⠃	⠉	⠙
a	⠁				
b	⠃				
c	⠉				
d	⠙				

Lesson
20-2

Understand It!
The order of the outcomes of an event may be important when counting the total number of possibilities.

Permutations and Combinations

How do you count arrangements when order matters?

Ken, Jon, Naomi, and Mindy are on the tennis team. They are playing a doubles match. How many possible ways can they be positioned on the tennis court to play?

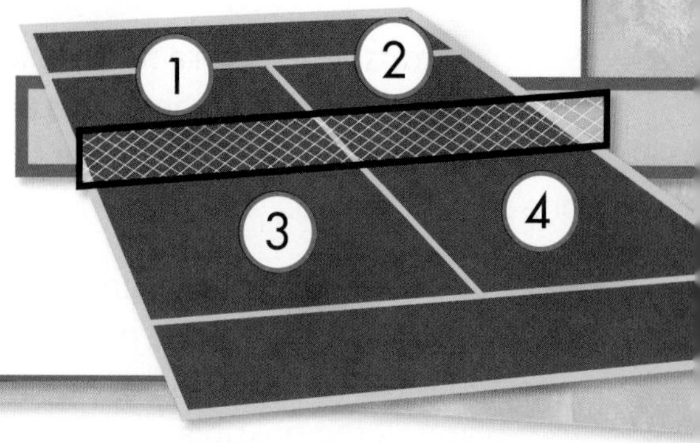

Another Example

How can you count arrangements when order does not matter?

Abby, Ginny, Joe, and Lars are badminton players. How many different pairs can they form to play in the tournament?

If order were important, there would be 12 possible pairs.

Abby and Ginny
Abby and Joe
Abby and Lars
Ginny and Abby
Ginny and Joe
Ginny and Lars
Joe and Abby
Joe and Ginny
Joe and Lars
Lars and Abby
Lars and Ginny
Lars and Joe

However, order is not important. Abby and Ginny and Ginny and Abby are the same pair.

So, when you make a list, eliminate duplicate pairs.

Abby and Ginny
Abby and Joe
Abby and Lars
Ginny and Joe
Ginny and Lars
Joe and Lars

When the order of the people or items is not important, each possible arrangement is called a combination.

There are 6 possible combinations of players.

Explain It

1. Why doesn't the order of the players on the team matter in the badminton tournament?

2. What if Abby, Ginny, and Joe are having a group picture taken? How many possible ways can they line up? Is this a permutation or a combination?

Find the number of choices for each position.

Think All four players are choices for the first position. Once the first player is chosen, the remaining three players are choices for the second position, and so on. Use the Counting Principle.

Choices for 1st position		Choices for 2nd position		Choices for 3rd position		Choices for 4th position		Total number of possible arrangements
4	×	3	×	2	×	1	=	24

When the order of people or items is important, each arrangement is called a permutation.

There are 24 possible permutations, or arrangements, of the tennis players.

Guided Practice*

Do you know HOW?

1. If Melany places 6 books on a shelf, how many possible ways can she line up the books on the shelf?

2. How many possible teams of 3 players can be formed from 4 players? Is this a combination or a permutation?

Do you UNDERSTAND?

3. Your teacher is putting the class in groups of three to work on a problem. Is the arrangement a combination or a permutation? Explain.

4. In the example at the top, if the coach joins the 4 players for a group photograph, how many possible ways could they all line up for the picture?

Independent Practice

Leveled Practice For **5** through **8**, decide whether the number of possible arrangements is a permutation or a combination.

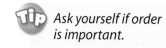

Tip *Ask yourself if order is important.*

5. Daryl has 4 frozen dinners in his freezer: chicken, beef, lasagna, and spaghetti. He eats one on Tuesday and one on Wednesday.

6. For a veggie pizza, Hugh is choosing 2 different toppings from 3 options: onion, peppers, and mushrooms.

7. Jennifer is arranging 8 different CDs in a row of her case.

8. Sharon has a bag with 8 soccer balls. She is giving 2 soccer balls to each team.

DIGITAL Animated Glossary **www.pearsonsuccessnet.com**

*For another example, Set B on page 541.

Independent Practice

For **9** through **16**, find the number of possible arrangements and state whether it is a permutation or combination.

9. Hugh and five friends are going to set a table for 6. How many possible seating arrangements are there?

10. There are 5 finalists in an art contest. In how many ways can the first, second, and third prizes be awarded?

11. Jose has 4 different shirts: red, blue, yellow and white. He wants to pack 2 shirts for camp. How many possible pairs of shirts can he pick?

12. For dinner, Jesse can choose 2 different side dishes from corn, potatoes, beans, rice, noodles, and peas. How many ways can he make his choices?

13. How many possible ways can 5 cars be lined up in a showroom?

14. In how many possible ways can 9 children line up to go down the water slide?

15. Seven friends arrive one at a time for Victor's picnic. In how many possible orders can they arrive?

16. Angelo has 5 jackets. How many possible pairs of 2 jackets can he give to a clothing drive for charity?

Problem Solving

Use the illustration of the birds on the telephone wire for **17** and **18**.

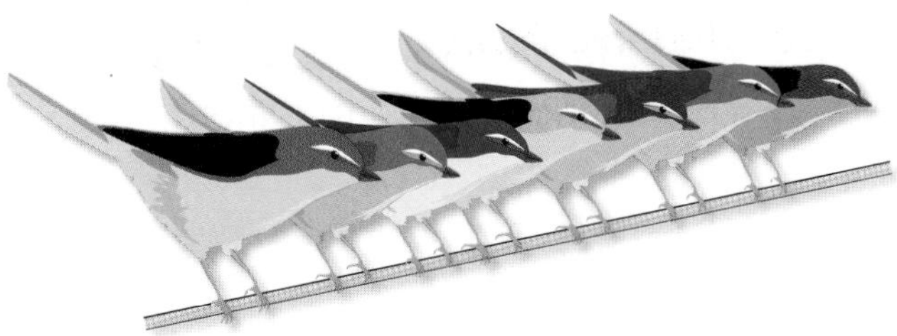

17. Suppose that 7 birds are landing on the wire. How many possible arrangements could the birds form on the wire?

A 38 **B** 5,040 **C** 10,080 **D** 20,160

18. If 2 birds fly away, how many possible arrangements could the remaining birds form on the wire?

A 38 **B** 64 **C** 120 **D** 40,320

19. **Reasoning** Which is less, the number of ways to choose 2 people from a group of 7 when order matters or when order doesn't matter?

20. **Writing to Explain** There are 24 ways to park *x* number of cars in order on the driveway. How many cars are there? Explain how you found your answer.

21. **Think About the Process** What numbers would you multiply to find the number of arrangements for 6 cows at a water trough? For 7 cows? Do you see a pattern? If so, describe it.

Algebra Connections

Repeating Patterns

Remember that a numerical pattern is a sequence of numbers that occurs in some predictable way. Numerical patterns can be based on one or more operations.

For **1** through **6**, find a pattern and the next three numbers in each sequence, using that pattern.

Example: Find a pattern and the next three numbers in the sequence 2, 3, 6, 7, 14, 15, 30, ...

Think $2 + 1 = 3$, $3 \times 2 = 6$, $6 + 1 = 7$, $7 \times 2 = 14$, $14 + 1 = 15$, $15 \times 2 = 30$.

The pattern is add 1, multiply by 2. The next three numbers are 31, 62, 63.

1. 7, 15, 23, 31, 39, ...

2. 50, 44, 38, 32, 26, ...

3. 12, 22, 20, 30, 28, 38, 36, ...

4. 65, 60, 63, 58, 61, 56, 59, ...

5. 2, 4, 8, 16, 32, ...

6. 3, 7, 15, 31, ...

7. 1, 3, 6, 10, ...
What is the 8th number in this pattern?

8. 75, 72, 69, 66, ...
What is the 7th number in this pattern?

9. 1, 4, 9, 16, ...
What is the *n*th number in this pattern?

10. The table shows the population for Green Mountain for 5 years. If this pattern in population growth continues, what will the population be in 2010?

Year	*Population*
2001	3,356
2002	3,399
2003	3,442
2004	3,485
2005	3,528

11. The table shows Jamie's savings account balances. If he continues his pattern of spending and saving, how much money will Jamie have in his bank on March 15?

Date	*Amount*
March 1	$15.00
March 2	$13.50
March 3	$18.50
March 4	$17.00
March 5	$22.00

12. Justyne sets her alarm clock for 5:45 A.M. on school days. Hitting "snooze" lets her sleep 3 more minutes before the alarm rings again. Today, Justyne hit "snooze" 4 times. What time did she finally wake up?

13. A train into the city stops 7 times. When the train starts, there are 35 passengers on board. At the first stop, 10 new passengers get on board. At the next stop, 6 passengers get off. This pattern continues all the way into the city. How many passengers are on the train when it arrives in the city?

Lesson
20-3

Understand It!
The likelihood that something will happen can be expressed as a fraction, a decimal, or a percentage.

Probability

How do you express probability?

A box contains the names of ten students from class. Anita draws a name without looking. What is the probability that she will draw a boy's name?

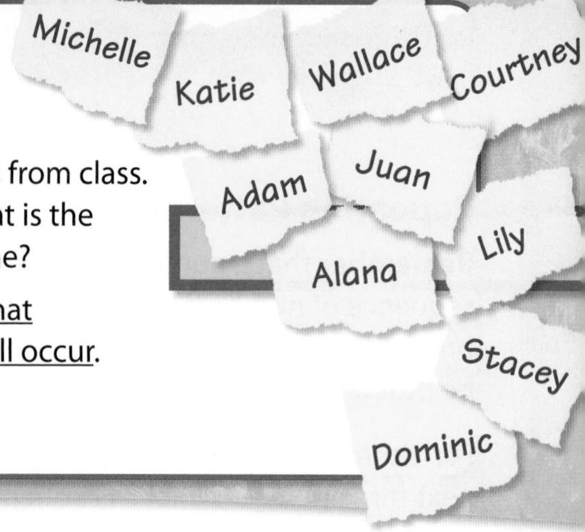

The probability of an event is a number that describes the likelihood that the event will occur.

$$P(\text{event}) = \frac{\text{number of favorable outcomes}}{\text{number of possible outcomes}}$$

Guided Practice*

Do you know HOW?

Use the spinner for **1** and **2**. Find each probability as a fraction, decimal, and percent.

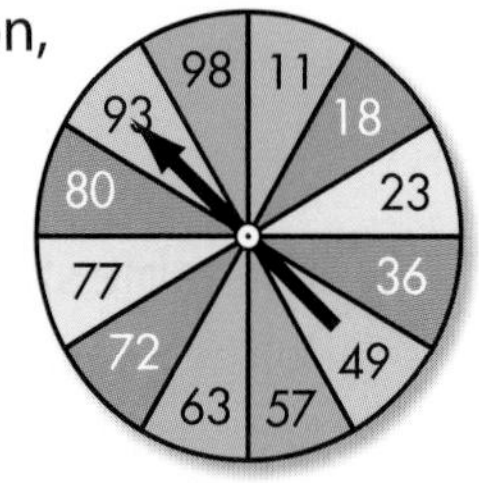

1. What is the probability of landing on a number less than 60?

2. What is the probability of landing on a number that is divisible by 9?

Do you UNDERSTAND?

3. If you know the probability of an event, how can you find the probability of the complement of that event?

4. When drawing from numbers 1–100, are you more likely to draw a number greater than 70 or an odd number? Explain.

Independent Practice

For **5** through **10**, use the spinner. Find each probability as a fraction, decimal, and percent rounded to the nearest whole percent.

5. P(not G, S, or V)

6. P(a letter in "Rebecca")

7. P(M or P)

8. P(a letter between F and W)

9. P(S)

10. P(consonant)

11. Use the same spinner to write a possible description for x, when $P(x) = 30\%$.

DIGITAL
Animated Glossary
www.pearsonsuccessnet.com

*For another example, see Set C on page 541.

Probabilities range from 0 to1.

certain		1 or 100%
more likely		
equally likely		$\frac{1}{2}$, 0.5, or 50%
less likely		
impossible		0 or 0%

$P(\text{boy}) = \frac{4}{10}$ ← There are 4 boys' names or favorable outcomes. ← There are 10 names or 10 possible outcomes.

The probability of choosing a boy's name is $\frac{4}{10}$ or $\frac{2}{5}$. This can also be expressed as a decimal, 0.4, or as a percent, 40%.

Not choosing a boy's name is the complement of choosing a boy's name. A complement is all of the unfavorable outcomes.

$P(\text{event}) + P(\text{complement}) = 1$

So, $P(\text{not a boy})$ is $\frac{3}{5}$, 0.6, or 60%.

Problem Solving

Use the picture of the grab bag for **12** through **14**. Assume that all drawings are done without looking.

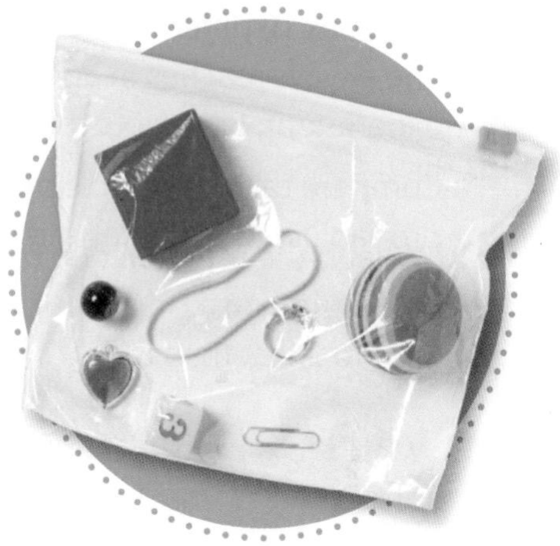

12. Writing to Explain If Mara draws any two items from the grab bag, how many possible outcomes could she have? Explain why this is a combination.

13. What is the probability of drawing the heart-shaped locket on the first try?

14. What is the probability of NOT drawing the ring or marble on the first try?

15. Draw a Picture Draw a set of 8 number cards that could yield this probability: $P(8) = 25\%$.

16. In the wild, there are about 4 times as many male Komodo dragons as there are females. Suppose you visited an island in Indonesia and saw a Komodo dragon in the wild. Which fraction shows the probability that it would be a male?

A $\frac{4}{5}$

B $\frac{5}{4}$

C $\frac{1}{5}$

D $\frac{1}{2}$

17. Think About the Process Suppose a zookeeper wants to schedule a check for each of 10 Komodo dragons. Which expression shows the number of different orders in which she can check them?

A 10^2

B $P(10)$

C $10 \times 10 \times 5$

D $10 \times 9 \times 8 \times 7 \times 6 \times 5 \times 4 \times 3 \times 2 \times 1$

Lesson
20-4

Understand It!
Theoretical and experimental probabilities can be used to make predictions about events.

Theoretical and Experimental Probability

What is experimental probability?

Lindsay is at the free-throw line. Look at the chart. Find a percent to estimate the probability that Lindsay will make her next free throw. Then use the probability to predict whether Lindsay will make her next free throw.

Data

Lindsay's Stats

Free throws attempted	Free throws made
48	32

Another Example

How do theoretical and experimental probability compare?

Belle has 10 differently colored pencils in her backpack. She always reaches in and gets one without looking. In an experiment, Belle gets the yellow pencil on 6 of 40 tries.

Compare the theoretical probability and the experimental probability of Belle getting a yellow pencil.

Probability	What It Means	Compute It
Theoretical	Theoretical probability tells the probability of an event based on what will likely happen in an experiment. $P(\text{event}) = \frac{\text{number of favorable outcomes}}{\text{number of possible outcomes}}$	$P(\text{yellow}) = \frac{1}{10} = 0.1 = 10\%$ Based on theoretical probability, Belle should pull out a yellow pencil 10% of the time.
Experimental	Experimental probability tells the probability based on what actually happens in an experiment. $P(\text{event}) = \frac{\text{number of successes}}{\text{number of trials}}$	$P(\text{yellow}) = \frac{6}{40} = \frac{3}{20} = 0.15 = 15\%$ Based on the experiment, Belle pulled out a yellow pencil 15% of the time.

Explain It

1. What is one possible reason that Belle gets a yellow pencil more often than the theoretical probability?
2. Which do you think would give an experimental probability that is closer to the theoretical probability of 10%, an experiment of 40 trials or an experiment of 400 trials? Explain.

Determine the experimental probability by comparing the number of successes to the number of trials, or experiments.

Lindsey has made 32 free throws in 48 trials.

$P(\text{Lindsay makes her next free throw}) \approx \frac{32}{48}$ ← number of successes / number of trials

$$\frac{32}{48} = \frac{2}{3} \approx 0.67 \approx 67\%$$

The experimental probability that Lindsay will make her next free throw is about 67%. The experimental probability that Lindsay will miss her next free throw is $1 - 0.67 \approx 0.33 \approx 33\%$.

Lindsay will probably make her next free throw.

Guided Practice*

Do you know HOW?

Find the experimental probability for **1** and **2**.

1. Ian was at batting practice. Out of 100 balls, he hit 30 of them. How many balls can he expect to hit in his next 30 tries?

2. Henri checked the number of seeds per grape in 40 grapes. He found a 60% chance that a grape would have two seeds. How many of the 40 grapes had two seeds?

Tip *A 60% chance means that 60% of the trial group had that trait.*

Do you UNDERSTAND?

3. Without looking, Jill is drawing the letters in the word "probability" from a bag. She said the probability of drawing the letter b is $\frac{2}{11}$. Is this the theoretical or experimental probability? Explain.

4. In 10 games, Lindsay attempted 55 field goals and made 25 of them. Use a percent to estimate the probability that she will make her next field goal.

Independent Practice

5. Three girls are playing a video game. The girls recorded the winners in the chart on the right. What is the experimental probabilities that each girl will win the next game?

Angie	*Emily*	*Gina*
30	7	13

6. Jon is playing Penny Toss at the school fair. He has tossed the penny 20 times, and it landed on the plate 8 times. What is the experimental probability that the next toss will land on the plate? How many times can he expect the penny to land on the plate in the next 10 throws?

DIGITAL Animated Glossary **www.pearsonsuccessnet.com**

*For another example, Set D on page 542.

Independent Practice

Use the picture for **7** through **9**.

7. What is the theoretical probability of drawing a red tile without looking?

8. If you draw a tile, put it back, and draw again, for a total of 40 draws, how many times might you expect to get a red tile?

9. Will you draw a red tile exactly that many times? Explain.

Problem Solving

10. If you toss a number cube (1–6) 360 times, how many times would you expect to get a number less than 4?

A 60 **B** 180 **C** 241 **D** 299

11. A snack manufacturer puts a prize in 90 out of every 600 bags of popcorn. What is the probability of finding a prize in a bag of popcorn?

A $\frac{6}{9}$ **B** 90% **C** $\frac{90}{100}$ **D** 15%

12. Cambria recorded how many red, green, yellow, purple, and blue purses were sold at her store. After selling 50 purses, she said there was a 30% chance that a shopper would buy a red purse. How many of the 50 purses sold were red?

Use these tiles for **13** through **15**.

13. Find *P*(S, N, or A).

14. Find *P*(vowel).

15. **Number Sense** If you scramble the tiles and pick one without looking, the probability of drawing the letter E is 20%. Do you think this probability is theoretical or experimental? Explain.

16. Jeff tossed a hook-and-loop dart 85 times, and he got 15 bull's-eyes. He missed the bull's-eye 70 times. What is the probability that Jeff's next toss will be a bull's-eye?

17. **Writing to Explain** When throwing a number cube, which do you think would give an experimental probability that is closer to the theoretical probability: 50 tosses or 500 tosses?

18. **Reasoning** Suppose a dartboard has 20 equal sections. Also suppose that Jeff is good enough, blindfolded, to hit the dartboard somewhere. What would be the theoretical probability of hitting one particular section?

Going Digital

Comparing Theoretical and Experimental Probability

Use eTools

Probability

A spinner has 4 equal sections colored red (R), blue (B), yellow (Y), and green (G). Find the theoretical and experimental probability of each outcome. Write probabilities as fractions in simplest form.

Step 1 Go to the Probability eTool. Then click on the one spinner tool. Under Number of Sections, click on 4 for the number of sections. At the top of the page, click to toggle on the probability column.

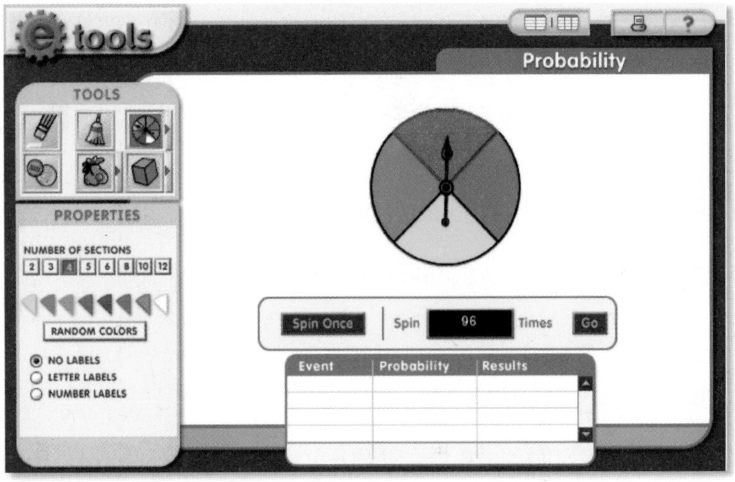

Step 2 Type 96 in the black box to spin 96 times. Then click on Go. The second column shows the theoretical probability of each event or outcome. The experimental probability written as a fraction is the number of favorable outcomes in the Results column over the number of possible outcomes, 96. Write each experimental probability fraction in simplest form.

Practice

1. Click on the pencil to start a new experiment. Find the experimental probabilities for 1,200 trials. What do you notice?

2. Click on the broom to erase the workspace. Click on the one spinner tool and select 5 Sections to start a new experiment. Find the experimental probabilities for 100 outcomes. Write each experimental probability as a fraction in simplest form, as a decimal, and as a percent.

Lesson

20-5

Understand It!
To find the probability that two events occur, you need to know whether the occurrence of one event effects the occurrence of the other.

Independent and Dependent Events

How do you find the probability that two events will occur?

Tom's aquarium has 4 platies and 3 mollies. If Tom nets one fish at a time randomly, what is the probability that the first two fish he nets are platies?

There are 4 platies and 3 mollies in the aquarium.

Guided Practice*

Do you know HOW?

You select one letter without looking, replace it, and then select another.

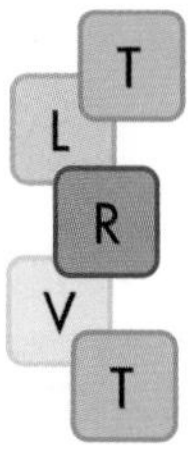

1. Find P(L, T). **2.** Find P(R, V).

For **3** and **4**, you do not replace the first letters selected.

3. Find P(L, T). **4.** Find P(R, V).

Do you UNDERSTAND?

5. In the example above, why is the probability of the netting a platy on first draw different from the probability of netting a platy on the second draw when Tom does not replace the first fish he nets?

6. In the example above, find P(molly, molly) without replacement between draws.

Independent Practice

In **7** through **11**, suppose that you put the 5 spheres and 3 cubes at the right in a bag and remove them without looking. Find each probability in two ways, with replacement and without replacement. Express probabilities as percents, rounded to the nearest whole percent.

7. P(red, blue) **8.** P(blue, red) **9.** P(blue, blue)

10. P(yellow or red cube, green sphere) **11.** P(red or green sphere, blue sphere or red cube)

12. Is the probability of a compound event always greater without replacement than it is with replacement? Explain.

DIGITAL Animated Glossary **www.pearsonsuccessnet.com**

*For another example, see Set E on page 542.

With Replacement

Suppose Tom replaces the first fish he nets back in the aquarium before netting a second fish. Since the outcome of the first event does not affect the outcome of the second event, the two nettings are independent events.

$P(\text{platy, platy}) = P(\text{platy on 1st draw}) \times P(\text{platy on 2nd draw})$

$\frac{4}{7} \times \frac{4}{7} = \frac{16}{49} \approx 33\%$

Without Replacement

Suppose Tom does not replace the first fish he nets before netting a second fish. Since the outcome of the first event affects the outcome of the second event, the two nettings are dependent events.

$P(\text{platy, platy}) = P(\text{platy on 1st draw}) \times P(\text{platy on 2nd draw})$

$\frac{4}{7} \times \frac{3}{6} = \frac{12}{42} = \frac{2}{7} \approx 29\%$

Problem Solving

13. Sam is drawing from a bag of 8 blocks—2 green, 1 yellow, 1 purple, 3 red, and 1 blue—without replacing them. Sam drew a green block the first time and a red block the second time. What is the probability that Sam will draw the purple block next?

14. **Number Sense** There are 8 pink socks and 16 blue socks loose in Chloe's drawer. If Chloe pulls out a sock without looking and then pulls out another sock, does she have at least a 50% chance of getting a pair of blue socks?

At a seashell shop, Adam and Niles drew 2 free shells from a grab bag. Before they drew, there were 20 augers, 15 cones, 15 cowries, 40 scallops, and 10 conchs in the bag. Use this information for **15** through **17**.

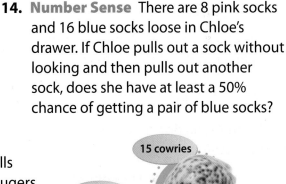

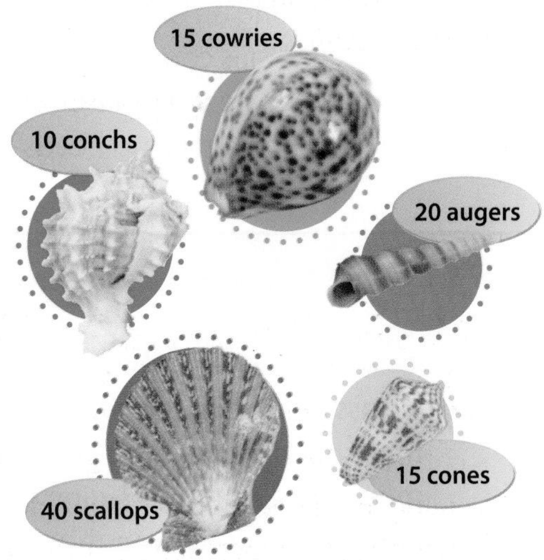

15. **Writing to Explain** Why is it logical to assume that Adam and Niles's draws were dependent events?

16. Find $P(\text{conch, cone})$ for Adam's draws, assuming Adam drew first.

17. Find $P(\text{auger, not cone})$ for Niles's draws, assuming Niles drew first.

The Fun Fair ball toss game gives a prize for each colored cup: a stuffed animal for a yellow cup, a pen for a red cup, and a key chain for a blue cup. Use the information to answer **18**.

The game has 10 yellow cups, 25 blue cups, and 15 red cup.

18. What are the chances that you will get a stuffed animal on your first try and a pen on your second try?

A 42% **B** 30% **C** 25% **D** 6%

Lesson
20-6

Understand It!
To solve some problems, you will need to make an organized list.

Problem Solving

Make an Organized List

Jeff and Fran are playing a game. They flip three coins at the same time. If the three coins land all heads up or all tails up, Jeff gets 1 point. Otherwise, Fran gets 1 point. Is this a fair game? Explain.

Guided Practice*

Do you know HOW?

1. Suppose you are flipping four coins. What is the first step in making an organized list to show the possible heads and tails combinations?

2. Begin making an organized list for the heads and tails combinations for four coins. What are the possibilities when the first coin comes up heads?

Do you UNDERSTAND?

3. In the example at the top, what pattern do you notice in the organized list of ways to get a mix of heads and tails?

4. **Write a Problem** Write a problem that can be solved using the organized list in Exercise 1.

Independent Practice

For **5** through **7**, make an organized list to solve.

5. A class of 25 students was given two numbers and three letters to use: 8, 3, T, L, and K. Each student must make a unique 3-digit password. No one student can use any number or letter more than once. Are there enough options for each student to have a unique password? Explain.

6. In Exercise 5, what would you have to do differently in an organized list if a password had to include at least one number and one letter?

7. A team was given the same five numbers and letters as in Exercise 5, but they were told to use only two of them in their passwords. How many unique passwords could be made?

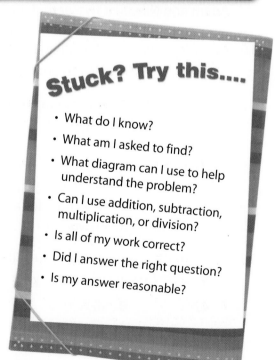

Stuck? Try this....

- What do I know?
- What am I asked to find?
- What diagram can I use to help understand the problem?
- Can I use addition, subtraction, multiplication, or division?
- Is all of my work correct?
- Did I answer the right question?
- Is my answer reasonable?

*For another example, see Set F on page 543.

Make an organized list.

There are two ways to get all heads or all tails.

Coin 1	Coin 2	Coin 3
H	H	H
T	T	T

There are six ways to get a mix of heads and tails.

Coin 1	Coin 2	Coin 3
H	H	T
H	T	H
H	T	T
T	H	H
T	H	T
T	T	H

In a fair game, both Jeff and Fran would have an equal chance to score a point.

There are 8 possible outcomes. Jeff can win with only 2 of these. The game is not fair.

One attraction at the Fun Fair was the beanbag toss shown at the right. Use the diagram at the right to answer **8** through **10**.

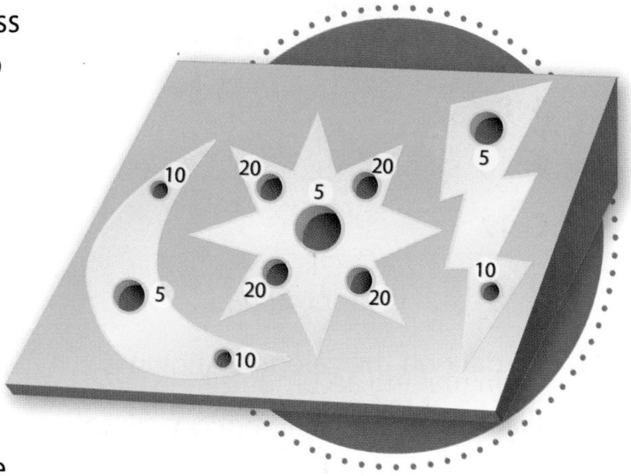

8. Make an organized list to show the possible number of points you could get in three throws if you hit a hole each time.

9. Suppose that your first throw hit a hole in the moon, your second throw hit a hole in the sun, and your third throw hit a hole in the lightning. Make an organized list to figure out how many different scores you could have.

10. Suppose that you toss five beanbags. Four of them hit holes in the same target, and one misses. Make an organized list to figure out how many different scores you could have.

For **11** and **12**, use the coins shown at right.

11. Draw a picture to solve this problem. In how many ways can you make 75¢ if you have the coins shown?

12. How many different groups of three types of coins can you make with the coins shown?

13. Beth started a petition. During the first hour, hers was the only signature. During the second hour, 5 people signed. After that, 20 more people signed per hour than had signed the previous hour. How many signatures were on the petition at the end of the 8th hour? Make a table with a pattern to solve the problem.

1. The table shows the different options available for a new car. How many possible outcomes are there from which to choose? (20-1)

Data

Model	Color	Engine
2 door	Blue	6 liter
4 door	Red	8 liter
	Silver	
	Black	

A 8

B 10

C 12

D 16

2. If a date on the calendar shown is chosen at random, which of the following shows the probability of choosing a Tuesday? (20-3)

September						
S	M	T	W	T	F	S
		1	2	3	4	5
6	7	8	9	10	11	12
13	14	15	16	17	18	19
20	21	22	23	24	25	26
27	28	29	30			

A $\frac{1}{7}$

B $\frac{5}{30}$

C $\frac{4}{30}$

D $\frac{1}{30}$

3. When rolling a number cube with numbers 1 to 6 two times, how many outcomes are possible for rolling the same numbers? (20-6)

A 36

B 30

C 6

D 1

4. Which of the following can be used to find the number of ways 6 bushes can be planted in a row? (20-2)

A 6×5

B 6×6

C $6 + 5 + 4 + 3 + 2 + 1$

D $6 \times 5 \times 4 \times 3 \times 2 \times 1$

5. Of 4 children, the oldest is a boy. How many outcomes are possible for the genders of the children? (20-6)

A 16

B 12

C 8

D 7

6. 20 different names are in a jar. What is the probability of choosing the same name twice if the name is replaced after the first drawing? (20-5)

A $\frac{1}{400}$

B $\frac{1}{40}$

C $\frac{1}{20}$

D $\frac{1}{10}$

7. Devin has thrown 36 darts. Nine hit in the black area of the target. What is the experimental probability that Devin's next dart will hit in the black area of the target? (20-4)

A 25%

B 33%

C 36%

D 75%

8. Pierre is choosing a tile from 3 tiles with letters X, Y and Z and then choosing a tile from 2 tiles with A and E. Which set shows all the possible outcomes? (20-1)

A {(X, A), (X, E), (Y, A), (Y, E), (Z, A), (Z, E)}

B {(X, A), (Y, E), (Z, A), (X, E), (X, Y), (A, E)}

C {(X, Y), (X, Z), (A, E)}

D {(X, A), (X, E), (Y, Y), (Z, Z)}

9. Mia has 2 quarters, 1 dime and 2 pennies in her pocket. The table shows the results of Mia reaching in her pocket 10 times and pulling out a coin without looking. The experimental probability of getting which type of coin is higher than expected, based on the theoretical probability? (20-4)

Data

Quarter	Dime	Penny
4	3	3

A Quarter

B Dime

C Penny

D None

10. How many possible 2-person teams can be formed from 6 students? (20-2)

A 6

B 12

C 15

D 30

11. A jar contains 4 blue marbles, 2 green marbles and 4 red marbles. One marble is chosen at random from the jar. Which of the following has a probability of 40%? (20-3)

A Not choosing a blue marble.

B Choosing a green marble.

C Choosing a blue marble.

D Not choosing a green marble.

12. Which shows the probability of choosing 2 white socks from a drawer having 6 white socks, 3 black socks, 3 brown socks, and 8 grey socks? (20-5)

A $\frac{6}{20} \times \frac{5}{20}$

B $\frac{6}{20} \times \frac{5}{19}$

C $\frac{6}{20} + \frac{5}{20}$

D $\frac{6}{20} + \frac{6}{20}$

13. Out of 12 golf balls, three are yellow and the rest are white. If Miguel chooses a ball at random, what is the probability it will be yellow? (20-3)

A 12%

B 25%

C 30%

D 75%

Set A, pages 520–522

A shirt comes in sizes S, M, and L. It comes in red, green, and yellow. It comes with and without sleeves. How many possible choices are there?

Method 1: Make an organized list.

S, R, W	S, R, Wo	S, G, W
S, G, Wo	S, Y, W	S, Y, Wo
M, R, W	M, R, Wo	M, G, W
M, G, Wo	M, Y, W	M, Y, Wo
L, R, W	L, R, Wo	L, G, W
L, G, Wo	L, Y, W	L, Y, Wo

Method 2: Make a tree diagram.

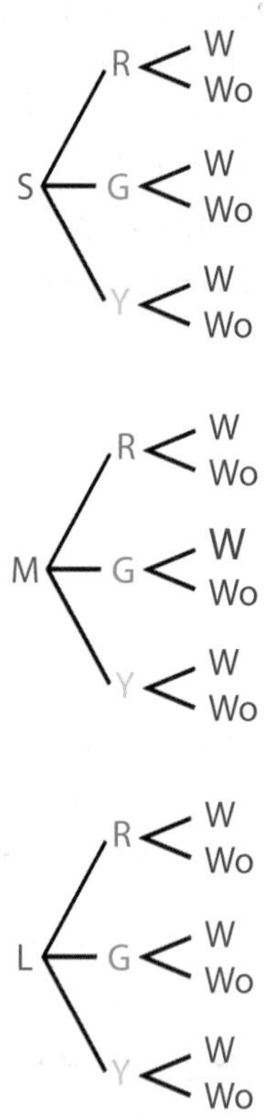

Method 3: Use the Counting Principle.

3 sizes $\times$ 3 colors $\times$ 2 sleeve styles $=$ 18 choices

By all three methods, there are 18 choices.

Remember that a compound event is a combination of two or more single events or outcomes. The set of all possible outcomes of an experiment is the sample space.

In **1** through **4**, find the number of possible outcomes.

1. The school chess team is selling caps. They are red, gold, or blue; large or small; and they say Kingsley School or Kingsley Chess. Make a tree diagram to find how many different caps are possible.

2. Suppose that you have two 8-sided letter cubes, one with the letters A through H and one with the letters J through Q. Use the Counting Principle to find how many possible outcomes there are if you toss each letter cube once.

3. You have two piles of pillows. One pile has green and yellow pillows, and one pile has red, green, and blue pillows. If you choose one pillow from each pile to go on your bed, how many possible outcomes are there? Make an organized list.

4. Katie must set a 4-digit password to use the school computer. Each digit may be any number from 0–9. How many passwords are possible if the digits may repeat?

Set B, pages 524–526

How many ways can Michael choose 2 hats from 4 different hats on a shelf? Is this a permutation or a combination?

Hat 1, Hat 2	Hat 3, Hat 1
Hat 1, Hat 3	Hat 3, Hat 2
Hat 1, Hat 4	Hat 3, Hat 4
Hat 2, Hat 1	Hat 4, Hat 1
Hat 2, Hat 3	Hat 4, Hat 2
Hat 2, Hat 4	Hat 4, Hat 3

Hats 1 and 2 are the same as hats 2 and 1. Order is not important; it is a combination. There are 6 different combinations.

How many ways can 4 hats be arranged on a shelf? Is this a permutation or a combination?

Use the Counting Principle with decreasing choices per position.

$4 \times 3 \times 2 \times 1 = 24$ possible arrangements

The first hat on the shelf and the second hat on the shelf are not the same. Order is important; it is a permutation.

Remember that you must first decide if order is important. Then decide how to solve.

For **1** through **4**, find the number of possible arrangements. Tell whether the arrangement is a permutation or a combination.

1. How many ways can you choose 3 flavors of yogurt from 5 flavors of yogurt?
2. How many ways can you choose 4 notebooks from an assortment of 6 different-colored notebooks?
3. How many ways can you line up 8 toy cars in a row?
4. How many ways can 1st-place, 2nd-place, and 3rd-place winners be selected from 4 finalists?

Set C, pages 528–529

A bag contains 20 marbles: 4 marbles are green, 6 are blue, 5 are red, and 5 are white. Jasmine draws a marble out of the bag without looking. What is the probability that she will choose a blue marble?

$$P(\text{drawing blue marble}) = \frac{\text{\# of blue marbles}}{\text{total \# of marbles}}$$

$$= \frac{6}{20} = \frac{3}{10} = 0.3 = 30\%$$

The probability of drawing a blue marble is 0.3 or 30%.

The probability of not choosing a blue marble is $1 - 0.3 = 0.7 = 70\%$

Remember that the probability of an event ranges from 0 for an impossible event to 1 for a certain event.

Find the probability as a fraction, decimal, and percent.

1. What is the probability of tossing a coin and having it land heads up? Is it more likely, equally likely, or less likely for the coin to land heads up than it is to land tails up?

Set D, pages 530–532

Theoretical probability $= \frac{\text{favorable outcomes}}{\text{possible outcomes}}$

There are 3 balls, 2 clips, and 4 pens in a grab bag. What is the chance of drawing a ball?

$\frac{3}{9} = \frac{1}{3} \approx 0.33$ or 33%

Experimental probability $= \frac{\text{successes}}{\text{trials}}$

There are 3 balls, 2 clips, and 4 pens in a grab bag. You drew 50 times, replacing each item after each draw, and got 20 balls, 20 clips, and 10 pens. What is the experimental probability of drawing a ball?

$\frac{20}{50} = \frac{4}{10} = 0.40 = 40\%$

Remember that experimental probability tells you what actually happened in an experiment.

Use the spinner for **1** and **2.** Write your answer as a percent, rounded to the nearest whole percent.

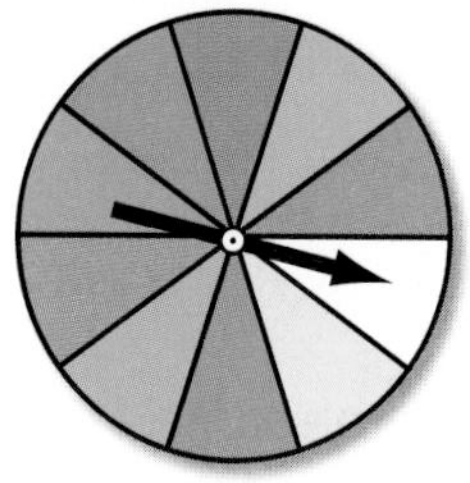

1. What is the theoretical probability of the spinner landing on green?

2. Phoebe spun the spinner 16 times and it landed on a green space 2 times. What is the experimental probability of the spinner landing on a green space?

Set E, pages 534–535

Independent events are compound events in which the outcome of the first event **does not** affect the outcome of the second event.

A bag of colored table-tennis balls contains 5 red, 4 yellow, 2 blue, and 1 white. Find *P*(red, yellow).

If the ball is replaced after the first pick:

$\frac{5}{12} \times \frac{4}{12} = \frac{20}{144}$, or $\frac{5}{36}$

Dependent events are compound events in which the outcome of the first event **does** affect the outcome of the second event.

If the ball is NOT replaced after the first pick:

$\frac{5}{12} \times \frac{4}{11} = \frac{20}{132}$, or $\frac{5}{33}$

Remember that probability events are either independent or dependent. If an object is not replaced, the possible results decrease by 1.

For **1** and **2**, tell whether each is dependent or independent.

1. Nina spins the dial of a spinner and then spins again.

2. George draws a card, keeps it, and draws again.

3. In the table-tennis ball problem at the left, find *P* (blue, blue) both with and without replacement.

Set F, pages 536–537

Nate and Alex are playing a game with a number cube. If Nate rolls an even number, he gets a point. If Alex rolls a factor of 3, he gets a point. Is this a fair game?

Make a list of all of the possibilities.

Outcome	Nate	Alex
1	–	–
2	1	–
3	–	1
4	1	–
5	–	–
6	1	1

There are 6 possible outcomes.

Nate has three possible winning outcomes and Alex has two possible winning outcomes.

The game is not fair.

Remember when you make a list, include column and row headings to identify your data.

Make an organized list to solve the problems.

1. Keri packed 4 shirts, 3 pairs of pants and 2 pairs of shoes for the weekend. How many different outfits can she make?

2. Remy is cooking on the grill for his family's barbeque. There are 5 different sandwich fillings, 2 types of bread and 3 different toppings. How many sandwich combinations can he make?

3. John and Nicole are playing the game Rock, Paper, or Scissors. The rock beats the scissors, the paper beats the rock, and the scissors beat the paper. How many possible outcomes are there? Is this a fair game?

A

absolute value The distance that an integer is from zero on the number line.

acute angle An angle with a measure between 0° and 90°.

acute triangle A triangle with three acute angles.

adjacent angles A pair of angles with a common vertex and a common side but no common interior points. *Example*: $\angle RSP$ and $\angle PST$

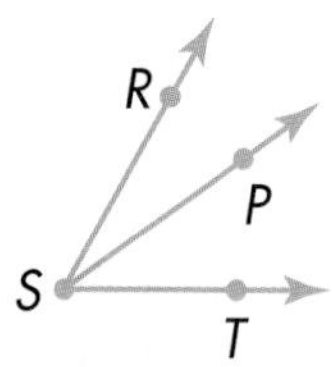

algebraic expression A mathematical phrase that has at least one variable and one operation. *Example*: $10 \times n$ or $10n$

angle Two rays with the same endpoint.

angle bisector A ray that divides an angle into two adjacent angles that are congruent.

arc A part of a circle connecting two points on the circle. *Example*:

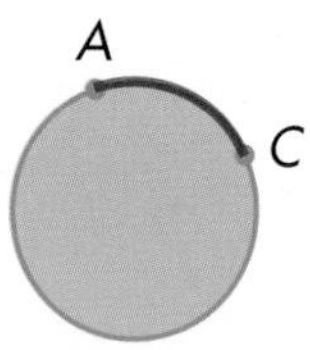

area The number of square units needed to cover a surface or figure.

associative properties Properties that state the way in which addends or factors are grouped does not affect the sum or product.

axis (*pl.* axes) Either of two lines drawn perpendicular to each other in a graph.

B

base (in geometry) A designated side of a polygon to which the height is drawn perpendicular; one of the two parallel and congruent faces on a prism; a particular flat surface of a solid, such as a cylinder or cone.

base (in numeration) A number multiplied by itself the number of times shown by an exponent. *Example*: $4 \times 4 \times 4 = 4^3$, where 4 is the base.

benchmark fraction Common fractions used for estimating, such as $\frac{1}{4}, \frac{1}{3}, \frac{1}{2}, \frac{2}{3}$, and $\frac{3}{4}$.

biased sample A sample which is not representative of the population from which it is drawn.

break apart Using the Distributive Property to compute mentally.

C

capacity The volume of a container measured in liquid units.

Celsius (°C) A metric unit for measuring temperature.

center The interior point from which all points of a circle are equally distant.

centi- Prefix meaning $\frac{1}{100}$.

central angle An angle with its vertex at the center of a circle. *Example*:

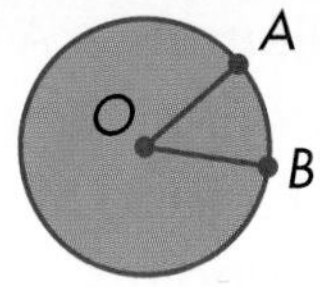

certain event An event that is sure to occur and has a probability of 1.

chord A line segment with both endpoints on a circle.

circle A closed plane figure with all points the same distance from a given point called the center.

circle graph A graph that represents a total divided into parts.

circumference The distance around a circle.

combination Each possible arrangement of the outcomes of an event where order is not important.

common denominator A denominator that is the same in two or more fractions.

common factor A factor that is the same for two or more numbers.

common multiple A multiple that is the same for two or more numbers.

commutative properties The properties that state the order of addends or the order of factors does not affect the sum or product.

compatible numbers Numbers that are easy to compute mentally.

compensation Choosing numbers close to the numbers in a problem, and then adjusting the answer to compensate for the numbers chosen.

complement of an event The unfavorable outcomes of an event. The sum of the probabilities of an event and its complement is 1.

complementary angles Two angles with measures that add up to 90°.

composite number A natural number greater than one that has more than two factors.

compound event A combination of two or more single events.

cone A three-dimensional figure that has one circular base. The points on this circle are joined to one point outside the base.

congruent angles Angles having the same measure.

congruent figures Figures that have the same size and shape.

congruent line segments Line segments that are the same length.

conjecture A generalization that you think is true.

construction A geometric drawing that uses a limited set of tools, usually a compass and a straightedge.

system in which a location is described by its distances from two perpendicular number lines called the *x*-axis and the *y*-axis.

Counting Principle If one choice can be made in *m* ways and a second choice can be made in *n* ways, then the two choices can be made together in $m \times n$ ways.

cross multiplication Multiplying the first term of the first ratio and the second term of the second ratio, and multiplying the second term of the first ratio and the first term of the second ratio. The products of cross multiplication are equal.

cubic unit A unit measuring volume, consisting of a cube with edges one unit long.

cylinder A three-dimensional figure that has two circular bases which are parallel and congruent. *Example:*

D

data Information that is gathered.

decagon A polygon with ten sides.

decimal A number with one or more digits to the right of the decimal point.

degree (°) A unit for measuring angles or temperatures.

denominator The number below the fraction bar in a fraction; the total number of equal parts in all.

dependent events Events for which the outcome of one affects the probability of the other.

two vertices of a polygon and is not a side. *Example:*

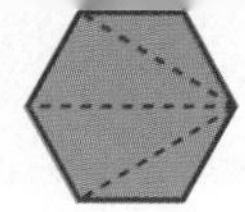

diameter A line segment that passes through the center of a circle and has both endpoints on the circle. *Example:*

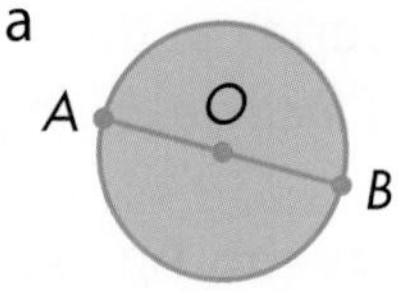

discount The amount by which the regular price of an item is reduced.

Distributive Property Multiplying a sum by a number produces the same result as multiplying each addend by the number and adding the products.
Example: $2 \times (3 + 4) = (2 \times 3) + (2 \times 4)$

dividend The number being divided by another number. *Example:* In $12 \div 3$, 12 is the dividend.

divisible A number is divisible by another number if its quotient is a whole number and the remainder is zero.

divisor The number used to divide another number. *Example:* In $12 \div 3$, 3 is the divisor.

double-bar graph A graph that uses pairs of bars to compare information.

double-line graph A graph that uses pairs of lines to compare information.

E

edge The line segment where two faces of a polyhedron meet.

elapsed time Total amount of time that passes from the beginning time to the ending time.

equation A mathematical sentence stating that two expressions are equal.

equilateral triangle A triangle with three sides of the same length.

equivalent fractions Fractions that name the same amount.

estimate To find a number that is close to an exact answer.

evaluate To find a value that an algebraic expression names by replacing a variable with a given value. *Example:* Evaluate $2n + 5$ when $n = 3$; $2(3) + 5 = 11$.

event An outcome or set of outcomes of an experiment or situation.

expanded form A number written as the sum of the place values of its digits.

expanded form using exponents A number written in expanded form with the place values written in exponential form. *Example:* $3{,}246 = (3 \times 10^3) + (2 \times 10^2) + (4 \times 10^1) + (6 \times 10^0)$

experimental probability A probability based on the statistical results of an experiment.

exponent The number that tells how many times the base is being multiplied by itself. *Example:* $8^3 = 8 \times 8 \times 8$, where 3 is the exponent and 8 is the base.

exponential form A way of writing repeated multiplication of a number using exponents. *Example:* 2^5

expression A mathematical phrase containing variables or constants and including at least one operation. *Example:* $12 - x$

F

face A flat surface of a polyhedron.

factor A number that divides another number without a remainder.

Fahrenheit (°F) A standard unit for measuring temperature.

formula A rule that uses symbols to relate two or more quantities.

fraction A number that can be used to describe a part of a whole, a part of a set, a location on a number line, or a division of whole numbers.

frequency table A table to organize data by showing the number of values that fall in particular groups.

function A relation in which each x-value is paired with exactly one y-value.

G

glide reflection The change in the position of a figure that moves it by a translation followed by a reflection.

gram (g) Metric unit of mass.

greatest common factor (GCF) The largest number that is a factor of two or more numbers.

H

height The segment from a vertex perpendicular to the line containing the opposite side; the perpendicular distance between the bases of a solid.

heptagon A polygon with seven sides.

hexagon A polygon with six sides.

histogram A graph that uses bars to show how equal ranges of data are distributed on a number line.

I

identity properties The properties that state the sum of any number and zero is that number and the product of any number and one is that number.

impossible event An event that will never occur and has a probability of 0.

improper fraction A fraction in which the numerator is greater than or equal to its denominator.

independent events Events for which the outcome of one does not affect the probability of the other.

inequality A statement that uses the symbols > (greater than), < (less than), ≥ (greater than or equal to), or ≤ (less than or equal to) to compare two expressions.

input/output table A table of related values.

integers The counting numbers, their opposites, and zero.

interest A charge for the use of money, paid by the borrower to the lender.

intersecting lines Lines that have exactly one point in common. *Example:*

interval A range of numbers used to represent data.

inverse relationships Relationships between operations that "undo" each other, such as addition and subtraction, or multiplication and division (except multiplication or division by 0).

isosceles triangle A triangle with at least two congruent sides.

K

kilo- Prefix meaning 1,000.

L

least common denominator (LCD) The least common multiple of the denominators of two or more fractions. *Example:* 12 is the LCD of $\frac{1}{4}$ and $\frac{1}{6}$.

least common multiple (LCM) The least number, other than zero, that is a multiple of two or more numbers.

like denominators Denominators in two or more fractions that are the same.

line A straight path of points that goes on forever in two directions.

line graph A graph used to show changes over a period of time.

line segment Part of a line that has two endpoints.

line of symmetry A line on which a figure can be folded into two congruent parts.

linear equation An equation whose graph is a straight line.

liter (L) Metric unit of capacity.

M

mass Measure of the amount of matter of an object.

mean The sum of the values in a data set divided by the number of values.

median The middle value when a set of numbers is listed from least to greatest.

meter (m) Metric unit of length.

metric system (of measurement) A system using decimals and powers of 10 to measure length, mass, and capacity.

midpoint The point that divides a segment into two segments of equal length.

milli- Prefix meaning $\frac{1}{1000}$.

mixed number A number that combines a whole number and a fraction.

mode The number or numbers that occur most often in a set of data.

multiple The product of a number and a whole number greater than zero.

multiplicative inverse (reciprocal) Two numbers whose product is one.
Example: The multiplicative inverse of $\frac{3}{4}$ is $\frac{4}{3}$ because $\frac{3}{4} \times \frac{4}{3} = 1$.

N

negative power of ten A number in exponential form where the base is ten and the exponent is a negative integer.

net A plane figure pattern which, when folded, makes a solid.

nonagon A polygon with nine sides.

numerator The number above the fraction bar in a fraction; the number of objects or equal parts being considered.

O

obtuse angle An angle with a measure between 90° and 180°.

obtuse triangle A triangle with an obtuse angle.

octagon A polygon with eight sides.

opposites The integer on the opposite side of zero from a given number, but at the same distance from zero. *Example:* 7 and −7 are opposites.

order of operations A set of rules mathematicians use to determine the order in which operations are performed.

ordered pair A pair of numbers (x, y) used to locate a point on a coordinate plane.

origin The point (0, 0), where the x- and y-axes of a coordinate plane intersect.

outcome The result in a probability experiment.

outlier A number that has a very different value from the other numbers in a data set.

P

parallel lines Lines in the same plane that do not intersect.

parallelogram A quadrilateral with both pairs of opposite sides parallel.

pentagon A polygon with five sides.

percent A ratio where the first term is compared to 100.

perimeter Distance around a figure.

permutation An arrangement of a group of things in a particular order.

perpendicular bisector A line, ray, or segment that intersects a segment at its midpoint and is perpendicular to it. *Example:*

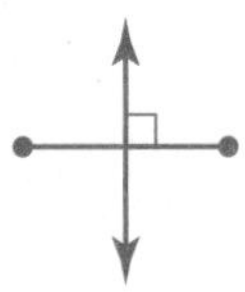

perpendicular lines Intersecting lines that form right angles.

pi (π) The ratio of the circumference of a circle to its diameter. Pi is approximately 3.14 or $\frac{22}{7}$.

plane A flat surface that extends forever in all directions.

point An exact location in space.

polygon A closed plane figure made up of three or more line segments.

polyhedron A three-dimensional figure made of flat surfaces that are polygons.

population The entire group of people or things that are being analyzed.

power The number of times a base number is multiplied by itself.

prime factorization The set of primes whose product is a given composite. *Example:* $60 = 2^2 \times 3 \times 5$

prime number A whole number greater than 1 with exactly two factors, 1 and itself.

principal An amount of money borrowed or loaned.

prism A polyhedron with two congruent and parallel polygon-shaped faces. *Examples:*

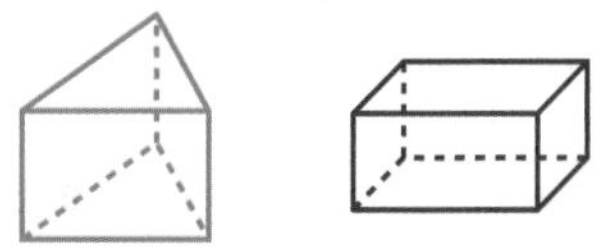

probability A ratio of the number of ways an event can happen to the total number of possible outcomes.

proper fraction A fraction less than 1; its numerator is less than its denominator.

properties of equality Properties that state performing the same operation to both sides of an equation keeps the equation balanced.

proportion A statement that two ratios are equal.

pyramid A polyhedron whose base can be any polygon and whose faces are triangles. *Examples:*

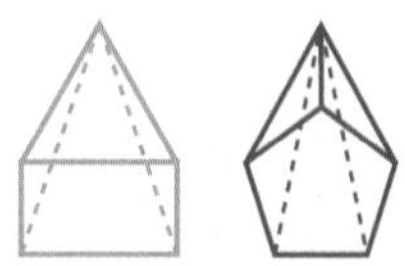

Q

quadrant One of the four regions into which the *x*- and *y*-axes divide the coordinate plane. The axes are not parts of the quadrant.

quadrilateral A polygon with four sides.

quotient The answer in a division problem. *Example:* In $45 \div 9 = 5$, 5 is the quotient.

R

radius Any line segment that connects the center of the circle to a point on the circle. *Example:*

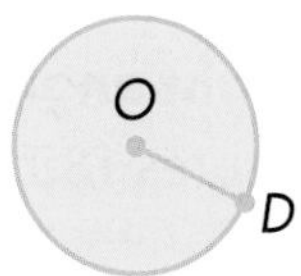

random sampling A sampling method that results in a representative sample, where each member of the population has an equal chance of being chosen.

range The difference between the greatest and least numbers in a set of data.

rate A ratio that compares two quantities with different units of measure.

ratio A relationship where for every *x* units of one quantity there are *y* units of another quantity.

rational number Any number that can be written as a quotient $\frac{a}{b}$, where *a* and *b* are integers and $b \neq 0$.

ray Part of a line with one endpoint, extending forever in only one direction.

reciprocals Two numbers whose product is one. *Example:* The reciprocal of $\frac{3}{4}$ is $\frac{4}{3}$ because $\frac{3}{4} \times \frac{4}{3} = 1$.

rectangle A parallelogram with four right angles.

reflection The change in the position of a figure that gives a mirror image over a line.

reflection symmetry Property of a figure that can be reflected onto itself.

regular polygon A polygon that has sides of equal length and angles of equal measure.

relation Any set of ordered pairs (x, y).

repeating decimal A decimal in which a digit or digits repeat endlessly.

representative sample A sample which fairly represents the population from which it is drawn.

rhombus A parallelogram with all four sides congruent.

right angle An angle which measures 90°.

right triangle A triangle with one right angle.

rotation The change in the position of a figure that moved it around a point.

rotational symmetry Property of a figure that rotates onto itself in less than a full turn.

round To give an approximation for a number to the nearest one, ten, hundred, thousand, or other place value.

S

sample Part of the population upon which an experiment or survey is conducted.

sample space The set of all possible outcomes of an experiment.

scale The ratio of the measurements in a drawing to the actual measurements of the object.

scale drawing A drawing made so that distances in the drawing are proportional to actual distances.

scalene triangle A triangle with no congruent sides.

scattergram A graph that compares data points for two variables.

scientific notation A number expressed as a product of a number greater than or equal to 1, but less than 10, and a power of 10. *Example:* $350 = 3.50 \times 10^2$

sector A region bounded by two radii and an arc. *Example:*

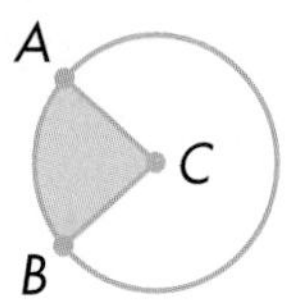

semicircle An arc that connects the endpoints of a diameter.

side A segment used to form a polygon; a ray used to form an angle.

similar figures Figures that have the same shape, but not necessarily the same size.

simple interest Interest paid only on the principal, found by taking the product of the principal, rate, and time.

simplest form A fraction for which the greatest common factor of the numerator and denominator is 1.

sphere A three-dimensional figure such that every point is the same distance from the center. *Example:*

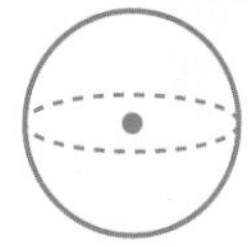

square A rectangle with all sides congruent.

squared When a number has been multiplied by itself.
Example: 5 squared $= 5^2 = 5 \times 5 = 25$

statistics Numerical data that have been collected and analyzed.

stem-and-leaf plot A frequency distribution that arranges data in order of place value. The leaves are the last digits of the numbers; the stems are the digits to the left of the leaves.

straight angle An angle which measures 180°.

substitution The replacement of the variable of an expression with a number.

supplementary angles Two angles with measures that add up to 180°.

surface area (SA) The sum of the areas of each face of a polyhedron.

survey Method to collect data from a sample to study some characteristic of the group.

T

T-table A table of *x*- and *y*-values used to graph an equation.

terminating decimal A decimal with a finite number of digits. *Example:* 0.375

terms The quantities *x* and *y* in a ratio.

theoretical probability Ratio of the favorable outcomes to the possible outcomes of an event.

transformation A move such as a translation, reflection, or rotation that moves a figure to a new position without changing its size or shape.

translation The change in the position of a figure that moves it up, down, or sideways in a straight direction.

trapezoid A quadrilateral with only one pair of opposite sides parallel.

tree diagram A diagram used to organize all the possible outcomes in a sample space or to find the prime factorization of a composite number.

trend A clear direction in a line graph suggesting how the data may behave in the future.

trial One of the instances of an experiment.

triangle A polygon with three sides.

trillions A place value or period of place values for numbers greater than billions.

U

unit rate A rate in which the comparison is to one unit. *Example:* 25 feet per second

unlike denominators Denominators in two or more fractions that are different.

V

variable A quantity that changes or varies, often represented with a letter.

vertex (in an angle) The common endpoint of two rays that form an angle.

vertex (in a polygon) The point of intersection of two sides of a polygon.

vertex (in a polyhedron) The point of intersection of the edges of a polyhedron.

vertical angles A pair of angles formed by intersecting lines, the angles have no side in common. Vertical angles are congruent. *Example:*

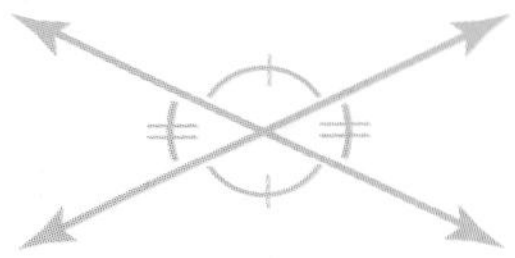

volume The number of cubic units needed to fill a solid figure.

X

***x*-axis** The horizontal line on a coordinate plane.

***x*-coordinate** The first number in an ordered pair that tells the position left or right of the *y*-axis.

Y

***y*-axis** The vertical line on a coordinate plane.

***y*-coordinate** The second number in an ordered pair that tells the position above or below the *x*-axis.

Illustrations

Cover: Luciana Navarro Powell

Photographs

Every effort has been made to secure permission and provide appropriate credit for photographic material. The publisher deeply regrets any omission and pledges to correct errors called to its attention in subsequent editions.

Unless otherwise acknowledged, all photographs are the property of Scott Foresman, a division of Pearson Education.

Photo locators denoted as follows: Top (T), Center (C), Bottom (B), Left (L), Right (R), Background (Bkgd)

2 (B) ©Myron Jay Dorf/Corbis 3 (L) Burnett/Palmer/Mira 6 (CR) ©Myron Jay Dorf/Corbis 9 (BL) ©Phillip Wallick/Corbis (BC) Nick Galante/PMRF/NASA 20 (TR) ©Robert Yin/Corbis 30 (L) ©Damian Dovargnes/AP Images (BR) AP Images (B) Getty Images 31 (L) ©Judy Hedding (T) ©Denis Scott/Corbis 44 (BR) ©Judy Hedding 60 (BL) ©Adam Jones/Alamy Images (BR) Jupiter Images (T) ©Richard T. Nowitz/Corbis 61 (L) ©Duncan McNicol/Getty Images 68 (CR) Jupiter Images 69 (TR) The Granger Collection, NY (TL) ©Tannen Maury/epa/Corbis 94 (C) ©Frank Whitney/Getty Images 95 (T) ©Mike Kelly/Getty Images 100 (R) ©Frank Whitney/Getty Images 118 (TR) ©Michael Freeman/Corbis (L) Bruce Lichtenberger/Peter Arnold, Inc. 119 (B) Soames Summerhayes/Photo Researchers, Inc. (T) Getty Images 142 (B) Nature Picture Library 146 ©Wolfgang Kaehler/Corbis 149 (B) Nature Picture Library 160 (B) ©James L. Amos/Corbis (TL) ©Philip Gould/Corbis (TR) Muench Photography, Inc 161 (TL) Prenzel Photo/Animals Animals/Earth Scenes 169 (T) Oxford Scientific/Jupiter Images (CL) Norbert Wu/Minden Pictures 184 (TL) Klaus Uhlenhut/Animals Animals/Earth Scenes 185 (L) Digital Vision 200 (B) NASA (TL) ©Kevin Schafer/zefa/Corbis 201 (T) ©George Diebold/Getty Images 207 (L, C) Jupiter Images (R) ©Kevin Schafer/zefa/Corbis 220 (B) Comstock Images/Jupiter Images (TR) Fritz Polking/Peter Arnold, Inc. 221 (B) Peter Christopher/Masterfile Corporation (T) MP Kahl/Okapia/Photo Researchers, Inc. 227 (BC) Howard Hall/OSF/Animals Animals/Earth Scenes (BR), (CL) ©Royalty-Free/Corbis (CR) ©Merlin D. Tuttle/Bat Conservation International, Inc. (T) MP Kahl/Okapia/Photo Researchers, Inc. 260 (BL) ESA/HST Moon Team/NASA (T) Getty Images (C) Georgette Douwma/Nature Picture Library (TR) Andrew J. Martinez/Photo Researchers, Inc. 261 (B) Creatas /Jupiter Images (TL) ©Cosmo CondinaChi/Alamy Images 272 (BR) Creatas /Jupiter Images 276 (TR) ©Cosmo CondinaChi/Alamy Images 283 (B) ESA/HST Moon Team/NASA 287 (BL) © Ralph A. Clevenger/Corbis (BR) ©Galen Rowell/Corbis (BC) GeckoStone®/©1998 John August. All Rights Reserved. 298 (T) ©Phillip Wallick/Corbis (B) Courtesy of Transrapid International-USA, Inc. (B) Getty Images 299 (T) Herve Berthoule/Jacana/Photo Researchers, Inc. (TL) Alan Sirulnikoff/Photo Researchers, Inc. 302 (TL) Corbis 304 (BR) Alan Sirulnikoff/Photo Researchers, Inc. 312 Courtesy of Transrapid International-USA, Inc. 320 (L) Getty Images (TR) ©Yann Arthus-Bertrand/Corbis (BR) ©Ron Kimball/PhotoLibrary 321 (L) Empire State Building art and photo ©Sean Kenney 337 (TR) Ancient Art & Architecture/Danita Delimont, Agent 342 (T) ©Ros Roberts/Getty Images (B) Reuters/Hugh Gentry/Landov LLC 343 (T) Jupiter Images (BL) ©Stefan Schuetz/zefa/Corbis 352 (BR) Getty Images 370 (T) Nature Picture Library (B) Getty Images 371 (T) Margarete Steiff GMbH ©Steiff North America, Inc. (T) Iconica/Getty Images 379 (BR) Iconica/Getty Images 384 (BR) Getty Images 398 (T) ©Holden Special Vehicles (T) Denis Paquin/AP Images 399 (B) Francois Gohier/Gaston Design/Photo Researchers, Inc. 406 (B) Francois Gohier/Gaston Design/Photo Researchers, Inc. 424 (T) Digital Vision (B) ©Tomas Kopecny/Alamy (TL) ©Theo Allofs/Getty Images 425 (T) STScI/NASA/Corbis 433 (BR) ©Tomas Kopecny/Alamy 441 (B) Courtesy of the Oriental Institute of the University of Chicago (T) Erich Lessing/Art Resource, NY (CR) ©Royalty-Free/Corbis (C) ©The Trustees of The British Museum 442 (BC), (BR) Getty Images (BL) Image Source/Getty Images 452 (T) ©Nick Hanna/Alamy Images (L) ©Brian Hagiwara/Jupiter Images 453 (T) Getty Images (B) NASA 457 Getty Images 465 (BR) NASA 474 ©Royalty-Free/Corbis 475 (T) ©John Bain (T) PhotoDisc (TL) Harrod Blank 504 (BR) ©Daniel J. Cox/Corbis 511 Getty Images 518 (B) ©Theo Allofs/Corbis (T) Blend Images/Jupiter Images 519 (T) Jupiter Images (C) ©Davies & Starr/Getty Images (BC) Michael Newton/Robert Harding World Imagery 522 (C) ©Davies & Starr/Getty Images (BC) Michael Newton/Robert Harding World Imagery 535 (B) Blend Images/Jupiter Images.

C

D

E

F

G

P

Q

R

S

U

V

W

X

Y